Fourth Edition

# INTERMEDIATE ACCOUNTING

## *STANDARD VOLUME*

**Harry Simons, M.A., C.P.A.**

Professor of Accounting
University of California, Los Angeles

**Wilbert E. Karrenbrock, Ph.D.**

Associate Professor of Accounting
University of California, Los Angeles

Published By

**SOUTH-WESTERN PUBLISHING COMPANY**

Cincinnati

Chicago

Burlingame, Calif.          Dallas          New Rochelle, N.Y.

A87

Library of Congress Catalog Card Number 65-10313

**K467**

Printed in the United States of America

# PREFACE

*Intermediate Accounting — Standard Volume* is a text for a second course in accounting to follow the introductory course in this subject. A companion book, *Intermediate Accounting — Comprehensive Volume*, has been developed for those schools that can devote sufficient time to an expanded treatment of the intermediate study. Although differing in scope, each book has been designed to serve the needs of two groups of students: (1) the general business student, for whom the intermediate course may be the final study in accounting; (2) the accounting major. Both groups must be thoroughly familiar with the basic assumptions that underlie modern accounting, the principles, procedures, and methods that are applied in the preparation of financial statements, and the proper uses that can be made of financial data. With this background, the business student is prepared to analyze and interpret the full product of accounting; the accounting major is prepared to continue with advanced studies that will enable him to achieve professional status.

The fourth edition *of Intermediate Accounting — Standard Volume* represents a major revision of the earlier work. Discussions recognize the accounting developments that have taken place since publication of the preceding edition in 1958. Special emphasis has been directed to subjects of high contemporary interest. Most recent opinions of the American Institute of Certified Public Accountants and the American Accounting Association are reflected in the theoretical discussions. Reference is made to the latest tax laws and other legislation affecting accounting practice. Modern terminology, statements, and forms are employed throughout the text. Problems have been revised and new problems have been added.

A summary of the major changes in subject matter that are found in the fourth edition follows.

*Part I — Fundamental Processes.* More attention is devoted to accounting postulates and principles, data-processing methods, and contemporary practices and forms in the development of financial statements.

*Part II — Working Capital.* Increased attention is directed to accounting controls. Discussions of the valuation of marketable securities, receivables, and inventories have been expanded. Inventory methods that have received increased attention in recent years are described, including standard costs, direct costing, unit lifo, and dollar-value lifo. The application of present-value concepts in valuing receivables and payables is described and illustrated. Income tax allocation procedures are fully considered and illustrated.

iii

*Part III — Noncurrent Assets and Liabilities.* Discussions relating to plant and equipment and intangible assets have been expanded significantly. Valuation problems receive particular emphasis. Alternative depreciation methods are fully evaluated. Group-rate and composite-rate methods receive special attention. Present-value concepts in the valuation of goodwill are considered.

*Part IV — Stockholders' Equity.* Legal factors governing accounting for the corporation receive particular emphasis. The special problems in the valuation of assets acquired upon corporate formation are considered. Legal requirements and their effects upon accounting for treasury stock receive careful attention. Stock subscription rights and stock option arrangements are described. Financial statements for the corporation are fully illustrated.

*Part V — Analytical Processes.* Additional analytical processes and techniques are introduced and illustrated. The chapter on the funds statement has been expanded to include consideration of the different definitions applied to funds — all financial resources, working capital, net monetary assets, and cash. The preparation of the funds statement employing each of the four concepts is described and illustrated.

The attempt is made throughout the text to present the theoretical setting for the practices and procedures that are described. When alternative positions can be taken on important matters of theory and practice, such alternatives are indicated and the positions that have been taken by leading authorities are described. But it is hoped that the discussions clearly indicate that answers acceptable today may require modification tomorrow; that continued inquiry may suggest different approaches and different emphases that will enable accounting to better serve society.

Each chapter concludes with a set of questions, exercises, and problems. Questions offer a review of theory. Exercises are provided to offer practice in the application of specific concepts and procedures. Problems are designed to enable the student to gain experience in applying his accounting skills. The first few problems in each set offer practice in applying the basic concepts that are developed within a chapter; remaining problems are of a more comprehensive nature that call for the application of the student's overall accounting maturity.

Every effort has been made to present the practices of accounting and the theoretical framework for such practices in a manner that is both clear and complete. When the instructor can depend upon the textbook to provide students with an adequate introduction to the accounting processes and procedures, he can devote classroom time to the critical examination and evaluation of the area that is covered. The instructor is afforded an opportunity to present his own position on matters of theory and practice and to make his own personal contribution to the group; students participating in classroom discussions can achieve growth and security in the use of the language of accounting and in the application of accounting concepts to business problems.

The authors are grateful to the many instructors and students who have contributed to the development and improvement of this text over the years. Preceding editions have named a number of persons who have made especially important contributions. The authors wish to name the following persons for their contributions to the fourth edition. Deep gratitude is expressed to Professor Anelise Mosich of San Fernando Valley State College who made important suggestions and offered valuable editorial assistance throughout the course of the revision. Sincere appreciation is expressed to Professor Allan Drebin of the University of California, Los Angeles, who contributed to parts of the revision. Thanks are also expressed to the following professors of accounting who made valuable suggestions: Wilton T. Anderson, Oklahoma State University; Bill J. Bishop, University of Missouri; Raymond C. Dein, University of Nebraska; W. C. Flewellen, Jr., Mississippi State University; H. Arthur Hoverland, Naval Postgraduate School; Ted M. Rabun, Pennsylvania State University; and John B. Ross, University of Tennessee.

The authors also wish to thank the American Accounting Association and the American Institute of Certified Public Accountants for permission to quote from their various publications and pronouncements.

Harry Simons

W. E. Karrenbrock

# CONTENTS

---

[1]Questions, exercises, and problems are given at the end of each chapter.

## Part III — Noncurrent Assets and Liabilities

## Part IV — Stockholders' Equity

## Part V — Analytical Processes

# Chapter 1

# FINANCIAL STATEMENTS

## THE BALANCE SHEET

### Need for an appreciation of accounting

The management of a business enterprise is responsible for planning and controlling the operations of the business. These responsibilities include the maintainance of an effective system of accounts. This system must provide not only the required information for management decision making in the areas of planning and control but also the data that are required for the financial statements that are to be made available to the owners of the business and to creditors and other interested parties.

Before management issues financial statements, it normally submits them, together with the supporting books and records, to a firm of independent public accountants for examination and review. The public accountants will express the opinion that the financial statements "present fairly the financial position of the company and the results of its operations" only if their examination shows that the statements were prepared in conformity with "generally accepted accounting principles."

If a person is to read and interpret intelligently the financial statements, he must be familiar with those "generally accepted accounting principles" that are applied in the development of accounting data. If a person is to undertake the preparation of financial statements, there is an even greater need for a thorough appreciation of the underlying principles. A study of accounting principles and procedures is necessary for those who expect to attain a responsible place in business. Such study is equally important for those who are interested in a thorough understanding of the business enterprise as the fundamental unit in economic society.

Accounting serves many groups and faces ever-increasing responsibilities. Although originally concerned with the demands made by the owners or the creditors of a business for financial data, the accountant now finds a number of different groups vitally concerned with his reports. Management requires accounting data in safeguarding business resources, in judging the results of past policies, and in planning future operations. Owners require reliable financial statements in evaluating their ownership interests and in appraising the performance of management. Creditors rely on financial statements in considering the degree of protection that is afforded their interests. Government, trade associations, labor unions, and the public also have special needs for accounting data of the business unit. Increasingly the products of accounting are being used as a basis for economic, political, and social policy and action. Modern accounting, thus, is called upon to meet public as well as private responsibilities.

Accounting principles and practices represent the response by the accounting profession to the needs and the expectations of the different groups calling for financial information. These principles and practices must be well defined and widely understood. Financial reports must be prepared within the framework of such standards with intelligence and integrity. Only under such circumstances can the products of accounting be received with confidence by those seeking information.

### Accounting and the corporation

The corporation is the dominant form of large business organization in the United States. Although there are more sole proprietorships and partnerships than corporations, the volume of business done by corporations exceeds by far that of the other forms of business organization. Furthermore, the value of properties owned by corporations is considerably greater than the value of properties owned by both sole proprietorships and partnerships.

By its very nature the corporate form calls for extended and accurate accounting. In large corporate enterprises the investment and the management groups are separated. Ownership interests are liquid and readily transferable. There are more than 17,000,000 stockholders in the United States today, and bondholders add to the total of the corporate investment group. The number of investors having any first-hand knowledge of the activities of the companies in which they have interests is small. Accounting becomes the only source of information concerning corporate financial status and progress for the investor. Absentee and scattered investment groups must be provided with financial data that tell the business story completely and dependably.

### Accounting defined

Transactions relating to the exchange of goods and services constitute the raw materials of accounting. It is through accounting that the transactions of the business unit are accumulated, summarized, and then communicated to those seeking facts concerning the activities of the business.

The Committee on Terminology of the American Institute of Certified Public Accountants has defined accounting in the following manner:

> Accounting is the art of recording, classifying, and summarizing in a significant manner and in terms of money, transactions and events which are, in part at least, of a financial character, and interpreting the results thereof.[1]

The Committee, faced with the problem of defining accounting as a science or an art, chose the latter to emphasize the knowledge, skill, experience, and constructive efforts that are applied by accountants in performing a service for society. The inclusion of the interpretive function in the definition of accounting is also worthy of special note. The accountant is in a position to render invaluable service to management by developing significant analyses that interpret activities of the past and provide guides for more effective utilization of business resources in the future.

## Accounting principles

Definition of accounting as an art does not rule out the fact that the accountant's work is practiced within a framework of fundamental doctrine. This body of doctrine consists of certain principles and practices that have won acceptance within the profession because of their logic as well as their proved usefulness. When reference is made to "accounting principles," it should be understood that the term is used to suggest, not natural laws of universal applicability, but rather, that body of standards that points to what may be considered good accounting practice.

The accounting profession engages continually in the re-examination and critical analysis of fundamental theory as well as the practices found in the field of accounting. From such study it seeks to define standards of sound practice in terms of contemporary problems. As agreement is reached on such standards, their wide application is encouraged by the profession.

Many groups have played important roles in the development and the expression of accounting principles and practices. Most prominent among these groups have been the American Institute of Certified Public Accountants (AICPA), the American Accounting Association (AAA), and the Securities and Exchange Commission (SEC).

The American Institute of Certified Public Accountants, in cooperation with governmental, business, and educational groups, has taken a leading role in this program. Arguments on matters of accounting theory and practice as well as the conclusions reached by special research committees of the Institute have been summarized in various pronounce-

---

[1] *Accounting Research and Terminology Bulletins,* 1961 (New York: American Institute of Certified Public Accountants), *Accounting Terminology Bulletin No. 1,* p. 9.

ments and official bulletins.[1] In the period 1939–1959 the Institute released a series of Accounting Research Bulletins setting forth the recommendations made by its Committee on Accounting Procedure. In 1959 an Accounting Principles Board was established to review contemporary accounting problems and to issue pronouncements expressing its opinions as to the preferred treatment of specific types of transactions. At the same time the Accounting Research Division was given authority to publish studies of current problems which could be considered by the Accounting Principles Board in establishing its position on these matters. In 1963 the research program was extended to provide for the identification and codification of accounting principles that have achieved general acceptance.[2] The objectives of the Institute program from the very beginning have been to further the development and recognition of generally accepted accounting principles and to narrow the areas of difference and inconsistency in accounting practice. The Institute has also made significant contributions to the ethical standards of the profession.

The American Accounting Association has made important contributions to the development of a coordinated body of basic doctrine through the publication of special studies and official pronouncements.[3] In 1936 the Executive Committee of this organization issued "A Tentative Statement of Accounting Principles Underlying Corporate Financial

---

[1]The American Institute of Certified Public Accountants, established in 1887, is the national organization of certified public accountants and is primarily concerned with professional public accounting. The objectives of the Institute are to unite the profession, to advance the interests of public accountants, to set standards for admission into the profession, to advance the art of accounting, and to improve accounting education. The Board of Examiners of the Institute prepares the Uniform Certified Public Accountant Examinations, which are now used by all of the 50 states, the District of Columbia, Puerto Rico, and the Virgin Islands. The Institute publishes a monthly journal, *The Journal of Accountancy*. The office of the American Institute of Certified Public Accountants is at 666 Fifth Avenue, New York 19, New York.

[2]*Accounting Research Bulletin No. 51* was the last bulletin issued by the Committee on Accounting Procedure. All of the research bulletins as well as the terminology bulletins issued prior to 1961 have been combined and published in a single volume, *Accounting Research and Terminology Bulletins — Final Edition* (1961). Several opinion statements have been issued since the formation of the Accounting Principles Board and a number of research studies have been issued by the Director of Accounting Research. The Director of Accounting Research, in a statement of policy relative to the research studies, observes, "The studies are intended to be informative, but tentative only. They furnish a vehicle for the exposure of matters for consideration and experimentation prior to the issuance of pronouncements by the Accounting Principles Board. . . . The conclusions and recommendations have not been approved, disapproved, or otherwise acted upon by the Accounting Principles Board, the only agency of the American Institute of Certified Public Accountants having authority to make or approve public pronouncements on accounting principles."

[3]The American Accounting Association is the successor organization to the American Association of University Instructors in Accounting established in 1916. The objectives of the organization are to encourage and sponsor accounting research, to develop accounting principles, to promote studies of accounting as an agency of control of business enterprise and of economic affairs, and to improve methods of accounting instruction. The Association publishes a quarterly magazine, *The Accounting Review*. The office of the Secretary-Treasurer of the American Accounting Association is at the College of Business Administration, University of Iowa, Iowa City, Iowa.

Statements." This statement was revised in 1941 and again in 1948. The study, development, and expression of accounting standards is viewed as a continuing activity, and in 1949 a special Committee on Concepts and Standards Underlying Corporate Financial Statements was appointed for this purpose. This committee has issued a number of statements supplementing the 1948 statement, and in 1957 issued a revision of the 1948 statement under the title, "Accounting and Reporting Standards for Corporate Financial Statements."[1]

The Securities and Exchange Commission has made extensive contribution to the development and the expression of accounting doctrine by issuing rules and regulations relating to the reports to be filed by registrants and rendering opinions on matters of theory and practice in its official decisions and reports and in its Accounting Series Releases. The issuance of the series of accounting releases by the Commission was announced as a "program for the publication, from time to time, of opinions on accounting principles for the purpose of contributing to the development of uniform standards and practices in major accounting questions."

It should be observed that the accounting organizations have felt that their conclusions should be regarded, not as rigid patterns and restraints, but rather as guides to good practice. The AICPA Committee on Accounting Procedure, for example, has stated with respect to its Accounting Research Bulletins:

> Except in cases in which formal adoption by the Institute membership has been asked and secured, the authority of opinions reached by the committee rests upon their general acceptability. The committee recognizes that in extraordinary cases fair presentation and justice to all parties at interest may require exceptional treatment. But the burden of justifying departures from accepted procedures, to the extent that they are evidenced in committee opinions, must be assumed by those who adopt another treatment.[2]

The Accounting Principles Board has made a similar statement with respect to the authority of its opinions.[3] Adherence to the recommended standards is thus encouraged; but it is recognized that in preparing reports that convey the financial story fully, clearly, and honestly, the doors must be left open to the exercise of judgment by the accountant in

---

[1]*Supplementary Statement No. 8*, issued in 1954, is the latest in the series of supplementary statements at this printing. The 1957 statement, earlier statements, and also the eight supplementary statements have been combined and published in a single pamphlet entitled, *Accounting and Reporting Standards for Corporate Financial Statements and Preceding Statements and Supplements* (1957).

[2]*Accounting Research and Terminology Bulletins*, 1961 (New York: American Institute of Certified Public Accountants), *Accounting Research Bulletin No. 43*, p. 9.

[3]*Opinions of the Accounting Principles Board, No. 1*, 1962 (New York: American Institute of Certified Public Accountants), p. 4.

the determination of the degree of conformity to standards that is proper under different circumstances. There is also recognition of the need for a continual re-examination of accepted standards and their restatement and revision to keep pace with changes in the economic environment.

The progress that has been made in defining the body of doctrine that is applicable to contemporary reporting has been highly important both to the accounting profession and to those who use the services offered by the profession. The practitioner, aware of standards that have general support, is afforded guidance as well as a sense of security in his performance. The product of accounting is improved and at the same time achieves greater uniformity and comparability. The reader of the financial report, familiar with the standards that have been applied in its preparation, can view it with confidence, interpret it properly, and compare it with other reports prepared within a common framework.

### The matching process

One of the most important duties of the accountant is to act as business historian. It is his function to record, classify, and summarize business activities. In fulfilling the historical function, the accountant must be impartial and systematic in seeking out the facts of business. His findings should be objective and verifiable.

Management of the business unit engages in exchange transactions directed to the increase of business resources through profits. Such transactions are carried on over a period of time. However, the recognition of business progress cannot be delayed until the termination of activities at some unascertainable future date but must be a continuing process. Accordingly, the life of the business unit is broken up into a succession of equal periods of time, and statements of financial progress are provided for each time segment. The preparation of statements within a business continuity may be no simple matter and normally involves both estimates and the exercise of judgment. Such statements must be recognized as no more than tentative reports or "test readings," since the full story is yet to be told and the future may modify the inferences made in the periodic analyses. Division of the life of a business into uniform periods of time is often referred to as the *time-period assumption*.

Business may be considered to consist of two streams of activities. First, there are the regular acquisitions of goods and services required for the performance of its objectives. These activities result in business *costs*. There follows the business accomplishments directed to the fulfillment of its objectives — to recover costs as well as to achieve a profit. Ordinarily, the test for business accomplishment is the sale of goods or services. These activities are the source of business *revenues*. The *net income* from operations for a specified period is determined by matching against the revenues for the period those costs that are considered applicable thereto. When revenues exceed costs, there is an increase in the business *net assets* — the difference between assets and liabilities — and an accompanying increase in the owner's equity; when revenues fail to equal costs, there is a decrease in net assets and a decrease in the owner's equity. The periodic application of costs against revenues is referred to as the *matching process* and is fundamental in accounting for the business unit.

Both costs and revenues in the matching process are expressed in terms of the homogeneous characteristic that is common to both — a money price. The price for the business effort, or cost, is found in the amount paid for the goods and services at the time these were originally acquired. The price that is assigned to the business accomplishment, or revenue, is the bargained amount arrived at between buyer and seller. As goods and services are acquired, then, their cost is established and recorded. These costs may be marshaled into different combinations where the business unites different acquisitions in the development of its services or products. Ultimately such costs, individually or as regrouped, are assigned to the revenue that they have produced.

The use of historical cost in the matching process is commonly referred to as application of the *cost principle*. Independent buyers and sellers through negotiation reach agreement as to the value of the economic utility that is exchanged. This bargained acquisition is the buyer's cost, his investment in the future. It is a value that is definite and immediately determinable, and is accepted as the starting point in the measurement process.

## Financial statements

The time segment generally selected for a comparison of costs and revenues and their effect upon the business position is one year, either the *calendar year* or some other selected *fiscal year*. At the end of each year two principal financial reports, the *balance sheet* and the *income statement*, are prepared. When the difference in the net assets for the year is not fully explained by the income statement, a third statement is usually provided to supplement profit and loss data and to offer a full reconciliation of the difference. This statement is known as the *statement of changes in capital*, or as applied to the corporation, the *retained earnings statement*.

The balance sheet, the income statement, and the statement of changes in capital or the retained earnings statement are referred to as *general purpose statements*. In addition to the general purpose statements, special statements may be prepared in forms that develop certain aspects of financial position and operations for management or owners or that meet requirements of governmental regulatory bodies, creditors, trade associations, etc. Such statements are referred to as *special purpose statements*.

## Nature and content of the balance sheet

The balance sheet, also variously called the *statement of financial position* and the *statement of condition*, shows the assets, liabilities, and capital of the business unit at a given date. The financial position is the cumulative result of all transactions of the business from its beginning. Since the balance sheet is basically historical, reporting the position growing out of a series of recorded transactions, only a thorough understanding of the principles and practices that are followed in the recording process offers an appreciation of the nature of the end product. Some of the basic concepts of balance sheet content, form, and presentation are considered in this chapter. Discussions of the individual asset, liability, and capital items in later chapters will serve to develop more fully the nature of the balance sheet.

The balance sheet is an expansion of the basic accounting equation, Assets = Liabilities + Proprietorship. The character and the amount of the assets are exhibited and the equities of the creditor and the ownership groups are listed. Creditor and ownership equities normally bear no relationship to specific assets and hence are presented as equities identified with the assets as a whole.

For accounting purposes, assets include those costs that have not been applied to revenues in the past and are considered to afford economic utility in the production of revenues in the future. Assets, then, include both monetary assets such as cash, marketable securities, and receivables, and those costs that are recognized as recoverable and hence properly assignable to revenues of future periods such as inventories, prepaid insurance, equipment, and patents.[1]

Liabilities measure the equities of the creditor group in the total assets. Such equities result from the extension of credit by this group. The method of liability liquidation varies. Claims may call for payment in cash or for settlement through goods to be delivered or services to be performed.

---

[1]The American Accounting Association defines assets as ". . . economic resources devoted to business purposes within a specific accounting entity; they are aggregates of service-potentials available for or beneficial to expected operations" (*Accounting and Reporting Standards for Corporate Financial Statements*). The American Institute of Certified Public Accountants defines an asset as "Something represented by a debit balance that is or would be properly carried forward upon a closing of books of account according to the rules or principles of accounting (provided such a debit balance is not in effect a negative balance applicable to a liability), on the basis that it represents either a property right or value acquired, or an expenditure made which has created a property right or is properly applicable to the future." (*Accounting Terminology Bulletin No. 1*, "Review and Resumé").

Proprietorship measures the equity of the ownership group in the total resources of the enterprise. Such equity originally arises as the result of investments by owners, and the equity changes with the change in net assets resulting from operations. An ownership equity does not call for settlement on a maturity date; in the event of business dissolution, it represents a claim on assets only after creditors have been paid in full.

Balance sheet items are generally classified in a manner that will facilitate the analysis and the interpretation of financial data. Information of primary concern to all parties is the business unit's solvency — its ability to meet current obligations. Accordingly, assets and liabilities are classified as (1) *current* or *short-term* items and (2) *noncurrent, long-term,* or *fixed* items. When assets and liabilities are classified, the difference between current assets and current liabilities may be determined. This is referred to as the company's *working capital* — the liquid buffer available in meeting financial demands and contingencies of the future.[1]

### Current assets and current liabilities

There have been important changes in the criteria for designating items as current or noncurrent in recent years. Originally, the "current" designation was applied to cash and those assets that would be realized in cash within one year and to liabilities that would be due within one year. This definition would call for the exclusion of inventories and receivables not expected to be converted into cash within one year and the exclusion of prepaid expenses that do not produce cash. Liabilities maturing after one year from balance sheet date would likewise be excluded from the current category. However, both the American Institute of Certified Public Accountants and the American Accounting Association have recommended a broadening of the definition of current items to emphasize a company's ability to meet its claims in the course of current operations rather than in the event of liquidation. Accordingly, current items are held to embrace those items relating to the particular company's "normal operating cycle." These groups conceive ordinary operations to involve the circulation of resources within the current group. Cash is converted into inventories, inventories into receivables, and receivables ultimately into cash again. Assets falling within this cycle are considered current. Prepaid expenses are included in the current grouping since they represent substitutes for expenditures that otherwise would require the use of current resources within the operating cycle. Current liabilities are conceived as those items making a claim against assets classified as current, and consist of: (1) payables for goods and services

---

[1]"Working capital" is used in this text to denote the excess of current assets over current liabilities. Sometimes this excess is referred to as "net working capital," the term "working capital" then being used to denote total current assets.

purchased, and (2) collections in advance of the delivery of goods or the performance of services sold.

The position of the AICPA Committee on Accounting Procedure on current assets follows:

> ... For accounting purposes, the term *current assets* is used to designate cash and other assets or resources commonly identified as those which are reasonably expected to be realized in cash or sold or consumed during the normal operating cycle of the business. Thus the term comprehends in general such resources as (a) cash available for current operations and items which are the equivalent of cash; (b) inventories of merchandise, raw materials, goods in process, finished goods, operating supplies, and ordinary maintenance material and parts; (c) trade accounts, notes, and acceptances receivable; (d) receivables from officers, employees, affiliates, and others, if collectible in the ordinary course of business within a year; (e) instalment or deferred accounts and notes receivable if they conform generally to normal trade practices and terms within the business; (f) marketable securities representing the investment of cash available for current operations; and (g) prepaid expenses such as insurance, interest, rents, taxes, unused royalties, current paid advertising service not yet received, and operating supplies. Prepaid expenses are not current assets in the sense that they will be converted into cash but in the sense that, if not paid in advance, they would require the use of current assets during the operating cycle.[1]

The Committee further suggests that the one-year period be used as a basis for current asset classification in those instances where the average operating cycle is less than twelve months; but where the operating cycle exceeds twelve months, as in the case of the tobacco, distillery, and lumber industries, that the longer period be used.

In accordance with the foregoing concept of current assets, the Committee lists the following items as noncurrent:

(a) Cash and cash claims restricted to use for other than current operations, designated for the acquisition of noncurrent assets, or segregated for the liquidation of noncurrent debts.

(b) Advances or investments in securities, whether marketable or not, made for the purposes of control, affiliation, or other continuing business advantage.

(c) Receivables not expected to be collected within twelve months arising from unusual transactions such as the sale of capital assets or advances to affiliates, officers, or employees.

(d) Cash surrender value of life insurance policies.

(e) Land and other natural resources.

(f) Depreciable assets.

(g) Unamortized costs fairly chargeable to the operations of several years.

Current liabilities are described as follows:

---

[1] *Accounting Research and Terminology Bulletins,* 1961 (New York: American Institute of Certified Public Accountants), *Accounting Research Bulletin No. 43,* p. 20. The American Accounting Association Committee on Concepts and Standards Underlying Corporate Financial Statements endorses the Institute's conclusions on working capital in its *Supplementary Statement No. 3,* "Current Assets and Current Liabilities," 1951.

The term *current liabilities* is used principally to designate obligations whose liquidation is reasonably expected to require the use of existing resources properly classifiable as current assets, or the creation of other current liabilities. As a balance-sheet category, the classification is intended to include obligations for items which have entered into the operating cycle, such as payables incurred in the acquisition of materials and supplies to be used in the production of goods or in providing services to be offered for sale; collections received in advance of the delivery of goods or performance of services; and debts which arise from operations directly related to the operating cycle, such as accruals for wages, salaries, commissions, rentals, royalties, and income and other taxes. Other liabilities whose regular and ordinary liquidation is expected to occur within a relatively short period of time, usually twelve months, are also intended for inclusion, such as short-term debts arising from the acquisition of capital assets, serial maturities of long-term obligations, amounts required to be expended within one year under sinking fund provisions, and agency obligations arising from the collection or acceptance of cash or other assets for the account of third persons.[1]

The current liability classification, however, does not include the following items, since these do not require the use of resources classified as current:

(a) Obligations due at an early date that are to be discharged by means of the issuance of new obligations in their places. There should, however, be parenthetical disclosure of the reason for continuing to report such items as noncurrent.

(b) Debts that are to be liquidated from funds that have been accumulated and are reported as noncurrent assets.

(c) Loans on life insurance policies made with the intent that these will not be paid but will be liquidated by deduction from the proceeds of the policies upon their maturity or cancellation.

(d) Obligations for advance collections that involve long-term deferment of the delivery of goods or services.

Current items are still classified in terms of a strict "one-year" concept on many statements. But there has been a steady movement towards acceptance of the AICPA's position since the release of its recommendations in 1947. There is sound logic in support of the broader interpretation for current assets and liabilities, and illustrations on the following pages are prepared in accordance with Institute recommendations.

Current assets are normally listed on the balance sheet in the order of their liquidity. These assets, with the exception of marketable securities and inventories, are usually reported at their estimated realizable values. Thus, current receivable balances are reduced by allowances for estimated bad debts. Marketable securities and inventories may be reported at cost or on the basis of "cost or market, whichever is lower."

Few problems are generally found in the valuation of current liabilities. Payables can usually be determined or accrued accurately.

---

[1]*Accounting Research and Terminology Bulletins*, 1961 (New York: American Institute of Certified Public Accountants), *Accounting Research Bulletin No. 43*, p. 21.

Some items may require estimates as to the amounts that will ultimately be paid. The claims, however determined, if payable currently must be included under the current heading.

### Noncurrent assets and liabilities

Assets and liabilities that do not qualify for presentation under the current headings are classified under a number of noncurrent headings. Noncurrent assets are generally listed under separate headings such as *Investments, Plant and Equipment, Intangibles,* and *Other Assets.* Noncurrent liabilities are listed under such headings as *Long-Term Debt, Deferred Revenues,* and *Other Liabilities.*

*Investments.* Investments held for such long-term purposes as regular income, appreciation, or ownership control are reported under the heading Investments. Examples of items properly reported under this heading are long-term stock, bond, and mortgage holdings; securities of affiliated companies as well as advances to such companies; sinking fund assets consisting of cash and securities held for the redemption of bonds, the redemption of stock, the replacement of buildings, or the payment of pensions; land held for future use or sale; the cash surrender value of life insurance; and other miscellaneous investments not used directly in the operations of the business. Long-term investments are normally reported at cost.

*Plant and equipment.* Properties of a tangible and relatively permanent character that are used in the normal business operations are reported under the heading Plant and Equipment. Land, buildings, machinery, equipment, tools, furniture, fixtures, and vehicles are included under this heading. Plant and equipment items are normally reported at cost less accumulated depreciation.

*Intangibles.* The long-term rights and privileges of a non-physical character acquired for use in business operations are reported under the heading Intangibles. Included in this class are such items as goodwill, patents, trademarks, franchises, copyrights, formulas, leaseholds, and organization costs. Intangible assets are normally reported at cost less amounts previously amortized.

The term *fixed assets* is frequently applied to all of those long-term properties that are used in the production of goods and services. As thus used, fixed assets would consist of two groups — *fixed tangibles* represented by plant and equipment items and *fixed intangibles* represented by the items named above.

*Other assets.* Those noncurrent assets that cannot be reported satisfactorily under any of the previous classifications are listed under special descriptive headings or under the general heading Other Assets. Such assets include cash funds representing deposits received from customers, deposits made with vendors to secure contracts, advances to officers, and construction in progress.

Prepayments for services or benefits that are to be received over a number of periods are properly regarded as noncurrent. Among these are such items as bond issuing costs and developmental and improvement costs. These long-term prepayments are frequently reported on the balance sheet under a *deferred costs* or *deferred charges* heading. However, serious objection can be raised to a deferred costs designation since this designation could be applied to all costs assignable to future periods including inventories, plant and equipment, and intangibles. The deferred costs heading may be avoided by reporting long-term prepayments under separate descriptive headings or within the Other Assets section of the balance sheet. Short-term prepayments are often listed together with long-term prepayments. But, as stated earlier, the trend in recent years has been to report these as current assets in accordance with the recommendations of the AICPA.

*Contingent assets.* Circumstances on the balance sheet date may indicate the existence of certain rights or claims that could materialize as valuable assets upon the favorable outcome of certain events. In the absence of a legal right to the properties at this time, these can be viewed only as contingent assets. Contingent assets may be reported by a special note or by appropriate comment under a separate contingent assets heading after other asset classifications. Tax claims, insurance claims, and claims against merchandise creditors may warrant such treatment. Reference to contingent assets is rare in practice.

*Long-term debt.* Long-term notes, bonds, mortgages, and similar obligations that will not require current funds for their retirement are generally reported under the Long-Term Debt heading on the balance sheet.

When an amount borrowed is not the same as the amount ultimately required in settlement of the debt and the debt is stated in the accounts at its maturity value, the debt discount or premium should be subtracted from or added to the amount of the debt. In practice, however, debt discount is frequently reported as a long-term asset and debt premium as a long-term debt item or as deferred revenue. When a note, a bond issue, or a mortgage formerly classified as a long-term obligation becomes payable within a year, it should be reclassified and presented as a current liability.

Frequently the term *fixed liabilities* is used to refer to the long-term obligations.

*Deferred revenues.* Cash may be received or other assets recognized for goods and services that are to be supplied in future periods. Such transactions are recognized in the accounts by charges to assets and credits to accounts reporting the advance payments. The latter balances are properly carried forward until the company meets its responsibilities through the delivery of goods or the performance of services. If, in subsequent periods, the costs of providing the goods and services are less than the obligations that are discharged thereby, a profit will be recognized; on the other hand, if costs are greater than the obligations that are discharged, it will be necessary to recognize a loss. Examples of transactions that call for revenue deferral and recognition as long-term obligations include leasehold and rental prepayments, interest prepayments, and fees received in advance on long-term service contracts. These prepayments are normally reported on the balance sheet under the heading of Deferred Revenues or Deferred Credits.

The deferred revenues heading is considered objectionable by some accountants on the grounds that it fails to suggest the liability character of the items that are listed thereunder. The use of an Advances by Customers heading might well clarify the nature of the items that are listed.

All prepayments for goods and services are frequently reported under the deferred revenues heading, including those calling for settlement in the near future. However, the noncurrent classification is appropriate only when an item represents no significant claim upon current assets. When significant costs are involved in satisfying a claim and these costs will be met from the company's current assets, the prepayment should be recognized as a current liability. Magazine subscriptions received in advance, for example, are properly recognized as a current liability in view of the claim that they make upon current assets.

*Other liabilities.* Certain noncurrent liabilities that cannot be reported satisfactorily under the long-term debt or deferred revenue headings are listed under special descriptive headings or under the general heading Other Liabilities. Such liabilities include obligations to customers in the form of long-term refundable deposits, long-term obligations to company officers or affiliated companies, matured but unclaimed bond principal and interest obligations, and amounts payable under pension plans.

*Contingent liabilities.* Past activities or circumstances may have given rise to possible future liabilities, although legal obligations do not exist on the date of the balance sheet. Such possible claims are known as contingent liabilities and are normally reported by a note or appropriate comment under a separate contingent liability heading. Possible obligations resulting from the discounting of customers' notes, accommodation endorsements on obligations of other parties, pending lawsuits, and taxes and other charges in dispute are examples of items frequently reported as contingent liabilities.

Careful distinction should be made between the contingent liabilities just described and liabilities that exist but that cannot be definitely measured in amount on the balance sheet date. For example, an income tax liability may have accrued although the exact amount of the obligation is not yet determinable; or payments may have to be made ultimately to employees under retirement plans although the costs of such plans cannot be finally determined. These claims must be arrived at by estimate but they cannot be ignored in setting forth the financial condition. The estimated liability for income taxes is payable currently and hence is properly reported under the current heading; the estimated liability for pensions is not payable currently and hence is reported under a non-current heading.

## Capital

In the case of a sole proprietorship, the owner's interest in assets is reported by means of a single capital account. The balance in this account is the cumulative result of the owner's investments and withdrawals as well as past profits and losses. In the partnership, capital accounts are established for each partner. Capital account balances summarize the investments and withdrawals and shares of past profits and losses of each partner and thus measure the partners' individual equities in the partnership assets.

In the corporation, the difference between assets and liabilities is referred to as the *stockholders' equity* or simply as *capital*. In presenting the stockholders' equity on the balance sheet, a distinction is made between capital originating from the stockholders' investment, referred to as *paid-in capital*, and the capital originating from earnings, referred to as *retained earnings*. In certain instances the stockholders' equity includes *appraisal capital* resulting from asset revaluation. Frequently the term *surplus* is applied to all corporate capital balances other than capital stock. Thus, paid-in capital other than that portion representing capital stock is designated *paid-in surplus* or *capital surplus*, retained earnings is designated *earned surplus*, and appraisal capital is designated *appraisal surplus*.

*Paid-in capital.* Paid-in capital is generally reported in two parts: (1) *Capital stock* representing that portion of the contribution by stockholders that is assignable to the shares of stock issued; (2) *additional paid-in capital* representing investments by shareholders in excess of the amounts assignable to capital stock as well as invested capital from other sources.

Capital stock outstanding, if it has a par value, is shown on the balance sheet at par. If it has no par value, it is stated at the amount received on its original sale or at some other value as set by law or as assigned by action of the board of directors of the corporation. When more than a single class of stock has been issued and is outstanding, the stock of each class is reported separately. *Treasury stock*, which is stock issued but subsequently reacquired by the corporation, is subtracted from the total stock issued or from the sum of the capital balances. The capital stock balance is viewed as the *legal capital* or *permanent capital* of the corporation.

A premium received on the sale of par-value stock or the amount received in excess of the value assigned to no-par stock is included as a part of paid-in capital. Capital arising from transactions other than the sale of stock, such as capital from the donation of property or from the sale of treasury stock at amounts in excess of cost, is also recognized as a part of the paid-in capital. Capital stock and other paid-in capital balances are normally totaled so that the full amount of the paid-in capital may be indicated. When stock is sold at less than par, capital stock is shown at par and the discount is reported as a subtraction item in arriving at paid-in capital.

*Retained earnings.* The amount of undistributed earnings of past periods is reported as retained earnings. An excess of dividends and losses over profits results in a negative retained earnings balance called a *deficit*. The balance of retained earnings is added to the paid-in capital total in summarizing the stockholders' equity; a deficit is subtracted from paid-in capital.

Portions of retained earnings are sometimes reported as restricted and unavailable as a basis for dividends. Restricted earnings are designated as *appropriations* or *reserves*. Appropriations are frequently made for such purposes as sinking funds, plant expansion, contingencies, and the reacquisition of capital stock. When appropriations have been made, retained earnings on the balance sheet consist of an amount reported as *Appropriated* and a balance designated as *Unappropriated* or *Free*.

*Appraisal capital.* An increase in asset balances to conform with values established by an independent appraisal of assets is accompanied by an increase in *appraisal capital*. Appraisal capital is added to paid-in capital and retained earnings balances in arriving at the total stockholders' equity.

## Form of the balance sheet

The form of the balance sheet varies in practice. Its form may be influenced by the nature and size of the business, by the character of the business properties, and, in some instances, by requirements set by regulatory bodies. The balance sheet is generally prepared in *account form*, assets being reported on the left-hand side and liabilities and capital on the right-hand side. It may also be prepared in *report form*, with assets, liabilities, and capital balances appearing in vertical arrangement.

The order of asset and liability classifications also varies. For example, where emphasis is placed upon a company's working capital position and liquidity, asset and liability groups, as well as the items within such groups, may be presented in the order of liquidity. This is the usual presentation for the mercantile unit. A balance sheet in account form with financial data reported in the order of liquidity is illustrated on pages 18 and 19.

When readers of a balance sheet are concerned primarily with such factors as total plant and the method of financing such plant, and when a satisfactory condition as to solvency is assumed, as in the case of public utilities for example, the order of presentation may emphasize plant investment and the financing of such investment. Class headings on the balance sheet may be reported in the following order:

| | |
|---|---|
| Plant and equipment | Paid-in capital |
| Intangibles | Retained earnings |
| Investments | Long-term debt |
| Current assets | Other liabilities |
| Other assets | Current liabilities |
| | Deferred revenues |

When the report form is used, liability and capital totals may be added together to form an amount equal to the asset total. In other instances total liabilities are subtracted from total assets, and capital is reported as the difference. A variation of the report form referred to as the *financial position form* has found some favor. This form emphasizes the current position and reports a working capital balance. The financial position form is illustrated at the top of page 20. (Individual assets and liabilities are omitted in the example.)[1]

Related balance sheet items are frequently combined so that the balance sheet may be prepared in condensed form. For example, land, buildings, equipment, and furniture may be reported as a single item; raw materials, goods in process, and finished goods inventories may be combined; and investments may be reported in total. Consolidation of similar items within reasonable limits may actually serve to clarify the business position and data relationships. Supporting detail for individual items, when considered of particular significance or when required by

---

[1] *Accounting Trends and Techniques in Published Annual Reports*, an annual publication issued by the AICPA, summarizes and analyzes the accounting practices that are found in the financial reports released to stockholders each year by 600 industrial companies. Analysis of the reports with fiscal years ending within the calendar year 1962 showed that 71 companies out of the 600 used the financial position form. This was down from the total of 79 companies that used this form in 1959. *Accounting Trends and Techniques in Published Annual Reports, Seventeenth Edition*, 1963 (New York: American Institute of Certified Public Accountants), p. 8.

Anderson
Balance
December

| Assets | | | |
|---|---|---|---|
| Current assets: | | | |
| Cash in bank and on hand...................... | | | $ 45,500 |
| Marketable securities (reported at cost; market value, $71,500)....................................... | | | 70,000 |
| Notes receivable, trade debtors*.................. | | $ 15,000 | |
| Accounts receivable.......................... | | 50,000 | |
| | | $ 65,000 | |
| Less allowance for bad debts.................. | | 5,000 | 60,000 |
| Creditors' accounts with debit balances........... | | | 750 |
| Advances to employees.......................... | | | 1,250 |
| Accrued interest on notes receivable.............. | | | 250 |
| Inventories (at lower of cost or market) ........... | | | 125,000 |
| Prepaid expenses: | | | |
| Supply inventories.......................... | | $ 3,000 | |
| Insurance.................................... | | 4,250 | 7,250 $310,000 |
| Investments: | | | |
| Cash and securities in preferred stock redemption fund | | | $ 22,500 |
| Cash surrender value of officers' life insurance policies. | | | 7,500 30,000 |

| Plant and equipment: | Cost | Allowance for Depreciation | Book Value |
|---|---|---|---|
| Equipment........................ | $100,000 | $ 45,000 | $ 55,000 |
| Buildings......................... | 150,000 | 35,000 | 115,000 |
| Land............................. | 80,000 | | 80,000 |
| | $330,000 | $ 80,000 | 250,000 |

| Intangibles: | | | |
|---|---|---|---|
| Organization costs............................ | | $ 6,500 | |
| Goodwill...................................... | | 18,500 | 25,000 |
| Other assets: | | | |
| Advances to officers........................... | | $ 15,000 | |
| Unamortized bond issue costs.................... | | 5,000 | 20,000 |
| Total assets...................................... | | | $635,000 |

*The Company is contingently liable on customers notes of $25,000 that have been discounted at the bank.

**Account Form**

law, may be supplied by means of special summaries referred to as *supplementary schedules.*

Balance sheet data are frequently presented in comparative form with changes in asset, liability, and capital balances reported in special increase-decrease columns. With comparative reports for two or more dates, information is made available concerning the nature and the trend of financial changes taking place within the periods between balance sheet dates. When a statement is presented in special form, the heading should designate such form, as, for example, "Condensed Balance Sheet," "Comparative Balance Sheet," etc.

Corporation
Sheet
31, 1964

### Liabilities and Stockholders' Equity
#### Liabilities

Current liabilities:

| | | | |
|---|---|---|---|
| Notes payable, trade creditors..................... | | $ 14,250 | |
| Accounts payable............................... | | 19,500 | |
| Dividends payable.............................. | | 5,000 | |
| Advances from customers........................ | | 5,750 | |
| Estimated income taxes payable.................. | | 23,000 | |
| Accrued expenses: | | | |
| Salaries and wages........................... | $ 1,000 | | |
| Taxes...................................... | 1,500 | 2,500 | $ 70,000 |

Long-term debt:

| | |
|---|---|
| 5½% First mortgage bonds due December 31, 1968. | 100,000 |

Deferred revenues:

| | |
|---|---|
| Unearned leasehold income...................... | 15,000 |

Total liabilities................................. 　　　　　　　　$185,000

#### Stockholders' Equity

Paid-in capital:

| | | | |
|---|---|---|---|
| 6% Preferred stock, $10 par, 5,000 shares authorized, issued, and outstanding....................... | $ 50,000 | | |
| Common stock, $5 stated value, 100,000 shares authorized, 40,000 shares issued and outstanding.... | 200,000 | | |
| Paid-in capital from sale of common stock in excess of stated value................................. | 45,000 | $295,000 | |

Retained earnings................................ 　　　　　155,000

Total stockholders' equity......................... 　　　　　　　　450,000

Total liabilities and stockholders' equity............. 　　　　　　　　$635,000

**Balance Sheet**

## Offsets on the balance sheet

A number of balance sheet items are frequently reported at gross amounts that call for the recognition of offset balances in arriving at proper valuations. Such offset balances are found in asset, liability, and capital categories. In the case of assets, for example, an allowance for bad debts is subtracted from the sum of the customers' accounts in reporting the net amount estimated collectible; an allowance for depreciation is subtracted from a related plant and equipment balance in reporting the cost of the asset still assignable to future revenues. In the case of liabilities, bonds reacquired, or *treasury bonds*, are subtracted from bonds

Anderson Corporation
Balance Sheet
December 31, 1964

| | | |
|---|---:|---:|
| Current assets.................................................... | | $310,000 |
| Less current liabilities........................................... | | 70,000 |
| Working capital................................................ | | $240,000 |
| Add: | | |
| Investments................................................... | | 35,000 |
| Plant and equipment............................................ | | 250,000 |
| Intangibles.................................................... | | 25,000 |
| Other assets................................................... | | 15,000 |
| | | $565,000 |
| Deduct: | | |
| Long-term debt......................................... | $100,000 | |
| Deferred revenues....................................... | 15,000 | 115,000 |
| Stockholders' equity — excess of assets over liabilities................... | | $450,000 |
| Stockholders' equity derived from: | | |
| Paid-in capital................................................ | | $295,000 |
| Retained earnings.............................................. | | 155,000 |
| Total equal to excess of assets over liabilities....................... | | $450,000 |

**Financial Position Form of Balance Sheet**

issued in reporting the amount of bonds outstanding; a bond discount is subtracted from the par value of bonds outstanding in reporting the net amount of the debt. In the case of capital, a discount on capital stock is subtracted from the par value of capital stock in reporting paid-in capital; a deficit is subtracted from paid-in capital in reporting the stockholders' equity.

The offsets described above are required in the proper reporting of particular balance sheet items. Offsets are improper, however, if applied to asset and liability balances or to asset and capital balances even when there is some relationship between the items. For example, a company may accumulate cash in a special fund to discharge certain tax liabilities; but as long as control of the cash is retained and the liabilities are still outstanding, the balance sheet must continue to report both the asset and the liabilities. Or a cash fund may have been accumulated for the purpose of redeeming preferred stock outstanding; but until the cash is applied to the reacquisition of the stock, the company must continue to report the asset as well as the capital item. A company may have made advances to certain salesmen while at the same time reporting accrued amounts payable to others; a net figure cannot be justified here, just as a net figure cannot be justified for the offset of trade receivables against trade payables.

## Balance sheet terminology

The accounting profession has engaged in a continuing effort to define the terms used in accounting. It has also directed attention to those terms that have been subject to misinterpretation because of an accounting use that differs from their popular use. Such efforts have been accompanied by a movement to modify terminology where modification might contribute to a better understanding of accounting.

*Net worth and surplus.* As early as 1941 the American Institute of Certified Public Accountants raised the question of more informative designations in reporting corporate capital. The use of "net worth" to designate capital was challenged on the grounds that "a balance sheet does not purport to reflect and could not usefully reflect the value of the enterprise or of equity interests therein." The need for designations that would emphasize *investment* rather than *value* was recognized. The use of the term "surplus" was also found to be objectionable on the grounds that its popular use to indicate "excess," "residue," "that which remains when use or need has been satisfied," was hardly in agreement with its accounting use. As indicated earlier, "surplus" as employed in an accounting sense has been used to suggest investment by owners, as in *paid-in surplus;* accumulated earnings, as in *earned surplus;* and unrealized profits, as in *appraisal surplus.* In order to clarify reporting, the AICPA Committee on Terminology in 1949 and again in 1953 recommended the discontinuance of the term "surplus" in the balance sheet presentation of the stockholders' equity, and the substitution of terms clearly indicating the sources from which capital was derived.[1]

*Reserves.* The use of the term "reserves" and classification problems relating to reserves have been subject to special inquiry and challenge. The term "reserve" is popularly interpreted to mean property that is held or retained for some purpose. For accounting purposes, such property would be referred to as a deposit, a temporary investment, or a sinking fund. The reserve designation, however, has been employed in the following conflicting ways on the balance sheet:

(1) As a valuation account — Reserve for Bad Debts, for example, to reduce a receivable balance to the estimated amount collectible.

(2) As a liability whose amount is uncertain — Reserve for Federal Income Taxes, for example, to indicate the amount of income taxes estimated to be payable.

(3) As an appropriation of retained earnings — Reserve for Bond Retirement Fund, for example, to represent an appropriation of retained earnings corresponding to the assets that have been segregated and that are to be used for bond retirement.

---

[1]See *Accounting Research and Terminology Bulletins,* 1961 (New York: American Institute of Certified Public Accountants), *Accounting Terminology Bulletin No. 1,* pp. 26–28. It may be observed that the American Institute continues to use the term "surplus" in its pronouncements. The Committee on Accounting Procedure states in its preface to *Accounting Research Bulletin No. 43,* "Although the committee has approved the objective of finding a better term than the word *surplus* for use in published financial statements, it has used *surplus* herein as being a technical term well understood among accountants, to whom its pronouncements are primarily directed."

The AICPA Committee on Terminology in 1953 recommended certain limitations in the use of the reserve designation. It pointed out that the term "reserve" is popularly interpreted to mean property that is held or retained for some special purpose. Since the generally accepted meaning of the term "reserve" relates only to appropriations of retained earnings, the Committee recommended that its use be limited to items within this class. The Committee further suggested that asset offsets be referred to by such titles as "less estimated losses on collection" and "less accrued depreciation," and that a liability involving an estimate be reported as "estimated liability" or "liability of estimated amount."[1]

The use of "reserve" as a valuation, a liability, and a capital designation should be discouraged. But even more objectionable is the practice of listing such diverse reserve elements under a common heading "Reserves" usually reported between the liabilities and the capital sections on the balance sheet. This practice results in a distortion of asset, liability, and capital balances, making necessary a full screening of the reserves and their identification with the appropriate balance sheet section in arriving at a summary of assets and related equities. Further, the use of such titles as "Miscellaneous Reserves," "General Reserves," and "Contingency Reserves" within a reserves section frequently makes accurate identification of the reserve item impossible. The American Accounting Association Committee on Concepts and Standards Underlying Corporate Financial Statements has taken a firm stand on this matter, recommending elimination of the "reserves section" on the balance sheet and the presentation of its elements as deduction-from-asset, or liability, or retained earnings amounts.[2]

The term "net worth" is rarely found in modern practice. However, the terms "surplus" and "reserve" are still found, although there is significant movement towards acceptance of the recommendations mentioned.[3] Most of the illustrations in the text employ statement forms and terminology that are recommended by leading accounting authorities. However, alternate forms and terms are used in the text questions, exercises, and problems, since these are still encountered in practice. It must be pointed out that in communicating the business story, move-

---

[1] *Ibid.*, pp. 26–28.

[2] *Accounting and Reporting Standards for Corporate Financial Statements and Preceding Statements and Supplements, Supplementary Statement No. 1*, "Reserves and Retained Income," 1950 (Iowa City: American Accounting Association), p. 19.

[3] In the AICPA list of 600 survey companies, the number using the term "surplus" in reporting paid-in capital ("capital surplus," for example), was 224 in 1962 as compared with 375 in 1948; the number using the term "surplus" in reporting accumulated earnings ("earned surplus," for example) was 150 in 1962 as compared with 501 in 1948. The term "reserve" was used in reporting accumulated depreciation by 100 companies in 1962 as compared with 275 companies in 1950. The term "reserve" was used in reporting the income tax liability by 15 companies in 1962 as compared with 48 companies in 1950. *Accounting Trends and Techniques, Seventeenth Edition*, 1963 (New York: American Institute of Certified Public Accountants), pp. 11–13, 63, 89.

ment towards more readily understood terminology is only one phase of the problem. The person who uses the statement must be educated so that he understands the nature of accounting, the service that it can legitimately perform, the limitations to which it is subject, and the kind of analysis and interpretation that is required under these circumstances.

### The simplified report

Along with the movement towards more descriptive terminology in accounting has come the attempt to improve the manner of presentation of financial data. Parenthetical remarks and notes are frequently employed to explain or to supplement the basic financial data. Careful classification of items under descriptive headings and the presentation of statements in comparative form provide more meaningful reports. Presentations in condensed forms and the elimination of cents, figures being stated to the nearest dollar, clarify relationships and facilitate analysis.

A number of companies have developed simplified reports that attempt to offer basic financial data in a nontechnical and explanatory manner. The development of original forms by different companies is movement away from an objective of the profession, which is to encourage uniformity so that statements may be generally comparable. Further, there is a real question as to whether the simplified reports have received a better response from users or have proved to be any more serviceable than reports prepared in the conventional manner.

A variety of different balance sheet forms are found in practice. Several selected statements are given in the Appendix of this textbook. These should be studied carefully, for they offer suggestions as to the different approaches that may be taken in the development of statements summarizing financial status.

### QUESTIONS

**1.** "From a convenient mechanical device, privately applied to the measurement of the status and results of a business enterprise, it (accounting) has grown into an important medium for the public expression of important facts about our vast and complex commercial and industrial society."

"In America the corporation is the dominant form of enterprise."

Are these two ideas related? Discuss.

**2.** How would you distinguish between accounting "principles" and accounting "methods"?

**3.** (a) What is meant by "the matching process"? (b) What is meant by the "cost principle"?

**4.** Distinguish between general purpose statements and special purpose statements.

**5.** Explain the two positions that have been taken in distinguishing items as current and noncurrent. Which position do you support? Why?

**6.** (a) Give examples of expense prepayments that are properly reported as (1) current items and (2) noncurrent items. What factors govern in the determination of the appropriate classification? (b) Give examples of revenue prepayments properly reported as (1) current items and (2) noncurrent items. What factors govern here?

**7.** Browne Liquidators, Inc. insists on reporting the cash surrender value of life insurance on company officials as a current asset in view of its immediate convertibility into cash. Do you support this treatment?

**8.** What major classifications may be applied to (a) assets, (b) liabilities, and (c) capital items? Indicate the nature of the data that is reported within each classification.

**9.** (a) What objections can be made to the use of the heading, Deferred Charges? (b) What objections can be made to the use of the heading Deferred Credits?

**10.** What two basic sequences may be employed in listing assets, liabilities, and capital on the balance sheet? What factors govern in making a choice between the two?

**11.** (a) Give an example of (1) an asset offset, (2) a liability offset, and (3) a capital offset. (b) When is offset improperly applied?

**12.** Give an example of (a) a contingent asset, (b) a contingent liability, and (c) contingent capital.

**13.** Indicate under what circumstances each of the following can be considered noncurrent: (a) cash, (b) receivables, (c) investments in securities, (d) inventories.

**14.** Under what circumstances would bonded indebtedness due in six months be reported as a noncurrent item?

**15.** Distinguish between the following: (a) contingent liabilities and estimated liabilities, (b) appropriated retained earnings and free retained earnings, (c) capital surplus and appraisal surplus.

**16.** (a) What objections are raised to the use of the terms (1) reserve, (2) net worth, and (3) surplus? (b) What suggestions have been made with respect to these terms in attempts to improve financial reporting?

## EXERCISES

**1.** Indicate the balance sheet classification for each of the following accounts. In the case of doubtful items, indicate what additional information would be required.

(a)  Retained Earnings
(b)  Accrued Vacation Pay
(c)  Cash Sinking Fund for Payment of Bonds Payable
(d)  Supplies Inventory
(e)  Receivables — U. S. Government Contracts
(f)  Investment in Bonds
(g)  Accrued Interest on Investment in Bonds
(h)  Treasury Stock
(i)  Reserve for Unclaimed Payroll Checks
(j)  Allowance for Depreciation
(k)  Accrued Interest on Bonds Payable
(l)  Dividends Payable on Preferred Stock
(m)  Raw Materials Inventory
(n)  Unearned Subscription Income
(o)  Federal Income Taxes Withheld from Employees

**2.** State how each of the following items should be classified:

(a)  Reserve for Patent Amortization
(b)  Reserve for Income Taxes
(c)  Reserve for Depletion
(d)  Reserve for Contingencies
(e)  Reserve for Doubtful Accounts
(f)  Reserve for Pension Payments
(g)  Marketable Securities
(h)  Premium on Sale of Stock
(i)  Unamortized Bond Issue Costs
(j)  Unearned Rental Income
(k)  Deficit
(l)  Advances to Salesmen
(m)  Customers' Accounts with Credit Balances
(n)  Creditors' Accounts with Debit Balances
(o)  Cash Representing Miscellaneous Refundable Deposits
(p)  Prepaid Rental Expense
(q)  Accrued Interest on Notes Receivable
(r)  Subscription Income Received in Advance
(s)  Treasury Stock
(t)  Factory Supplies
(u)  Tools
(v)  Postage Stamps
(w)  Loans to Officers
(x)  Leasehold Improvements
(y)  Patents

**3.** Indicate how each of the following items should be classified on the balance sheet:

(a) Cash surrender value of life insurance.
(b) Sinking fund cash for retirement of bonds.
(c) Bonds payable in six months out of sinking fund cash.
(d) Note receivable that will be collected in 10 annual installments.
(e) Cash deposited with broker on option to buy real estate.
(f) Land held as future plant site.
(g) Warehouse in process of construction.
(h) Cash fund representing customers' deposits on returnable containers.
(i) Cash fund representing sales tax collections.
(j) Advances from customers on orders being produced.

**4.** The bookkeeper for Crocker-Crossett, Inc. submitted the following balance sheet as of June 30, 1964:

Balance Sheet
Crocker-Crossett, Inc.
June 30, 1964

| | | | |
|---|---|---|---|
| Cash.......................... | $15,000 | Accounts Payable — Trade...... | $35,000 |
| Receivables — Trade........... | 30,000 | Capital | 60,000 |
| Inventories.................... | 40,000 | | |
| Goodwill...................... | 10,000 | | |
| | $95,000 | | $95,000 |

Reference to the records of the company indicated the following:

(a) Cash included a check for $450 that was returned by the bank marked "maker unknown"; it is doubtful whether payment will ever be recovered on this check.

(b) State and local taxes of $800 were accrued on June 30. However, $800 had been deposited in a special cash account to be used to pay these and neither cash nor the accrued taxes were reported on the balance sheet.

(c) Goods costing $1,250 were shipped to customers on June 29 and 30, at a sales price of $2,400. Goods shipped were not included in the inventory as of June 30. However, receivables were not recognized for the shipments since invoices were not sent out until July 3.

(d) The corporation had been organized on January 1, 1964, by exchanging 10,000 shares of no par stock with stated value of $10 per share for the net assets of the partnership of Crocker and Crossett.

Prepare a corrected balance sheet for the corporation as of June 30, 1964.

## PROBLEMS

**1-1.** From the account balances given below for the Carter Corporation, as of December 31, 1964, prepare a balance sheet with information properly classified:

| | | | |
|---|---|---|---|
| Accounts Payable | $ 53,000 | Interest Receivable | $ 1,500 |
| Accounts Receivable | 77,500 | Inventories | 142,000 |
| Accrued Interest and Property | | Land | 60,000 |
| Taxes | 3,050 | Land for Future Plant Site | 35,000 |
| Accrued Salaries | 1,400 | Notes Payable | 25,000 |
| Advances to Officers | 10,000 | Notes Receivable | 30,000 |
| Allowance for Bad Accounts | 3,000 | Paid-In Capital from Sale of | |
| Allowance for Depreciation of | | Common Stock in Excess of | |
| Buildings | 36,000 | Stated Value | 110,450 |
| Allowance for Depreciation of | | Preferred Stock, $100 par | 120,000 |
| Equipment | 12,000 | Preferred Stock Redemption | |
| 6% Bonds Payable, due Sept. 1, | | Fund | 40,000 |
| 1973 | 100,000 | Premium on Bonds Payable | 5,000 |
| Buildings | 128,000 | Prepaid Taxes, Insurance, and | |
| Cash | 36,500 | Miscellaneous Services | 2,600 |
| Cash Dividends Payable | 16,000 | Retained Earnings | 68,000 |
| Cash Surrender Value of Life | | Supplies Inventory | 3,500 |
| Insurance | 3,850 | Temporary Investments in Mar- | |
| Common Stock, $25 Stated | | ketable Securities | 24,000 |
| Value | 150,000 | Trademarks | 10,000 |
| Discount on Preferred Stock | 4,500 | Treasury Stock, Common, 1,000 | |
| Dividends Receivable | 1,200 | shares | 25,000 |
| Equipment | 42,000 | Unamortized Developmental | |
| Estimated Income Taxes Pay. | 6,200 | Costs | 5,400 |
| F.I.C.A. Taxes Payable | 300 | Unearned Rental Income | 950 |
| Goodwill | 28,800 | Withholding Taxes Payable | 1,000 |

**1-2.** Prepare a properly classified balance sheet for the Andrews Sales Corp. from the information that follows as of March 31, 1964:

| | | | |
|---|---:|---|---:|
| Accounts Payable | $ 24,150 | Land | $ 50,000 |
| Accounts Receivable | 46,000 | Machinery and Equipment | 65,000 |
| Accrued Interest on Notes Receivable | 300 | Misc. Accrued Expenses | 2,100 |
| | | Misc. Prepaid Expenses | 1,600 |
| Advances from Customers on Contracts in Progress | 9,000 | Misc. Supplies Inventories | 2,600 |
| | | Notes Payable (current) | 15,000 |
| Allowance for Depreciation of Buildings | 50,000 | Notes Payable (due 1969) | 20,000 |
| | | Notes Receivable | 10,500 |
| Allowance for Depreciation of Machinery and Equipment | 21,000 | Patents | 15,000 |
| | | Preferred Stock, $10 par | 100,000 |
| Allowance for Doubtful Notes and Accounts | 1,600 | Premium on Issue of Common Stock | 40,000 |
| Buildings | 100,000 | Raw Materials Inventory | 26,000 |
| Cash in Banks | 18,500 | Retained Earnings (debit balance) | 60,500 |
| Cash on Hand | 500 | | |
| Cash Value of Life Insurance Policies | 4,000 | Salaries and Wages Payable | 1,500 |
| | | 4% Serial Bonds Payable (due March 1, 1965) | 10,000 |
| Common Stock, $10 par | 300,000 | | |
| Dividends Receivable | 150 | 4% Serial Bonds Payable (due in 1966 and thereafter) | 90,000 |
| Estimated Inc. Taxes Payable | 6,000 | | |
| Finished Goods Inventory | 19,500 | Temporary Investments in Marketable Securities | 15,600 |
| Goods in Process Inventory | 30,000 | | |
| Interest Received in Advance | 200 | Tools | 6,000 |
| Investment in Stock of Subsidiary Company | 85,000 | Unamortized Bond Issue Costs | 5,200 |
| | | Withholding Taxes Payable | 1,400 |
| Investment in Undeveloped Properties | 130,000 | | |

**1-3.** The following accounts appear in the ledger of the Kay Stores, Inc. on June 30, 1964:

| | Dr. | Cr. |
|---|---:|---:|
| Accounts payable — trade | | $ 62,500 |
| Accounts receivable — trade | $ 80,000 | |
| Accrued interest | 1,500 | |
| Accrued salaries and wages | | 4,000 |
| Advance to affiliated company | 12,500 | |
| Allowance for customer sales discounts | | 1,600 |
| Allowance for doubtful accounts | | 2,500 |
| Allowance to reduce inventories to lower of cost or market | | 5,200 |
| Cash surrender value of life insurance | 2,800 | |
| Bonds, payable in installments of $15,000 on September 1 of each year | | 135,000 |
| Estimated employee retirement benefits | | 80,000 |
| Estimated income taxes payable | | 28,000 |
| First National Bank — Fund for employee retirement benefits | 45,000 | |
| First National Bank — General account | 21,500 | |
| First National Bank — Payroll account | 14,000 | |
| F.I.C.A. taxes payable | | 800 |
| Income taxes withheld from employee salaries | | 1,500 |
| Inventories | 205,000 | |
| Investment in affiliated company | 140,000 | |
| Marketable securities | 16,500 | |
| Office supplies | 3,500 | |
| Returnable containers | 15,000 | |
| Unamortized organization costs | 20,000 | |
| Unamortized bond issue costs | 6,500 | |
| Unexpired insurance | 2,200 | |
| Unearned leasehold income | | 42,000 |

*Instructions:* Select the current assets and the current liabilities and present these as they would appear on a balance sheet prepared in financial position form.

**1-4.** The bookkeeper for the Squires Corporation prepares the following condensed balance sheet. A review of the account balances disclosed the data listed below.

Balance Sheet
Squires Corporation
December 31, 1964

| | |
|---|---:|
| Current assets................................................. | $91,800 |
| Less current liabilities...................................... | 55,000 |
| Working capital............................................. | $36,800 |
| Add other assets............................................. | 42,800 |
| | $79,600 |
| Deduct other liabilities..................................... | 5,200 |
| Investment in business..................................... | $74,400 |

An analysis of the current asset grouping revealed the following:

| | |
|---|---:|
| Cash......................................................... | $ 8,500 |
| Trade accounts receivable (fully collectible).............. | 21,500 |
| Notes receivable (notes of customer who has been declared bankrupt and is unable to pay anything on his obligations) | 1,500 |
| Marketable securities, at cost (market value, $5,150)........ | 12,200 |
| Inventory.................................................... | 45,300 |
| Cash surrender value of insurance on officers' lives......... | 2,800 |
| Total current assets..................................... | $91,800 |

The inventory account was found to include the cost of supplies of $750, a delivery truck acquired at the end of 1964 at a cost of $3,400, and fixtures at a depreciated value of $15,000. The fixtures had been acquired in 1961 at a cost of $17,500.

The total for other assets was determined as follows:

| | |
|---|---:|
| Land and buildings, at cost of acquisition on July 1, 1962... | $84,000 |
| Less balance due on mortgage, $40,000, and accrued interest on mortgage, $1,200 (mortgage is payable in annual installments of $10,000 on July 1 of each year together with interest for the year at that time at 6%.)................ | 41,200 |
| Total other assets..................................... | $42,800 |

It was estimated that the land, at the time of purchase, was worth $50,000. Buildings as of December 31, 1964 were estimated to have a remaining life of $17\frac{1}{2}$ years.

Current liabilities represented balances that were payable to trade creditors. Other liabilities consisted of withholding, payroll, real estate and other taxes payable to the federal, state, and local governments. However, no recognition was given to accrued salaries, utilities, and other miscellaneous items totaling $920.

The company was originally organized in 1960 when 10,000 shares of no par stock with a stated value of $2.50 per share were issued in exchange for business assets which were recognized on the books at their fair market value of $100,000.

*Instructions:* Prepare a corrected balance sheet in financial position form with the items properly classified.

**1-5.** The balance sheet below is submitted to you for inspection and review. In the course of the review you find the data listed below. Using the balance sheet and the information that follows, prepare a corrected balance sheet with accounts properly classified.

Balance Sheet
Benson Corporation
December 31, 1964

| Assets | | Liabilities and Stockholders' Equity | |
|---|---|---|---|
| Cash............................ | $ 20,500 | Accrued expenses.............. | $ 2,500 |
| Accounts receivable........... | 65,000 | Loan payable.................. | 20,000 |
| Inventories.................... | 80,000 | Accounts payable............. | 65,000 |
| Unexpired insurance........... | 3,500 | Capital stock................. | 100,000 |
| Plant and equipment.......... | 115,000 | Surplus...................... | 96,500 |
| | $284,000 | | $284,000 |

(a) The possibility of bad debts on accounts receivable has not been considered. It is estimated that bad debts will total $2,000.

(b) $15,000 representing the cost of a large-scale newspaper advertising campaign completed in 1964 has been added to the inventories, since it is believed that this campaign will benefit sales of 1965. It is also found that inventories include merchandise of $6,500 received on December 31 that has not yet been recorded as a purchase.

(c) Unexpired insurance consists of $400, the cost of fire insurance for 1965, and $3,100, the cash surrender value on officers' life insurance policies.

(d) The books show that plant and equipment has a cost of $200,000 with depreciation of $85,000 recognized in prior years. However, these balances include fully depreciated equipment of $15,000 that has been scrapped and is no longer on hand.

(e) Accrued expenses of $2,500 represent accrued salaries of $3,500, less noncurrent advances of $1,000 made to company officials.

(f) Loan payable represents a loan from the bank that is payable in regular quarterly installments of $2,000. Interest of $200 is accrued on the loan on December 31 but has not been recorded on the books.

(g) Tax liabilities not shown are estimated at $4,500.

(h) Capital stock consists of 6,000 shares of 4% preferred stock, par $10, and 8,000 shares of common stock, stated value $5 per share.

(i) Capital stock had been issued for a total consideration of $185,000, the amount received in excess of the par and stated values of the stock being reported as surplus.

**1-6.** The bookkeeper for the Franklin Corporation submits the following condensed balance sheet. A review of the account balances reveals the data listed below. Using the balance sheet and the related data, prepare a corrected balance sheet reporting individual asset, liability, and capital balances properly classified.

Balance Sheet
Franklin Corporation
June 30, 1964

| | | | | |
|---|---:|---|---:|
| Current assets.............. | $ 67,500 | Current liabilities............ | $ 30,000 |
| Other assets............... | 95,000 | Other liabilities.............. | 20,000 |
| | | Capital..................... | 112,500 |
| | $162,500 | | $162,500 |

An analysis of current assets discloses the following:

| | |
|---|---:|
| Cash......................................... | $15,000 |
| Marketable securities held as temporary investment...... | 10,000 |
| Franklin Corporation Preferred Stock, 500 shares........ | 5,000 |
| Trade accounts receivable........................... | 20,000 |
| Inventories, including advertising supplies of $500........ | 17,500 |
| | $67,500 |

Other assets include:

| | |
|---|---:|
| Plant and equipment, cost $110,000, depreciated value.... | $ 75,000 |
| Deposit with a supplier for merchandise ordered for August delivery........................................ | 5,500 |
| Goodwill recorded on the books to cancel losses incurred by the company in prior years...................... | 14,500 |
| | $95,000 |

Current liabilities include:

| | |
|---|---:|
| Accrued payrolls.................................... | $ 2,500 |
| Accrued taxes...................................... | 2,000 |
| Trade accounts payable, $27,500, less a $2,000 debit balance reported in the account of a vendor to whom merchandise had been returned after the account had been paid in full. | 25,500 |
| | $30,000 |

Other liabilities include:

| | |
|---|---:|
| 6% mortgage on plant and equipment, payable in semi-annual installments of $2,500 through June 30, 1968.... | $20,000 |

Capital includes:

| | |
|---|---:|
| 5,000 shares of preferred stock, $10 par................. | $50,000 |
| 20,000 shares of common stock at stated value.......... | 62,500 |
| | $112,500 |

Common shares were originally issued at a price of $87,500, but the paid-in capital in excess of the share stated value was applied against losses of the company for past years.

# Chapter 2

# FINANCIAL STATEMENTS
## THE INCOME AND RETAINED EARNINGS STATEMENTS

### Nature of the income statement

The income statement, also variously called the *earnings statement*, the *statement of profit and loss*, and the *statement of operations*, summarizes revenues and expenses for a given period and reports the profit or the loss from operations. The statement thus explains the financial progress of the company and accounts for the changes in the net assets.

The importance of the income measurement function of the income statement cannot be overemphasized. Reference is made to this statement in evaluating the results of business activities. Reference is also made to this statement in arriving at the worth of a business, for it is business earnings that validate asset values. As earnings rise, a higher value is assigned to the source of such earnings; as earnings shrink, the value of the business shrinks accordingly. The income statement, then, assumes broad importance, not only as a report that is used in the analysis of business progress, but also as a complement to the balance sheet in the measurement of business worth.

It has already been suggested that a business commences activities in the attempt to increase its net assets through profitable operations. Generally, as a first step in this process, cash or other assets are given up in the acquisition of goods or services. Costs are thus incurred. Goods and services may now be sold. This means the acquisition of new assets (or reductions in liabilities) and the realization of revenue. With such realization comes a need for recognizing those costs that have expired. Profit or loss emerges from the comparison of revenue and those costs that are related to such revenue. Profit or loss from normal and recurring activities may be accompanied by other gains or losses from the sale or exchange of property items, or from the liquidation of debt.

Revenue is recognized for accounting purposes when a sale of goods is made or when services are performed for customers. In special instances involving long-term contracts, revenue may be recognized in accordance with the degree of progress made towards contract fulfillment. Cost expiration is recognized when an asset is consumed, as in the sale of merchandise and in the payment of rent; when there is a decline in the economic utility represented by an asset, as in the wear and tear of equipment through use or its loss by fire; and when there is the emergence of a liability, as in the case of the accrual of salaries and the issue of product guarantees.

## Nature of the retained earnings statement

In providing a full record of the activities of the period, there should be an explanation for the change in capital as reported on beginning and ending balance sheets. The income statement is the vehicle for the revenue and expense summary. For the sole proprietorship or partnership, the *statement of changes in capital* explains the change in capital, reconciling beginning and ending balances; for the corporation, the *retained earnings statement* serves this purpose. The statement of changes in capital lists the opening capital balances, owners' investments and withdrawals, the result of operations as summarized on the income statement, and any other changes that were reported directly in capital during the period. The retained earnings statement lists the opening retained earnings balance, the result of operations as summarized on the income statement, the distributions of earnings to stockholders, and any other changes that were reported directly in retained earnings during the period. When, in a corporation, there are changes in the paid-in capital as a result of the sale of additional shares, stock dividends, the retirement of shares, etc., a *paid-in capital statement* can be prepared to explain such changes.

## Content of the income statement

The income statement generally consists of a series of sections that develop the net income for the period. Such sections include (1) revenue from the sale of goods (or revenue from the sale of services), (2) cost of goods sold (or expenses of providing services), (3) operating expenses, (4) other revenue and expense items, and (5) income taxes.

(1) *Sales.* Revenue from sales reports the total sales to customers for the period. This total should not include additions to billings for sales and excise taxes that the business is required to collect on behalf of the government. Such billing increases are properly recognized as a current liability. Sales returns and allowances and sales discounts should be subtracted from gross sales in arriving at net sales revenue. When the sales price is increased to cover the cost of freight to the customer and the customer is billed accordingly, freight charges paid by the company should also be subtracted from sales in arriving at net sales. Freight charges that are not absorbed by the buyer are recognized as selling expenses.

(2) *Cost of goods sold.* When merchandise is acquired from outsiders, the cost of goods relating to sales of the period must be determined. Cost

of goods available for sale is first determined. This is the sum of the beginning inventory, purchases, and all other buying, freight, and storage costs relating to the acquisition of goods. A net purchases balance is developed by subtracting purchases returns and allowances and purchases discounts from gross purchases. Cost of goods sold is calculated by subtracting the ending inventory from the cost of goods available for sale.

When the goods are manufactured by the seller, the cost of goods manufactured must first be calculated. Cost of goods manufactured replaces purchases in the summary just described. The determination of cost of goods manufactured begins with the cost of goods in process at the beginning of the period. To this is added the cost of materials put into production, the cost of labor applied to material conversions, and all of the other costs for services and facilities utilized in manufacturing, including factory superintendence, indirect labor, depreciation and other costs relating to factory buildings and equipment, factory supplies used, patent amortization, and factory light, heat, and power. The total thus obtained represents the cost of goods completed and goods still in production. The goods in process inventory at the end of the period is subtracted from this total in arriving at the cost of the goods finished and made available for sale.

(3) *Operating expenses.* Operating expenses may be reported in two categories: (1) selling expenses and (2) general and administrative expenses. Selling expenses include such items as sales salaries and commissions and related payroll taxes, advertising and store displays, store supplies used, depreciation of store furniture and equipment, and delivery expenses. General and administrative expenses include officers' and office salaries and related payroll taxes, office supplies used, depreciation of office furniture and fixtures, telephone, postage, business licenses and fees, legal and accounting services, contributions, and similar items. Charges related to the use of buildings, such as rent, depreciation, taxes, insurance, light, heat, and power, should be allocated in some equitable manner to manufacturing activities and to selling and general and administrative activities. In the case of the trading concern, charges relating to buildings are generally reported in full in the general and administrative category.

(4) *Other revenue and expense items.* Other revenue and expense items include items identified with financial management and other miscellaneous recurring items not related to the central operations. Other revenue includes earnings in the form of interest and dividends, and miscellaneous earnings from rentals, royalties, and service fees. Other expense includes interest expense and other expenses related to the miscel-

laneous revenue items reported. In practice purchases and sales discounts are frequently regarded as financial management items and reported in the other revenue and expense group rather than as reductions in sales and purchases.

(5) *Income taxes.* Earnings of the corporate unit may be subject to federal, state, and local income taxes. Such taxes are generally listed as a separate item in arriving at net income.

## The current operating performance income statement vs. the all-inclusive income statement

There is general agreement that there should be a clear distinction on statements summarizing activities between those charges and credits that are normal and recurring and those that are extraordinary and non-recurring. The latter consist of two classes of items: (1) unusual gains and losses and (2) charges and credits arising from the recognition of errors made in reporting activities of prior periods. There is not full agreement, however, as to how such a distinction should be made. Should the income statement be restricted to a presentation of normally recurring profit and loss items, extraordinary items being presented on the retained earnings statement, or should the income statement summarize both ordinary and extraordinary items? The income statement restricted to normally recurring items, commonly referred to as the *current operating performance* statement, has been supported by the American Institute of Certified Public Accountants. The income statement that includes extraordinary items, commonly referred to as the *all-inclusive* statement, has found strong advocates in both the American Accounting Association and the Securities and Exchange Commission. Because extraordinary items are cleared through profit and loss and retained earnings or earned surplus is freed of such charges or credits, all-inclusive reporting is commonly referred to as the *clean retained earnings* or *clean surplus* approach.

*The current operating performance statement.* The current operating performance statement finds its support in the following arguments:

(1) The income statement should show as clearly as possible what the company was able to earn under normal conditions for the period so that sound comparisons can be made with similar summaries for prior periods as well as with summaries of other companies.

(2) Use of the all-inclusive statement may result in misleading inferences as to the level of sustained earning power, since many persons reading the statement may be unable to eliminate those items that distort operating results. The reader, unfamiliar with the full story behind the items indicated, is less qualified than the accountant to determine what

items should be rejected in measuring the basic earning power of the enterprise.

Those supporting the current operating performance statement would designate the result of normally recurring activities summarized on the income statement as "net income."

*The all-inclusive statement.* Those supporting the all-inclusive statement offer the following arguments in support of their position:

(1) A statement purporting to show operating results for a fiscal period should provide the full story of activities so that annual statements since the start of the enterprise will offer the total income history for the life of the enterprise. Whether gain or loss is the product of one year or of several years, it deserves recognition on the income statement so that the total business and management performance may be evaluated. The all-inclusive statement is simple to prepare, is not subject to variations in judgment as to treatment of special items, is easy to understand and less subject to misunderstandings, and can be accepted with confidence as a complete report of the administration of business properties.

(2) The current operating performance statement carries with it a number of difficulties and dangers:

(a) The reader of financial statements untrained in accounting may be unaware of the fact that an income statement can be prepared in a manner incomplete as to activities of the period, and by failing to analyze the change in retained earnings will not have a full appreciation of current activities as well as the long-run earning capacity of the enterprise.

(b) Permitting the omission of extraordinary items opens the doors to possible manipulation of current earnings by burying significant information in retained earnings.

(c) Use of distortion as a criterion for the omission of items means the adoption of standards for normalizing income rather than measuring income.

(d) Differences in judgment will be found in the treatment of borderline cases.

(e) The presentation of profit and loss data in this form carries with it implications as to future earnings. However, the past is only of limited help in forecasting; furthermore, unusual events are a part of the past and should be considered in arriving at estimates concerning the future.

Those supporting the all-inclusive statement would generally use the net income designation for the final effect of all of the items that are recognized on the income statement.

*Modified all-inclusive form.* Many accountants support the inclusion on the income statement of all extraordinary items except corrections in profits of prior periods. For this group the income statement should be the vehicle for reporting fully on current profit and loss activities but the retained earnings statement should report past accounting failures.

*Combined income and retained earnings statement.* The preparation of a combined income and retained earnings statement has been encouraged as a means of recognizing both normal and extraordinary items on a single report, while still providing for the classification of the extraordinary items as adjustment in retained earnings. Presentation of normal and extraordinary items in the single report offers a current earnings picture plus an appreciation of the modifications of earnings on a long-term basis. Extraordinary items add emphasis to the income report as a tentative installment in the continuing story of financial progress. A disadvantage of the combined statement is that net income is reported within the body of the statement, and special care must be taken to provide clear and descriptive item and total designations. The combined statement has won wide acceptance in recent years.

The authors favor use of the all-inclusive form or the combined form. In employing these, they would designate the result of normal and recurring items as "net income" and would show extraordinary items following the net income summary. These practices are followed in the illustrations in the text.

## Allocation of income taxes between normal and extraordinary items

When both normal and extraordinary items enter into the calculation of the income taxes, an allocation of the taxes should be made between the two classes of items. Both normal activities and extraordinary activities including the income tax consequences related to each of these activities can then be clearly reported.

Satisfactory allocation of income taxes is ordinarily achieved by assigning to net income the taxes that would apply to this balance in the absence of any other items and assigning to extraordinary items the difference between the full amount of the taxes and the amount related to normal income. Normal activities, then, neither enjoy tax benefit nor suffer tax penalty as a result of the extraordinary items; net income after taxes is both a meaningful balance and a balance that is comparable with similar presentations of prior periods. Extraordinary activities, in turn, are summarized together with the tax effects emerging from such activities; the actual effect that these items have upon capital is thus clearly set forth.

When both normal and extraordinary items report positive balances contributing to the total income tax payment, the tax allocation involves a division of the total tax between the separate profit sources. When either normal or extraordinary items report a loss balance, thus serving to reduce the taxes that would otherwise be payable, a tax allocation is still required if the two types of activities are to be satisfactorily presented and evaluated. However, allocation here involves the assignment of a tax charge that is larger than the actual tax payment to the positive or profit balance accompanied by a tax credit counterbalancing the excessive tax charge to the negative balance. Favorable activities of the period, then, carry their normal tax burden; unfavorable activities which served to reduce the taxes that otherwise would have been payable are summarized in terms of their net effect upon capital.

When extraordinary items are reported after normal items on the income statement, the tax allocation affects only sections on the income statement. When extraordinary items are reported on the retained earnings statement, the tax allocation affects both the income statement and the retained earnings statement, taxes related to extraordinary items being reported on the latter statement. In either case, it is desirable to report on the income statement the actual amount of the income taxes for the period together with the adjustment that was made in this amount in effecting the tax allocation. The actual amount of taxes and the increase or decrease in this amount carried to other sections of the income statement or to the retained earnings statement may be indicated parenthetically, or the two amounts may be listed in reporting the taxes assigned to net income.

It should be pointed out that there may be special instances when allocations are not practical. Furthermore, there are some who prefer to report income taxes on the income statement as a single charge without adjustment. When income taxes are reported as a single charge, a note should be provided to point out the nature of the deduction and its implications in the evaluation of net income and extraordinary balances reported on the income and retained earnings statements.

### Form of the income statement

The income statement may be prepared in either *multiple-step* or *single-step* form. Profit and loss data are presented in a multiple-step statement on page 39 and in a single-step statement on page 38. In each case, the presentation is all-inclusive summarizing both normal and extraordinary items. In the multiple-step form, the result of normal activities is first summarized and designated as net income, and this is followed by a listing of the extraordinary items. Profit and loss items are grouped to provide different profit or income measurements as follows:

*Gross profit on sales (or gross margin)* — the difference between sales and costs directly related to such sales.
*Net operating income* — the gross profit on sales less operating expenses.
*Net income before income taxes* — the net operating income and other revenue and expense items.
*Net income* — net income less the income taxes applicable to ordinary and recurring items.
*Net income and extraordinary items* — net income plus extraordinary gains and minus extraordinary losses together with related income taxes.

Many accountants are averse to the use of multiple-step income statements. They point out that the various profit designations have no universal meaning and may prove a source of confusion to the reader. Quoting such designations in the absence of a complete income statement may prove ambiguous or actually misleading. They further maintain that multiple-step presentation implies certain cost priorities and an order for cost recoveries. But there is no such order and there can be no profit unless all costs are recovered. These persons support the single-step form that avoids sectional labeling. The single-step form has won wide adoption in recent years.[1]

Anderson Corporation
Condensed Income Statement
For Year Ended December 31, 1964

| | | |
|---|---:|---:|
| Revenues and extraordinary gains: | | |
| Net sales. . . . . . . . . . . . . . . . . . . . . . . . . . . . | $500,000 | |
| Other revenue — interest and dividends. . . . . . . . . . . . . . . | 8,000 | |
| Extraordinary items — gain on sale of securities. . . . . . . . . . . . | 20,000 | $528,000 |
| | | |
| Expenses and extraordinary losses: | | |
| Cost of goods sold. . . . . . . . . . . . . . . . . . . . . . . . . | $300,000 | |
| Selling expenses. . . . . . . . . . . . . . . . . . . . . . . . . . | 60,000 | |
| General and administrative expenses. . . . . . . . . . . . . . . . . | 95,500 | |
| Other expense — interest. . . . . . . . . . . . . . . . . . . . . . | 7,500 | |
| Extraordinary items — corrections in profits of prior periods — understatement of depreciation. . . . . . . . . . . . . . . . . . . | 7,000 | |
| Income taxes. . . . . . . . . . . . . . . . . . . . . . . . . . . . | 23,000 | 493,000 |
| | | |
| Net income and extraordinary items. . . . . . . . . . . . . . . . . . | | $ 35,000 |

**Single-Step Income Statement**
**(All-inclusive)**

The income statement is frequently prepared in condensed form and simply reports totals for certain classes of items, such as cost of goods sold, selling expenses, general expenses, other revenue and expense, and extraordinary items. This was done in the single-step statement shown above. Additional detail may be provided by means of supporting schedules.

When goods are manufactured by the seller, the cost of goods manufactured must be determined before the cost of goods sold can be measured. If this information is made available with the regular reports, it is generally displayed on a separate schedule because it involves so much

---

[1] In the AICPA list of 600 survey companies, there has been a steady increase in the number of companies using the single-step income statement. The number using the single-step income statement rose from 125 in 1946 to 342 in 1962, while the number using the multiple-step form declined from 468 to 257 during this period. Seven companies failed to provide an income statement in their annual reports in 1946 as compared with one in 1962. It should be observed that some companies offered a variation of the single-step form that included a separate last section setting forth tax items or special nonrecurring items, or both. *Accounting Trends and Techniques, Seventeenth Edition,* 1963 (New York: American Institute of Certified Public Accountants), p. 6.

Anderson Corporation
Income Statement
For Year Ended December 31, 1964

| | | | |
|---|---:|---:|---:|
| Gross sales............................................. | | | $510,000 |
| Less: Sales returns and allowances..................... | | $ 7,500 | |
| Sales discounts............................... | | 2,500 | 10,000 |
| Net sales........................................ | | | $500,000 |
| **Cost of goods sold:** | | | |
| Merchandise inventory, January 1, 1964.............. | | $ 95,000 | |
| Merchandise purchases............................. | $320,000 | | |
| Freight in........................................ | 15,000 | | |
| Delivered cost of purchases........................ | $335,000 | | |
| Less: Purchases returns and allowances....... $1,000 | | | |
| Purchases discounts................. 4,000 | 5,000 | 330,000 | |
| Merchandise available for sale...................... | | $425,000 | |
| Deduct merchandise inventory, December 31, 1964..... | | 125,000 | 300,000 |
| Gross profit on sales................................. | | | $200,000 |
| **Operating expenses:** | | | |
| Selling expenses: | | | |
| Sales salaries.................................... | $ 30,000 | | |
| Advertising...................................... | 15,000 | | |
| Depreciation of selling and delivery equipment....... | 5,000 | | |
| Miscellaneous selling expense..................... | 10,000 | $ 60,000 | |
| General and administrative expenses: | | | |
| Officers and office salaries....................... | $ 48,000 | | |
| Taxes, insurance, etc............................. | 20,000 | | |
| Miscellaneous supplies used...................... | 5,000 | | |
| Depreciation of office furniture and fixtures........ | 5,000 | | |
| Bad debts........................................ | 2,500 | | |
| Miscellaneous general expense.................... | 15,000 | 95,500 | 155,500 |
| Net operating income............................... | | | $ 44,500 |
| **Other revenue and expense items:** | | | |
| Interest income.................................. | $ 3,000 | | |
| Dividend income................................. | 5,000 | $ 8,000 | |
| Interest expense................................. | | 7,500 | 500 |
| Net income before income taxes...................... | | | $ 45,000 |
| Income taxes applicable to net income (total tax provision, $23,000, less $5,000 applicable to gain on sale of securities, reported below)................................... | | | 18,000 |
| Net income........................................ | | | $ 27,000 |
| **Extraordinary items:** | | | |
| Gain on sale of securities........................... | $ 20,000 | | |
| Less income taxes applicable to gain................ | 5,000 | $ 15,000 | |
| Corrections in profits of prior periods — understatement of depreciation.................................... | | 7,000 | 8,000 |
| Net income and extraordinary items.................... | | | $ 35,000 |

**Multiple-Step Income Statement**
**(All-inclusive)**

detail. Assuming that the goods available for sale were obtained by manufacture rather than by purchase as in the example on page 39, the cost of goods sold section of the income statement and the supporting schedule would be prepared as shown below.

Cost of goods sold:

| | | |
|---|---:|---:|
| Finished goods inventory, January 1, 1964.................... | $ 40,000 | |
| Add cost of goods manufactured per manufacturing schedule...... | 310,000 | |
| Merchandise available for sale............................... | $350,000 | |
| Deduct finished goods inventory, December 31, 1964........... | 50,000 | |
| Cost of goods sold........................................ | | $300,000 |

**Cost of Goods Sold Section of Income Statement for a Manufacturing Business**

Anderson Corporation
Manufacturing Schedule
To Accompany Income Statement
For Year Ended December 31, 1964

| | | | |
|---|---:|---:|---:|
| Goods in process inventory, January 1, 1964........... | | | $ 25,000 |
| Raw materials: | | | |
| Inventory, January 1, 1964....................... | | $ 30,000 | |
| Purchases....................................... | $105,000 | | |
| Freight in....................................... | 10,000 | | |
| Delivered cost of raw materials.................... | $115,000 | | |
| Less: Purchases returns and allowances....... $1,000 | | | |
| Purchases discounts.................. 4,000 | 5,000 | 110,000 | |
| Total cost of raw materials available for use........... | | $140,000 | |
| Deduct inventory, December 31, 1964............... | | 40,000 | 100,000 |
| Direct labor........................................ | | | 140,000 |
| Manufacturing overhead: | | | |
| Indirect labor.................................... | | $ 20,000 | |
| Factory superintendence........................... | | 14,500 | |
| Depreciation of factory buildings and equipment....... | | 12,000 | |
| Light, heat, and power............................ | | 10,000 | |
| Factory supplies used............................. | | 8,500 | |
| Miscellaneous factory overhead.................... | | 15,000 | 80,000 |
| Total goods in process during 1964.................... | | | $345,000 |
| Deduct goods in process inventory, December 31, 1964.... | | | 35,000 |
| Cost of goods manufactured......................... | | | $310,000 |

**Manufacturing Schedule**

Frequently, only the cost of goods sold total is reported on the income statement. A supporting cost of goods sold schedule then summarizes the cost of goods manufactured as well as the change in finished goods inventories. Instead of reporting beginning and ending inventories, it is possible to report the inventory variation for the period in arriving at cost of goods sold and cost of goods manufactured; for example, an increase in the finished goods inventory would be subtracted from the cost of goods manufactured in arriving at cost of goods sold; a decrease in the finished goods inventory would be added to the cost of goods manufactured in arriving at cost of goods sold.

## Form of the retained earnings statement

When the income statement reports extraordinary items, including corrections in profits of prior periods, beginning and ending retained earnings balances on the retained earnings statement are reconciled by the change in retained earnings as reported by the income statement, and dividends declared during the period. Such a statement is shown below.

Anderson Corporation
Retained Earnings Statement
For Year Ended December 31, 1964

| | |
|---|---|
| Retained earnings, January 1, 1964.................................... | $140,000 |
| Add net income and extraordinary items per income statement............... | 35,000 |
| | $175,000 |
| Deduct dividends declared.............................................. | 20,000 |
| Retained earnings, December 31, 1964.................................. | $155,000 |

**Retained Earnings Statement to
Accompany "All-Inclusive" Income Statement**

When the income statement is limited to normally recurring items, extraordinary items must be reported on the retained earnings statement. The order of presentation of net income, extraordinary items, corrections in profits of prior periods, and dividends declared varies. In the form below, retained earnings is first corrected for errors in profits of prior periods.

Anderson Corporation
Retained Earnings Statement
For Year Ended December 31, 1964

| | | | |
|---|---|---|---|
| Retained earnings, January 1, 1964............................. | | | $140,000 |
| Corrections in retained earnings applicable to prior periods — understatement of depreciation.................................... | | | 7,000 |
| Corrected balance of retained earnings at beginning of year......... | | | $133,000 |
| Add: Net income per income statement........................ | | $ 27,000 | |
| Gain on sale of securities....................... | $20,000 | | |
| Less income taxes applicable to gain............. | 5,000 | 15,000 | 42,000 |
| | | | $175,000 |
| Deduct dividends declared..................................... | | | 20,000 |
| Retained earnings, December 31, 1964.......................... | | | $155,000 |

**Retained Earnings Statement to
Accompany "Current Operating Performance" Income Statement**

In preparing the combined income and retained earnings statement, profit and loss data are first listed and summarized. The net change in retained earnings for the period is then combined with the retained earnings balance at the beginning of the period. This total is reduced by the dividends declared during the period in arriving at the retained earnings balance at the end of the period. Profit and loss data can be presented in either single-step or multiple-step form. The combined statement listing profit and loss data in multiple-step form can be prepared as follows:

Anderson Corporation
Income and Retained Earnings Statement
For Year Ended December 31, 1964

| | | |
|---|---:|---:|
| Sales revenues: | | |
| Gross sales.................................................... | | $510,000 |
| Less: Sales returns and allowances.............................. | $7,500 | |
| Sales discounts......................................... | 2,500 | 10,000 |
| Net sales ................................................ | | $500,000 |
| | | |
| Net income and extraordinary items......................................... | | $ 35,000 |
| Add retained earnings, January 1, 1964................................. | | 140,000 |
| | | $175,000 |
| Deduct dividends declared................................................ | | 20,000 |
| Retained earnings, December 31, 1964................................. | | $155,000 |

**Combined Income and Retained Earnings Statement**

Dividends in the illustrations in this chapter have been recognized as reductions in retained earnings. Some companies prefer to add a section to the income presentation that reports the disposition of net income. When such a form is employed, dividends declared during the period are subtracted from net income. The difference is designated as the increase or decrease in retained earnings after dividends. Dividends on preferred stock may be listed separately to develop the portion of current earnings related to the common equity. Sometimes bond interest is excluded in arriving at net income and is reported together with dividends as a disposition of income. Such presentation emphasizes management's success in the use of all business resources — resources provided by the creditors as well as the owners.

### The simplified income statement

Some companies depart from the conventional forms of the income statement in the attempt to display profit and loss data in simplified or more popular and readable form. Data may be presented in narrative or graphic form to help the reader grasp significant relationships.

A variety of income statements and retained earnings statements are included in the Appendix of this textbook.

## Basic postulates and principles forming the theoretical structure of accounting

Serious attention has been redirected in recent years to the basic concepts that should form the theoretical structure for accounting activities. Teachers and practitioners as well as committees of the different accounting societies, concerned with conflicting doctrines and diversity in definitions and terminology, have agreed that highest priority should be assigned to the development of a statement of basic concepts that can be accepted as an authoritative guide for all accounting activity. Changing economic conditions, the increasing complexities of business operations, and an ever-widening scope of services undertaken by accountants have intensified the need for such a statement. With the basic propositions clearly stated, objectives of accounting might be clarified, uncertainties as to accounting methods that are appropriate under given circumstances resolved, and greater uniformity in financial accounting achieved.

In attempting to develop the basic concepts, theorists have frequently distinguished between *postulates* and *principles*. Postulates have generally been regarded as those basic assumptions that are required in developing a theoretical structure; principles have been regarded as those general standards that would guide accounting activities.

Certain concepts that are generally recognized as basic in accounting activity have already been described, for example: the time-period assumption — reporting in terms of a clearly defined period of time which is only a segment of the business unit's life; the quantification approach — expression of business activities in terms of quantitative data in comparing business effort with business achievement; the cost principle — the use of cost as a basis for the initial recognition of goods and services. Other basic propositions that are generally regarded as important parts of the basic theoretical structure and are applied in modern practice are described in the remaining pages of this chapter.

### The business entity

The accountant normally views the business enterprise as a specific entity separate and distinct from its owners and any other business unit. It is this entity and its activities that assume the focus of his attention. This unit owns resources contributed by creditors and its owners, whether sole proprietor, partners, or stockholders. It has as its objective to make a profit, and periodic reports are means of bringing to the attention of the ownership the progress that has been made in this objective. Such reports are limited to the effects of all of the business transactions upon the assets and equities of the entity.

### Objective, verifiable evidence

Accounting seeks to present its findings on a foundation of facts determined objectively and subject to verification. Cash receipts and disbursements can be adequately supported by vouchers, and cash on hand is determined by count; full support and verification for this element and its changes are available. Findings here can be fully objective. Purchases of goods and services as well as sales are also generally well supported by evidence and subject to verification. There are a number of areas in accounting, however, where determinations must be based in part upon judgment, estimate, and other subjective factors. The recognition of depreciation is an example of the latter. But the degree of estimate can be minimized by the attempt to develop evidence that will lend objective support to conclusions. Objective determinations are encouraged as means of closing the doors to possible error, bias, or even intentional fraud, and achieving an accounting that can be accepted with confidence.

### The continuity assumption

When the future is unpredictable, one can only assume a continuity of existence and a business environment to follow that is similar to that in which the enterprise finds itself currently. The business unit, thus, is viewed as a "going concern" in the absence of evidence to the contrary. The continuity assumption is support for the preparation of a balance sheet that reports costs that are assignable to future activities rather than realizable values that would attach to properties in the event of voluntary liquidation or forced sale. The continuity assumption calls for the preparation of an income statement that reports only such portions of costs as are allocable to current activities. Obviously, the assumption of a going concern may be invalidated by future experience. Financial statements, then, should be regarded as of a provisional nature, with support for their conclusions still to be found in the events of the future. If business termination were anticipated, a "quitting concern" assumption would be called for; the implications of such change of status would then require recognition.

In applying the assumption of continuity, the intent of management must frequently be recognized in problems of valuation and presentation. For example, if it is the policy of management to trade in automotive equipment at three-year intervals even though such equipment may have a materially longer life, the intent of management governs the allocation of cost. Or if management has taken steps to replace a currently maturing bond issue with a new issue, the maturing issue continues to be reported as a noncurrent obligation since it will make no claim upon current assets.

## The conservative approach

Alternative approaches may frequently be indicated in resolving certain problems relative to the measurement of financial position and progress. When alternatives exist, accountants have generally felt that they can serve business best by adopting a "conservative approach" — choosing the alternative with the least favorable effect upon capital.

The doctrine of conservatism is illustrated in the application of practices such as the following: increases in the values of assets and anticipated gains are normally ignored until realized by means of sale; declines in asset values and anticipated losses, however, are normally recognized. Marketable securities, for example, are normally valued at cost or market, whichever is lower. A market value in excess of cost is ignored or shown only parenthetically, recognition of the gain awaiting realization through sale. A decrease in market, however, although not yet incurred through sale, is recognized. Again, certain expenditures are charged in full against current revenue despite the possibility of future benefits. For example, a large-scale advertising campaign may contribute to future revenues; however, in view of the indeterminate character of the contribution, conservatism would suggest no deferral of the expenditure but rather the recognition of the entire amount as expense.

A conservative approach in the measurement process is desirable. However, the deliberate and arbitrary understatement of asset values or overstatement of liabilities simply to achieve conservatism on the balance sheet is hardly the appropriate application of this concept. There are instances where, as a means of arriving at conservative appraisals of business worth or business debt-paying ability, inventories have been deliberately understated, plant and intangibles have been reported at nominal amounts, and reserves for possible losses and future contingencies have been established and reported among the liabilities. Conservatism expressed in this manner results in financial statements that no longer serve to report a revenue-cost matching process. The understatement of inventories to achieve a conservative working capital position carries with it an understatement of current income; the current understatement of inventories results further in the understatement of cost of goods sold and the overstatement of net income in the next period. The arbitrary reduction of plant items in the interest of a conservative asset position results in the understatement of depreciation charges in future periods and the overstatement of net incomes; balance sheet conservatism here has been accompanied by a contrary effect on subsequent income statements. The recognition of fictitious liabilities to achieve a conservative capital results in the misrepresentation of financial condition until such balances are canceled; further, if payment of expenses in the future is applied against such liability balances, net incomes of these periods will be overstated. Departures from sound measurement procedures to achieve balance sheet conservatism serve to distort net income as well as net asset and capital measurements.

The concept of balance sheet conservatism carries over from an earlier day when the accounting process was considered to be concerned largely with the preparation of a statement of financial condition for creditors and owners. The income statement occupied a supporting role by linking successive balance sheets, income measurement being determined by the values assigned to assets. But with a growing recognition of the importance of earnings both as a progress and a value indicator, the income statement has now become the center of attention. With emphasis upon accuracy in earnings measurement, there has come a regard for the balance sheet as "the connecting link between successive income statements and as the vehicle for the distribution of charges and credits between them."[1] Conservatism is now accepted as a moderating and refining influence to be applied to the matching process as a whole.

### Consistency

In view of variations such as the different procedures for cost allocation in measuring depreciation, the different approaches for pricing inventories in developing cost of goods sold, and the different forms and classifications for the presentation of operating and financial data, methods that are adopted should be consistently employed if there is to be continuity and comparability in the accounting presentations. In analyzing statements one constantly seeks to identify and evaluate the changes and trends within the enterprise. Conclusions concerning financial position and progress may be seriously wrong if, for example, straight-line depreciation is applied against the revenue of one year and reducing-charge depreciation against the revenue of the next year, or if marketable securities are reported under long-term investments in one year and under current assets in the following year. Consistency in the application of accounting procedures is also recognized as a means of insuring integrity in financial reporting; the use of alternate procedures

---

[1] *Accounting Research Bulletin No. 1*, "General Introduction and Rules Formerly Adopted," 1939 (New York: American Institute of Certified Public Accountants), p. 2.

in succeeding periods opens the doors to possible manipulation of net income and asset and equity measurements.

This is not to suggest that methods once adopted should not be changed. A continuing analysis of the business activities as well as changing conditions may suggest changes in accounting methods and presentations that will lead to more informative statements. Such changes should be incorporated in the accounting system and statements. But the financial statements should be accompanied by a clear explanation of the nature of the changes and their effects, where material, so that current reporting can be properly interpreted and related to past reporting. When comparative statements are presented, it is normally desirable either (1) to restate the statement for the periods prior to the change in terms of current reporting so that statements are comparable, or (2) to offer the statements in noncomparable form but with an accompanying note or exhibit indicating the comparable results that would have been obtained if either the old practice or the new practice had been used consistently.

It may further be observed that a company may adopt certain practices and apply these consistently. However, alternative practices offering materially different results may be in common use by other companies. Under these circumstances, special disclosure of the method that is followed and data required in applying alternative practices may well be provided through accompanying notes and exhibits.

**Full disclosure**

One finds constant reference in accounting literature to the concept of *full disclosure*. It has already been suggested that a great many groups rely on accounting statements as their only source of information concerning the financial progress of an enterprise. The accountant, aware of the needs of these groups, can meet his responsibility to them only by making known all of those facts that are required in reaching informed opinions. These facts are not limited to matters of the past and the present, but, under certain circumstances, include matters relating to the future, either anticipated or actually accomplished.

The concept of full disclosure calls not only for disclosure of all financial facts, but also for the presentation of such facts in a manner that will lead to their proper interpretation. Care should be taken in developing data classifications, arrangements, and summaries, and in employing supporting schedules and supplementary exhibits.

It should be pointed out that full disclosure calls for setting forth all matters of a material nature, not simply more detail. Excessive detail, descriptions, and qualifications may only serve to obscure certain significant facts and relationships and thus act as an impairment to the appreciation of the complete financial story. Obviously, the goal of full disclosure will continue to be a product of accounting convention and individual judgment on the part of the accountant.

It may be possible to provide all significant financial information within the body of the financial statements through the use of descriptive account titles and supporting data developed in parenthetical form. Frequently, however, certain matters can better be handled by means of (1) special notes to accompany the statements, or (2) explanations in the auditor's report accompanying the statements. Whenever the data are not included on the face of the statements, the statements should make reference to such supporting material as representing an integral part of financial reporting.

Matters that should be recognized and developed in an appropriate manner on the financial statements include the following:

(1) Methods of arriving at cost and valuation bases for marketable securities and inventories.

(2) Methods of valuation for noncurrent assets, including particulars for any departures from the normal cost and cost allocation procedures.

(3) Material differences between costs reported on the statements and current market values.

(4) Hypothecation, pledge, or mortgage of any asset.

(5) Maturity dates for noncurrent receivables.

(6) Legal aspects of property reported on the statements but not owned.

(7) Long-term leases, including particulars with respect to period covered, annual rentals, rental guarantees, and other significant terms involved in the contracts.

(8) Purchase commitments outstanding involving material amounts and significant market price fluctuation.

(9) Policies and procedures used in consolidating subsidiary companies.

(10) Particulars as to long-term debt, including amounts authorized and outstanding, maturity date or dates for installment obligations, conversion and redemption rights, interest rates, assets securing debt, redemption fund or other requirements, defaults on scheduled redemption fund contributions or principal and interest payments, etc.

(11) Basis for estimating income tax liabilities, including reference to tax audits, tax settlements, taxable years under review by taxing authorities, and the status of any taxes in dispute.

(12) Particulars concerning provisions for retirement, bonus, and separation plans.

(13) Contingent claims, with analysis of the nature of contingencies, sums of money involved, etc.

(14) Particulars as to classes of stock issued including par or no-par features; amounts authorized, reacquired, and outstanding; dividend preferences, redemption and liquidation values on senior issues; dividends in arrears on preferred cumulative stock; conversion features; stock purchase options outstanding; etc.

(15) Particulars as to special limitations on the use of retained earnings as a basis for dividends, including references to legal requirements, contractual agreements with creditor groups, etc.

(16) Effects on income taxes of extraordinary gains and losses, and also the consequences emerging from differences between financial accounting and tax accounting.

(17) Methods of income measurement where income is recognized at some time other than at time of sale and on a basis other than the conventional accrual basis.

(18) Major accounting policies with respect to depreciation, depletion, and amortization procedures.

(19) Departures from consistency in methods of valuation and presentation, including the effects of such changes in the development of comparative statements.

(20) Departures from "generally accepted accounting principles" in the development of the financial summaries.

(21) Contemplated future actions of material significance where supporting evidence is adequate to assume such projects will be consummated, including proposed expansion, financing, reorganization, and liquidation.

(22) Occurrences between the end of the previous period and the date of completion of statements that have a material effect upon the company and are of significance in projecting the financial facts disclosed by the statements into the future. Post-statement disclosures frequently include such items as:

- (a) Financing operations, including long-term debt increase or retirement.
- (b) Changes in the capital structure, including stock issuance, retirement, or conversion.
- (c) Significant changes in the market value of inventories, securities, real property, etc.
- (d) Major property acquisitions or sales.
- (e) Union negotiations and settlements.
- (f) Legal suits filed, appealed, or settled.
- (g) Death, resignation, and appointment of officers and directors.
- (h) Sales, orders, earnings statistics and trends.
- (i) Action taken by the board of directors on major policy.
- (j) Involuntary conversion of property items.
- (k) Significant events that modify inferences that might otherwise be drawn from financial statements.

## Assumption of a stable monetary unit

Business consists of exchange transactions. Accounting requires the preparation of statements that reflect these changes in terms of some unit of measurement. Thus, revenue is expressed as the number of dollars received or the dollar equivalent of the commodities or services received; cost is expressed as the number of dollars paid out or the dollar equivalent of the items given up. Fluctuations in the value of the dollar and differences in purchasing power are ignored; the dollar is assumed to represent a stable unit of value, an acceptable yardstick for financial measurements.

With significant price-level changes in recent years, conventional accounting presentations are being challenged. It is charged that the assembly of dollars of different values on the balance sheet cannot provide a satisfactory statement of position; the matching of dollars of different purchasing power on the income statement cannot provide a satisfactory measurement of income. It is further charged that comparative financial data have lost their validity and usefulness when dollar amounts reflect widely different price levels.

Suggestions have been made by responsible groups who use the product of accounting as well as by accounting authorities that, in view of marked changes in the price level, accountants must now assume a new major responsibility, that of making available statements reflecting dollars adjusted for purchasing power. Such *common-dollar statements* would offer significant data relating to economic position and progress. They would attempt to report the story behind the dollars. Proponents of common-dollar statements recognize that definition of the methods and the procedures for the development of such statements still requires considerable study. They are also aware that the conventional financial statements reflecting historical-dollar reporting are so firmly embedded in law, business relationships, and general understanding that these will continue to represent the basic reports and that common-dollar reports will assume a position as interpretive supplements.

There is little question as to the usefulness of supplementary statements to clarify the effect of changing dollar values upon financial position and operating results. It should be observed that some progress has been made in this direction. Modern corporate reporting frequently includes supplementary explanations pointing out the nature and limitations of conventional reporting together with the modifications that apply to these data in considering the effects of price-level changes.

### Statement limitations

The framework for modern reporting has been suggested in the first two chapters. An appreciation of what accounting seeks to do also affords an understanding of certain difficulties and limitations identified with this process. One must be aware of the judgment, opinion, and estimate involved in the development of financial statements that represent no more than interim reports in the continuing and indeterminate life of the business. Furthermore, in the measurement process the use of different procedures may give rise to different answers, yet each answer can be supported as the product of "generally accepted accounting principles." One must be familiar with the nature of the values presented and with the need for other approaches to value in using statements for certain specialized purposes. The need for comparative statements in evaluating progress and trend should be recognized. One needs to be aware of the shortcomings and the distortions of a varying standard of measurement — the dollar. Finally, it must be recognized that financial statements fail to give the full story. Certain very real assets never appear on the balance sheet — capable management, the demand for a company's services and products, good management-employee relationships, and other valuable intangibles built up through years of operations. And one must look beyond the statements for certain matters that explain operations and affect the financial position both present and future — the business cycle, governmental tax and regulatory policies, changes in demand, etc. An appraisal of business position and progress can be obtained only through the intelligent use of basic reports together with an appreciation of the economic and political environment.

## QUESTIONS

**1.** "There has been a shift from the balance sheet to the income statement as the statement of primary accounting importance." What reasons can you offer for the change in emphasis?

**2.** It has been suggested that the balance sheet is subject to certain "major limitations." It has also been said that the balance sheet is "a statement of non-homogeneous residuals." (a) Give arguments in favor of each of these contentions. (b) In view of these arguments would you suggest that the importance of the balance sheet be discounted in modern accounting?

**3.** How would you define (a) revenue, (b) cost, (c) expense?

**4.** Describe the nature of each of the following: (a) cost of goods manufactured, (b) cost of goods sold, (c) operating expenses, (d) financial management expense, (e) extraordinary losses.

**5.** How would you distinguish between ordinary items and extraordinary items in profit and loss analysis?

**6.** What are the arguments for and against use of: (a) the current operating performance income statement? (b) the all-inclusive income statement?

**7.** What are the advantages and the disadvantages that are found in the use of the combined income and retained earnings statement?

**8.** (a) What objections can be raised to the multiple-step income statement? (b) What objections can be raised to the single-step statement?

**9.** What two positions are taken with respect to reporting income taxes when these accrue as a result of regular activities and extraordinary activities? What position do you favor?

**10.** What procedures are followed when income taxes are to be allocated between net income reported on the income statement and special items reported on the retained earnings statement?

**11.** Distinguish between the proper application of accounting conservatism and the improper application of this concept. Give reasons in support of your conclusions.

**12.** (a) What is meant by accounting consistency? (b) Are changes in method ever permissible? (c) How would you develop and present comparative data where changes in accounting methods had been effected?

**13.** (a) What is meant by the concept of full disclosure? (b) Accounting reports have been criticized as affording insufficient disclosure and as offering too much detail. Are these contentions contradictory? Evaluate.

**14.** (a) Give five significant items relating to past or current financial matters that might be reported in special notes accompanying the financial statements. (b) Give five significant items relating to prospective financial matters that might be reported in the special notes. (c) Give five significant post-statement occurrences that might be reported in the special notes.

**15.** (a) What is meant by common-dollar statements? (b) What advantages are claimed for such reporting? (c) Is such reporting expected to replace conventional procedures?

## EXERCISES

**1.** List each of the following as an asset, expense, or extraordinary item:
  (a) Loss on sale of marketable securities.
  (b) Loss on sale of securities by security dealer.
  (c) Write-off of goodwill and patents in the interest of conservatism.
  (d) Installation costs for new machinery.
  (e) Payments representing organization costs.
  (f) Costs of rehabilitating plant just purchased.
  (g) Cost of grading land for construction.
  (h) Additional federal income tax assessment for prior years.
  (i) Landscaping costs upon completion of new building.
  (j) Charges on suits arising from breach of contract.
  (k) Purchase and retirement of bonds outstanding at an amount in excess of their book value.
  (l) Contributions to Community Chest.
  (m) Loss from flood.
  (n) Loss on sale of shopworn merchandise.

**2.** Indicate which of the following items involves the realization of revenue or gain and give the reasons for your answer.
  (a) Land acquired in 1946 at $15,000 is now conservatively appraised at $40,000.
  (b) Stock acquired as an investment at $40 per share now has a market value of $52.

(c) Timberlands show a growth in timber valued at $40,000 for the year.

(d) An addition to a building was self-constructed at a cost of $3,600 after two offers from private contractors for the work at $4,650 and $5,000.

(e) Certain valuable franchise rights were received from a city for payment of annual licensing fees.

(f) A customer owing $4,600, which was delinquent for one year, gave securities valued at $5,000 in settlement of his obligation.

(g) Merchandise, cost $1,000, is sold for $1,600 with a 50% down payment on a conditional sales contract, title to the merchandise being retained by the seller until the full contract price is collected.

(h) Cash is received on the sale of gift certificates redeemable in merchandise in the following period.

**3.** Changes in account balances for the Sloan Sales Co. during 1964 were as follows:

| | | | |
|---|---|---|---|
| Cash.................. | +$ 25,000 | Accounts payable........ | −$ 15,000 |
| Accounts receivable..... | −$ 5,000 | Bonds payable.......... | +$100,000 |
| Mdse. inventory........ | +$ 60,000 | Capital stock........... | +$ 50,000 |
| Plant and equipment (net) | +$120,000 | Additional paid-in capital. | +$ 5,000 |

Dividends paid during 1964 were $20,000. Calculate the net income for the year.

**4.** Calculate the retained earnings balance on December 31, 1964, from the following data:

| | |
|---|---|
| Balance of retained earnings, January 1, 1964...................... | $140,000 |
| Dividends declared, 1964........................................ | 60,000 |
| Net income for 1964........................................... | 102,500 |
| Uninsured fire loss (net of income tax credit)....................... | 45,000 |
| Gain on sale of marketable securities (net of income tax charge)....... | 12,500 |
| Write-off of goodwill........................................... | 10,000 |
| Sale of common stock, par $100,000, at premium of $20,000 .......... | 120,000 |
| Receipt of income tax refund.................................... | 14,000 |
| Discovery of errors in prior years' net income: | |
| Charges to purchases instead of to plant and equipment in 1962–1963.. | 4,500 |
| Understatement of depreciation 1960–1963....................... | 12,000 |
| Sales of 1962 reported as sales of 1963.......................... | 8,000 |

**5.** E and E, Inc. shows a retained earnings balance on January 1, 1964, of $160,000. For 1964, the net income before income taxes was $40,000. The following extraordinary gains and losses were also recognized during the year:

| | |
|---|---|
| Gain on sale of long-term investments............................. | $14,000 |
| Refund of tax payments by federal government...................... | 6,000 |
| Understatement of depreciation charges of prior years................ | 10,000 |
| Understatement of accrued expenses at end of 1963.................. | 2,000 |

Income taxes for 1964 were $15,800, of which $3,500 accrued as a result of the gain on the sale of investments. Dividends of $16,000 were declared by the company during the year.

Assuming that the income statement shows extraordinary items and that income taxes are allocated between normal income and extraordinary items, complete the lower section of the income statement, beginning with the item "Net income before income taxes," and prepare an accompanying retained earnings statement.

**6.** Using the data in Exercise 5, prepare a retained earnings statement for E and E, Inc., assuming that extraordinary items are reported on this statement, only normal operations being reported on the income statement.

**7.** The selling expenses of F and M, Inc. for 1964 are 10% of sales. General expenses, excluding bad debts, are 25% of cost of sales but only 15% of sales. Bad debts are 2% of sales. The beginning merchandise inventory was $62,000 and it decreased 25% during the year. Net income for the year before income taxes of 40% is $52,000. Prepare an income statement, giving supporting computations.

## PROBLEMS

**2-1.** The following data were taken from the ledger of the Robinson Co. at the end of 1964:

| | | | |
|---|---|---|---|
| Retained earnings, January 1.... | $ 16,250 | Dividends received............. | $ 1,200 |
| Sales......................... | 210,500 | Selling and general expenses..... | 22,000 |
| Purchases.................... | 160,000 | Federal and state income taxes, | |
| Increase in inventory, 1964...... | 12,000 | 1964....................... | 12,600 |
| Purchases discounts............ | 3,000 | Additional federal income taxes | |
| Sales discounts................ | 3,600 | assessed for prior years........ | 4,400 |
| Dividends declared............. | 40,000 | Corrections in profits of prior | |
| Interest expense............... | 500 | years — additions to plant reported as repairs............. | 15,000 |

*Instructions:* Prepare a multiple-step income statement in all-inclusive form accompanied by a retained earnings statement.

**2-2.** The Coldwell Co. on July 1, 1963, reported a retained earnings balance of $818,500. The books of the company showed the following account balances on June 30, 1964:

| | |
|---|---|
| Sales........................................................ | $1,220,000 |
| Inventory: July 1, 1963....................................... | 80,000 |
| June 30, 1964....................................... | 82,500 |
| Sales returns and allowances.................................... | 15,000 |
| Purchases.................................................... | 850,000 |
| Discounts on purchases........................................ | 12,000 |
| Gain on sale of securities....................................... | 40,000 |
| Dividends declared on common stock............................. | 65,000 |
| Selling and general expenses..................................... | 140,000 |
| Income taxes: Applicable to net income........................... | 95,000 |
| Applicable to gain on sale of securities.............. | 10,000 |
| Collection of income tax refund for prior years.................... | 26,000 |
| Corrections in profits of prior years — understatement of depreciation. | 58,500 |

*Instructions:* Prepare a single-step income statement accompanied by a retained earnings statement. (The income statement is to include extraordinary items.)

**2-3.** The following account balances are taken from the books of the Pearson Corp. on December 31, 1964:

| | | | |
|---|---|---|---|
| Corrections in Profits of Prior Years — Understatement of Depreciation | $ 32,000 | Rental Income | $ 4,800 |
| | | Income Taxes — 1964 | 12,000 |
| | | Income Tax Refunds for Prior Years | 20,000 |
| Cost of Goods Sold | 275,000 | Interest Expense | 6,350 |
| Dividend Income | 1,250 | Interest Income | 3,000 |
| Dividends Declared | 25,000 | Sales | 450,500 |
| General and Admin. Exp. | 35,000 | Selling Expenses | 80,000 |

The retained earnings balance on January 1, 1964, was $121,200.

*Instructions:* (1) Assuming that the income statement reports ordinary and extraordinary items including corrections in profits of prior periods, prepare an income statement in multiple-step form and a retained earnings statement for the year ended December 31, 1964.

(2) Assuming that the income statement reports only normally recurring items, prepare a retained earnings statement for the year ended December 31, 1964.

**2-4.** The Torrance Outlet Co. prepares a multiple-step income statement that summarizes normal operations as well as extraordinary items and corrections in profits of prior periods. The statement is supported by (1) a manufacturing schedule, (2) a selling expense schedule, and (3) a general and administrative expense schedule. Prepare an income statement with supporting schedules and a retained earnings statement using the data for the year ended April 30, 1964 listed below. Retained earnings on May 1, 1963, were $62,950.

Federal income taxes for the current year were as follows:

| | |
|---|---|
| Applicable to net income | $25,050 |
| Applicable to gains on sale of securities | 2,000 |
| Total taxes | $27,050 |

Inventory balances at the end of the fiscal period as compared with balances at the beginning of the fiscal period were as follows:

| | |
|---|---|
| Finished goods | $7,900 increase |
| Goods in process | 4,500 increase |
| Raw materials | 3,000 decrease |

Other account balances include the following:

| | | | |
|---|---|---|---|
| Advertising | $ 6,500 | Factory Taxes | $ 14,000 |
| Bad Debts Expense | 1,600 | Freight In on Raw Materials | 2,500 |
| Delivery Expense | 12,200 | | |
| Depreciation of Machinery | 5,600 | Gain on Sale of Securities | 8,000 |
| Direct Labor | 76,000 | Indirect Labor | 24,000 |
| Dividend Income | 300 | Interest Expense | 10,200 |
| Dividends Declared | 30,000 | Misc. Factory Costs | 6,000 |
| Factory Heat, Light, Power | 20,100 | Misc. General Expense | 3,200 |
| Factory Maintenance | 2,600 | Misc. Selling Expense | 2,150 |
| Factory Superintendence | 20,000 | Office Salaries | 15,200 |
| Factory Supplies Used | 4,000 | Office Salaries | 12,000 |

| | | | |
|---|---|---|---|
| Office Supplies Used..... | $ 2,200 | Sales Discounts.......... | $ 4,000 |
| Raw Materials Purchases. | 84,000 | Sales Returns and Allow- | |
| Raw Materials Returns... | 2,000 | ances................ | 4,700 |
| Royalty Income......... | 2,700 | Sales Salaries........... | 25,000 |
| Sales................. | 402,000 | | |

**2-5.** The following balances were taken from the books of Marine Supply Corporation on December 31, 1964:

| | | | |
|---|---|---|---|
| Cash Dividends Declared. | $ 45,700 | Merchandise Purchases...$ | 855,500 |
| General and Administra- | | Purchases Discounts...... | 22,350 |
| tive Expenses......... | 211,250 | Pur. Returns and Allow... | 11,150 |
| Interest Income......... | 13,500 | Sales................. | 1,500,000 |
| Interest Expense........ | 21,250 | Sales Discounts.......... | 28,250 |
| Loss on the Retirement of | | Sales Returns and Allow.. | 16,750 |
| Company Bonds....... | 95,500 | Selling Expenses........ | 178,500 |

Income taxes for 1964 amounted to $36,100, however, the income taxes applicable to net income, exclusive of the loss on the retirement of the company bonds, amounted to $85,760.

Merchandise inventory: January 1, 1964................. $210,000
December 31, 1964.............. $150,000
Retained earnings: January 1, 1964.................... $482,000

*Instructions:* Prepare a combined statement of income and retained earnings for the year ended December 31, 1964. (Summarize income in multiple-step form.)

**2-6.** The Washburn Corporation was organized on March 21, 1964, 15,000 shares of no-par stock being issued in exchange for plant and equipment valued at $60,000 and cash of $15,000. Data below summarize activities for the initial fiscal period ending December 31, 1964:

(a) Net income for the period ending December 31, 1964, was $12,000.
(b) Raw materials on hand on December 31 were equal to 25% of raw materials purchased in 1964.
(c) Manufacturing costs in 1964 were distributed as follows:
Materials used...... 50%
Direct labor........ 30%
Manufacturing over-
head............. 20% (includes depreciation of plant, $2,500)
(d) Goods in process remaining in the factory on December 31 were equal to $33\frac{1}{3}$% of the goods finished and transferred to stock.
(e) Finished goods remaining in stock were equal to 25% of the cost of goods sold.
(f) Operating expenses were 30% of sales.
(g) Cost of goods sold was 150% of the operating expenses total.
(h) Ninety per cent of sales were collected in 1964; the balance was considered collectible in 1965.
(i) Seventy-five per cent of the raw materials purchased were paid for; there were no expense accruals or prepayments at the end of the year.

*Instructions:* (1) Prepare a balance sheet, an income statement, and a supporting manufacturing schedule. (Disregard income taxes.)
(2) Prepare a summary of cash receipts and disbursements to support the cash balance reported on the balance sheet.

# Chapter 3

# THE ACCOUNTING PROCESS

## Phases of the accounting process

The first two chapters described the nature, the form, and the content of the financial statements. Attention is now directed to the accounting process that makes possible the preparation of these reports.

The accounting process is composed of two parts: (1) the recording phase and (2) the summarizing phase. During the fiscal period it is necessary to engage in a continuing activity — the recording of transactions in the various books of record. At the end of the fiscal period the recorded data are brought up to date and summarized and the financial reports are prepared. The recording and summarizing activities are described in this chapter. The accounting process as applied to a particular business unit is then illustrated in the next chapter.

## Recording transactions

Accurate statements can be prepared only if transactions have been properly recorded. A transaction is an action that results in a change in the assets, the liabilities, or the proprietorship of a business. There are two general classes of transactions that require accounting recognition: (1) *business transactions*, or transactions entered into with outsiders; and (2) *internal transactions*, or accountable transfers of costs within the business. Among the latter, for example, are the transfers of materials, labor, and manufacturing overhead costs to goods in process and transfers of goods in process to finished goods, in manufacturing activities.

## Bookkeeping systems

The bookkeeping records of a business consist of: (1) the original documents evidencing the transactions, called *business papers* or *vouchers;* (2) the media for classifying and recording the transactions, known as the *books of original entry* or *journals;* and (3) the media for summarizing the effects of transactions upon individual asset, liability, and proprietorship accounts, known as the *ledgers* or *ledger records.* The bookkeeping records of the business are referred to as its *bookkeeping system.* The various recording routines in such a system are developed to meet the special needs of the business unit. Recording processes must be designed to provide information accurately and efficiently, while at the same time, serving as effective controls in preventing mistakes and guarding against dishonesty.

### Business papers

A business paper or voucher is prepared as a first record for each transaction. Such a document offers detailed information concerning the transaction and also fixes responsibility for such information by naming the parties identified with the transaction. The business papers are support for the data that are to be recorded in the books of original entry. Copies of sales invoices or the cash register tapes, for example, are the evidence in support of the sales record; purchases invoices support the purchases or invoice record; debit and credit memorandums support adjustments in debtor and creditor balances; check stubs or duplicate checks provide data concerning cash disbursements; the corporation minutes book supports entries authorized by action of the board of directors; *journal vouchers* prepared and approved by appropriate officers are a source of data for adjustments or corrections that are to be reported in the accounts. Documents underlying each recorded transaction provide a means of verifying the accounting records and thus form a vital part of the information and control system.

### Books of original entry

Transactions are analyzed from the information provided on the business papers. They may then be recorded in chronological order in the appropriate books of original entry. Transactions are analyzed in terms of accounts to be maintained for (1) assets, (2) liabilities, (3) proprietorship, (4) revenue and gains, and (5) expenses and losses. Classes (4) and (5) are temporary proprietorship accounts summarizing profit and loss data for the current period. The analysis is expressed in terms of *debit* and *credit*. Asset, expense, and loss accounts have left-hand or debit balances and are decreased by entries on the right-hand or credit side. Liabilities, proprietorship, revenue, and gain accounts have credit balances and are decreased by entries on the debit side.

Although it would be possible to record every transaction in a single book of original entry, this is rarely done. Whenever a number of transactions of the same character take place, special journals may be designed in which such transactions can be conveniently entered and summarized. Special journals eliminate much of the repetitive work involved in recording routine transactions. In addition, they permit the recording function to be divided among bookkeeping personnel, each individual being responsible for a separate record. Such specialization often results in greater efficiency as well as a higher degree of control.

Some examples of special journals are the *sales journal*, the *purchases journal*, the *cash receipts journal*, the *cash disbursements journal*, the *payroll register*, and the *voucher register*. Regardless of the number and nature of the special journals, there are certain transactions that cannot be recorded in the special journals, and these are recorded in the *general journal*.

Sales on account are recorded in the sales journal. The subsequent collections on account as well as cash sales and other transactions involving the receipt of cash are recorded in the cash receipts journal. Merchandise purchases on account are entered in the purchases journal. Subsequent payments on account as well as all other transactions involving the payment of cash are recorded in the cash disbursements journal or in the *check register*. A *payroll record* may be employed to accumulate payroll information including special payroll withholdings for tax and other purposes; in certain instances, this record may be used as a book of original entry providing the debits to salaries and wages and the credits to accrued payroll and other liability accounts.

Column headings in the various journals specify the accounts to be debited or credited and account titles and explanations may be omitted in recording routine transactions. A "miscellaneous" column is usually provided for transactions that are relatively infrequent and account titles are specially designated in recording such transactions.

The use of special columns facilitates recording and also serves to summarize the effects of a number of transactions upon individual account balances. The subsequent transfer of information from the books of original entry is thus simplified as this process is performed with the aggregates of many transactions rather than with separate data for each transaction. Certain data must be transferred individually — data affecting individual accounts receivable and accounts payable and data reported in the "miscellaneous" columns — but the volume of transcription is substantially reduced.

Transactions that do not occur frequently enough to justify a special journal are recorded in the general journal. The general journal provides debit and credit columns and space for designating account titles and it can be used in recording any transaction. A particular business unit may not need certain special journals, but it must have a general journal.

## Accounts and the ledger

Information as reported on a business paper and analyzed, classified, and summarized in terms of debits and credits in the books of original entry is transferred to accounts in the ledger. Such transfer is referred to as *posting*. The accounts then summarize the full effects of the transactions upon assets, liabilities, and proprietorship and are used as a basis for the preparation of the financial statements.

Accounts are sometimes referred to as *real* (or *permanent*) accounts and *nominal* (or *temporary*) accounts. The balance sheet accounts are referred to as real accounts; the profit and loss accounts are referred to as nominal accounts. If during the course of the accounting period a balance sheet or a profit and loss account balance represents both real and nominal elements, it may be described as a *mixed account*. The store supplies account, for example, is composed of two elements: (1) the store supplies used, and (2) the store supplies still on hand. There is no need to analyze mixed accounts until financial statements are prepared. At this time the real and nominal portions of each mixed account must be determined.

When accounts are set up to record subtractions from related accounts reporting positive balances, such accounts are termed *offset*, *contra*, or *negative accounts*. Allowance for Bad Debts is an offset to Accounts Receivable and is a negative asset account. Treasury Stock is an offset to Capital Stock and is a negative capital account. Sales Returns and Allowances is an offset to Sales and is a negative revenue account. Certain accounts that are related to others and are to be added to them are sometimes referred to as *adjunct accounts*. Examples of these are Freight In that is added to the purchases balance and Premium on Capital Stock that is added to the capital stock balance.

The real and nominal accounts required by a business unit vary depending upon the nature of the business, its properties and activities, the information to be provided on the financial statements, and the controls to be employed in carrying out the accounting functions. The accounts to be maintained by a particular business are usually expressed in the form of a *chart of accounts*. Such a chart lists in systematic form the accounts with identifying numbers or symbols that are to form the framework for summarizing business operations.

It is often desirable to establish separate ledgers for detailed information in support of balance sheet or profit and loss items. The *general ledger* then carries summaries of all of the accounts appearing on the financial statements, while separate *subsidiary ledgers* afford additional detail in support of general ledger balances. For example, a single accounts receivable account is usually carried in the general ledger, and individual customers' accounts are shown in a subsidiary *accounts receivable ledger;* the capital stock account in the general ledger is normally supported by individual stockholders' accounts in a subsidiary *stockholders ledger;* selling and general and administrative expenses may be summarized in a single account in the general ledger, individual expenses being carried in a subsidiary *expense ledger*. The account in the general ledger that summarizes the detailed information reported elsewhere is known as a *controlling account*.

Whenever possible, individual postings to subsidiary accounts are made directly from the business paper evidencing the transaction. This practice saves time and avoids errors that might arise in summarizing and transferring this information. A business paper also provides the basis for the journal entry that authorizes the postings to the controlling account in the general ledger. In many instances business papers themselves are used to represent a book of original entry. When this is done, business papers are assembled and summarized, and the summaries are transferred directly to the appropriate controlling accounts as well as to the other accounts affected in the general ledger. Whatever the procedure may be, if postings to the subsidiary records and to the controlling accounts are made accurately, the sum of the detail in a subsidiary record will agree with the balance in the controlling account. A reconciliation of each subsidiary record with its related controlling account should be made periodically, and any discrepancies investigated and corrected.

The use of subsidiary records results in a number of advantages: (1) the number of accounts in the general ledger is reduced, thus making the general ledger more useful as a basis for preparing reports; (2) errors in the general ledger are minimized because of fewer accounts and fewer postings; (3) the accuracy of the posting to a large number of subsidiary accounts may be tested by comparing the total of the balances of the accounts with the balance of one account in the general ledger; (4) totals relating to various items are readily obtained; (5) specialization of bookkeeping duties and individual bookkeeping responsibilities is made possible; and (6) daily posting is facilitated for accounts that must be kept up to date, such as customer and creditor accounts.

### The voucher system

A relatively large organization ordinarily provides for the control of purchases and cash disbursements through adoption of some form of a *voucher system*. With the use of a voucher system, checks may be drawn only upon a written authorization in the form of a *voucher* approved by some responsible official.

A voucher is prepared, not only in support of each payment that is to be made for goods and services purchased on account, but also for cash purchases, retirement of debt, replenishment of petty cash funds, payrolls, dividends, etc. The voucher identifies the person authorizing the expenditure, explains the nature of the transaction, and names the accounts that are affected by the transaction. Vouchers related to purchases invoices should be compared with receiving reports. Upon verification, the voucher and the related business papers are submitted to the appropriate official for final approval. Upon such approval, the voucher is numbered and recorded in a *voucher register*. The voucher register is a book of original entry. Charges on each voucher are classified and summarized in appropriate columns and the amount to be paid is listed in an Accounts Payable or Vouchers Payable column. After a voucher is entered in the register, it is placed in an unpaid vouchers file together with its supporting papers.

Checks are written in payment of individual vouchers. The checks are recorded in a check register as debits to Accounts Payable or Vouchers Payable and credits to Cash. Charges to the various asset, liability, or expense accounts, having been recognized when the payable was recorded in the voucher register, need not be listed in the payments record. When a check is issued, payment of the voucher is reported in the voucher register by entering the check number and the payment date. Paid vouchers and invoices are removed from the unpaid vouchers file, marked "Paid," and placed in a separate paid vouchers file. The balance of the payable account after the credit for total vouchers issued and the debit for total vouchers paid should be equal to the sum of the unpaid vouchers as reported in the voucher register and as found in the unpaid vouchers file. The voucher register, thus, while representing a book of original entry, also serves as a subsidiary ledger affording the detail in support of the accounts or vouchers payable total, and the need for a ledger reporting the individual payable accounts is eliminated.

### Recording methods: from manual operation to electronic data-processing

As a business grows in size and complexity, the recording process becomes more involved and means are sought for improving efficiency and reducing costs. Some business units may find that a system involving primarily manual operations is adequate in meeting their needs. Others may find that recording requirements can be handled effectively only through the introduction of mechanical devices or elaborate electronic data-processing equipment.

In a manual bookkeeping system all operations are carried on by hand. Original documents — invoices, checks, and other business papers — are written out, and the data they contain are transferred by hand to the journals, the ledgers, and the trial balance. Many small businesses rely solely on manual methods of processing accounting data.

As the volume of record keeping expands, machines may be added to the system. Machines to supplement manual operations often include posting machines, bookkeeping machines, and billing machines. By using special papers, these machines are able to prepare original documents and journal and ledger records at one time, thus saving the work of transferring data. They also can perform a few routine arithmetic operations, such as adding journal columns and computing ledger balances.

Companies requiring great speed and accuracy in processing large amounts of accounting data may utilize an electronic system. The heart of the electronic system is a *computer* that is capable of storing and recalling vast quantities of data, performing many arithmetic functions, and making certain routine decisions based on arithmetic comparisons. The system normally includes various other machines which can "read" data from magnetic tapes or punched cards, and print information in a variety of forms, all under the control of the computer.

The installation of an electronic system normally entails many basic changes in the business papers and the accounting records that are used. Data on original documents must be transferred by *input* preparation equipment to magnetic tapes or punched cards so that the computer can read them at high speeds. For this purpose, the business papers may be encoded with magnetic characters or punch holes which allow the input equipment to process this information directly, reducing the amount of human intervention in the process.

Complete accounting records equivalent to journals, ledgers, and subsidiary files may be maintained on reels of magnetic tape or in the electronic "memory" of the computer. The computer can search through these to recall any needed information almost instantaneously. But in such form these records cannot be read by humans so information must be printed by *output* devices for use outside of the electronic system.

Under the direction of a series of instructions called a *program*, the computer performs the desired operations at electronic speeds. The program may be changed in a short time to make the computer perform different functions. As a result the computer is extremely versatile and may be used in practically every phase of the accounting process.

For example, the computer can prepare the weekly payroll. It may have information stored in its memory concerning hourly wages, accumulated wages for the year to date, tax status, and deductions for each employee. Upon reading the current week's employee hours, the computer calculates all wages and deductions, adjusts the cumulative wage record for each employee, aggregates wages and deductions so that proper ledger balances can be determined, and directs the automatic printer to prepare payroll checks.

The computer system may maintain accounts with customers. It can print invoices, analyze sales data, adjust inventory records, and prepare lists of goods to be reordered. Accounts with creditors may also be maintained by the system. It can check the accuracy of purchases invoices, calculate discounts, print checks for the proper amount when payments are due, and adjust cash and accounts payable records.

Despite their tremendous capabilities, electronic systems cannot replace skilled accountants. In fact, their presence places increased demands on the accountant in directing the operations of the system to assure the use of appropriate procedures. Although all arithmetical operations can be assumed to be done accurately by the computer, the validity of the output data depends upon the adequacy of the instructions that are given it. Unlike a human bookkeeper, a computer cannot think for itself, but must be given explicit instructions in performing each operation. This has certain advantages in that the accountant can be sure that every direction will be carried out precisely. On the other hand, this places a great responsibility on the accountant to anticipate any unusual situations that might require special consideration or judgment. Particular techniques must also be developed for checking and verifying data recorded in electronic form.

The remainder of this chapter is concerned with the summarizing activities which are required in preparing periodic financial statements. The exact manner in which these activities are carried out may vary somewhat, depending upon the degree of mechanization of the particular bookkeeping system. The underlying objectives of these procedures are the same, however, whether the operations are performed manually or with a high-speed computer.

## The periodic summary

The accounting routine at the close of the fiscal period is frequently referred to as the *periodic summary* and normally consists of the following steps:

1. *A trial balance of the accounts in the ledger is taken.* The trial balance offers a summary of the information as classified and summarized in the ledger, as well as a check on the accuracy of recording and posting.
2. *The data required to bring the accounts up to date are compiled.* Before financial statements can be prepared, all of the accountable information that has not been recorded must be determined.
3. *A work sheet is prepared.* By means of the work sheet, data in steps (1) and (2) are summarized and classified.
4. *Financial statements are prepared from the work sheet.* Statements that summarize operations and that show the financial condition are prepared from the information supplied on the work sheet.
5. *Accounts are adjusted and closed.* Accounts in the ledger are brought up to date. Balances in nominal accounts are then closed, and the profit and loss detail is summarized in appropriate summary accounts. The results

of operations as calculated in summary accounts are finally transferred to the appropriate proprietorship account.

6. *A post-closing trial balance is taken.* A trial balance is taken to check the equality of the debits and credits after posting the adjusting and closing entries.

7. *Accounts are reversed.* Accrued and prepaid balances that were established by adjusting entries are returned to the nominal accounts that are to be used in accounting for activities involving these items in the new period.

The last step is not required but is often desirable as a means of facilitating recording and adjusting routines in the succeeding period.

## Adjusting the accounts

The division of the life of a business into periods of arbitrary length creates many important problems for the accountant who must measure the financial progress for a certain period and report on the financial position at the end of this period. Transactions during the period have been recorded in balance sheet and profit and loss accounts. At the end of the period, mixed accounts require adjustment. At this time, too, other financial data not recognized currently must be entered in the accounts in bringing the books up to date. The special problems that arise in bringing the accounts up to date and in summarizing their effects are considered under the following headings:

Asset Depreciation and Cost Amorti-
    zation
Probable Uncollectible Accounts
Accrued Expenses
Accrued Revenues

Prepaid Expenses (expenses paid in
    advance)
Prepaid Revenues (revenues received
    in advance)
Inventories

It should be observed that although the discussion of adjustments is based upon their treatment in the books of account during the adjusting and closing phase of the accounting process, each adjustment would first be recognized in preparing the work sheet.

## Asset depreciation and cost amortization

Charges to operations for the use of plant and equipment items and intangibles must be recorded at the end of the period. In recording asset depreciation or amortization, operations are charged with a portion of the asset cost and the carrying value of the asset is reduced by that amount. A reduction in an asset for depreciation is usually recorded by a credit to a valuation account. Adjustments at the end of a period for depreciation and amortization may be made as follows:

| | | |
|---|---:|---:|
| Depreciation of Machinery................................. | 12,500 | |
|     Allowance for Depreciation of Machinery........ | | 12,500 |
| Amortization of Patents......................... | 1,500 | |
|     Patents......................................... | | 1,500 |

## Probable uncollectible accounts

Provision is ordinarily made for the probable expense that will result from failure to collect receivables. In recognizing the probable expense arising from the policy of granting credit to customers, operations are charged with the estimated expense, and receivables are reduced by means of a valuation account. When there is positive evidence that receivables are uncollectible, receivables are written off against the valuation account. To illustrate the adjustment at the end of the period, assume that receivables of $5,000 are estimated to be uncollectible. An adjustment is made as follows:

| | | |
|---|---|---|
| Bad Debts........................................ | 5,000 | |
| Allowance for Bad Debts...................... | | 5,000 |

## Accrued expenses

During the period, certain expenses may have been incurred although payment is not to be made until a subsequent period. At the end of the period, it is necessary to determine and record the expenses that have not yet been recognized. In recording an accrued expense, an expense account is debited and a liability account is credited.

At the beginning of the new period, the adjustment may be reversed by a charge to the liability and a credit to the expense. The reversing entry makes it possible for the bookkeeper to record the expense payments in the new period in the usual manner, the entry on the credit side of the expense account absorbing that part of the payments recognized as expense in the prior period. If a reversing entry is not made, expense payments will have to be analyzed as to (1) the amount representing payment of an accrued liability, and (2) the amount representing expense of the current period.

*Accounting for accrued expense illustrated.* To illustrate accounting for an accrued expense when (1) reversing entries are made and (2) reversing entries are not made, assume that accrued salaries on December 31 are $350. Payment of salaries for the week ending January 4 is $1,000. Adjustments are made and the books are closed annually on December 31. The entries that may be made are shown on the opposite page.

## Accrued revenues

During the period, certain amounts may have been earned although collection is not to be made until a subsequent period. At the end of the period, it is necessary to determine and record the earnings that have not yet been recognized. In recording accrued revenue, an asset account is debited and a revenue account is credited.

| | (1) Assuming Liability Account Is Reversed | (2) Assuming Liability Account Is Not Reversed |
|---|---|---|
| December 31<br>Adjusting entry to record accrued salaries. | Salaries......... 350<br>   Salaries Payable    350 | Salaries.......... 350<br>   Salaries Payable.    350 |
| December 31<br>Closing entry to transfer expense to the profit and loss account. | Profit and Loss... xxx<br>   Salaries.......    xxx | Profit and Loss.... xxx<br>   Salaries........    xxx |
| January 1<br>Reversing entry to transfer balance to the account that will be charged when payment is made. | Salaries Payable.. 350<br>   Salaries.......    350 | No entry |
| January 4<br>Payment of salaries for week ending January 4. | Salaries...... 1,000<br>   Cash.......    1,000 | Salaries Payable. 350<br>Salaries........ 650<br>   Cash........    1,000 |

At the beginning of the new period, the adjustment may be reversed by a charge to revenue and a credit to the asset. The reversing entry makes it possible for the bookkeeper to record the revenue receipts in the new period in the usual manner, the entry on the debit side of the revenue account absorbing that part of the receipts recognized as revenue in the prior period. If a reversing entry is not made, receipts will have to be analyzed as to (1) the amount representing collection of an accrued asset, and (2) the amount representing revenue of the current period.

*Accounting for accrued revenue illustrated.* To illustrate accounting for accrued revenue when (1) reversing entries are made and (2) reversing entries are not made, assume that on December 31, accrued interest on bonds held as an investment is $100. Adjustments are made and the books are closed annually on December 31. The entries that may be made are shown on the following page.

## Prepaid expenses

During the period, charges may have been recorded on the books for commodities or services that are not to be received or used up currently. At the end of the period it is necessary to determine the portions of such charges that are applicable to subsequent periods and hence require recognition as assets.

The method of adjusting for prepaid expenses depends upon how the expenditures were originally entered in the accounts The charges for the commodities or services may have been recorded as debits to (1) an expense account or (2) an asset account.

*Original debit to an expense account.* If an expense account was originally debited, an asset account is debited for the expense applicable to a future

|  | (1) Assuming Asset Account Is Reversed | (2) Assuming Asset Account is Not Reversed |
|---|---|---|
| December 31<br>Adjusting entry to record accrued interest. | Accrued Interest on Investment in Bonds.......... 100<br>    Interest Income.    100 | Accrued    Interest on Investment in Bonds........... 100<br>    Interest Income.    100 |
| December 31<br>Closing entry to transfer revenue to the profit and loss account. | Interest Income.. xxx<br>    Profit and Loss.    xxx | Interest Income.... xxx<br>    Profit and Loss..    xxx |
| January 1<br>Reversing entry to transfer balance to the account that will be credited when collection is made. | Interest Income.. 100<br>    Accrued Interest on   Investment in Bonds......    100 | No entry |
| May 1<br>Collection of interest for six-month period. | Cash............ 300<br>    Interest Income.    300 | Cash............ 300<br>    Accrued   Interest on Investment in Bonds.........    100<br>    Interest Income.    200 |

period and the expense account is credited. The expense account then remains with a debit balance representing the amount applicable to the current period.

The balance in the asset account is ordinarily returned to the expense account at the beginning of the new period by a reversing entry. This is desirable, since expenditures of the same character will continue to be recorded in the expense account, and the expense account at the end of the next period should show all of the relevant data for determining the adjustment at that time.

*Original debit to an asset account.* If an asset account was originally debited, an expense account is debited for the expense applicable to the current period and the asset account is credited. The asset account remains with a debit balance that shows the amount applicable to future periods. In this instance, no reversing entry is needed since expenditures for the same purpose will continue to be recorded in the asset account.

*Accounting for prepaid expense illustrated.* To illustrate the two methods of accounting, assume that a 3-year insurance policy, dated July 1, is purchased for $900. Adjustments are made and the books are closed annually on December 31. The required entries are shown on the opposite page.

## Prepaid revenues

During the period, cash or other assets may have been received from customers in advance of fulfillment of the company's obligation to deliver goods or services. In recording the transactions, assets are debited

|  | (1) Assuming that the Charge is Made to an Expense Account | (2) Assuming that the Charge is Made to an Asset Account |
|---|---|---|
| July 1<br>Payment of premium | Insurance Expense  900<br>    Cash. . . . . . . . . .    900 | Unexpired<br>Insurance. . . . . . . .  900<br>    Cash. . . . . . . . . .    900 |
| December 31<br>Adjusting entry to record:<br>  (1) unexpired portion.<br>  (2) expired portion. | Unexpired<br>Insurance. . . . . . . .  750<br>    Insurance<br>    Expense. . . . . . .    750 | Insurance Expense.  150<br>    Unexpired<br>    Insurance. . . . . . .    150 |
| December 31<br>Closing entry to transfer expense to the profit and loss account. | Profit and Loss. . .  150<br>    Insurance<br>    Expense. . . . . . .    150 | Profit and Loss. . . .  150<br>    Insurance<br>    Expense. . . . . . . .    150 |
| January 1<br>Reversing entry to transfer balance to the account that will be charged with subsequent expenditures. | Insurance Expense  750<br>    Unexpired<br>    Insurance. . . . . .    750 | No entry |

and accounts reporting such receipts are credited. The latter balances must be analyzed at the end of the period to determine the portions that are applicable to future periods and hence require recognition as liabilities.

The method of adjusting for prepaid revenues depends upon how the receipts were originally entered in the accounts. The receipts may have been recorded as credits to (1) a revenue account or (2) a liability account.

*Original credit to a revenue account.* If a revenue account was originally credited, this account is debited and a liability account is credited for the revenue applicable to a future period. The revenue account remains with a credit balance representing the earnings applicable to the current period.

The balance in the liability account is ordinarily returned to the revenue account at the beginning of the new period by a reversing entry. This is desirable, since receipts of the same character will continue to be recorded in the revenue account, and the revenue account at the end of the next fiscal period should show all of the relevant data for determining the adjustment at that time.

*Original credit to a liability account.* If a liability account was originally credited, this account is debited and a revenue account is credited for the revenue applicable to the current period. The liability account remains with a credit balance that shows the amount applicable to future periods. In this instance, no reversing entry is needed, since receipts of the same character will continue to be recorded in the liability account.

*Accounting for prepaid revenue illustrated.* To illustrate the two methods of accounting, assume that on October 1, $600 is collected representing rents for a period of one year from this date. Adjustments are made and the books are closed annually on December 31. The required entries are as follows:

| | (1) Assuming that the Credit Is Made to a Revenue Account | (2) Assuming that the Credit Is Made to a Liability Account |
|---|---|---|
| October 1<br>Collection of rents. | Cash............ 600<br>   Rental Income .     600 | Cash............ 600<br>   Rents Received<br>   in Advance.....     600 |
| December 31<br>Adjusting entry to record:<br>  (1) unearned portion.<br>  (2) earned portion. | Rental Income... 450<br>   Rents Received<br>   in Advance....     450 | Rents Received in<br>  Advance........ 150<br>   Rental Income..     150 |
| December 31<br>Closing entry to transfer revenue to the profit and loss account. | Rental Income... 150<br>   Profit and Loss.     150 | Rental Income.... 150<br>   Profit and Loss..     150 |
| January 1<br>Reversing entry to transfer balance to the account that will be credited with subsequent receipts. | Rents Received in<br>Advance........ 450<br>   Rental Income.     450 | No entry |

## Inventories

When perpetual or book inventory records are not maintained, physical inventories must be taken at the end of the period to determine the inventory to be reported on the balance sheet and the cost of goods sold amount to be reported on the income statement. When perpetual or book inventories are maintained, the ending inventory and the cost of goods sold balance appear in the ledger and no adjustment is required. The two practices are described for trading and manufacturing concerns in the following paragraphs.

*Physical inventories — the trading enterprise.* In a trading concern, the beginning inventory and the purchases account may be closed into the profit and loss account. The ending inventory is then recorded by a debit to the inventory account and a credit to the profit and loss account. The asset account now reports the inventory balance at the end of the period; the profit and loss account shows the cost of goods sold. To illustrate, assume the following facts: merchandise on hand, January 1, 1964, $95,000; purchases, 1964, $330,000; merchandise on hand, December 31, 1964, $125,000. The entries to close the beginning inventory and to record the ending inventory follow:

| To close the beginning inventory: | Profit and Loss......................... | 95,000 | |
| | Merchandise Inventory................ | | 95,000 |
| To record the ending inventory: | Merchandise Inventory.................. | 125,000 | |
| | Profit and Loss....................... | | 125,000 |

After Purchases has been closed into Profit and Loss, the inventory and profit and loss accounts appear as follows:

**Merchandise Inventory**

| Beginning Inventory | 95,000 | To Profit and Loss | 95,000 |
| Ending Inventory | 125,000 | | |

**Profit and Loss**

| Beginning Inventory | 95,000 | Ending Inventory | 125,000 |
| Purchases | 330,000 | | |

(Balance: Cost of Goods Sold, $300,000)

*Physical inventories — the manufacturing enterprise.* In a manufacturing organization, three inventories are recognized: raw materials, goods in process, and finished goods. If cost of goods manufactured is to be summarized separately, beginning and ending raw materials and goods in process inventories are recorded in a manufacturing account, and beginning and ending finished goods inventories are recorded in the profit and loss account. To illustrate the entries to close beginning inventories and to record ending balances, assume the following data:

Inventories, January 1, 1964: Raw Materials, $30,000; Goods in Process, $25,000; Finished Goods, $40,000.

Charges incurred during 1964: Raw Materials Purchases, $110,000; Direct Labor, $140,000; Manufacturing Overhead, $80,000.

Inventories, December 31, 1964: Raw Materials, $40,000; Goods in Process, $35,000; Finished Goods, $50,000.

The entries to close the beginning inventories and to record the ending inventories follow:

| To close the beginning inventories: | Manufacturing........................... | 30,000 | |
| | Raw Materials Inventory................ | | 30,000 |
| | Manufacturing........................... | 25,000 | |
| | Goods in Process Inventory............. | | 25,000 |
| | Profit and Loss........................... | 40,000 | |
| | Finished Goods Inventory.............. | | 40,000 |
| To record the ending inventories: | Raw Materials Inventory.................. | 40,000 | |
| | Manufacturing......................... | | 40,000 |
| | Goods in Process Inventory............... | 35,000 | |
| | Manufacturing......................... | | 35,000 |
| | Finished Goods Inventory................. | 50,000 | |
| | Profit and Loss........................ | | 50,000 |

After manufacturing costs are closed into the manufacturing account, the balance in this account summarizes the cost of goods manufactured. The cost of goods manufactured is transferred to the profit and loss account and the latter then reports cost of goods sold. Inventory and summary accounts will appear as follows:

### Raw Materials Inventory

| | | | |
|---|---|---|---|
| Beginning Inventory | 30,000 | To Manufacturing | 30,000 |
| Ending Inventory | 40,000 | | |

### Goods in Process Inventory

| | | | |
|---|---|---|---|
| Beginning Inventory | 25,000 | To Manufacturing | 25,000 |
| Ending Inventory | 35,000 | | |

### Finished Goods Inventory

| | | | |
|---|---|---|---|
| Beginning Inventory | 40,000 | To Profit and Loss | 40,000 |
| Ending Inventory | 50,000 | | |

### Manufacturing

| | | | |
|---|---|---|---|
| Beginning Raw Materials Inventory | 30,000 | Ending Raw Materials Inventory | 40,000 |
| Beginning Goods in Process Inventory | 25,000 | Ending Goods in Process Inventory | 35,000 |
| Raw Materials Purchases | 110,000 | Cost of Goods Manufactured to Profit and Loss | 310,000 |
| Direct Labor | 140,000 | | |
| Manufacturing Overhead | 80,000 | | |
| | 385,000 | | 385,000 |

### Profit and Loss

| | | | |
|---|---|---|---|
| Beginning Finished Goods Inventory | 40,000 | Ending Finished Goods Inventory | 50,000 |
| Cost of Goods Manufactured | 310,000 | | |

(Balance: Cost of Goods Sold, $300,000)

*Perpetual inventories — the trading enterprise.* When the perpetual inventory plan is maintained, a separate purchases account is not used. The inventory account is charged whenever goods are acquired. When a sale takes place, two entries are required: (1) the sale is recorded in the usual manner, and (2) the merchandise sold is recorded by a debit to Cost of Goods Sold and a credit to the inventory account. Subsidiary records for inventory items are normally maintained. Detailed increases and decreases in the various inventory items are reported in the subsidiary accounts, and the costs of goods purchased and sold are summarized in the inventory controlling account. At the end of the period, the inventory account reflects the inventory on hand; the cost of goods sold account is closed into Profit and Loss. These accounts appear as follows:

### Merchandise Inventory

| | | | |
|---|---|---|---|
| Beginning Inventory | 95,000 | To Cost of Goods Sold | 300,000 |
| Purchases | 330,000 | | |

(Balance: Ending Inventory, $125,000)

### Cost of Goods Sold

| | | | |
|---|---|---|---|
| Cost of Goods Sold | 300,000 | To Profit and Loss | 300,000 |

### Profit and Loss

| | | | |
|---|---|---|---|
| Cost of Goods Sold | 300,000 | | |

Even if a perpetual inventory system is not used, a closing procedure similar to the foregoing may be preferred. Purchases can be closed into the inventory account. The inventory account would then be reduced to the ending inventory figure and Cost of Goods Sold charged with the inventory decrease. Cost of Goods Sold is then closed into Profit and Loss.

*Perpetual inventories — the manufacturing enterprise.* When perpetual inventories are maintained by a manufacturing enterprise, material purchases are recorded by charges to Raw Materials Inventory. Materials removed from stores for processing are recorded by debits to Goods in Process Inventory and credits to Raw Materials Inventory. Labor and manufacturing overhead costs, likewise, are charged to Goods in Process Inventory. Finished Goods Inventory is debited and Goods in Process Inventory is credited for the cost of goods completed and transferred into the finished goods stock. The entry to record a sale is accompanied by an entry to record the cost of goods sold, Cost of Goods Sold being debited and Finished Goods Inventory credited. At the end of the period, inventory accounts report ending balances; Cost of Goods Sold is closed into Profit and Loss. Normally, raw materials, goods in process, and finished goods inventory accounts are controlling accounts, individual changes in the various inventory items being reported in the respective subsidiary ledgers. Frequently, such procedures are maintained as a part of a system designed to offer detailed information concerning costs. Perpetual inventory accounts, together with the other accounts affected in the closing process, will appear as follows:

Raw Materials Inventory

| | | | |
|---|---|---|---|
| Beginning Inventory | 30,000 | Materials Transferred to Factory | |
| Raw Materials Purchases | 110,000 | to Goods in Process Inventory | 100,000 |

(Balance: Ending Inventory, $40,000)

Goods in Process Inventory

| | | | |
|---|---|---|---|
| Beginning Inventory | 25,000 | Cost of Goods Manufactured to | |
| Materials Transferred to Factory | 100,000 | Finished Goods Inventory | 310,000 |
| Direct Labor | 140,000 | | |
| Manufacturing Overhead | 80,000 | | |

(Balance: Ending Inventory, $35,000)

Finished Goods Inventory

| | | | |
|---|---|---|---|
| Beginning Inventory | 40,000 | To Cost of Goods Sold | 300,000 |
| Cost of Goods Manufactured | 310,000 | | |

(Balance: Ending Inventory, $50,000)

Cost of Goods Sold

| | | | |
|---|---|---|---|
| Cost of Goods Sold | 300,000 | To Profit and Loss | 300,000 |

Profit and Loss

| | | | |
|---|---|---|---|
| Cost of Goods Sold | 300,000 | | |

Even if the perpetual inventory system is not used, a closing procedure similar to the foregoing may be preferred. The raw materials purchases account can be closed into the raw materials inventory account. The inventory account would then be reduced to the ending inventory balance, Goods in Process Inventory being charged with the decrease in raw materials. Direct labor and manufacturing overhead accounts are closed into Goods in Process Inventory. Goods in Process Inventory is then reduced to the ending inventory figure and Finished Goods Inventory is debited. Finished Goods Inventory is finally reduced to its ending balance and a cost of goods sold account is opened and charged for the inventory decrease. Cost of Goods Sold is closed into Profit and Loss.

## Closing the accounts with provision for income taxes

After the accounts have been adjusted and the ending inventories recorded, nominal accounts are closed into the profit and loss account. In a sole proprietorship and partnership, the balance in the profit and loss account is transferred to appropriate capital accounts. In a corporation, provision must be made for income taxes before activities can be summarized and the result of activities transferred to retained earnings.

When nominal accounts include extraordinary gains and losses and income taxes are allocated between normal and extraordinary items, separate nominal accounts may be established to report taxes applicable to net income and taxes applicable to special items. When extraordinary items have been recorded directly in the retained earnings account, taxes related to net income are reported in a nominal account and taxes related to the special items are recorded directly in Retained Earnings. The entries that follow illustrate the allocation of taxes between net income and extraordinary items. Assume that income taxes on a corporation's taxable income are 30% on the first $25,000 and 52% on amounts in excess of $25,000, or stated differently, the rate is 52% less $5,500; however, taxes on gains from the sale of assets qualifying as "long-term capital gains" are limited to 25%.[1] In case (a) a company has a taxable net income of $100,000 and also a gain from the sale of an investment of $50,000 that qualifies as a long-term capital gain. In case (b) a company has a taxable net income of $100,000 and also a loss from fire of $50,000 that is fully deductible for tax purposes.

---

[1] Income tax rates for the corporation that are used in this and succeeding illustrations in the text are based upon federal tax rates in effect for 1963. The Revenue Act of 1964, enacted in February, 1964, makes the following changes in the corporate tax rate schedule:

|  | Taxable income beginning in | |
|---|---|---|
|  | 1964 | 1965 and later |
| On the first $25,000 of taxable income | 22% | 22% |
| On taxable income in excess of $25,000 | 50% | 48% |

Taxes on gains qualifying as long-term capital gains are still limited to 25%.

| Summary of Transactions for Year | Entries to Record Tax Provision Assuming Extraordinary Items are Reported on the Income Statement | Entries to Record Tax Provision Assuming Extraordinary Items are Reported on the Retained Earnings Statement |
|---|---|---|
| (a) Net income........ $100,000<br>Extraordinary gain, qualifying as long-term capital gain.... 50,000<br>——————<br>$150,000<br>========<br><br>Taxes applicable to net income:<br>$100,000 @ 52%, less $5,500............ $ 46,500<br>Taxes on extraordinary gain, $50,000 @ 25%.. 12,500<br><br>Tax liability.... ...... $ 59,000<br>======== | Income Taxes Applicable to Net Income. 46,500<br>Income Taxes Applicable to Extraordinary Gain........ 12,500<br>Estimated Income Taxes Payable... 59,000 | Income Taxes Applicable to Net Income. 46,500<br>Retained Earnings.. 12,500<br>Estimated Income Taxes Payable.... 59,000 |
| (b) Net income........ $100,000<br>Extraordinary loss, fully deductible..... 50,000<br>——————<br>$ 50,000<br>========<br><br>Taxes applicable to net income:<br>$100,000 @ 52%, less $5,500............ $ 46,500<br>Taxes applicable to net income after fire loss:<br>$50,000 @ 52%, less $5,500............ 20,500<br><br>Tax credit related to fire loss............. $ 26,000<br>======== | Income Taxes Applicable to Net Income. 46,500<br>Income Tax Credit Applicable to Extraordinary Loss.. 26,000<br>Estimated Income Taxes Payable.... 20,500 | Income Taxes Applicable to Net Income. 46,500<br>Retained Earnings. 26,000<br>Estimated Income Taxes Payable... 20,500 |

To illustrate the application of the foregoing procedures in the accounts at the end of the period, assume that nominal accounts after adjustment report the following balances:

| Debits | | Credits | |
|---|---|---|---|
| Cost of Goods Sold | $300,000 | Sales | $500,000 |
| Operating Expenses | 155,500 | Other Revenues | 8,000 |
| Other Expenses | 7,500 | Extraordinary Gain | 20,000 |
| Corrections in Profits of Prior Periods | 7,000 | | |

The total income tax liability on the total taxable income of $65,000 ($528,000 less $463,000) is estimated at $23,000. However, assume that the extraordinary gain qualified as a long-term capital gain resulting in a tax limited to 25% of the gain, or $5,000. Estimated Income Taxes Payable is credited for $23,000 and charges are made to Income Taxes Applicable to Net Income, $18,000, and Income Taxes Applicable to Extraordinary Gain, $5,000.

When the tax provision has been recorded, nominal accounts may be closed into Profit and Loss, and Profit and Loss closed into Retained Earnings. These accounts will appear as follows after the accounts are closed:

Profit and Loss

| | | | |
|---|---:|---|---:|
| Cost of Goods Sold | 300,000 | Sales | 500,000 |
| Operating Expenses | 155,500 | Other Revenues | 8,000 |
| Other Expenses | 7,500 | Extraordinary Gain | 20,000 |
| Corrections in Profits of Prior Periods | 7,000 | | |
| Income Taxes Applicable to Net Income | 18,000 | | |
| Income Taxes Applicable to Extraordinary Gain | 5,000 | | |
| Net Income and Extraordinary Items to Retained Earnings | 35,000 | | |
| | 528,000 | | 528,000 |

Estimated Income Taxes Payable

| | | |
|---|---|---:|
| | Estimated Income Taxes | 23,000 |

Retained Earnings

| | | |
|---|---|---:|
| | Net Income and Extraordinary Items | 35,000 |

## Financial reports on cash versus accrual basis

In the preceding pages of this chapter, adjustments were made at the end of the period in an attempt to measure accurately revenues and expenses of the fiscal period. In the case of revenues, amounts *earned* rather than amounts collected, and in the case of expenses, amounts *incurred* rather than amounts *paid*, were recognized and given effect in the measurement of profit and loss. Statements recognizing revenues in the period when earned and expenses in the period when incurred are said to be prepared on the *accrual basis*. For most businesses, satisfactory measurement of operating results can be achieved only through accounting on the accrual basis.

Statements are said to be prepared on a *cash basis* when revenues and expenses are recognized only upon the receipt and the disbursement of cash. In the case of a pure cash basis, revenues from the sale of goods and services are recognized at the time collections from customers are made; expenses are recognized only when payments are made for equipment, goods, services, and other operating items. There is no recognition of bad debts, since revenue is not recognized unless cash is received; there is no recognition of depreciation, since the entire cost of the equipment is recognized as expense at the time of payment.

The federal government permits the filing of income tax returns on the accrual basis or on the cash basis. But the cash basis for tax purposes is actually a combination cash-accrual basis, since it is recognized that the application of a strictly cash approach as described might result in serious distortions in net income measurement. Furthermore, a strictly cash approach would offer a means of shifting significant amounts of revenues and expenses from one year to another by control of cash receipts and disbursements. The following requirements must be observed by a taxpayer reporting on a cash basis:

1. When goods are sold, income from sales must include full recognition of sales on account, and cost of goods sold must include full recognition of purchases on account and also inventories. In the case of trading or manufacturing companies, then, the gross profit on sales is the same on the cash basis and the accrual basis. But professional men or companies selling services may disregard receivables from clients and recognize as revenues only amounts actually collected.
2. When receivables must be recognized, the taxpayer is given the option of recognizing as bad debts expense either (a) those amounts actually written off as uncollectible during the period or (b) amounts anticipated to be uncollectible established through satisfactory valuation procedures.
3. In the case of acquisitions of plant and equipment items and intangibles, deductions are allowed only to the extent of the depreciation or amortization allocable to the current period.
4. The reporting policy that is adopted must be employed consistently each period.

Use of the cash basis, then, generally means the use of a hybrid system, with sales, purchases, depreciation, and bad debts being reported as on the accrual basis, but with remaining revenue and expense items being measured by cash receipts and disbursements. The cash basis offers certain advantages in simpler and more economical bookkeeping. A summary of operations prepared on the cash basis may be acceptable when failure to recognize accruals and prepayments results in relatively minor misstatements that are largely counterbalanced in periodic reporting. But when accruals and prepayments are material in amount and vary significantly from period to period, satisfactory net income measurement would call for adoption of the accrual basis.

### From transactions to statements

Preceding pages have stressed the importance of financial reports in modern economic society. The usual procedures for recording transactions and the sequence of events incident to the preparation of such reports have been briefly reviewed. The treatment applied to these transactions and events is called the *accounting process*.

The accounting process includes the entire field of analyzing, classifying, recording, and summarizing. It includes the successive steps that constitute the bookkeeping or accounting cycle. It starts with the first written record of the transactions of the business unit and concludes with the final summarized financial statements.

The significance of the accounting process and its applicability to every business unit, regardless of size, in our economic society must be appreciated. Although the procedures may be modified to meet special conditions, the process that has been reviewed here is basic in accounting for every business unit.

## QUESTIONS

**1.** What is the accounting function supplied by (a) the business paper? (b) the book of original entry? (c) the ledger?

**2.** Distinguish between: (a) real and nominal accounts, (b) general journal and special journal, (c) general ledger and subsidiary ledger.

**3.** What advantages are provided through the use of (a) special journals, (b) subsidiary ledgers, and (c) the voucher system?

**4.** (a) Describe the nature and the operation of the voucher system. (b) How does the voucher register serve as a combined book of original entry and subsidiary ledger?

**5.** "The computer will ultimately take the place of the accountant." Do you agree?

**6.** List and describe the steps in the periodic summary. State why each step is necessary.

**7.** Explain the nature and the purpose of (a) adjusting entries, (b) closing entries, and (c) reversing entries.

**8.** (a) State a general rule that may be applied in determining when to reverse adjusting entries. (b) Give examples for both accrued revenue and accrued expense items where exceptions to the rule can be supported.

**9.** Payment of insurance in advance may be recorded in either (a) an expense account or (b) an asset account. Which method would you recommend? What periodic entries are required under each method?

**10.** The bookkeeper for the Walls Co. does not reverse accrued and prepaid balances at the beginning of the period. At the end of the period he charges or credits these accounts to bring them to the appropriate balances as of the end of the fiscal period, and the offsetting debits and credits are made to the related revenue and expense accounts. Revenue and expense accounts at the end of the year thus report receipts and disbursements and the adjustments resulting from variations in the accrued and prepaid balances. Evaluate this procedure.

**11.** (a) Distinguish between reporting on a cash basis and reporting on an accrual basis. (b) What are the advantages and disadvantages of reporting on a cash basis?

## EXERCISES

**1.** On February 15, 1964, G. C. Cummings paid insurance for a three-year period beginning March 1. He recorded the payment as follows:

Prepaid Insurance............................. 1,080
Cash........................................      1,080

(a) What adjustment is required on December 31? What reversing entry, if any, would you make? (b) What nominal account could be debited instead of Prepaid Insurance? What adjustment would then be necessary? What reversing entry, if any, would you make?

**2.** Stanley Reed received rent of $1,800 for one year beginning February 1. He recorded the transaction as follows:

Cash......................................... 1,800
Rent Received in Advance......................      1,800

(a) What adjustment is required on December 31? What reversing entry, if any, would you make? (b) What nominal account could have been credited instead of Rent Received in Advance? What adjustment would then be necessary? What reversing entry, if any, would you make?

**3.** In analyzing the accounts of Dick Roberts, the adjusting data listed below are determined on December 31, the end of an annual fiscal period. (a) Give the adjusting entry for each item. (b) What reversing entries would be appropriate? (c) What sources would provide the information for each adjustment?

(1) The unexpired insurance account shows a debit of $450, representing the cost of a 3-year fire insurance policy dated September 1.

(2) On November 1, Rental Income was credited for $600, representing income from a subrental for a 3-month period beginning on that date.

(3) Purchase of advertising materials for $400 during the year was recorded in the advertising expense account. On December 31 advertising materials of $60 are on hand.

(4) On August 1, $750 was paid as rent for a 6-month period beginning on that date. The expense account, Rent, was debited.

(5) Miscellaneous Office Expense was debited for office supplies of $860 purchased during the year. On December 31 office supplies of $280 are on hand.

(6) Interest of $45 is accrued on notes payable.

**4.** Account balances before and after adjustment on December 31 follow. Give the adjustment that was made for each account.

| Account Title | Before Adjustment | | After Adjustment | |
|---|---|---|---|---|
| | Dr. | Cr. | Dr. | Cr. |
| (a) Merchandise Inventory.......... | $35,500 | | $32,000 | |
| (b) Allowance for Bad Debts........ | 1,150 | | | $ 4,000 |
| (c) Allowance for Depreciation...... | | $16,000 | | 18,500 |
| (d) Sales Salaries.................. | 24,200 | | 24,650 | |
| (e) Taxes......................... | 5,600 | | 5,450 | |
| (f) Royalty Income................ | | 8,000 | | 7,500 |
| (g) Interest Income................ | | 550 | | 600 |

**5.** In analyzing the accounts for Charles Cox, Inc., you find the following data. Give any entries that are required to correct and bring the books up to date on December 31, 1964. State which entries may appropriately be reversed at the beginning of the new fiscal period.

(a) The rental income account had been credited for rental receipts of $8,000. On December 31, $400 is unearned. In addition it is found that certain property was rented on November 1, 1964 at $250 per month, but the rent for November and December will not be received until February 1, 1965.

(b) Advertising Expense was debited for $1,500, the cost of advertising materials purchased. There are advertising materials of $200 on hand. In addition, a contract for radio advertising for 1 year beginning December 1, 1964, was made. The rate is $480 for a 3-month period payable at the end of each such period.

(c) It is found that the following adjustments were overlooked in closing the books on December 31, 1963:

(1) Depreciation on store equipment, $250.
(2) Accrued interest on notes payable, $140.
(3) Rentals collected in advance, $275.
(4) Insurance paid in advance, $180 (Miscellaneous Expense was debited for insurance payments).

**6.** Some of the accounts that appear in the ledger of the Mills Manufacturing Co. on November 30, the end of a fiscal year, follow:

| | | | |
|---|---|---|---|
| Raw Materials Inventory... | $ 60,000 | Direct Labor... | $130,000 |
| Goods in Process Inventory.. | 50,000 | Manufacturing Overhead... | 100,000 |
| Finished Goods Inventory... | 70,000 | Sales... | 800,000 |
| Raw Materials Purchases... | 340,000 | Operating Expenses... | 150,000 |

Physical inventories on November 30 are: Raw Materials, $80,000; Goods in Process, $60,000; Finished Goods, $60,000. The federal income tax liability is estimated at $46,500.

Assuming no further adjustments, give the entries required to adjust and close the accounts according to two different methods.

**7.** Accounts for the Bennett Co. show a taxable net income for 1963 of $150,000, a loss from fire that is deductible for income tax purposes of $20,000, and taxable gains from the sales of investments during the year of $45,000. Income taxes for 1963 are calculated at $73,350; in analyzing the tax provision, the company determines that the fire loss resulted in a tax savings of $10,400 while the sale of securities resulted in additional taxes of $11,250. (a) Give the entry that is required in recording the tax allocation, assuming that the company reports the special gains and losses on the income statement. (b) Give the entry that would be required if the company reports the special gains and losses directly in Retained Earnings.

## PROBLEMS

**3-1.** The trial balance of Remington, Inc. shows among other items the following balances on December 31, 1964, the end of a fiscal year:

| | | |
|---|---:|---:|
| Accounts Receivable............................ | $ 80,000 | |
| 4½% Panorama City Bonds.................... | 50,000 | |
| Buildings..................................... | 90,000 | |
| Allowance for Depreciation of Buildings.......... | | $ 31,500 |
| Land......................................... | 100,000 | |
| 6% First Mortgage Bonds Payable.............. | | 100,000 |
| Rental Income................................ | | 26,000 |
| Office Expense................................ | 800 | |

The following facts are ascertained on this date upon inspection of the records of the company:

(a) It is estimated that approximately 3% of accounts receivable may prove uncollectible.

(b) Interest is receivable semiannually on the Panorama City bonds on March 1 and September 1.

(c) Buildings are depreciated at 2½% a year; however, there were building additions of $20,000 during the year. The company computes depreciation on asset acquisitions during the year at one half the annual rate.

(d) Interest on the first mortgage bonds is payable semiannually on February 1 and August 1.

(e) Rental income includes $1,800 that was received on October 1, representing rent on part of the buildings for the period October 1, 1964, to September 30, 1965.

(f) Office supplies of $350 are on hand on December 31. Purchases of office supplies were charged to the office expense account.

*Instructions:* (1) Prepare the journal entries to adjust the books on December 31, 1964.

(2) Give the reversing entries that may appropriately be made at the beginning of 1965.

**3-2.** The Parker Company was organized in 1964 and transactions during the year included the following:

(a) Paid a premium of $780 for a fire insurance policy covering the period April 1, 1964–April 1, 1967.

(b) Received $900 representing advance rent for the use of a portion of the company's properties for the period September 1, 1964–March 1, 1965.

(c) Purchased office supplies during the year, $1,415; supplies on hand on December 31 amounted to $680.

*Instructions:* Give the necessary adjusting entries as of December 31, 1964, and appropriate reversing entries, assuming:

(1) Transactions are originally recorded in revenue and expense accounts.

(2) Transactions are originally recorded in asset and liability accounts.

**3-3.** The bookkeeper for the Brooks Co. has submitted an income statement for the year ended December 31, 1963, with results as follows:

| | |
|---|---|
| Net income from operations............................... | $120,350 |
| Gain on sale of securities................................ | 18,000 |
| Net income and extraordinary item........................ | $138,350 |

Accounts have not yet been closed, and a review of the books discloses the need for the following additional adjustments:

(a) The account Office Expense shows the cost of all purchases of office supplies for the year. At the end of 1963 there are supplies of $450 on hand.

(b) The allowance for bad debts account shows a debit balance of $350. It is estimated that 4% of the accounts receivable as of December 31 will prove uncollectible. The accounts receivable balance on this date is $22,500.

(c) The ledger shows a balance for accrued salaries and wages of $1,200 as of December 31, 1962, which was left unadjusted during 1963. No recognition was made in the accounts at the end of 1963 for accrued salaries and wages which amounted to $1,350.

(d) The ledger shows a balance for accrued interest on investments of $375 as of December 31, 1962, which was left unchanged during 1963. No recognition was made in the accounts at the end of 1963 for accrued interest on investments which amounted to $325.

(e) The account Unexpired Insurance was debited during the year for amounts paid for insurance and shows a balance of $1,550 at the end of 1963. The unexpired portions of the policies on December 31, 1963, total $350.

(f) A portion of a building was subleased for 3 months, November 1, 1963, to February 1, 1964. Unearned Rental Income was credited for $900 and no adjustment was made in this account at the end of 1963.

(g) The account Interest Expense was charged for all interest charges incurred during the year and shows a balance of $2,050. However, of this amount, $250 represents charges applicable to 1964.

(h) Provision for income taxes for 1963 is to be made at the following rates: 30% on taxable income up to $25,000; 52% on taxable income in excess of $25,000. However, the income taxes applicable to the sale of securities are limited to 25% of the gain. Income taxes are to be allocated in the accounts between net income and the extraordinary item.

*Instructions:* (1) Give the entries that are required on December 31, 1963, to bring the books up to date. (In recording income taxes, provide a schedule to show how the corrected net income subject to tax was determined.)

(2) Prepare a revised summary of the results from 1963 activities.

**3-4.** The bookkeeper for the Hollingsworth Corporation submits an income statement for the year ended December 31, 1963, which reports the following:

| | |
|---|---|
| Net income from normal activities....................... | $43,300 |
| Deduct fire loss........................................ | 18,500 |
| Net income and extraordinary item....................... | $24,800 |

An inspection of the books before they are closed reveals the following accounting failures:

(a) A balance of $1,200 for accrued salaries established at the end of 1962 was left unchanged during 1963, with no recognition of accrued salaries as of December 31, 1963, which totaled $1,475.

(b) A balance of $350 for accrued interest on customer notes established at the end of 1962 was left unchanged during 1963, with no recognition of accrued interest as of December 31, 1963, which amounted to $275.

(c) Prepaid insurance was debited for insurance premiums paid during 1963 and was left at the end of 1963 with a balance of $660. The unexpired insurance balance at the end of 1963 was $210.

(d) On December 1, 1963, part of a building was sublet by the company for 6 months; $1,200 was collected and was recorded as Rental Income. No adjustment was made in this balance at the end of 1963.

(e) On November 1, 1963, the company borrowed cash on a $7,500 one-year non-interest-bearing note. The note was discounted by the bank at 6%. The discount was reported as Interest Expense. No adjustment was made for this item at the end of 1963.

(f) Bonds of $100,000 are outstanding. Interest at $4\frac{1}{2}\%$ is payable semi-annually on February 1 and August 1. No entry was made for accrued interest as of December 31, 1963.

(g) Income taxes for 1963 are to be calculated at the following rates: 30% on taxable income up to $25,000; 52% on all income in excess of $25,000. (The fire loss is fully deductible from other taxable income in arriving at the net income subject to tax.) Income taxes are to be allocated in the accounts between net income and special items.

*Instructions:* (1) Give the entries that are required on December 31, 1963, to bring the books up to date. (In recording income taxes, provide a schedule to show how the corrected net income figure subject to tax was determined.)

(2) Prepare a revised summary of the results from 1963 activities.

**3-5.** A balance sheet for the Cameron Supply Company on January 1, 1964, reports the following balances:

| | | | | | |
|---|---|---|---|---|---|
| Cash................... | | $16,750 | Accounts payable.............. | | $ 9,300 |
| Accounts receivable..... | $6,000 | | Salaries payable............... | | 200 |
| Less allowance for bad | | | Taxes payable................. | | 150 |
| debts............... | 350 | 5,650 | P. L. Cameron, capital......... | | 30,350 |
| Inventories............ | | 14,500 | | | |
| Unexpired insurance..... | | 100 | | | |
| Furniture.............. | $3,600 | | | | |
| Less allowance for de- | | | | | |
| preciation........... | 600 | 3,000 | | | |
| | | $40,000 | | | $40,000 |

Transactions for 1964 are summarized below:

| | |
|---|---|
| Sales on account..................................... | $102,000 |
| Purchases on account................................. | 67,500 |
| Sales returns (credits were made to customers' accounts)... | 1,500 |
| Cash collected on accounts receivable................... | 97,000 |
| Discounts allowed on accounts collected................. | 1,200 |
| Uncollectible accounts written off against allowance....... | 300 |
| Cash paid on accounts payable......................... | 64,000 |
| Discounts taken on accounts paid...................... | 800 |
| Operating expenses paid............................... | 24,000 |

Withdrawals for personal use:

| | | |
|---|---|---|
| Merchandise (cost)........................... | $ 2,000 | |
| Cash...................................... | 16,000 | 18,000 |

Cash borrowed from the bank on a note dated
November 1, 1964, and payable 6 months from
this date together with interest at 6%.................... 6,000

In addition to the foregoing information, the following data are to be considered on December 31: inventories, $18,000; unexpired insurance, $250; accrued salaries, $300; and accrued taxes, $200. Depreciation of furniture for the year is $300. The balance in the allowance for bad debts account is increased by $150.

*Instructions:* Prepare an income statement, a balance sheet, and a statement of changes in the owner's capital account for the year ended December 31, 1964. (T accounts or working papers should be used in developing statement data.)

**3-6.** The Walton Sales Co. is organized on January 2, 1964, selling its total authorized stock of 7,500 shares for cash at par, $75,000. Transactions for the next six months follow:

| | |
|---|---|
| Payments for equipment............................... | $ 20,000 |
| Sales on account...................................... | 152,000 |
| Purchases on account................................. | 166,000 |
| Cash borrowed on long-term notes..................... | 40,000 |
| Operating expenses paid............................... | 42,000 |
| Purchases returns and allowances (charges were made to creditors' accounts)................................ | 2,000 |

A cash dividend of $2,000 is declared in June, payable July 15. On June 30, there are accounts of trade debtors of $50,000 that have not been collected; sales discounts of $1,200 were allowed on accounts collected. On June 30, there are also accounts of trade creditors of $30,000 that have not been paid. An allowance for bad debts of $650 is to be established on accounts receivable on hand. The merchandise inventory on this date is $76,500. Depreciation for the six months is estimated at $600. In addition, adjustments are to be made for the following prepaid and accrued items as of June 30:

| | |
|---|---|
| Unexpired insurance................................... | $500 |
| Advances to employees................................ | 550 |
| (Insurance and advances were recorded as operating expenses during the period.) | |
| Accrued interest on notes payable........................ | 750 |
| Accrued salaries...................................... | 350 |
| Accrued payroll and property taxes..................... | 400 |

The income taxes for 1964 are estimated at 30% of the net income.

*Instructions:* Prepare an income statement, a balance sheet, and retained earnings statement for the six-month period ended June 30, 1964. (T accounts or working papers should be used in developing statement data.)

# Chapter 4

# THE ACCOUNTING
# PROCESS ILLUSTRATED

### Steps in the accounting process

The accounting process as described in the preceding chapter is composed of a number of steps in well-defined sequence. To review, these steps consist of:

1. Making a first record of each transaction on an appropriate business paper or form.
2. Recording the transactions in chronological order in the books of original entry.
3. Posting the transactions as classified and summarized in the journals to the appropriate accounts in the ledgers.
4. Preparing a trial balance of the accounts in the general ledger and reconciling supporting data in the subsidiary ledgers with respective controlling accounts.
5. Compiling the data to bring the accounts up to date.
6. Preparing the work sheet.
7. Preparing the financial statements and supporting schedules.
8. Adjusting and closing the accounts.
9. Preparing a post-closing trial balance.
10. Reversing the adjustments that established accrued and prepaid revenue and expense balances.

The entire course of the accounting process is illustrated in the example that appears on the following pages. The books of original entry for a hypothetical manufacturing company, the Mitchell Corporation, are described. Data in the journals are transferred to the ledger, and the work involved in the periodic summary at the end of a fiscal year is then illustrated.

### Books of original entry

The Mitchell Corporation maintains the following books of original entry: a sales journal, a sales returns and allowances journal, a cash receipts journal, a voucher register, a cash payments journal, and a general journal.

*Sales journal.* The sales journal as summarized at the end of the month appears as follows:

Sales Journal

| Cash Dr. | Accounts Receivable Dr. | Date | Description | Sales Cr. | Sales Taxes Payable Cr. |
|---|---|---|---|---|---|
| | 780 00 | 31 | Sales on account for day.... | 750 00 | 30 00 |
| 250 00 | | 31 | Cash sales for day....... | 240 00 | 10 00 |
| 8,800 00 | 24,500 00 | 31 | Totals................. | 32,000 00 | 1,300 00 |
| ( √ ) | (116) | | | (41) | (218) |

One entry is made to record the sales on account for each day. Accounts Receivable is debited; Sales and Sales Taxes Payable are credited. Debits are posted to the individual customers' accounts in the accounts receivable ledger directly from the sales invoices.

One entry is also made for the cash sales for each day. Cash is debited and Sales and Sales Taxes Payable are credited.

*Sales returns and allowances journal.* The sales returns and allowances journal appears as follows:

Sales Returns and Allowances Journal

| Date | Description | Accounts Receivable Cr. | Sales Returns and Allowances Dr. | Sales Taxes Payable Dr. |
|---|---|---|---|---|
| 31 | Sales returns and allowances for day..................... | 26 00 | 25 00 | 1 00 |
| 31 | Totals..................... | 520 00 | 500 00 | 20 00 |
| | | (116) | (041) | (218) |

One entry is made to record the sales returns and allowances for each day. Sales Returns and Allowances and Sales Taxes Payable are debited; Accounts Receivable is credited. Credits are posted to the individual customers' accounts in the accounts receivable ledger directly from the credit memorandums.

*Cash receipts journal.* The cash receipts journal appears as shown at the top of the following page.

One entry is made each day for the total amount collected on accounts receivable. In this entry Cash and Sales Discounts are debited and Accounts Receivable is credited. Credits are posted to the individual customers' accounts in the accounts receivable ledger from a separate list of receipts on account maintained by the cashier.

Cash Receipts Journal

| Cash Dr. | Sales Discounts Dr. | Date | Description | Post. Ref. | General Cr. | Sales Cr. | Accounts Receivable Cr. |
|---|---|---|---|---|---|---|---|
| 6,565 00 | | 31 | Notes Receivable. | 113 | 6,500 00 | | |
| | | | Interest Income.. | 72 | 65 00 | | |
| 10,000 00 | | 31 | Notes Payable ... | 211 | 10,000 00 | | |
| 1,020 00 | 20 00 | 31 | K. T. Nelson..... | √ | | | 1,040 00 |
| 250 00 | | 31 | Sales........... | √ | | 250 00 | |
| 48,460 00 | 255 00 | 31 | Totals.......... | √ | 16,565 00 | 8,800 00 | 23,350 00 |
| (111) | (042) | | | | ( √ ) | ( √ ) | (116) |

In order to maintain the cash receipts journal as a complete record of all cash received, an entry for cash sales is made each day. This entry is also made in the sales journal so that the sales journal provides a complete record of sales. To avoid double posting of the transaction, the total of the Cash Dr. column in the sales journal and the total of the Sales Cr. column in the cash receipts journal are checked and are not posted. As a result, the debit to Cash for cash sales is posted from the cash receipts journal as a part of the total of the Cash Dr. column, and the credit to Sales for cash sales is posted from the sales journal as a part of the total of the Sales Cr. column.

*Voucher register.* The voucher register maintained by the company appears across the top of pages 88 and 89.

The company does not maintain an expenses control account and therefore a number of separate columns are provided for expenses in its voucher register. The total of each amount column is posted to the corresponding account, with the exception of the Payroll Dr. column and the General Dr. and Cr. columns.

The debits to the various accounts for salaries and wages are posted directly from the payroll records. The total of the amounts thus posted equals the total of the Payroll Dr. column in the voucher register.

The debits posted from the payroll records to the various salaries and wages accounts for the month of December are as follows:

| | |
|---|---|
| Direct Labor..... | $ 6,500 |
| Indirect Labor..... | 1,900 |
| Sales Salaries and Commissions..... | 2,100 |
| Delivery Salaries..... | 800 |
| Factory Superintendence..... | 1,700 |
| Officers Salaries..... | 1,400 |
| Office Salaries..... | 900 |
| | $15,300 |

Voucher Register

| Date | Vchr. No. | Name | Paid Date | Chk. No. | Accounts Payable Cr. | Raw Materials Purchases Dr. | Freight In Dr. | Payroll Dr. | |
|---|---|---|---|---|---|---|---|---|---|
| 21 | 31 | 5154 | First National Bank | 12/31 | 4207 | 8,120 | | | | 21 |
| 22 | | | | | | | | | | 22 |
| 23 | 31 | 5155 | Payroll | 12/31 | 4208 | 1,780 | | | 2,000 | 23 |
| 24 | | | | | | | | | | 24 |
| 25 | 31 | 5156 | Midwest G. & E. | | | 1,700 | | | | 25 |
| 26 | 31 | 5157 | Jack's Hardware | | | 300 | | | | 26 |
| 27 | 31 | 5158 | Jarris Supply Co. | | | 1,200 | 1,200 | | | 27 |
| 28 | 31 | 5159 | Petty Cash | 12/31 | 4210 | 160 | | | | 28 |
| 29 | 31 | | Totals | | | 37,020 | 6,800 | 400 | 15,300 | 29 |
| | | | | | | (213) | (51) | (52) | Posted to accounts as indicated by payroll records | |

One payroll record is kept for direct labor, indirect labor, sales salaries and commissions, and delivery salaries; another, for factory superintendence, officers salaries, and office salaries. The first group is paid weekly; the second, semimonthly. The entry for the payroll on December 31 in the voucher register is for the second group only.

General debits reported in the voucher register for December total $14,010 and are composed of the following items (the first five items represent vouchers recorded prior to December 31 and are not shown in the partial record):

| | |
|---|---|
| Income Tax Withholdings Payable (November)............ | $ 2,000 |
| F.I.C.A. Taxes Payable (November)..................... | 440 |
| Sales Taxes Payable (November)....................... | 720 |
| Prepaid Insurance.................................... | 250 |
| Building Maintenance and Repair...................... | 480 |
| Notes Payable....................................... | 8,000 |
| Interest Expense — Other............................. | 120 |
| Factory Heat, Light, and Power....................... | 1,700 |
| Tools............................................... | 300 |
| | $14,010 |

General credits reported in the voucher register for December represent payroll income tax and federal social security tax withholdings. These are summarized for the month as follows:

| | |
|---|---|
| Income Tax Withholdings Payable...................... | $ 2,130 |
| F.I.C.A. Taxes Payable............................... | 210 |
| | $ 2,340 |

*Cash payments journal.* The cash payments journal is illustrated on the opposite page. This cash payments journal accounts for all of the checks that are issued during the period. Checks are issued only in payment of vouchers that have been properly approved. In entering a check, the

For Month of December, 1964

| Factory Supplies Dr. | Misc. Factory Overhead Dr. | Advertising Dr. | Misc. Selling Expense Dr. | Misc. Del. Expense Dr. | Office Supplies Dr. | Misc. Gen. Exp. Dr. | General Account | P. R. | Amount Dr. | Cr. | |
|---|---|---|---|---|---|---|---|---|---|---|---|
| | | | | | | | Notes Payable | 211 | 8,000 | | 21 |
| | | | | | | | Interest Expense—Other | 83 | 120 | | 22 |
| | | | | | | | Income Tax Withhold. Pay. | 214 | | 200 | 23 |
| | | | | | | | F.I.C.A. Taxes Pay. | 215 | | 20 | 24 |
| | | | | | | | Factory Ht., Lt., & Power | 624 | 1,700 | | 25 |
| | 20 | | 60 | | 80 | | Tools | 131 | 300 | | 26 |
| | | | | | | | | | | | 27 |
| | | | | | | | | | | | 28 |
| 400 | 300 | 800 | 200 | 180 | 750 | 220 | Totals | | 14,010 | 2,340 | 29 |
| (1110) | (626) | (632) | (633) | (642) | (1111) | (653) | | | (√) | (√) | |

Cash Payments Journal

| Date | Check No. | Description | Vchr. No. | Accounts Payable Dr. | Purchases Discounts Cr. | Cash Cr. |
|---|---|---|---|---|---|---|
| 31 | 4207 | First National Bank.... | 5154 | 8,120 00 | | 8,120 00 |
| 31 | 4208 | Payroll.............. | 5155 | 1,780 00 | | 1,780 00 |
| 31 | 4209 | Pat Hay............. | 5006 | 500 00 | 10 00 | 490 00 |
| 31 | 4210 | Petty Cash........... | 5159 | 160 00 | | 160 00 |
| 31 | | Totals.............. | | 29,480 00 | 160 00 | 29,320 00 |
| | | | | (213) | (71) | (111) |

payee is designated together with the number of the voucher authorizing the payment. The cash payments record when prepared in this form is frequently called a *check register*.

*General journal.* The general journal with the entries for the month of December is given on page 90. This company's general journal is prepared in three-column form. A pair of columns is provided for the entries that are to be made to the general ledger accounts. A "detail" column is provided for the individual debits and credits to subsidiary records that accompany entries affecting general ledger controlling accounts.

## Posting; preparation of trial balance

Data in the journals are transferred to the accounts in the ledger at the end of December, and a trial balance is then taken. In order to conserve space here, the complete ledger of the Mitchell Corporation is not reproduced. Instead, the information that would appear in the ledger

### General Journal

| Date | Description | Post. Ref. | Detail | Debits | Credits |
|------|-------------|-----------|--------|--------|---------|
| 1964 Dec. 1 | Notes Receivable............... | 113 | | 6,000 00 | |
| | Accounts Receivable........... | 116 | | | 6,000 00 |
| | T. A. Wellman............... | AR | 6,000 00 | | |
| | Received note from customer. | | | | |
| 12 | Allowance for Bad Debts........... | 0116 | | 120 00 | |
| | Accounts Receivable........... | 116 | | | 120 00 |
| | B. B. Bartlett.................. | AR | 120 00 | | |
| | To write off uncollectible customer's account. | | | | |
| 22 | Accounts Payable.................. | 213 | | 200 00 | |
| | Case and Downs, Inc............ | AP | 200 00 | | |
| | Raw Materials Returns and Allow.... | 051 | | | 200 00 |
| | Materials returned to supplier. | | | | |
| 31 | Taxes............................ | 625 | | 210 00 | |
| | F.I.C.A. Taxes Payable........... | 215 | | | 210 00 |
| | To record employer's taxes payable for month under Federal Insurance Contributions Act. (Social Security legislation). | | | | |
| 31 | Taxes............................ | 625 | | 200 00 | |
| | S.U.I. Taxes Payable............. | 216 | | | 200 00 |
| | To record employer's taxes payable for month under State Unemployment Insurance plan. | | | | |
| 31 | Taxes............................ | 625 | | 30 00 | |
| | F.U.T.A. Taxes Payable........... | 217 | | | 30 00 |
| | To record employer's taxes payable for month under Federal Unemployment Tax Act. | | | | |

has been summarized in tabular form on page 91. The tabulation shows: (1) a trial balance of the accounts in the ledger on November 30, (2) the effects upon account balances of the information transferred from the books of original entry for the month of December, and (3) a trial balance as of December 31 formed by combining the trial balance of November 30 and the transactions for December.

The letters in the parentheses preceding each amount in the transactions columns of the tabulation refer to the books of original entry on the previous pages from which the information was obtained. The identification letters are: Voucher Register (VR); Cash Receipts Journal (CR); Cash Payments Journal (CP); Sales Journal (S); Purchases Journal (P); Sales Returns and Allowances Journal (SR); and General Journal (J). These are the letters that are customarily used to indicate the sources of information that is posted.

| Accounts | Trial Balance November 30, 1964 | | Transactions December, 1964 | | Trial Balance December 31, 1964 | |
|---|---|---|---|---|---|---|
| | Dr. | Cr. | Dr. | Cr. | Dr. | Cr. |
| Cash........................................ | 22,770 | | (CR) 48,460 | (CP) 29,320 | 41,910 | |
| Petty Cash.................................. | 200 | | | | 200 | |
| Notes Receivable ........................... | 6,500 | | (J) 6,000 | (CR) 6,500 | 6,000 | |
| Accounts Receivable ....................... | 57,490 | | (S) 24,500 | (SR) 520 | | |
| | | | | (CR) 23,350 | 52,000 | |
| | | | | (J) 6,000 | | |
| | | | | (J) 120 | | |
| Allowance for Bad Debts.................... | | 730 | (J) 120 | | | 610 |
| Finished Goods Inventory................... | 36,000 | | | | 36,000 | |
| Goods in Process Inventory ................ | 21,000 | | | | 21,000 | |
| Raw Materials Inventory ................... | 17,000 | | | | 17,000 | |
| Factory Supplies .......................... | 5,100 | | | (VR) 400 | 5,500 | |
| Office Supplies............................. | 2,050 | | | (VR) 750 | 2,800 | |
| Prepaid Insurance.......................... | 4,750 | | | (VR) 250 | 5,000 | |
| Bailey, Inc. Common Stock ................. | 24,300 | | | | 24,300 | |
| Tools...................................... | 9,700 | | | | 10,000 | |
| Delivery Equipment........................ | 8,000 | | | (VR) 300 | 8,000 | |
| Allowance for Depreciation of Delivery Equip... | | 3,600 | | | | 3,600 |
| Office Furniture and Fixtures............... | 5,000 | | | | 5,000 | |
| Allowance for Depreciation of Office Furniture and Fixtures ............................. | | 1,600 | | | | 1,600 |
| Machinery and Equipment.................. | 64,000 | | | | 64,000 | |
| Allowance for Depreciation of Machinery and Equipment................................ | | 9,300 | | | | 9,300 |
| Buildings ................................. | 42,500 | | | | 42,500 | |
| Allowance for Depreciation of Buildings........ | | 6,800 | | | | 6,800 |
| Land....................................... | 40,000 | | | | 40,000 | |
| Patents.................................... | 6,500 | | | | 6,500 | |
| Goodwill................................... | 40,000 | | | | 40,000 | |
| Notes Payable.............................. | | 18,000 | (VR) 8,000 | (CR) 10,000 | | 20,000 |
| Accounts Payable........................... | | 20,370 | (CP) 29,480 | (VR) 37,020 | | 27,710 |
| | | | (J) 200 | | | |
| Income Tax Withholdings Payable........... | | 2,000 | (VR) 2,000 | (VR) 2,130 | | 2,130 |
| F.I.C.A. Taxes Payable..................... | | 440 | (VR) 440 | (VR) 210 | | 420 |
| | | | | (J) 210 | | |
| S.U.I. Taxes Payable....................... | | 530 | | (J) 200 | | 730 |
| F.U.T.A. Taxes Payable..................... | | 250 | | (J) 30 | | 280 |
| Sales Taxes Payable........................ | | 720 | (VR) 720 | (S) 1,300 | | 1,280 |
| | | | (SR) 20 | | | |
| 6% First Mortgage Bonds .................. | | 100,000 | | | | 100,000 |
| 6% Preferred Stock, $100 par .............. | | 50,000 | | | | 50,000 |
| Common Stock, $20 par .................... | | 150,000 | | | | 150,000 |
| Treasury Stock — Common.................. | 30,000 | | | | 30,000 | |
| Paid-in Capital — Premium on Preferred Stock.. | | 2,000 | | | | 2,000 |
| Retained Earnings ......................... | | 50,450 | | | | 50,450 |
| Sales...................................... | | 333,000 | | (S) 32,000 | | 365,000 |
| Sales Returns and Allowances .............. | 4,500 | | (SR) 500 | | 5,000 | |
| Sales Discounts............................ | 2,845 | | (CR) 255 | | 3,100 | |
| Raw Materials Purchases ................... | 78,600 | | (VR) 6,800 | | 85,400 | |
| Raw Materials Returns and Allowances........ | | 1,900 | | (J) 200 | | 2,100 |
| Purchases Discounts ....................... | | 2,020 | | (CP) 160 | | 2,180 |
| Freight In................................. | 4,300 | | (VR) 400 | | 4,700 | |
| Direct Labor............................... | 69,700 | | (VR) 6,500 | | 76,200 | |
| Indirect Labor............................. | 20,700 | | (VR) 1,900 | | 22,600 | |
| Factory Superintendence.................... | 18,300 | | (VR) 1,700 | | 20,000 | |
| Building Maintenance and Repairs........... | 2,520 | | (VR) 480 | | 3,000 | |
| Factory Heat, Light, and Power............. | 18,780 | | (VR) 1,700 | | 20,480 | |
| Taxes ..................................... | 15,960 | | (J) 210 | | 16,400 | |
| | | | (J) 200 | | | |
| | | | (J) 30 | | | |
| Miscellaneous Factory Overhead............. | 3,000 | | (VR) 300 | | 3,300 | |
| Sales Salaries and Commissions.............. | 21,900 | | (VR) 2,100 | | 24,000 | |
| Advertising ............................... | 7,300 | | (VR) 800 | | 8,100 | |
| Miscellaneous Selling Expense .............. | 2,000 | | (VR) 200 | | 2,200 | |
| Delivery Salaries........................... | 8,200 | | (VR) 800 | | 9,000 | |
| Miscellaneous Delivery Expense ............. | 1,920 | | (VR) 180 | | 2,100 | |
| Officers Salaries........................... | 14,600 | | (VR) 1,400 | | 16,000 | |
| Office Salaries............................. | 9,100 | | (VR) 900 | | 10,000 | |
| Miscellaneous General Expense.............. | 2,080 | | (VR) 220 | | 2,300 | |
| Interest Income............................ | | 635 | | (CR) 65 | | 700 |
| Dividend Income .......................... | | 300 | | | | 300 |
| Royalty Income ........................... | | 1,750 | | | | 1,750 |
| Interest Expense — Bonds.................. | 5,000 | | | | 5,000 | |
| Interest Expense — Other.................. | 2,230 | | (VR) 120 | | 2,350 | |
| | 756,395 | 756,395 | 149,335 | 149,335 | 798,940 | 798,940 |

## Compilation of adjusting data

In considering the adjustments that are required in preparing statements at the end of 1964, it is found that the accounts do not show the following information:[1]

(1) A dividend of $1.50 per share, payable January 15 to stockholders of record December 31, was declared on Bailey, Inc. common stock. The Mitchell Corporation holds 200 shares of Bailey, Inc. common stock as a long-term investment.

(2) Dividends on Mitchell Corporation's stock were declared and are payable on January 10 to stockholders of record December 26 as follows:

Regular quarterly dividend of $1.50 on 500 shares of 6% preferred stock outstanding, $100 par.

Forty cents per share on 6,000 shares of common stock outstanding, $20 par (7,500 shares of stock were originally issued, 1,500 shares being reacquired and held as treasury stock.)

The following adjusting data as of December 31, 1964, were compiled upon thorough examination of the company's books and records:

*Physical Inventories:*
(6) Finished goods inventory, $49,000.
(7) Goods in process inventory, $28,000.
(8) Raw materials inventory, $20,000.
(9) Factory supplies, $1,200.
(10) Office supplies, $700.

*Bad Debts:*
(11) The allowance for bad debts is to be increased by $1,800.

*Depreciation and amortization:*
(12) Tools on hand are valued at $7,500.
(13) Delivery equipment depreciation, 20% a year.
(14) Office furniture and fixtures depreciation, 10% a year.
(15) Machinery and equipment depreciation, 5% a year.
(16) Buildings depreciation, 4% a year.
(17) Patents are to be reduced by $500, the amortization for the year.

*Accrued Expenses:*
(18) Salaries and wages:
Direct labor, $1,400.
Indirect labor, $300.
Sales salaries and commissions, $400.
Delivery salaries, $200.
(19) Accrued interest on bonds payable, $1,000.
(20) Accrued interest on notes payable, $600.

*Prepaid Expenses:*
(21) Prepaid insurance, $2,600
(22) Prepaid taxes, $300.

---

[1] The adjusting data are numbered to correspond to the numbers given the adjustments on the work sheet on pages 94 to 97. Numbers (3), (4), and (5) do not appear in this list because the data for these adjustments, representing transfers of beginning inventories, already appear on the work sheet trial balance.

*Accrued Revenue:*
   (23) Accrued interest on notes receivable, $200.

*Prepaid Revenue:*
   (24) Royalties received in advance, $350.

*Income Taxes:*
   (25) Provision of $10,000 is to be made for federal and state income taxes.

Building expenses, expired insurance, and taxes are to be distributed as follows: to manufacturing operations, 85%; to general and administrative operations, 15%.

Retained earnings of the company were $52,700 on January 1, 1964, and have been affected only by dividends declared on preferred stock prior to recording the foregoing data.

### Preparation of the work sheet

The adjusting data must be combined with the information on the trial balance in bringing the accounts up to date. This is done and the financial statements are developed through the preparation of a work sheet. In the construction of the work sheet, trial balance data are listed in the first two amount columns. The adjusting entries are listed in the second pair of columns. Sometimes a third pair of columns is included to show the trial balance after adjustment. Account balances as adjusted are carried to the appropriate statement columns. A work sheet for a manufacturing concern usually includes a pair of columns for (a) manufacturing accounts, (b) profit and loss accounts, and (c) balance sheet accounts. A similar work-sheet form would be used for a trading concern except for the absence of manufacturing columns.

The work sheet for the Mitchell Corporation is shown on pages 94 to 97.

The adjustments to the inventory accounts should be particularly noted. Items (4) and (5) are entered as debits to Manufacturing and as credits to Goods in Process Inventory and Raw Materials Inventory respectively. These entries transfer the beginning inventory costs to the manufacturing account. Entries (7) and (8) are debits to Goods in Process Inventory and Raw Materials Inventory respectively and credits to Manufacturing. These entries record the goods in process and raw material inventories at the end of the fiscal period and reduce manufacturing costs by the ending inventories. Both the debit and the credit amounts in the manufacturing account are carried to the manufacturing columns. The manufacturing columns then include all of the information that is required in developing cost of goods manufactured on the manufacturing schedule.

Mitchell
Work
For Year Ended

| | Name of Account | Trial Balance | | Adjustments | | |
|---|---|---|---|---|---|---|
| | | Dr. | Cr. | Dr. | Cr. | |
| 1 | Cash..................... | 41,910 | .......... | .......... | .......... | 1 |
| 2 | Petty Cash.................. | 200 | .......... | .......... | .......... | 2 |
| 3 | Notes Receivable........... | 6,000 | .......... | .......... | .......... | 3 |
| 4 | Accounts Receivable........ | 52,000 | .......... | .......... | .......... | 4 |
| 5 | Allowance for Bad Debts..... | .......... | 610 | .......... | (11) 1,800 | 5 |
| 6 | Finished Goods Inventory..... | 36,000 | .......... | (6) 49,000 | (3) 36,000 | 6 |
| 7 | Goods in Process Inventory... | 21,000 | .......... | (7) 28,000 | (4) 21,000 | 7 |
| 8 | Raw Materials Inventory..... | 17,000 | .......... | (8) 20,000 | (5) 17,000 | 8 |
| 9 | Factory Supplies............. | 5,500 | .......... | .......... | (9) 4,300 | 9 |
| 10 | Office Supplies.............. | 2,800 | .......... | .......... | (10) 2,100 | 10 |
| 11 | Prepaid Insurance........... | 5,000 | .......... | .......... | (21) 2,400 | 11 |
| 12 | Bailey, Inc. Common Stock... | 24,300 | .......... | .......... | .......... | 12 |
| 13 | Tools..................... | 10,000 | .......... | .......... | (12) 2,500 | 13 |
| 14 | Delivery Equipment.......... | 8,000 | .......... | .......... | .......... | 14 |
| 15 | Allow. for Depr. of Del. Equip. | .......... | 3,600 | .......... | (13) 1,600 | 15 |
| 16 | Office Furniture and Fixtures.. | 5,000 | .......... | .......... | .......... | 16 |
| 17 | Allowance for Depreciation of Office Furniture and Fixtures | .......... | 1,600 | .......... | (14) 500 | 17 |
| 18 | Machinery and Equipment.... | 64,000 | .......... | .......... | .......... | 18 |
| 19 | Allowance for Depreciation of Machinery and Equipment.. | .......... | 9,300 | .......... | (15) 3,200 | 19 |
| 20 | Buildings.................. | 42,500 | .......... | .......... | .......... | 20 |
| 21 | Allow. for Depr. of Buildings.. | .......... | 6,800 | .......... | (16) 1,700 | 21 |
| 22 | Land...................... | 40,000 | .......... | .......... | .......... | 22 |
| 23 | Patents.................... | 6,500 | .......... | .......... | (17) 500 | 23 |
| 24 | Goodwill.................. | 40,000 | .......... | .......... | .......... | 24 |
| 25 | Notes Payable.............. | .......... | 20,000 | .......... | .......... | 25 |
| 26 | Accounts Payable........... | .......... | 27,710 | .......... | .......... | 26 |
| 27 | Income Tax Withholdings Pay. | .......... | 2,130 | .......... | .......... | 27 |
| 28 | F.I.C.A. Taxes Payable...... | .......... | 420 | .......... | .......... | 28 |
| 29 | S.U.I. Payable.............. | .......... | 730 | .......... | .......... | 29 |
| 30 | F.U.T.A. Taxes Payable...... | .......... | 280 | .......... | .......... | 30 |
| 31 | Sales Taxes Payable.......... | .......... | 1,280 | .......... | .......... | 31 |
| 32 | 6% First Mortgage Bonds..... | .......... | 100,000 | .......... | .......... | 32 |
| 33 | 6% Preferred Stock, $100 par.. | .......... | 50,000 | .......... | .......... | 33 |
| 34 | Common Stock, $20 par...... | .......... | 150,000 | .......... | .......... | 34 |
| 35 | Treasury Stock — Common.... | 30,000 | .......... | .......... | .......... | 35 |
| 36 | Paid-in Capital — Premium on Preferred Stock............. | .......... | 2,000 | .......... | .......... | 36 |
| 37 | Retained Earnings........... | .......... | 50,450 | (2) 3,150 | .......... | 37 |
| 38 | Sales..................... | .......... | 365,000 | .......... | .......... | 38 |
| 39 | Sales Returns and Allowances. | 5,000 | .......... | .......... | .......... | 39 |
| 40 | Sales Discounts.............. | 3,100 | .......... | .......... | .......... | 40 |
| 41 | Raw Materials Purchases..... | 85,400 | .......... | .......... | .......... | 41 |
| 42 | Raw Mat. Returns and Allow.. | .......... | 2,100 | .......... | .......... | 42 |
| 43 | Purchases Discounts.......... | .......... | 2,180 | .......... | .......... | 43 |
| 44 | Freight In.................. | 4,700 | .......... | .......... | .......... | 44 |
| 45 | Direct Labor................ | 76,200 | .......... | (18) 1,400 | .......... | 45 |
| 46 | Indirect Labor.............. | 22,600 | .......... | (18) 300 | .......... | 46 |
| 47 | Factory Superintendence..... | 20,000 | .......... | .......... | .......... | 47 |
| 48 | Bldg. Maintenance & Repairs. | 3,000 | .......... | .......... | .......... | 48 |
| 49 | Factory Heat, Light, and Power | 20,480 | .......... | .......... | .......... | 49 |
| 50 | Taxes..................... | 16,400 | .......... | .......... | (22) 300 | 50 |
| 51 | Misc. Factory Overhead...... | 3,300 | .......... | .......... | .......... | 51 |
| 52 | Sales Salaries and Commissions | 24,000 | .......... | (18) 400 | .......... | 52 |
| 53 | Advertising................. | 8,100 | .......... | .......... | .......... | 53 |
| 54 | Miscellaneous Selling Expense. | 2,200 | .......... | .......... | .......... | 54 |
| 55 | Delivery Salaries............. | 9,000 | .......... | (18) 200 | .......... | 55 |

Corporation
Sheet
December 31, 1964

| | Manufacturing | | Profit and Loss | | Balance Sheet | | |
|---|---|---|---|---|---|---|---|
| | Dr. | Cr. | Dr. | Cr. | Dr. | Cr. | |
| 1 | | | | | 41,910 | | 1 |
| 2 | | | | | 200 | | 2 |
| 3 | | | | | 6,000 | | 3 |
| 4 | | | | | 52,000 | | 4 |
| 5 | | | | | | 2,410 | 5 |
| 6 | | | | | 49,000 | | 6 |
| 7 | | | | | 28,000 | | 7 |
| 8 | | | | | 20,000 | | 8 |
| 9 | | | | | 1,200 | | 9 |
| 10 | | | | | 700 | | 10 |
| 11 | | | | | 2,600 | | 11 |
| 12 | | | | | 24,300 | | 12 |
| 13 | | | | | 7,500 | | 13 |
| 14 | | | | | 8,000 | | 14 |
| 15 | | | | | | 5,200 | 15 |
| 16 | | | | | 5,000 | | 16 |
| 17 | | | | | | 2,100 | 17 |
| 18 | | | | | 64,000 | | 18 |
| 19 | | | | | | 12,500 | 19 |
| 20 | | | | | 42,500 | | 20 |
| 21 | | | | | | 8,500 | 21 |
| 22 | | | | | 40,000 | | 22 |
| 23 | | | | | 6,000 | | 23 |
| 24 | | | | | 40,000 | | 24 |
| 25 | | | | | | 20,000 | 25 |
| 26 | | | | | | 27,710 | 26 |
| 27 | | | | | | 2,130 | 27 |
| 28 | | | | | | 420 | 28 |
| 29 | | | | | | 730 | 29 |
| 30 | | | | | | 280 | 30 |
| 31 | | | | | | 1,280 | 31 |
| 32 | | | | | | 100,000 | 32 |
| 33 | | | | | | 50,000 | 33 |
| 34 | | | | | | 150,000 | 34 |
| 35 | | | | | 30,000 | | 35 |
| 36 | | | | | | 2,000 | 36 |
| 37 | | | | | | 47,300 | 37 |
| 38 | | | | 365,000 | | | 38 |
| 39 | | | 5,000 | | | | 39 |
| 40 | | | 3,100 | | | | 40 |
| 41 | 85,400 | | | | | | 41 |
| 42 | | 2,100 | | | | | 42 |
| 43 | | 2,180 | | | | | 43 |
| 44 | 4,700 | | | | | | 44 |
| 45 | 77,600 | | | | | | 45 |
| 46 | 22,900 | | | | | | 46 |
| 47 | 20,000 | | | | | | 47 |
| 48 | 2,550 | | 450 | | | | 48 |
| 49 | 20,480 | | | | | | 49 |
| 50 | 13,685 | | 2,415 | | | | 50 |
| 51 | 3,300 | | | | | | 51 |
| 52 | | | 24,400 | | | | 52 |
| 53 | | | 8,100 | | | | 53 |
| 54 | | | 2,200 | | | | 54 |
| 55 | | | 9,200 | | | | 55 |

Work Sheet (Continued)

| | Name of Account | Trial Balance | | Adjustments | | |
|---|---|---|---|---|---|---|
| | | Dr. | Cr. | Dr. | Cr. | |
| 56 | Miscellaneous Delivery Expense | 2,100 | .......... | .......... | .......... | 56 |
| 57 | Officers Salaries............. | 16,000 | .......... | .......... | .......... | 57 |
| 58 | Office Salaries............. | 10,000 | .......... | .......... | .......... | 58 |
| 59 | Miscellaneous General Expense | 2,300 | .......... | .......... | .......... | 59 |
| 60 | Interest Income............. | .......... | 700 | .......... | (23) 200 | 60 |
| 61 | Dividend Income............. | .......... | 300 | .......... | (1) 300 | 61 |
| 62 | Royalty Income............. | .......... | 1,750 | (24) 350 | .......... | 62 |
| 63 | Interest Expense — Bonds..... | 5,000 | .......... | (19) 1,000 | .......... | 63 |
| 64 | Interest Expense — Other..... | 2,350 | .......... | (20) 600 | .......... | 64 |
| 65 | | 798,940 | 798,940 | .......... | .......... | 65 |
| 66 | Dividends Receivable........ | .......... | .......... | (1) 300 | .......... | 66 |
| 67 | Div. Pay. on Preferred Stock.. | .......... | .......... | .......... | (2) 750 | 67 |
| 68 | Div. Pay. on Common Stock.. | .......... | .......... | .......... | (2) 2,400 | 68 |
| 69 | Profit and Loss............. | .......... | .......... | (3) 36,000 | (6) 49,000 | 69 |
| 70 | Manufacturing............. | .......... | .......... | (4) 21,000 | (7) 28,000 | 70 |
| 71 | ............. | .......... | .......... | (5) 17,000 | (8) 20,000 | 71 |
| 72 | Factory Supplies Used........ | .......... | .......... | (9) 4,300 | .......... | 72 |
| 73 | Office Supplies Used......... | .......... | .......... | (10) 2,100 | .......... | 73 |
| 74 | Bad Debts............. | .......... | .......... | (11) 1,800 | .......... | 74 |
| 75 | Depreciation of Tools........ | .......... | .......... | (12) 2,500 | .......... | 75 |
| 76 | Depreciation of Delivery Equip. | .......... | .......... | (13) 1,600 | .......... | 76 |
| 77 | Depr. of Office Fur. and Fix... | .......... | .......... | (14) 500 | .......... | 77 |
| 78 | Depr. of Machinery and Equip. | .......... | .......... | (15) 3,200 | .......... | 78 |
| 79 | Depreciation of Buildings..... | .......... | .......... | (16) 1,700 | .......... | 79 |
| 80 | Amortization of Patents...... | .......... | .......... | (17) 500 | .......... | 80 |
| 81 | Accrued Salaries and Wages... | .......... | .......... | .......... | (18) 2,300 | 81 |
| 82 | Accrued Interest on Bonds Pay. | .......... | .......... | .......... | (19) 1,000 | 82 |
| 83 | Accrued Interest on Notes Pay. | .......... | .......... | .......... | (20) 600 | 83 |
| 84 | Insurance............. | .......... | .......... | (21) 2,400 | .......... | 84 |
| 85 | Prepaid Taxes............. | .......... | .......... | (22) 300 | .......... | 85 |
| 86 | Accrued Interest on Notes Rec. | .......... | .......... | (23) 200 | .......... | 86 |
| 87 | Royalties Received in Advance | .......... | .......... | .......... | (24) 350 | 87 |
| 88 | Income Taxes............. | .......... | .......... | (25) 10,000 | .......... | 88 |
| 89 | Estimated Income Taxes Pay... | .......... | .......... | .......... | (25) 10,000 | 89 |
| 90 | | | | 209,800 | 209,800 | 90 |
| 91 | Cost of Goods Manufactured.. | .......... | .......... | .......... | .......... | 91 |
| 92 | | | | | | 92 |
| 93 | Net Income............. | .......... | .......... | .......... | .......... | 93 |
| 94 | ............. | .......... | .......... | .......... | .......... | 94 |

Adjustment (3) is a debit to Profit and Loss and a credit to Finished Goods Inventory, whereas adjustment (6) is a debit to Finished Goods Inventory and a credit to Profit and Loss. Entry (3) transfers the beginning inventory of finished goods to profit and loss; entry (6) records the ending inventory of finished goods and reports this item as a deduction from costs. Both the debit and credit amounts in the profit and loss

Work Sheet (Continued)

| | Manufacturing | | Profit and Loss | | Balance Sheet | | |
|---|---|---|---|---|---|---|---|
| | Dr. | Cr. | Dr. | Cr. | Dr. | Cr. | |
| 56 | | | 2,100 | | | | 56 |
| 57 | | | 16,000 | | | | 57 |
| 58 | | | 10,000 | | | | 58 |
| 59 | | | 2,300 | | | | 59 |
| 60 | | | | 900 | | | 60 |
| 61 | | | | 600 | | | 61 |
| 62 | | | | 1,400 | | | 62 |
| 63 | | | 6,000 | | | | 63 |
| 64 | | | 2,950 | | | | 64 |
| 65 | | | | | | | 65 |
| 66 | | | | | 300 | | 66 |
| 67 | | | | | | 750 | 67 |
| 68 | | | | | | 2,400 | 68 |
| 69 | | | 36,000 | 49,000 | | | 69 |
| 70 | 21,000 | 28,000 | | | | | 70 |
| 71 | 17,000 | 20,000 | | | | | 71 |
| 72 | 4,300 | | | | | | 72 |
| 73 | | | 2,100 | | | | 73 |
| 74 | | | 1,800 | | | | 74 |
| 75 | 2,500 | | | | | | 75 |
| 76 | | | 1,600 | | | | 76 |
| 77 | | | 500 | | | | 77 |
| 78 | 3,200 | | | | | | 78 |
| 79 | 1,445 | | 255 | | | | 79 |
| 80 | 500 | | | | | | 80 |
| 81 | | | | | | | 81 |
| 82 | | | | | | 2,300 | 82 |
| 83 | | | | | | 1,000 | 83 |
| 84 | 2,040 | | 360 | | | 600 | 84 |
| 85 | | | | | | | 85 |
| 86 | | | | | 300 | | 86 |
| 87 | | | | | 200 | | 87 |
| 88 | | | 10,000 | | | 350 | 88 |
| 89 | | | | | | 10,000 | 89 |
| 90 | 302,600 | 52,280 | | | | | 90 |
| 91 | | 250,320 | 250,320 | | | | 91 |
| 92 | 302,600 | 302,600 | 397,150 | 416,900 | 469,710 | 449,960 | 92 |
| 93 | | | 19,750 | | | 19,750 | 93 |
| 94 | | | 416,900 | 416,900 | 469,710 | 469,710 | 94 |

account are carried to the profit and loss columns. The profit and loss columns then include all of the information that is required in developing cost of goods sold on the income statement.

A number of methods may be used in recording inventory data on the work sheet. A simple procedure would be the following:

| Name of Account | Trial Balance | | Adjustments | | Manufacturing | | Profit and Loss | | Balance Sheet | |
|---|---|---|---|---|---|---|---|---|---|---|
| | Dr. | Cr. | Dr. | Cr. | Dr. | Cr. | Dr. | Cr. | Dr. | Cr. |
| Finished Goods Inventory 1/1, 1964 | 36,000 | | | | | | 36,000 | | | |
| Goods in Process Inventory 1/1, 1964 | 21,000 | | | | 21,000 | | | | | |
| Raw Materials Inventory 1/1, 1964 | 17,000 | | | | 17,000 | | | | | |
| Finished Goods Inventory 12/31, 1964.. | | | | | | | | 49,000 | 49,000 | |
| Goods In Process Inventory 12/31, 1964 | | | | | | 28,000 | | | 28,000 | |
| Raw Materials Inventory 12/31, 1964... | | | | | | 20,000 | | | 20,000 | |

Mitchell
Balance
December

## Assets

Current assets:

Cash on hand and in bank.................................. $42,110

Notes receivable......................................... 6,000

Accounts receivable.............................$52,000

Less allowance for bad debts........................ 2,410    49,590

Accrued interest and dividends receivable..................... 500

Inventories:

Finished goods.................................$49,000

Goods in process............................... 28,000

Raw materials................................. 20,000

Factory supplies............................... 1,200    98,200

Prepaid expenses:

Office supplies, insurance, and taxes....................... 3,600

Total current assets........................................ $200,000

Investments:

Bailey, Inc., common stock.................................. 24,300

| Plant and equipment: | Cost | Allowance for Depreciation | Book Value |
|---|---|---|---|
| Tools.............................. | $ 7,500 | — | $ 7,500 |
| Delivery equipment.................. | 8,000 | $ 5,200 | 2,800 |
| Office furniture and fixtures........... | 5,000 | 2,100 | 2,900 |
| Machinery and equipment............ | 64,000 | 12,500 | 51,500 |
| Buildings.......................... | 42,500 | 8,500 | 34,000 |
| Land.............................. | 40,000 | — | 40,000 |
| Total plant and equipment............ | $167,000 | $28,300 | 138,700 |

Intangibles:

Patents...................................................... $ 6,000

Goodwill..................................................... 40,000

Total intangibles........................................... 46,000

Total assets........................................................... $409,000

In this example, beginning inventories in the trial balance are carried to the manufacturing and the profit and loss columns; ending inventories are listed separately as credits in the manufacturing and the profit and loss columns and as debits in the balance sheet columns without inclusion in the adjustments columns.  An even simpler procedure would be to report the ending inventory balances on the same lines used for beginning

Corporation — Exhibit A
Sheet
31, 1964

### Liabilities and Stockholders' Equity

#### Liabilities

Current liabilities:

| | | |
|---|---:|---:|
| Notes payable............................................... | $20,000 | |
| Accounts payable............................................ | 27,710 | |
| Estimated income taxes payable.............................. | 10,000 | |
| Misc. sales, payroll, and withholding taxes payable............. | 4,840 | |
| Accrued salaries and wages.................................. | 2,300 | |
| Accrued interest on notes and on bonds payable................ | 1,600 | |
| Dividends payable on preferred and common stock ............. | 3,150 | |
| Total current liabilities..................................... | | $ 69,600 |

Long-term debt:

| | | |
|---|---:|---:|
| 6% First mortgage bonds, due Nov. 1, 1973................... | | 100,000 |

Deferred revenues:

| | | |
|---|---:|---:|
| Royalties received in advance................................ | | 350 |
| Total liabilities............................................. | | $169,950 |

#### Stockholders' Equity

Paid-in capital:

Capital stock:

| | | | |
|---|---:|---:|---:|
| 6% Preferred stock, $100 par, 500 shares issued and outstanding................................. | | $ 50,000 | |
| Common stock, $20 par (7,500 shares issued)............................... | $150,000 | | |
| Less treasury stock (1,500 shares reacquired, carried at par)............. | 30,000 | | |
| Common stock, 6,000 shares outstanding......... | | 120,000 | |
| Paid-in capital — premium on preferred stock........ | | 2,000 | |
| Total paid-in capital....................................... | | | $172,000 |
| Retained earnings........................................... | | | 67,050 |
| Total stockholders' equity.................................... | | | 239,050 |
| Total liabilities and stockholders' equity........................ | | | $409,000 |

inventories; beginning balances would then be carried as debits to the manufacturing and the profit and loss columns, while ending balances would be entered directly as credits in the manufacturing columns and as debits in the balance sheet columns. Although procedures for recording adjustments directly in the statement columns are acceptable, adjusting entries are still required in the journal to bring accounts up to date and to transfer profit and loss data to the appropriate summary account. It is generally desirable to assemble all adjusting data and to summarize this information in informal journal form before making formal entries in the general journal. When such a procedure is followed, it may prove convenient to recognize adjustments on the working papers in exactly the same form that is to be followed in recognizing the adjustments in the journal. This procedure was followed on the work sheet on pages 94 to 97 even though this involves more work than a direct method of adjustment as described above.

It was indicated earlier that building expenses, expired insurance, and taxes are allocated 85% to manufacturing activities and 15% to general and administrative activities. The percentage used in the distribution of the charges resulted from an analysis of expenses during the period. The building maintenance and repairs account is shown on the trial balance at $3,000; 85% of $3,000, or $2,550, is entered in the manufacturing columns and 15%, or $450, is entered in the profit and loss columns. The charges for taxes, depreciation of buildings, and expired insurance are similarly distributed on the work sheet.

### Preparation of financial statements

*Balance sheet.* The balance sheet of the Mitchell Corporation, shown on pages 98 and 99, is prepared from the balance sheet columns on the work sheet. A number of items reported in the balance sheet columns of the work sheet have been combined for balance sheet presentation. Such a procedure may be followed when items can be combined under a descriptive title and when amounts involved for the individual items are not material. Items that have been combined include: accrued interest and dividends receivable; office supplies, prepaid insurance, and prepaid taxes; income tax withholdings, federal insurance contributions taxes, state unemployment insurance taxes, federal unemployment taxes, and state sales taxes; accrued interest on notes and bonds payable; and dividends payable on preferred and common stock. The retained earnings balance on the balance sheet is composed of retained earnings reported in the trial balance columns, minus the charge for dividends shown in the adjustments column, plus the net income found in summarizing the work sheet.

*Income statement.* The income statement is prepared from the profit and loss columns on the work sheet. The income statement follows:

Mitchell Corporation — Exhibit B
Income Statement
For Year Ended December 31, 1964

| | | | |
|---|---:|---:|---:|
| Gross sales........................................................ | | $365,000 | |
| Less: Sales returns and allowances...................... | $5,000 | | |
| Sales discounts.................................. | 3,100 | 8,100 | |
| Net sales........................................... | | | $356,900 |
| **Cost of goods sold:** | | | |
| Finished goods inventory, January 1, 1964..................... | | $ 36,000 | |
| Cost of goods manufactured (Schedule B-1)...................... | | 250,320 | |
| Total cost of finished goods available for sale.................... | | $286,320 | |
| Deduct finished goods inventory, December 31, 1964.............. | | 49,000 | 237,320 |
| Gross profit on sales........................................... | | | $119,580 |
| **Operating expenses:** | | | |
| Selling expenses: | | | |
| Sales salaries and commissions....................... | $24,400 | | |
| Advertising....................................... | 8,100 | | |
| Miscellaneous selling expense....................... | 2,200 | | |
| Delivery salaries.................................. | 9,200 | | |
| Depreciation of delivery equipment.................. | 1,600 | | |
| Miscellaneous delivery expense...................... | 2,100 | $ 47,600 | |
| General and administrative expenses: | | | |
| Officers salaries................................... | $16,000 | | |
| Office salaries..................................... | 10,000 | | |
| Office supplies used............................... | 2,100 | | |
| Bad debts......................................... | 1,800 | | |
| Depreciation of office furniture and fixtures........... | 500 | | |
| Depreciation of buildings........................... | 255 | | |
| Insurance......................................... | 360 | | |
| Building maintenance and repairs.................... | 450 | | |
| Taxes............................................. | 2,415 | | |
| Miscellaneous general expense...................... | 2,300 | 36,180 | |
| Total operating expenses....................................... | | | 83,780 |
| Net operating income.......................................... | | | $ 35,800 |
| **Other revenue and expense items:** | | | |
| Interest expense — bonds........................... | $6,000 | | |
| Interest expense — other............................ | 2,950 | $8,950 | |
| Interest income.................................... | $ 900 | | |
| Dividend income................................... | 600 | | |
| Royalty income.................................... | 1,400 | 2,900 | 6,050 |
| Net income before income taxes ................................ | | | $ 29,750 |
| Income taxes................................................... | | | 10,000 |
| Net income.................................................... | | | $ 19,750 |

*Manufacturing schedule.* The manufacturing schedule is prepared from the manufacturing columns of the work sheet and is shown below:

Mitchell Corporation — Schedule B-1
Manufacturing Schedule
To Accompany Income Statement
For Year Ended December 31, 1964

| | | | | |
|---|---:|---:|---:|---:|
| Goods in process inventory, January 1, 1964...................... | | | | $21,000 |
| Raw materials: | | | | |
| Raw materials inventory, January 1, 1964...................... | | | $17,000 | |
| Raw materials purchases..................... | $85,400 | | | |
| Freight in................................ | 4,700 | $90,100 | | |
| Less: Raw materials returns and allowances ..... | $2,100 | | | |
| Purchases discounts.................... | 2,180 | 4,280 | 85,820 | |
| Total cost of raw materials available for use.................... | | | $102,820 | |
| Deduct raw materials inventory, December 31, 1964............. | | | 20,000 | |
| Cost of raw materials consumed................................ | | | $82,820 | |
| Direct labor.................................................. | | | 77,600 | |
| Manufacturing overhead: | | | | |
| Indirect labor........................................ | $22,900 | | | |
| Factory superintendence............................. | 20,000 | | | |
| Building maintenance and repairs.................... | 2,550 | | | |
| Factory heat, light, and power...................... | 20,480 | | | |
| Taxes................................................ | 13,685 | | | |
| Factory supplies used............................... | 4,300 | | | |
| Depreciation of tools............................... | 2,500 | | | |
| Depreciation of machinery and equipment............ | 3,200 | | | |
| Depreciation of buildings........................... | 1,445 | | | |
| Amortization of patents............................. | 500 | | | |
| Insurance............................................ | 2,040 | | | |
| Miscellaneous factory overhead...................... | 3,300 | 96,900 | 257,320 | |
| Total goods in process during period........................... | | | $278,320 | |
| Deduct goods in process inventory, December 31, 1964............. | | | 28,000 | |
| Cost of goods manufactured..................................... | | | $250,320 | |

*Retained earnings statement.* The retained earnings statement is prepared as follows:

Mitchell Corporation — Exhibit C
Retained Earnings Statement
For Year Ended December 31, 1964

| | | |
|---|---:|---:|
| Retained earnings, January 1, 1964............................. | | $52,700 |
| Add net income per income statement............................ | | 19,750 |
| | | $72,450 |
| Deduct: Dividends on preferred stock........................... | $3,000 | |
| Dividends on common stock............................ | 2,400 | 5,400 |
| Retained earnings, December 31, 1964.......................... | | $67,050 |

### Adjusting and closing the accounts

Upon completing the work sheet and statements, entries are made in the journal to bring the accounts up to date and to close the accounts. Before closing the accounts, any current, correcting, and adjusting entries are recorded. Although such entries may first have been prepared in informal form in the course of preparing the work sheet, these are now entered formally in the journal. Closing entries may be conveniently prepared by using as a basis for the entries the balances as shown in the manufacturing and profit and loss columns of the work sheet. The following entries are required for the Mitchell Corporation:

(current entries)<br>December 31

| | | |
|---|---:|---:|
| (1) Dividends Receivable.............................. | 300 | |
|     Dividend Income................................. | | 300 |
|        To record announcement of $1.50 dividend on investment in 200 shares of Bailey, Inc. common stock. | | |

31

| | | |
|---|---:|---:|
| (2) Retained Earnings................................. | 3,150 | |
|     Dividends Payable on Preferred Stock............... | | 750 |
|     Dividends Payable on Common Stock............... | | 2,400 |
|        To record declaration of dividends payable on January 10 to stockholders of record December 26. | | |

(adjusting entries)<br>31

| | | |
|---|---:|---:|
| (3) Profit and Loss.................................... | 36,000 | |
|     Finished Goods Inventory.......................... | | 36,000 |
|        To transfer beginning finished goods inventory to profit and loss. | | |

31

| | | |
|---|---:|---:|
| (4) Manufacturing.................................... | 21,000 | |
|     Goods in Process Inventory........................ | | 21,000 |
|        To transfer beginning goods in process inventory to manufacturing. | | |

31

| | | |
|---|---:|---:|
| (5) Manufacturing.................................... | 17,000 | |
|     Raw Materials Inventory........................... | | 17,000 |
|        To transfer beginning raw materials inventory to manufacturing. | | |

31

| | | |
|---|---:|---:|
| (6) Finished Goods Inventory.......................... | 49,000 | |
|     Profit and Loss.................................. | | 49,000 |
|        To record ending finished goods inventory. | | |

31

| | | |
|---|---:|---:|
| (7) Goods in Process Inventory......................... | 28,000 | |
|     Manufacturing.................................. | | 28,000 |
|        To record ending goods in process inventory. | | |

31

| | | |
|---|---:|---:|
| (8) Raw Materials Inventory........................... | 20,000 | |
|     Manufacturing.................................. | | 20,000 |
|        To record ending raw materials inventory. | | |

31

(9) Factory Supplies Used.............................. 4,300
    Factory Supplies.................................. 4,300
        To record cost of factory supplies used.

31

(10) Office Supplies Used............................... 2,100
    Office Supplies................................... 2,100
        To record cost of office supplies used.

31

(11) Bad Debts........................................ 1,800
    Allowance for Bad Debts.......................... 1,800
        To provide for estimated bad debts.

31

(12) Depreciation of Tools.............................. 2,500
    Tools........................................... 2,500
        To record depreciation on tools.

31

(13) Depreciation of Delivery Equipment.................. 1,600
    Allowance for Depreciation of Delivery Equipment..... 1,600
        To record depreciation on delivery equipment.

31

(14) Depreciation of Office Furniture and Fixtures ........... 500
    Allowance for Depreciation of Office Furniture and Fix-
    tures......................................... 500
        To record depreciation on office furniture and fixtures.

31

(15) Depreciation of Machinery and Equipment............. 3,200
    Allowance for Depreciation of Machinery and Equipment 3,200
        To record depreciation on machinery and equipment.

31

(16) Depreciation of Buildings........................... 1,700
    Allowance for Depreciation of Buildings.............. 1,700
        To record depreciation on buildings.

31

(17) Amortization of Patents............................ 500
    Patents......................................... 500
        To record amortization of patents.

31

(18) Direct Labor...................................... 1,400
    Indirect Labor ................................... 300
    Sales Salaries and Commissions...................... 400
    Delivery Salaries................................. 200
    Accrued Salaries and Wages....................... 2,300
        To record accrued salaries and wages.

31

(19) Interest Expense — Bonds........................... 1,000
    Accrued Interest on Bonds Payable.................. 1,000
        To record accrued interest on bonds.

31

(20) Interest Expense — Other........................... 600
    Accrued Interest on Notes Payable.................. 600
        To record accrued interest on notes payable.

31

(21) Insurance......................................... 2,400
    Prepaid Insurance................................ 2,400
        To record expired insurance.

31

(22) Prepaid Taxes.................................... 300
 Taxes............................................    300
  To record prepaid taxes.

31

(23) Accrued Interest on Notes Receivable................. 200
 Interest Income..................................    200
  To record accrued interest on notes receivable.

31

(24) Royalty Income.................................... 350
 Royalties Received in Advance.....................    350
  To record royalties received in advance.

31

(25) Income Taxes..................................... 10,000
 Estimated Income Taxes Payable...................    10,000
  To record estimated income taxes.

(*closing entries*)

31

Manufacturing........................................ 260,320
Raw Materials Returns and Allowances.................... 2,100
Purchases Discounts................................... 2,180
 Raw Materials Purchases............................    85,400
 Freight In.........................................    4,700
 Direct Labor.......................................    77,600
 Indirect Labor.....................................    22,900
 Factory Superintendence............................    20,000
 Building Maintenance and Repairs....................    2,550
 Factory Heat, Light, and Power......................    20,480
 Taxes.............................................    13,685
 Miscellaneous Factory Overhead.....................    3,300
 Factory Supplies Used..............................    4,300
 Depreciation of Tools..............................    2,500
 Depreciation of Machinery and Equipment............    3,200
 Depreciation of Buildings..........................    1,445
 Amortization of Patents............................    500
 Insurance.........................................    2,040
  To close manufacturing accounts into Manufacturing.

31

Sales................................................ 365,000
Interest Income...................................... 900
Dividend Income...................................... 600
Royalty Income....................................... 1,400
 Profit and Loss....................................    367,900
  To close revenue accounts into Profit and Loss.

31

Profit and Loss....................................... 361,150
 Manufacturing......................................    250,320
 Sales Returns and Allowances.......................    5,000
 Sales Discounts....................................    3,100
 Building Maintenance and Repairs....................    450
 Taxes.............................................    2,415
 Sales Salaries and Commissions.....................    24,400
 Advertising........................................    8,100
 Miscellaneous Selling Expense......................    2,200
 Delivery Salaries..................................    9,200
 Miscellaneous Delivery Expense.....................    2,100
 Officers Salaries..................................    16,000
 Office Salaries....................................    10,000
 Miscellaneous General Expense......................    2,300
 Interest Expense — Bonds...........................    6,000
 Interest Expense — Other...........................    2,950
 Office Supplies Used...............................    2,100

| | | |
|---|---|---|
| Bad Debts............................................ | | 1,800 |
| Depreciation of Delivery Equipment...................... | | 1,600 |
| Depreciation of Office Furniture and Fixtures.............. | | 500 |
| Depreciation of Buildings.............................. | | 255 |
| Insurance............................................. | | 360 |
| Income Taxes......................................... | | 10,000 |
| To close expense accounts into Profit and Loss. | | |

31

| | | |
|---|---|---|
| Profit and Loss....................................... | 19,750 | |
| Retained Earnings.................................... | | 19,750 |
| To transfer the balance in Profit and Loss after income taxes to Retained Earnings. | | |

### Preparation of post-closing trial balance

After the adjusting and closing entries are posted, a post-closing trial balance is prepared to verify the equality of the debits and credits. The post-closing trial balance is given on the opposite page.

### Reversing the accounts

The adjustments establishing accrued and prepaid balances may now be reversed. The reversing entries follow:

January 1

| | | |
|---|---|---|
| Accrued Salaries and Wages............................. | 2,300 | |
| Direct Labor....................................... | | 1,400 |
| Indirect Labor..................................... | | 300 |
| Sales Salaries and Commissions...................... | | 400 |
| Delivery Salaries................................... | | 200 |

1

| | | |
|---|---|---|
| Accrued Interest on Bonds Payable...................... | 1,000 | |
| Interest Expense — Bonds........................... | | 1,000 |

1

| | | |
|---|---|---|
| Accrued Interest on Notes Payable...................... | 600 | |
| Interest Expense — Other........................... | | 600 |

1

| | | |
|---|---|---|
| Taxes............................................... | 300 | |
| Prepaid Taxes..................................... | | 300 |

1

| | | |
|---|---|---|
| Interest Income...................................... | 200 | |
| Accrued Interest on Notes Receivable................. | | 200 |

1

| | | |
|---|---|---|
| Royalties Received in Advance.......................... | 350 | |
| Royalty Income.................................... | | 350 |

The post-closing trial balance is frequently prepared after the reversing entries have been posted. When such practice is followed, a check is offered on the accuracy of adjusting, closing, and reversing the accounts.

### Interim statements

Statements are prepared at least once a year, and at that time the accounts in the ledger are adjusted and closed. Many business units,

Mitchell Corporation
Post-Closing Trial Balance
December 31, 1964

| | | |
|---|---:|---:|
| Cash | 41,910 | |
| Petty Cash | 200 | |
| Notes Receivable | 6,000 | |
| Accounts Receivable | 52,000 | |
| Allowance for Bad Debts | | 2,410 |
| Dividends Receivable | 300 | |
| Accrued Interest on Notes Receivable | 200 | |
| Finished Goods Inventory | 49,000 | |
| Goods in Process Inventory | 28,000 | |
| Raw Materials Inventory | 20,000 | |
| Factory Supplies | 1,200 | |
| Office Supplies | 700 | |
| Prepaid Insurance | 2,600 | |
| Prepaid Taxes | 300 | |
| Bailey, Inc. Common Stock | 24,300 | |
| Tools | 7,500 | |
| Delivery Equipment | 8,000 | |
| Allowance for Depreciation of Delivery Equipment | | 5,200 |
| Office Furniture and Fixtures | 5,000 | |
| Allowance for Depreciation of Office Furniture and Fixtures | | 2,100 |
| Machinery and Equipment | 64,000 | |
| Allowance for Depreciation of Machinery and Equipment | | 12,500 |
| Buildings | 42,500 | |
| Allowance for Depreciation of Buildings | | 8,500 |
| Land | 40,000 | |
| Patents | 6,000 | |
| Goodwill | 40,000 | |
| Notes Payable | | 20,000 |
| Accounts Payable | | 27,710 |
| Estimated Income Taxes Payable | | 10,000 |
| Income Tax Withholdings Payable | | 2,130 |
| F.I.C.A. Taxes Payable | | 420 |
| S.U.I. Taxes Payable | | 730 |
| F.U.T.A. Taxes Payable | | 280 |
| Sales Taxes Payable | | 1,280 |
| Accrued Salaries and Wages | | 2,300 |
| Accrued Interest on Bonds Payable | | 1,000 |
| Accrued Interest on Notes Payable | | 600 |
| Dividends Payable on Preferred Stock | | 750 |
| Dividends Payable on Common Stock | | 2,400 |
| 6% First Mortgage Bonds | | 100,000 |
| Royalties Received in Advance | | 350 |
| 6% Preferred Stock, $100 par | | 50,000 |
| Common Stock, $20 par | | 150,000 |
| Treasury Stock — Common | 30,000 | |
| Paid-in Capital — Premium on Preferred Stock | | 2,000 |
| Retained Earnings | | 67,050 |
| | 469,710 | 469,710 |

however, require statements during the fiscal year at one-month, three-month, or six-month intervals. Such statements may be prepared for management and internal use, or they may also be made available to stockholders as a means of keeping this group informed on financial progress during the year.

When interim statements are desired, they are prepared by means of a work sheet. The accounts in the ledger may be adjusted but they are not closed. In preparing the work sheet, balances in the ledger are first listed in trial balance form. Because accounts have not been closed since the end of the previous year, nominal accounts reflect balances to date. Adjustments are listed on the work sheet to bring the account balances up to date, and adjusted balances are carried to the appropriate statement columns. Financial statements are then drawn up from the work sheet.

For example, in preparing the interim statements at the end of March, the adjusting data are reported on the working papers just as though the fiscal period were one quarter. Inventories and accrued and prepaid items as of March 31 are recorded. Amortization and depreciation are stated for a three-month period. The balance sheet prepared from the work sheet shows the financial position as of March 31; the income statement reports cumulative results for the three months ended March 31. To obtain an income statement covering operations for the month of March alone, it is necessary to subtract revenue and expense balances on the income statement for the two-month period ended February 28 from cumulative balances on the income statement for the three-month period ended March 31. Inventory figures as of February 28 and March 31 are reported, and a statement showing the net income for the month of March is then available. By following the procedure just outlined, monthly statements, as well as cumulative income statements, can be made available.

## QUESTIONS

**1.** Describe the kind of work sheet that would be employed for:
    (a) A trading company.
    (b) A manufacturing company.
    (c) A departmentalized business, the gross profit to be ascertained for each department.
    (d) A manufacturing organization with departmentalized retail sales departments, a net operating income to be determined for each department.

**2.** The bookkeeper for the R. C. Folsom Store, after completing all adjustments except those for the merchandise inventories, makes the entry reported on top of the next page to close the beginning inventory, to set up the ending inventory, to close all nominal accounts, and to report the net result of operations in the capital account.

    (a) Would you regard this procedure acceptable?
    (b) What alternate procedure could be followed in adjusting and closing the accounts?

| | | |
|---|---:|---:|
| Merchandise Inventory, December 31, 1964...... | 18,000 | |
| Sales........................................ | 200,000 | |
| Purchases Discounts.......................... | 2,000 | |
| Merchandise Inventory, January 1, 1964....... | | 20,000 |
| Purchases.................................... | | 140,000 |
| Selling Expenses............................. | | 20,000 |
| General and Administrative Expenses.......... | | 15,000 |
| Interest Expense............................. | | 1,500 |
| R. C. Folsom, Capital........................ | | 23,500 |

**3.** The Beverly Corporation prepares financial statements and adjusts and closes the accounts at the end of each month. The Burke Corporation prepares financial statements monthly, but adjusts and closes the accounts only at the end of each year.

(a) Will the reports of each company be the same?
(b) Can a cumulative "year-to-date" income statement be made available for the Beverly Corporation? How?
(c) Can income statements covering single months be made available for the Burke Corporation? How?
(d) Which procedure, monthly or annual closing, do you consider preferable? Why?

**4.** State the effect upon the balance sheet and the income statement of each of the following errors:

(a) Accrued expenses are overstated at the end of the period.
(b) Prepaid revenues are understated at the end of the period.
(c) Prepaid expenses are understated at the end of the period.
(d) Accrued revenues are overstated at the end of the period.
(e) The inventory is understated at the end of the period.
(f) Depreciation on an equipment item is overstated at the end of the period.

## EXERCISES

**1.** Accounts of Super Products Co. at the end of the first year of operations show the following balances:

| | | |
|---|---:|---:|
| Cash....................................... | $ 13,200 | |
| Investments................................ | 20,000 | |
| Machinery.................................. | 50,000 | |
| Factory buildings........................... | 80,000 | |
| Land....................................... | 40,000 | |
| Accounts payable........................... | | $ 30,000 |
| Capital stock............................... | | 200,000 |
| Paid-in capital — premium on stock........... | | 40,000 |
| Sales...................................... | | 300,000 |
| Raw materials purchases..................... | 140,000 | |
| Direct labor............................... | 100,000 | |
| Manufacturing overhead..................... | 75,500 | |
| Operating expenses......................... | 52,000 | |
| Income on investments...................... | | 700 |
| | $570,700 | $570,700 |

At the end of the year physical inventories are: raw materials, $40,000; goods in process, $30,000; finished goods, $30,000. Prepaid operating expenses are $1,500 and accrued manufacturing overhead is $500. Accrued income on investments is $300. Depreciation for the year on buildings is $2,000, apportioned $1,500 to the factory and $500 to general operations. Depreciation of machinery is $2,500. Federal and state income taxes for the year are estimated at $10,000. Give the entries to adjust and close the books.

**2.** E. S. Barnett fails to adjust the accounts for the following items in closing the books on December 31, 1964. Assume that the omissions are never discovered but that adjustments are properly made at the end of 1965. What effect does each omission have on the net incomes for 1964 and for 1965?

    (a) Sales salaries accrued, $30.
    (b) Prepaid advertising, $200. Advertising Expense was debited for advertising payments.
    (c) Depreciation of office machine, $100.
    (d) Accrued interest on notes receivable, $20.
    (e) Office supplies inventory, $100. Office Supplies, an asset account, was charged for purchases and has a balance of $300.

**3.** Upon inspecting the books and records for the Melcombe Manufacturing Co. for the year ended December 31, 1964, you find the following data. What entries are required to bring the accounts up to date?

    (a) A receivable of $150 from L. A. Case is determined to be uncollectible. The company maintains no allowance for such losses.
    (b) A creditor, the Williams Co., has just been awarded damages of $2,200 as a result of breach of contract by Melcombe Manufacturing Co. Nothing appears on the books in connection with this matter.
    (c) Furniture and fixtures, cost $12,000, book value, $1,800, had been sold for salvage of $250, the salvage proceeds being credited to Miscellaneous Income.
    (d) Advances of $1,500 to salesmen have been recorded as Sales Salaries.
    (e) Machinery at the end of the year shows a balance of $24,500. It is discovered that additions to this account during the year totaled $6,000, but of this amount $2,500 should have been recorded as expense. Depreciation is to be recorded at 10% on machinery owned throughout the year; at one half this rate on machinery purchased during the year.

**4.** The Waring Sales Co. shows a credit balance in the profit and loss account of $16,600 after the revenue and expense items have been transferred to this account at the end of a fiscal year. Give the remaining entries to close the books, assuming:

    (a) The business is a sole proprietorship; the owner, A. C. Waring, has made withdrawals of $12,000 during the year and this is reported in a drawing account.
    (b) The business is a partnership; the owners, A. C. Waring and P. H. Waring, share profits 5:3; they have made withdrawals of $15,000 and $5,000 respectively and these amounts are reported in drawing accounts.

(c) The business is a corporation; the ledger reports additional paid-in capital, $150,000, and retained earnings, $15,000; dividends during the year of $18,000 were charged to a dividends paid account.

**5.** A. L. James began operations in 1964 with cash of $15,000. During the year his sales were $50,000, $36,000 being collected from customers during the year. Accounts receivable on December 31 are believed fully collectible. Purchases for the year were $40,000, payments of $27,500 being made on account. All sales were made at double the cost of the merchandise. Operating expenses were all paid in cash. The income statement reported net income for 1964 of $6,500. (a) Prepare a balance sheet as of December 31, 1964. (b) Submit a summary of cash receipts and disbursements for the year.

**6.** Sales for the Parallel Products Co. were $150,000 for 1964. The beginning inventory was 30% of the cost of goods sold. The ending inventory was 50% of the beginning inventory. Selling expenses were 10% of sales and absorbed 30% of the gross profit on sales. Net income before income taxes was 12% of sales. Income taxes were 30% of net income before taxes. Prepare an income statement for 1964.

## PROBLEMS

**4-1.** The following data are assembled from the books and records of the McQueen Corporation:

(a) The company borrowed $20,000 from the bank on November 5, issuing a note that is payable in 90 days with interest at 6%.
(b) The company paid $1,350 for a fire insurance policy covering a three-year period beginning October 1, 1964. The charge was made to Prepaid Insurance.
(c) A $6,000 note dated November 10, 1964, and due in 90 days with interest at 5% was received from a customer in payment of account.
(d) The company received $2,700 representing rent for parking privileges granted to a neighboring business for the period July 1, 1964–June 30, 1965. The credit was made to Unearned Rental Income.

*Instructions:* (1) Give the adjusting journal entries as of November 30, 1964, assuming that he books are adjusted monthly but are closed at the end of each calendar year.
(2) Give the adjusting journal entries as of December 31, 1964, assuming that the books are adjusted monthly but are closed at the end of each calendar year.
(3) Give the adjusting journal entries as of December 31, 1964, assuming that the books are adjusted and closed only at the end of each calendar year.

**4-2.** Data from the books of the Woodruff Company are compiled as follows:

(a) On August 1, payment of $2,100 was made for a fire insurance policy covering a three-year period beginning on this date. The charge for the premium was made to a real account.
(b) Five percent first-mortgage bonds of $1,000,000 were issued on October 1, 1964. Interest is payable semiannually on April 1 and October 1.

(c) A non-interest bearing 90-day note dated November 15 for $10,150 was received from a customer who owed the company $10,000. The company reported the note at its full amount and credited Unearned Interest Income for $150.

(d) The company purchased $15,000 U.S. 4% Treasury Bonds on April 1. Interest on the bonds is payable semiannually on February 1 and August 1.

*Instructions:* (1) Give the adjusting journal entries as of November 30, 1964, assuming that the books are adjusted monthly but are closed at the end of each calendar year.

(2) Give the adjusting journal entries as of December 31, 1964, assuming that the books are adjusted monthly but are closed at the end of each calendar year.

(3) Give the adjusting journal entries as of December 31, 1964, assuming that the books are adjusted and closed only at the end of each calendar year.

**4-3.** Account balances taken from the ledger of the Neill Supply Corporation on December 31, 1964, follow:

| | | | |
|---|---|---|---|
| Accounts payable | $ 27,500 | Land | $ 55,000 |
| Accounts receivable | 56,000 | Long-term investments | 10,500 |
| Advertising | 4,000 | Mortgage payable | 40,000 |
| Allowance for depreciation of | | Notes payable—short term | 12,500 |
| buildings | 16,500 | Office expense | 13,400 |
| Allowance for doubtful accounts | 1,150 | Purchases | 115,400 |
| Buildings | 60,000 | Purchases discounts | 950 |
| Capital stock, $10 par | 150,000 | Retained earnings, Dec. 31, 1963 | 11,200 |
| Cash | 20,000 | Sales | 205,000 |
| Dividends | 12,000 | Sales returns | 2,800 |
| Freight in | 3,000 | Sales discounts | 4,500 |
| Insurance | 1,200 | Selling expense | 41,200 |
| Interest expense | 2,200 | Supplies expense | 3,500 |
| Interest income | 550 | Taxes — real estate, payroll, etc. | 6,650 |
| Inventory, Dec, 31, 1963 | 54,000 | | |

Adjustments on December 31 are required as follows:

(a) The inventory on hand is $72,850.

(b) The allowance for doubtful accounts is to be increased to a balance of $2,500.

(c) Buildings are depreciated at the rate of $3\frac{1}{3}$% per year.

(d) Accrued selling expenses are $2,200.

(e) There are supplies of $650 on hand.

(f) Unexpired nsurance relating to 1965 and 1966 totals $350.

(g) Accrued interest on long-term investments is $200.

(h) Accrued real estate, payroll and other taxes are $750.

(i) Accrued interest on the mortgage is $400.

(j) Income taxes are estimated at 30% of the net income before income taxes.

*Instructions:* (1) Prepare an eight-column work sheet.

(2) Prepare a balance sheet, income statement, and retained earnings statement.

(3) Prepare adjusting, closing, and reversing entries.

**4-4.** The account balances taken from the ledger of Alan White and Jerome Young at the end of the first year's operations on December 31, 1964, and the data for adjustments are given below:

| | | | |
|---|---:|---|---:|
| Accounts Payable | $12,600 | Personal—Alan White (dr.). | $ 2,400 |
| Accounts Receivable | 2,500 | Personal — Jerome Young | |
| Capital — Alan White | 10,000 | (dr.) | 900 |
| Capital — Jerome Young | 7,350 | Purchases | 67,000 |
| Cash | 4,650 | Purchases Discounts | 2,300 |
| Interest Expense | 500 | Purchases Ret. and Allow. | 1,650 |
| Interest Income | 150 | Sales | 65,000 |
| Miscellaneous General Ex- | | Sales Salaries | 8,000 |
| pense | 12,600 | Store Furniture | 3,700 |
| Notes Payable | 6,000 | Store Supplies | 600 |
| Notes Receivable | 1,600 | Taxes | 600 |

Data for adjustments, year ended December 31, 1964:
(a) Inventories: merchandise, $23,600; store supplies, $280.
(b) Depreciation of store furniture, 10% a year. Additions to store furniture were made on March 1 costing $900.
(c) Accrued advertising, $65.
(d) Taxes paid in advance, $100.
(e) Accrued taxes, $215.
(f) Accrued interest on notes payable, $75.
(g) Accrued interest on notes receivable, $105.
(h) 5% of the accounts receivable are expected to prove uncollectible.
(i) White and Young divide profits and losses in the ratio 3:2.

*Instructions:* (1) Prepare an eight-column work sheet.
(2) Prepare an income statement, a statement of changes in partners' capital accounts, and a balance sheet.
(3) Prepare adjusting, closing, and reversing entries.

**4-5.** The following account balances are taken from the books of the Carr Manufacturing Co on December 31, 1964, the end of the first year of operations:

| | | | |
|---|---:|---|---:|
| Cash | $ 22,000 | Indirect Labor | $ 25,500 |
| Accounts Receivable | 92,800 | Heat, Light, and Power | 9,000 |
| Factory Supplies | 1,200 | Maintenance and Repairs | 5,000 |
| Office Supplies | 700 | Miscellaneous Factory | |
| Plant and Equipment | 205,000 | Overhead | 3,500 |
| Accounts Payable | 61,200 | Sales Salaries and Commis- | |
| 4½% Bonds Payable | 150,000 | sions | 24,000 |
| Capital Stock, $20 par | 100,000 | Advertising | 15,000 |
| Sales | 470,000 | Miscellaneous Selling Ex- | |
| Sales of Raw Materials (at | | pense | 20,000 |
| cost) | 26,100 | Office Salaries | 17,000 |
| Raw Materials Purchases | 247,100 | Miscellaneous General and | |
| Freight In | 7,000 | Administrative Expense. | 4,125 |
| Direct Labor | 105,000 | Interest Expense — Bonds. | 3,375 |

The following adjustments are to be made on December 31:
(a) Inventories:

| | | | |
|---|---:|---|---:|
| Finished Goods | $18 000 | Factory Supplies | $500 |
| Goods in Process | 14,000 | Office Supplies | 250 |
| Raw Materials | 20,000 | | |

(b) Provision for bad debts, 1% of sales of finished product.
(c) Depreciation, 8%, chargeable ¾ to manufacturing, ⅛ to selling, ⅛ to office.

(d) Accrued salaries and wages:

Direct Labor . . . . $2,200      Sales Salaries . . . . . $300
Indirect Labor . . .    500

(e) A dividend of $1 per share had been declared December 28 and is payable January 10, 1965.

(f) Bond interest payment dates are March 1 and September 1.

(g) Provision of $12,200 is to be made for income taxes for 1964.

*Instructions:* (1) Prepare a ten-column work sheet.

(2) Prepare a balance sheet, an income statement and a manufacturing schedule, and a retained earnings statement.

(3) Prepare the adjusting, closing, and reversing entries.

**4-6.** The following account balances are taken from the general ledger of the Walker Manufacturing Co. on December 31, 1964, the end of its fiscal year. The corporation was organized January 2, 1958.

| | | | |
|---|---|---|---|
| Cash on Hand and in Banks . . . . . . . . . . . . . . . | $ 35,625 | 6% Preferred Stock, $100 par . . . . . . . . . . . . . . . . . | $ 100,000 |
| Notes Receivable . . . . . . . | 18,500 | Common Stock, $100 par . . | 100,000 |
| Accounts Receivable . . . . . | 56,000 | Paid-In Capital — Premium on Common Stock . . . . . . . . . . . . . . | 10,000 |
| Allowance for Bad Debts . . | 650 | | |
| Finished Goods Inventory January 1, 1964 . . . . . . | 40,500 | Retained Earnings . . . . . . . | 125,000 |
| | | Sales . . . . . . . . . . . . . . . . . | 520,000 |
| Goods in Process Inventory, January 1, 1964 . . . | 42,000 | Sales Ret. and Allow. . . . . | 10,000 |
| | | Sales Discounts . . . . . . . . . | 6,500 |
| Raw Materials Inventory, January 1, 1964 . . . . . . . | 24,000 | Raw Materials Purchases . | 110,200 |
| Factory Supplies . . . . . . . . | 12,500 | Freight and Cartage In . . . | 8,800 |
| Shipping Supplies . . . . . . . | 8,500 | Purchases Ret. and Allow. | 3,000 |
| Office Supplies . . . . . . . . . | 6,200 | Purchases Discounts . . . . . | 3,400 |
| Tools . . . . . . . . . . . . . . . . . | 10,000 | Direct Labor . . . . . . . . . . . | 103,700 |
| Patterns and Dies . . . . . . . | 20,000 | Indirect Labor . . . . . . . . . | 24,000 |
| Shipping Department Equipment . . . . . . . . . . . | 12,000 | Plant Superintendence . . . . | 20,000 |
| Allow. for Depr. of Shipping Department Equipment . . . . . . . . . . . . . . . . | 7,200 | Maintenance and Repairs of Buildings . . . . . . . . . . | 6,300 |
| | | Maintenance and Repairs of Machinery . . . . . . . . . | 4,500 |
| Office Furniture and Fixtures . . . . . . . . . . . . . . . | 15,000 | Heat, Light, and Power (Factory) . . . . . . . . . . . . | 11,000 |
| Allow. for Depr. of Office Furniture and Fixtures. | 9,000 | Taxes . . . . . . . . . . . . . . . . . | 10,200 |
| Machinery and Equipment | 160,000 | Sundry Factory Overhead. | 3,600 |
| Allow. for Depr. of Machinery and Equipment. | 30,000 | Sales Salaries . . . . . . . . . . . | 30,000 |
| | | Sales Commissions . . . . . . . | 12,300 |
| Buildings . . . . . . . . . . . . . . | 125,000 | Traveling Expense . . . . . . . | 8,500 |
| Allow. for Depr. of Bldgs. | 18,000 | Advertising Expense . . . . . . | 24,000 |
| Land . . . . . . . . . . . . . . . . . | 20,000 | Shipping Dept. Salaries . . . | 6,000 |
| Patents . . . . . . . . . . . . . . . | 27,500 | Sundry Shipping Dept. Expense . . . . . . . . . . . . . | 1,000 |
| Notes Payable . . . . . . . . . . | 20,000 | | |
| Accounts Payable . . . . . . . . | 45,700 | Officers Salaries . . . . . . . . | 30,000 |
| 4½% First Mortgage Bonds . . . . . . . . . . . . . . | 100,000 | Office Salaries . . . . . . . . . . | 14,000 |
| | | Insurance . . . . . . . . . . . . . . | 8,500 |

| Postage, Telephone, and | | Interest Income......... | $    800 |
| Telegraph........... | $1,400 | Interest Expense — Bonds. | 2,625 |
| Sundry Office Expense... | 1,500 | Interest Expense — Other. | 800 |

The following adjustments are to be made on December 31, 1964, before the books are closed:

(a) Inventories:
Finished Goods, $49,500; Goods in Process, $55,200; Raw Materials $36,600; Factory Supplies, $2,700; Shipping Supplies, $1,800; Office Supplies, $1,000.

(b) Depreciation and Amortization:
Shipping department equipment, $12\frac{1}{2}\%$.
Office furniture and fixtures, 10%.
Machinery and equipment, 5%. New machinery and equipment costing $60,000 was installed on March 1, 1964.
Buildings, 4%. Additions to the buildings costing $50,000 were completed June 30, 1964.
Patents were acquired on January 2, 1958. A charge for patent amortization for 1964 is to be made at 1/17 of the original patents cost.
A charge for patterns and dies amortization for 1964 is to be made at 15% of the balance in the patterns and dies account.
A charge for tools used during the year is to be made at 20% of the balance in the tools account.

(c) The allowance for bad debts is to be increased to a balance of $3,200.

(d) Accrued Expenses:
Salaries and wages: direct labor, $1,400; indirect labor, $300; sales salaries, $400; shipping department salaries, $100.
Interest on bonds is payable semiannually on February 1 and August 1.
Interest on notes payable, $50.
Property taxes, $2,000.

(e) Prepaid Expenses: Insurance, $2,500.

(f) Accrued Revenue: Interest on notes receivable, $300.

(g) The following information is also to be recorded:
(1) It is discovered that sales commissions of $1,200 were charged in error to the account Shipping Department Salaries.
(2) On December 30 the board of directors declared a quarterly dividend on preferred stock and a dividend of $1.50 on common stock, payable January 25, 1965, to stockholders of record January 15, 1965.
(3) Income taxes for 1964 are estimated at $20,000.
Taxes, expired insurance, and building expenses are to be distributed as follows: to manufacturing operations, 70%; to selling operations, 20%; to general operations, 10%.
The only charges to retained earnings during the year resulted from the declaration of the regular quarterly dividends on preferred stock. The balance of Retained Earnings on January 1, 1964 was $129,500.

*Instructions:* (1) Prepare a ten-column work sheet. There should be a pair of columns for trial balance, adjustments, manufacturing, profit and loss, and balance sheet.

(2) Prepare (a) a balance sheet, (b) an income statement supported by schedules showing the cost of goods manufactured, selling expenses, and general and administrative expenses, and (c) a retained earnings statement.

(3) Prepare all of the journal entries necessary to give effect to the foregoing information and to adjust and close the books of the corporation.

(4) Prepare the reversing entries that may appropriately be made.

# Chapter 5

# CASH AND
# TEMPORARY INVESTMENTS

### Importance of working capital

The nature of working capital and the importance that attaches to a satisfactory working capital position have already been mentioned. A business may not be able to survive in the absence of a satisfactory relationship between current assets and current liabilities. Furthermore, its ability to prosper is largely determined by the composition of the current asset pool. There must be a satisfactory balance between liquid assets in the form of cash and temporary investments, and receivables and inventories. Activities of the business center around these assets. Cash and temporary investments, representing immediate purchasing power, are used to meet current claims and purchasing, payroll, and expense requirements; receivables are the outgrowth of sales effort and provide cash in the course of operations; merchandise is also a source of cash as well as the means of achieving a profit. Management in setting policies with respect to selling, purchasing, financing, expansion, and dividends must work within the limitations set by the company's working capital position. This chapter and the four that follow direct attention to the working capital items and to the problems of income measurement related thereto.

### Nature of cash

Cash is the most active item on the accounting statements. The movement of cash completes almost all purchases and sales transactions. Purchases of goods and services normally result in cash payments; sales normally result in cash receipts. Cash, more often than any other asset, is the item involved in business transactions. This is due to the nature of the business transactions, which include a price and conditions calling for settlement in terms of the medium of exchange.

In striking contrast to the activity of cash is its unproductive nature. Since cash is the measure of value, it cannot expand or grow unless it is converted into other properties. Excessive balances of cash on hand are often referred to as "idle cash." To be most useful to a business enterprise, cash must be kept moving.

## Composition of cash

Cash is represented by those monetary as well as nonmonetary items that are immediately available to management for business purposes. Cash includes commercial and saving deposits in banks and elsewhere that are available upon demand, and money items on hand that can be used as a medium of exchange or that are acceptable for deposit at face value by a bank. Cash on hand would include petty cash funds, change funds, and other regularly used and unexpended monetary funds, together with nonmonetary items consisting of personal checks, travelers' checks, cashiers' checks, bank drafts, and money orders.

"Acceptance at face value on deposit" is a satisfactory test in classifying as cash the items that may be found in the cash drawer. It is assumed that deposits in a bank are made regularly, and that deposits become the basis for disbursements by the depositor. Although postage stamps may in some instances pass for mail payments of small amounts, they are not accepted for deposit and should be classified as office supplies. Postdated checks are in effect notes receivable and should not be recognized as cash until the time they can be deposited. Checks deposited but returned by the bank because of insufficient funds in the debtor's account are receivables. Cash-due memorandums for money advanced to officers and employees are receivable items, in some instances less satisfactory receivables than those of trade customers. Paper left at a bank for collection represents a receivable until collection is made and the amount is added to the depositor's account. Stocks, bonds, and United States securities, although immediately convertible into cash, cannot be used as a means for making payments, hence do not constitute cash but should be recognized as investments.

Deposits in foreign banks subject to immediate and unrestricted withdrawal qualify as cash. Such balances should be converted into their U. S. dollar equivalents as of the date of the balance sheet. However, cash in foreign banks that is blocked or otherwise restricted as to use or withdrawal and cash in closed banks should be designated as claims or receivables of a current or noncurrent character and should be reported subject to allowances for losses on their realization.

Cash balances that have been specifically designated by management for special purposes may be separately reported. But those cash balances that are to be applied to some current purpose or current obligation are properly reported in the current section on the balance sheet. For example, cash funds for employees' travel, for payment of current interest and dividends, or for payment of taxes or other obligations included in the current liabilities may be separately reported but are still classified as current.

Cash restricted as to use by agreement should be separately designated and reported. Such cash should be reported as a current item only if it is to be applied to some current purpose or obligation. Cash representing refundable deposits collected from customers, for example, requires separate reporting. Classification of the cash balance as current or noncurrent should parallel the classification applied to the liability balance.

Cash balances that are not available for current purposes require separate designation and classification under a noncurrent heading on the balance sheet. The noncurrent classification applies to items such as the following: time deposits not currently available as a result of withdrawal restrictions; cash deposits on bids or options that may be applied to the acquisition of noncurrent assets; and cash funds held by trustees for plant acquisitions, bond retirement, and pension payments.

Since the concept of cash embodies the standard of value, no valuation problem is encountered in reporting those items qualifying as cash.

## Internal control

*Internal control* has been broadly defined by the Committee on Auditing Procedure of the AICPA as ". . . the plan of organization and all of the coordinate methods and measures adopted within a business to safeguard its assets, check the accuracy and reliability of its accounting data, promote operational efficiency, and encourage adherence to prescribed managerial policies."[1] This definition may be considered to embrace both *accounting controls* and *administrative controls*. Accounting controls dealing with the safeguarding of assets and the reliability of records are expressed in the form of systems of authorization and approval, separation of duties concerned with record keeping and reporting from those concerned with operations and asset custody, physical controls over assets, and internal auditing. Administrative controls dealing with operational efficiency and adherence to managerial policies are expressed in the form of statistical analyses, time and motion studies, performance reports, employee training programs, and quality controls.[2]

Obviously, the system of internal control must be developed with appropriate regard to the size and nature of the particular unit that is to be served. Its design should provide the maximum contributions practicable considering the special risks that are faced as well as the costs of providing controls.

---

[1] *Internal Control — Elements of a Coordinated System and Its Importance to Management and the Independent Public Accountant*, 1949 (New York: American Institute of Certified Public Accountants), p. 6.

[2] *Statement on Auditing Procedure No. 33*, "Auditing Standards and Procedures," 1963 (New York: American Institute of Certified Public Accountants), p. 28.

In any system of internal accounting control, special emphasis must be placed on the procedures for handling and accounting for cash.

## Control of cash

Because of the characteristics of cash — its small bulk, its lack of owner identification, and its immediate transferability — it is the asset most subject to misappropriation. Losses can be avoided only by careful control of cash from the time it is received until the time it is spent.

Control over business cash normally requires as a minimum the separation of cash custodial functions and cash recording functions. When the same persons have access to cash and also to the cash records, the business becomes vulnerable to the misappropriation of cash and to the manipulation or falsification of cash records. The following are representative of the practices that have been found under these circumstances: (1) cash receipts from sales, from recoveries of accounts previously written off, from refunds on invoice overpayments, and from other sources are understated, the unrecorded cash being pocketed; (2) receivables are not entered on the books and cash collected on such receivables is withheld; (3) customers' accounts are credited for remittances but Sales Returns or Bad Debts is charged and the cash is withheld; (4) checks for personal purposes are charged to business expense; (5) invoices, vouchers, receipts, payroll records, or vouchers once approved and paid are used in support of fictitious charges, and endorsements on checks issued in payment of such charges are subsequently forged; (6) the cash balance is misstated by erroneous footings in the cash receipts and disbursement records, cash equivalent to the misstatement being withheld.

Two additional practices, *check kiting* and *lapping*, are found when those who handle cash also maintain the cash records of the business.

Check kiting occurs when at the end of a month a transfer of funds is made by check from one bank to another to cover a cash shortage, and the entry to record the issue of the check is held over until the beginning of the new period. A cash increase in the customer's balance is recognized by the second bank in the current month as a result of the receipt of the check but a corresponding decrease in the customer's balance is not recognized by the first bank in the absence of current clearance of the check affecting the transfer. When the bank statements are received, the balance in the bank in which the check was deposited shows an increase. At the same time, the balance shown in the bank on which the check was drawn remains unchanged, because the check has not yet been presented to that bank for payment. A cash shortage is thus temporarily concealed.

Lapping occurs when a customer's remittance is misappropriated, the customer's account being credited when cash is collected from another customer at a later date. This process may be continued with further misappropriations and increasing delays in postings. To illustrate lapping, assume that on successive days, cash is received from customers A, B, and C in amounts of $75, $125, and $120. A's payment is misappropriated. A is subsequently credited with $75 out of B's payment and the difference, $50, is misappropriated. B is credited for $125 upon C's $120 payment and $5 is returned on the amounts originally "borrowed." The shortage at this point is $120, the unrecorded credit to C's account. This procedure can be continued with but slight delay in recording any customer's payment. The embezzler usually intends to return the money and avoid the strain of lapping after he has made a "profit on his investments." Unable to make restitution, he may resort to a fictitious entry charging Bad Debts or some other expense account and crediting the customers' balances to bring these up to date.

A system of accounting control over cash funds should serve to disclose cash discrepancies as well as to fix responsibility for any possible misappropriations or mistakes in handling and recording cash. When misuse of funds or errors are indicated, it is only fair to members of an organization that the causes be determined and the responsibility be fixed so that innocent parties may be spared any embarrassment. Responsibilities for the handling and recording functions should be specifically defined and scrupulously observed and carried out.

The system for the control of cash must be adapted to the particular business that it is to serve. It is not feasible to attempt to describe all of the features and techniques that might be employed in businesses of various kinds and sizes. In general, however, systems of cash control deny access to the records to those who handle cash. This reduces the possibility of improper entries to conceal the misuse of cash receipts and cash payments. The misappropriation of cash is greatly reduced if two or more employees must conspire in the embezzlement. Further, systems normally provide for separation of the receiving and paying functions. The basic characteristics of a system of cash control are listed and described below:

1. Separation of handling and recording cash receipts.
2. Daily deposit of all cash received.
3. Voucher system to control cash payments.
4. Internal audit at irregular intervals.

*Separation of handling and recording cash receipts.* An adequate system normally requires that cash from sales and cash remittances from customers be made available directly to the treasurer or the cashier for deposit, while records related to such transactions as well as records related to bank deposits be made available directly to the bookkeeping division. It is also desirable that comparisons of bank deposits with the book records of cash be made regularly by a third party who is engaged neither in the cash handling nor in the cash recording functions. Frequently, for example, a clerk opens the mail, prepares lists of remittances in duplicate, and then sends the cash and one copy of the list of remittances to the cashier and the second copy of the list to the bookkeeping division. Readings of cash registers are made by some responsible individual other than the cashier at the end of the day. The cash together with a summary of the receipts is sent to the cashier; a summary of the receipts is also sent to the bookkeeping division. Although deposits in the bank are made by the cashier or treasurer, entries on the books are made from lists of remittances and register readings prepared by individuals not otherwise involved in handling or recording cash. Members of the accounting or auditing staff compare periodic bank statements with related data on the books to determine whether the data are in agreement. If customers' remittances are not listed and the cash is misused, statements to customers will report excessive amounts and protests will lead to sources of the discrepancies; if cash receipts listed are not deposited properly, the bank record will not agree with cash records.

*Daily deposit of all cash received.* The daily deposit of all cash received prevents sums of cash from lying around the office and being used for other than business purposes. Officers and employees have less opportunity to borrow on I.O.U.'s. Both the temptation for misappropriation of cash and the risk of theft of this item are avoided. The bank now protects company funds and releases these only upon proper company authorization. When the full receipts are deposited daily, the bank's record of deposits must agree with the depositor's record of cash receipts. This double record of cash provides an automatic check over cash receipts.

*Voucher system to control cash payments.* The use of the voucher system to control cash payments is a desirable feature of cash control. Vouchers authorizing disbursements of cash by check are made at the time goods or services are received and found acceptable. Entries in the voucher register recording the expenditures and the authorizations for payment are made by the bookkeeping division. Checks are also prepared here and are sent, together with the documents supporting the disbursements, to the person specifically authorized to make payment, normally the official designated as treasurer. This party signs and issues checks only after careful inspection of the vouchers supporting and authorizing payments. The bookkeeping department, upon notification of the issuance of checks, makes appropriate records of this fact. Receiving and paying functions of the business are maintained as two separate systems. In each instance, custodial and recording activities are exercised by different parties.

*Internal audit at irregular intervals.* Internal audits at irregular and unannounced intervals may be made a part of the system of cash control. A member of the internal auditing staff verifies the records and checks upon the activities of those employees handling cash to make sure that the provisions of the system are being carried out. Such control is particularly desirable over petty cash and other cash funds where cash handling and bookkeeping are generally combined.

### Double record of cash

The preceding section listed the daily deposit of all cash received as an important factor in the control of cash. If all cash receipts are deposited daily, then the bank record of deposits will agree with the depositor's record of cash receipts. As a complementary device, all cash payments should be made by check, the bank then maintaining a record for checks that will agree with the depositor's record of cash payments. Two complete cash summaries are thus available, one in the cash account and the other on the monthly bank statement. In addition to the advantages resulting from organized and consistent routines applied to cash receipts and disbursements, a duplicate record of cash maintained by an outside agency is made available as a check upon the accuracy of the records kept by the company.

Maintenance of the double record of cash involves two special business and accounting procedures described in the following sections: (1) the adoption of a system of cash disbursements from a petty cash fund, and (2) reconciliation of the bank balance with the cash account balance at regular intervals.

### Imprest system of cash funds

Immediate cash payments and payments that are too small to be made by check may be made from a petty cash fund. Under the *imprest system* the petty cash fund is created by drawing a check to Petty Cash for the amount of the fund. In recording the establishment of the fund, Petty Cash Fund is charged and Cash is credited. The cash is then turned over to a cashier or some person who is to be responsible for payments made out of the fund. The cashier generally requires a signed receipt for all payments made. Such receipts may be printed in prenumbered form. Frequently, a bill or other memorandum is submitted when a payment is requested. A record of petty cash payments may be kept in a *petty cash journal*.

Whenever the amount of cash in the fund runs low and also at the end of each fiscal period, the fund is replenished by writing a check to Petty Cash equal to the payments that have been made. In recording replenishment, expenses and other appropriate accounts are charged for petty cash disbursements and Cash is credited. Replenishment is necessary whenever statements are to be prepared, since petty cash disbursements are recognized on the books only when the fund is replenished.

The request for cash to replenish the fund is supported by a summary and analysis of the signed receipts that were required at the time of the payments from the fund. This analysis is the basis for the charges that are recognized on the books when the replenishing check is issued. The signed receipts, together with appropriate supporting documents, are filed as evidence supporting petty cash disbursements.

The cashier of the petty cash fund is held accountable for the total amount of the fund in his care. He must have on hand at all times cash and signed receipts equal in amount to the original balance of the fund. He should be discouraged from cashing employees' checks from petty cash or otherwise engaging in a banking function. If a banking function is to be undertaken, it should represent a separate activity with a fund established for this purpose. Inasmuch as the cashier normally keeps the petty cash records, the rule of separating the recording and handling of cash is not here enforced.

Methods other than the imprest system are sometimes employed in handling petty cash. These may provide for checks of fixed amounts to be given to the petty cashier upon his request. Replenishing checks would not have to agree with the disbursements. Records of petty cash payments may be used as books of original entry for posting purposes. In establishing the fund, Petty Cash is debited and Cash is credited. Disbursements from the fund are recorded by debits to expenses and credits to Petty Cash. Replenishment is recorded by a debit to Petty Cash and a credit to Cash. This method is sometimes called the *fluctuating fund method* to distinguish it from the imprest system that provides for a nonfluctuating fund.

The imprest system may be employed not only for petty cash but for other cash funds in a large organization. For example, a branch office or agency may be allowed a fund that is subsequently replenished for amounts equal to disbursements out of the fund. Evidence concerning payments out of the fund is submitted with the request for replenishment, and fund disbursements are recorded on the books at the time of fund replenishment.

The petty cash operation should be maintained apart from other cash funds employed for particular business purposes. For example, a business may require funds for making change. Certain sums of coins and currency are withheld from deposit at the end of each day to be carried forward as the change funds for the beginning of business on the next day. A separate account should be established to report a cash supply always on hand. Also, special funds or bank accounts may be established for payrolls, dividend distributions, and bond interest payments. Each fund would call for a separate accounting.

### Reconciliation of bank balances

When daily receipts are deposited and payments other than those from petty cash are made by check, the bank's account of its transactions with the depositor provides a record that may be compared with the record of cash on the depositor's books. A comparison of the bank balance with the balance reported on the books is usually made monthly by means of a summary known as a *bank reconciliation statement*. The reconciliation statement is prepared to disclose any errors or irregularities existing in either the bank's records or those maintained by the business unit. It is developed in a form that points out the reasons for discrepancies in the two balances. It should be prepared by an individual who neither handles nor records cash, preferably by a member of the internal audit staff. Any discrepancies should be brought to the immediate attention of appropriate company officials.

An understanding of the reciprocal relationship that exists between the records of the depositor and of the bank is necessary in the preparation of the reconciliation statement. All debits to the bank on the books of the depositor should be matched by credits to the depositor on the books of the bank; all credits to the bank on the books of the depositor should be matched by debits to the depositor on the books of the bank. To illustrate, cash from sales is recorded on the books of the depositor by a debit to the account with the bank, for example, Cash — State First National Bank, and a credit to Sales; the bank upon receiving the deposit debits Cash and credits the account with the depositor. A check in payment of an account is recorded on the books of the depositor by a debit to Accounts Payable, and a credit to the account with the bank; the bank upon clearing the check debits the account with the depositor and credits Cash.

When the two records are compared, certain items may appear on one record and not on the other, resulting in a difference in the two balances. Discrepancies in depositor and bank balances may be classified as follows:

(1) *Debits on the depositor's records without corresponding credits on the bank records.* For example, a deposit recognized on the depositor's records on the last day of the month may have been mailed, put into an after-hours depository, or held for transfer to the bank on the next day, and does not appear on the bank statement.

(2) *Credits on the depositor's records without corresponding debits on the bank records.* For example, checks that were drawn and are recognized on the depositor's records may not yet have cleared and do not appear on the bank statement.

(3) *Debits on the bank records without corresponding credits on depositor's records.* For example, the bank may have charged the depositor's account for bank services, check books, interest, collections, and other items, but the depositor has not been notified of these before receiving his bank statement and these do not appear on his books.

(4) *Credits on the bank records without corresponding debits on the depositor's records.* For example, the bank may have credited the depositor's

Mason, Inc.
Bank Reconciliation Statement
November 30, 1964

| | | |
|---|---:|---:|
| Balance per bank statement, November 30, 1964................ | | $2,979.72 |
| Add: Receipts for November 30 not yet deposited... | $658.50 | |
| Charge for interest made to depositor's account by bank in error....................... | 12.50 | 671.00 |
| | | $3,650.72 |
| Deduct outstanding checks: | | |
| No. 1125.................................... | $ 58.16 | |
| No. 1138.................................... | 100.00 | |
| No. 1152.................................... | 98.60 | |
| No. 1154.................................... | 255.00 | |
| No. 1155.................................... | 192.07 | 703.83 |
| Corrected bank balance............................. | | $2,946.89 |
| Balance per books, November 30, 1964..................... | | $2,552.49 |
| Add: Proceeds of draft collected by bank November 30 ($500 face less $1.50 bank charges)... | $498.50 | |
| Check No. 1116 for $46 recorded by depositor as $64 in error....................... | 18.00 | 516.50 |
| | | $3,068.99 |
| Deduct: Bank service charges.................... | $ 3.16 | |
| Customer's check deposited November 25 found to be uncollectible.............. | 118.94 | 122.10 |
| Corrected book balance............................. | | $2,946.89 |

**Reconciliation of Bank and Book Balances to Corrected Balances**

account for amounts collected on his behalf, but the depositor has not been notified of these before receiving his bank statement and these do not appear on his books.

If, after considering the items mentioned, the bank statement and the book balances cannot be reconciled, a detailed analysis of both the bank's records and the depositor's books may be necessary to determine whether errors or other irregularities exist on the records of either party.

There are two forms of the bank reconciliation statement. One form is prepared in two sections, the bank statement balance being adjusted to the corrected cash balance in the first section, and the book balance being adjusted to the same corrected cash balance in the second section. The first section, then, contains items that the bank has not recognized as well as any corrections for errors that were made by the bank; the second section contains items that the depositor has not yet recognized and any corrections for errors that were made by the depositor. Another form begins with the bank statement balance and reports the adjustments that must be applied to this balance to obtain the cash balance on the depositor's books. The second form, then, simply reports the items that account for the discrepancy between the bank and book balances. The first form is illustrated on the preceding page; the second is illustrated below.

Mason, Inc.
Bank Reconciliation Statement
November 30, 1964

| | | | |
|---|---:|---:|---:|
| Balance per bank statement, November 30, 1964............... | | | $2,979.72 |
| Add: Receipts for November 30 not yet deposited... | $658.50 | | |
| Charge for interest made to depositor's account by bank in error....................... | | 12.50 | |
| Bank service charges....................... | | 3.16 | |
| Customer's check deposited November 25 found to be uncollectible...................... | | 118.94 | 793.10 |
| | | | $3,772.82 |
| Deduct: Outstanding checks: | | | |
| No. 1125.................... | $ 58.16 | | |
| No. 1138.................... | 100.00 | | |
| No. 1152.................... | 98.60 | | |
| No. 1154.................... | 255.00 | | |
| No. 1155.................... | 192.07 | $703.83 | |
| Check No. 1116 for $46 recorded by depositor at $64 in error................. | | 18.00 | |
| Proceeds of draft collected by bank on November 30........................ | | 498.50 | 1,220.33 |
| Balance per books, November 30, 1964...................... | | | $2,552.49 |

**Reconciliation of Bank Balance to Book Balance**

Although the first form of bank reconciliation may be considered preferable because it develops a corrected cash figure and shows separately all of the items requiring adjustment on the depositor's books, some accountants prefer to use the second form, which is consistent with the nature of the analysis that is required in many other accounting situations.

After preparing the reconciliation, the depositor should record any items appearing on the bank statement and requiring recognition on his books, as well as any corrections for errors discovered on his own books. The bank should be notified immediately of any bank errors. The following entries are required on the books of Mason, Inc., as a result of the reconciliation just made:

| | | |
|---|---:|---:|
| Cash......................................... | 498.50 | |
| Miscellaneous General Expense.................. | 1.50 | |
| Notes Receivable........................... | | 500.00 |
| To record collection of a $500 time draft by the bank on which bank charges were $1.50. | | |
| Cash......................................... | 18.00 | |
| Advertising................................. | | 18.00 |
| To record correction for check in payment of advertising that was recorded as $64 instead of the actual amount, $46. | | |
| Accounts Receivable......................... | 118.94 | |
| Miscellaneous General Expense.................. | 3.16 | |
| Cash....................................... | | 122.10 |
| To record customer's uncollectible check and bank charges for November. | | |

After these entries are posted, the cash account will show a balance of $2,946.89. This is the amount to be reported on the balance sheet.

### Misrepresentation of current condition

Although a system of internal control may provide for the effective safeguarding of cash, careful examination of the records is still necessary at the end of the accounting period to determine whether transactions have been satisfactorily recorded and cash and the current position of the business are properly presented. Certain practices designed to present a more favorable financial condition than is actually the case may be encountered. Such practices are sometimes referred to as "window dressing." For example, cash records may be held open for a few days after the close of the fiscal period, and cash received from customers during this period reported as receipts of the preceding period. An improved cash position is thus reported. If this balance is then used as a basis for drawing predated checks in payment of accounts payable, the ratio of current assets to current liabilities is improved. For example, if current assets are $30,000 and current liabilities are $20,000 providing a current ratio of 1.5 to 1, recording payment to creditors of $10,000 will produce balances of $20,000 and $10,000, a current ratio of 2 to 1. The current ratio is also improved by writing checks in payment of obligations and entering these on the books even though checks are not to be mailed until the following period. Or the current position as well as net income and capital are overstated by predating sales made at the beginning of the new period. A careful review of the records will disclose whether any improper practices have been employed. If such practices are discovered, the accounts should be corrected.

## Cash overdrafts

A credit balance in the cash account resulting from the issuance of checks in excess of the amount on deposit is known as a *cash overdraft* and should be reported as a current liability. An overdraft may not necessarily embarrass the company if a number of checks are outstanding and deposits are made to cover the checks before they are actually cleared. When a company has two balances with a single bank, there can be no objection to the offset of the overdraft against an account with a positive balance; failure by the depositor to meet the overdraft will actually result in bank action to effect such offset. However, when a company has accounts with two different banks and there is a positive balance in one account and an overdraft in the other, both an asset balance and a liability balance should be recognized in view of the claim against one bank and an obligation to the other; if recognition of an overdraft is to be avoided, cash should actually be transferred to cover the deficiency.

## Cash forecasts

Management, in meeting its responsibilities and in achieving successful business operations, needs to develop intelligent objectives and means for the realization of such objectives. The instrument that management employs to express its objectives and to define the guides and controls for achieving these is the business *budget*. A comprehensive operating budget offers an integrated and detailed plan for the future. Standards are set for sales, production, and expenses. The inflow and outgo of cash are planned. Statements are prepared reporting the estimated earnings and financial position in terms of projected operations, financing, and earnings distributions. With a well-organized master plan for integrated and coordinated action by all parts of the organization, operations may be channeled toward achievement of individual and collective goals. Continuous comparisons are made between the standards that have been set by the budget and the results actually achieved through operations.

Variations between budgetary standards and actual results are evaluated, and adjustment and revision of the standards are made when appropriate.

Although the budget expresses the objectives set by top management and those in charge of operations, its preparation as well as subsequent analyses indicating the degree to which objectives have been realized are normally the responsibilities of the controller and his staff. The accounting staff is technically qualified to organize and present operational plans in the most satisfactory form. The accountants, too, are best qualified to develop the analyses that are required by management in evaluating the past and setting plans for the future.

An important part of any budget is the forecast and planning of cash. Cash is the beginning and the end of all business activity, and any plans for the future must be directly related to cash. Even in the absence of a comprehensive budgetary program, attention must be directed to cash, its expected movement, and methods for its proper utilization and control, if financial chaos is to be avoided. Adequate cash must be available for all current needs; at the same time, any cash in excess of current needs and reasonable reserves must be profitably employed.

The preparation of a *cash forecast* requires estimates of future cash receipts and cash disbursements. In projecting the cash flow, it is necessary to refer to forecasts and plans that have been made by management relative to sales, inventory acquisitions, operational costs, and plant and equipment acquisitions. Appropriate consideration must also be given to commitments with creditors and owners and probable actions of the board of directors that will affect the cash position.

Cash receipts and disbursements may not be matched in the months to come as the result of a number of factors, the most important of which are the following:

1. Purchases and payments to creditors predate sales and collections from customers. Cyclical factors call for heavy seasonal expenditures that are recovered only at some later date.
2. Acquisition of plant and equipment items are made at various intervals.
3. Long-term debt is retired at various intervals.

With a full consideration of these factors, management may set plans for establishing and maintaining a satisfactory cash balance. In meeting the requirements of (1) above, steps may be taken to provide for a supply of cash through short-term borrowing or through the conversion of marketable securities held for such purposes. Upon the recovery of cash through sales, excess cash may be applied to the payment of loans, to the acquisition of marketable securities, to the increase of the cash balance, or to the payment of dividends. In meeting the requirements of (2) and

(3), planning may be directed towards the acquisition of cash through long-term borrowing, through the issuance of additional stock, or through the accumulation of cash from the operations of the business unit.

A cash forecast prepared in statement form as a part of a budgetary program is illustrated below. The illustration covers only a part of a year. Ordinarily the forecast would be developed for a period of a year.

The statement is usually accompanied by schedules that offer detailed support for the various data summarized thereon. Although the example makes reference to a number of schedules, only the schedules in support of collections on trade accounts receivable and payments on trade accounts payable are illustrated on the opposite page.

Carver Co.

Cash Forecast

For Three Months Ending December 31, 1964

|  | October | November | December |
|---|---|---|---|
| Cash sales..................................... | 10,000 | 15,000 | 25,000 |
| Collections on accounts receivable (see schedule).. | 50,000 | 61,000 | 80,500 |
| Other receipts (interest and dividend income, see schedule)................................. | 2,500 | 2,000 | 3,000 |
|  | 62,500 | 78,000 | 108,500 |
| Merchandise payments (see schedule)........... | 68,600 | 44,100 | 19,600 |
| Expense payments (see schedule)............... | 25,000 | 27,500 | 30,000 |
| Other payments (acquisition of furniture and equipment, see schedule).................... | 7,500 |  |  |
|  | 101,100 | 71,600 | 49,600 |
| Cash increase (decrease) for month............. | (38,600) | 6,400 | 58,900 |
| Cash balance at beginning of month............ | 16,500 | 7,900 | 14,300 |
| Cash requirements: |  |  |  |
| Obtained through loans..................... | 10,000 |  |  |
| Obtained through sale of marketable securities.. | 20,000 |  |  |
|  | 7,900 | 14,300 | 73,200 |
| Cash applications: |  |  |  |
| To payment of loans....................... |  |  | (25,000) |
| To purchase of marketable securities.......... |  |  | (35,000) |
| Cash balance carried into succeeding month...... | 7,900 | 14,300 | 13,200 |

## Nature of temporary investments

A company with an excess of available cash may deposit such funds as a time deposit or under a certificate of deposit at a bank, or it may

## Cash Forecast
### Schedule Reporting Collections on Accounts Receivable*
### For Three Months Ending December 31, 1964

|  | Estimated Sales | October | November | December |
|---|---|---|---|---|
| August........................ | 40,000 | 4,000 | | |
| September..................... | 50,000 | 40,000 | 5,000 | |
| October....................... | 60,000 | 6,000 | 48,000 | 6,000 |
| November..................... | 80,000 | | 8,000 | 64,000 |
| December..................... | 105,000 | | | 10,500 |
| Total monthly collections......... | ......... | 50,000 | 61,000 | 80,500 |

*Terms of sale — no cash discounts, payments due by the tenth of the month following sale. It is assumed that collections on charge sales will be made as follows:

Month of sale......................................... 10%
First month following sale............................ 80%
Second month following sale.......................... 10%

## Cash Forecast
### Schedule Reporting Payments on Accounts Payable*
### For Three Months Ending December 31, 1964

|  | Estimated Purchases | Purchases Discounts | Net Purchases | October | November | December |
|---|---|---|---|---|---|---|
| September.. | 60,000 | 1,200 | 58,800 | 19,600 | | |
| October.... | 75,000 | 1,500 | 73,500 | 49,000 | 24,500 | |
| November.. | 30,000 | 600 | 29,400 | | 19,600 | 9,800 |
| December.. | 15,000 | 300 | 14,700 | | | 9,800 |
| Total monthly payments.......... | ......... | | | 68,600 | 44,100 | 19,600 |

*A 2% cash discount is allowed by vendors on payments made within 10 days from date of purchase. It is assumed that discounts will be taken on all purchases, payments to be made as follows:

Month of purchase................................ 66⅔%
Month following purchase (first 10 days)............. 33⅓%

purchase securities. Income will thus be produced that would not be available if cash were left idle. Investments made during seasonal periods of low activity can be converted into cash in periods of expanding operations. Asset items arising from temporary conversions of cash are commonly reported in the current asset section of the balance sheet under the heading, Temporary Investments. Temporary investments are frequently limited to marketable securities.

Securities that are purchased as temporary investments should be marketable on short notice. There should be a day-to-day market for them, and the volume of trading in the securities should be sufficient to absorb a company's holdings without materially affecting the market price. Although there may be no definite assurance that the securities will be disposed of without loss, it is essential that any possible loss resulting from such disposal be kept at a minimum. Securities that have a limited market and fluctuate widely in price are not suitable for temporary investments. The prices of United States government securities tend to be relatively stable and the market for these securities is quite broad. Because of these factors, short-term government securities are widely favored despite their relatively low interest rates.

## Composition of temporary investments

Investments qualify for reporting as temporary investments as long as (1) there is a ready market for converting such securities into cash and (2) it is management's intention to sell them if the need for cash arises. Such investments may be converted into cash within a relatively short period after being acquired, or they may be carried for some time. In either case, however, they are properly shown under the current heading. The following types of investments do not qualify as marketable securities, and should not be included in the current section: (a) reacquired shares of the company's own stock, (b) securities acquired for control of a company, (c) securities held for maintenance of business relations, and (d) other securities that cannot be used or are not intended to be used as a ready source of cash.

## Recording purchase and sale of marketable securities

Stocks and bonds acquired as temporary investments are recorded at cost, which includes brokers' fees, taxes, and other charges incurred in their acquisition. Shares are normally quoted at a price per single share; bonds are quoted at a price per $100 face value although they are normally issued in $1,000 denominations. The purchase of 100 shares at $5\frac{1}{8}$, then, would indicate a purchase price of $512.50; the purchase of a $1,000 bond at $104\frac{1}{4}$ would indicate a purchase price of $1,042.50.

When bonds are acquired between interest payment dates, the bond price is increased by a charge for accrued interest to the date of purchase. Such a charge should not be reported as part of investment cost. Two assets have been acquired — bonds and accrued interest — and the purchase price may be reported in two separate asset accounts. Upon the receipt of bond interest, the accrued interest account is closed and Interest Income is credited for the excess. Interest Income may be charged for the accrued interest paid. The subsequent collection of interest would then be credited in full to Interest Income. The latter procedure is usually more convenient.

When bonds are acquired at a price that is more or less than their maturity value and it is expected that they will be held until maturity, periodic amortization of the premium or accumulation of the discount with corresponding adjustments to income is appropriate. However, when bonds are acquired as a temporary investment and it is not likely that the bonds will be held until maturity, such procedures are normally not necessary.

When an investment is sold, the difference between the sales price and the value at which it is carried is reported as a gain or loss on the sale.

## Valuation of marketable securities

Three different methods for the valuation of marketable securities have been advanced: (1) cost, (2) cost or market, whichever is lower, and (3) market.

*Cost.* Marketable securities held as temporary investments are frequently carried at cost. The recognition of either gain or loss is deferred until the asset is sold, and at this time investment cost is matched against investment proceeds. Disclosure of the market value of securities is made parenthetically or by special note on the balance sheet so that the immediate current position can be determined for analysis purposes. The cost basis is consistent with income tax procedures that recognize neither a change in asset value nor gain or loss until there is a sale or exchange.

*Cost or market, whichever is lower.* Cost or market, whichever is lower, is the valuation method most commonly applied. Current market prices are regarded as affording an objective appraisal of the values of marketable securities. When market is lower than cost, security values are written down to the lower value; when market is higher than cost, securities are maintained at cost, profits awaiting confirmation through sale. In applying the lower of cost or market procedure, marketable securities may be reported at cost at one time and at market at another time, securities being valued regularly at the lower of the two alternative values.

The AICPA Committee on Accounting Procedure supports the use of a lower market. The Committee states:

> In the case of marketable securities where market value is less than cost by a substantial amount and it is evident that the decline in market value is not due to a mere temporary condition, the amount to be included as a current asset should not exceed the market value.[1]

The lower of cost or market rule may be employed in two ways: (1) it may be applied to securities in the aggregate or (2) it may be

---

[1] Accounting Research and Terminology Bulletins, 1961 (New York: American Institute of Certified Public Accountants), *Accounting Research Bulletin No. 43*, p. 23.

applied to the individual items.    To illustrate, assume marketable securities with costs and market values on December 31, 1964, as follows:

|  | Cost | Market | Lower of Cost or Market on Individual Basis |
|---|---|---|---|
| 1,000 shares of Carter Co. Common. | $20,000 | $16,000 | $16,000 |
| $25,000 Emerson Co. 5% Bonds.... | 25,000 | 26,500 | 25,000 |
| $10,000 Gardner Co. 4% Bonds..... | 10,000 | 7,500 | 7,500 |
|  | $55,000 | $50,000 | $48,500 |

The lower of cost or market value on an aggregate basis above is $50,000; on an individual basis, $48,500.  It would appear that sufficient conservatism is exercised in reporting securities at $50,000, the amount that would become available upon conversion of all the securities.

Recognition of the decline in value on the books calls for the reduction of the asset and a charge to a loss account; however, the loss is not recognized for income tax purposes and the basis of the securities for measurement of gain or loss continues to be cost.  Cost can be preserved on the books by the use of a valuation account to reduce the securities to market.  The following entry may be made in the example above:

| | | |
|---|---|---|
| Recognized Decline in Value of Marketable Securities..... | 5,000 | |
| Allowance for Decline in Value of Marketable Securities. | | 5,000 |

The balance sheet would show:

| | | |
|---|---|---|
| Marketable securities, at cost......................... | $55,000 | |
| Less allowance for decline in value of marketable securities. | 5,000 | |
| Securities at market value, December 31, 1964........... | | $50,000 |

This information could also be reported:

| | |
|---|---|
| Marketable securities at market (cost $55,000)........... | $50,000 |

The $5,000 loss may be reported on the income statement as a financial management expense or as an extraordinary loss, whichever may be considered appropriate.

When securities have been reduced to the lower of cost or market, adjustments are normally considered to be necessary in future periods only in the event of further declines.  Having established a lower basis, this is considered as replacing cost for further comparisons with market.  A market in excess of such substitute for cost is thus ignored until sale of the asset takes place.

Assume in the preceding example that the securities are sold in 1965 for $51,500.  An entry is made as follows:

| Cash.......................................... | 51,500 | |
| Allowance for Decline in Value of Marketable Securities.. | 5,000 | |
| Marketable Securities — Carter Co. Common......... | | 20,000 |
| Marketable Securities — Emerson Co. 5% Bonds....... | | 25,000 |
| Marketable Securities — Gardner Co. 4% Bonds....... | | 10,000 |
| Gain on Sale of Marketable Securities............... | | 1,500 |

Neither the $5,000 loss nor the $1,500 gain is recognized for income tax purposes; instead, a $3,500 loss is reported on the tax return for 1965 when securities that cost $55,000 are sold for $51,500.

It was assumed in the entry above that all of the securities were sold requiring full cancellation of the allowance. Assume, however, that only some of the holdings are sold. If the lower of cost or market had been applied on an individual basis, the allowance would be composed of amounts related to specific securities and sale of a security would be accompanied by a charge to the allowance for the amount related to the security sold. When the lower of cost or market is applied on an aggregate basis and there can be no identification of the allowance with specific securities, losses are normally charged against the allowance until this balance is canceled. Further losses would be reported in nominal accounts. At the end of the period, if the aggregate market for securities on hand is less than their cost, an allowance for the decline would be established once more.

To illustrate, assume securities valued at the lower of cost or market at the end of 1964 as shown on page 134, but sale in 1965 of only the Carter Co. stock for $17,000. The following entry would be made:

| Cash............................................... | 17,000 | |
| Allowance for Decline in Value of Marketable Securities..... | 3,000 | |
| Marketable Securities — Carter Co. Common........... | | 20,000 |

This entry leaves the valuation account with a balance of $2,000. Assuming that the market value of the remaining securities remains unchanged at $34,000 at the end of 1965, they would still be reported at cost, $35,000, less the allowance for decline carried over from the preceding period, $2,000, or $33,000.

On the other hand, assume sale of the Carter Co. stock for $14,000. The sale would be recorded as follows:

| Cash............................................... | 14,000 | |
| Allowance for Decline in Value of Marketable Securities..... | 5,000 | |
| Loss on Sale of Marketable Securities..................... | 1,000 | |
| Marketable Securities — Carter Co. Common........... | | 20,000 |

Assuming again that the remaining securities have a market value of $34,000 at the end of 1965, the following entry would be required in reporting these at the lower market:

| Recognized Decline in Value of Marketable Securities....... | 1,000 | |
| Allowance for Decline in Value of Marketable Securities.. | | 1,000 |

*Market.* There are some who insist that marketable securities should be valued at market: securities on the balance sheet should be reported at their current values whether higher or lower than cost; capital on the balance sheet should reflect not only the gains and losses on securities sold, but also the changes in values of securities still held. In applying market, it would be possible to recognize changes in security values by adjusting asset account balances and recognizing profit and loss from such asset restatement. However, to preserve investment cost data for income tax purposes, asset increases may be reported in special asset accounts; decreases may be reported in special valuation accounts. Furthermore, if it is felt that any increase in retained earnings should await sale of the securities, appraisal capital may be credited. To illustrate the procedure that may be followed, assume that at the end of 1964 securities costing $50,000 have quoted values of $60,000. The securities are sold in 1965 for $62,000. An unrealized gain is reported at the end of 1964. This is canceled when the securities are sold in 1965 and the effect of the sale is reported in profit and loss. The entries are:

December 31, 1964

| | | |
|---|---|---|
| Marketable Securities — Increase to Current Market Value.. | 10,000 | |
| Appraisal Capital — Increase in Marketable Securities to Current Market Value............................... | | 10,000 |

March 5, 1965

| | | |
|---|---|---|
| Cash.................................................... | 62,000 | |
| Appraisal Capital — Increase in Marketable Securities to Current Market Value.................................... | 10,000 | |
| Marketable Securities (at cost)........................ | | 50,000 |
| Marketable Securities — Increase to Current Market Value | | 10,000 |
| Gain on Sale of Marketable Securities................. | | 12,000 |

Although changes in market values must be disregarded for general income tax purposes, regulations do permit recognized dealers in securities to value periodic security "inventories" at cost, cost or market, whichever is lower, or market. The valuation procedure that is adopted must be applied consistently in successive tax reportings.

*Evaluation of methods.* Valuation at cost finds support on the grounds that it is an extension of the cost principle; the asset is carried at cost until a sale or exchange provides an alternative asset and confirms a gain or loss. The cost method offers valuation on a consistent base from period to period. It is the simplest method to apply and adheres to income tax requirements. However, certain objections to cost can be raised. The use of cost means that investments are carried at amounts that are more or less than values that can be objectively established at the date of the balance sheet, and the integrity of both balance sheet and income statement measurements can be challenged. The party using the financial statement must refer to parenthetical notes or other accompanying data in reaching conclusions relative to business position and operations. Overlooking supplementary data or failing to adjust properly for these, the person using the statements may reach conclusions that are seriously in error. The use of cost also means that identical securities are reported at different values because of purchases at different prices. A further objection is that management in controlling the sale of securities can determine the periods in which gains or losses are to be recognized even though such changes may have accrued over a number of periods.

The lower of cost or market procedure provides for the recognition of market declines and serves to prevent the mistakes that might arise in analyzing statements when these are not reported. The lower of cost or market is supported as a conservative procedure. But this approach is challenged on a number of grounds. It can be maintained that the recognition of price increases is no less important than the recognition of price decreases in stating financial condition and the result of operations. Valuation at the lower of cost or market may be the most complicated method to apply in the accounts. It fails to provide consistency in valuation — cost at the end of one period may be replaced by a lower of cost or market at the end of the next. As indicated earlier, in certain instances the lower of cost or market procedure may be overly conservative, providing valuations that are less than the aggregate lower market. Also, among its limitations, the lower of cost or market does not conform with income tax requirements and requires the maintenance of supplementary tax records.

When the market value for marketable securities is less than cost, little objection is made to recognizing the decline on the financial statements; consistency would call for recognizing market value when this is more than cost. With valuation at market, those referring to the financial statements can satisfactorily appraise the relationship of monetary assets and current assets to current liabilities; they can properly evaluate managerial decisions and activities relative to purchases, sales, and holdings of marketable securities. However, valuation at market is not as simple to apply as the cost method. It is also challenged as a departure from the cost principle and as lacking in conservatism. Furthermore, market is not acceptable for general income tax purposes and requires the maintenance of supplementary records for tax reporting.

The importance of information concerning market values for items included in the working capital pool is obvious. It should be emphasized that when market values are not actually introduced into the accounts, this information should be incorporated in the financial statements by parenthetical remark or note. The Securities and Exchange Commission requires that the following rules be applied in reporting securities as a current asset in statements that are filed with the Commission:

> Include only securities having a ready market. . . . State the basis of determining the amount at which carried. The aggregate cost, and aggregate amount on the basis of current market quotations, shall be stated parenthetically or otherwise.[1]

### Presentation of cash and temporary investments on the balance sheet

For statement purposes, cash may be reported as a single item or it may be summarized under several descriptive headings, such as cash on hand, commercial deposits, and savings deposits. Since current assets are normally reported in the order of their liquidity, cash is listed first, followed by temporary investments, receivables, and inventories. When temporary investments are pledged for some particular purpose, the nature and the purpose of such a pledge should be disclosed parenthetically or by note.

Cash and temporary investments may be reported on the balance sheet in the following manner:

Current assets:

| | | | |
|---|---|---|---|
| Cash on hand and demand deposits in banks.............................. | | | $ 46,000 |
| Special cash deposits (to pay interest and dividends).......................... | | | 24,000 |
| Temporary investments: | | | |
|    Time deposits in banks.............. | | $100,000 | |
|    Marketable securities: | | | |
|       U.S. Government obligations, at cost, which is approximate market value ($50,000 in bonds has been pledged as security on short-term bank loan). | $150,000 | | |
|       Other stocks and bonds at cost (quoted market price, $44,200)........... | 35,000 | 185,000 | |
|    Total temporary investments........... | | | 285,000 |

---

[1]Regulation S-X. This regulation is issued by the Securities and Exchange Commission and states the basic rules as to form and content that are to be observed in the preparation of reports that are required to be filed with the Commission under federal laws. The Commission has released a number of other instruction books and regulations that give the different rules and procedures adopted by the Commission.

## QUESTIONS

**1.** State how each of the following items should be reported on the balance sheet: (a) demand deposits with bank, (b) blocked cash deposits in foreign banks, (c) payroll fund to pay off accrued salaries, (d) change funds on hand, (e) cash on deposit in escrow on purchase of property, (f) cash in a special cash account to be used currently for the construction of a new building.

**2.** (a) Define internal control. (b) Suggest the different techniques that might be employed in adopting a system of internal control for cash.

**3.** (a) Explain check kiting and lapping. (b) Mention at least six other practices that result in misappropriations of cash in the absence of an adequate system of internal control.

**4.** (a) What is the nature of a budget? (b) What is a cash forecast? (c) Describe the preparation of the cash forecast and the nature of the problems encountered in maintaining a healthy cash status.

**5.** On reconciling the cash account with the bank statement, it is found that the general cash fund is overdrawn $436 but that the bond redemption account has a balance of $5,400. The treasurer wishes to show cash as a current asset at $4,964. Discuss.

**6.** Define temporary investments. Distinguish between temporary investments and marketable securities.

**7.** (a) What positions are held with respect to the valuation of marketable securities? (b) What arguments can be advanced in support of each and which position do you feel has greatest merit?

**8.** The Brooks Co. reports marketable securities on the balance sheet at the lower of cost or market. What adjustments are required on the books at the end of the year in each case below:

(a) Securities are purchased in 1961 and at the end of 1961 their market value is more than cost.
(b) At the end of 1962 the market value of the securities is less than cost.
(c) At the end of 1963 the market value of the securities is greater than at the end of 1962 but is still less than cost.
(d) At the end of 1964 the market value of the securities is more than the amount originally paid.

**9.** The accountant for the Goodwin Co. in preparing a balance sheet has made certain offsets as follows:

An overdraft of $120 in the Payroll Fund kept with the Second National Bank has been offset against the general cash balance kept with the same bank.

Advances of $500 to buyers have been offset against accrued salaries of $1,200.

$1,000 receivable from Jones Wholesalers has been offset against a note payable of $1,200 that was sent to Jones Wholesalers as a result of a previous purchase.

Comment on the foregoing practices.

## EXERCISES

**1.** In auditing the books of McDonald, Inc. for 1964, you find that a petty cash fund of $250 is maintained on the imprest basis, but the company has failed to replenish the fund on December 31. Replenishment was made and recorded on January 15, 1965, when a check for $185 was drawn to petty cash for expenses paid. Your analysis discloses that $125 had been spent out of petty cash in 1964. What entry would be made in correcting the records, assuming that the books for 1964 have been closed?

**2.** The Wilson Co. receives its bank statement for the month ending June 30 on July 2. The bank statement shows a balance of $231. The cash account as of the close of business on June 30 shows a credit balance of $123. In reconciling the balances, the auditor discovers the following:

Receipts on June 30, $1,860, were not deposited until July 1.
Checks outstanding on June 30 were $2,215.
The bank has charged the depositor for overdrafts, $10.
A canceled check to S. S. Dohr for $56 was entered in cash payments in error as $65.

Prepare a bank reconciliation statement. (Use the form that reconciles bank and depositor figures to corrected cash balance.)

**3.** Sales on account for the Meadows Company for March amount to $10,000 and they are estimated to increase by $3,000 in each succeeding month. Terms of the sales are 2/10, E.O.M. It is estimated that no collections will be made in the month of the sale, 80% will be collected within the discount period, 10% after the discount period in the month following the sale, and 8% in the second month following the sale. What are the estimated cash collections from customers for the month of July?

**4.** The Weldon Co. completed the transactions in marketable securities listed below during 1964. What are the entries to record the transactions?

(a) Purchased $10,000 Moore Co. 5½% bonds paying 96½ plus accrued interest of $40.
(b) Purchased 300 shares of Scott Co. common stock at 21.
(c) Received semiannual interest on Moore Co. bonds.
(d) Sold 100 share lot of Scott Co. common at 22½.
(e) Sold $5,000 Moore Co. bonds at 95 plus accrued interest of $15.

**5.** Marketable securities held by the Tepper Co. on December 31, 1964, have the following cost and market values.

| | Cost | Market |
|---|---|---|
| 500 shares Roote Corp. Common | $14,000 | $10,500 |
| 1,000 shares Starr Co. Common | 16,000 | 10,000 |
| $25,000 Union Gas 4½% Bonds | 26,000 | 27,500 |

Show how this information would be presented on the balance sheet following three different valuation procedures that might be adopted.

**6.** Walsh and Werner acquire marketable securities in 1962 at a cost of $80,000. Market values of the securities at the end of each year are as follows: 1962, $85,000; 1963, $75,000; 1964, $82,000. Give the entries that would be made at the end of 1962, 1963, and 1964 and indicate how the securities would be reported on the balance sheet at the end of each year under each of the following assumptions:

(a) Securities are reported at cost.
(b) Securities are reported at the lower of cost or market.
(c) Securities are reported at market.

**7.** Marketable securities are acquired by the Webster Co. during 1964 at a cost of $15,000. Marketable securities are to be reported on the balance sheet at the lower of cost or market. (a) What entry would be made at the end of the year assuming that the securities have a market value of $12,500? (b) What entry would be made at the end of the next year assuming: (1) that the market value of the securities has declined to $12,000? (2) The market value has recovered to $14,000? (3) The market value is $16,000?

## PROBLEMS

**5-1.** Martin, Inc. received its bank statement for the month ending June 30, 1964. The auditor, in attempting to reconcile the statement with the books, discovered the following:

The cashier, who was also the bookkeeper, had misappropriated $305 by lapping and an additional $185 by passing a noncash credit through the sales returns and allowances account.

The bank had charged the depositor with: protest fee, $3.00; collection charges, $4.10; and telegram, $2.60.

A check made payable to C. H. Kelly in payment of an account for $35 was incorrectly recorded as $25.

Outstanding checks were as follows:

| No.  405....... | $370.00 | No. 1153...... | $  289.76 |
| 1112....... | 74.25 | 1154...... | 587.33 |
| 1138....... | 384.90 | 1155...... | 1,225.50 |

Receipts of June 30 for $1,183.55 were not deposited until July 1.

The balance on the bank statement was $1,446.84. The cash account showed an overdraft of $281.65.

Check No. 405 has been outstanding for ten months; the company decides to notify the bank to stop payment on the check and to establish a liability for the amount of the check.

*Instructions:* (1) Prepare a bank reconciliation statement, using the form where the bank balance is reconciled with the cash balance per books (the form illustrated on page 126).

(2) Give all of the required journal entries indicated by the preceding.

**5-2.** The cash account of Lathrop Co. showed a balance of $4,112.78 on April 30, 1964. The bank statement as of April 30 showed a balance of $3,329.13. Upon comparing the statement with the cash records, the following facts were developed:

(a) The Lathrop Co.'s account had been charged for a customer's uncollectible check amounting to $457.20 on April 26.

(b) A two-month, 6%, $1,000 customer's note dated February 25, discounted on April 12, had been protested April 26, and the bank had charged the Lathrop Co. for $1,012.90, which included a protest fee of $2.90.

(c) A customer's check for $90 had been entered as $70 both by the depositor and the bank but was later corrected by the bank.

(d) Check No. 742 for $392 had been entered in the cashbook as $329, and check No. 747 for $47.10 had been entered as $471.

(e) There were bank service charges for March of $19.72.

(f) A bank memo stated that J. J. West's note for $600 and interest of $18 had been collected on April 29, and the bank had made a charge of $2.50 on the collection. (No entry had been made on the books when the note was sent to the bank for collection.)

(g) Receipts of April 30 for $1,735 were not deposited until May 2.

The following checks were outstanding on April 30:

| No. 718 | $153.46 | No. 785 | $112.00 |
|---|---|---|---|
| 743 | 43.20 | 786 | 160.00 |
| 782 | 135.00 | 787 | 139.43 |
| 784 | 389.50 | 788 | 312.18 |

*Instructions:* (1) Construct a bank reconciliation statement, using the form where both bank and book balances are brought to a corrected cash balance (the form illustrated on page 125).

(2) Give the journal entries required as a result of the information given above. (Assume that the company makes use of the voucher system.)

**5-3.** A bank statement for Regal, Inc. shows a balance as of December 31, 1964, of $1,845.59. The cash account for the company as of this date shows an overdraft of $305.74. In reconciling the statement with the books, the following items are discovered:

(a) The cash balance includes $200 representing change cash on hand. When the cash on hand is counted, only $187.35 is found.

(b) The cash balance includes $250 representing a petty cash fund. Inspection of the petty cash fund reveals cash of $210 on hand and a replenishing check drawn on December 31 for $40.

(c) Proceeds from cash sales of $345 for December 27 were stolen. The company expects to recover this amount from the insurance company and has made no entry for the loss.

(d) The bank statement shows the depositor charged with a customer's N.S.F. check for $62.92, bank service charges of $19.75, and a check for $68 drawn by Regan, Inc. and incorrectly cleared through this account.

(e) The bank statement does not show receipts of December 31 of $918.50, which were deposited on January 2.

(f) Checks outstanding were found to be $4,015.50. This includes the check transferred to the petty cash fund and also two checks for $91 each payable to T. L. Russo. Russo had notified the company that he had lost the original check and had been sent a second one, the company stopping payment on the first check. Among the checks outstanding, one for $60 has been outstanding for fourteen months, and it is decided to cancel this item since the payee cannot be found and payment may never be claimed.

*Instructions:* (1) Prepare a bank reconciliation statement, using the form where both bank and book balances are brought to a corrected cash balance (form illustrated on page 125).

(2) Give the correcting entries required by the foregoing.

(3) List the cash items as they should appear on the balance sheet on December 31.

**5-4.** Parmley and Webb, Inc. carry marketable securities on their books at the lower of cost or market. On December 31, 1963, their balance sheet showed:

Marketable securities, at cost.................... $51,500
Less allowance for decline in value of marketable
   securities.................................... 2,850  $48,650

The following analysis was made in establishing the allowance.

|  | No. of Shares or Face Value | Cost | Market |
|---|---|---|---|
| U.S. Gas Co. Common......... | 500 shares | $26,500 | $24,000 |
| Wallace Stores Common........ | 100 shares | 6,500 | 5,400 |
| Barlow Gas and Electric 4½'s.... | $20,000 | 18,500 | 19,250 |
|  |  | $51,500 | $48,650 |

On June 30, 1964, the shares of Wallace Stores were sold for $5,000. On December 31, 1964, U.S. Gas Co. shares were quoted at $43.50 per share; Barlow Gas and Electric 4½'s were quoted at $987.50 per thousand dollar bond.

*Instructions:* Give the entries that are required to record the sale of securities in 1964 and to adjust the valuation account at the end of 1964.

**5-5.** Wheeler and Woods, Inc., made the following investments in marketable securities in 1962:

| United Hardware.............. | 400 shares @ 40 ¾ | $16,300 |
|---|---|---|
| Gardner Instruments............ | 400 shares @ 25 ⅛ | 10,050 |
| Superior First Mortgage 5% Bonds. | 50 $1,000 bonds at par | 50,000 |
|  |  | $76,350 |

Gardner Instruments was sold at the end of 1964 for $6,200. Securities had market values at the end of 1962, 1963, and 1964 as follows:

|  | 1962 | 1963 | 1964 |
|---|---|---|---|
| United Hardware.................... | $17,250 | $14,200 | $15,350 |
| Gardner Instruments................ | 9,600 | 6,450 |  |
| Superior First Mortgage 5% Bonds..... | 51,000 | 51,500 | 50,400 |

*Instructions:* Give whatever entries are required in 1962, 1963, and 1964 for the valuation and for the sale of securities, and show how the securities would be reported on the balance sheet prepared at the end of 1962, 1963, and 1964 under each of the following assumptions:

(1) Securities are valued at cost.
(2) Securities are valued at the lower of cost or market.
(3) Securities are valued at market.

**5-6.** The Leeds Novelty Co. asks the controller to prepare a cash forecast for the first three months of 1965. The following information is assembled in developing the forecast:

| Sales: | | | Purchases: | | |
|---|---|---|---|---|---|
| | January..... | $45,000 | | January...... | $36,000 |
| | February.... | 60,000 | | February.... | 48,000 |
| | March...... | 85,000 | | March....... | 30,000 |

All sales are made on a credit basis as follows: 2% cash discount if paid by the tenth of the month following the sale; credit period 30 days from end of month in which sale is made. Past experience has shown that 70% of the billings are collected within the first ten days of the month following the sale and credited with the discount, 20% of the billings are collected during the remainder of the month following sale, and 10% are collected in the second month following sale.

All purchases are made on terms of 2/10, n/30, and the company follows the practice of taking all discounts on the tenth day following the invoice date. It is assumed that purchases will be distributed evenly throughout the month, purchases for the last third of the month being paid in the first third of the succeeding month.

Selling and general and administrative expenses, excluding depreciation, will be paid as incurred and are anticipated as follows: fixed expenses, $5,000 per month; variable expenses, 12½% of gross sales.

The following balances taken from a trial balance on December 31 are to be considered in developing the cash summary:

| | | |
|---|---|---|
| Cash...................................... | | $ 1,580 |
| Accounts receivable: | | |
| November.............................. | $ 8,500 | |
| December.............................. | 90,000 | 98,500 |
| | | |
| Accounts payable: | | |
| December.............................. | | 15,000 |
| Bank loan due January 15, 1965.............. | | 14,000 |
| Estimated federal income tax for 1964 (the company expects to make payment in two installments of $16,750 on 3/15/65 and 6/15/65)............. | | 33,500 |

*Instructions:* Prepare a forecast of the cash position by months supported by receipts and payments schedules in forms similar to those illustrated on pages 130 and 131.

# Chapter 6

# RECEIVABLES

### Nature of receivables

In its broadest sense, the term *receivables* is applicable to all claims against others, whether these be claims for money, for goods, or for services. For accounting purposes, however, the term is employed in a narrower sense to designate claims that will be settled by the receipt of money.

Usually, the chief source of receivables is found in the normal activities of the operating cycle of the business. Business today is largely based on credit. Goods and services are sold on account, the collection of the accounts following some time after the sales. In the meantime, the seller has claims against the buyers. Other receivables arise as a result of such diverse activities as advances made by a company, the sale of plant and equipment items, and the sale of capital stock.

### Composition of receivables

Receivables are composed of two classes: (1) those supported by formal promises to pay in the form of notes, referred to as *notes receivable*, and (2) those not so supported, referred to as *accounts receivable*. Accounts receivable may be divided into groupings as follows: (a) receivables from customers, (b) receivables from others, and (c) accrued receivables. Receivables should be established in the accounts only when supportable claims exist and it can be assumed that the claims will be realized.

### Notes receivable

A note is an unconditional written promise by one party to another to pay a certain sum of money at a specified time. The note may be negotiable or nonnegotiable. It is negotiable or legally transferable by endorsement and delivery only if it provides for payment to the order of the second party or bearer. Such notes are commonly accepted by commercial banks for discount; hence they are considered more liquid than are other classes of receivables.

The term "notes" is commonly used to include not only promissory notes but also time drafts and trade acceptances. If the time drafts and the trade acceptances are material in amount, they may be summarized separately.

The notes receivable designation for reporting purposes should be limited to negotiable short-term instruments that are acquired from trade debtors and that are not yet due. When a written instrument fails to meet these requirements, it should be reported separately under an appropriately descriptive title. For example, notes arising from loans to customers, officers, employees, and affiliated companies should be reported separately.

## Accounts receivable

As previously indicated, accounts receivable broadly include all receivables other than those supported by some form of commercial paper. Although it would be appropriate to refer to open accounts with customers arising from the sale of goods and services as "Trade Debtors" or "Trade Receivables" to distinguish these from other receivables, it has become established practice to use the designation "Accounts Receivable" to represent these claims. Accounts Receivable for reporting purposes should be limited to trade accounts that are expected to be converted into cash in the regular course of business. This balance, for example, should not include receivables arising from charges for containers that will be canceled when containers are returned.

A receivable arising from the sale of goods is properly recognized when the title to goods passes to the buyer. However, the time that title passes may vary with the terms of the sale, and it is general practice to recognize the receivable when goods are shipped to the customer. Receivables should not be recognized for goods shipped on approval where the shipper retains title to the goods until there is a formal acceptance, or for goods shipped on consignment where the shipper retains title to the goods until they are sold by the consignee. Under these circumstances only a memorandum entry is appropriate until title to the goods passes.

Receivables for services to customers are properly recognized when the services are performed. When work under a contract has not been completed at the end of the period, the amount due as of the balance sheet date will have to be calculated. Receivables should be recognized for the portion of work completed under construction contracts and for reimbursable costs and accrued fees on cost-plus-fixed-fee contracts.

Ordinarily, detailed records of customer transactions and customers' balances are carried in subsidiary records. Entries to subsidiary records may be made from original business papers evidencing the transactions. With machine methods, subsidiary records are frequently maintained simultaneously with the preparation of invoices and remittance records.

Nontrade receivables should be summarized in appropriately titled accounts and should be reported separately. The following are examples of the receivables that should be carried separately: claims arising from the sale of securities or property other than goods or services; advances to stockholders, directors, officers, employees, and affiliated companies; deposits with creditors, utilities, and other agencies; purchase prepayments; deposits to guarantee contract performance or expense payment; claims for losses or damages; claims for rebates and tax refunds; subscriptions for capital stock; and dividends receivable.

Certain revenues for services or goods accrue with the passage of time and are most conveniently recognized when collections are made. At the end of the period, it is necessary to calculate the amounts accrued since the last collections and to establish appropriate accrued receivables. Accrued interest is recognized on bank deposits, notes, bonds, annuities, etc. Rentals may accrue on real estate holdings. Royalties and patent fees may accrue on certain rights and properties. Salaries and commissions may accrue as a result of services that have been received. For some business units accrued receivables may be small in total; for others, they may involve large amounts.

It was indicated in an earlier chapter that the current asset classification as broadly conceived comprehends all receivables identified with the normal operating cycle. Installment and other deferred collection contracts are current regardless of their terms. But receivables arising outside of the inventory-to-cash cycle qualify as current only if they are expected to be collected within one year. For classification purposes, then, each nontrade item requires separate analysis to determine whether it is reasonable to assume that it will be collected within one year. Noncurrent receivables are reported under the Investments or Other Assets caption, whichever may be considered appropriate.

Amounts due from officers, directors, and major stockholders arising out of sales and subject to the usual credit terms are normally considered current; however, when claims have arisen from transactions other than sales and current recovery is not assured, such items are properly classified as noncurrent. Sales to affiliated companies give rise to current claims, but advances are generally regarded as long-term in nature. Deposits on materials and merchandise ordered will soon represent inventories and are reported as current, but deposits on utility contracts are reported as long-term. Deposits for machinery and equipment ordered are noncurrent in view of the ultimate application of the deposit. Claims from the sale of assets other than merchandise and calling for collections over a period exceeding one year require special analysis to determine the portion of the claim to be reported as current and the portion to be reported as noncurrent.

Subscriptions to capital stock are current only if they are currently collectible; when current collection is not probable or when payments may be deferred indefinitely, such balances are reported as noncurrent assets or in some instances more appropriately as subtractions from capital balances so that no more than the amount actually paid in by stockholders and subscribers is reported as paid-in capital.

When income tax refund claims or other claims have been granted and collection is expected within one year, they qualify for current presentation. When claims are still being processed and recovery is assured although the period required for such processing is uncertain, they are shown under a noncurrent heading. Certain claims may be in dispute. When a claim does not involve a material amount and there is little likelihood of recovery, no reference needs to be made to it on the balance sheet. On the other hand, if a material amount is involved and there is prospect of a favorable settlement, the claim is properly viewed as a contingent receivable and should be disclosed by a special note or by an appropriate comment under a separate contingent asset heading. If a contingent receivable becomes an actual receivable, an asset account is established and a special gain account is credited.

Creditor and customer accounts with contra balances require special attention. These balances are found by an analysis of subsidiary ledger detail. For example, assume that the accounts payable controlling account reports a balance of $10,000. Inspection of subsidiary account detail reveals accounts with credit balances of $10,500 and accounts with debit balances of $500. The nature of the debit balances should be investigated. If the debit balances have arisen as a result of overpayments or returns and allowances after payment, they are reportable as current assets in view of the claims that they represent for cash or merchandise from vendors. Such balances are properly reported under a title such as "Creditors' Accounts with Debit Balances" or "Sundry Claims." If debit balances represent advance payments on the purchase of raw materials or merchandise, these too, are current assets reportable under some descriptive title such as "Advances on Purchase Contracts." In either case, Accounts Payable is reported at $10,500. Although both an asset and a liability are reported, no adjustment to the controlling account or the subsidiary ledger detail is required. Debit balances in the subsidiary ledger are carried forward and are ultimately canceled by purchases or cash settlement.

Customer ledger detail needs similar analysis. Customers' accounts with credit balances may result from overpayments, from customer returns after full payment, or from advance payments by customers. Such credits should be recognized as current liabilities, and accounts receivable should be reported at the sum of the debit balances in the subsidiary ledger.

It may be pointed out that when contra balances in customer and creditor accounts are not material in amount, they are frequently disregarded and only the net receivable or payable balance is reported on the balance sheet.

### Valuation of receivables

Theoretically, receivables should be carried at their net realizable or cash value. Receivables, thus, are properly reported at their present discounted values — claim balances reduced by the application of a discount rate for the period from the balance sheet date to the date of expected collection. Such adjustments are normally small and are generally ignored in practice. Notes receivable are usually reported at their face value. Thus, non-interest-bearing notes are shown at face values although, theoretically, they are not worth such amounts until their maturity. Accounts receivable are usually reported at the amounts collectible according to the terms of the sale even though such collections may not be made for some time. Interest-bearing receivables call for the recognition of accrued interest to the balance sheet date.

Almost invariably some of the receivables arising from sales will prove uncollectible. Uncollectible amounts will have to be anticipated if the charge for them is to be related to the period of the sale, and receivables are to be stated at their estimated realizable amounts.

The amount of receivables estimated uncollectible is recorded by a charge to Bad Debts and a credit to Allowance for Bad Debts. The bad debts charge may be treated as a deduction from sales on the theory that it is net sales — sales after bad debts shrinkage — that must cover current charges and yield a profit. Instead of being treated as a contra-sales balance, however, the bad debts item is usually regarded as emerging from a failure of management and, hence, is reported as a selling, general and administrative, or financial charge, depending upon the division that is held responsible for approving sales on account. The allowance account is reported as a subtraction from accounts receivable. Use of the allowance account avoids premature adjustments to individual receivable accounts while making possible a continuing control of subsidiary ledger detail by the accounts receivable account in the general ledger.

When positive evidence is available concerning the partial or complete worthlessness of an account, a charge is made to the allowance and the receivable is credited. Positive evidence of worthlessness is found in the bankruptcy, death, or disappearance of a debtor, failure to enforce collection legally, or a barring of collection by the statute of limitations. Write-offs should be supported by evidence of the uncollectibility of the accounts from appropriate parties — courts, lawyers, credit agencies, etc., and should be authorized in writing by appropriate company officers.

### Bases for estimating charge for bad debts

The estimate for bad debts may be based upon (1) the amount of sales or (2) the amount of receivables. When sales are used as the basis for calculation, the problem of estimating bad debts is viewed as one involving primarily the accurate measurement of income. Basing the adjustment on receivables considers the problem from the point of view of satisfactory asset valuation. A description of the methods employed under each of these bases is described in the paragraphs that follow.

### Bad debts adjustment based on sales

Bad debts of recent periods are related to sales of such periods in developing a percentage of bad debts to sales. This percentage may be modified by expectations in the light of current experience. Since bad debts occur only on credit sales, it would seem logical to develop a percentage of bad debts to charge sales of past periods. This percentage would be applied to charge sales of the current period. However, since extra work may be required in maintaining records of cash and credit sales or in analyzing sales data, the percentage is frequently developed in terms of total sales. Unless there is considerable fluctuation in the proportion of cash and credit sales periodically, the total sales method will give satisfactory results.

The sales percentage method for anticipating bad debts is widely used in practice because it is sound in theory and simple to apply. Although normally offering a satisfactory approach to income measurement by providing equitable charges to periodic revenue, the method may not offer a "cash realizable" valuation for receivables. This shortcoming can be overcome by analyzing receivables at different intervals and correcting the allowance for any significant excess or deficiency.

### Bad debts adjustment based on receivables

There are two methods of establishing and maintaining an allowance for bad debts when receivables are used as the base for the adjustment:

1. The allowance is raised to a certain percentage of receivables.
2. The allowance is raised to an amount determined by aging the accounts.

*Raising allowance to a certain percentage of receivables.* The bad debts experiences of recent periods are related to accounts outstanding in such periods and these data are considered in terms of special current conditions. An estimate of the probable uncollectibles is developed and Bad Debts is charged and Allowance for Bad Debts credited for an amount that brings the allowance to the desired balance. To illustrate, assume receivables of $60,000 and a credit balance of $200 in the allowance account at the end of the period. Bad debts are estimated at 2% of accounts receivable, or $1,200. The following entry brings the allowance to the desired amount:

Bad Debts. . . . . . . . . . . . . . . . . . . . . . . . . . . . . . . . . . . . . . . .     1,000
    Allowance for Bad Debts. . . . . . . . . . . . . . . . . . . . . .                   1,000

Although this method provides a satisfactory approach to the valuation of receivables, it may fail to provide equitable periodic charges to revenue. This is particularly true in view of the irregular determinations of bad debts as well as the lag in their recognition. After the first year, periodic bad debt provisions are directly affected by the current reductions in the allowance resulting from a recognition of bad accounts originating in prior periods.

*Raising allowance to an amount determined by aging the accounts.* The most commonly used method for establishing an allowance in terms of receivables is that which involves *aging receivables.* Individual accounts are analyzed to determine those that are not yet due and those that are past due. Past-due accounts are classified in terms of the length of the period past due. An analysis sheet may be used in aging accounts receivable, as follows:

Parker and Pope
Analysis of Receivables — December 31, 1964

| Customer | Amount | Not Yet Due | Not More Than 30 Days Past Due | 31–60 Days Past Due | 61–90 Days Past Due | 91–180 Days Past Due | 181–365 Days Past Due | More Than One Year Past Due |
|---|---|---|---|---|---|---|---|---|
| A. B. Andrews. . | $ 450 | | | $ 450 | | | | |
| B. T. Brooks. . . | 300 | | | | $ 100 | $ 200 | | |
| B. Bryant. . . . . . | 200 | | $ 200 | | | | | |
| L. B. Devine. . . | 2,100 | $ 2,100 | | | | | | |
| K. Flood . . . . . . | 200 | | | | | | | $ 200 |
| M. A. Young. . . | 1,400 | 1,000 | | 100 | 300 | | | |
| Total . . . . . . . . . | $47,550 | $40,000 | $3,000 | $1,200 | $ 650 | $ 500 | $ 800 | $1,400 |

It is desirable to review each overdue balance with some appropriate company official and to arrive at estimates concerning the degree of collectibility of each item listed. An alternative procedure is to develop a series of estimated loss percentages and to apply these to the different receivable classifications. The calculation of the allowance on the latter basis is illustrated below:

Parker and Pope

Estimated Amount of Uncollectible Accounts — December 31, 1964

| Classification | Balances | Bad Debt Experience Percentage | Estimated Amount of Uncollectibles |
|---|---|---|---|
| Not yet due................... | $40,000 | 2% | $    800 |
| Not more than 30 days past due. | 3,000 | 5% | 150 |
| 31–60 days past due............ | 1,200 | 10% | 120 |
| 61–90 days past due............ | 650 | 20% | 130 |
| 91–180 days past due........... | 500 | 30% | 150 |
| 181–365 days past due.......... | 800 | 50% | 400 |
| More than one year past due.... | 1,400 | 80% | 1,120 |
|  | $47,550 |  | $2,870 |

Bad Debts is now debited and Allowance for Bad Debts is credited for an amount that will bring the allowance account up to the required balance. Assuming bad debts estimated at $2,870 as shown in the tabulation and a credit balance of $620 in the allowance before adjustment, the following entry would be made:

Bad Debts......................................... 2,250
    Allowance for Bad Debts.......................     2,250

The aging method provides the most satisfactory approach to the valuation of receivables at their cash realizable amounts. Furthermore, data developed through aging receivables may be quite useful to management for purposes of credit analysis and control. On the other hand, application of this method may require considerable time and may prove expensive. The method still involves estimates, and the added refinement that is achieved by the aging process may not warrant the additional cost. Also, it should be noted that here, as in the preceding instance, charges based upon the recognizable impairment of asset values rather than upon sales may fail to provide equitable periodic charges against revenue.

### Corrections in allowance for bad debts

As previously indicated, the allowance for bad debts balance is established and maintained by means of adjusting entries at the close of each accounting period. If the allowance provisions are too large, the allowance account balance will be unnecessarily inflated and earnings will be understated; if the allowance provisions are too small, the allowance account balance will be inadequate and earnings will be overstated.

Care must be taken to see that the allowance balance follows the credit experience of the particular business. The process of aging receivables at different intervals may be employed as a means of checking the allowance balance to be certain that it is being maintained satisfactorily. Such periodic reviews may indicate the need for a correction in the allowance as well as a change in the rate or in the method.

When the bad debt experience approximates the anticipation of the losses, the allowance procedure may be considered satisfactory and no adjustment is called for. When it appears that there has been a failure to estimate bad debts satisfactorily resulting in an allowance balance that is clearly inadequate or excessive, a correcting entry is in order. The nature of the correcting entry depends upon the statement that is to be used in reporting the correction. If corrections in profits of prior periods are to be reported on the income statement, a nominal account is established for corrections. If the corrections are to appear on the retained earnings statement, retained earnings is charged or credited; this account is subsequently analyzed in developing detail for the retained earnings statement.

The recognition of current period receivables as bad debts by charges to the allowance may result in a debit balance in the allowance account. A debit balance arising in this manner does not indicate that the allowance is inadequate; charges to the allowance simply predate the current provision for uncollectible accounts, and the adjustment at the end of the period should cover uncollectibles already determined as well as those yet to be recognized.

Occasionally, accounts that have been charged off as worthless are unexpectedly collected. The original entry whereby the customer's account was written off against the allowance should be reversed. The receipt of cash is then recorded in the usual manner.

## Bad debts recognition in period of discovery

Many small businesses may feel that the accounting refinement to be gained by anticipating uncollectibles hardly warrants the additional work required. Certain large businesses may encounter serious problems in developing reliable estimates of uncollectibles. These units, then, instead of anticipating bad debts, may prefer simply to recognize bad debts in the periods in which accounts are determined to be uncollectible. When bad debts are not anticipated by the establishment of an allowance, bad accounts are written off by a charge to Bad Debts and a credit to the customer's account. If an account written off is unexpectedly recovered in the same period, the entry to record the loss may be reversed and the collection recorded in the usual manner. If recovery is made in a subsequent period, it is necessary to restore the receivable balance and to credit a nominal account such as Recoveries of Accounts Written Off in Prior Periods; the collection is then recorded in the usual manner. The balance of the account Recoveries of Accounts Written Off in Prior Periods may be reported as a subtraction from Bad Debts in arriving at the net charge for bad debts made currently, or it may be reported as an extraordinary item.

Although theory supports the anticipation of uncollectibles so that current revenue may carry its full burden of expenses, the recognition of bad debts in the period of their discovery is widely practiced because of its simplicity and convenience. Either method can be used for income tax purposes. However, the method that is elected must be employed consistently on successive tax returns.

### Anticipation of discounts and other charges in valuation of receivables

The foregoing discussion has been restricted to the provision for uncollectible items. Conditions of sales and collections may suggest the anticipation of other charges that will emerge in the realization of accounts receivable and hence are properly matched against current revenue.

For example, if customers generally take cash discounts in making remittances, it may be argued that reporting income and receivables in terms of customer billings involves some overstatement of these balances. Under these circumstances, it may be desirable to anticipate discounts by a charge to Sales Discounts and a credit to Allowance for Sales Discounts. Allowance for Sales Discounts would be subtracted from Accounts Receivable so that receivables are reflected at their estimated cash realizable value. Discounts on the collection of old accounts in the new period can be charged against the allowance account. However, it would be more convenient to transfer the allowance to the sales discounts account by a reversing entry at the beginning of the new period. All discounts can then be charged to the sales discounts account.

Similar recognition may be suggested for probable allowances yet to be made to customers for shipment shortages and defects, for price adjustments, and also for probable losses on sales returns. Claims that customers may make for freight charges that they pay on the receipt of goods or on the return of goods may call for consideration. Probable future expenses involved in the realization of accounts such as billing and collection expenses and attorneys' fees may likewise warrant consideration. It may be pointed out that the anticipation of charges for the items just mentioned is seldom found in practice and is not allowed for income tax purposes. When these charges are not anticipated and the volume of activities and experiences with respect to such charges does not vary significantly from period to period, the recognition of such charges in the period in which they are finally determined will have little effect upon periodic net income, although the receivables balance may include some minor overstatement.

The preceding discussion has considered charges relating to the realization of accounts receivable. The realization of notes receivable may involve similar charges. When sales are used as a basis for estimating future charges, allowances may be considered applicable to both accounts receivable and notes receivable received from customers. When accounts receivable are analyzed and used as a basis for developing related allowances, notes receivable would require similar treatment.

### Use of receivables in raising cash

A business may require cash for current purposes that exceeds the amount on hand and the amount to become available in the normal course of operations. The business may use accounts receivable or notes receivable as a basis for a cash advance from a bank or a finance company. These procedures are described in the sections that follow.

### Customers' accounts as a source of cash

In order to obtain immediate cash, accounts receivable owned by the business may be (1) pledged, (2) assigned, or (3) sold.

*Pledge of accounts receivable.* Advances are frequently obtained from banks or other lending institutions by pledging accounts receivable as security on the loan. Ordinarily, collections are made by the borrower who is required to use this cash in meeting his obligation to the lender. The lender, in such instances, may be given access to the borrower's records to determine whether remittances are being properly made on pledged accounts.

*Assignment of accounts receivable.* Finance companies may agree to advance cash over a period of time as accounts receivable are assigned to them. The assignments carry a guarantee on the part of the assignor that he will make up any deficiency if the accounts fail to realize required amounts. Assignments thus represent, in effect, sale of accounts on a *recourse* basis. The cash advanced by the finance company is normally less than the assigned accounts by a percentage that is considered adequate to cover uncollectible items, returns and allowances, offsets, and amounts subject to dispute. When amounts actually recovered on assigned accounts exceed the sum of the advance and the finance company's charges, such excess accrues to the assignor. Charges made by the finance company frequently consist of a commission on the amount advanced, plus interest on the unrecovered balance of the advance computed on a daily basis. Assignments are usually made on a *non-notification basis*, customers remaining uninformed concerning the assignment; customers, then, make payment to the assignor who is required to turn collections over to the assignee. When assignments are on a *notification basis*, customers are instructed to make payments directly to the finance company.

*Sale of accounts receivable.* Certain dealers or finance companies purchase accounts receivable outright on a *without recourse* basis. This is known as accounts receivable *factoring*, and the buyer is referred to as a *factor*. Customers are notified that their bills are payable to the factor, and this party assumes the burden of billing and collecting accounts. In many instances, factoring may involve more than simply the purchase and collection of accounts receivable. Factoring frequently involves a continuing agreement whereby a financing institution assumes the credit function as well as the collection function. Under such an arrangement, the factor grants or denies credit, handles the accounts receivable bookkeeping, bills customers, and makes collections. The business unit is relieved of all of these activities. The sale of goods provides immediate cash for business use. Because the factor absorbs the losses from bad accounts and frequently assumes credit and collection responsibilities, the charge that he makes exceeds the interest charge involved in borrowing cash or the commission and interest charges involved in the assignment of receivables. In some instances the factor may withhold a portion of the purchase price for possible future charges for customer returns and allowances or other special adjustments. Final settlement is made after receivables have been collected.

*Accounting procedures for accounts receivable financing.* No special accounting problems are encountered in the pledge or the sale of receivables. When receivables are pledged, the books simply report the loan and the subsequent settlement. Disclosure should be made on the balance sheet by parenthetical comment or note of the receivables pledged to secure the obligation to the lending agency. When receivables are sold outright, Cash is debited, receivables and related allowance balances are closed, and an expense account is charged for factoring charges. When part of the purchase price is withheld by the factor, a receivable is established pending final settlement.

The assignment of accounts receivable is comparable to the discounting of customers' notes and similar accounting may be employed. To illustrate, assume that the Bronson Co. on March 1 assigns accounts receivable of $25,000 to the Weber Finance Co. and receives $19,500 representing an advance of 80% of receivables less a commission on the advance of $2\frac{1}{2}\%$. Collections are to be made by the assignor who is to deposit such receipts intact to the credit of the assignee. The entries on the books of the assignor and assignee during the course of the relationship are given on page 158.

It will be observed that the assignor makes two entries at the time of assignment: one entry sets the assigned accounts receivable apart under separate control; a second entry establishes a credit to an assignment balance representing the reduction in the receivables arising from the assignment, accompanied by charges to cash for the cash received, to an equity in accounts receivable balance for the equity in assigned accounts retained by the assignor, and to assignment expense for the charges made by the assignee. Thereafter as cash is collected on assigned accounts and transferred to the assignee, the assignment balance is applied against the assigned receivables. Entries reducing the assigned receivables balance for returns, allowances, write-offs, etc., are accompanied by offset of the assignment balance against the assignor's equity in receivables. Upon settlement with the assignee, the assignment balance and the assignor's equity balance are offset, and the balance in accounts receivable assigned is returned to the unassigned accounts control.

On the books of the assignee, the advance of cash is recorded by a charge to an asset account for the total receivables assigned, a credit to an account with the assignor for the latter's equity in this total, a credit to commission income for the charges made, and a credit to cash for the cash paid. As cash is received, cash is debited and assigned accounts and income are credited. Reductions in assigned accounts involving charges that are to be absorbed by the assignee are recognized by reductions in the assignor's equity. Upon final settlement, any balance remaining in the assignor's equity in assigned accounts is offset against the assigned receivables balance.

If a balance sheet is prepared before the finance company has received full payment, the assignor recognizes the difference between the total accounts assigned and the portion required to cover the claim of the finance company as an asset. Disclosure is also made of the responsibilities to the finance company if assigned accounts do not realize enough to liquidate the loan. The assignee in preparing a balance sheet would report his interest in assigned accounts as an asset.

To illustrate, if in the preceding example balance sheets are prepared on March 31, information relating to assigned accounts may be reported as shown on page 159.

| Transaction | Entries on Assignor's Books (Bronson Company) | | | Entries on Assignee's Books (Weber Finance Co.) | | |
|---|---|---|---|---|---|---|
| **March 1**<br><br>Bronson Co. assigned accounts receivable of $25,000 to Weber Finance Co. receiving $19,500 representing an advance of 80% of receivables less a commission on the advance of 2½%. | Accounts Rec.<br>Assigned....... | 25,000 | | Bronson Co.<br>Accounts....... | 25,000 | |
| | Accounts<br>Receivable... | | 25,000 | Equity of<br>Bronson Co.<br>in Assigned<br>Accounts.... | | 5,000 |
| | Cash.......... | 19,500 | | Commission | | |
| | Equity in<br>Accounts Rec.<br>Assigned....... | 5,000 | | Income...... | | 500 |
| | Assignment<br>Expense....... | 500 | | Cash........ | | 19,500 |
| | Accounts Rec.<br>Assigned to<br>Weber<br>Finance Co... | | 25,000 | | | |
| **March 31**<br><br>Bronson Co. collected $15,000 on assigned accounts. This amount together with interest at 6% for one month on this amount, or $75, was remitted to Weber Finance Co. | Accounts Rec.<br>Assigned to<br>Weber<br>Finance Co..... | 15,000 | | Cash.......... | 15,075 | |
| | Accounts Rec.<br>Assigned..... | | 15,000 | Bronson Co.<br>Accounts..... | | 15,000 |
| | Interest Expense | 75 | | Interest<br>Income...... | | 75 |
| | Cash........ | | 75 | | | |
| **March 31**<br><br>Sales returns and allowances granted by Bronson Co. on assigned accounts during March totaled $1,000. | Sales<br>Returns and<br>Allowances..... | 1,000 | | Equity of<br>Bronson Co.<br>in Assigned<br>Accounts....... | 1,000 | |
| | Accounts Rec.<br>Assigned..... | | 1,000 | Bronson Co.<br>Accounts..... | | 1,000 |
| | Accounts Rec.<br>Assigned to<br>Weber<br>Finance Co..... | 1,000 | | | | |
| | Equity in<br>Accounts Rec.<br>Assigned..... | | 1,000 | | | |
| **April 30**<br><br>Bronson Co. collected $8,500 on assigned accounts. Balance due, $5,000, together with interest at 6% for two months on this amount, or $50, was remitted to Weber Finance Co. in final settlement; $3,500 was retained. Remaining account balances relative to assignment were closed. | Accounts Rec.<br>Assigned to<br>Weber<br>Finance Co..... | 5,000 | | Cash.......... | 5,050 | |
| | Accounts Rec.<br>Assigned..... | | 5,000 | Bronson Co.<br>Accounts..... | | 5,000 |
| | Interest Expense | 50 | | Interest<br>Income...... | | 50 |
| | Cash........ | | 50 | | | |
| | Cash.......... | 3,500 | | Equity of<br>Bronson Co.<br>in Assigned<br>Accounts....... | 4,000 | |
| | Accounts Rec.<br>Assigned..... | | 3,500 | Bronson Co.<br>Accounts..... | | 4,000 |
| | Accounts Rec.<br>Assigned to<br>Weber<br>Finance Co..... | 4,000 | | | | |
| | Equity in<br>Accounts Rec.<br>Assigned..... | | 4,000 | | | |
| | Accounts<br>Receivable..... | 500 | | | | |
| | Accounts Rec.<br>Assigned..... | | 500 | | | |

Bronson Company

Current assets:
Accounts receivable–unassigned . . . . . . . . . . . . . . .     $50,000

Company's equity in assigned accounts
receivable:
    Assigned accounts. . . . . . . . . . . . . . . .     $9,000
    Less equity of Weber Finance Co.
    in assigned accounts (company is
    contingently liable as guarantor of
    assigned accounts) . . . . . . . . . . . . . . .     5,000      4,000

Total accounts receivable . . . . . . . . . . . . . . . . . . . . . . . . . . .     $54,000

Weber Finance Company

Current assets:
Bronson Co. accounts . . . . . . . . . . . . . . . . . . . . . .     $9,000
Less equity of Bronson Co. in assigned accounts     4,000     $5,000

When collections are made by the finance company, procedures similar to those illustrated can still be employed. In such instances, however, entries are made by the assignor when information is received from the finance company concerning collections, interest charges, and the return of accounts in excess of claims.

Management may employ accounts receivable financing as a temporary or emergency matter after exhausting the limited line of unsecured credit that may be available from a lending institution. On the other hand, management may engage in accounts receivable financing as a continuing policy. Recent years have witnessed an increasing number of factoring arrangements involving the full delegation of credit and collection responsibilities to specialists. Financial assistance to business through the factoring of open accounts today runs into billions of dollars.

## Customers' notes as a source of cash

Cash may be obtained by selling customers' notes to a bank or to some other agency willing to accept such instruments. If a customer's note is non-interest-bearing, cash is received for the face value of the note less a charge for interest, known as *discount*, for the period from the date the note is discounted to the date of its maturity. If the note is interest-bearing, the maturity value of the note is first determined. The amount that is received from the bank is the maturity value of the note less discount calculated on this maturity value from the date the note is discounted to its maturity.

To illustrate entries for a non-interest-bearing note, assume that such a 90-day $1,000 note dated December 1 is received from a customer, and the note is discounted on December 16 at 6%. The following entries are made:

Dec. 1 Notes Receivable.................... 1,000.00
      Accounts Receivable............... 1,000.00

Dec. 16 Cash............................. 987.50
      Interest Expense.................... 12.50
      Notes Receivable.................. 1,000.00
        Interest: $1,000 \times .06 \times 75/360$, or $12.50.

It should be observed that theoretical objections can be raised to the foregoing entries on the grounds that interest expense emerges from the failure to recognize a sales discount implicit in the acceptance of the note. If money is worth 6%, settlement of the account by a $1,000, 90-day, non-interest-bearing note is properly regarded as settlement by note with a cash equivalent value of $985.22 ($1,000 $\div$ 1.015). Either of the following entries, then, is appropriate:

| (a) | | | (b) | | |
|---|---|---|---|---|---|
| Notes Receivable....... | 985.22 | | Notes Receivable..... | 1,000.00 | |
| Sales Discount......... | 14.78 | | Sales Discount........ | 14.78 | |
|   Accounts Receivable.. | | 1,000.00 |   Accounts Receivable | | 1,000.00 |
| | | |   Discount on Notes | | |
| | | |     Receivable......... | | 14.78 |

Assuming that the note reported at $985.22 is sold for $987.50, the difference would be recognized as interest income. If the note is reported on the balance sheet before its sale or collection, an adjustment should be made to recognize the accrual of interest at 6% to the balance sheet date. If the note is recorded as in (a) above, the interest accrual is recorded by a debit to Notes Receivable and a credit to Interest Income. If the note is recorded as in (b), Discount on Notes Receivable is debited and Interest Income is credited; the balance of the discount should be subtracted from notes receivable in reporting the asset on the balance sheet. As indicated earlier, however, discounted values are seldom recognized in establishing accounts and notes on the books. The sale of a receivable prior to its maturity date, then, involves the recognition of a charge for the difference between its carrying value and the amount realized; collection of the receivable at its maturity is recognized as no more than recovery of the balance originally reported.

To illustrate the accounting for an interest-bearing note, assume that the note received from a customer in the previous example provides for the payment of interest at 6% at its maturity and that it is discounted at 6%. Under these circumstances, the following entries are appropriate:

Dec. 1 Notes Receivable.................... 1,000.00
      Accounts Receivable.............. 1,000.00

Dec. 16  Cash. . . . . . . . . . . . . . . . . . . . . . . . . . . . . .    1,002. 31
    Notes Receivable. . . . . . . . . . . . . . . . .          1,000. 00
    Interest Income. . . . . . . . . . . . . . . . . .              2. 31
   Maturity value of note: $1,000 + interest ($1,000 $\times$ .06 $\times$ 90/360), or $1,015.
   Discount: $1,015 $\times$ .06 $\times$ 75/360, or $12.69.

When a person endorses a note "without recourse," he is relieved of any liability for the inability of the maker of the note or any prior endorser to pay the note upon its maturity. When he endorses a note without making any qualification, he becomes liable to subsequent holders of the note if it is not paid at maturity. However, if he is held liable on the note, he has the right to recover amounts he has paid from the maker of the note or prior endorsers who failed to comply with its terms.

Normally, endorsement without qualification is required in discounting a note, and the endorser becomes contingently liable on the note. Under these circumstances Notes Receivable Discounted instead of Notes Receivable may be credited when the note is discounted. Pending final settlement on the note, Notes Receivable would be regarded as a contingent asset. Notes Receivable Discounted, in turn, would be an accompanying contingent liability. When the person who holds the note at maturity receives payment from the maker, both payment and recovery contingencies are ended, and Notes Receivable Discounted can be applied against Notes Receivable.

The use of the notes receivable discounted account gives the same final result as that obtained when Notes Receivable is credited for notes that are discounted. Since data concerning the contingent liability are of concern only on the balance sheet date and these can be determined readily at the end of the period from an examination of the detailed record of notes discounted, the extra work involved in maintaining a notes receivable discounted account may not be warranted. When a notes receivable discounted balance is carried in the accounts, this balance is subtracted from notes receivable in reporting the notes receivable balance. Information concerning the contingent liability is provided on the balance sheet by means of a parenthetical remark or note or by special reference under a separate contingent liabilities heading.

If a note is not paid when it is due, the holder of the note must give the endorser prompt notice of such dishonor. The endorser is then required to make payment to the holder. Payment consists of the face value of the note plus interest and plus any fees and costs relating to collection. The full amount paid is recoverable from the maker of the note, and Accounts Receivable, Notes Receivable Dishonored, or Notes Receivable Past-Due is charged. If Notes Receivable Discounted was credited at the time the note was discounted, this balance, together with the original notes receivable balance, should be canceled. Subsequent recovery on the note is recorded by a charge to cash and a credit to the account with the debtor; failure to recover any portion of the balance due would call for writing off the unpaid balance.

### Presentation of receivables on the balance sheet

Normally, the receivables that qualify as current items are grouped for presentation in the following classes: (1) notes — trade debtors, (2) accounts — trade debtors, (3) other receivables, and (4) accrued receivables. Reporting should disclose notes that are nonnegotiable. The detail reported for other and accrued receivables depends upon the relative significance of the various items included. When trade accounts or installment contracts are properly reported as current but involve collections beyond one year, particulars of such deferred collections should be provided. Valuation accounts are deducted from the individual receivable balance or combined balances to which they relate. Notes receivable may be reported gross with notes receivable discounted shown as a deduction from this balance, or notes may be reported net with appropriate reference to the contingent liability arising from notes discounted. Accounts receivable assigned may be reported gross with the interest of the assignee in such balance shown as a subtraction item, or the company's interest in receivables may be reported net; here too, appropriate reference would be made to the contingent liability involved. When receivables are supported by pledges of collateral to assure their collectibility, the nature of the pledge and the fact that the receivables are wholly or partly secured should be disclosed. On the other hand, when receivables have been pledged or otherwise hypothecated on obligations of the company, these facts, too, should be disclosed and reference made to the obligation that is thus secured.

Current receivable items as they might appear on the balance sheet are shown below:

| | | |
|---|---:|---:|
| Receivables: | | |
| Trade notes and drafts receivable (notes of $20,000 have been pledged to secure bank borrowing) . . . . . . . . . . . . . . . . . . . . . . . . . . . . | | $ 38,000 |
| Trade accounts receivable (including install-ment contracts not due for 12–18 months of approximately $30,000) . . . . . . . . . . . . . . . . | $112,000 | |
| Less allowance for bad debts and reposses-sion costs . . . . . . . . . . . . . . . . . . . . . . . . . . . | 2,500 | 109,500 |
| Miscellaneous notes and accounts, including short-term loans to employees of $6,500. . . . | | 12,000 |
| Accrued receivables . . . . . . . . . . . . . . . . . . . . . | | 4,500 |
| Total receivables . . . . . . . . . . . . . . . . . . . . . | | $164,000 |

## QUESTIONS

**1.** The Proctor Corporation shows on its balance sheet one receivable balance that includes the following items: (a) advances to officers, (b) deposits on machinery and equipment being produced by various companies for the Proctor Corporation, (c) traveling expense advances to salesmen, (d) damage claims against transportation companies approved by such companies, (e) estimated federal income tax refunds, (f) accrued interest on notes receivable, (g) United States Treasury Tax Anticipation Bills, (h) overdue notes, (i) receivables from a foreign subsidiary company, (j) subscriptions receivable on a new bond issue, and (k) creditor overpayments. Suggest the proper treatment of each item.

**2.** An analysis of the accounts receivable balance of $8,702 on the books of Burke, Inc. on December 31 reveals the following:

| | |
|---|---:|
| Accounts from sales of last three months (appear to be fully collectible) | $7,460 |
| Accounts from sales prior to October 1 (of doubtful value)......... | 1,312 |
| Accounts known to be worthless................................. | 320 |
| Dishonored notes charged back to customers' accounts............. | 800 |
| Credit balances in customers' accounts......................... | 1,190 |

(a) What adjustments are required? (b) How should the various balances be shown on the balance sheet?

**3.** (a) Give three methods for the establishment and the maintenance of an allowance for bad debts. (b) What are the advantages and the disadvantages of each method? (c) Which do you feel is the preferable method?

**4.** The bookkeeper for Wells, Inc. believes he can show a more accurate valuation of notes and accounts receivable by aging the notes and accounts and establishing an allowance on this basis than he can by crediting the allowance account with a percentage of net sales on account. Do you agree? Give the advantages of each procedure.

**5.** List and explain the nature of at least four deductions that may be applied under certain circumstances in the valuation of accounts receivable.

**6.** In what section of the income statement would you report (a) bad debts, (b) sales discounts, (c) recovery of accounts written off in prior periods?

**7.** (a) Distinguish between the practices of (1) pledging, (2) assigning, and (3) selling accounts receivable. (b) Describe the accounting procedure to be followed in each instance.

**8.** Indicate several methods for presenting information on the balance sheet relating to (a) notes receivable discounted, and (b) accounts receivable assigned.

## EXERCISES

**1.** The accounts receivable controlling account for the Armour Co. shows a debit balance of $34,550; the allowance for bad debts account shows a credit balance of $600. Subsidiary ledger detail reveals the following:

| | |
|---|---:|
| Trade accounts receivable in 30 days.......................... | $12,000 |
| Installment receivables, due 1 month-18 months hence............ | 3,500 |
| Trade receivables from officers, due currently..................... | 1,250 |
| Customers' accounts reporting credit balances arising from sales returns..................................................... | 150 |
| Advance payments to creditors on purchase orders............... | 3,000 |
| Advance payments to creditors on orders for machinery........... | 5,000 |
| Customers' accounts reporting credit balances arising from advance payments..................................................... | 1,000 |
| Accounts known to be worthless................................ | 450 |
| Trade accounts on which post-dated checks are held (no entries were made on receipt of checks)................................... | 500 |
| Advances to affiliated companies................................ | 10,000 |

Show how this information would be reported on the balance sheet.

**2.** The trial balance before adjustment for the Moore Sales Co. shows the following balances:

| | Dr. | Cr. |
|---|---:|---:|
| Accounts Receivable............................... | $26,000 | |
| Allowance for Bad Debts.......................... | 150 | |
| Sales............................................ | | $215,000 |
| Sales Returns and Allowances....................... | 1,000 | |

Give the adjustment for estimated bad debts, assuming:

(a) The allowance is maintained at 2% of accounts receivable.
(b) The allowance is to provide for bad debts of $680 arrived at by aging accounts.
(c) The allowance is to be increased by ½ of 1% of net sales.

**3.** The Barnett Co. decides to employ accounts receivable as a basis for financing. Its current position at this time is as follows:

| | | | |
|---|---:|---|---:|
| Accounts Receivable...... | $30,000 | Cash Overdraft......... | $ 750 |
| Inventories.............. | 45,000 | Accounts Payable........ | 32,000 |

Prepare a statement of its current position, assuming that cash is obtained as indicated in each case below:

(a) Cash of $20,000 is borrowed on short-term notes and $18,000 is applied to the payment of creditors; accounts of $25,000 are pledged to secure the loan.
(b) Cash of $20,000 is advanced to the company by Wells Finance Co., the advance representing 80% of accounts assigned to it; assignment is made on a "with recourse" basis, and amounts collected in excess of the loan balance and charges accrue to the Barnett Co.
(c) Cash of $20,000 is received on the sale of accounts receivable of $22,500 on a "no recourse" basis.

**4.** Wallace Sales Co. assigns accounts of $80,000 to the Brothers Finance Co. guaranteeing these accounts and receiving an 80% advance less a flat commission of 5% on the amount of the advance. Accounts of $60,000 are collected and remittance is made to the finance company. Bad accounts of $2,000 are written off against an allowance for bad debts; remaining accounts are collected and settlement is made with the finance company together with payment of $1,200 for interest. What entries are required on the books of Wallace Sales Co. and on the books of Brothers Finance Co. to record the assignment and the subsequent transactions?

**5.** Joe Bailey received from John Clark a 60-day, 6% note for $3,000, dated November 6, 1963. On December 6, Bailey had Clark's note discounted at 6% and recorded the contingent liability. The bank protested nonpayment of the note and charged the endorser with protest fees of $2.75 in addition to the amount of the note. On January 29, 1964, the note was collected with interest at 8% from the maturity date on the face value of the note. What entries would appear on Bailey's books as a result of the foregoing?

## PROBLEMS

**6-1.** The balance sheet for the Werden Co. on December 31, 1963, includes the following receivable balances:

| | | |
|---|---:|---:|
| Notes receivable including accrued interest of $150....... | $19,200 | |
| Less notes receivable discounted.................... | 12,000 | $ 7,200 |
| | | |
| Accounts receivable............................... | $45,200 | |
| Less allowance for bad debts....................... | 2,200 | 43,000 |

Transactions during 1964 included the following:

(a) Sales on account were $318,500.
(b) Cash collected on accounts totaled $231,000, which included accounts of $58,500 on which cash discounts of 2% were allowed.
(c) Notes received in payment of accounts totaled $79,000.
(d) Notes receivable discounted as of December 31, 1963, were paid at maturity with the exception of one $5,000 note on which the company has to pay $5,053, which included interest and protest fees. It is expected that recovery will be made on this note in 1965.
(e) Customers' notes of $50,000 were discounted during the year, proceeds from their sale being $49,200. Of this total, $34,500 matured during the year without notice of protest.
(f) Customers' accounts of $4,150 were written off during the year as worthless.
(g) Recoveries of bad debts written off in prior years were $725.
(h) Notes receivable collected during the year totaled $12,500 and interest collected was $850.
(i) On December 31, accrued interest on notes receivable was $220.

(j) Aging the accounts on December 31, 1964, revealed the need for an allowance for bad debts of $2,775.

(k) Cash of $20,000 was borrowed from the bank, accounts receivable of $25,000 being pledged on the loan. Collections of $12,500 had been made on these receivables (included in the total given in transaction [b]) and this amount was applied on December 31, 1964, to payment of accrued interest on the loan of $300, and the balance to partial payment of the loan.

*Instructions:* (1) Prepare journal entries summarizing the transactions and information given above.

(2) Prepare a summary of current receivables for balance sheet presentation.

**6-2.** Accounts receivable for the Compton Co. were reported on the balance sheet prepared at the end of 1963 as follows:

| | | | |
|---|---|---|---|
| Accounts receivable.................. | | $46,600 | |
| Less allowance for doubtful accounts... | $1,950 | | |
| Allowance for sales discounts......... | 830 | 2,780 | $43,820 |

The company sells goods on terms of 2/10 e.o.m, n/30. At the end of the year accounts receivable are aged and the following percentages are applied in arriving at an estimate of the charge for doubtful accounts:

| | Estimated Loss |
|---|---|
| Accounts not more than two months overdue.......... | 5% |
| Accounts more than two months but not more than six months overdue...................................... | 20% |
| Accounts more than six months but not more than one year overdue...................................... | 50% |
| Accounts more than one year overdue................. | 100% |

At the end of the year the company also anticipates sales discounts on all receivables not yet due for payment.

In 1964 the following transactions took place:

| | |
|---|---|
| Sales on account....................................... | $412,405 |
| Cash collected on account............................. | 395,615 |
| Cash discounts allowed............................... | 5,540 |
| Sales returns and allowances.......................... | 2,320 |
| Bad debts written off................................. | 1,280 |
| Bad debts previously written off but recovered.......... | 225 |

At the end of the year overdue accounts are as follows:

| | |
|---|---|
| Accounts not more than two months overdue............ | $5,200 |
| Accounts more than two months but not more than six months overdue...................................... | 1,250 |
| Accounts more than six months but not more than one year overdue...................................... | 1,050 |
| Accounts more than one year overdue................. | 1,500 |

*Instructions:* (1) Give the entries required to record the transactions listed above and also to adjust the accounts.

(2) Calculate the balances for accounts receivable and the related allowances as of December 31, 1964, and show these as they will appear on the balance sheet.

**6-3.** Matson, Inc. assigned $70,000 in accounts to the Atlas Finance Co. on March 1. Seventy-five per cent of this amount was advanced, less a 2% commission charged by the finance company. Interest on the amount paid back is to be figured at 6%. The assignor continues to make collections on the accounts and makes monthly remittances of amounts collected.

Collections of $34,500 were made in March, remittance for this amount being made on March 31 plus the charge for interest.

Collections of $9,500 were made in April, remittance being made on April 30 of collections and interest.

Accounts of $1,900 were written off against an allowance for bad debts in May, collections were made on the balance of accounts, and settlement was made with the finance company on May 31.

*Instructions:* Give the entries on the books of the assignor and the assignee to record the foregoing transactions.

**6-4.** Huddle, Inc. assigns certain accounts receivable to the Harris Finance Co. on the following basis: 80% is advanced, a charge of 4% being made on the amount advanced, and interest at 8% is charged on the amount owed; the finance company makes collections, the assignor guaranteeing all accounts. Transactions in June and July follow:

June   1. Received remittance upon the assignment of $56,000 in accounts to the finance company.
June 30. Received notice that accounts of $40,000 were collected and that $180 was due for interest. Sent check to Harris Finance Co. for interest charge.
July 31. Received check in settlement from finance company, together with a summary reporting that all accounts were collected with the exception of one from Wayne Gross for $650 that was being returned. In making settlement, the Harris Finance Co. deducted $100 as its charge for interest.

*Instructions:* Give the entries that would appear on the books of the assignor and the assignee for the foregoing transactions.

**6-5.** J. A. Torres completed the following transactions, among others:

Oct.   1. Received a $3,000, 60-day, 6% note dated October 1 from R. T. Holmes, a customer.
      20. Received a $1,000, 90-day, non-interest-bearing note dated October 19 from F. C. Hamilton, a customer.
      21. Had Holmes' note discounted at the bank at 6%.
Nov.   4. Had Hamilton's note discounted at the bank at 6%.
      21. Received from B. C. Marshall, a customer, a $5,000, 90-day, 6% note dated November 1, payable to Marshall and signed by the Young Corporation. Upon endorsement, gave the customer credit for the maturity value of the note less discount at 7%.
      25. Received a $1,000, 60-day, 6% note dated November 24 from G. H. Robbins, a customer.

Dec.  1. Received notice from the bank that Holmes' note was not paid at maturity. Protest fees of $2.50 were charged by the bank.
     16. Received payment from Holmes on his dishonored note, including interest at 8% on the face value of the note from the maturity date.

*Instructions:* (1) Give the journal entries to record the above transactions, showing contingent liabilities in the accounts. (Show data used in calculations with each entry.)

(2) Give the adjusting entries that would be necessary on December 31.

(3) Indicate the adjustments that may appropriately be reversed.

**6-6.** The following are some of the transactions completed by W. C. Rasmussen over a three-month period:

Oct. 10. Received from P. M. Cory, a customer, a $1,500, 60-day, 7% note dated October 9.
     11. Received from D. A. Hart on account, a $3,000, 60-day, 7% note dated October 10.
     13. Had Cory's note discounted at the bank at 6%.
     27. Had Hart's note discounted at the bank at 6%.
Nov.  3. Received a $950, 30-day, non-interest-bearing note dated November 1 from J. R. Morton, crediting the customer's account at face value.
      7. Had Morton's note discounted at the bank at 6%.
     28. Received from M. L. Wade, a customer, a $300, 60-day, 6% note dated November 14 and made by the Miles Company. Gave the customer credit for the maturity value of the note less discount at 6%.
     29. Received a $2,200, 15-day, 7% note dated November 29 from B. Sharp, a customer.
Dec. 10. Received notice from the bank that Cory's note was not paid at maturity. Protest fees of $2.50 were charged by the bank.
     22. Received a $12,000, 60-day, 6% note dated December 22, from C. C. Stamp, a customer.
     27. Received payment on Sharp's note, including interest at 8%, the legal rate, on the face value from the maturity date.

*Instructions:* (1) Give the entries to record the above transactions showing the contingent liabilities in the accounts. (Show data used in calculations with each entry.)

(2) Give the necessary adjusting entries on December 31.

(3) Indicate the adjustments that may appropriately be reversed.

**6-7.** Current assets for the Thornton Company are listed as follows on the balance sheet prepared on December 31, 1964:

Current assets:
| | |
|---|---|
| Cash | $  9,150 |
| Marketable securities | 25,920 |
| Notes receivable | 21,450 |
| Accounts receivable | 74,485 |
| Merchandise inventory | 93,200 |
| | $224,205 |

An examination of the books revealed the following information concerning the current assets:

Cash included:

| | |
|---|---:|
| Petty cash funds (of which $450 is cash, $170 is in the form of employees' I.O.U.'s, and $30 is in the form of postage stamps). . . . | $   650 |
| Customers' checks not yet deposited. . . . . . . . . . . . . . . . . . . . . . . . . | 1,150 |
| Demand deposit at the First National Bank . . . . . . . . . . . . . . . . . . | 7,200 |
| An overdraft at the Central City Bank. . . . . . . . . . . . . . . . . . . . . . . | (450) |
| Customer's non-interest-bearing note (due January 2, 1965) deposited at the First National Bank for collection. . . . . . . . . . . . . | 600 |
| | $ 9,150 |

Marketable securities included:

| | |
|---|---:|
| Glendale Company Common (a subsidiary company), reported at cost. . . . . . . . . . . . . . . . . . . . . . . . . . . . . . . . . . . . . . . . . . . . . . . | $15,500 |
| Thornton Company Preferred (treasury stock), reported at cost | 7,200 |
| 6% Hamilton Company Bonds (interest payable Jan. 1 and July 1), $3,000 face value, purchased Sept. 1, 1964 as a temporary investment, reported at cost plus accrued interest to date of purchase. . | 3,220 |
| | $25,920 |

Notes receivable included:

| | |
|---|---:|
| Customers' notes (due in 1965). . . . . . . . . . . . . . . . . . . . . . . . . . . . . | $ 8,750 |
| Glendale Company note (due March 1, 1965). . . . . . . . . . . . . . . . . | 11,000 |
| Note receivable from sale of equipment (due July 1, 1966). . . . . . . | 5,700 |
| Notes receivable discounted (customers' notes). . . . . . . . . . . . . . . . | (4,000) |
| | $21,450 |

Accounts receivable included:

| | |
|---|---:|
| Creditors' accounts with debit balances. . . . . . . . . . . . . . . . . . . . . . | $   700 |
| Customers' accounts (regular). . . . . . . . . . . . . . . . . . . . . . . . . . . . . . | 37,070 |
| Dividends receivable on investments. . . . . . . . . . . . . . . . . . . . . . . . . | 500 |
| Deposit on equipment (ordered for delivery in December, 1966). . | 2,000 |
| Installment accounts receivable ($17,800 due in 1965; $6,200 due in 1966). . . . . . . . . . . . . . . . . . . . . . . . . . . . . . . . . . . . . . . . . . . | 24,000 |
| Interest receivable on bond investment. . . . . . . . . . . . . . . . . . . . . . . | 60 |
| Interest receivable on notes. . . . . . . . . . . . . . . . . . . . . . . . . . . . . . . . | 330 |
| Receivables from consignees (representing the merchandise at cost transferred to consignees and still unsold on December 31, 1964) | 4,100 |
| Refundable income taxes of prior periods (believed to be collectible in 1965). . . . . . . . . . . . . . . . . . . . . . . . . . . . . . . . . . . . . . . . . . . . | 2,250 |
| Salary advances to employees. . . . . . . . . . . . . . . . . . . . . . . . . . . . . . | 975 |
| Subscriptions receivable on capital stock (due in 1966). . . . . . . . . | 4,500 |
| Allowance for bad debts (on regular and installment accounts). . . | (2,000) |
| | $74,485 |

| | |
|---|---:|
| Merchandise inventory (representing a physical count of goods on hand), at cost. . . . . . . . . . . . . . . . . . . . . . . . . . . . . . . . . . . . . . . . . . | $93,200 |

*Instructions:* Revise the current asset section of the balance sheet presenting individual items appropriately included therein in a proper manner. Prepare schedules stating what disposition was made of those items excluded in the revised presentation.

# Chapter 7

# INVENTORIES

## GENERAL VALUATION PROCEDURES

### Nature of inventories

The term *inventories* is a designation for goods that are held for sale in the normal course of business, as well as for goods that are in production or are to be placed in production. Practically all tangible items fall into this classification at one time or another. Gasoline, oil, and automotive supplies are included in the inventory of a service station; crops and livestock are included in the inventory of a farmer; machinery and equipment are included in the inventory of a manufacturer producing such items for sale. It is the sale of inventories that normally provides a business with its chief source of revenue.

Inventories represent one of the most active elements in business operations, being continuously acquired, converted, and resold. A large part of a company's resources is frequently tied up in goods that are purchased or manufactured. The cost of such goods must be recorded, grouped, and summarized during the period. At the end of the period, costs must be allocated to current activities and to future activities. Such allocation normally occupies a central role in the measurement of periodic operating results as well as in the determination of financial position. Failure to allocate costs properly can result in serious distortions of financial progress and position.

Accounting for inventory costs presents a number of theoretical and practical problems. Members of the accounting profession have directed much thought to these problems in recent years, but there is still no general agreement on many important matters. This chapter and the chapter that follows consider these problems.

### Classes of inventories

The term *merchandise inventory* is generally applied to goods held by a trading concern, either wholesale or retail, when such goods have been acquired in a condition for resale. The terms *raw materials, goods in process*, and *finished goods* refer to the inventories of a manufacturing concern. The latter items require description.

*Raw materials.* Raw materials are those tangible goods that are acquired for use in the productive process. Raw materials may be obtained directly from natural sources. Ordinarily, however, raw materials are acquired from other companies and represent the finished products of the companies from which they were purchased. For example, news-print is the finished product of the paper mill but represents raw material to the printer who acquires it.

Although the term *raw materials* can be used broadly to cover all of the materials used in manufacturing, this designation is frequently restricted to materials that will be physically incorporated in the products being manufactured. The term *factory supplies* or *manufacturing supplies* is then used to refer to auxiliary materials, that is, materials that although necessary in the productive process are not directly incorporated in the products. Oils, fuels, cleaning supplies, etc., fall into this grouping since these items are not incorporated in a product but simply facilitate production as a whole; paint, nails, bolts, etc., although physically embodied in the final product, are normally of such minor significance as to warrant inclusion within the auxiliary grouping. Raw materials that can be directly associated with the production of certain goods are frequently referred to as *direct materials*; factory supplies are referred to as *indirect materials*.

Although factory supplies may be summarized separately, they should be reported as a part of the company's inventories since they will ultimately be applied to the productive process. Factory supplies should be distinguished from other supplies that make contributions to the delivery, sales, and general administrative functions of the enterprise. Such other supplies should not be reported as part of the inventories but as prepaid expenses.

*Goods in process.* Goods in process, alternately referred to as *work in process*, consist of materials partly processed and requiring further work before they can be sold. This inventory is considered to be made up of three cost elements: (1) *direct materials*, (2) *direct labor*, and (3) *manufacturing overhead* or *burden*. The cost of materials that can be directly identified with the goods in production is included under (1). The cost of labor that can be directly identified with goods in production is included under (2). The portion of manufacturing overhead assignable to goods still in production forms the third element in cost.

Manufacturing overhead consists of all manufacturing costs other than direct materials and direct labor. It includes factory supplies and labor not directly identified with the production of specific products. It also includes general manufacturing costs such as depreciation, main-tenance, repairs, property taxes, insurance, and light, heat, and power, as well as a reasonable share of the managerial costs other than those relating solely to the selling and administrative functions of the business. Overhead may be designated as *fixed, variable,* or *semivariable.* Over-head charges that remain constant in amount regardless of the volume of production are referred to as fixed. Depreciation, insurance, rent, and property taxes normally fall into this category. Charges that fluctuate in proportion to the volume of production are called variable. Indirect materials, indirect labor, and repairs vary with production. Some charges vary, but the variations are not in direct proportion to the volume. These charges have both fixed and variable components and are designated as semivariable items. Factory supervision is an example of a semivariable item when it is fixed within a certain range of production but changes when production is not within this range.

*Finished goods.* Finished goods are the manufactured products awaiting sale. The cost of the finished product consists of the direct material, direct labor, and manufacturing overhead costs assigned to it. Finished parts that were purchased and that are to be used in the production of the finished product are normally classed as raw materials; finished parts that are held for purposes of sale may be reported as finished goods.

### Inventories in the measurement of income

When goods that are purchased or manufactured are all sold within a fiscal period, the determination of the gross profit on sales is a simple matter. The total cost of goods purchased or manufactured is also the cost of goods sold that is properly chargeable to revenue. Such a situation, however, is seldom found in practice. Normally, a part of the goods acquired remains on hand at the end of the period. A value must be assigned to these goods. This value is subtracted from the total merchandise acquisition costs and is carried into the subsequent period to be charged against future revenue. Adequate records are required in providing cost data for statement purposes. Such records are also required for the proper internal control of goods on hand.

Two classes of questions arise in the determination of the inventory to be reported on the statements: (1) what items are properly included in the inventory? and (2) what values are to be assigned to such items?

### Inventory methods

Quantities of inventories on hand are ascertained either through a *periodic system* that calls for *physical inventories* at the end of each period, or a *perpetual system* that involves *perpetual* or *book inventories*.

The periodic system calls for counting, measuring, or weighing goods at the end of the period to determine the quantities on hand. Values are then assigned to such quantities in arriving at the portion of the recorded costs to be carried forward.

The perpetual inventory system requires the maintenance of records that offer a running summary of inventory items on hand. Individual accounts are kept for each class of goods. Inventory increases and decreases are recorded in the individual accounts, the resulting balances representing the amounts on hand. In the manufacturing organization, a perpetual system applied to inventories calls for recording the full movement of goods through individual accounts for raw materials, goods in process, and finished goods. Perpetual records may be kept in terms of quantities only or in terms of both quantities and costs.

When the perpetual system is employed, physical counts of the units on hand should be made at least once a year, and preferably at more frequent intervals, to confirm the balances that are found on the books. The frequency of physical inventories will vary depending upon the nature of the goods as well as their rate of turnover. A plan of continuous checking of inventory items on a rotation basis is frequently employed. Variations between the book record and the amounts actually on hand resulting from errors in recording, shrinkage, breakage, theft, and other causes should be recognized, and the book inventories should be brought into agreement with the physical count with offsetting charges and credits to an inventory adjustment account. The explanation for the discrepancy will determine whether the inventory adjustment balance should be regarded as an adjustment to cost of goods sold, an operating expense, or an extraordinary item on the income statement.

Practically all large trading and manufacturing enterprises, as well as many relatively small organizations, have adopted the perpetual inventory system as an integral part of their record keeping and internal control. This system offers a continuous check and control over inventories, as well as immediate data concerning inventory position. Purchasing and production planning are facilitated, adequate supplies on hand are assured, and losses through damage and theft are fully disclosed. The additional costs of maintaining such a system are usually well repaid by the services provided to management through its adoption.

### Items to be included in inventory

As a general rule, goods should be included in the inventory of the party holding title. The "passing of title" is a legal term designating the point at which ownership changes. There are instances where the legal rule may be waived for practical reasons or because of certain limitations that are found in its application. When the circumstances are such that the rule of passing of title does not need to be observed, there should be appropriate disclosure on the statements of the special practice that is followed and the factors that support such practice. Application of the legal test under a number of special circumstances is described in the following paragraphs.

*Goods in transit.* When terms of sale are "f.o.b. shipping point," title passes to the buyer with the loading of goods at the point of shipment. Application of the legal rule to a year-end shipment calls for recognition of a sale and an accompanying decrease in goods on hand on the books of the seller. On the other hand, the buyer should recognize such goods in transit as a purchase and an accompanying inventory increase even though there is no physical possession at this time. A determination of the goods in transit as of the year-end is made by a review of the incoming orders during the early part of the new period. The purchases records may be kept open beyond the fiscal period to permit the recognition of goods in transit as of the end of the period, or goods in transit may be recorded by means of an adjusting entry. Although no objection to the application of the legal rule can be raised by a seller, the buyer, in the interests of expediency, may prefer to ignore such a rule and employ "receipt" as a basis for the recognition of a purchase and the related inventory increase. The latter approach is not objectionable when amounts in transit are not material and the inclusion of such items before their receipt and acceptance offers practical difficulties.

When terms of a sale are "f.o.b. destination," application of the legal test calls for no recognition of the transaction until goods are received by the buyer. In this case, it is the seller who may prefer to ignore the legal rule and employ "shipment" as a basis for booking a sale and the accompanying inventory decrease. In view of the practical difficulties involved in ascertaining whether goods have reached their destination at year-end, application of a "shipment" rule is not objectionable under normal circumstances.

*Segregated goods.* When goods are prepared on special order and segregated for shipment, title may pass with such segregation. When goods are segregated at the end of the period and title has passed, the vendor may properly recognize a sale and exclude segregated goods from his inventory, while the vendee may properly recognize both a purchase and an inventory increase. Frequently, one encounters many practical problems in arriving at the portion of the inventory that is segregated as well as perplexing legal problems in defining the precise status of such goods. These difficulties normally lead to the adoption of a policy whereby entries for both sale and purchase await formal shipment of goods by the vendor.

*Goods on consignment.* Goods are frequently transferred to dealers on a consignment basis, the consignor retaining title to such goods until their sale by the consignee. Until the goods are sold and cash or a receivable can be recognized, the goods should continue to be reported as a part of the inventory of the consignor. Consigned goods are properly reported at the sum of their cost and the handling and shipping costs involved in their transfer to the consignee.   The goods may be separately designated on the balance sheet as "Merchandise on Consignment."   The consignee does not own the consigned goods; hence he reports neither consigned goods nor an obligation for such goods on his financial statements.   Other merchandise owned by a business but in the possession of others, such as goods in the hands of salesmen and agents, goods held by customers on approval, and goods held by others for storage, processing, or shipment, should also be shown as a part of the ending inventory of the owner.

*Conditional and installment sales.*   Conditional sales and installment sales contracts may provide for a retention of title by the seller until the sales price is fully recovered.   Under these circumstances, it would be possible for the seller to continue to show the goods to which he has title, reduced by the buyer's equity in such goods as established by collections from the latter; the buyer, in turn, can report an equity in the goods accruing through payments that have already been made.   However, when the possibilities of returns and default are negligible, the test of passing of title is generally relinquished and the transaction is recorded in terms of the expected outcome: the seller, anticipating completion of the contract and the ultimate passing of title, recognizes the transaction as a regular sale involving deferred collections; the buyer, intending to comply with the contract and acquire title, recognizes the transaction as a regular purchase.

## Inventory valuation

In viewing the inventory in its dual position as (1) a value that is reported on the income statement in developing charges properly applicable to current revenue and (2) a value reported on the balance sheet that represents the charges properly assignable to future revenues, cost must be accepted as the primary basis for inventory valuation. A marked change in the value of the inventory between the purchase date and the date of inventory raises the question as to whether some recognition should be given to current inventory replacement values. With a rise in prices, accountants generally answer this question in the negative, insisting that income must await sale of the goods; with a decline in prices, there is wide support for recognizing such decline by applying the "cost or market, whichever is lower" valuation procedure. In a few special instances full departure from cost and the use of a sales price or a modified sales price basis is considered acceptable.

Income measurement rather than balance sheet valuation is generally regarded as the major criterion in accounting for inventories.   The

American Institute of Certified Public Accountants has taken this position. The AICPA has also held that although inventories should be reported at cost in keeping with the cost principle, modifications in cost may be appropriate under certain circumstances. The Committee on Accounting Procedure, in discussing inventory pricing, has expressed the following view:

> ... In accounting for the goods in the inventory at any point of time, the major objective is the matching of appropriate costs against revenues in order that there may be a proper determination of the realized income. Thus, the inventory at any given date is the balance of costs applicable to goods on hand remaining after the matching of absorbed costs with concurrent revenues. This balance is appropriately carried to future periods provided it does not exceed an amount properly chargeable against the revenues expected to be obtained from ultimate disposition of the goods carried forward.[1]

The principal inventory valuation methods and their special applicabilities will be considered in detail. Attention is directed first to the measurement of cost when cost is required for inventory valuation as well as when cost is to be used as the first step in the development of a lower of cost or market value.

### Inventory cost

The determination of the cost of the inventory may be no simple matter. First, it involves a determination of the expenditures that actually entered into the cost of the goods that were acquired. Second, it involves the application of a method for relating the different costs of the goods acquired to periodic revenue.

Inventory cost consists of all expenditures, both direct and indirect, relating to inventory acquisition, preparation, and placement for sale. In the case of raw materials or goods acquired for resale, cost includes, in addition to the purchase price, buying, freight, receiving, storage, and all other expenditures incurred to the time goods are ready for sale. Certain expenditures can be traced to specific acquisitions or can be allocated to inventory items in some equitable manner. Other expenditures may be relatively small and difficult to allocate. Such items are normally excluded in the calculation of inventory cost and are thus charged in full against current revenue.

The charges to be included in the cost of manufactured products have already been mentioned. Proper accounting for materials, labor, and manufacturing overhead items and their identification with goods in process and finished goods inventories may be best achieved through

---

[1]*Accounting Research and Terminology Bulletins,* 1961 (New York: American Institute of Certified Public Accountants), *Accounting Research Bulletin No. 43,* p. 28.

adoption of a cost accounting system designed to meet the needs of the business unit. Overhead at a predetermined rate may be assigned to goods being produced during the period. At the end of the period, when the actual overhead is determined, appropriate adjustments are made for any under-applied or over-applied overhead amount. Certain costs relating to the acquisition or the manufacture of goods may be considered abnormal and may be excluded in arriving at inventory cost. For example, costs arising from idle capacity, excessive spoilage, and reprocessing are normally considered extraordinary items chargeable to current revenue. Only that portion of selling, general, and administrative costs that is clearly related to procurement or production should be included in inventory cost.

### Discounts as reductions in cost

Discounts that are treated as a reduction of cost in recording the acquisition of goods should likewise be treated as a reduction in the cost assigned to the inventory. *Trade discounts* are discounts that convert a printed price list to the prices actually to be charged to the particular buyer. Cost, then, is list price less the trade discount; purchases should be reported at such cost with no accounting recognition given to the discount, and the inventory should be stated on an equivalent basis. *Cash discounts* are reductions in prices allowed only upon payment of invoices within a limited period. Inventory treatment depends upon whether cash discounts are regarded as a reduction in cost or as a source of revenue. If cash discounts are treated as a subtraction from purchases, the inventory balance should be correspondingly reduced; if cash discounts are reported as other revenue, inventories should be reported at invoice cost without reference to the discounts.

Treatment of purchases discounts as revenue is frequently found in practice and is defended on the grounds that the buyer takes special measures in liquidating a claim in advance of its due date to secure such discounts. There may be expenses attached to raising capital for the advance liquidation of debts. Financial management is charged with such expenses; discounts earned, then, may be properly credited to financial management and matched against such expenses.

Serious objection, however, can be raised to the foregoing practice wherein revenue arises from the act of buying. Sound accounting provides for income recognition from the sale of goods or services, not from their purchase. The buyer is offered goods at a net or cash price, and no more than this actually needs to be paid. Settlement is almost invariably made on a cash basis in view of the difference between the cash discount and the cost of borrowing money to make prompt payment.

In fact, when settlement is not made within the discount period, a failure on the part of financial management is indicated either through carelessness in considering payment alternatives or through financial inability to avoid the extra charge.

Treatment of purchases discounts taken as a subtraction from purchases recognizes the discounts as an adjustment in purchase price. But this practice offers only partial recognition of the cost view just developed. Full agreement with the preceding analysis calls for recording purchases net and recognizing any amounts paid in excess of these amounts as Purchases Discounts Lost, a financial management expense item. When such a practice is to be followed, two methods may be employed: (1) accounts payable may be reported net or (2) accounts payable may be reported at the gross invoice price with a payable offset balance or liability valuation account reporting the purchases discounts available. The two methods are illustrated below.

| Transaction | Accounts Payable Reported Net | Accounts Payable Reported Gross |
|---|---|---|
| Purchase of merchandise priced at $2,500 less trade discount of 30%—20% and a cash discount of 2%:<br><br>$2,500 less 30% = $1,750<br>$1,750 less 20% = $1,400<br>$1,400 less 2% = $1,372 | Purchases (or Inventory)....1,372<br>  Accounts<br>    Payable......... 1,372 | Purchases (or Inventory)....1,372<br>Allowance for Purchases Discounts..... 28<br>  Accounts<br>    Payable......... 1,400 |
| (a) Assuming payment of the invoice within discount period. | Accounts Payable......1,372<br>  Cash........... 1,372 | Accounts Payable......1,400<br>  Allowance for Purchases Discounts....... 28<br>  Cash.......... 1,372 |
| (b) Assuming payment of the invoice after discount period. | Accounts Payable......1,372<br>Purchases Discounts Lost........ 28<br>  Cash.......... 1,400 | Accounts Payable......1,400<br>  Cash.......... 1,400<br>Purchases Discounts Lost........ 28<br>  Allowance for Purchases Discounts....... 28 |
| (c) Required adjustment at the end of the period assuming that the invoice was not paid and the discount period has lapsed. | Purchases Discounts Lost........ 28<br>  Accounts Payable......... 28 | Purchases Discounts Lost........ 28<br>  Allowance for Purchases Discounts....... 28 |

Although recording purchases net and recognizing cash discounts lost as an expense is of obvious merit, it has failed to gain wide adoption. Chief objection is made on practical grounds. Use of this method calls for converting gross amounts stated on invoices into net amounts relating to individual acquisitions and using converted values throughout the accounting for inventories. This is normally less convenient than accounting in terms of gross invoice charges.

### Specific identification of costs with inventory items

Revenue may be charged for goods sold on the basis of identified costs of the specific items sold. Such practice calls for the identification of a cost with each item acquired. When perpetual inventories are maintained, the sale of goods calls for the transfer of articles and their identified costs to the cost of goods sold. When a system of physical inventories is maintained, goods on hand require identification with specific invoices. In each instance, costs related to units sold are reported as cost of goods sold and costs identified with goods on hand remain to be reported as the ending inventory.

Although such identification procedure may be considered a highly satisfactory approach in matching costs with revenues in view of its objectivity and adherence to empirical fact, the practice may be difficult or impossible to apply or may be considered inadequate in view of special existing conditions. When an inventory is composed of a great many items, some being similar items acquired at different times and at different prices, cost identification procedures may prove to be slow, burdensome, and costly. When identical items have been acquired at different times, their identities may be lost and cost identification thus denied. Furthermore, when units are identical and interchangeable, this method opens the doors to possible profit manipulation through the choice of particular units for delivery. Finally, marked changes in costs during a period may warrant charges to revenue on a basis other than past identifiable costs.

When specific identification procedures are considered inappropriate, it is necessary to adopt some assumption with respect to the flow of costs that is to be associated with the movement of goods. Three methods, each with a different assumption as to an orderly flow of costs, have achieved widest application. These are: (1) *first-in, first-out*, (2) *weighted average*, and (3) *last-in, first-out*.

### First-in, first-out method

The first-in, first-out method (*fifo* method) is based on the assumption that costs should be charged out in the order in which incurred. Inventories are thus stated in terms of most recent costs. To illustrate the application of this method, assume the following data for a commodity:

| | | | | | |
|---|---|---|---|---|---|
| January | 1 | Inventory | 200 units at $10 | $ 2,000 |
| | 12 | Purchase | 400 units at 12 | 4,800 |
| | 26 | Purchase | 300 units at 11 | 3,300 |
| | 30 | Purchase | 100 units at 12 | 1,200 |
| | | Totals | 1,000 | $11,300 |

A physical inventory on January 31 shows 300 units on hand. The inventory would be considered to be composed of the most recent costs as follows:

| | | |
|---|---|---|
| Most recent purchase, January 30 | 100 units at $12 | $1,200 |
| Next most recent purchase, Jan. 26 | 200 units at 11 | 2,200 |
| Totals | 300 | $3,400 |

If the ending inventory is recorded at $3,400, cost of goods sold is $7,900 ($11,300–$3,400), and revenue is charged with the earliest costs.

When perpetual inventory accounts are maintained, a form similar to that illustrated below is kept to record the cost of units issued and the cost relating to the goods on hand. The first column is used for memorandum entries reporting amounts ordered. Remaining columns show the quantities and values relating to goods acquired, goods issued, and balances on hand. It should be observed that identical values for physical and perpetual inventories are obtained when fifo is applied.

COMMODITY X (FIFO)

| Ordered | Date | Received | | Issued | | Balance | |
|---|---|---|---|---|---|---|---|
| Memo- | Jan. 1 | | | | | 200 at $10 | 2,000 |
| randum | 12 | 400 at $12 | 4,800 | | | 200 at $10 | 2,000 |
| | | | | | | 400 at $12 | 4,800 |
| Entries | 16 | | | 200 at $10 | 2,000 | | |
| | | | | 300 at $12 | 3,600 | 100 at $12 | 1,200 |
| | 26 | 300 at $11 | 3,300 | | | 100 at $12 | 1,200 |
| | | | | | | 300 at $11 | 3,300 |
| | 29 | | | 100 at $12 | 1,200 | | |
| | | | | 100 at $11 | 1,100 | 200 at $11 | 2,200 |
| | 30 | 100 at $12 | 1,200 | | | 200 at $11 | 2,200 |
| | | | | | | 100 at $12 | 1,200 |

## Weighted average method

The weighted average method is based on the assumption that goods should be charged out at an average cost, such average being influenced by the number of units acquired at each price. Inventories are stated at the same weighted average cost. Assuming the cost data in the preceding section, the weighted average cost of a physical inventory of 300 units on January 31 would be as follows:

| January | 1 | Inventory | 200 units at $10 | $ 2,000 |
|---|---|---|---|---|
| | 12 | Purchase | 400 units at 12 | 4,800 |
| | 26 | Purchase | 300 units at 11 | 3,300 |
| | 30 | Purchase | 100 units at 12 | 1,200 |
| | | Totals | 1,000 | $11,300 |

Weighted average cost: $11,300 ÷ 1,000, or $11.30.
Ending inventory: 300 units at $11.30 = $3,390.

If the ending inventory is recorded at a cost of $3,390, cost of goods sold is $7,910 ($11,300 − $3,390), and revenue is charged with a weighted average cost.

Calculations above were made for costs of one month. Calculations could be developed in terms of data for a quarter or for a year.

When perpetual inventories are maintained but the costs of units issued are not recorded until the end of a period, a weighted average cost for the period may be calculated at that time and the accounts may be credited for the cost of total units issued. Frequently, however, costs relating to issues are recorded currently, and it is necessary to calculate costs on the basis of the weighted average on the date of issue. This requires the calculation of a new weighted average cost immediately after the receipt of each additional lot of merchandise. This method, which involves successive average recalculations, is referred to as a *moving average method*. The use of this method is illustrated below.

### COMMODITY X (MOVING AVERAGE)

| Ordered | Date | Received | | Issued | | Balance | |
|---|---|---|---|---|---|---|---|
| Memo- | Jan. 1 | | | | | 200 at $10.00 | 2,000 |
| randum | 12 | 400 at $12 | 4,800 | | | 600 at $11.33 | 6,800 |
| Entries | 16 | | | 500 at $11.33 | 5,665 | 100 at $11.35 | 1,135 |
| | 26 | 300 at $11 | 3,300 | | | 400 at $11.09 | 4,435 |
| | 29 | | | 200 at $11.09 | 2,218 | 200 at $11.09 | 2,217 |
| | 30 | 100 at $12 | 1,200 | | | 300 at $11.39 | 3,417 |

On January 12 the new unit cost of $11.33 was found by dividing $6,800, the total cost, by 600, the number of units on hand. On January 16, the dollar balance, $1,135, represented the previous balance, $6,800, less $5,665, the cost assigned to the 500 units issued on this date. New unit costs were calculated on January 26 and 30 when additional units were acquired.

It should be observed that with successive recalculations of cost and the use of such different costs during the period, the cost identified with the ending inventory will differ from that determined when cost is assigned to the ending inventory in terms of the average cost for all goods available during the period. A physical inventory and use of the weighted average method resulted in a value for the ending inventory of $3,390; a perpetual inventory and use of the moving average method resulted in a value for the ending inventory of $3,417.

## Last-in, first-out method

The last-in, first-out method (*lifo* method) is based on the assumption that the latest costs should be the first that are charged out. Inventories are thus stated in terms of earliest costs. Assuming the cost data in the preceding section, a physical inventory of 300 units on January 31 would have a cost as follows:

| | | |
|---|---|---|
| Earliest costs relating to goods, January 1 | 200 units at $10 | $2,000 |
| Next earliest cost, January 12 | 100 units at $12 | 1,200 |
| Totals | 300 | $3,200 |

If the ending inventory is recorded at a cost of $3,200, cost of goods sold is $8,100 ($11,300−$3,200), and revenue is charged with the latest costs.

When perpetual inventories are maintained but the cost of units issued is not recorded until the end of the period, the most recent costs relating to the total units issued may be determined and the inventory account credited for this cost. Cost, then, is the same as reported above. Frequently, however, costs relating to issues are recorded currently, and it is necessary to calculate costs on a last-in, first-out basis using the cost data as shown on the date of issue. This is illustrated on page 183.

It should be noted that in applying lifo, physical and perpetual inventory values are not the same. In the example, a cost of $3,200 was obtained for the periodic inventory, whereas $3,300 was obtained when costs were calculated as goods were issued. This difference is due to the fact that it was necessary to charge out 100 units at $10 in the issue of January 16. The ending inventory thus reflects only 100 units of the beginning inventory.

## COMMODITY X (LIFO)

| Ordered | Date | Received | | Issued | | Balance | |
|---|---|---|---|---|---|---|---|
| Memo- | Jan.  1 | | | | | 200  at  $10 | 2,000 |
| randum | 12 | 400 at $12 | 4,800 | | | 200 at $10<br>400 at $12 | 2,000<br>4,800 |
| Entries | 16 | | | 400 at $12<br>100 at $10 | 4,800<br>1,000 | 100 at $10 | 1,000 |
| | 26 | 300 at $11 | 3,300 | | | 100 at $10<br>300 at $11 | 1,000<br>3,300 |
| | 29 | | | 200 at $11 | 2,200 | 100 at $10<br>100 at $11 | 1,000<br>1,100 |
| | 30 | 100 at $12 | 1,200 | | | 100 at $10<br>100 at $11<br>100 at $12 | 1,000<br>1,100<br>1,200 |

With large and diversified inventories, application of the lifo procedures just illustrated may prove extremely burdensome. To reduce clerical work and to simplify the valuation process, procedures referred to as *unit lifo* are frequently employed. Goods making up the inventory are first segregated into a number of groups or pools based on their similarity in type if purchased or their similarity in degree of processing if manufactured. Having made the choice to adopt lifo as of a certain date, the number of units within each pool and the total costs of such units are determined. Average unit costs for goods within each pool are then calculated, units being regarded as all having been, acquired at the same time. At the end of a period, units in each pool equal to the beginning number are assigned the beginning unit costs. An increase in the number of units in an inventory pool during a period is regarded as an incremental layer, and such incremental layer is valued at current costs applied on the basis of (1) actual costs of earliest acquisitions within the period, (2) the average cost of acquisitions within the period, or (3) actual costs of the latest acquisitions within the period. Increments in subsequent periods form successive inventory layers. A decrease in the number of units in an inventory pool during a period is regarded as a reduction in the most recently added or top layer, then in successively lower layers, and finally in the original or base quantity.

To illustrate the valuation process, assume inventory pools and changes in pools as listed on the next page. The inventory calculations that follow are based on the assumption that average costs are used in valuing annual incremental layers.

Inventory pool increments and liquidations:

|  | Class A Goods | Class B Goods | Class C Goods |
|---|---|---|---|
| Inv., Dec. 31, 1962 | 3,000@$6 | 3,000@$5 | 2,000@$10 |
| Purchases — 1963 | 3,000@$7 | 2,000@$6 | 3,000@$11 |
|  | 1,000@$9 |  |  |
|  | 7,000 | 5,000 | 5,000 |
| Sales — 1963 | 3,000 | 1,000 | 3,500 |
| Inv., Dec. 31, 1963 | 4,000 | 4,000 | 1,500 |
| Purchases — 1964 | 1,000@$8 | 2,000@$6 | 3,000@$11 |
|  | 3,000@$10 |  |  |
|  | 8,000 | 6,000 | 4,500 |
| Sales — 1964 | 3,500 | 2,500 | 2,000 |
| Inv., Dec. 31, 1964 | 4,500 | 3,500 | 2,500 |

Unit-lifo inventory valuations:

|  | Class A Goods | | Class B Goods | | Class C Goods | |
|---|---|---|---|---|---|---|
| Inv., Dec. 31, 1962: | 3,000@$6 | $18,000 | 3,000@$5 | $15,000 | 2,000@$10 | $20,000 |
| Inv., Dec. 31, 1963: | 3,000@$6 | $18,000 | 3,000@$5 | $15,000 | 1,500@$10 | $15,000 |
|  | 1,000@$7.50[1] | 7,500 | 1,000@$6 | 6,000 |  |  |
|  | 4,000 | $25,500 | 4,000 | $21,000 | 1,500 | $15,000 |
| Inv., Dec. 31, 1964: | 3,000@$6 | $18,000 | 3,000@$5 | $15,000 | 1,500@$10 | $15,000 |
|  | 1,000@$7.50 | 7,500 | 500@$6 | 3,000 | 1,000@$11 | 11,000 |
|  | 500@$9.50[2] | 4,750 |  |  |  |  |
|  | 4,500 | $30,250 | 3,500 | $18,000 | 2,500 | $26,000 |

[1]Cost of units acquired in 1963, $30,000, divided by number of units acquired, 4,000, or $7.50.
[2]Cost of units acquired in 1964, $38,000, divided by number of units acquired, 4,000, or $9.50.

## Effects of cost flow procedures compared

In using the first-in, first-out procedure, inventories are reported at or near current costs. In using last-in, first-out, inventories that do not change significantly in quantity are reported at more or less fixed amounts. Use of the average method generally provides inventory values that closely parallel first-in, first-out values, since purchases during a period are normally several times the opening inventory balance and average costs are thus heavily influenced by current costs. When the prices paid for merchandise do not fluctuate significantly, the alternative inventory methods may provide only minor differences on the financial statements. However, in periods of steadily rising or falling prices, the alternative methods may produce relatively material differences. Differences in inventory valuations on the balance sheet are accompanied by differences in earnings on the income statement.

Use of first-in, first-out in a period of rising prices matches oldest low-cost inventory with rising sales prices, thus expanding the gross profit margin. In a period of declining prices, oldest high-cost inventory is matched with declining sales prices, thus narrowing the gross profit margin. On the other hand, use of last-in, first-out in a period of rising prices relates current high costs of acquiring goods with rising sales prices, and in a period of falling prices, low costs of acquiring goods with declining sales prices.

Average methods that provide inventory costs that are closely comparable with first-in, first-out costs offer operating results that approximate first-in, first-out results.

### Evaluation of cost flow procedures

Fifo assumes a procession of costs that are assignable to revenue in exactly the same order in which they were incurred. The average method assumes a complete commingling of costs for units acquired with costs for units on hand, such commingled costs being assignable to revenue. Lifo assumes that first costs are identified with the inventory, subsequent costs bypassing the inventory and being assignable to revenue.

Fifo can be supported as a logical and realistic approach to the flow of costs when it is impractical or impossible to achieve cost identification with goods as these move forward. An assumed cost flow is achieved which normally parallels closely the actual physical flow of goods. Revenue is charged with costs considered applicable to those goods involved in revenue realization; ending inventories are reported in terms of most recent costs — costs that fairly present the latest acquisitions and that may equitably be assigned to revenues of the subsequent period. Fifo affords no opportunity for profit manipulation; assignment of costs against revenue is determined by the order in which costs are incurred.

The average cost approach, too, can be supported as realistic and as paralleling the physical flow of goods particularly where there is an intermingling of identical inventory units. Unlike the other methods, the average approach provides the same cost for similar items of equal utility. The method does not permit profit manipulation. Limitations ascribed to the average method are inventory values that perpetually contain to some minor degree the influence of earliest costs, and inventory values that may lag significantly behind current prices in periods of rising or falling prices.

The cost assignment resulting from the application of lifo cannot normally be considered in harmony with a movement of goods through the business. One would seldom encounter a practice of priorities for the use or transfer of goods representing latest acquisitions. Sequences involved in the physical movement of goods are disregarded so that charges may be made to revenue in terms of most-current costs, that is, costs that are more nearly representative of the cost of replacing the gap in the inventory resulting from sales.[1]

However, it is argued that lifo offers a more accurate statement of earnings accruing to the ownership group than alternate methods. When fifo is used in a period of rising prices, for example, earnings are reported that are not fully available to owners but rather must be applied in part or in whole to higher-cost inventory replacement; in a period of falling prices, earnings are reported that fail to show the full resources accruing to owners from sales activities plus the amounts made available through lower cost inventory replacement. Lifo, on the other hand, by charging revenue with latest costs, avoids the recognition of "paper profit or loss" on an inventory that the company must continue to hold as long as it operates as a going concern. This aspect of the measurement process may be illustrated as follows:

|  | Inventory Cost | Sales Price | Latest Purchase Price | Fifo "Profit" | Lifo "Profit" | Dollars Available After Unit Replacement |
|---|---|---|---|---|---|---|
| With rising prices: | $10 | $15 | $12 | $5 | $3 | $3 |
| With falling prices: | $10 | $12 | $ 8 | $2 | $4 | $4 |

Under lifo, that portion of sales proceeds that is required for the replacement of the inventory at higher costs receives recognition as net income only when it is freed through a subsequent replacement of inventories at lower costs. Lifo is acceptable for income tax purposes. Its use for tax purposes in a period of rising prices serves to postpone taxes until earnings are reflected in a company's net monetary assets.

Although arguments for lifo as a means of achieving satisfactory income measurement are impressive, one must consider the deficiencies of this method as applied to the recognition of inventory position for balance sheet purposes. The lifo inventory consists of an assembly of congealed costs or cost layers dating back to original acquisitions — costs that may differ materially from current prices. Such inventory costs enter into the determination of working capital and may seriously distort this measurement. Inventory position is also a determinant of total assets and capital. Adoption of lifo in a period of rising prices results in inventory understatement, a practice that is normally rational-

---

[1] It may be noted that some accountants would go beyond lifo and charge revenue with the replacement cost of goods sold (next-in, first-out, or *nifo*) rather than with latest acquisition costs.

ized as acceptable on conservative grounds. Adoption of lifo in a period of falling prices results in inventory overstatement; here, it is fair to assume, there would be strong pressure for special action to write down inventory balances to replacement cost.

In certain instances, the use of lifo may produce highly unrealistic operating results. Assume, for example, that special conditions make it necessary for a company to liquidate a significant part or an entire inventory carried at costs that are materially different from current costs. Under these circumstances, the lifo gross profit margin would not be the steady percentage offered by the recurring application of current costs to current revenues but instead a highly distorted figure resulting from the need to charge off original inventory costs. Lifo may also invite profit manipulation practices. For example, purchases, though required to maintain an inventory position, may be postponed at the end of the period so that costs of prior periods may be used in measuring net income. On the other hand, purchases may be made at the end of the period, though goods are not required, so that costs of such latest purchases may be used in arriving at net income.

Last-in, first-out has been widely adopted largely because of its ability to smooth the profit curve and its income tax advantages in a period of steadily rising prices. However, it is not the effects of a procedure but its merit as a means of sound measurement that should determine its acceptance for general accounting purposes. Depreciation and amortization charges, for example, could be recorded in accordance with the ability of revenue to absorb such charges in smoothing the profit curve. Such practices would not lead to measurements of what actually took place; they would serve to obscure measurements and thus contradict the aim of accounting to report financial activities fairly.

Support for lifo must be found in its merit as a means of charging current revenue with current costs. But lifo can be challenged on the grounds that it is no more than an artifice resorted to because of failures of accounting theory to provide a satisfactory and cohesive approach to the problem of price level changes. In supporting the alternative methods one can insist that it is historical costs, as best determined, that should be used to measure cost of goods sold. Net income emerges from a comparison of revenues with those costs that made such revenues possible. In periods of changing prices, such accounting needs to be supplemented by special analyses in arriving at conclusions concerning economic gain, changes in resources, and the availability of resources for continued operations and for distribution to owners.

### Other cost procedures

The methods previously described for arriving at inventory cost are the ones most widely used. Several other procedures are also encountered and deserve mention.

### Cost of latest purchases

Sometimes goods are valued at cost of the latest purchase regardless of quantities on hand. When the inventory consists largely of recent purchases, this method may give results closely approximating those obtained through specific cost identification or first-in, first-out procedures with considerably less work. However, when the quantities of goods on hand are significantly in excess of the latest quantities purchased and major price changes have taken place, use of latest costs may result in significant cost misstatement.

### Simple average of costs

Goods on hand are sometimes valued at a simple average of all of the costs for the period without regard to the number of units acquired on each purchase. With significant differences in quantities acquired, the disregard of the weight factor may result in unrepresentative costs.

### Base stock method

Some companies employ the *base stock* or *normal stock* method. This method assumes that a minimum stock is a normal and permanent requirement of the business; current purchases are means of satisfying current sales requirements, and hence their cost is properly applicable to revenues. The base stock inventory is regarded as fixed as to quantity and fixed as to price. The price is frequently the lowest cost experienced for the stock by the business unit. At the end of the period the amount of goods on hand is determined. The base stock quantity is valued at the original base cost. An amount in excess of the base stock quantity is regarded as a temporary inventory increase and is valued at current costs, applied on a first-in, first-out, average, or other basis. A reduction in the base stock quantity is viewed as an amount temporarily "borrowed" to meet sales requirements, and this is charged to sales at current replacement value in view of the cost to be incurred in restoring the inventory deficiency.

The base stock is thus regarded as a permanent asset; operations are charged with the costs of maintaining the normal stock. Results obtained through the base stock method are closely comparable with those obtained by the last-in, first-out method and the arguments for and against last-in, first-out can be applied here. Charges to revenue are costs currently experienced. The inventory, normally reported at the lowest value in the experience of the organization, may be seriously understated in terms of current prices. Use of the base stock method is not permitted for income tax purposes.

## Standard costs

Manufacturing inventories are frequently reported at *standard costs*, which are predetermined costs based upon representative or normal conditions of efficiency and volume of operations. Differences between actual costs and standard costs for material, labor, and manufacturing overhead give rise to *standard cost variances* indicating favorable and unfavorable operational or cost experiences. Excessive material usage, inefficient labor application, excessive spoilage, and idle time, for example, produce unfavorable variances, and these would be separately summarized in variance accounts.

Standard costs are developed from a variety of sources. Past manufacturing experiences may be carefully analyzed; time and motion studies as well as job and process studies may be undertaken; data from industry and economy-wide sources may be referred to. Standards should be reviewed at frequent intervals to determine whether they continue to offer reliable cost criteria. Changes in conditions will call for adjustment in the standards.

## Direct costing

A practice that has been widely debated in recent years is referred to as *direct costing, marginal costing,* or *variable costing.* Inventories under direct costing are assigned only the variable costs that are incurred in production — direct materials, direct labor, and the variable component of manufacturing overhead. Fixed costs are treated as periodic charges and assigned to current revenue. Only costs that can be directly related to output, then, are assigned to goods and charged to the period in which the goods are sold; costs that are a function of time and that are continuing regardless of the volume of output — for example, supervisory salaries, depreciation, and property taxes — are charged against revenue of the period in which they are incurred.

Support for direct costing is made on the grounds that it provides more meaningful and useful data to management than conventional costing procedures referred to as *full costing* or *absorption costing.* Direct costing enables management to appraise the effects of sales fluctuations on net income. Sales, current and potential, can be evaluated in terms of out-of-pocket costs to achieve such sales. The direct costing approach becomes a valuable tool for planning and control.

With direct costing applied to inventories, cost of goods sold varies directly with sales and a high earnings rate emerges in a period of high sales; with full costing, a high earnings rate may emerge in a period of high production even though sales are declining. Changes in the volume of production have no effect upon earnings when inventories are valued at no more than the direct costs related to their production.

Direct costing can offer management highly useful approaches to cost, price, and volume relationships. No objection can be raised to the use of direct costing when it is used for internal reporting and as a means for assisting management in decision-making. However, objection can be raised to the extension of direct costing procedures to the annual financial statements. It is fair to maintain that in measuring financial position and the results of operations, inventories must carry their full costs including a satisfactory allocation of the fixed overhead costs. Fixed costs, no less than variable costs, are incurred in contemplation of future benefits and should be matched against the revenues that are ultimately produced through such efforts. Inventories, then, when arrived at by direct costing procedures for internal reporting, should be restated in terms of full costing whenever financial statements are to be prepared.

### Inventory valuation at cost or market, whichever is lower

Replacement costs for goods that are held may fall below original acquisition costs, suggesting sales prices that are less than those anticipated when the goods were purchased. Such circumstances are considered to justify departure from cost and the use of the lower replacement costs in valuing the inventory. Recognition of an inventory decline identifies the loss with the period in which it was incurred; goods are reported at an amount that measures the contribution carried into the next period. This practice is referred to as valuation at "cost or market, whichever is lower," or valuation at "the lower of cost or market."

"Market" in "cost or market" is generally interpreted to be inventory replacement cost by purchase or manufacture. Federal Income Tax Regulations offer the following definition: "Under ordinary circumstances and for normal goods in an inventory, 'market' means the current bid price prevailing at the date of the inventory for the particular merchandise in the volume in which usually purchased by the taxpayer. . . ."[1] Replacement cost includes freight, duties, and other costs incidental to the acquisition of goods.

---

[1]Regulations, Sec. 39.22 (c) –4.

## Methods of applying lower of cost or market procedure

The lower of cost or market procedure may be applied to each inventory item or it may be applied to major inventory groupings or to the inventory as a whole. Application of this procedure to the individual inventory items will result in the lowest inventory value. However, application to inventory groups or to the inventory as a whole may provide a sufficiently conservative valuation with considerably less effort. For example, assume that balanced stocks of raw materials are on hand, some of which have gone down and others have gone up. When such raw materials are used as components of a single finished product, a loss in the value of certain materials may be considered to be counterbalanced by the gains that are found in other materials, and the lower of cost or market applied to this category as a whole may provide an adequate measure of the utility of the goods.

The illustration below shows the valuation procedure applied to (1) individual inventory items, (2) independent classes of the inventory, and (3) inventory as a whole.

| | Quantities | Unit Cost | Market | Totals | | Cost or Market, Whichever Is Lower | | |
|---|---|---|---|---|---|---|---|---|
| | | | | Cost | Market | (1) If Applied to Individual Inventory Items | (2) If Applied to Inventory Classes | (3) If Applied to Inventory as a Whole |
| Material A.......... | 4,000 | $1.20 | $1.10 | $ 4,800 | $ 4,400 | $ 4,400 | | |
| Material B.......... | 5,000 | .50 | .40 | 2,500 | 2,000 | 2,000 | | |
| Material C.......... | 2,000 | 1.00 | 1.10 | 2,000 | 2,200 | 2,000 | | |
| | | | | $ 9,300 | $ 8,600 | | $ 8,600 | |
| Goods in Process D... | 10,000 | 1.60 | 1.40 | $16,000 | $14,000 | 14,000 | | |
| Goods in Process E.... | 12,000 | 1.00 | 1.20 | 12,000 | 14,400 | 12,000 | | |
| | | | | $28,000 | $28,400 | | 28,000 | |
| Finished Goods F..... | 3,000 | 2.00 | 1.70 | $ 6,000 | $ 5,100 | 5,100 | | |
| Finished Goods G..... | 2,000 | 1.50 | 1.60 | 3,000 | 3,200 | 3,000 | | |
| | | | | $ 9,000 | $ 8,300 | | 8,300 | |
| | | | | $46,300 | $45,300 | | | $45,300 |
| Inventory valuation... | | | | | | $42,500 | $44,900 | $45,300 |

In valuing manufacturing inventories, raw materials declines are applicable to the raw materials inventory and also to raw material costs in goods in process and finished goods inventories. Declines in direct labor and manufacturing overhead costs also affect the values of goods in process and finished goods, but these are usually ignored when they are relatively minor.

The method that is chosen for reducing an inventory to a lower market should be applied consistently in successive valuations. A lower market value assigned to goods at the end of a period is considered to be its cost for purposes of inventory valuation in subsequent periods; cost reductions once made, then, would not be restored in subsequent inventory determinations.

For federal income tax purposes, taxpayers, except those who use lifo, may value their inventories at either cost or the lower of cost or market. Tax requirements provide for the application of cost or market to individual items; however, this rule may not be rigidly enforced when it involves certain practical difficulties. The valuation method that is elected must be applied on successive tax returns.

## Evaluation of lower of cost or market procedure

Inventory valuation at the lower of cost or market is commonly employed in practice. However, such valuation is subject to serious criticism.

Valuation of inventories at the lower of cost or market can be challenged on the grounds that it violates the cost concept. Is it proper to distinguish between "favorable" and "unfavorable" costs and to adjust the latter to provide a more satisfactory showing in the period when these produce revenue? There would normally be no modification in charges for depreciation because of a decline in the replacement cost of plant and equipment; nor would there be a modification in charges for bond interest, because bonds can be issued at a lower interest rate. Should, then, cost of goods sold be reduced in response to a decline in the replacement value of merchandise? Profit and loss measurements involve actual and not "fair" or "ideal" costs and revenues, some costs emerging currently from policies and transactions that date back to the time the company was organized.

Objection to valuation at the lower of cost or market is also raised on the grounds that it produces inconsistencies in the measurements of both the financial position and the operations of the enterprise. Market decreases are recognized but increases are not; with changes in the direction of market prices, a lower of cost or market valuation at the end of one year may be followed by a strictly cost valuation the next. Furthermore, serious income distortions may emerge when assumptions of future lower sales prices fail to materialize. To illustrate, assume that activities summarized in terms of cost provide the following results over a three-year period:

| | 1962 | | 1963 | | 1964 | |
|---|---|---|---|---|---|---|
| Sales................. | | $200,000 | | $225,000 | | $250,000 |
| Cost of goods sold: | | | | | | |
| Beginning inventory... | $ 60,000 | | $ 80,000 | | $127,500 | |
| Purchases........... | 120,000 | | 160,000 | | 90,000 | |
| | $180,000 | | $240,000 | | $217,500 | |
| Less ending inventory.. | 80,000 | 100,000 | 127,500 | 112,500 | 92,500 | 125,000 |
| Gross profit on sales..... | | $100,000 | | $112,500 | | $125,000 |
| Operating expenses..... | | 80,000 | | 90,000 | | 100,000 |
| Net income........... | | $ 20,000 | | $ 22,500 | | $ 25,000 |
| Rate of income to sales.. | | 10% | | 10% | | 10% |

Assume, now, that estimates as to the future utility of ending inventories indicated market values as follows:

| 1962 | 1963 | 1964 |
|---|---|---|
| $ 75,000 | $110,000 | $ 92,500 |

Inventory valuation at the lower of cost or market would provide the following results:

| | 1962 | | 1963 | | 1964 | |
|---|---|---|---|---|---|---|
| Sales................. | | $200,000 | | $225,000 | | $250,000 |
| Cost of goods sold: | | | | | | |
| Beginning inventory... | $ 60,000 | | $ 75,000 | | $110,000 | |
| Purchases........... | 120,000 | | 160,000 | | 90,000 | |
| | $180,000 | | $235,000 | | $200,000 | |
| Less ending inventory.. | 75,000 | 105,000 | 110,000 | 125,000 | 92,500 | 107,500 |
| Gross profit on sales..... | | $ 95,000 | | $100,000 | | $142,500 |
| Operating expenses..... | | 80,000 | | 90,000 | | 100,000 |
| Net income........... | | $ 15,000 | | $ 10,000 | | $ 42,500 |
| Rate of income to sales.. | | 7.5% | | 4.4% | | 17.0% |

Reduction of an inventory below cost reduces the net income of the period in which the reduction is made and increases the net income of a subsequent period. In the example just given, total net income for the three-year period is the same under either set of calculations. But the reduction of inventories to lower market values reduced the incomes for 1962 and 1963 and increased the income for 1964. The fact that inventory reductions were not followed by decreases in the sales prices resulted in net income determinations that varied considerably from those that might reasonably have been expected from increasing sales and costs that normally vary with sales volume.

Application of the lower of cost or market procedure requires careful analysis of the underlying market conditions and care in arriving at the values to be used.

## Application of lower of cost or market in the accounts

If beginning and ending inventories are reported on the income statement at amounts that are less than cost as a result of inventory pricing at the lower of cost or market, the cost of goods sold determination will include the effects of fluctuations in inventory replacement values. With unusual and substantial adjustments resulting from application of the cost or market rule, it is normally desirable to show these separately so that the reader of the income statement is fully informed on these matters and is able to make comparisons of operating results for successive periods. This may be done by reporting the ending inventory in the cost of goods sold section at cost and listing separately the loss on inventory decline. To illustrate, assume an ending inventory with a cost of $50,000 but with a replacement value of only $40,000. An entry to record the inventory may be made as follows:

| | | |
|---|---|---|
| Merchandise Inventory................................ | 40,000 | |
| Loss on Reduction of Inventory to Market.......... | 10,000 | |
|     Profit and Loss (Ending Inventory at Cost)........ | | 50,000 |

Cost of goods sold is calculated on the basis of an ending inventory cost of $50,000 in the profit and loss account and on the income statement. The inventory loss of $10,000 is closed into the profit and loss account and is reported on the income statement as an expense or an extraordinary loss, whichever may be appropriate. In the foregoing example, if the ending inventory were simply reported at $40,000, net income would be accurately stated but cost of goods sold would be overstated by the amount of the loss.

## Deteriorated goods, trade-ins, repossessions

A decline in market conditions may not be the only factor suggesting the use of values that are less than cost for inventories. There may be goods on hand that are deteriorated, obsolete, damaged, or shopworn. If such goods are unsaleable, they should be excluded from the inventory. If the goods are saleable but only at reduced prices, the lower of cost or market criterion should be applied in their valuation. When inventory cost shrinkages are significant, they should not be buried in cost of goods sold but should be reported under appropriate expense or loss headings. Thus, physical deterioration of goods arising from normal activities would be reported either as a special cost of goods sold item or as a selling expense, whichever might be considered more appropriate under the circumstances.

When goods are acquired in secondhand condition as a result of repossessions and trade-ins, they should be recorded at their estimated "cash purchase price." However, when this is difficult or impossible to define, the consistent application of "floor" values — amounts which after increase by reconditioning charges will permit the recognition of normal profits — would be appropriate. Sales efforts are required in the sale of repossessions and trade-ins just as in the sale of new items; recording the goods at floor values will permit the recognition of normal profits when goods are sold.

## Losses on purchase commitments

Commitments are frequently made for the future purchase of goods at fixed prices. When price declines take place subsequent to such commitments, it is considered appropriate to measure and recognize such losses on the books just as losses on goods on hand. A decline is recorded by a charge to a special loss account and a credit to an accrued liability. Acquisition of the goods in a subsequent period is recorded by a credit to cash, a charge canceling the accrued liability, and a charge to purchases for the difference. The loss is thus assigned to the period in which the decline took place, and subsequent periods are charged for no more than the economic utilities of the goods they receive. Current loss recognition would not be appropriate when commitments can be canceled, when commitments provide for price adjustments, when hedging transactions prevent losses, or when declines do not suggest reductions in sales prices. Losses that are expected to arise from commitments for the sale of goods would suggest similar current recognition.

## Valuation at sales price

In special instances there is support for reporting goods at sales prices less costs to be incurred in their sale even though such values may exceed cost. Valuation at sales price must be regarded as exceptional treatment since earnings are recognized prior to time of sale. Such valuation can be justified only when it is a regular trade practice and arises from either (1) assured market conditions that make possible the immediate sale of the goods at stated prices, or (2) standard products, a ready market, plus the inability to arrive at reasonable assignments of costs. Inventories such as gold, silver, and certain other metals may be accorded this exceptional treatment in view of their immediate marketability at a fixed sales price. Similar treatment may be accorded a farmer's inventory in view of the difficulty of arriving at satisfactory costs. When inventories are reported at more than cost, the special valuation procedure should be disclosed on the financial statements.

### Valuation at market

There has been some support, particularly in recent years, for reporting inventories on the financial statements at their net realizable values or current replacement costs. Such valuation would recognize gains as well as losses when market or replacement costs differ from the costs of purchase or production. Earnings would emerge in two stages: (1) part of the earnings would be related to the periods in which goods are acquired, processed, and held; (2) the balance of the earnings would be related to the period in which goods are sold. Supporters of market insist that such valuation is necessary if inventories and working capital are to be fairly stated on the balance sheet. They also argue that valuation at market is necessary if net income is to be measured in a fair and consistent manner. Should price decreases be recognized but price increases ignored? Should net income be related only to the period of the sale when it actually emerges from productive, holding, and sales efforts?

Little tendency to accept valuation at market has been shown by the accounting profession. Such procedure has been challenged chiefly on the grounds that it represents a departure from the cost concept and would violate accounting conservatism.

### QUESTIONS

**1.** (a) Why is so much importance attached to the satisfactory valuation of inventories? (b) What criteria might be adopted for inventory valuation? What criterion would you support?

**2.** (a) What are the three cost elements entering into goods in process and finished goods? (b) What items enter into manufacturing overhead? (c) Define fixed overhead, variable overhead, and semivariable overhead and give an example of each.

**3.** (a) How does title passing affect the current sections of a balance sheet? (b) Distinguish between a purchase "f.o.b. destination" and a purchase "f.o.b. shipping point." (c) What circumstances would suggest that exception be made from the legal rule of "passing title"?

**4.** State how you would report each of the following items on the financial statements:
- (a) Manufacturing supplies.
- (b) Goods on hand received on a consignment basis.
- (c) Materials of a customer held for processing.
- (d) Goods received but without an accompanying invoice.
- (e) Goods in stock to be delivered to customers in subsequent periods.
- (f) Goods in hands of agents and consignees.
- (g) Deposits with vendors for merchandise to be delivered next period.
- (h) Goods in hands of customers on approval.
- (i) Defective goods requiring reprocessing.

**5.** What objections can be raised to inventory valuation by specific cost identification procedures?

**6.** Describe and give the arguments in support of each of the following inventory cost methods: (a) fifo, (b) average, (c) lifo.

**7.** Compare the effects of the use of fifo and lifo upon inventory valuation and upon net income measurement in a period of rapidly rising prices.

**8.** It has been stated that lifo may produce highly unrealistic operating results in certain instances, and further, that it opens the doors to profit manipulation. What is your understanding of these assertions?

**9.** Describe the application of unit lifo in the accounts.

**10.** (a) Describe the base stock method. (b) How does this method differ from inventory valuation by lifo?

**11.** (a) Describe the valuation of inventories in terms of standard costs. (b) What precautions are necessary in the use of standard costs?

**12.** What is direct costing? Would you approve of this costing procedure for financial statement purposes?

**13.** Define "market" for purposes of inventory valuation at "cost or market, whichever is lower."

**14.** (a) Describe the application of the lower of cost or market valuation to (1) each inventory item, (2) inventory classes, (3) the inventory as a whole. (b) State the conditions that would indicate the use of each of these methods.

**15.** What conditions might suggest caution in the application of the rule of cost or market, whichever is lower? Why?

**16.** What treatment would you recommend when substantial losses are indicated in connection with certain purchase commitments outstanding at the end of the period? Give reasons for your answer.

**17.** What factors might call for inventory valuation at sales prices?

**18.** How should repossessed goods be valued for inventory purposes? Give reasons for your proposal.

## EXERCISES

**1.** Transactions of the Barlow Co. relating to goods purchased during December are summarized below:

> Purchases were $10,000, terms 2/10, n/30.
> Accounts of $8,500 were paid, including accounts of $8,000 paid within the discount period on which discounts of $160 were received.

Give the entries to record purchases and invoice payments in December, assuming that:

(a) Accounts payable are recorded at invoice price and purchases discounts earned are summarized in the accounts.

(b) Accounts payable are recorded net and purchases discounts lost are summarized in the accounts.
(c) Accounts payable are recorded at invoice price and purchases discounts lost are summarized in the accounts.

**2.** Changes in Commodity X during January are:

| Jan. 1 | Balance 400 units @ $5 | Jan. 10 | Sale 300 units @ $10 |
|---|---|---|---|
| 12 | Purchase 200 units @ 6 | 30 | Sale 200 units @ 12 |
| 28 | Purchase 200 units @ 7 | | |

(a) Assuming that perpetual inventories are maintained and that accounts are kept up to date currently, what is the cost of the ending inventory for Commodity X using: (1) fifo; (2) lifo; (3) average?
(b) Assuming that perpetual inventories are not maintained and that a physical count at the end of the month shows 300 units to be on hand, what is the cost of the ending inventory using each of the three methods listed in part (a)?

**3.** The Woods Company decided to use unit lifo in valuing its inventories beginning in 1962. Commodity Z, included in its inventory on January 1, 1962, consisted of 6,000 units at a total cost of $6,600. Purchases and sales of Commodity Z during the next three years were as follows:

| | Purchases | | Sales | |
|---|---|---|---|---|
| | No. of Units | Amount | No. of Units | Amount |
| 1962 | 25,000 | $29,000 | 23,500 | $38,000 |
| 1963 | 30,000 | 38,400 | 34,000 | 57,500 |
| 1964 | 32,500 | 39,000 | 28,000 | 49,200 |

Calculate the value to be assigned to Commodity Z at the end of 1962, 1963, and 1964.

**4.** The Allen Manufacturing Co. has the following items in its inventory on December 31, 1964:

| | Quantities | Unit Cost | Market |
|---|---|---|---|
| Raw Material A........ | 2,000 | $1.10 | $1.00 |
| Raw Material B........ | 7,000 | 2.40 | 2.50 |
| Raw Material C........ | 5,000 | 3.00 | 3.20 |
| Goods in Process #1..... | 8,000 | 3.75 | 3.80 |
| Goods in Process #2..... | 6,000 | 5.00 | 5.10 |
| Finished Goods X....... | 4,000 | 7.00 | 7.20 |
| Finished Goods Y....... | 2,500 | 8.00 | 7.50 |

Calculate the value of the company's inventory using cost or market, whichever is lower, assuming that this valuation procedure is applied:

(a) To individual inventory items.
(b) To each class of inventory.
(c) To the inventory as a whole.

## PROBLEMS

**7-1.** Records of the Burgess Sales Co. show the following data relative to Commodity X:

| | | | |
|---|---|---|---|
| Balance: | January | 1 | 350 units at $20.50 |
| Purchases: | January | 3 | 400 units at 21.00 |
| | | 12 | 200 units at 22.00 |
| | | 24 | 100 units at 21.50 |
| Sales: | January | 2 | 250 units at 30.00 |
| | | 18 | 300 units at 30.25 |
| | | 29 | 100 units at 31.50 |

*Instructions:* Calculate the inventory balance and the gross profit on sales for the month on each of the following bases:
  (1) First-in, first-out. Perpetual inventories are maintained and costs are charged out currently.
  (2) First-in, first-out. No book inventory is maintained.
  (3) Last-in, first-out. Perpetual inventories are maintained and costs are charged out currently.
  (4) Last-in, first-out. No book inventory is maintained.
  (5) Moving average. Perpetual inventories are maintained.
  (6) Weighted average.

**7-2.** The Cummings Co. reports sales and purchases of Commodity A as follows:

| | Purchases | | Sales |
|---|---|---|---|
| | Units | Unit Cost | Units |
| January 6......... | | | 100 |
| January 7......... | 200 | $4.20 | |
| January 10........ | | | 150 |
| January 12........ | 100 | 4.35 | |
| January 15........ | | | 200 |
| January 20........ | 200 | 4.40 | |
| January 27........ | | | 100 |

Commodity A inventory on hand on January 1 consisted of 300 units that cost $1,215.

*Instructions:* Calculate the cost of goods sold for January and the cost of the ending inventory balance assuming use of:
  (1) The first-in, first-out basis.
  (2) The last-in, first-out basis, costs calculated at time of sale.
  (3) The last-in, first-out basis, costs calculated at end of month.
  (4) Moving average basis, costs calculated at time of sale.
  (5) Weighted average basis, costs calculated at end of month.

**7-3.** Allendale, Inc. sells a single commodity. Purchases, sales, and expenses for January, February, and March are summarized on top of the next page.

*Instructions:* Prepare a comparative income statement summarizing operations for the months of January, February, and March for each case below:
  (1) Assume that monthly inventories are calculated at cost on a first-in, first-out basis.
  (2) Assume that monthly inventories are calculated at cost on a last-in, first-out basis.
  (3) Assume that monthly inventories are calculated at cost on a weighted average basis. (Unit costs are calculated to the nearest cent.)

| | | Purchases | |
| --- | --- | --- | --- |
| | | Units | Cost Per Unit |
| January | 1–15 | 1,000 | $ 5.00 |
| | 16–31 | 2,000 | 5.75 |
| February | 1–15 | 1,000 | 6.00 |
| | 16–28 | 1,500 | 6.50 |
| March | 1–15 | — | — |
| | 16–31 | 1,000 | 5.75 |

| | Sales | | |
| --- | --- | --- | --- |
| | Units | Sales Price Per Unit | Operating Expenses |
| January | 1,500 | $ 8.75 | $2,700 |
| February | 2,400 | 9.50 | 4,100 |
| March | 1,500 | 9.50 | 2,950 |

**7-4.** The Brooks Mfg. Co. was organized in 1961 to produce a single product. Its production and sales records for the period 1961–1964 are summarized below:

| | Units Produced | | | Sales | |
| --- | --- | --- | --- | --- | --- |
| | No. of Units | Production Costs | Unit Cost | No. of Units | Sales Revenue |
| 1961 | 240,000 | $ 96,000 | $.40 | 200,000 | $122,500 |
| 1962 | 300,000 | 138,000 | .46 | 290,000 | 175,000 |
| 1963 | 280,000 | 140,000 | .50 | 310,000 | 210,000 |
| 1964 | 250,000 | 120,000 | .48 | 260,000 | 175,000 |

*Instructions:* Calculate the gross profit for each of the four years assuming that inventory balances are calculated in terms of:

(1) first-in, first-out;
(2) last-in, first-out.

**7-5.** The Compton Sales Company reports its inventories at lifo. Inventories are composed of three classes of goods. Values are assigned to each class as follows: units equal to the number on hand when lifo was adopted are assigned average costs as of this date; annual incremental layers thereafter are assigned the average cost for the period. Lifo was adopted in 1961. The inventory on January 1, 1964, and purchases and sales for 1964 were as follows:

Inventory, Jan. 1, 1964:

| | Model 600 | | Model 610 | | Model 620 | |
| --- | --- | --- | --- | --- | --- | --- |
| | Units | Amount | Units | Amount | Units | Amount |
| 1961 balance | 60,000@$.12 | $ 7,200 | 12,000@$.80 | $ 9,600 | 5,000@$2.50 | $12,500 |
| 1962 increment | 14,000@$.15 | 2,100 | 2,000@$.90 | 1,800 | | |
| 1963 increment | 10,000@$.16 | 1,600 | | | 1,000@$3.25 | 3,250 |
| Total | 84,000 | $10,900 | 14,000 | $11,400 | 6,000 | $15,750 |
| Purchases, 1964 | 250,000 | $45,000 | 60,000 | $61,200 | 12,500 | $42,500 |
| Sales, 1964 | 265,000 | $66,200 | 64,500 | $88,200 | 12,200 | $48,800 |

*Instructions:* Prepare a statement reporting sales, cost of goods sold (including purchases and inventory detail), and gross profits for each class of goods handled and for combined activities. Provide supporting schedules to show how the ending inventory balances are developed for each class of goods.

**7-6.** First-in, first-out has been used for inventory valuation by the Washburn Co. since it was organized in 1961. Using the data that follow, redetermine the net incomes for each year on the assumption of inventory valuation on the last-in, first-out basis:

|  | 1961 | 1962 | 1963 | 1964 |
|---|---|---|---|---|
| Reported net income............ | $ 17,500 | $ 30,000 | $ 32,500 | $ 45,000 |
| Reported inventories — fifo basis. | 82,000 | 115,000 | 132,500 | 140,000 |
| Inventories — lifo basis......... | 80,000 | 95,000 | 105,000 | 100,000 |

**7-7.** Sanders, Inc. carries five products. Units on hand, costs, and market prices of these items on January 31, 1964, are as follows:

| | Units | Cost Per Unit | Current Market Price Per Unit |
|---|---|---|---|
| Product A............. | 4,300 units | $2.00 | $1.90 |
| B............. | 2,500 units | 4.80 | 5.40 |
| C............. | 5,000 units | 5.00 | 5.20 |
| D............ | 2,200 units | 3.80 | 3.50 |
| E............. | 5,600 units | 1.85 | 1.80 |

*Instructions:* Prepare a statement to show the calculation of the inventory for statement purposes on the basis of cost or market, whichever is lower.

**7-8.** The inventory for Gardner and Associates on December 31, at cost using first-in, first-out, and at market is as follows:

| Article No. | Units and Costs | Current Market Price Per Unit |
|---|---|---|
| 101........................ | 1,600 @ $1.40⎫<br>1,100 @  1.60⎬ | $1.55 |
| 165........................ | 700 @  1.85 | 1.70 |
| 202........................ | 3,000 @  1.90⎫<br>1,000 @  2.10⎬ | 2.30 |
| 345........................ | 3,000 @   .80 | .70 |
| 410........................ | 400 @   .80⎫<br>600 @   .70⎬ | .75 |
| 503........................ | 500 @  4.00 | 4.50 |
| 611........................ | 1,000 @  1.20⎫<br>1,200 @  1.30⎬ | 1.30 |

*Instructions:* Calculate the value of the inventory, assuming valuation on the basis of (1) cost, and (2) cost or market, whichever is lower, applied to individual inventory items.

**7-9.** The Stuart Sales Co. sells three products. Inventories and purchases during May and the market prices of these goods on May 31 are as follows:

| | Product A | Product B | Product C |
|---|---|---|---|
| Inventory, May 1 | 200 units @ $ 65 | 200 units @ $110 | 60 units @ $150 |
| Purchases, May 1–31 | 50 units @ 55 | 120 units @ 100 | 50 units @ 135 |
| Total available for sale | 250 | 320 | 110 |
| Sales, May 1–31 | 40 units @ 105 | 30 units @ 150 | 20 units @ 240 |
| | 140 units @ 100 | 100 units @ 145 | 30 units @ 225 |
| Total sales | 180 | 130 | 50 |
| Units on hand, May 31 | 70 | 190 | 60 |
| Market values per unit, May 31 | $55 | $90 | $140 |

Selling, general, and administrative expenses for May were $15,500.

*Instructions:* (1) Prepare an income statement for May, assuming that the ending inventory is valued at cost on a first-in, first-out basis.

(2) Prepare an income statement for May, assuming that the inventory is reduced to cost or market, whichever is lower, applied to individual products, and the inventory loss is reported separately on the income statement. (First-in, first-out is used in arriving at cost.)

**7-10.** Westchester Co. carries three classes of inventory items. Inventory data as of December 31, 1964, are summarized below.

| | | | Per Unit |
|---|---|---|---|
| | Quantity | Cost | Replacement Cost |
| Raw Materials | | | |
| #1 | 150 | $ 8.00 | $ 7.60 |
| #2 | 500 | 10.40 | 9.05 |
| #3 | 100 | 16.85 | 17.50 |
| #4 | 125 | 10.00 | 8.40 |
| #5 | 615 | 5.00 | 4.20 |
| Goods in Process | | | |
| #10 | 200 | 15.50 | 14.50 |
| #11 | 305 | 6.00 | 5.00 |
| #12 | 150 | 3.20 | 3.30 |
| Finished Goods | | | |
| #101 | 6,000 | 3.40 | 3.75 |
| #102 | 3,200 | 3.10 | 3.25 |
| #103 | 1,500 | 2.00 | 2.20 |
| #104 | 10,500 | 1.50 | 1.40 |

*Instructions:* Prepare summaries to develop inventory valuation at the lower of cost or market, assuming this valuation procedure is applied:

(1) To individual inventory items.
(2) To separate inventory classes.
(3) To the inventory as a whole.

# Chapter 8

# INVENTORIES
## ESTIMATING PROCEDURES IN VALUATION

### Estimated costs

Estimates are frequently employed in developing inventory quantities and inventory costs. Certain estimating procedures must be applied when inventories are lost by fire or other casualty. Estimating procedures are frequently employed in arriving at inventories of the mercantile enterprise when such procedures can offer satisfactory measurements without the counting and costing routines that would otherwise be necessary. Widely used estimating procedures and the circumstances under which they are employed are described in the following pages.

### Gross profit method

Estimates of merchandise on hand may be developed by means of the *gross profit method*. In using the gross profit method, the company's gross profit percentage is applied to sales in developing cost of goods sold; cost of goods sold is subtracted from the cost of goods available for sale in arriving at an estimated inventory balance.

The gross profit method of arriving at an inventory is applicable in the following instances:

1. When an inventory has been destroyed by fire or other cause and the specific data required for its valuation are not available.
2. When inventories are required for interim statements, or for the determination of the week-to-week or month-to-month inventory position, and the cost of taking inventories would be excessive for such purposes.
3. When it is desired to test or check on the validity of inventory figures determined by other means. Such application is referred to as the *gross profit test*.

The gross profit percentage that is used in reducing sales to a cost of goods sold balance must be a reliable measure of current sales experience. In developing a reliable rate, reference is usually made to past rates and these are adjusted for variations that are considered to exist currently.

Past gross profit rates may require adjustment when they are affected by inventory valuations expressed in terms of the lower of cost or market; rates affected by reductions applied to beginning or ending inventories may not be regarded as applicable under current experiences. Past gross profit rates may also require adjustment when inventories are valued at last-in, first-out, and significant fluctuations in inventory position and in prices have affected gross profits in a manner that is not representative of current experiences. Current changes in cost-price relationships will further create need for modifying past rates.

The calculation of cost of goods sold depends upon whether the gross profit percentage is developed and stated in terms of sales or in terms of cost. The procedures to be followed in each case are illustrated below:

*Example 1 — Given: Gross profit as a percentage of sales.* Assume that sales are $100,000 and goods are sold at a gross profit of 40% of sales.

If gross profit is 40% of sales, then cost of goods sold must be 60% of sales:

| Sales...................... | 100% | Sales........................ | 100% |
|---|---|---|---|
| Cost of goods sold........... | ? | =Cost of goods sold............. | 60% |
| Gross profit............... | 40% | Gross profit................... | 40% |

Cost of goods sold, then, is 60% of $100,000, or $60,000. Goods available for sale less the estimated cost of goods sold gives the estimated cost of the remaining inventory. Assuming that the cost of goods available for sale is $85,000, this balance less the estimated cost of goods sold, $60,000, gives an estimated inventory of $25,000.

*Example 2 — Given: Gross profit as a percentage of cost.* Assume that sales are $100,000 and goods are sold at a gross profit that is 60% of their cost.

(a) If sales are made at a gross profit of 60% of cost, then sales must be equal to the sum of cost, considered 100%, and the gross profit on cost, 60%. Sales, then, are 160% of cost:

| Sales...................... | ? | Sales........................ | 160% |
|---|---|---|---|
| Cost of goods sold........... | 100% | =Cost of goods sold............. | 100% |
| Gross profit............... | 60% | Gross profit................... | 60% |

To find cost, or 100%, sales may be divided by 160 and multiplied by 100, or sales may simply be divided by 1.60. Cost of goods sold, then, is $100,000 ÷ 1.60, or $62,500. This amount is subtracted from the cost of goods available for sale in arriving at the estimated inventory.

(b) The cost of goods sold can be developed through an alternate calculation. If sales are 60% above cost, then the cost relationship to sales must be 100/160, or 62.5%.

| Sales............ | 160% | But in terms | Sales............ | 100.0% | |
|---|---|---|---|---|---|
| Cost of goods sold. | 100% | of sales as | Cost of goods sold. | 62.5% | (100/160) |
| Gross profit...... | 60% | 100% | Gross profit...... | 37.5% | ( 60/160) |

Cost of goods sold, then, is 62.5% of $100,000, or $62,500.

*Example 3 — Given: Sales as a percentage increase above cost.* Assume that sales are $100,000 and goods are sold at 20% above cost. This is the same as saying that the gross profit is 20% of cost, and the answer would be developed as in Example 2 above. Sales, then, would be divided by 1.20, as in (a) above, or multiplied by .83⅓ (100/120), as in (b) above, in arriving at the estimated cost of goods sold.

When various lines of merchandise are sold at different gross profit rates, it may be possible to develop a reliable inventory value only by making separate calculations for each of the different lines. Under such circumstances, it would be necessary to develop summaries of sales, goods available, and gross profit data for the different sections of the inventory.

## Retail inventory method

The *retail inventory method* is widely employed by retail concerns, particularly by department stores, as a means of arriving at reliable estimates of the business unit's inventory position whenever desired. When this method is employed, records of goods placed in stock are maintained in terms of costs and also at marked retail prices. The goods on hand at retail may be calculated at any time by subtracting sales for the period from the total goods available at retail. Cost and retail pricings of goods available are used in developing the percentage that cost bears to retail, and this percentage is applied to the goods on hand at retail in arriving at the estimated cost of such goods.

The determination of a company's inventory at the end of a month by using the procedure described follows:

|  | At Cost | At Retail |
|---|---|---|
| Inventory, January 1.......................... | $30,000 | $45,000 |
| Purchases in January.......................... | 20,000 | 35,000 |
| Goods available for sale....................... | $50,000 | $80,000 |
| Deduct sales for January...................... |  | 25,000 |
| Inventory, January 31, at retail sales price....... |  | $55,000 |
| Inventory, January 31, at estimated cost: $55,000× 62½% (percentage of cost to sales price, $50,000 ÷ $80,000)[1]................................ | $34,375 |  |

It should be observed that the effect of the above procedure is to provide an inventory valuation in terms of average cost. No cost sequence is recognized; the percentage of cost to retail for the ending inventory is the same as the percentage of cost to retail for goods sold.

---

[1]Instead of calculating the percentage that total cost bears to total retail price and then applying this percentage to the ending inventory at retail, it is possible to compute the cost of the inventory by a single arithmetical calculation as follows:

$$50,000/80,000 \times \$55,000 = \$34,375.$$

Use of the retail inventory method offers the following advantages:

1. Estimated interim inventories can be obtained without a physical count.
2. When a physical inventory is actually taken for periodic statement purposes, it can be taken at retail and then converted to cost without reference to individual costs and invoices, thus saving time and expense.
3. Checks are afforded on the movement of goods, since physical counts at retail should compare closely with inventories calculated at retail.

A physical inventory in support of the inventory balance to be reported on the annual statements is required at least once a year. Relatively significant discrepancies between a physical inventory and the inventory position as derived from book calculations should be investigated. Such inquiry may lead to sources of inventory misappropriations. Retail inventory records should be adjusted for variations shown by the physical count so that records reflect the actual status of the inventory for purposes of future estimates and control.

The earlier inventory calculation assumed that, after the goods were originally marked at retail prices, no further changes in such prices were made. Frequently, however, because of changes in the price level, changes in consumer demand, or other reasons, original retail prices are changed. The following items must ordinarily be considered in employing the retail method:

1. *Original retail* — the established sales price, including the original increase over cost variously referred to as the *markon* or *initial markup*.
2. *Additional markups* — increases that raise sales prices above original retail.
3. *Markup cancellations* — decreases in additional markups that do not reduce sales prices below original retail.
4. *Markdowns* — decreases that reduce sales prices below original retail.
5. *Markdown cancellations* — decreases in the markdowns that do not raise the sales prices above original retail.

The difference between cost and retail as adjusted for the changes described above is referred to as the *maintained markup*.

To illustrate the use of the data listed, assume that goods originally placed for sale are marked at 50% above cost. Certain merchandise costing $4 a unit, then, is marked at $6, which is termed the original retail. This increase in cost is variously referred to as a "50% markon on cost" or a "33⅓% markon on sales price." In anticipation of a heavy demand for the article, the goods are subsequently increased to $7.50. This represents an additional markup of $1.50. At a later date the goods are reduced to $7. This is a markup cancellation of 50 cents and not a markdown, since the retail price has not been reduced below the original sales price. But assume that goods originally marked to sell at $6 are subsequently marked down to $5. This represents a markdown of $1. At a later date the goods are marked to sell at $5.25. This is a markdown cancellation of 25 cents and not a markup, since sales price does not exceed the original retail.

In determining the goods on hand without a physical inventory, a record of each of the foregoing adjustments is required. The beginning inventory and purchases at retail are increased by net markups and decreased by net markdowns to arrive at goods available for sale at retail. Subtractions from goods available at retail are then made for sales, discounts to employees, inventory breakage, spoilage, and other losses. The ending inventory at retail as thus calculated may now be reduced to cost by applying the percentage that cost bears to retail.

In obtaining the cost percentage, the cost of goods available for sale is normally related to the original retail plus the net markups, without taking into account the net markdowns. Calculation of the inventory in this manner is illustrated below.

|  | At Cost | At Retail |
|---|---|---|
| Beginning inventory | $ 8,600 | $ 14,000 |
| Purchases | 69,000 | 110,000 |
| Freight in | 3,100 |  |
| Additional markups |  | 13,000 |
| Markup cancellations |  | (2,500) |
| Goods available for sale | $ 80,700 | $134,500 |
| Deduct: Sales |  | $108,000 |
| Markdowns |  | 4,800 |
| Markdown cancellations |  | (800) |
|  |  | $112,000 |
| Ending inventory at retail |  | $ 22,500 |

Ending inventory at estimated cost:
$22,500×60% (percentage of cost to retail before markdowns, $80,700÷$134,500) . . . . . . . .    $ 13,500

Failure to recognize markdowns in calculating the cost percentage results in a lower cost percentage and consequently a lower inventory figure than would otherwise be obtained. Markdowns may be made for special sales or clearance purposes, or they may be made as a result of market fluctuations and a decline in the replacement cost of goods. In either case their omission in calculating the cost percentage is justified. This is illustrated in the two examples that follow:

*Example 1 — Markdowns for special sales purposes:* Assume that merchandise which cost $50,000 is marked to sell for $100,000. To dispose of part of the goods immediately, one fourth of the stock is marked down $5,000 and is sold. The cost of the ending inventory is calculated as follows:

|  | At Cost | At Retail |
|---|---|---|
| Purchases........................................... | $50,000 | $100,000 |
| Deduct: Sales......................................... |  | $ 20,000 |
| Markdowns...................................... |  | 5,000 |
|  |  | $ 25,000 |
| Ending inventory at retail.............................. |  | $ 75,000 |
| Ending inventory at estimated cost:<br>$75,000×50% (percentage of cost to retail before mark-<br>downs, $50,000÷$100,000).......................... | $37,500 |  |

If cost, $50,000, had been related to sales price after markdowns, $95,000, a cost percentage of 52.6 per cent would have been obtained, and the inventory, which is three fourths of the merchandise originally acquired, would have been reported at 52.6 per cent of $75,000, or $39,450. The inventory would thus be overstated and cost of goods sold understated. A markdown relating to goods no longer on hand would have been recognized in the development of a cost percentage to be applied to the inventory. Reductions in the goods available at sales price resulting from shortages, damaged goods, or employees' discount should likewise be disregarded in calculating the cost percentage.

*Example 2 — Markdowns as a result of market declines:* Assume that merchandise which cost $50,000 is marked to sell for $100,000. With a drop in replacement cost of the merchandise to $40,000, sales prices are marked down to $80,000. One half of the merchandise is sold. The cost of the ending inventory is calculated as follows:

|  | At Cost | At Retail |
|---|---|---|
| Purchases............................................ | $50,000 | $100,000 |
| Deduct: Sales......................................... |  | $ 40,000 |
| Markdowns...................................... |  | 20,000 |
|  |  | $ 60,000 |
| Ending inventory at retail.............................. |  | $ 40,000 |
| Ending inventory at estimated cost:<br>$40,000×50% (percentage of cost to retail before mark-<br>downs, $50,000÷$100,000).......................... | $20,000 |  |

If cost, $50,000, had been related to sales price after markdowns, $80,000, a cost percentage of 62.5 per cent would have been obtained and the inventory would have been reported at 62.5 per cent of $40,000, or $25,000. Although this procedure reduces the inventory to cost, ignoring markdowns results in a cost percentage that reduces the inventory to a lower of cost or market basis. The use of the 50 per cent cost percentage in the example reduces the inventory to $20,000, a balance that will provide the usual gross profit if current prices prevail in subsequent periods.

It should be recognized that the calculation of a cost percentage for all of the goods carried is valid only when goods on hand can be regarded as a representative slice of the total goods handled. Varying markon percentages and sales of high and low-margin items in proportions that differ from purchases will require separate records and the development of separate cost percentages for the different classes of goods. In some cases the subdivision of the inventory by departments and by lines within such departments will be necessary.

The retail method is acceptable for income tax purposes, provided the taxpayer maintains adequate and satisfactory records in support of inventory calculations and applies the method consistently on successive tax returns.

### Cost apportionment by relative sales value method

Mention needs to be made of a special accounting problem that arises when different commodities are purchased for a lump sum. Such purchase calls for the apportionment of the single cost to the units in some equitable manner. This cost apportionment should recognize the utility that is found in the different units. Ordinarily, the estimated sales value of the different units provides the best measure of respective utilities, and accordingly cost is allocated on the basis of such estimated sales value. This procedure is referred to as the *relative sales value method*. Costs derived through apportionment in terms of sales value are charged to revenue as units are sold.

To illustrate application of the relative sales value method, assume the purchase by a realty company of 60 acres of land for $220,000. The costs of grading, landscaping, streets, walks, water mains, lighting, and other improvements total $300,000. The property is divided into three groups of lots as follows: Class A, 100 lots to sell for $2,000 each; Class B, 200 lots to sell for $2,500 each; and Class C, 20 lots to sell for $5,000 each. The total cost of the property, $520,000, is apportioned to the lots on the basis of their relative sales values. The cost apportionment is made as follows:

| | |
|---|---:|
| Class A lots, 100 at $2,000 | $200,000 |
| Class B lots, 200 at $2,500 | 500,000 |
| Class C lots, 20 at $5,000 | 100,000 |
| Total sales value of Class A, B, and C lots | $800,000 |

| | Total | No. of Lots | Cost Assigned to Each Lot |
|---|---|---|---|
| Cost apportioned to Class A lots: | | | |
| 200,000/800,000 × $520,000 = $130,000 | | 100 | $1,300 |
| Cost apportioned to Class B lots: | | | |
| 500,000/800,000 × $520,000 = 325,000 | | 200 | $1,625 |
| Cost apportioned to Class C lots: | | | |
| 100,000/800,000 × $520,000 = 65,000 | | 20 | $3,250 |
| Total..................... | $520,000 | | |

The sale of a lot of any class results in a constant gross profit of 35% of sales.[1] Sale of a Class A lot would be recorded as follows:

Contracts Receivable............................ 2,000
    Real Estate — Lot A-56........................ 1,300
    Gross Profit on Sale of Real Estate................ 700

## Dollar-value lifo procedures

Lifo valuation described in Chapter 7 included reference to unit lifo. Unit-lifo procedures called for a determination of the number of physical units comprising the inventory and the application of last-in, first-out costing to such quantities. Although unit-lifo procedures reduce the clerical routines, these still may be tedious, involved, and costly. Alternative procedures referred to as *dollar-value lifo*, using dollar values identified with the inventory rather than physical units as a basis for computing the lifo inventory, can simplify the valuation process. These procedures are widely used and are acceptable for income tax purposes.

Dollar-value lifo views all goods in the inventory or in the separate pools to which it is to be applied as homogeneous. Inventories are taken in terms of current replacement prices. Beginning and ending inventory values are then converted by means of appropriate price indexes to base-year prices, prices at the time the lifo method was adopted. The difference between beginning and ending balances as converted is regarded as a measure of the inventory quantity change for the year. An inventory increase is recognized as an inventory layer to be added to the beginning inventory, and such increase is converted at the current price index and added to the dollars identified with the beginning balance. An inventory decrease is recognized as a shrinkage to be applied to the most recent or top layer and to successively lower layers of the beginning inventory, and such decrease is converted at the price indexes applying to such layers and subtracted from the dollars identified with the beginning inventory.

[1]The same cost allocation can be developed by calculating the percentage of total cost to total estimated sales value, and applying such percentage to the sales price for the individual unit. In the example, cost is 65% of the total estimated sales value of the properties (520,000 ÷ 800,000). Each lot, then, is assigned a cost equal to 65% of its sales value: Class A lots have a cost of 65% of $2,000, or $1,300; Class B lots a cost of 65% of $2,500, or $1,625; Class C lots a cost of 65% of $5,000, or $3,250.

The following example illustrates dollar-value lifo calculations.

*January 1, 1961 — date of adoption of dollar-value lifo:*
January 1, 1961 inventory at base prices (cost) ........................... $38,000

*December 31, 1961 — end of first year:*
(a) December 31, 1961 inventory at year-end prices........................ $54,000
(b) December 31, 1961 inventory at base prices............................ $45,000
(c) January 1, 1961 inventory at base prices.............................. $38,000
(d) 1961 inventory increase at base prices, $45,000–$38,000 (b−c)......... $ 7,000
(e) Price index applying to 1961 layer, $54,000 ÷ $45,000 (a÷b).......... 120
(f) 1961 layer increase, $7,000 × 1.20 (d × e)........................... $ 8,400
(g) December 31, 1961 inventory at dollar-value lifo, $38,000 + $8,400 (c+f)... $46,400

| | Base prices | Index | Cost |
|---|---|---|---|
| Inventory composition: 1961 layer...................... | $ 7,000 | 120 | $ 8,400 |
| Base quantity.................... | 38,000 | 100 | 38,000 |
| Totals....................... | $45,000 | | $46,400 |

*December 31, 1962 — end of second year:*
(a) December 31, 1962 inventory at year-end prices........................ $66,000
(b) December 31, 1962 inventory at base prices............................ $50,000
(c) January 1, 1962 inventory at base prices.............................. $45,000
(d) 1962 inventory increase at base prices, $50,000–$45,000 (b−c)......... $ 5,000
(e) Price index applying to 1962 layer, $66,000 ÷ $50,000 (a÷b).......... 132
(f) 1962 layer increase, $5,000 × 1.32 (d×e)............................. $ 6,600
(g) December 31, 1962 inventory at dollar-value lifo, $46,400 + $6,600 (1961g+f). $53,000

| | Base prices | Index | Cost |
|---|---|---|---|
| Inventory composition: 1962 layer...................... | $ 5,000 | 132 | $ 6,600 |
| 1961 layer...................... | 7,000 | 120 | 8,400 |
| Base quantity.................... | 38,000 | 100 | 38,000 |
| Totals....................... | $50,000 | | $53,000 |

*December 31, 1963 — end of third year:*
(a) December 31, 1963 inventory at year-end prices........................ $56,000
(b) December 31, 1963 inventory at base prices............................ $40,000
(c) January 1, 1963 inventory at base prices.............................. $50,000
(d) 1963 inventory decrease at base prices, $50,000−$40,000 (c−b).......... $10,000
(e) 1963 decrease: 1962 layer, $5,000 × 1.32 $6,600
     1961 layer, $5,000 × 1.20   6,000........................... $12,600
(f) December 31, 1963 inventory at dollar-value lifo, $53,000−$12,600 (1962g−e). $40,400

| | Base prices | Index | Cost |
|---|---|---|---|
| Inventory composition: 1961 layer...................... | $ 2,000 | 120 | $ 2,400 |
| Base quantity.................... | 38,000 | 100 | 38,000 |
| | $40,000 | | $40,400 |

*December 31, 1964 — end of fourth year:*
(a) December 31, 1964 inventory at year-end prices........................ $55,000
(b) December 31, 1964 inventory at base prices............................ $44,000
(c) January 1, 1964 inventory at base prices.............................. $40,000
(d) 1964 inventory increase at base prices, $44,000−$40,000 (b−c) .......... $ 4,000
(e) Price index applying to 1964 layer, $55,000 ÷ $44,000 (a÷b).......... 125
(f) 1964 layer increase, $4,000 × 1.25 (d×e)............................. $ 5,000
(g) December 31, 1964 inventory at dollar-value lifo, $40,400+$5,000 (1963f+f). $45,400

| | Base prices | Index | Cost |
|---|---|---|---|
| Inventory composition: 1964 layer...................... | $ 4,000 | 125 | $ 5,000 |
| 1961 layer...................... | 2,000 | 120 | 2,400 |
| Base quantity.................... | 38,000 | 100 | 38,000 |
| | $44,000 | | $45,400 |

The following items should be observed in the example:

December 31, 1961 — With an ending inventory of $45,000 in terms of base prices, the inventory has gone up in 1961 by $7,000; however, the $7,000 increase is stated in terms of the pricing when lifo was adopted and needs to be restated in terms of year-end prices which are 120% of the base level.

December 31, 1962 — With an ending inventory of $50,000 in terms of base prices, the inventory has gone up in 1962 by another $5,000; however, the $5,000 increase is stated in terms of the pricing when lifo was adopted and needs to be restated in terms of year-end costs which are 132% of the base level.

December 31, 1963 — With an ending inventory of $40,000 in terms of base prices, the inventory has gone down in 1963 by $10,000; however, the $10,000 decrease is stated in terms of pricing when lifo was adopted and needs to be restated in terms of the pricing of the inventory layers that are eliminated or reduced. The decrease is applied first to elimination of the 1962 $5,000 layer and next to the reduction of the 1961 $7,000 layer; decreases are restated in terms of the percentages at which these layers were included in the inventory cost — for 1962, 132% of the base level, and for 1961, 120% of the base level.

December 31, 1964 — The ending inventory of $44,000 in terms of base prices indicates an inventory increase for 1964 of $4,000; this increase requires restatement in terms of year-end prices which are 125% of the base level.

It is assumed in the example that, instead of referring to industry or government sources for price indexes, indexes are most satisfactorily developed by comparing the prices of goods on hand at the end of each period with the prices assigned to such classes at the time of the adoption of lifo. In developing inventory values, goods may first be subdivided into reasonably homogeneous groupings and samples selected within these groupings; price relatives for the selected samples may then be employed in arriving at values assigned to groups and ultimately to the aggregate of goods on hand. In developing a value for the ending inventories in terms of base year prices after the first year, two steps may be employed: (1) a balance for the inventory in terms of beginning-of-year prices may be developed; (2) this balance may be converted to a base year value by dividing it by the index expressing the price change from the time of adoption of lifo until the beginning of the current year. To illustrate, in the example the price index was 120 at the end of 1961 and 132 at the end of 1962, or 10% above the 1961 level. If the December 31, 1962 inventory is found to be $66,000 on an end-of-year pricing basis and $60,000 at a beginning-of-year pricing basis, a base price valuation of $50,000 is arrived at by dividing $60,000 by 1.20, the cumulative price change from the time of adoption of lifo to January 1, 1962.

### Uncompleted contracts — profits based on degree of completion

A special valuation problem is encountered in those instances where a contractor engages in certain construction work requiring months or perhaps years for completion and the projects are found in various degrees of completion at the end of the contractor's fiscal period.

It is possible for a contractor engaged in a long-term project to carry such "work in process" at cost until it is completed, accepted by the customer, and the full profit can be calculated. This practice, referred to as the *completed-contract method*, is in conformity with the concept that revenue is not realized until a sale is completed and there can be formal recognition of new assets; revenue emerges from sales, not production.

However, the application of a sales basis concept of revenue for long-term contracts may lead to serious distortions of periodic achievement. If profit recognition is to await contract completion, the full profit will be related to the year in which the project is completed even though only a small part of the earnings may be attributable to productive effort in that period. Previous periods receive no credit for their productive efforts; as a matter of fact, they may be penalized through the absorption of selling, general and administrative, and other overhead costs relating to construction in progress but not considered chargeable to the construction inventory. Authorities are in general agreement that circumstances such as those described may justify departure from the sales standard as a basis for the recognition of revenue. Accordingly, they would support a valuation procedure that provides for an accrual of profit over the life of the contract in some equitable and systematic manner.

A satisfactory approach to periodic profit recognition on long-term construction contracts may be achieved by use of the *percentage-of-completion* method. Use of the percentage-of-completion method calls for the selection of either of the following approaches:

(1) The degree of completion is developed by comparing costs already incurred with the most recent estimates as to total estimated costs to complete the project. The percentage that costs incurred bear to total estimated costs is applied to the estimated net profit on the project in arriving at the earnings to date. Profit is thus recognized in terms of a *percentage-of-cost-completion.*

(2) Estimates of the progress of a project in terms of the work performed are obtained from qualified engineers and architects. Such estimates are applied to total contract price, and costs incurred to date are subtracted from estimated revenue in arriving at current earnings.

To illustrate the application of the percentage-of-completion method using the first approach, assume that a dam is to be constructed over a two-year period commencing in September, 1962, at a contract price of $750,000. Summaries of construction progress and the estimated earnings for each year calculated on a degree of completion basis follow:

| | | |
|---|---:|---:|
| 1962: Contract price............................... | | $750,000 |
| Less estimated cost: | | |
| Cost to date................................ | $ 50,000 | |
| Estimated cost to complete project.............. | 550,000 | 600,000 |
| Estimated total income........................ | | $150,000 |
| Estimated income — 1962: | | |
| 50,000/600,000 × $150,000................ | | $ 12,500 |
| | | |
| 1963: Contract price............................... | | $750,000 |
| Less estimated cost: | | |
| Cost to date................................ | $450,000 | |
| Estimated cost to complete project.............. | 175,000 | 625,000 |
| Estimated total income........................ | | $125,000 |
| Estimated income to date: | | |
| 450,000/625,000 × $125,000................. | | $ 90,000 |
| Less income recognized in 1962................ | | 12,500 |
| Estimated income — 1963...................... | | $ 77,500 |
| | | |
| 1964: Contract price............................... | | $750,000 |
| Less total cost: | | |
| Cost of prior periods......................... | $450,000 | |
| Current cost to complete...................... | 167,500 | 617,500 |
| Total income............................... | | $132,500 |
| Less income recognized to date ($12,500 + $77,500). | | 90,000 |
| Estimated income — 1964...................... | | $ 42,500 |

---

[1] The same estimated earnings are developed if the relationship of cost incurred to total estimated cost is applied to the total contract price in arriving at the contract price considered earned, and this balance is then reduced by cost incurred to date. Calculations in the example would be:

| | |
|---|---:|
| Contract price considered earned: 50,000/600,000 × $750,000.............. | $62,500 |
| Cost to date.......................................................... | 50,000 |
| Estimated income — 1962............................................. | $12,500 |

In the preceding example, recognition of profit only upon project completion would have resulted in income of $132,500 in 1964. Recognition of profits on the basis of degree of completion is compared with recognition of profits only upon project completion in the series of entries below based upon the facts in the example just given.

| Transaction | Income Recognition by Percentage-of-Completion Method | | Income Recognition by Completed-Contract Method | |
|---|---|---|---|---|
| **1962:** —— Costs of construction. | Construction in Progress..... Materials, Cash, etc. .... | 50,000  50,000 | Construction in Progress..... Materials, Cash, etc. .... | 50,000  50,000 |
| Advances from customer on contract. | Cash.......... Customer Advances..... | 60,000  60,000 | Cash.......... Customer Advances..... | 60,000  60,000 |
| Recognition of income for year. | Construction in Progress..... Recognized Income on Long-Term Construction.. | 12,500  12,500 | | |
| **1963:** —— Costs of construction. | Construction in Progress..... Materials, Cash, etc. .... | 400,000  400,000 | Construction in Progress..... Materials, Cash, etc. .... | 400,000  400,000 |
| Advances from customer on contract. | Cash.......... Customer Advances..... | 425,000  425,000 | Cash.......... Customer Advances..... | 425,000  425,000 |
| Recognition of income for year. | Construction in Progress..... Recognized Income on Long-Term Construction. | 77,500  77,500 | | |
| **1964:** —— Cost of construction in completing contract. | Construction in Progress..... Materials, Cash, etc. .... | 167,500  167,500 | Construction in Progress..... Materials, Cash, etc. .... | 167,500  167,500 |
| Completion of contract: (a) Recognition of income for year. | Construction in Progress..... Recognized Income on Long-Term Construction. | 42,500  42,500 | Construction in Progress..... Income on Construction.. | 132,500  132,500 |
| (b) Advances including payment in settlement. | Cash.......... Customer Advances..... | 265,000  265,000 | Cash.......... Customer Advances..... | 265,000  265,000 |
| (c) Approval of completed projects by customer. | Customer Advances...... Construction in Progress.... | 750,000  750,000 | Customer Advances...... Construction in Progress.... | 750,000  750,000 |

Assume in the example that profits are measured on a percentage-of-completion basis using the second approach on page 214, and engineers and architects provide estimates of physical completion of the project at the end of each year as follows: 1962, 8%; 1963, 73%; 1964, 100%. Estimated earnings to be recognized in the accounts would be as follows:

| Year | Revenue | Costs | Income |
|------|---------|-------|--------|
| 1962 | 8% × $750,000..................... | $ 60,000 | $ 50,000 | $ 10,000 |
| 1963 | (73% × $750,000) − $60,000....... | 487,500 | 400,000 | 87,500 |
| 1964 | $750,000 − ($60,000 + $487,500)... | 202,500 | 167,500 | 35,000 |
| | | $750,000 | $617,500 | $132,500 |

It should be observed that the practice of recognizing earnings on a job still in progress is a departure from normal valuation procedures and should be applied only when the circumstances are considered to warrant exceptional treatment. Estimates of the costs to complete a project or the degree of project completion should be developed from adequate data supplied by qualified architects and engineers. When reliable estimates cannot be obtained or when possible future contingencies may operate to reduce or cancel what appear to be accruing profits, conservatism would require the recognition of profit only upon project completion. In the event that estimates indicate an ultimate loss on the contract, the full amount of such loss should be recognized in the accounts.

Financial statements should disclose the valuation method that is used for construction in progress as well as the full implications of such a method. When sales or transfers of partnership interests or of capital stock are involved, the status of contracts in progress and the degree of recognition of profits on such contracts in the asset and the capital sections assume vital significance.

In preparing the balance sheet, Construction in Progress summarizing construction costs and recorded income on construction to date is properly recognized as a current asset. The credit balance in the account with the customer summarizing advance and progress payments is properly reported as a subtraction from the construction in progress balance. An excess of customer advances over the balance in the asset account should be recognized as a current liability. Advances from customers representing loans or deposits should be reported as liabilities.

When a building, installation, or construction contract covers more than one year, federal income tax regulations permit the taxpayer to recognize profits on a percentage of completion basis over the life of the project or in the year when the project is completed and accepted.

Salaries, taxes, and other expenses not directly attributable to the contract must be deducted in the year in which incurred. Consistent application of the method of accounting chosen is required for tax purposes, a change from the percentage-of-completion basis to the completed-contract basis, or *vice versa*, requiring special permission.

### Inventories on the balance sheet

It is customary for business units to report trading as well as manufacturing inventories as current assets, even though in some instances it may take considerable time before parts of such inventories are realized in cash  Among the items that are generally reported separately under the inventories heading are merchandise inventory or finished goods, goods in process, raw materials, factory supplies, goods and materials in transit, goods on consignment, and goods in the hands of agents and salesmen. Inventories are normally listed in the order of their liquidity.

Purchase orders should not be treated as additions to inventories, nor should sales orders be treated as deductions as long as title to goods has not passed. When goods have been formally set aside and the title is transferred, purchases or sales may be recognized with proper recognition of the effect of such transactions on the inventory position. Advance payments on purchase commitments should not be included in inventories but should be reported separately. Such advances are preferably listed after inventories in the current asset section since they still await entry into the inventory phase of the operating cycle.

A number of parenthetical remarks or notes may be required in disclosing the valuation procedures employed. The basis of valuation (cost, lower of cost or market, etc.), together with the method of arriving at cost (lifo, fifo, average, or other method), should be indicated. The reader of a statement may assume that the valuation procedures that are indicated have been consistently applied and financial statements are comparable with those of past periods. If this is not the case, a special note should be provided stating the change in the method and the effects of the change upon the financial statements.

When the inventory method provides values that are materially less than current replacement costs, parenthetical disclosure of replacement costs should be offered. The use of lifo and base stock methods, for example, may result in serious distortions of working capital measurements. Data concerning replacement costs should be given if the reader of the statement is to be adequately informed on financial position.

An inventory allowance to reduce an inventory to a lower of cost or market basis is reported as a subtraction from the inventory at cost. However, an appropriation of retained earnings to preserve earnings within the business for possible future market decline in the inventory value is reported as a part of the stockholders' equity. If the decline fails to materialize, the appropriation balance is no longer required and is returned to the retained earnings account. If the decline does materialize, the appropriation is still returned to the retained earnings account where it will absorb the inventory loss that is ultimately carried to the latter account.

If significant inventory price declines take place between the balance sheet date and the date the statement is actually prepared, mention of such declines should be made by parenthetical remark or note. When relatively large orders for merchandise have been placed in a period of widely fluctuating prices but the title to such goods has not yet passed, such commitments should be described by special note. Information should also be provided concerning possible losses on purchase commitments. Similar information may be appropriate for possible losses on sales commitments.

When inventories or sections of an inventory have been pledged as security on loans from banks, finance companies, or factors, the amounts pledged should be mentioned parenthetically in the inventory section.

Inventory items may be reported on a balance sheet as follows:

Inventories (valuation on the basis of cost or market, whichever is lower, cost being obtained by the first-in, first-out method):

| | | |
|---|---|---|
| Finished goods: | | |
| On hand (goods of $100,000 have been pledged as security on loan of $75,000 from First State Bank) | $300,000 | |
| On consignment | 15,000 | $315,000 |
| Finished parts | | 25,000 |
| Goods in process | | 300,000 |
| Raw materials: | | |
| On hand | $210,000 | |
| In transit from suppliers | 30,000 | 240,000 |
| Factory supplies | | 12,000 |
| Total inventories | | $892,000 |

## Prepaid expenses

It has been indicated that the current assets classification is composed of: (1) monetary assets — cash, temporary investments, and receivables; and (2) non-monetary assets — inventories and prepaid expenses. Prepaid expenses representing rights to services have sometimes been referred to as "service receivables." However, these cannot be classified with receivables for they will not be converted into cash but rather will be applied to revenue of the operating cycle. This quality indicates a closer relationship to inventories and a more satisfactory designation as "service inventories." But prepaid expenses do not qualify as "items of tangible property held for sale" and hence should not be included as a part of a company's inventories. Prepaid expenses should be separately shown below inventories on the balance sheet.

Prepayments may be found for such items as insurance, rents, taxes, advertising, royalties, and supplies. When payment is made in advance of the receipt of a service or when supplies are acquired and not fully utilized, recognition of a prepayment is in order. Such prepayment should be assigned to future revenue in accordance with the expiration of the service or the consumption of the supplies.

## QUESTIONS

**1.** Give certain instances in which estimates of inventory costs are necessary or appropriate and state what procedure would be followed in developing satisfactory estimates of such costs.

**2.** Distinguish between: (a) gross profit as a percentage of cost and gross profit as a percentage of sales; (b) markup cancellation and markdown; (c) the gross profit method of calculating estimated inventory cost and the retail inventory method of calculating estimated inventory cost.

**3.** What is your understanding of the meaning of the "gross profit test"?

**4.** In using the gross profit method, what circumstances might indicate a need for adjusting past period rates?

**5.** Define (a) initial markup, (b) additional markup, (c) markup cancellation, (d) markdown, (e) markdown cancellation, and (f) maintained markup.

**6.** What are the advantages of the retail inventory method?

**7.** Describe cost apportionment by the relative sales method.

**8.** Distinguish between unit-lifo and dollar-value lifo procedures.

**9.** Describe the application of dollar-value lifo procedures.

**10.** What valuation procedure is applied for an increase in inventory using dollar-value lifo? What procedure is applied for a decrease?

**11.** (a) Describe the percentage-of-completion method for recognition of profits on long-term construction contracts. (b) What problems are involved in the application of this method? (c) How would you report the following account balances: (1) Construction in Progress; (2) Customer Advances on Construction in Progress; (3) Deposits by Customers on Construction Contracts.

**12.** How would you recommend that the following items be reported on the balance sheet:

(a) Unsold goods in the hands of consignees.

(b) Purchase orders outstanding.
(c) Advance payments on purchase commitments.
(d) Raw materials pledged by means of warehouse receipts on notes payable to bank.
(e) Raw materials in transit from suppliers.
(f) An allowance to reduce the inventory cost to market.
(g) An appropriation of retained earnings for possible future inventory declines.
(h) Materials received from a customer for processing.
(i) Merchandise produced by special order and set aside to be picked up by customer.
(j) Raw materials set aside and to be used in connection with plant rehabilitation activities.
(k) Finished parts to be used in the assembly of final products.

## EXERCISES

**1.** (a) What is the percentage of profit on the basis of cost when the gross profit margin is 25% of selling price? 50% of selling price? 60% of selling price?

(b) What is the percentage of profit on the basis of sales price when the gross profit percentage is 25% of cost? 33⅓% of cost? 50% of cost? 100% of cost?

**2.** Assume sales for a period of $100,000. What is the cost of goods sold under each assumption below:
(a) Gross profit on sales is 25%.
(b) Gross profit on cost of sales is 60%.
(c) Goods are marked up ⅓ above cost.
(d) Gross profit on cost of sales is 200%.
(e) Goods are marked up 150% above cost.
(f) Gross profit on sales is 18%.
(g) Gross profit on cost is 18%.

**3.** R. T. Fellows requires an estimate of the cost of goods lost by fire on March 7. Merchandise on hand on January 1 was $50,000. Purchases since January 1 were $35,000; freight in, $3,000; purchases returns and allowances, $2,000. Sales are made at 25% above cost and totaled $42,000 to March 7. Goods costing $12,250 were left undamaged by the fire; remaining goods were destroyed. (a) What was the cost of goods destroyed? (b) What would your answer be if sales are made at a gross profit of 25% of sales?

**4.** From the information that follows for the Forrest Co., calculate by the gross profit method the value to be assigned to the inventory as of September 30, 1964, and prepare an interim statement summarizing operations for the nine-month period ending on this date. Disregard income taxes.

|  | 1/1/63–12/31/63 | 1/1/64–9/30/64 |
|---|---|---|
| Sales (net of returns)................ | $1,250,000 | $750,000 |
| Beginning inventory................ | 210,000 | 365,000 |
| Purchases......................... | 1,076,000 | 530,500 |
| Freight in......................... | 58,000 | 36,000 |
| Purchases discounts................. | 15,000 | 7,500 |
| Purchases returns.................. | 20,000 | 6,500 |
| Purchases allowances............... | 4,000 | 2,500 |
| Ending inventory................... | 365,000 |  |
| Selling and general expenses........ | 225,000 | 160,000 |

**5.** From the records kept by the Lovett Department Store, the following information is available for the month of January:

|  | At Cost | At Retail |
|---|---|---|
| Inventory, January 1..................... | $  8,400 | $ 12,000 |
| Purchases............................. | 48,810 | 80,000 |
| Freight in............................. | 2,000 |  |
| Additional markups..................... |  | 4,300 |
| Markup cancellations................... |  | 800 |
| Markdowns............................ |  | 6,600 |
| Markdown cancellations................. |  | 200 |
| Sales................................. |  | 72,600 |

(a) Calculate the inventory on January 31 at (1) retail, and (2) a conservative cost figure.

(b) Assuming that a physical count on January 31 shows inventory at retail of $15,500, how would this be explained and what effect does this have on the calculation of the ending inventory?

**6.** The Graham Development Company acquires land at a cost of $50,000. Twenty per cent of the land is used for streets and alleys, and the remainder is subdivided into lots as follows:

| Class | No. of Lots | Sales Price Per Lot |
|---|---|---|
| Class A | 10 | $2,500 |
| Class B | 20 | 1,500 |
| Class C | 25 | 1,000 |

What costs are to be assigned to the individual lots of each class if cost is allocated on the basis of relative sales values?

**7.** Best Brands, Inc. employs dollar-value lifo for periodic inventories. The inventory on January 1, 1964, was reported at $60,000; the inventory on December 31, 1964, was $84,000. The December 31 inventory at January 1 prices was $80,000. What cost would be assigned to the ending inventory?

**8.** The Whitney Construction Company recognizes profits on long-term construction periodically in the proportion that annual costs bear to total estimated costs of the project. Costs incurred on project #18–56 and remaining costs estimated to complete the project as summarized at the end of each year are listed below. The contract price of the project is $250,000.

|  | Costs | Estimated Remaining Costs |
|---|---|---|
| 1962 | $ 60,000 | $140,000 |
| 1963 | 120,000 | 45,000 |
| 1964 | 47,500 | —— |

What profit would be recognized by the Whitney Construction Company each year?

**9.** Annual earnings for the Webster Co. for the period 1960–1964 appear below. However, a review of the records for the company reveals inventory misstatements as listed. Calculate corrected net earnings for each year.

|  | 1960 | 1961 | 1962 | 1963 | 1964 |
|---|---|---|---|---|---|
| Reported net income (loss).. | $19,500 | $20,000 | $2,000 | ($4,500) | $15,000 |
| Inventory overstatement, end of year | 1,500 | | 2,800 | | 1,600 |
| Inventory understatement, end of year | | | | 4,000 | |

## PROBLEMS

**8-1.** Quarterly purchases and sales for Western Products, Inc. for 1964 are listed below. The corporation began 1964 with a merchandise inventory of $41,515. Goods have been sold at a uniform markup of 66 ⅔%.

|  | Purchases | Sales |
|---|---|---|
| January 1 — March 31 | $36,300 | $43,150 |
| April 1 — June 30 | 27,900 | 51,620 |
| July 1 — September 30 | 43,815 | 66,550 |
| October 1 — December 31 | 27,000 | 72,275 |

*Instructions:* Calculate the inventory for the end of each quarter.

**8-2.** Records for the Morrisey Store for the calendar year 1964 show the following:

|  | Cost | Retail |
|---|---|---|
| Merchandise inventory Jan. 1, 1964 | $30,400 | $40,000 |
| Purchases | 64,200 | 80,600 |
| Freight | 2,400 | |
| Net markups | | 4,400 |
| Net markdowns | | 12,600 |
| Sales | | 78,000 |

A physical inventory was taken on December 31, 1964, and this disclosed goods on hand at retail of $32,500.

*Instructions:* Calculate the inventory at a conservative cost price using the retail inventory method.

**8-3.** The records of the appliance department for the Bay Discount Store show the following data for the month of March:

| | | | |
|---|---|---|---|
| Sales................... | $178,500 | Purchases returns (at cost price)............... | $ 2,500 |
| Sales returns........... | 3,500 | | |
| Additional markups...... | 14,000 | Purchases returns (at sales price)............... | 3,800 |
| Markdowns............. | 30,000 | Markup cancellations.... | 4,000 |
| Markdown cancellations.. | 5,000 | Beginning inventory (at cost price)........... | 105,000 |
| Freight on purchases..... | 2,000 | | |
| Purchases (at cost price).. | 55,500 | Beginning inventory (at sales price)........... | 160,000 |
| Purchases (at sales price).. | 83,800 | | |

*Instructions:* Calculate the inventory at a conservative cost price using the retail inventory method.

**8-4.** Ross and Swain employ dollar-value lifo. Inventories at base prices and at year-end prices for 1962–1964 follow:

| | Base Price | Year-End Price |
|---|---|---|
| January 1, 1962......................... | $30,000 | |
| December 31, 1962...................... | 40,000 | $44,000 |
| December 31, 1963...................... | 50,000 | 57,500 |
| December 31, 1964...................... | 45,000 | 54,000 |

*Instructions:* Calculate the cost to be assigned to the inventory at the end of 1962, 1963, and 1964.

**8-5.** Peters Construction Co. reports its income for tax purposes on a completed-contract basis and income for financial statement purposes on a degree-of-completion basis. A record of construction activities for 1964 follows:

| | | As of Dec. 31, 1963 | | January 1, 1964– December 31, 1964 | |
|---|---|---|---|---|---|
| | Contract Price | Costs Incurred | Percent Completed | Costs Incurred | Percent Completed |
| Project A | $1,450,000 | $715,000 | 60% | $505,000 | Completed in April |
| Project B | 1,200,000 | 850,000 | 75% | 310,000 | Completed in July |
| Project C | 1,650,000 | 350,000 | 20% | 1,030,000 | 75% |
| Project D | 900,000 | | | 515,000 | 65% |
| Project E | 215,000 | | | 35,000 | 15% |

General and administrative expenses for 1964 were $80,000.

*Instructions:* (1) Calculate the net income before income taxes for 1964 to be reported for financial statement purposes.

(2) Calculate the net income for 1964 to be reported for income tax purposes.

**8-6.** The 20th Century Engineering Associates undertakes the construction of a bridge at a contract price of $750,000. Construction begins in 1962 and is completed in 1964. Construction transactions are summarized below:

1962: Construction costs incurred total $100,000; remaining costs to complete the project are estimated at $500,000. Collections from the public authority ordering such construction are $75,000.

1963: Construction costs for the year total $450,000; remaining costs to complete the project are estimated at $75,000. Collections from the public authority are $500,000.

1964: Construction costs in completing the project total $65,000. Collections are made from the public authority for the balance owed.

*Instructions:* (1) Give the entries for each year that would appear on the books of the company assuming that construction profit is recognized only when the project is completed.

(2) Give the entries for each year that would appear on the books of the company assuming that construction profit is recognized periodically in the proportion that costs to date bear to the total estimated cost of the project.

**8-7.** The errors listed below were made by the Marshall Co. in 1964.

(a) The company failed to record a sale on account of $210 at the end of 1964. The merchandise had been shipped and was not included in the ending inventory. The sale was recorded in 1965 when cash was collected from the customer.

(b) The company failed to recognize $400 due from a consignee as a result of goods sold by this party at the end of 1964. The consignee had failed to report the sale of consigned goods and the company included their cost of $260 in inventory as Goods on Consignment.

(c) The company failed to recognize a purchase on account of $1,350 at the end of 1964 and also failed to include the goods purchased in the ending inventory. The purchase was recorded when payment was made to the creditor in 1965.

(d) The company failed to make an entry for a purchase on account of $60 at the end of 1964, although it included this merchandise in the inventory count. The purchase was recorded when payment was made to the creditor in 1965.

(e) The company overlooked goods of $360 in the physical count of goods at the end of 1964.

*Instructions:* Give the entry required in 1965 to correct each error. Assume that the company arrives at its inventory position by physical count and that the books for 1964 have been closed.

**8-8.** The Riley Metal Products Co. adjusted and closed its books at the end of 1964, the summary of 1964 activities showing a net loss of $6,500. The following errors relating to 1964 are discovered upon an audit of the books of the company made in March, 1965:

(a) Merchandise, cost $4,500, was recorded as a purchase at the end of 1964 but was not included in the ending inventory since it was received on January 3, 1965.

(b) Merchandise, cost $400, was received in 1964 and included in the ending inventory; however, the entry recording the purchase was made on January 4, 1965, when the invoice was received.

(c) 1,200 units of Commodity Z, costing $4.25 per unit, were recorded at a per unit cost of $2.45 in summarizing the ending inventory.

(d) Goods in the hands of a consignee costing $6,000 were included in the inventory; however, $3,600 of such goods had been sold as of December 31, and the sale was not recorded until January 31 when the consignee made a full remittance of $4,800 on this item.

(e) Merchandise, cost $600, sold for $760 and shipped on December 31, 1964, was not included in the ending inventory; however, the sale was not recorded until January 12, 1965, when the customer made payment on the sale.

*Instructions:* (1) Calculate the corrected net income or loss for 1964.

(2) Give the entries that are required in 1965 in correcting the accounts.

# Chapter 9

# CURRENT LIABILITIES

### Nature of liabilities

In an economic system based so largely on credit, one finds many evidences of credit on the balance sheet. Most goods and services are purchased on account. Funds are borrowed from commercial banks for working capital purposes. Large sums are provided by bond issues to finance new plant and equipment. During the life of such obligations, interest accrues as an additional liability. Taxes accrued but not yet due appear as liabilities until paid. Employees working for the enterprise are creditors until paid for their services.

Liabilities of the business unit must be fully recognized and properly measured on the balance sheet if both the creditors' equity and the owners' equity in business assets are to be reported accurately. In presenting liabilities, appropriate distinction must be made between current and noncurrent items if the company's working capital position is to be accurately defined.

Full recognition on the balance sheet of contingent liabilities, those liabilities that may materialize in the event of certain acts or circumstances, is also essential. If contingent liabilities become actual liabilities, creditor and ownership equities will change. Current payment will normally be required with a change in the status of the liability. Contingent liabilities, therefore, must be considered along with presently existing liabilities in arriving at conclusions concerning a company's ability to meet its financial commitments.

This chapter considers the problems relating to determination, measurement, and presentation of current and contingent liabilities. The problems relating to long-term liabilities are considered in a later chapter.

### Current liabilities

It was indicated in Chapter 1 that current liabilities are broadly defined to include (1) all obligations arising from operations related to the operating cycle, and (2) all other obligations that are to be paid within a year. These liabilities make a claim against resources classified as current. Current liabilities are subtracted from current assets in arriving at working capital.

Liabilities entering into the current grouping may be reported under the following headings: (1) notes and accounts currently payable, (2) current maturities of long-term obligations, (3) cash dividends payable, (4) deposits and agency obligations, (5) accrued liabilities, and (6) prepayments from customers for goods and services making claims upon current assets.

## Notes and accounts currently payable

Both notes and accounts that are currently payable originate from the purchase of goods and services and from short-term borrowings. Notes currently payable may include notes issued to trade creditors for the purchase of goods and services, notes issued to banks for loans, notes issued to officers and stockholders for advances, and notes issued to others for the purchase of equipment. Accounts currently payable may consist of a wide variety of items, including obligations to trade creditors for the purchase of goods and services, obligations for the purchase of property items and securities, credit balances in customers' accounts, customers' refundable deposits, advances from officers and stockholders, and guaranteed interest and dividends on securities of affiliated companies.

In presenting current payables on the balance sheet, it is normally desirable to classify notes and accounts in terms of their origin. Such presentation affords information concerning the sources of business indebtedness as well as the extent to which the business has relied upon each source in financing its activities.

In arriving at the total amount owed trade creditors, particular attention must be given to the purchase of goods and services at the end of the fiscal period. Both the goods and the services acquired, as well as the accompanying obligations, must be reported on the statements even though invoices evidencing the charges are not received until the following period.

Individual notes and accounts are frequently secured by the pledge of certain assets. Assets pledged may consist of marketable securities, notes receivable, accounts receivable, inventories, or plant and equipment items. The pledge of an asset limits the use or the disposition of the asset or its proceeds until the related obligation is liquidated. In the event of bankruptcy, the cash that is realized on a pledged asset must first be applied to the satisfaction of the related obligation. A liability is *partly secured* or *fully secured* depending upon whether the value of the pledged property is less than the amount of the obligation or whether such value is equal to or in excess of the obligation. It has already been stated that reference is made to a lien on an asset by parenthetical remark in the asset section of the balance sheet. It is also desirable to provide a parenthetical comment or note in connection with the liability item that identifies the asset pledged and indicates its present market value.

## Valuation of payables

Valuation problems arise in the measurement of payables just as they do in the measurement of receivables. In reporting receivables, valuation accounts were established for uncollectibles and for other reductions that might apply in the course of their realization. It was further recognized that theoretical accuracy in valuing receipts that will become available subsequent to the balance sheet date would require that these be stated at their present values. In reporting payables, similar considerations apply. Valuation accounts should be established for reductions in payables that are expected in the course of their settlement. Here, too, theoretical accuracy in valuing payments to be made subsequent to the balance sheet date would call for recognizing these at their present values. However, the latter refinement is generally ignored for payables as it is for receivables. Consider the cases that follow.

(1) Assume that goods are purchased on terms calling for the issue of a $10,000 non-interest bearing note for one year. A purchase under these circumstances is generally recorded by a charge to Purchases and a credit to Notes Payable for $10,000, and payment of $10,000 at maturity is recognized as settlement of an obligation for this amount. Such procedure, however, fails to recognize the charge for interest implicit in the deferred payment arrangement. If money is worth 5% per year, theoretical accuracy would require that the purchase as well as the obligation be recognized at a cash-equivalent value of $9,523.81 ($10,000.00 ÷ 1.05). Either of the following entries would be appropriate:

| (a) Reporting the obligation in terms of the cash-equivalent value | | (b) Reporting the obligation at maturity value | |
|---|---|---|---|
| Purchases.........9,523.81 | | Purchases........9,523.81 | |
| Notes Payable... | 9,523.81 | Discount on | |
| | | Notes Payable.... 476.19 | |
| | | Notes Payable.. | 10,000.00 |

If either of the foregoing procedures is employed and the note is reported on the balance sheet before its payment, an adjustment should be made to recognize the accrual of interest at 5% to the date of the balance sheet. If the note is recorded as in (a) above, the interest accrual is recorded by a debit to Interest Expense and a credit to Notes Payable. If the note is recorded as in (b), Interest Expense is debited and Discount on Notes Payable is credited. The balance of the discount on notes payable should be subtracted from notes payable in reporting the liability on the balance sheet.

(2) Assume that a company discounts a $10,000 one-year non-interest bearing note at the bank, receiving $10,000 less discount at 5%, or $9,500. A loan

under these circumstances is generally recorded by a debit to Cash, $9,500, a debit to Prepaid Interest, $500, and a credit to Notes Payable, $10,000. The prepaid interest balance would be transferred to interest expense over the term of the loan. Such procedure, however, overstates both asset and liability balances: interest has not been paid in advance but is still to be paid; the obligation at the time of borrowing is no greater than the amount borrowed. Either of the following alternatives offers a more accurate accounting:

| (a) Reporting the obligation at the amount borrowed | (b) Reporting the obligation at maturity value |
|---|---|

| | | | | |
|---|---|---|---|---|
| Cash ............. 9,500.00 | | | Cash ............ 9,500.00 | |
| Notes Payable... | 9,500.00 | | Discount on | |
| | | | Notes Payable .... 500.00 | |
| | | | Notes Payable .. | 10,000.00 |

In reporting the note on the balance sheet prior to its payment, adjustments should be made to recognize the accrual of interest just as in (1) above. However, the discount of 5% is in effect a charge for interest at the rate of 5.26% ($500 ÷ $9,500), and 5.26% should be used in recognizing the accrual of interest.

## Current maturities of long-term obligations

Bonds, mortgage notes, and other long-term indebtedness are reported as current liabilities if they are to be paid within a twelve-month period. When only a part of a long-term obligation is to be paid currently, as in the case of bonds that are payable in a series of annual installments, the maturing portion of the debt is reported as current, the balance as noncurrent. But if the maturing obligation is payable out of a special retirement fund or if it is to be retired from the proceeds of a new bond issue or by conversion into capital stock, the obligation will not call for the use of current funds and therefore should continue to be listed as noncurrent. Reference to the plan for liquidation should be made parenthetically or by special note.

## Dividends payable

A cash dividend that is declared by appropriate action of the board of directors is recorded by a charge to Retained Earnings and a credit to Cash Dividends Payable. The latter balance is reported as a current liability. The declaration of a dividend payable in the form of additional shares of stock is recorded by a charge to Retained Earnings and a credit to Stock Dividends Distributable. The latter balance is not recognized as a liability but is reported in the stockholders' equity section, since it represents Retained Earnings in the process of transfer to paid-in capital.

A company with cumulative preferred stock outstanding may have sufficient retained earnings to legally declare a dividend but may fail to declare a dividend in order to preserve cash for other purposes. A liability is not recognized here, for dividends are not payable until formal action is taken by the corporate board of directors authorizing the distribution of earnings. Nevertheless, the amount of cumulative dividends unpaid should be reported on the balance sheet. This amount may be shown parenthetically in the stockholders' equity section following a description of the stock or it may be reported by a special note.

## Deposits and agency obligations

Current resources of a company may include monies deposited with it and returnable to depositors, or monies that have been collected or otherwise accumulated and that are to be paid to third parties. A company may have received deposits as guarantees of contract performance; here a current liability needs to be recognized until the deposits are returned. In other instances, companies will make payroll deductions for employees' income taxes, payroll taxes, hospital protection, saving plans, etc.; here current liability balances to the third parties need to be recognized until payments are made and the company fulfils its responsibilities as an agent.

## Accrued liabilities

A subsection under current liabilities may be devoted to those liabilities that have accrued as of the balance sheet date. An examination of the expense accounts as well as of the obligations is required in determining the accrued liabilities. Some of the most common accrued items are considered in the sections that follow.

## Sales and use taxes

With the passage of sales and use tax laws by state and local governments, additional duties are required of the business unit. Laws generally provide that the business unit must act as an agent for the governmental authority in the collection from customers of *sales taxes* on the transfers of tangible personal properties. Laws may also provide that the business unit is additionally liable for *use taxes* on goods that it buys for its own use. Use taxes are applied against the vendee because the vendor is outside of the tax authority's jurisdiction. Provision must be made in the accounts for the liability to the government for the taxes collected from customers and the additional taxes that the business must absorb.

*Sales tax collections included in sales balance.* The sales taxes payable are generally a stated percentage of sales. When the sales tax collections as well as sales are recorded in total in the sales account, it becomes necessary to divide this amount into its component parts, sales and sales taxes payable. For example, if the sales tax is 3% of sales, then the amount recorded in the sales account is equal to sales + .03 of sales, or 1.03 times the sales total. The amount of sales is obtained by dividing the sales account balance by 1.03, and 3% of the sales amount as thus derived is the tax liability. To illustrate, assume that the sales account balance is $100,000, which includes sales taxes of 3%. Sales, then, are $100,000 ÷ 1.03, or $97,087.38. The sales tax liability is then 3% of $97,087.38 or $2,912.62. The liability can also be determined by subtracting the sales figure, $97,087.38, from $100,000.00. To record the liability, Sales would be debited and Sales Taxes Payable credited for $2,912.62.

*Sales tax collections recorded separately.* Frequently the actual sales total and the sales tax collections are recorded separately at the time of sale. The sales taxes payable account then accumulates the sales tax liability. If sales tax collections are not exactly equal to the sales tax liability for the period as computed under the law, the payable account will require adjustment to bring it to the balance due. In making this adjustment a gain or a loss on sales tax collections is recognized, and this balance is ultimately closed into profit and loss.

*Obligation for use taxes.* The recognition in the accounts of obligations for use taxes should be accompanied by charges to the asset or expense balances in which the original purchases are recorded. For example, use taxes on the purchase of furniture and fixtures are recorded as a part of the cost of this asset; use taxes on supplies that are charged to selling expense would be reported as selling expense.

## Payroll taxes and income tax withholdings

Social security and income tax legislation impose four taxes based upon payrolls:

(1) *Federal old-age and survivor insurance.* The Federal Insurance Contributions Act, generally referred to as the federal old-age retirement legislation, provides for equal taxes on employer and employee to provide funds for federal old-age and survivor insurance benefits for certain individuals and members of their families. At one time only employees were covered by this legislation; however, coverage in recent years has been broadened to include most individuals who are self-employed.

As originally enacted, the legislation provided for a tax of 1% on employer and employee to begin on January 1, 1937, with increases in rates to take effect in later years. Beginning January 1, 1963, the rate was $3\frac{5}{8}$%. Under current legislation, an employee contributes $3\frac{5}{8}$% on wages up to $4,800 a year received from any number of employers, although he will be entitled to a refund of the taxes he has paid on wages that exceed $4,800 received from two or more employers. The employer pays the same rate on wages up to $4,800 paid to each employee during the year.[1] An employer is not entitled to a refund.

Employers of one or more persons, with certain exceptions, come under the law. The amount of the employee's tax is withheld from the wage payment by the employer. The employer remits this amount together with his own tax. The employer is required to maintain complete records and submit detailed support for the tax remittance. He is responsible for the full amount of the tax even when he fails to withhold from employees amounts representing their contributions.

Since 1951 a tax has been levied on self-employed persons who carry on a trade or business as sole proprietors or partners or render services as independent contractors. Certain services, however, are specifically excluded from coverage. The tax rate on the self-employed beginning January 1, 1963, was 5.4%. The tax is applicable only when self-employment income is at least $400; the rate is applied to a maximum of $4,800 of self-employment income.

(2) *Federal unemployment insurance.* The Federal Social Security Act and the Federal Unemployment Tax Act provide for the establishment of unemployment insurance plans. Employers with 4 or more covered workers employed in each of 20 weeks during a calendar year are affected.

Under provisions of the law effective in 1964, the federal government taxes eligible employers on the first $3,000 paid to every employee during the calendar year at 3.1% but allows the employer a tax credit limited to 2.7% for taxes paid under state unemployment compensation laws. No tax is levied on the employee by the federal government. When an employer is subject to a tax of 2.7% or more as a result of state unemployment legislation, the federal unemployment tax, then, is 0.4% of the wages. Payment to the federal government is required on or before January 31 following the taxable calendar year. Unemployment benefits are provided by the systems created by the individual states. Revenues of the federal government under the acts are used to meet the cost of administering state and federal unemployment plans as well as to provide supplemental unemployment benefits.

(3) *State unemployment insurance.* State unemployment compensation laws are not the same in all states. In most states laws provide for taxes only on employers; but in a few states taxes are applicable to both employers and employees. Each state law specifies the classes of employees

---

[1]The rate on both employee and employer is scheduled to rise to $4\frac{1}{8}\%$ in 1966 and to $4\frac{5}{8}\%$ in 1968 and thereafter. However, Congress may act to modify both the rate schedule and also the wage limits, as it has done in the past.

that are exempt, the number of employees that are required or the amount of wages that must be paid before the tax is applicable, and the contributions that are to be made by employers and employees. In some states the tax is applicable only when 4 or more persons are employed, as in the case of the federal legislation; in other states the tax applies when there are one or more employees. Exemptions are frequently similar to those under the federal act. Tax payment is generally required on or before the last day of the month following each calendar quarter.

Although the normal tax on employers may be 2.7%, states have merit rating or experience plans that provide for lower rates based upon employers' individual employment experiences. Thus employers with stable employment records are taxed at a rate in keeping with the limited amount of benefits required for their employees; employers with less satisfactory employment records contribute at a rate more nearly approaching 2.7% in view of the greater amount of benefits paid to their employees. Savings under state merit systems are allowed as credits in the calculation of the federal contribution, so that the federal tax does not exceed 0.4% even though payment of less than 2.7% is made by an employer entitled to a lower rate under the merit rating system.

(4) *Income tax withholding.* Since 1943 federal income taxes on the earnings of an individual have been collected in the period of such earnings instead of in the calendar year following the earnings. With the change to the "pay-as-you-go" plan, employers were required to withhold income taxes from wages paid to their employees. Withholding is required not only of employers engaged in a trade or business, but also of religious and charitable organizations, educational institutions, social organizations, and governments of the United States, the states, the territories, and their agencies, instrumentalities, and political subdivisions. Certain classes of wage payments are exempt from withholding, although these are still subject to income taxes.

An employer must meet withholding requirements under the law even if wages of no more than one employee are subject to such withholding. The amounts to be withheld by the employer are developed from formulas provided by the law or from tax withholding tables made available by the government. Withholding is based upon the length of the payroll period, the amount earned, and the number of withholding exemptions claimed by the employee. Taxes that are required under the Federal Insurance Contributions Act (both employees' and employer's portions) and income taxes that have been withheld by the employer are paid at the same time. When federal insurance contributions and income tax withholdings for a month do not exceed $100, such amount is accumulated to be paid on a quarterly basis. Payment is required on or before the last day of the month following the calendar quarter. When the total for a month exceeds $100, this total must be deposited in an authorized bank within fifteen days after the close of the calendar month. A Federal Depository Receipt is validated by the bank and is attached to the quarterly return.

## Accounting for payroll taxes and income tax withholdings

To illustrate the accounting procedures for payroll taxes and income tax withholdings, assume that in January, 1964, salaries for a retail store with 20 employees are $10,000. The state unemployment compensation law provides for a tax on employers of 2.7%. Income tax withholdings for the month are $1,020.

Entries for the payroll and the employer's payroll taxes follow:

| | | |
|---|---:|---:|
| Salaries.................................. | 10,000.00 | |
|     F.I.C.A. Taxes Payable.................... | | 362.50 |
|     Income Tax Withholdings Payable.......... | | 1,020.00 |
|     Cash.................................. | | 8,617.50 |

    To record payment of payroll of $10,000 after deduction of $3\frac{5}{8}\%$ for employees' contribution for federal old-age benefits and $1,020 for income tax withholdings.

| | | |
|---|---:|---:|
| Payroll Taxes................................ | 672.50 | |
|     F.I.C.A. Taxes Payable..................... | | 362.50 |
|     S.U.I. Taxes Payable...................... | | 270.00 |
|     F.U.T.A. Taxes Payable.................... | | 40.00 |

    To record the payroll tax liability of the employer:

    (1) Taxes under Federal Insurance Contributions Act — $3\frac{5}{8}\%$ of $10,000, or $362.50.

    (2) Taxes under state unemployment insurance legislation — 2.7% of $10,000, or $270.

    (3) Taxes under Federal Unemployment Tax Act — 0.4% (3.1% less credit of 2.7%) of $10,000, or $40.

When tax payments are made to the proper agencies, the tax liability accounts are debited and Cash is credited.

The employer's payroll taxes, as well as the taxes withheld from employees, are based upon amounts paid to employees during the period regardless of the basis employed for measuring income. When financial reports are prepared on the accrual basis, the employer will have to recognize both accrued payroll and the employer's payroll taxes relating thereto by adjustments at the end of the accounting period. In adjusting the accounts for accrued payroll, however, recognition of the amounts to be withheld for employees' taxes may be ignored. The entries recording the accrued payroll and the employer's payroll taxes may be reversed at the start of the new period. The next regular payment of wages can then be recorded in the usual manner, giving recognition to the employees' taxes based upon the entire payroll and the balances payable to employees; a second entry is made at this time recording the accrual of the employer's payroll taxes based upon the full amount of the payroll. The accrual of payroll and taxes at the end of the period as indicated provides accurate statements while deferring the analysis of payroll as to amounts payable to the government and to employees until the wage payment date.

Agreements with employees may provide for payroll deductions and employer contributions for such other items as group insurance plans, pension plans, savings bonds purchases, union dues, etc. Such agreements call for accounting procedures that are similar to those described for payroll taxes and income tax withholdings.

### Prepayments from customers for goods and services making claim on current assets

Advances from customers for goods and services that are to be supplied in the future are recorded as liabilities. When significant costs are involved in meeting customer commitments and such costs are to be met from resources classified as current, the advances should be recognized as current liabilities. Tuition fees received in advance by a school and subscriptions received in advance by a publisher are current liabilities; advances received from customers on purchase orders are likewise current. When the services or the goods are applied to liquidation of the obligation, profit or loss emerges for the difference between the amount of the advance that has now become revenue and the costs that have been incurred in its realization.

### Estimated liabilities

The amount of an obligation is generally established by contract or accrues at a certain rate. There are instances, however, when an obligation definitely exists on a balance sheet date but the amount ultimately payable cannot definitely be determined. The fact that the amount to be paid is not certain does not mean that the liability can be ignored or even given a "contingent" status. Such claim must be estimated from whatever data are available. The amount to be paid in the form of income taxes, for example, must be estimated in the preparation of interim statements, or at the end of the period if the tax return has not yet been prepared. Although the exact amount ultimately payable is not known, the obligation is unquestioned and requires recognition. Expenditures to emerge from current operations and the realization of current revenue, as, for example, the cost of meeting guarantees for servicing and repairs on goods sold, also call for estimates. Here, uncertainty as to the amount to be expended is accompanied by inability to identify the payees as well as to determine the time of payments; but the fact that there are charges yet to be absorbed is certain. Liabilities established to meet estimated charges arising from current activities are sometimes referred to as *operating reserves*. These liabilities generally call for current liquidation and hence are classified under the current heading.

Certain long-term liabilities also call for estimates. A self-administered pension plan calls for estimates as to the amount ultimately payable. Long-term guarantees and agreements calling for severance payments to employees also involve estimates.

Liabilities definite in existence but estimated in amount are frequently designated as "reserves." However, it was pointed out in an earlier chapter that this practice should be discouraged and account titles should be used that indicate the exact nature of the item. The designation "Estimated Income Taxes Payable" is preferable to "Reserve for Income Taxes"; "Estimated Amounts Payable under Retirement Plans" is preferable to "Reserve for Retirement Plans." When a separate "Reserves" heading is found in the liability section of a balance sheet, it is important to determine what practices were followed in classifying items. Sometimes such diverse items as asset valuation accounts, short and long-term liabilities, and appropriations of retained earnings are found under this heading. When this is the case, restatement of account groupings may be necessary in analyzing balance sheet position. Special investigation is necessary when account titles such as "General Reserve," "Special Reserve," and "Contingency Reserve" are listed in the "reserves" section on the balance sheet. Such designations offer no information as to the real nature of the account.

Representative of short-term estimated liabilities that are frequently found on financial statements are the following:

*Estimated Taxes Payable,* reporting the estimated income, state franchise, property, and other tax obligations.

*Estimated Premium Claims Outstanding,* reporting the estimated value of premiums or prizes that are to be distributed as a result of past sales or sales promotion activities.

*Estimated Liabilities under Guarantees for Service and Replacements,* reporting the estimated future claims by customers as a result of past guarantees of services or product or product part replacement.

*Estimated Liabilities on Tokens, Tickets, and Gift Certificates Outstanding,* reporting the estimated obligations in the form of merchandise or services arising from the receipt of cash in past periods.

Some of the problems arising in the development of the balances to be reported for these items are described in the sections that follow.

### Estimated tax liabilities

Estimates are required for all taxes that are related to current operations but that are not finally known at the time financial statements are prepared. Estimates may thus be called for in the case of federal income taxes, state income or franchise taxes, real and personal property taxes, and various other licenses and fees. Tax rates may vary from year to year. Normally, the best guide as to current tax rates is found in rates that were applicable in the preceding period. When legislative bodies are considering revisions in tax rates and their application, the best available information should be used in developing estimates. Not only may rates have to be estimated, but also the bases to which such rates are applicable. In the case of real and personal property taxes, for example, the valuation to be assigned to properties owned may have to be estimated in arriving at an estimated tax liability. In the case of income taxes, estimates of the income subject to taxes are required unless tax data are fully compiled before the financial statements are drawn up.

Estimated taxes are recorded by debits to expense and credits to liability accounts. Liabilities are closed when the taxes are paid. Any difference between the amount paid and the obligation originally recognized, if of relatively minor amount, may be reported in the expense account in the period of payment; if the difference is material, it should be recognized as an extraordinary item.

### Inter-period allocations of income taxes

It has already been suggested that when income taxes apply to both ordinary and extraordinary items, taxes should be allocated between the two classes of items. Such allocations were limited to the statements for a single period and involved the assignment of taxes to separate sections on the income statement or to the income statement and the retained earnings statement. Allocation resulted in a full matching of revenue, expense, and income tax elements and provided summaries that were meaningful and directly comparable with similar summaries of the past.

In some instances there are significant differences between reported or book income and taxable income. Some differences arise because certain revenue items are not taxable and certain expense items are not deductible under income tax laws. Such differences are permanent and the resulting tax advantages or disadvantages are likewise permanent. Other differences arise, however, because the timing for revenue and expense items for income tax purposes is not the same as that employed for reporting purposes.  Taxable income in one period is greater or less than the reported income for the same period and such difference is counterbalanced in subsequent periods.  As a consequence, the charge for the income taxes to be paid in one period is greater or less than the charge that would otherwise be applicable to reported income, with the tax advantage or disadvantage ultimately counterbalanced by the opposite effect in subsequent periods.  Under the latter circumstances, there has been strong support for extending tax allocation procedures to embrace successive statements and to provide for the assignment of tax charges to reported income in terms of the amounts that may be regarded as allocable thereto rather than in terms of the amounts actually payable.

Differences between financial reporting and tax reporting that suggest inter-period tax allocation procedures may be classified as follows:

1. Book income before taxes is less than taxable income because:
   a. Certain revenue is deferred for book purposes but is currently recognized for tax purposes.
   b. Certain expense is currently recognized for book purposes but is deferred for tax purposes.

2. Book income before taxes is more than taxable income because:
   a. Certain revenue is currently recognized for book purposes but is deferred for tax purposes.
   b. Certain expense is deferred for book purposes but is currently recognized for tax purposes.

Each of these is illustrated below.

(*1-a*) *Revenue that is deferred for book purposes but is currently recognized for tax purposes.*  Assume that a company collects advance rents for a three-year period and recognizes such collection as deferred revenue.  For income tax purposes, however, the rents must be recognized as revenue and are taxed in the period they are received.  If income taxes are recognized on the books at the amounts actually payable, the current period is penalized by a charge for taxes on revenue not currently recognized while subsequent periods are correspondingly favored by the absence of taxes on revenue that emerges from the balance originally deferred.  Tax allocation procedures, here, call for reducing the charge for taxes by the portion related to the taxable income that exceeds book income; this portion of the tax charge should be assigned to future periods concurrent with the recognition of the deferred revenue as realized.

(*1-b*) *Expense that is currently recognized for book purposes but is deferred for tax purposes.*  Assume that a company charges initial organization costs to revenues of the first year of operations.  For income tax purposes, however, these costs must be capitalized and are amortizable over a period of not less than 60 months. The charge for taxes currently payable, then, will exceed the tax charge applicable to book income because of the expense that is not recognized for tax purposes; taxes in subsequent periods will be correspondingly less than the taxes applicable to book income because of deductions that are recognized for tax purposes but that do not appear on the books. Here, as in the preceding example, the charge for taxes in the first year should be reduced by the portion related to the taxable income that exceeds book income; this portion of the tax charge should be assigned to future periods concurrent with the recognition of organization costs as a deduction for tax purposes.

*(2-a) Revenue that is currently recognized for book purposes but is deferred for tax purposes.* Assume that a company engages in a long-term construction contract requiring three years for its completion and for book purposes recognizes income on a percentage-of-completion basis. For income tax purposes, however, the company elects to report the full contract income and pay income taxes in the year of contract completion. If income taxes are recognized on the books at the amounts actually payable, periods in which the contract is still in progress and in which portions of the income are recognized are favored through the absence of income taxes and the period in which the contract is completed is correspondingly penalized by a charge for taxes on the entire contract income. Tax allocation procedures, here, call for increasing the charge for taxes payable by taxes on the portion of book income that exceeds taxable income; the tax charge in the period in which the contract is completed, then, can be limited to the amount applicable to the income recognized on the books in the period of completion.

*(2-b) Expense that is deferred for book purposes but is currently recognized for tax purposes.* Assume that a company acquires property with a five-year life and reports depreciation on the books on a straight-line basis or at the rate of 20% per year. For income tax purposes, however, it elects to recognize depreciation by the sum of years'-digits method and reports annual charges for the five-year period of 5/15, 4/15, 3/15, 2/15, and 1/15 of cost. Charges for taxes payable in the first and second years, then, are less than the charges applicable to book income because depreciation recognized on the tax return exceeds that per books; taxes that are payable in the fourth and fifth years are correspondingly greater than the taxes applicable to book income because depreciation per books exceeds the depreciation recognized for tax purposes. In applying tax allocation procedures, charges for taxes in the first two years should be increased by taxes on the portions of the book income that exceed taxable income; tax charges in the fourth and fifth years, then, can be limited to the amounts that are applicable to the income recognized per books.

When circumstances involve factors such as summarized in (1-a) and (1-b) above, inter-period tax allocation calls for the recognition of a deferred tax expense balance that is assignable to later periods when book income will exceed taxable income. When circumstances involve factors such as summarized in (2-a) and (2-b), allocation calls for the recognition of a deferred tax liability balance that will relieve tax charges of later periods when taxable income will exceed book income. Deferred tax asset and liability balances relating to a number of subsequent periods would be reported on the balance sheet as non-current items. The procedures for inter-period tax allocations that may be employed in the accounts are illustrated in the sections that follow.

*When book income before taxes is less than taxable income:*

Assume book and taxable incomes for a corporation for a three-year period as follows, a taxable income excess in the first year being counter-balanced by an equal amount in the second and third years.

|  | Book income before income taxes | Taxable income |
|---|---|---|
| 1961................... | $100,000 | $120,000 |
| 1962................... | 100,000 | 90,000 |
| 1963................... | 120,000 | 110,000 |
|  | $320,000 | $320,000 |

Assume also that throughout this period the tax rate is 30% on the first $25,000 of taxable income and 52% on amounts in excess of $25,000, or stated differently, 52% of the total taxable income less $5,500. Entries to record the taxes to be paid each year as well as the allocation of taxes between periods are listed below:

1961: To record accrued taxes on taxable income, 52% of $120,000, less $5,500.

Income Taxes....... 56,900
    Income Taxes Pay..                56,900

To defer portion of income taxes estimated to be applicable to subsequent periods, 52% of $20,000, taxable income in excess of book income.

Deferred Income Tax
Expense............ 10,400
    Income Taxes.....                10,400

1962: To record accrued taxes on taxable income, 52% of $90,000, less $5,500.

Income Taxes....... 41,300
    Income Taxes Pay..                41,300

To recognize portion of tax expense deferral as an addition to current tax charge, 52% of $10,000, book income in excess of taxable income.

Income Taxes....... 5,200
    Deferred Income
    Tax Expense......                5,200

1963: To record accrued taxes on taxable income, 52% of $110,000, less $5,500.

Income Taxes....... 51,700
    Income Taxes Pay..                51,700

To recognize balance of tax expense deferral as addition to current tax charge, 52% of $10,000, book income in excess of taxable income.

Income Taxes....... 5,200
    Deferred Income
    Tax Expense......                5,200

A comparison of book results in the absence of the adjustments for differences between financial reporting and tax reporting with results when adjustments are made is given at the top of the next page.

| | Book results unadjusted | | | Book results adjusted | | |
|---|---|---|---|---|---|---|
| | Net Income before Income Taxes | Income Taxes | Net Income | Net Income before Income Taxes | Income Taxes | Net Income |
| 1961.. | $100,000 | $ 56,900 | $ 43,100 | $100,000 | $ 46,500 | $ 53,500 |
| 1962.. | 100,000 | 41,300 | 58,700 | 100,000 | 46,500 | 53,500 |
| 1963.. | 120,000 | 51,700 | 68,300 | 120,000 | 56,900 | 63,100 |
| | $320,000 | $149,900 | $170,100 | $320,000 | $149,900 | $170,100 |

*When book income before taxes is more than taxable income:*

Assume book and taxable incomes as follows for a three-year period, a book income excess in the first year being counterbalanced by an equal amount in the second and third years.

| | Book income before income taxes | Taxable income |
|---|---|---|
| 1961................... | $100,000 | $ 80,000 |
| 1962................... | 100,000 | 110,000 |
| 1963................ | 120,000 | 130,000 |
| | $320,000 | $320,000 |

Assume the same tax rates indicated previously. Entries to record the taxes to be paid each year as well as the allocation of taxes between periods are listed below:

1961: To record accrued taxes on taxable income, 52% of $80,000, less $5,500.

Income Taxes....... 36,100
   Income Taxes Pay.. 36,100

To accrue income taxes estimated to be applicable to income not currently reported, 52% of $20,000, book income in excess of taxable income.

Income Taxes....... 10,400
   Deferred Income
   Tax Liability...... 10,400

1962: To record accrued taxes on taxable income, 52% of $110,000, less $5,500.

Income Taxes....... 51,700
   Income Taxes Pay.. 51,700

To apply portion of tax accrual as a reduction in current tax charge, 52% of $10,000, taxable income in excess of book income.

Deferred Income Tax
Liability........... 5,200
   Income Taxes..... 5,200

1963: To record accrued taxes on taxable income, 52% of $130,000, less $5,500.

Income Taxes ...... 62,100
   Income Taxes Pay.. 62,100

To apply balance of tax accrual as a reduction in current tax charge, 52% of $10,000, taxable income in excess of book income.

Deferred Income Tax
Liability........... 5,200
   Income Taxes..... 5,200

A comparison of book results in the absence of tax adjustments with results when adjustments are made is given below:

| | Book results unadjusted | | | Book results adjusted | | |
|---|---|---|---|---|---|---|
| | Net Income before Income Taxes | Income Taxes | Net Income | Net Income before Income Taxes | Income Taxes | Net Income |
| 1961.. | $100,000 | $ 36,100 | $ 63,900 | $100,000 | $ 46,500 | $ 53,500 |
| 1962.. | 100,000 | 51,700 | 48,300 | 100,000 | 46,500 | 53,500 |
| 1963.. | 120,000 | 62,100 | 57,900 | 120,000 | 56,900 | 63,100 |
| | $320,000 | $149,900 | $170,100 | $320,000 | $149,900 | $170,100 |

Those who support the inter-period allocation of income taxes admit that this involves difficulties and creates special problems. They are faced with such questions as: How can the allocation procedures and the recognition of a tax charge that is more or less than that actually paid be made comprehensible to the statement reader? What theoretical support can be offered for the recognition of tax prepayments and tax accruals as assets and liabilities in the conventional sense? Furthermore, what tax prepayments and accruals are appropriate in view of the uncertainties related to future tax rates as well as to future business profits or losses that will determine the amounts to be paid?

Some accounting authorities, while supporting the recognition on the financial statements of material differences in reported income and taxable income, feel that such recognition should take the form of supplementary notes accompanying the financial statements rather than entries in the account structure. Supplementary remarks would offer a description of the causes for differences in financial and tax reporting and would state the full implications of such differences on net income.

### Estimated liability on customer premium offers

Many companies offer special premiums to those purchasing their products. Such offers to stimulate the regular purchase of certain products may be open for a limited time or they may be of a continuing nature. The premium is normally made available when the customer submits the required number of product labels, box tops, wrappers, or certificates. In certain instances the premium offer may provide for an optional cash payment.

When a company purchases premiums that it is to distribute in accordance with premium offers, an appropriate asset is charged for the premiums acquired and Cash is credited. The distribution of premiums to customers is recorded by a charge to premium expense and a credit to the premiums account. If a premium offer expires at the end of the company's fiscal period, adjustments in the accounts are not required.

Premium requirements are fully met and the premium expense account summarizes the full charge for the period. However, when a premium offer is continuing, an adjustment must be made at the end of the period to recognize the liability that is found in the continuing costs of the offer. Premium Expense is debited and an appropriate liability account is credited. The expense is thus charged to the period that benefits from the premium plan and current liabilities reflect the claim for premiums outstanding. If premium distributions are charged to expense, the liability balance may be reversed at the start of the new period. Experience that indicates a redemption percentage that differs from the assumed rate will call for appropriate correcting entries and the revision of future redemption estimates.

Many organizations have adopted plans for the issue to customers of trading stamps, cash register tapes, or other media redeemable in merchandise, premiums, or cash. The accounting that is followed will depend upon the nature of the plan. A business may establish its own plan, prepare its own stamps or other trading media, and assume redemption responsibilities. Under these circumstances, the accounting would parallel that just illustrated for specific premium offers. On the other hand, the business unit may enter into an agreement for a stamp plan with a trading-stamp company. The latter normally assumes full responsibility for the redemption of stamps and sells the trading stamps for a set unit price whether they are redeemed or not. The business would report stamps purchased as an asset and stamps issued as a selling expense; the trading-stamp company would recognize on its books the sale of stamps, purchase of premiums, distributions of premiums, and the estimated redemptions identified with stamps outstanding.

### Estimated liability under guarantees for service and replacements

Some companies agree to provide free service on units failing to perform satisfactorily or to replace goods that are defective. When agreements involve only minor costs, it may be decided to recognize such costs in the periods in which they are incurred. When agreements involve significant future costs, estimates of such costs are in order. Such estimates are recorded by a charge to an expense account and a credit to a liability account. Subsequent costs of fulfilling guarantees are charged to the liability account. The anticipation of costs results in charges to the period that is credited for the revenue and in recognition of the obligation that is outstanding.

In certain cases customers are charged special fees for a service or replacement guarantee covering a specific period. In such cases, a customers' advances account is credited. Expenditures in meeting contract requirements are charged to expense, and the advances balance is recognized as revenue over the guarantee period. Recognition of revenue in excess of expenses indicates a net profit on such service contracts; revenue that is less than expenses indicates a net loss on such contracts. The customers' advances balance should be reported as a current liability in view of the claim that it makes upon current assets.

### Estimated liability on tickets, tokens, and gift certificates outstanding

Many companies sell tickets, tokens, certificates, etc., that entitle the owner to services or goods. For example, railroads issue tickets that are used for travel; local transit companies issue tokens that are good for fares; department stores sell gift certificates that are redeemable in merchandise.

When instruments redeemable in services or goods are outstanding at the end of the period, accounts should be adjusted to reflect the obligations under such arrangements. The nature of the adjustment will depend upon the entries that were originally made in recording the sale of the instruments.

Ordinarily, the sale of instruments redeemable in services or goods is recorded by a debit to Cash and a credit to a liability account. As instruments are redeemed, the liability balance is debited and Sales or an appropriate revenue account is credited. Certain claims may be rendered void by lapse of time or for some other reason as defined by the sales agreement. In addition, experience may indicate that a certain percentage of outstanding claims will never be presented for redemption. These factors must be considered at the end of the period. At this time, the liability balance is reduced to the balance of the claim estimated to be outstanding and a revenue account is credited for the gain that is indicated from forfeitures. If Sales or a special revenue account is originally credited on the sale of the redemption instrument, the adjustment at the end of the period calls for a charge to the revenue account and a credit to a liability account for the claim still outstanding.

### Contingent liabilities

Contingent liabilities represent possible future liabilities; certain acts or circumstances have created conditions that may result in liabilities in the event of future developments that are considered possible though not probable. The question of whether a liability is contingent or actual is not related to whether it involves an amount that is determinable or indeterminable; a determinable amount may be involved, yet if the claim is uncertain, it is recognized as a contingent liability; an indeterminable amount may be involved, but if the claim is certain, an actual liability, though estimated in amount, must be reported. Although a contingent liability involves no legal obligation on the date of the balance sheet, reference must be made to the possibility of such claim materializing in the future if the company's financial condition is to be fully shown. If a contingent liability should become an actual liability, the liability is recognized in the accounts at the later date, and a charge is made to an asset account, a loss account, or Retained Earnings, whichever is appropriate.

Examples of the contingent liabilities that call for recognition on the balance sheet are described in the following paragraphs.

*Notes receivable discounted and accounts receivable assigned.* The discounting of customers' notes and the assignment of customers' accounts involves a liability on the part of the transferor for payment of the claim in the event that the original debtor fails to make settlement. In the event that a liability ultimately materializes and is paid, the payment gives rise to a claim against the original debtor. Failure to recover such a claim calls for the recognition of a loss.

*Accommodation endorsements.* A party may become an accommodation endorser on a note by endorsing it for purposes of transfer. Such an endorsement creates a contingent liability as in the preceding case, and any ultimate payment on such an instrument should be treated as described above. If a person signs an accommodation note as maker, an entry should be made charging the party accommodated and crediting Notes Payable. These balances are closed if the accommodated party pays the note at maturity; if the accommodation maker is required to pay the note, he will attempt to recover the amount paid from the party originally accommodated.

*Lawsuits pending.* When there is litigation relative to matters such as patent infringement, breach of contract, or additional income tax liability, and advice of legal counsel indicates doubt as to the outcome of the litigation, amounts that are claimed may be regarded as contingent liabilities. If counsel is of the opinion that current litigation will ultimately result in a judgment against the company, an estimate of the amount payable should be made. The estimated liability is recorded by a debit to a nominal account or to Retained Earnings and a credit to a liability account.

*Additional taxes.* Certain tax items may be under review by tax authorities, giving rise to the possibility of additional tax assessments. If additional assessments are ultimately confirmed, the liabilities are recognized and a nominal account or Retained Earnings is charged.

*Guarantee of debt service of affiliated companies.* A company may guarantee the payment of interest and principal on long-term debt of affiliated companies. If this contingency materializes and payments are required, such payments will be accompanied by claims against the company whose obligations were assumed.

*Customer service guarantees.* In many instances, product or service guarantees may be considered of a contingent nature rather than calling for the recognition of a liability of a stated amount. If charges are subsequently incurred, these are recognized as expenses or as extraordinary items.

*Guarantees to customers against price declines.* Guarantees may be made to customers for refunds on goods purchased in the event of price declines or other specified contingencies. If conditions develop that call for customer reimbursement, a nominal account or Retained Earnings is charged, and the customer's account or Cash is credited.

### Appropriations of retained earnings for possible future losses

When a liability is certain and of a definite amount, it is presented as a part of the creditors' equity. When it is certain but of an indefinite amount, it is still presented as a part of the creditors' equity, although it is designated as an estimate. When the liability is uncertain, it is reported as a contingent liability. In the latter instance, management may authorize an appropriation of retained earnings until the contingency is resolved. Such action will preserve earnings within the business to absorb a loss if it develops. An appropriation to cover a possible loss arising in connection with a contingent claim is frequently designated as an appropriation for contingencies. This balance remains a part of the stockholders' equity as long as the liability item to which it relates is only of a contingent nature. If the liability fails to materialize, the appropriated balance is returned to Retained Earnings. If the liability does materialize, the loss should be charged to a nominal account or to Retained Earnings. The appropriated balance is then returned to Retained Earnings. The direct application of the loss against the appropriated balance would not be proper; such action would conceal the loss without recognition on either the income statement or the retained earnings statement.

### Current and contingent liabilities on the balance sheet

The nature of the detail to be presented for current liabilities depends upon the use that is to be made of the statement. A balance sheet prepared for stockholders might report little detail; on the other hand, creditors may insist on full detail concerning current debt.

Current assets are normally recorded in the order of their liquidity, and consistency would suggest that liabilities be reported in the order of their maturity. The latter practice may be followed only to the extent that it is practical; observance of such procedure would require an analysis of the different classes of obligations and separate reporting for classes with varying maturity dates. A bank overdraft should be listed first in view of the immediate demand that it makes on cash. In some cases a distinction is made between liabilities that have matured and are presently payable and others that have not matured though they are current. Disclosure as to future debt liquidation may be provided by appropriate parenthetical reference or note. Disclosure of liabilities that are secured by specific assets should also be made by parenthetical reference or note.

Contingent liabilities are generally reported on the balance sheet by means of (1) parenthetical remarks, (2) accompanying notes, or (3) descriptions under a special contingent liabilities heading. When the third method is used and amounts are indicated, the amounts are reported "short," that is, they are not included in the totals on the liability side since they have not been established as obligations on the balance sheet date. Contingent liabilities presented in a separate section of the balance sheet are preferably reported immediately after the current liabilities since these will normally require current liquidation if they materialize. When a lengthy explanation is required for a contingent claim, such an explanation is best provided by the second method above.

Foregoing discussions dealt with liabilities as of the balance sheet date, both current and contingent. Business commitments that will result in liabilities in succeeding periods that are material in amount, should be disclosed. Commitments for the purchase of goods, services, and equipment, and for the construction, purchase, or lease of properties, for example, may warrant disclosure by special notes accompanying the balance sheet.

Current and contingent liabilities sections on a balance sheet prepared on December 31, 1964, might appear as shown on page 247.

## QUESTIONS

**1.** (a) Distinguish between current and noncurrent liabilities. (b) Indicate the major classifications for current liabilities.

**2.** "Contingent claims require careful consideration in the evaluation of a company's working capital position." Explain.

**3.** What problems arise in the valuation of liabilities?

Liabilities

Current liabilities:

Notes payable:

| | | |
|---|---:|---:|
| Trade creditors......................... | $12,000 | |
| Banks (secured by assignment of monies to become due under certain contracts totaling $36,000 included in asset section).......... | 20,000 | |
| Officers................................. | 10,000 | |
| Miscellaneous............................ | 2,500 | $44,500 |

Accounts payable:

| | | |
|---|---:|---:|
| Trade creditors.......................... | $30,500 | |
| Credit balances in customers' accounts........ | 1,250 | |
| Miscellaneous........................... | 3,500 | 35,250 |
| Long-term debt installments due in 1965........ | | 10,000 |
| Cash dividends payable...................... | | 4,500 |
| Estimated income taxes payable............... | $16,000 | |
| Less U. S. Treasury tax anticipation bills...... | 10,000 | 6,000 |

Accrued liabilities:

| | | |
|---|---:|---:|
| Salaries and wages......................... | $ 1,250 | |
| Real and personal property taxes............. | 1,550 | |
| Miscellaneous accruals...................... | 1,400 | 4,200 |

Other:

| | | |
|---|---:|---:|
| Customer advances........................ | $ 7,500 | |
| Estimated repair costs on goods sold with service guarantees................................ | 2,500 | 10,000 |
| Total current liabilities........................ | | $114,450 |

Contingent liabilities:

| | |
|---|---:|
| Guarantors on employees' loans................ | $ 7,500 |
| Customers' drafts discounted.................. | 12,000 |
| Additional income tax assessments proposed by the Treasury Department for 1962 that have been protested by the company............... | 4,500 |
| Total contingent liabilities.................... | $24,000 |

**4.** The Walker Co. issues a non-interest bearing note due in one year in payment of merchandise. Describe alternate accounting procedures that may be employed for the purchase. Which procedure is best in your opinion?

**5.** (a) What factors suggest the desirability for income tax allocations within a single set of statements? What factors suggest the desirability of income tax allocations affecting successive periodic statements? (b) What are the arguments for and against inter-period income tax allocation? (c) What is the alternative to such inter-period allocation?

**6.** In adopting tax allocation procedures for timing differences between financial and taxable income, what adjustments are made when (a) book income before taxes is less than taxable income, and (b) book income before taxes is more than taxable income?

**7.** (a) Define contingent liabilities. (b) Give five examples of contingent liabilities. (c) Indicate for each example in (b) the accounting treatment to be followed in the event that a real liability emerges from the item previously considered of a contingent nature.

**8.** What methods may be employed on the balance sheet for disclosure of contingent liabilities?

**9.** (a) When in your opinion would commitments for future expenditures call for special disclosure? (b) How would you recommend that such disclosure be made?

**10.** Where would each of the following items be reported on the balance sheet?

    (a) Bank overdraft.
    (b) Cash dividends declared.
    (c) Dividends in arrears on preferred stock.
    (d) Estimated income taxes.
    (e) Insurance premiums received in advance for a 5-year period by an insurance company.
    (f) Stamps that were issued and that are redeemable by customers for certain premiums.
    (g) Deposits received in connection with meter installations by a public utility.
    (h) Personal injury claim pending.
    (i) Notes receivable discounted.
    (j) Current maturities of a serial bond issue.
    (k) Customer accounts with credit balances.
    (l) Purchase money obligation maturing in five annual installments.
    (m) Gift certificates sold to customers but not yet presented for redemption.
    (n) Service guarantees on equipment sales.
    (o) Accommodation endorsement on a note issued by an affiliated company.
    (p) Contract entered into with contractors for the construction of a new building.
    (q) Stock dividend payable.
    (r) Accrued vacation pay.
    (s) Strike settlement calling for retroactive wage payments.

## EXERCISES

**1.** Phillip Thompson, certified public accountant, has 3 employees. The weekly payroll is $400. Give the entries to record payment of the salaries if: (a) the employer is responsible for remitting $7\frac{1}{4}\%$ quarterly to the Federal Government for federal insurance contributions, $3\frac{5}{8}\%$ being deducted from employees' salaries and $3\frac{5}{8}\%$ representing the employer's contribution; (b) the employer is responsible for remitting a total of 3.7% quarterly to the state for unemployment and disability insurance, 1% being deducted from employees' salaries and 2.7% representing the employer's contribution; and (c) income tax withholdings are $65.

**2.** The Burton Corporation accrues certain revenue on its books in 1962 and 1963 of $4,500 and $5,500 respectively, but such revenue is not subject to income taxes until 1964. Book income before taxes and taxable income for the three-year period, then, are as follows:

|       | Book income | Taxable income |
|-------|-------------|----------------|
| 1962. | $14,000     | $ 9,500        |
| 1963. | 16,500      | 11,000         |
| 1964. | 15,000      | 25,000         |

Assume that the rate that is applicable to taxable income is 30% in each year. What entries would be made for each year to recognize the tax liability and to provide for a proper allocation of taxes in view of the differences in book and taxable income?

**3.** The Wakefield Co. includes 1 coupon in each box of soap powder that it packs, 10 coupons being redeemable for a premium consisting of a kitchen utensil. In 1964, the Wakefield Co. purchases 5,000 premiums at 65 cents, and sells 80,000 boxes of soap powder. 15,000 coupons are presented for redemption. It is estimated that 60% of the coupons issued will be presented for redemption. What entries would be made relating to the premium plan in 1964?

**4.** Prepare the current liabilities section of the balance sheet for the Parks Co. on December 31, 1964, from the data that follow:

Notes payable: arising from purchases of goods, $28,500; arising from loans from banks, $15,000, on which marketable securities valued at $19,500 have been pledged as security; arising from advances by officers, $10,000.

Accounts payable: arising from purchases of goods, $22,000.

Cash balance with Farmers Bank, $6,500; cash overdraft with Merchants Bank, $8,750.

Dividends in arrears on preferred stock, $12,000.

Income tax withholdings payable, $650.

First-mortgage serial bonds, $100,000, payable in semiannual installments of $5,000 due on March 1 and September 1 of each year.

Advances received from customers on purchase orders, $1,500.

Customers' accounts with credit balances arising from purchases returns, $900.

Estimated costs of meeting guarantee for service requirements on goods sold, $3,600.

Estimated damages to be paid as a result of unsatisfactory performance on a contract, $1,200.

## PROBLEMS

**9-1.** The Pak-Rite Co. shows book income before income taxes and taxable income for 1962 and 1963 as follows:

|       | Book income | Taxable income |
|-------|-------------|----------------|
| 1962. | $ 84,600    | $122,400       |
| 1963. | 120,100     | 111,700        |

The reason for the discrepancies is found in the fact that the company, organized in the middle of 1962, wrote off against revenue of that year organization costs totaling $42,000. For federal income tax purposes, however, the organization costs can be written off ratably over a period of not less than 60 months. For income tax purposes, then, the company deducted 6/60 of the costs in 1962 and 12/60 of the costs in 1963. Corporate income tax rates in 1962 and 1963 were 30% on all taxable income and an additional 22% on taxable income in excess of $25,000.

*Instructions:* Give the entries that would be made on the books of the company at the end of 1962 and 1963 to recognize the income tax liability and to provide for a proper allocation of taxes in view of the differences in book and income tax reporting.

**9-2.** Decker Sales, Inc., was incorporated at the beginning of 1962. The books of the company for 1962 and 1963 reported net incomes before income taxes of $150,000 and $280,000 respectively. In arriving at net income each year, the company charged revenue and credited a liability account for costs estimated to be incurred in the following year as a result of guarantees on products sold. At the end of 1962, the liability was reported at $20,000; at the end of 1963, the liability balance was $30,000. For income tax purposes, charges for guarantees cannot be anticipated but must be recognized in the year costs are incurred. Corporate income tax rates for 1962 and 1963 were 30% on all taxable income and an additional 22% on taxable income in excess of $25,000.

*Instructions:* Give the entries that would be made on the books of the company at the end of 1962 and 1963 to recognize the income tax liability and to provide for a proper allocation of taxes in view of the differences in book and income tax reporting.

**9-3.** The Ruggles Co. was organized at the beginning of 1959 and at that time acquired machinery and equipment at a cost of $150,000. The asset had a five-year life and no salvage value, and a depreciation rate of 20% was used for book purposes. However, for income tax purposes the company employed the sum of years'-digits method and decreasing annual charges were recognized for the five-year period of $50,000, $40,000, $30,000, $20,000, and $10,000. All of the revenue of the company was taxable; all of the expenses were deductible for tax purposes. Income tax rates throughout the five-year period were 30% on the first $25,000 of taxable income, 52% on amounts in excess of $25,000.

*Instructions:* Assuming that the net income before income taxes per books is $100,000 each year for the period 1959–1963 inclusive, give the entries that would be made at the end of each year in recording the tax accrual in a manner that charges book income with the income taxes allocable to such income.

**9-4.** The Kansas Mills Corp. manufactures a cake mix that is packaged and sold. A cake knife is offered to customers sending in 2 box tops from these packages accompanied by a remittance of 50 cents. Data with respect to the premium offer are summarized below:

|                                                      | 1963      | 1964      |
|------------------------------------------------------|-----------|-----------|
| Cake mix sales (70¢ per package)                     | $175,000  | $210,000  |
| Cake knife purchases (75¢ per knife) . . . . . . . . | $ 10,125  | $ 11,250  |
| Number of knives distributed as premiums. . . . .    | 10,000    | 14,500    |
| Estimated number of knives to be distributed in      |           |           |
|   subsequent periods. . . . . . . . . . . . . . . . . . . . . . . | 2,000     | 4,000     |

Mailing costs are 20¢ per cake knife.

*Instructions:* (1) Give the entries that would be made in 1963 and 1964 to record product sales, premium purchases and redemptions, and year-end adjustments.

(2) List the account balances that will appear on the balance sheet and the income statement at the end of 1963 and 1964 as a result of the foregoing.

**9-5.** Suburbia Services, Inc. sells a television warranty policy covering all parts and labor for $50 per year. Warranties begin as of the first of the month following issuance of the policy. Policies were first issued in September, 1963. In reviewing the records before closing the accounts for 1964, you find that revenues and expenses on such contracts have been recognized in 1963 and 1964 on the cash basis. The accounts show revenues and expenses for the two years as follows:

|            | Revenue 1963 | Revenue 1964 | Expense 1963 | Expense 1964 |
|------------|--------------|--------------|--------------|--------------|
| January. . . . . . . . . . . . . . . . . . . . |          | $ 4,950  |          | $ 1,750  |
| February. . . . . . . . . . . . . . . . . . |          | 4,800    |          | 1,925    |
| March. . . . . . . . . . . . . . . . . |          | 4,350    |          | 1,900    |
| April . . . . . . . . . . . . . . . . . |          | 4,200    |          | 2,350    |
| May. . . . . . . . . . . . . . . . . . |          | 4,800    |          | 2,700    |
| June. . . . . . . . . . . . . . . . . . |          | 3,300    |          | 2,800    |
| July. . . . . . . . . . . . . . . . . |          | 3,000    |          | 2,950    |
| August. . . . . . . . . . . . . . . . . |          | 2,850    |          | 3,000    |
| September. . . . . . . . . . . . . . . | $ 1,500  | 3,000    |          | 3,050    |
| October. . . . . . . . . . . . . . . . . | 2,250    | 3,450    | $    450  | 3,250    |
| November . . . . . . . . . . . . . . . | 3,000    | 3,600    | 850      | 3,075    |
| December. . . . . . . . . . . . . . | 3,450    | 3,600    | 1,225    | 2,975    |
|            | $10,200  | $45,900  | $ 2,525  | $31,725  |

*Instructions:* (1) List monthly revenue, expense, and net income balances for 1963 and 1964, assuming that proper recognition is given to prepaid revenue on the service policies. (Submit working paper summaries that show calculation of the monthly net income figures listed.)

(2) Assuming that financial statements are to be prepared for 1964 that report the earnings with appropriate recognition of prepaid revenue at the beginning and the end of the period, give (a) the correcting entry to be made in recognition of the prepaid revenue balance at the beginning of the year and (b) the adjusting entry to be made in recognition of the prepaid revenue balance at the end of the year.

**9-6.** The following data are made available for purposes of stating the financial position of the San Fernando Corp. on December 31, 1964.

| | |
|---|---:|
| Cash in bank.................................................. | $37,000 |
| Petty cash, which includes IOU's of employees totaling $250 that are to be repaid to the petty cash fund............. | 750 |
| Marketable securities, valued at $43,250, securities valued at $12,500 having been pledged on a note payable to the bank for $10,000, reported on books at cost.................. | 41,125 |
| Notes receivable, which have been reduced by notes discounted of $12,000 that are not yet due and on which the company is contingently liable........................ | 14,500 |
| Accounts receivable, which include accounts with credit balances of $250 and past-due accounts of $3,250 on which a loss of 50% is anticipated........................... | 30,500 |
| Merchandise inventory, which includes goods held on a consignment basis, $3,200, and goods received on December 31, $2,150, neither of these items having been recorded as a purchase...................................... | 26,200 |
| Prepaid insurance, which includes cash surrender value of life insurance policies, $6,500........................ | 7,250 |
| Rents paid in advance.................................... | 450 |

Furniture and fixtures, which include fixtures that were fully depreciated and that have just been scrapped, $3,600:

| | | |
|---|---:|---:|
| Cost...................................... | $12,500 | |
| Allowance for depreciation................... | 8,250 | 4,250 |

| | |
|---|---:|
| Notes payable, which are trade notes with the exception of a 6-month, $10,000 note payable to Bank of Commerce on June 15, 1965....................................... | 25,800 |
| Accounts payable, which include accounts with debit balances of $425......................................... | 27,400 |
| Miscellaneous accrued expenses, which include $3,500 representing estimated costs of premiums in connection with a special sales offer made in December.................... | 9,150 |
| Long-term notes, which are payable in annual installments of $2,500 on February 1 of each year..................... | 7,500 |
| 6% cumulative preferred stock, $10 par, on which dividends for 3 years are in arrears......................... | 50,000 |
| No-par common stock, 40,000 shares authorized and outstanding......................................... | 52,500 |
| Retained earnings (debit balance)...................... | (10,325) |

The following data are not included in the above account balances:

(a) A suit has been filed against the company for $50,000; legal counsel has informed the company that while it is probable that the company will lose the suit, the award for damages will not be in excess of $15,000.

(b) There are product replacement guarantees outstanding that are estimated to result in costs to the company of $5,000.

*Instructions:* Prepare a classified balance sheet, including whatever notes are appropriate in support of balance sheet data.

# Chapter 10

# INVESTMENTS

## STOCKS

### Nature of investments

A company must invest funds in inventories, receivables, plant and equipment, and other assets in order to engage in the sale of goods and services. But a portion of its available funds may be applied to assets not directly identified with primary activities. Assets that occupy an auxiliary relationship to central revenue-producing activities are referred to as *investments*. Investments are expected to contribute to the success of the business either by exercising certain favorable effects upon sales and operations generally, or by making an independent contribution to business earnings over the long term.

### Classification of investments

From the standpoint of the owner, investments are either temporary or long-term. As suggested earlier, investments are classified as current only where they are readily marketable and it is management's intent to use them in meeting current cash requirements. Investments that do not meet these tests are considered *long-term* or *permanent investments* and are reported on the balance sheet under a separate noncurrent heading. The purpose that is to be served by the investment governs its classification.

### Composition of long-term investments

Long-term or permanent investments include a variety of items. For discussion purposes, long-term investments will be classified in four groupings: (1) investments in stocks, both preferred and common; (2) investments in bonds, mortgages, and similar debt instruments; (3) funds for bond retirement, stock redemption, and other special purposes; and (4) miscellaneous investments including real estate held for appreciation or for future use, advances to affiliates, interests in life insurance contracts, ownership equities in partnerships and joint ventures, and interests in trusts and estates. The accounting problems relating to long-term investments in stocks are considered in this chapter; the problems relating to the remaining long-term investments are considered in the next chapter.

### Investments in stocks

Although long-term investments in corporate stocks may involve the risk of price decline, they may afford significant rewards in the form of periodic revenue and price appreciation. Frequently investments in stock are made to secure certain continuing business advantages. For example, stock ownership may be a means of obtaining suppliers for required materials and services or outlets for sales products. Here the income factor of the investment is only incidental to the other considerations. In certain instances, ownership of a controlling interest in the voting stock of a company may be sought. With control, activities of the related companies may be integrated towards the achievement of greater profits. A company exercising control over another through majority ownership of its voting stock is called a *holding* or *parent company;* the company controlled is referred to as a *subsidiary company.*

Investments may be made in preferred or common stock. Preferred stock has certain preferences as to dividends and frequently as to assets upon dissolution. Sometimes preferred stock is convertible at the option of the stockholder into some other security, usually common stock. When this is the case, the preferred stock may be exchanged into common stock should corporate activities prove sufficiently profitable to make the common stock the more attractive equity.

The accounting procedures that are outlined on the following pages are equally applicable to short-term and long-term investments except when variations in treatment are indicated. Furthermore, the procedures would be employed by individual investors with single holdings in stock as well as by banks, investment companies, insurance companies, and other financial enterprises with many holdings.

Shares of stock may be acquired on the New York Stock Exchange, the American Stock Exchange, and other exchanges in the different regions of the country. Stock that is not listed on the exchanges is acquired "over the counter" through brokers. Stock may also be acquired directly from an issuing company or from a private investor.

When stock is purchased for cash, it is recorded at the amount paid, including brokers' commissions, taxes, and other fees incidental to the purchase. When stock is acquired "on margin," the stock should be recorded at its full cost and a liability should be recognized for the unpaid balance; to report only the amount invested would be, in effect, to offset the obligation to the broker against the investment account. An agreement or *subscription* entered into with a corporation for the purchase of stock gives rise to an asset representing the security to be received and a liability for the amount to be paid. A charge for interest on an obligation arising from a stock purchase should be reported as expense. When stock is acquired in exchange for properties or services, the fair market value of such considerations or the value at which the stock is currently selling, whichever may be more clearly ascertainable, should be used as a basis for recording the investment. In the absence of clearly defined values for assets or services exchanged or a market price for the security acquired, appraisals and estimates are required in arriving at cost.

When two or more securities are acquired for a lump-sum price, this cost should be allocated in some equitable manner to the different acquisitions. When market prices are available for each security, cost may be apportioned on the basis of the relative market prices. When there is a market price for one security but not for the other, it may be reasonable to assign the market price to the one and the cost excess to the other. When market prices are not available, it may be necessary to postpone cost apportionment until support for an equitable division becomes available. In certain instances it may be desirable to carry the two securities in a single account and to treat the proceeds from the sale of one as a subtraction from total cost, the residual cost then to be identified with the other. To illustrate the foregoing procedures, assume the purchase of 100 units of preferred and common stock at $75 per unit; each unit consists of one share of preferred and two shares of common. Market prices at the time the stock is acquired are $60 and $10 per share for preferred and common shares, respectively. The investment cost is recorded in terms of the relative market values of the securities:

| | | |
|---|---|---|
| Investment in Preferred Stock..................... | 5,625 | |
| Investment in Common Stock..................... | 1,875 | |
| Cash....................................... | | 7,500 |

| | | | |
|---|---|---|---|
| Value of preferred: | 100×$60 | $6,000 | |
| Value of common: | 200×$10 | 2,000 | $8,000 |

Cost assigned to preferred: 6,000/8,000×$7,500=$5,625.
Cost assigned to common: 2,000/8,000×$7,500=$1,875.

If only a value for preferred of $60 is available, the investment is recorded as follows:

| | | |
|---|---|---|
| Investment in Preferred Stock..................... | 6,000 | |
| Investment in Common Stock..................... | 1,500 | |
| Cash....................................... | | 7,500 |

| | |
|---|---|
| Cost of preferred and common.......... | $7,500 |
| Cost identified with preferred (market) ........................ | 6,000 |
| Remaining cost identified with common ........................ | $1,500 |

If the division of cost must be deferred, the following entry is made:

| | | |
|---|---|---|
| Investment in Preferred and Common Stock......... | 7,500 | |
| Cash....................................... | | 7,500 |

The joint investment balance may be closed when a basis for apportionment is established and costs can be assigned to individual issues.

When stock is subject to special calls or assessments and such payments are made to the corporation, these are recorded as additions to the costs of the holdings. Prorata contributions by the stockholders to the corporation to enable it to eliminate a deficit, to retire bonds, or to effect a reorganization, are also treated as additions to investment cost.

For federal income tax purposes, the sale of securities gives rise to a *capital gain* or *capital loss*. Such gain or loss is the difference between the cost of the securities sold, and their sales proceeds. When securities are sold from lots acquired at different dates and prices and the identity of the lots cannot be determined, the cost of the securities must be calculated on a first-in, first-out basis. Tax laws further provide that capital gains and losses must be classified in terms of the holding period of the securities sold: if the period from the date the securities were acquired to the date they were sold is not more than six months, a *short-term* gain or loss is recognized; if the holding period exceeds six months, a *long-term* gain or loss is recognized. Certain tax advantages are granted to taxpayers with an excess of long-term capital gains over capital losses: (1) only 50% of such excess is included in gross income subject to tax; (2) the tax rate applicable to this portion of income is limited to 50%. Income taxes on an excess of long-term capital gains are thus limited to 25% of gains.

In accounting for securities on the books, care should be taken to preserve costs of the individual purchases as well as the dates of purchases and sales. Although the use of an average cost might be supported when securities have been acquired at different prices and identification is not possible, first-in, first-out is acceptable and is normally employed. The use of tax procedures in the accounts permits the preparation of the income tax returns from the books without the analyses and adjustments that would otherwise be necessary, and also provides the taxpayer with data that he requires in planning the sale of securities in a manner that will offer him maximum tax advantages.

### Stock valuation

Reference was made in an earlier chapter to the valuation of securities held as a temporary investment. Management's intent to use securities as a source of cash gives support to the recognition of current market values. But when management intends to hold securities, market values do not assume the significance that they would otherwise have. As in the case of other long-term assets, securities held as a long-term investment may be reported at cost. In making the statements more informative, costs may be supplemented by parenthetical disclosure of the aggregate market value of the securities when such data are available.

When a significant and apparently permanent decline in the value of securities held as a long-term investment takes place, recognition of the loss is necessary if financial position is not to be misrepresented. For example, assume that stock is held in companies that have discontinued dividends or that face the possibility of creditor control as a result of continued losses, or assume that stock is held in companies in foreign countries where war has broken out. With cost no longer considered recoverable, the investment should be written down. Writing down an investment is preferably accomplished by a valuation account so that cost is preserved for income tax purposes.

## Dividends

The receipt of cash dividends by a stockholder is recorded by a debit to Cash and a credit to Dividend Income. Three dates are generally included in the formal dividend announcement: (1) date of declaration, (2) record date, and (3) date of payment. The formal dividend announcement may read somewhat as follows: "The Board of Directors at their meeting on November 5, 1964, declared a regular quarterly dividend on outstanding common stock of 50 cents per share payable on January 15, 1965, to stockholders of record at the close of business, December 29, 1964." The stockholder becomes aware of the dividend action upon its announcement. But if he sells his holdings and a new owner is recognized by the corporation prior to the record date, the dividend is paid to the new owner. If the stockholder retains his holdings until the record date, he will be entitled to the dividends when paid. After the record date, stock no longer carries a right to dividends and sells "ex-dividend."[1] Accordingly, a stockholder is justified in recognizing the corporate dividend action on the record date. At this time a receivable account may be debited and Dividend Income credited. Upon receipt of the dividend, Cash is debited and the receivable credited.

There are some who would accrue dividends in the same manner as interest when the declaration of a regular dividend at a certain date is virtually assured by the nature of the security, the position and earnings of the company, and the policies of the board of directors. The recognition of accrued dividends under such circumstances is not objectionable if disclosure is made on the statements that such special practice is followed.

Federal income tax regulations provide that dividends are taxable only when unqualifiedly made subject to the demand of the stockholder.

---

[1]Stock on the New York Stock Exchange is normally quoted ex-dividend or ex-rights two full trading days prior to the record date because of the time required to deliver the stock and to record the stock transfer.

Hence, even though preparing the tax return on an accrual basis, the taxpayer recognizes dividends as revenue only when these become available. Ordinarily, the taxpayer maintains his books in accordance with the tax rule and recognizes revenue at the time the dividend check is received.

## Property dividends

Dividends in the form of property or assets other than cash are referred to as *property dividends* or *dividends in kind*. The corporation in distributing earnings by means of a property dividend credits an asset account for the cost of the asset distributed and charges retained earnings. The stockholder charges an asset account and credits dividend income. The stockholder, however, recognizes the dividend in terms of the value of the property item at the date of its distribution. To illustrate, assume that the Wells Corporation with 1,000,000 shares of common stock outstanding distributes as a dividend in kind its holdings of 50,000 shares of Barnes Co. stock. The distribution of one share of Barnes Co. stock on every 20 shares of Wells Corporation held is made when Barnes Co. shares are selling at $16. A stockholder owning 100 shares of Wells Corporation stock would make the following entry in recording the receipt of the dividend:

| | | |
|---|---|---|
| Investment in Barnes Co. Stock | 80 | |
| Dividend Income | | 80 |

Received 5 shares of Barnes Co. stock, market price $16 per share, as a dividend on 100 shares of Wells Corporation stock.

Income tax requirements for a property dividend agree with the foregoing.

## Stock dividends

A company may distribute a dividend in the form of additional shares that are the same as those held by its stockholders. Such a dividend does not affect company assets but results in the transfer of retained earnings to invested capital. The increase in total shares outstanding is distributed prorata to individual stockholders. The receipt of additional shares by stockholders leaves their respective equities exactly as they were; although the number of shares held by individual stockholders has gone up, there are now a greater number of shares outstanding and proportionate interests remain unchanged. The division of equities into a greater number of parts cannot be regarded as giving rise to revenue. Only a memorandum entry needs to be made in recognizing the receipt of additional shares. Original investment cost applies to a greater number of shares, and this cost is divided by the total shares now held in arriving at the cost per share to be used upon subsequent disposition of holdings. The new per-share cost basis is indicated in the memorandum entry.

It may be noted that market recognition of the stock dividend will result in a similar restatement in the market price of the security. For example, assume that shares sell for $45 just before the record date for a 50 per cent stock dividend. Such shares would be expected to sell at a lower market in view of the dividend that now puts into the hands of stockholders 50 per cent more shares with no increase in company assets. After the dividend, 1½ shares carry the book value and represent the equity previously attached to a single share; 1½ shares are now worth $45, or each share has a value of $30 ($45÷1.5).

When stock has been acquired at different dates and at different costs, the stock dividend will have to be related to such different acquisitions. Adjusted costs for shares comprising each lot held can then be developed. To illustrate, assume that H. C. Smith owns stock of the Banner Corporation acquired as follows:

| | Shares | Cost per Share | Total Cost |
|---|---|---|---|
| Lot 1........ | 50 | $120 | $6,000 |
| Lot 2........ | 30 | 90 | 2,700 |

A stock dividend of 1 share for every 2 held is distributed by the Banner Corporation. A memorandum entry on Smith's books to report the number of shares now held and the cost per share of each lot follows:

> Received 40 shares of Banner Corporation stock, representing a 50% stock dividend on 80 shares held. Number of shares held and costs assigned to shares are now as follows:

| | Shares | Cost per Share | Total Cost |
|---|---|---|---|
| Lot 1........ | 75 (50 + 25) | $80 ($6,000 ÷ 75) | $6,000 |
| Lot 2........ | 45 (30 + 15) | 60 ($2,700 ÷ 45) | 2,700 |

These costs assume significance upon the sale of shares. The sale of the 75 shares comprising Lot 1, for example, would be charged with a cost of $6,000. The sale of only part of the shares identified with this lot would call for use of a cost of $80 per share. If shares sold are identified as those of Lot 2, cost would be figured at $60 per share. Assuming that 100 shares are sold at $100 and stock is unidentifiable as to lot, the following entry is made to show cost calculated on the first-in, first-out basis:

| | | |
|---|---|---|
| Cash.................................................. | 10,000 | |
|     Investment in Banner Corporation Stock.......... | | 7,500 |
|     Gain on Sale of Banner Corporation Stock........ | | 2,500 |
|     Sold 100 shares, cost calculated on the first-in, first-out basis as follows: | | |
|     75 shares at $80..................... | $6,000 | |
|     25 shares at $60..................... | 1,500 | |
|     Total cost assigned to sale............. | $7,500 | |

The foregoing analysis assumes maintenance of cost data in the investment accounts in accordance with income tax requirements. The use of an average cost on the books would result in a charge of $72.50 for each share sold ($8,700 ÷ 120). However, $72.50 cannot be used for tax purposes, and analysis by lot as illustrated would still be required in calculating the taxable gain or loss.

When a stock of a class different from that held is received as a stock dividend, such a dividend, too, should not be regarded as revenue. As in the case of a like dividend, a portion of the retained earnings relating to the original holdings has now been formally labeled invested capital. All owners of the stock on which the dividend is declared participate prorata in the distribution. The respective equity of each owner in the corporate capital remains unchanged, although it is now composed of two classes of stock instead of a single class. A book value is now identified with the new stock, but this is accompanied by a corresponding decrease in the book value identified with the original holdings. A similar position can be taken when an investor receives dividends in the form of bonds or other contractual obligations of the corporation.

One difference between the receipt of stock of the same class and securities of a different class needs to be noted. When common stock is received on common, all shares are alike and original cost may be equitably assigned in terms of the total number of units held after the dividend. When different securities are received whose value is not the same as that of the shares originally held, it would not be proper to assign an equal amount of original cost to both old and new units. Instead, equitable apportionment of cost would require use of the relative market values of the two classes of securities.

For federal income tax purposes, receipt by a stockholder of shares of any kind, common or preferred, as a stock dividend is nontaxable except when the distribution is made in lieu of cash. The distribution is regarded as having been made in lieu of cash if (1) it is made in discharge of preference dividends for the current or preceding taxable year, or (2) the stockholder is given the option of receiving cash or other property instead of stock.

### Stock splits

A corporation may effect a *stock split* by reducing the par or the stated value of capital stock and increasing the number of shares outstanding accordingly. For example, a corporation with 1,000,000 shares outstanding may decide to split its stock on a 3-for-1 basis. After the split the corporation will have 3,000,000 shares outstanding; each stockholder will have three shares for every share originally held. However, each share will now represent only one-third of the interest previously represented; furthermore, each share of stock can be expected to sell for approximately one-third of its previous value.

The stock split requires no change in capital stock and retained earnings balances on the corporate books; however, the stockholders' ledger is revised to show the increased number of shares identified with each stockholder. Accounting for a stock split on the books of the investor is the same as that for a stock dividend. With an increase in the number of shares, each share now carries only a portion of the original cost. When shares have been acquired at different dates and at different prices, the shares received in a split will have to be associated with the original acquisitions and per-share costs for each lot revised. A memorandum entry is made to report the increase in the number of shares and the allocation of cost to the shares held after the split.

Income tax requirements for stock splits agree with the foregoing.

## Stock rights

A corporation that wishes to raise cash by the sale of additional stock must first offer existing stockholders the right to subscribe to the new stock. This privilege attaching to stock is called the *pre-emptive right* and is designed to enable a stockholder to retain his respective interest in the corporation. For example, assume that a stockholder owns 50 per cent of a company's outstanding stock. If the stock is doubled and the additional shares are offered and sold to other parties, his interest in the company would drop to 25 per cent. With the right to subscribe to his prorata share of any new offering, the stockholder can maintain his proportionate interest in the corporation. It should be noted, however, that pre-emptive rights generally apply only to the issue of the same kind of stock held by the stockholders. The statutes of some states allow the corporation to limit stockholders' pre-emptive rights by suitable provisions in the corporate charter.

Because of the possibility of failure to dispose of an entire new offering by sale to holders of rights, many corporations follow the policy of having the offering underwritten by an investment house. With such an arrangement, the underwriters agree to purchase at a fixed price all of the shares that are not sold through the exercise of rights.

In order to make subscription privileges attractive and to insure sale of the stock, it is customary for corporations to offer the additional issues to its stockholders at less than the market price of the stock. Certificates known as *warrants* or *rights* are issued to stockholders enabling them to subscribe for stock in proportion to the holdings on which they are issued. One right is offered for each share held. But more than one right is generally required in subscribing for one share. Rights may be sold by stockholders who do not care to exercise them.

As in the case of cash and other dividends, the directors of the corporation in declaring rights to subscribe for additional shares designate a record date that follows the declaration date. All stockholders on the record date are entitled to the rights. Up to the record date, stock sells "rights-on," since parties acquiring the stock will receive the rights when they are issued; after the record date, the stock sells "ex-rights," and the rights may be sold separately by those owning the rights as of the record date. A date on which the rights expire is also designated when the rights are declared. Rights that are not exercised are worthless beyond the expiration date.

## Accounting for stock rights

The receipt of stock rights is comparable to the receipt of a stock dividend. The corporation has made no asset distribution; stockholders' equities remain unchanged. However, the stockholders' investment is evidenced by shares originally acquired and rights that have a value of their own since they permit the purchase of shares at less than market price. These circumstances call for an allocation of cost between original shares and the rights. Since shares and rights have different values, apportionment should be made in terms of relative market values. A separate accounting for each class of security is subsequently followed. The accounting for stock rights is illustrated in the example that follows.

Assume that in 1960 W. C. Warner acquires 100 shares of Superior Products no-par common at $180 per share. In 1964 the corporation issues rights to purchase 1 share of common at $100 for every 5 shares owned. Warner thus receives 100 rights — one right for each share owned. However, since 5 rights are required for the acquisition of a single share, the 100 rights enable him to subscribe for only 20 new shares. Warner's original investment of $18,000 now applies to two assets, the shares and the rights. This cost is apportioned on the basis of the relative market values of each security as of the date that the rights are distributed to stockholders. The cost allocation may be expressed as follows:

$$\text{Cost assigned to rights:} \quad \frac{\text{Market Value of Rights}}{\text{Market Value of Stock Ex-Rights} + \text{Market Value of Rights}} \times \begin{array}{c}\text{Original}\\\text{Cost of}\\\text{Stock}\end{array}$$

$$\text{Cost assigned to stock:} \quad \frac{\text{Market Value of Stock Ex-Rights}}{\text{Market Value of Stock Ex-Rights} + \text{Market Value of Rights}} \times \begin{array}{c}\text{Original}\\\text{Cost of}\\\text{Stock}\end{array}$$

Calculation of the cost assigned to stock by the application of the formula above is not actually required; original cost less the cost assigned to rights gives the cost allocable to the original holdings.

Assume that Superior Products Common is selling ex-rights at $121 per share and rights are selling at $4 each. The cost allocation is made as follows:

To rights: $\dfrac{4}{121 + 4}$ × $18,000 = $576 ($576 ÷ 100 = $5.76, cost per right)

To stock (balance): $18,000 − $576 = $17,424 ($17,424 ÷ 100 = $174.24, cost per share)

The following entry may be made at this time:

Superior Products Stock Rights. . . . . . . . . . . . . . . . . . . . . . .    576
    Investment in Superior Products Common Stock. . . . . . .            576
    Received 100 rights permitting the purchase of 20
    shares at $100. Cost of stock was apportioned on the
    basis of the relative market values of stock and rights
    on the date rights are distributed.

A corporation issuing rights generally notifies individual stockholders of the portion of cost to be applied to rights. While stockholders' cost assignments to rights will vary as a result of the different amounts that were originally paid for stock, the cost apportionment formula is the same in each case. Instead of notifying stockholders of an assignment of $4/125$ of the original cost to rights, as above, the corporate notice would normally instruct stockholders to calculate rights cost at 3.2% of their respective investment cost (4 ÷ 125).

The cost apportioned to the rights is used in determining the gain or the loss arising from the sale of rights. Assume that the rights in the preceding example are sold at $4\frac{1}{2}$. The following entry would be made:

Cash. . . . . . . . . . . . . . . . . . . . . . . . . . . . . . . . . . . . . . . . . . . . . . .    450
Loss on Sale of Superior Products Stock Rights. . . . . . . . . .    126
    Superior Products Stock Rights. . . . . . . . . . . . . . . . . . . . .            576
    Sold 100 rights at $4\frac{1}{2}$.

If the rights are exercised, the cost of the new shares acquired consists of the cost assigned to the rights plus the cash that is paid in the exercise of the rights. Assume that, instead of selling the rights, Warner exercises his privilege to purchase 20 additional shares at $100. The following entry is made:

Investment in Superior Products Common Stock. . . . . . .    2,576
    Superior Products Stock Rights. . . . . . . . . . . . . . . . . .            576
    Cash. . . . . . . . . . . . . . . . . . . . . . . . . . . . . . . . . . . . . . . . . .          2,000
    Exercised rights acquiring 20 shares at $100.

Upon exercising the rights, Warner's records show an investment balance of $20,000 consisting of two lots of stock as follows:

Lot 1 (1962 acquisition) 100 shares
   ($17,424 ÷ 100 = $174.24, cost per share as adjusted)... $17,424
Lot 2 (1964 acquisition) 20 shares
   ($2,576 ÷ 20 = $128.80, cost per share acquired through
   rights)........................................................ 2,576
Total......................................................... $20,000

These costs provide the basis for calculating gains or losses upon subsequent sales of the stock.

When rights are received on stock that was acquired through several purchases at different costs, special care is required in tracing costs. Rights must be related to the different stock lots owned. Cost of each lot is then allocated between the stock and the rights emerging from the ownership of the particular lot. These costs are used in the future sale or exercise of the various lots of stock rights.

Frequently the receipt of rights includes one or more rights that cannot be used in the purchase of a whole share. For example, assume that the owner of 100 shares receives 100 rights; 6 rights are required for the purchase of 1 share. Here the holder uses 96 rights in purchasing 16 shares. He may allow the remaining 4 rights to lapse, sell these and report a gain or a loss on such sale, or supplement these by the purchase of 2 more rights making possible the purchase of an additional share of stock.

If the owner of valuable rights allows them to lapse, it would appear that the cost assigned to such rights should be written off as a loss. This can be supported on the theory that the issuance of stock by the corporation at less than current market price results in some dilution in the equities identified with original holdings. However, when changes in the market price of the stock make the exercise of rights unattractive and the rights cannot be sold, any cost of rights reported separately should be returned to the investment account.

Frequently, no entry is made at the time of acquisition of rights, the reduction in the cost attaching to the original stock being made at the time the rights are sold or exercised. Although the transfer of cost through a stock rights account is not shown, investment balances would be the same after the sale or the exercise of rights.

## Liquidating dividends

When a company consumes natural resources in its operations, sales revenue includes earnings as well as a recovery of the cost of such natural resources. When natural resources are limited and irreplaceable, the company may choose to distribute full proceeds becoming available from operations. Dividends paid, then, represent in part a distribution of earnings and in part a distribution of invested capital. Distributions involving both earnings and invested capital may also be found when a company makes full distribution of the proceeds from the sale of certain properties such as land or securities, or when a distribution represents the proceeds from business liquidation. Dividends representing a return of invested capital are known as *liquidating dividends.*

A stockholder receiving a dividend that consists of both a distribution of earnings and a return of invested capital credits revenue for the amount representing earnings and the investment account for the amount representing invested capital. To illustrate, assume that Lucky Mines, Inc., pays a dividend of $500,000, 60% representing a distribution of earnings and 40% representing a distribution of the cost recovery of certain wasting assets. A stockholder receiving a dividend of $1,200 makes the following entry:

| | | |
|---|---|---|
| Cash. . . . . . . . . . . . . . . . . . . . . . . . . . . . . . . . . . . . . . . . . . . | 1,200 | |
| Dividend Income. . . . . . . . . . . . . . . . . . . . . . . . . . . . . . . . . | | 720 |
| Investment in Lucky Mines, Inc. Stock. . . . . . . . . . . . . | | 480 |

Information regarding the portion of dividends representing earnings and the portion representing invested capital is reported to the stockholder by the corporation making the distribution. This report may not accompany each dividend check but instead may be provided annually and may cover the total dividends paid during the year. If dividends have been recorded as revenue during the year, the revenue account is charged and the investment account is credited when notification is received of the amount that is to be recognized as a distribution of invested capital.

When liquidating dividends exceed investment cost, excess distributions are reported as a gain from the investment. If liquidation is completed and the investment cost is not fully recovered, the balance of the investment account should be written off as a loss.

## Sale of stock

When stock is sold, the investment account should be credited for the carrying value of the shares, which is original cost adjusted for any past stock assessments, liquidating dividends, stock dividends, splits, rights, etc. If stock transactions have been properly recorded in the past, adjusted cost is readily available; if there have been past accounting failures, appropriate account correction will be required. The difference between cash or the fair market value of other assets received and the adjusted cost of the shares is reported as a gain or loss on the sale.

## Redemption of stock

Stock, particularly preferred issues, may be called in for redemption and cancellation by the corporation under conditions set by the issue.

The call price is ordinarily set at a figure higher than the price at which the stock was originally issued, but this call price may be more or less than the cost to the holder who acquired the stock from another person after its original issue. When stock is surrendered to the corporation, an entry is made charging cash and crediting the investment account. Any difference between the cash proceeds and the investment cost is recorded as a gain or a loss. For example, assume that an investor acquires 100 shares of Y Co. 6 per cent preferred stock, par $100, at 97. These shares are subsequently called in at 105. The stockholder makes the following entry:

| | | |
|---|---|---|
| Cash......................................... | 10,500 | |
| Investment in Y Co. 6% Preferred Stock......... | | 9,700 |
| Gain on Redemption of Y Co. Preferred Stock.... | | 800 |
| Received $10,500 on call of Y Co. preferred stock, cost $9,700. | | |

## Exchange of stock

When shares of stock are exchanged for other securities, the investor opens an account for the newly acquired security and closes the account of the security originally held. The new securities should be recorded at their fair market value or at the fair market value of the shares given up, whichever may be more clearly determinable, and a gain or loss is recognized on the exchange for the difference between the value assigned to the securities acquired and the carrying value of the shares given up. In the absence of a market value for either old or new securities, the carrying value of the shares given up will have to be recognized as the cost of the new securities. To illustrate, assume that the Z Co. offers its preferred stockholders two shares of no-par common stock in exchange for each share of $100 par preferred. An investor exchanges 100 shares of preferred stock carried at a cost of $10,000 for 200 shares of common stock. Common shares are quoted on the market at the time of exchange at $65. The exchange is recorded on the books of the stockholder by the following entry:

| | | |
|---|---|---|
| Z Co. Common Stock.......................... | 13,000 | |
| Z Co. Preferred Stock........................ | | 10,000 |
| Gain on Conversion of Z Co. Preferred Stock..... | | 3,000 |
| Acquired 200 shares of common stock valued at $65 in exchange for 100 shares of preferred stock costing $100. | | |

Recognition of a gain or a loss on a security exchange can be supported on the grounds that the exchange closes the transaction cycle relating to the original asset and opens a new cycle, the newly acquired asset requiring valuation in terms of current market. However, there are some who object to the recognition of gain or loss on the exchange of stock for other securities. These hold that there is no actual realization of gain or loss as there would be upon the outright sale of stock; here an asset has been replaced by a similar asset, such exchange calling for a transfer of cost from the asset originally held to the newly acquired asset.

## Ownership of controlling interest in stock

The acquisition of a majority interest in the stock of another company raises the question of whether such a relationship calls for special accounting in view of the control that is exercised and the effects that favorable and unfavorable operations have upon the welfare of the parent. There are two positions that are taken with respect to carrying investments in subsidiaries: (1) investments may be carried on a cost or a modified cost basis, comparable to investments in companies not so controlled, and (2) investments may be carried in a manner that reflects the degree of success or failure of the controlled unit. The first method emphasizes the legal factors in the relationship by recognizing only investment cost and is referred to as the *cost method;* the second method emphasizes the economic factors in the relationship by recognizing changes in the parent's equity in the subsidiary and is referred to as the *equity method.*

*Cost method.* When the cost method is used, the investment account reports the original cost of the investment in the subsidiary. Increases and decreases in the capital of the subsidiary resulting from profit and loss are disregarded on the books of the parent. Dividends representing distributions of subsidiary earnings are recorded by credits to Dividend Income. Earnings of a subsidiary, then, are recognized only as these are distributed in the form of dividends.

*Equity method.* When the equity method is used, the investment account reports investment cost modified by changes in the parent's equity in the subsidiary after subsidiary acquisition. The subsidiary is viewed as though it were a branch. Subsidiary net income increasing subsidiary net assets is recognized by the parent by a charge to the investment account and a credit to capital; a subsidiary net loss reducing subsidiary net assets is recognized by a credit to the investment and a charge to capital. Dividends reducing subsidiary net assets are recognized by a decrease in the investment balance.

Since earnings of a subsidiary are not legally realized by the parent until they are made available in the form of dividends, the capital credit should be made originally to an appraisal capital account. Losses would be recorded as decreases in such a balance. When dividends are received, two entries are called for: (1) the receipt of cash is recorded by a debit to Cash and a credit to the investment account, the increase in the subsidiary equity previously recognized now becoming available in the form of cash, and (2) appraisal capital equal to the amount of the dividend may now be recognized as Dividend Income, subsidiary earnings previously recognized as appraisal capital now having been realized by the parent. Dividend Income is closed into Profit and Loss at the end of the period and is ultimately reflected as an increase in Retained Earnings. The equity method thus consists of the periodic recognition of subsidiary profit or loss by the application of appraisal accounting.

The cost method and the equity method of accounting for a controlling interest in the stock of a subsidiary are illustrated in the following:

| Transaction | Cost Method of Carrying Investment | | Equity Method of Carrying Investment | |
|---|---|---|---|---|
| Jan. 1, 1964 Investment in 80,000 shares of Co. S stock at $5. (Co. S has 100,000 shares outstanding.) | Investment in Co. S Stock .....400,000<br>Cash ......... | 400,000 | Investment in Co. S Stock .....400,000<br>Cash ......... | 400,000 |
| June 30, 1964 Announcement by Co. S of net income of $30,000 for six-month period. (Parent's share of net income, 80% of $30,000.) | No entry | | Investment in Co. S Stock ..... 24,000<br>Appraisal Capital — Parent's Share of Undistributed Earnings of Co. S....... | 24,000 |
| Dec. 10, 1964 Payment of dividend by Co. S, $10,000. (Parent's share of dividend, 80% of $10,000.) | Cash............ 8,000<br>Dividend Income......... | 8,000 | Cash.......... 8,000<br>Investment in Co. S Stock ... 8,000<br>Appraisal Capital — Parent's Share of Undistributed Earnings of Co. S. 8,000<br>Dividend Income......... | 8,000 |
| Dec. 31, 1964 Announcement by Co. S of net loss of $5,000 for six-month period. (Parent's share of net loss, 80% of $5,000.) | No entry | | Appraisal Capital — Parent's Share of Undistributed Earnings of Co. S ........ 4,000<br>Investment in Co. S Stock.... | 4,000 |

The effect of subsidiary operations upon parent company earnings is the same in each case above. In each instance the parent recognizes revenue and a retained earnings increase of $8,000. However, when the cost method is used, the investment account remains unchanged at $400,000. When the equity method is used, the investment balance is $412,000, reflecting the net increase that has taken place in the parent's equity in the subsidiary as a result of the recognition of undistributed earnings of the subsidiary since date of acquisition, 80% of $15,000, or $12,000. The $12,000 increase in the investment balance is matched by a similar balance in the appraisal capital account.

If both the legal and the economic aspects of the relationship are to be disclosed on the statements of the parent company, cost method accounting should be accompanied by data provided in parenthetical or other appropriate form concerning net changes in the parent's equity in subsidiary earnings since control of the subsidiary was achieved; equity method accounting should be accompanied by data concerning original investment cost. Investment data might be shown on the balance sheet as follows:

(Cost Method)

Investment in Subsidiary Co. S
  (Investment is carried at original cost of 80,000 shares representing an 80% interest. The parent's share in undistributed earnings of Co. S since date of acquisition, Jan. 1, 1964, not included in the accounts, is 80% of $15,000, or $12,000.) . . . . . . . . . . . . . . . . . . . . .    $400,000

(Equity Method)

Investment in Subsidiary Co. S
  (Investment is carried at cost of 80,000 shares representing an 80% interest, $400,000, increased by the parent's share in undistributed earnings of Co. S since date of acquisition, Jan. 1, 1964, 80% of $15,000, or $12,000.). . . . . . . . . . . . . . . . . . . . . . . . . . . . . . . . . . .    $412,000

The use of the equity method calling for an investment balance that follows changes in subsidiary capital brings an economic interpretation of the relationship between parent and subsidiary into the separate accounts of the parent. However, the full economic implications to the parent of subsidiary ownership and operations can be presented only through the preparation of consolidated statements. Assets and liabilities of the subsidiary replace the investment account and are combined with assets and liabilities of the parent and increases or decreases in retained earnings of the subsidiary are combined with retained earnings of the parent in developing a consolidated balance sheet; income and expense balances of the subsidiary are combined with similar balances of the parent in developing a consolidated income statement. Statements are prepared as though parent and subsidiary were a single entity. Financial position and progress are reported for affiliated units from an overall economic point of view, and the legal realities underlying the relationships are disregarded. The detailed problems involved in the development of consolidated statements are beyond the scope of this discussion.

## Investments and tax accounting

Previous discussions have indicated that federal income tax laws may call for the use of a certain method when a number of methods, including the one prescribed, may be considered theoretically sound for financial reporting purposes. In other instances tax laws call for the use of methods that differ from those that might warrant application on theoretical grounds. Normally, the procedures that are to be required in the calculation of taxable income are applied in the accounts so that analysis of income and its restatement for tax purposes may be avoided. Such practice may be supportable when tax methods are acceptable, or when their application offers measurements that do not differ materially from those obtained through the use of alternative methods considered sounder under the circumstances. But the use in the books of tax methods that result in significant misstatements of net income and financial position cannot be condoned. In the event of conflict between acceptable reporting procedures and income tax procedures, financial statements should be developed in terms of the former, and supplementary records should be maintained to accumulate the data required for tax purposes.

## QUESTIONS

**1.** Distinguish between temporary investments and long-term investments.

**2.** How should each of the following be classified on the balance sheet?
   (a) Stock held for purposes of controlling the activities of a subsidiary.
   (b) Listed stock rights that are to be sold.
   (c) Stock that is intended to be transferred to a supplier in cancellation of an amount owed.

**3.** How would you record an investment in stock when it is acquired: (a) by exchange for an asset whose value is known? (b) by exchange for an asset whose value is not known, stock for patents, for example?

**4.** (a) Describe stock rights, stock dividends, and stock splits. (b) Distinguish between stock sold rights-on and stock sold ex-rights.

**5.** B. A. Beard receives $400 representing a dividend of $4.00 per share on Atlas Securities Co. stock, accompanied by a statement that $1.56 represents a distribution of income and $2.44 represents a dividend in partial liquidation. (a) What is the meaning of this statement? (b) What entry should Beard make in recording the dividend?

**6.** State how each of the following situations should be treated on the books and on the income tax return:
   (a) Announcement of dividends on stock and arrival of "record" date.
   (b) Sale of part of security holdings acquired in three lots.
   (c) Receipt of stock dividend of common on common.
   (d) Receipt of stock dividend of preferred stock on common.
   (e) Exchange of 1 share of common for 3 shares in a stock split-up.
   (f) Receipt of a dividend of 1 share of Z Co. stock for every 10 shares of Y Co. stock held.

**7.** (a) Define: (1) parent company, (2) subsidiary company. (b) How much stock ownership is required to exercise control?

**8.** (a) Describe the two methods for carrying investments in subsidiary companies and indicate how they differ. (b) What arguments can you give pro and con for each method?

## EXERCISES

**1.** R. T. Welding acquired 100 shares of Walsh Co. stock at 15. At a later date he received a stock dividend of 25 shares, which he sold at 12. Proceeds from the sale were recorded as income. What correction in the accounts would you make assuming: (a) the transaction took place currently and accounts are still open? (b) the transaction was recorded in the previous period and accounts are closed?

**2.** M. A. Parks holds stock of A-B Trading Co. acquired as follows:

| | | |
|---|---|---|
| Jan. 2, 1962 | 100 shares at $40 | $4,000 |
| Mar. 30, 1963 | 100 shares at $46 | 4,600 |

In 1964 Parks receives a 50% stock dividend. He then sells 150 shares at 34½. What entry would be made to record the sale? (Assume the use of first-in, first-out in recording the sale of shares.)

**3.** On April 1, N. N. Andrews purchased 1,000 shares of Doyle Corp. common stock, par $5, at 24. On July 7 Andrews received a stock dividend of 1 share for every 5 owned. On September 10 he received a cash dividend of 60 cents on the stock and was granted the right to purchase 1 share at $10 for every 4 shares held. On this date stock had a market value ex-rights of $15, and each right had a value of $1; stock cost was allocated on this basis. On December 12 Andrews sold 400 rights at 1⅛ and exercised the remaining rights. What entries will appear on Andrews' books as a result of the foregoing?

**4.** A. M. Peet owns 100 shares in Fabulous Prospectors, Inc., acquired in 1956 at a cost of $5 per share. Beginning in 1960, Peet received dividends of $2 per share each year, the corporation notifying him that a portion of this amount represented earnings and the balance a liquidating dividend, the allocation to be made as follows:

| | Income | Depletion Proceeds — Liquidating |
|---|---|---|
| 1960. . . . . . . . . . . . . . . | $.728 | $1.272 |
| 1961. . . . . . . . . . . . . . . | .68 | 1.32 |
| 1962. . . . . . . . . . . . . . . | .642 | 1.358 |
| 1963. . . . . . . . . . . . . . . | .44 | 1.56 |
| 1964. . . . . . . . . . . . . . . | .61 | 1.39 |

(a) What entries should Peet have made each year in recording the dividends? (b) How would you report the investment on Peet's balance sheet at the end of 1964?

**5.** The Wharton Co. acquires 425,000 shares of Bagby, Inc. in 1963 at a total cost of $1,600,000. Bagby, Inc. has 500,000 shares outstanding. What entries would be made by the Wharton Co. in 1964 for the following data, assuming the investment account is carried on (a) the cost basis? (b) the equity basis?

(1) Bagby, Inc. announces net income of $80,000 for the first six months and pays a cash dividend of 10 cents per share.

(2) Bagby, Inc. announces a net loss of $15,000 for the second six months and distributes a 5% stock dividend.

(3) The Wharton Co. acquires an additional 26,250 shares of Bagby, Inc. stock at 4.

## PROBLEMS

**10-1.** Transactions of Walter C. Young during 1964 included the following:

January 20   Purchased 300 shares of Wilson Steel Corp. at 80½ plus brokerage charges of $150.

June 10      Received a 50% stock dividend.

November  1  Received stock rights permitting the purchase of one share at $60 for every 4 shares held. On this date rights were being traded at $3 each and stock was being traded at $72 per share.

November 18  Exercised 400 rights which pertained to the stock acquired on January 20, and sold remaining rights at 2½ less brokerage charges of $3.

December 28  Sold 100 shares from the holdings acquired on January 20 at 70¼ less brokerage charges of $47.

*Instructions:* (1) Give journal entries to record the foregoing transactions. (Give computations in support of your entries.)

(2) Give the investment account balance on December 31, 1964, and the shares and costs making up this balance.

**10-2.** John A. Parks holds shares of Woodland, Ltd. acquired as follows:

| | | |
|---|---|---|
| 1960 | 200 shares | $28,800 |
| 1962 | 50 shares | 8,100 |

In 1964 the following takes place with respect to these holdings:

March  4  Stock was split on a 3 for 1 basis, Parks receiving 500 additional shares.

June   1  Received a fifty-cent cash dividend, and also rights to subscribe for additional shares as follows: 1 share could be purchased at $60, for every 5 shares held. On the date of rights issue, stock was selling ex-rights for 72½; and rights were selling for 2½; stock cost was apportioned on this basis.

June  15  Parks purchased 100 shares exercising rights identified with the 1960 stock purchase and sold remaining rights at 2 less brokerage charges of $20.

Nov.  30  Parks sold 100 shares acquired in 1960 at 58¼ less brokerage charges of $45.

*Instructions:* (1) Give journal entries to record the foregoing transactions. (Give computations in support of your entries.)

(2) Give the investment account balance on December 31 and the shares and costs making up this balance.

**10-3.** P. R. Coleman owns 640 shares of Dennison, Inc. acquired on May 1, 1960, for $30,000.

During 1963 and 1964 the following transactions take place with respect to this investment:

March 1, 1963   Received cash dividend of fifty cents and stock dividend of 25%.

Oct.   15, 1963   Received stock rights offering the purchase of 1 share at 75 for every 4 shares held. At this time stock was quoted ex-rights at 95 and rights were quoted at 5; stock cost was apportioned on this basis. Rights were exercised.

March 1, 1964   Received a cash dividend of fifty cents and a stock dividend of 25%.

Dec.    5, 1964   Received stock rights offering the purchase of 1 share at 70 for every 4 shares held. At this time stock was quoted ex-rights at 78 and rights were quoted at 2; stock cost was apportioned on this basis. Rights were sold at 2, less brokerage charges of $90.

*Instructions:* (1) Give journal entries to record the foregoing transactions.

(2) Give the investment account balance as of December 31, 1964, including shares and costs in support of this balance.

**10-4.** The following balances appeared in the ledger of the Holmes Company on December 31, 1961:

Investment in Murphy Co. Common, par $100, 200 shares.....   $19,500
Investment in Murphy Co. 5% Preferred, par $100, 100 shares.   $ 9,175

The Holmes Company uses the first-in, first-out method in accounting for stock transactions. In 1962, 1963, and 1964 the following transactions took place relative to the above investments:

Jan. 20, 1962   Holders of Murphy Co. 5% preferred were given the right to exchange their holdings into an equal number of Murphy Co. common, and the Holmes Co. made such exchange. Common shares on the date of exchange were quoted on the market at $130.50 per share.

Dec. 28, 1962   Received cash dividends of $2 per share on Murphy Co. common.

July 30, 1963   Received additional shares of Murphy Co. common in a 2-for-1 stock split. (Par value of common was reduced to $50.)

Dec. 28, 1963   Exercised option to receive one share of Murphy Co. common for each 20 shares held in lieu of a cash dividend of $2.40 per share held. The market value of Murphy Co. common on the date of distribution was $50 per share. Dividend income was recognized at the value of the shares received.

July  1, 1964   Received a stock dividend of 20% on Murphy Co. common.

Oct. 15, 1964   Received warrants representing right to purchase at par 1 share of Murphy Co. common for every 4 shares held. On date of warrants issue, the market value of shares ex-rights was $60, and of rights was $2.50; cost of the stock was allocated on this basis.

Oct. 30, 1964   Exercised 400 rights identified with the first lot of stock acquired and sold remaining rights at $2 per right less brokerage charges of $30.

Dec. 31, 1964   Sold 300 shares of Murphy Co. common at $52 per share less brokerage charges of $140.

*Instructions:* (1) Prepare journal entries to record the transactions in Murphy Co. holdings.

(2) Prepare a schedule showing the balance of Murphy Co. common held by Holmes Company on December 31, 1964.

**10-5.** You have instructed the bookkeeper for Wright Imports, Inc., to record all proceeds from security transactions directly in the investment accounts so that all of this data will be summarized there and will be available for analysis and proper disposition at the time of your audit. You find the following data in the account summarizing the investment with Northern Steel Common:

### Northern Steel Common

| | | | | | |
|---|---|---|---|---|---|
| 1/12/63 | Purchased 100 shares at 40 | 4,000 | 2/15/64 | Cash dividend | 400 |
| 7/15/63 | Purchased 100 shares at 44 | 4,400 | 3/25/64 | Proceeds from sale of 50 rights at 3 | 150 |
| 3/20/64 | Payment on purchase of 50 shares through exercise of 150 rights | 2,500 | 12/20/64 | Proceeds from sale of 100 shares at 60 | 6,000 |

Further analysis discloses that rights were received in March permitting the purchase of 1 share of stock at $50 for every 3 shares held. In May the company was informed that 5.125% of original stock cost was applicable to the rights.

*Instructions:* (1) Assuming the use of first-in, first-out in calculating cost on sales, give individual entries for each correction required in the investment account on December 31, 1964.

(2) Give the corrected balance for the investment account on December 31, 1964, and the shares and costs making up this balance.

**10-6.** The Warner and York Corporations each have 120,000 shares of no-par stock outstanding. Abbott, Inc. acquired 102,000 shares of Warner stock and 114,000 shares of York stock in 1960. Changes in retained earnings for Warner and York for 1963 and 1964 are as follows:

| | Warner Corporation | York Corporation |
|---|---|---|
| Retained earnings (deficit), Jan. 1, 1963 | $50,000 | ($10,000) |
| Cash dividends, 1963 | (30,000) | |
| | $20,000 | ($10,000) |
| Net income, 1963 | 50,000 | 80,000 |
| | $70,000 | $70,000 |
| Cash dividends, 1964 | | (15,000) |
| | $70,000 | $55,000 |
| Net income (loss), 1964 | (15,000) | (20,000) |
| Retained earnings, Dec. 31, 1964 | $55,000 | $35,000 |

*Instructions:* (1) Give any entries required on the books of Abbott, Inc. for 1963 and 1964, assuming that investments in subsidiaries are carried at cost.

(2) Give any entries required on the books of the parent for 1963 and 1964, assuming that investments in subsidiaries are carried on the equity basis.

# Chapter 11

# INVESTMENTS

## BONDS, FUNDS, AND MISCELLANEOUS ITEMS

### Investments in bonds

Bonds and related obligations such as long-term notes and mortgages are means of raising capital used by trading, manufacturing, transportation, real estate, and utility enterprises as well as by the various governmental units — federal, state, and local. Investments in securities evidencing such obligations are made by the individual investor. Business units acquire securities of this class both for short-term and long-term investment purposes. Large blocks of these securities are held by insurance companies, banks, trust companies, various investment organizations, and educational and charitable institutions. Such securities also make up a large part of the holdings of pension, bond retirement, and other funds maintained by corporations. Bonds and long-term notes provide for the payment of interest at periodic intervals and principal sums at stated maturity dates. The probability of fluctuation in price during the time these securities are held is generally less than that in the case of stock, and the receipt of revenue is more regular and assured.

### Kinds of bonds

A bond issue arises from a group contract known as an *indenture* between the borrowing corporation and investors. The bond issue is usually divided into a number of individual bonds of $1,000 denomination or par value. Bond interest payments are usually made at semi-annual intervals by the corporation or by an agent designated by the company. When all of the bonds mature on a single date, they are called *term bonds*; when bonds mature in installments, they are known as *serial bonds*.

Bonds issued by private corporations are classified as *secured* or *unsecured*. Secured bonds provide protection to the investor in the form of a mortgage covering the company's real estate and perhaps other property, or a pledge in the form of certain collateral. A *first-mortgage bond* represents a first claim against the property of a corporation in the event of the company's inability to meet bond interest and principal payments. A *second-mortgage bond* is a secondary claim ranking only after the claim of the first-mortgage bonds or senior issue has been completely satisfied. A *collateral trust bond* is usually secured by stocks and bonds of other corporations owned by the issuing company. Such securities are generally transferred to a trustee who holds them as collateral on behalf of the bondholders and, if necessary, will sell them to satisfy the bondholders' claim.

Bonds that are not protected by the pledge of certain property are frequently termed *debenture bonds*. Holders of debenture bonds simply rank as general creditors with other unsecured parties. The risk involved in such securities varies with the financial strength of the debtor. Debentures issued by a strong company may involve little risk; debentures issued by a weak company whose properties are already heavily mortgaged may involve considerable risk.

When another party promises to make payment on bonds if the issuing company fails to do so, the bonds are referred to as *guaranteed bonds*. A parent company, for example, may guarantee payment of the bonds issued by its subsidiaries.

Obligations known as *income bonds* have been issued when business failure has resulted in corporate reorganization. Such bonds require the payment of interest only to the extent of a company's current earnings. Income bonds may be cumulative or noncumulative. If cumulative, interest that cannot be paid in one year is carried over as a lien against future earnings; if noncumulative, no future lien arises from inability to meet interest payments.

The investor acquiring governmental obligations looks to the taxing authority of the issuing unit for the measure of its ability to raise money to meet debt service requirements. Certain government obligations are identified with government-owned enterprises, and principal and interest payments are made from the revenues accruing from such operations. These are known as *revenue bonds*.

Bonds may provide for their conversion into some other security at the option of the bondholder. Such bonds are known as *convertible bonds*. The conversion feature generally permits the owner of bonds to exchange his holdings into common stock. The bondholder is thus able to exchange his claim into an ownership interest if corporate operations prove successful and conversion becomes attractive; in the meantime he maintains the special rights of a creditor.

Other bond features may serve the issuer's interests. For example, bond indentures frequently give the issuing company the right to call and retire the bonds prior to their maturity. Such bonds are termed *callable bonds*. When a corporation wishes to reduce its outstanding indebtedness, bondholders are notified of the portion of the issue to be surrendered, and they are paid in accordance with call provisions. Interest does not accrue after the call date.

Bonds may be classified as (1) *registered bonds* and (2) *bearer* or *coupon bonds*. Registered bonds call for the registry of the owner's name on the corporation books. Transfer of bond ownership is similar to that for stock. When a bond is sold, the corporate transfer agent cancels the bond certificate surrendered by the seller and issues a new certificate to the buyer. Interest checks are mailed periodically to the bondholders of record. Bearer or coupon bonds are not recorded in the name of the owner, title to such bonds passing with delivery. Each bond is accompanied by coupons for individual interest payments covering the life of the issue. Coupons are clipped by the owner of the bond and presented to a bank for deposit or collection. The issue of bearer bonds eliminates the work of recording bond ownership changes and preparing and mailing periodic interest checks. But coupon bonds fail to offer the bondholder the protection found in registered bonds in the event bonds are lost or stolen. In some cases bonds provide interest coupons but require registry as to principal. Here, ownership safeguards are afforded while the routines involved in making interest payments are avoided.

## Bond yield

The yield that is offered on the purchase of bonds varies with the safety of the investment. When the financial condition and earnings of a corporation are such that payment of interest and principal on bonded indebtedness is assured, the interest rate that the company must offer to dispose of a bond issue is relatively low. As the risk factor increases, a higher interest return is necessary to attract investors. The interest rate stated on the bonds is known as the *contract rate* or *nominal rate*. Although bonds provide for the payment of interest at a certain rate, this rate may not be the same as the prevailing or *market rate* for bonds of similar quality at the time the issue is sold. Furthermore, the market rate constantly fluctuates. It is these factors that result in the difference between bond face values and the prices at which bonds sell on the market.

The purchase of bonds at face value implies agreement between the bond rate of interest and the prevailing market rate of interest. If the bond rate exceeds the market rate, then bonds will sell at a premium; if the bond rate is less than the market rate, the bonds will sell at a discount. The premium or the discount is the discounted value of the difference between the contract rate and the market rate of the series of interest payments. A declining market rate of interest subsequent to issuance of the bonds results in an increase in market value of the bonds; a rising market rate of interest results in a decrease in market value. The nominal rate corrected for the premium or the discount on the purchase gives the actual yield on the bonds, known as the *effective rate*.

Bond tables are available in determining the price to be paid for bonds if they are to provide a certain yield.

### Bond acquisition

Bonds may be acquired directly from the issuer or they may be purchased on the open market through securities exchanges or investment bankers.

An investment in bonds, whether short-term or long-term, is initially recorded at cost, which includes brokerage fees and any other costs incident to the purchase. Bonds acquired in exchange for assets or services are recorded at the fair market value of such consideration. When bonds and other securities are acquired for a lump sum, an apportionment of such cost among the securities is required. Purchase of bonds on a deferred payment basis calls for recognition of both asset and liability balances.

The purchase as well as the sale of bonds when made between interest payment dates requires calculation of the accrued interest which is added to the bond price. The amount paid for accrued interest on a purchase is subtracted from subsequent interest collections in measuring interest income; the amount received for accrued interest on a sale is recognized as interest income for the portion of the period that the bonds were held. In the calculation of accrued interest on bonds other than those issued by the United States Government, each month is considered to have 30 days. For example, the purchase on September 10 of bonds that pay interest on January 1 and July 1 requires calculation of interest for two months and 9 days or 69/360 year. In the case of U.S. Government bonds, the exact number of days must be determined and the year is considered to have 365 days in calculating the fractional part of the annual interest that has accrued. In the preceding example, then, calculation of interest would be made for 71/365 year.

### Amortization and accumulation procedures

When bonds are acquired as a temporary investment, investment cost is maintained in the accounts without adjustment. Interest is reported at amounts actually received. Upon disposition of the bonds, original cost is applied against net sales proceeds in arriving at the gain or the loss on the sale. If a similar procedure were to be followed on long-term bonds and these were held until maturity, a loss would emerge if bonds had been acquired at a premium and a gain if bonds had been acquired at a discount. But such "gains" and "losses" are in effect adjustments in interest of prior periods. Bonds are acquired at a premium in recognition of an interest rate that exceeds the rate prevailing at the time of bond purchase; hence interest income is properly viewed as consisting of the interest received less the portion of the receipt that may be considered to be a recovery of the premium originally paid. Bonds are acquired at a discount in view of an interest rate that is less than the prevailing rate; here interest income is properly viewed as interest received increased by a portion of the bond discount that will be realized at bond maturity. Although the attempt to refine income measurement by recognizing the change in bond value over its life is not warranted in the case of bonds acquired as a temporary investment, systematic adjustment for this factor is desirable when bonds are acquired as long-term holdings.

*Bond premium amortization.* A premium on bonds acquired is charged against interest received over the life of the bonds. The bond account is credited and Interest Income is charged each period for the part of the premium that is written off. The investment, then, moves towards its maturity value, and interest is reported periodically at the amount actually earned — the interest collected decreased by that part of the premium considered to have been recovered. The reduction of bonds to par by periodic charges to income is referred to as *bond premium amortization.*

*Bond discount accumulation.* A discount on bonds acquired is added to bond interest received over the life of the bonds. The bond account is charged and Interest Income is credited each period for the part of the discount that is accumulated. Here, too, the investment moves towards its maturity value, and interest is reported periodically at the amount actually earned — the interest collected increased by that part of the discount considered realized. Increase of bonds to par by periodic credits to income is called *bond discount accumulation.*

## Methods of amortization and accumulation

The *straight-line* method of amortization or accumulation provides for the recognition of an equal amount of premium or discount each period. Use of the *compound-interest* or *scientific* method requires that the effective earnings rate on the purchase of the bonds first be determined; interest income is then reported periodically at the effective rate, the difference between the amount earned and the amount actually received being recognized as an adjustment to the investment account. To illustrate, assume the purchase of 5-year bonds of $100,000, interest at 6% payable semiannually, at a price of 104⅜. Reference to bond tables indicates a yield of approximately 5% at this price. The tabulations on page 280 show the differences in use of the two methods.

The straight-line method of amortization offers a uniform interest amount for each period. The compound-interest method offers a uni-

### AMORTIZATION OF PREMIUM — STRAIGHT-LINE METHOD
$100,000 5-Year Bonds, Interest at 6% Payable Semiannually, Purchased at $104,375

| Interest Payment | A Interest (3% of Face Value) | B Premium Amortization (1/10 x $4,375) | C Effective Interest (A—B) | D Bond Carrying Value (D—B) |
|---|---|---|---|---|
| | | | | $104,375.00 |
| 1 | $3,000.00 | $437.50 | $2,562.50 | 103,937.50 |
| 2 | 3,000.00 | 437.50 | 2,562.50 | 103,500.00 |
| 3 | 3,000.00 | 437.50 | 2,562.50 | 103,062.50 |
| 4 | 3,000.00 | 437.50 | 2,562.50 | 102,625.00 |
| 5 | 3,000.00 | 437.50 | 2,562.50 | 102,187.50 |
| 6 | 3,000.00 | 437.50 | 2,562.50 | 101,750.00 |
| 7 | 3,000.00 | 437.50 | 2,562.50 | 101,312.50 |
| 8 | 3,000.00 | 437.50 | 2,562.50 | 100,875.00 |
| 9 | 3,000.00 | 437.50 | 2,562.50 | 100,437.50 |
| 10 | 3,000.00 | 437.50 | 2,562.50 | 100,000.00 |

### AMORTIZATION OF PREMIUM — COMPOUND-INTEREST METHOD
$100,000 5-Year Bonds, Interest at 6% Payable Semiannually, Purchased at $104,375
To Yield Approximately 5%

| Interest Payment | A Interest (3% of Face Value) | B Effective Interest ($2\frac{1}{2}$% of Bond Carrying Value) | C Premium Amortization (A—B) | D Bond Carrying Value (D—C) |
|---|---|---|---|---|
| | | | | $104,375.00 |
| 1 | $3,000.00 | $2,609.38 ($2\frac{1}{2}$% of $104,375.00) | $390.62 | 103,984.38 |
| 2 | 3,000.00 | 2,599.61 ($2\frac{1}{2}$% of $103,984.38) | 400.39 | 103,583.99 |
| 3 | 3,000.00 | 2,589.60 ($2\frac{1}{2}$% of $103,583.99) | 410.40 | 103,173.59 |
| 4 | 3,000.00 | 2,579.34 ($2\frac{1}{2}$% of $103,173.59) | 420.66 | 102,752.93 |
| 5 | 3,000.00 | 2,568.82 ($2\frac{1}{2}$% of $102,752.93) | 431.18 | 102,321.75 |
| 6 | 3,000.00 | 2,558.04 ($2\frac{1}{2}$% of $102,321.75) | 441.96 | 101,879.79 |
| 7 | 3,000.00 | 2,546.99 ($2\frac{1}{2}$% of $101,879.79) | 453.01 | 101,426.78 |
| 8 | 3,000.00 | 2,535.67 ($2\frac{1}{2}$% of $101,426.78) | 464.33 | 100,962.45 |
| 9 | 3,000.00 | 2,524.06 ($2\frac{1}{2}$% of $100,962.45) | 475.94 | 100,486.51 |
| 10 | 3,000.00 | 2,513.49 ($3,000 — $486.51)[1] | 486.51 | 100,000.00 |

[1] $2\frac{1}{2}$% of $100,486.51 would be $2,512.16. However, use of 5% when the effective rate was not exactly 5% has resulted in a small discrepancy that requires compensation upon recording the final receipt of interest. The bond account is reduced to face value, interest income being reduced by the premium balance at the time of bond maturity.

form earnings rate based upon a declining investment balance; since each interest payment represents a partial return of the premium, the investment is reduced each period and earnings, in turn, are correspondingly less.

The use of the two methods when bonds are acquired at a discount is illustrated in the tables that follow. Here it is assumed that 5-year bonds of $100,000, interest at 4% payable semiannually, are purchased to yield 5%, or at a price as shown by bond tables of $95,623.93.

The compound-interest method offers a uniform earnings rate based upon a successively higher investment balance. Periodic earnings are composed of the cash received plus the increase that is considered to have taken place in the investment balance. As the investment balance goes up each period, earnings are correspondingly greater.

The compound-interest method may be favored over the straight-line method because of the accuracy that it affords in income measurement.

### ACCUMULATION OF DISCOUNT — STRAIGHT-LINE METHOD
$100,000 5-Year Bonds, Interest at 4% Payable Semiannually, Purchased at $95,623.93

| Interest Payment | A Interest (2% of Face Value) | B Discount Accumulation (1/10 x $4,376.07) | C Effective Interest (A+B) | D Bond Carrying Value (D+B) |
|---|---|---|---|---|
| 1 | $2,000.00 | $437.61 | $2,437.61 | $ 95,623.93 |
| 2 | 2,000.00 | 437.61 | 2,437.61 | 96,061.54 |
| 3 | 2,000.00 | 437.61 | 2,437.61 | 96,499.15 |
| 4 | 2,000.00 | 437.61 | 2,437.61 | 96,936.76 |
| 5 | 2,000.00 | 437.61 | 2,437.61 | 97,374.37 |
| 6 | 2,000.00 | 437.61 | 2,437.61 | 97,811.98 |
| 7 | 2,000.00 | 437.61 | 2,437.61 | 98,249.59 |
| 8 | 2,000.00 | 437.61 | 2,437.61 | 98,687.20 |
| 9 | 2,000.00 | 437.61 | 2,437.61 | 99,124.81 |
| 10 | 2,000.00 | 437.58 | 2,437.58 | 99,562.42 |
|  |  |  |  | 100,000.00 |

### ACCUMULATION OF DISCOUNT — COMPOUND-INTEREST METHOD
$100,000 5-Year Bonds, Interest at 4% Payable Semiannually, Purchased at $95,623.93
To Yield 5%

| Interest Payment | A Interest (2% of Face Value) | B Effective Interest ($2\frac{1}{2}$% of Bond Carrying Value) | C Discount Accumulation (B—A) | D Bond Carrying Value (D+C) |
|---|---|---|---|---|
| 1 | $2,000.00 | $2,390.60 ($2\frac{1}{2}$% of $95,623.93) | $390.60 | $ 95,623.93 |
| 2 | 2,000.00 | 2,400.36 ($2\frac{1}{2}$% of $96,014.53) | 400.36 | 96,014.53 |
| 3 | 2,000.00 | 2,410.37 ($2\frac{1}{2}$% of $96,414.89) | 410.37 | 96,414.89 |
| 4 | 2,000.00 | 2,420.63 ($2\frac{1}{2}$% of $96,825.26) | 420.63 | 96,825.26 |
| 5 | 2,000.00 | 2,431.15 ($2\frac{1}{2}$% of $97,245.89) | 431.15 | 97,245.89 |
| 6 | 2,000.00 | 2,441.93 ($2\frac{1}{2}$% of $97,677.04) | 441.93 | 97,677.04 |
| 7 | 2,000.00 | 2,452.97 ($2\frac{1}{2}$% of $98,118.97) | 452.97 | 98,118.97 |
| 8 | 2,000.00 | 2,464.30 ($2\frac{1}{2}$% of $98,571.94) | 464.30 | 98,571.94 |
| 9 | 2,000.00 | 2,475.91 ($2\frac{1}{2}$% of $99,036.24) | 475.91 | 99,036.24 |
| 10 | 2,000.00 | 2,487.85 ($2,000+$487.85)[1] | 487.85 | 99,512.15 |
|  |  |  |  | 100,000.00 |

[1] $12\frac{1}{2}$% of $99,512.15 would be $2,487.80. By earlier computations to the nearest cent, an element of error was introduced. Compensation for the error is made when the final receipt of interest is recorded. The bond account is raised to face value, interest income being increased by the discount balance at the time of bond maturity.

However, because of its simplicity the straight-line procedure is normally preferred except in those instances where large blocks of bonds are acquired at a substantial premium or discount and use of this method would give results that differ materially from the scientific procedures. Straight-line amortization is accepted for income tax purposes. Use of this method is assumed in the remaining illustrations of this chapter.

## Accounting for long-term investments in bonds

The entries for a long-term investment in bonds are illustrated in the example that follows. Assume that an investor acquires 6% bonds, face value $100,000, for $107,000, with interest payable semiannually on April 1 and October 1. Bonds are acquired on July 1, 1963, and mature on April 1, 1972. Books are to be adjusted and closed at the end of each calendar year.

A schedule may be prepared by the investor to summarize premium amortization and earnings over the period the bonds are to be held. This schedule can then be used in making periodic adjustments. The bond premium is to be spread over the period that bonds will be earning interest, July 1, 1963, to April 1, 1972, or 105 months. An amortization schedule is prepared as follows:

AMORTIZATION SCHEDULE — STRAIGHT-LINE METHOD

| Period | A<br>Interest Received (including adjustments for accruals) | Number of Months | Premium Amortization | | | E<br>Bond Carrying Value (E−C) |
|---|---|---|---|---|---|---|
| | | | B<br>Fraction of Premium to be Amortized | C<br>Amount of Premium Amortization (Bx$7,000) | D<br>Effective Interest (A−C) | |
| | | | | | | $107,000 |
| July 1 (acquisition date) to Dec. 31, 1963 | $3,000 | 6 | 6/105 | $ 400 | $2,600 | 106,600 |
| Year Ended Dec. 31, 1964 | 6,000 | 12 | 12/105 | 800 | 5,200 | 105,800 |
| Year Ended Dec. 31, 1965 | 6,000 | 12 | 12/105 | 800 | 5,200 | 105,000 |
| Year Ended Dec. 31, 1966 | 6,000 | 12 | 12/105 | 800 | 5,200 | 104,200 |
| Year Ended Dec. 31, 1967 | 6,000 | 12 | 12/105 | 800 | 5,200 | 103,400 |
| Year Ended Dec. 31, 1968 | 6,000 | 12 | 12/105 | 800 | 5,200 | 102,600 |
| Year Ended Dec. 31, 1969 | 6,000 | 12 | 12/105 | 800 | 5,200 | 101,800 |
| Year Ended Dec. 31, 1970 | 6,000 | 12 | 12/105 | 800 | 5,200 | 101,000 |
| Year Ended Dec. 31, 1971 | 6,000 | 12 | 12/105 | 800 | 5,200 | 100,200 |
| Jan. 1 to Apr. 1, 1972 (maturity date) | 1,500 | 3 | 3/105 | 200 | 1,300 | 100,000 |
| | | 105 | 105/105 | $7,000 | | |

Entries for bond ownership in 1963 and 1964 appear below:

| Transaction | Entry |
|---|---|
| JULY 1, 1963<br>Purchased 100, $1,000, 6% bonds of Hope Corp. at 106¾, bonds maturing on April 1, 1972. Interest is payable semiannually on April 1 and October 1. Payment was made as follows:<br>  Bonds of $100,000 at 106¾.... $106,750<br>  Costs of purchase.......... 250<br>  Accrued interest, April 1–July 1................. 1,500<br><br>  $108,500 | Investment in Hope Corp. 6's............. 107,000<br>Interest Income........ 1,500[1]<br>Cash..............  108,500 |
| OCTOBER 1, 1963<br>Received semiannual interest. | Cash................ 3,000<br>Interest Income......  3,000 |
| DECEMBER 31, 1963<br>(a) To record accrued interest for 3 months, and (b) to amortize bond premium applicable to current year. Amortization: period held in current year, 6 months; total life of bond issue, 8¾ years or 105 months; current amortization, $\frac{6}{105}$ x $7,000, or $400 (or 6 x $66.66⅔, monthly amortization=$400). | (a) Accrued Interest on Investment in Bonds............ 1,500<br>    Interest Income...  1,500<br><br>(b) Interest Income.... 400<br>    Investment in Hope Corp. 6's...  400 |

[1]As indicated in Chapter 5, payment for accrued interest can be recorded by a charge to an accrued receivable balance; this account would be closed when interest is collected.

| Transaction | Entry |
|---|---|
| JANUARY 1, 1964<br>To reverse 1963 accrued interest. | Interest Income........ 1,500<br>  Accrued Interest on<br>  Investment in Bonds.. 1,500 |
| APRIL 1, 1964<br>Received semiannual interest. | Cash................ 3,000<br>  Interest Income...... 3,000 |
| OCTOBER 1, 1964<br>Received semiannual interest. | Cash................ 3,000<br>  Interest Income...... 3,000 |
| DECEMBER 31, 1964<br>(a) To record accrued interest for 3 months, and (b) to amortize bond premium applicable to current year, $\frac{12}{105}$ x $7,000, or $800 (or 12 x $66.66$\frac{2}{3}$, monthly amortization = $800). | (a) Accrued Interest<br>   on Investment in<br>   Bonds............ 1,500<br>    Interest Income... 1,500<br>(b) Interest Income.... 800<br>    Investment in<br>    Hope Corp. 6's... 800 |

Entries similar to those for 1964 will be made until 1972. The reversing entry required on January 1, 1972, and the entries on April 1, 1972, when the last interest payment is received, will be as follows:

| Transaction | Entry |
|---|---|
| JANUARY 1, 1972<br>To reverse 1971 accrued interest. | Interest Income........ 1,500<br>  Accrued Interest on<br>  Investment in Bonds.. 1,500 |
| APRIL 1, 1972<br>(a) To record amortization for last 3-month period, $\frac{3}{105}$ x $7,000, or $200 (or 3 x $66.66$\frac{2}{3}$, monthly amortization = $200), and (b) to record receipt of semiannual interest and principal amount. | (a) Interest Income.... 200<br>    Investment in<br>    Hope Corp. 6's... 200<br>(b) Cash............. 103,000<br>    Investment in<br>    Hope Corp. 6's... 100,000<br>    Interest Income... 3,000 |

When bonds are acquired at a discount, the investment account is raised to par by discount accumulation as illustrated below:

| Transaction | Entry |
|---|---|
| OCTOBER 11, 1963<br>Purchased 100, $1,000, 5$\frac{1}{4}$% bonds of Atlas, Inc. at 96$\frac{1}{2}$, bonds maturing on March 1, 1969. Interest is payable semiannually on March 1 and September 1.<br>Payment was made as follows:<br>  Bonds of $100,000 at 96$\frac{1}{2}$... $96,500.00<br>  Costs of purchase......... 250.00<br>  Interest, Sept. 1–Oct. 11,<br>  40 days, at 5$\frac{1}{4}$%.......... 583.33<br>                 $97,333.33 | Investment in Atlas,<br>  Inc. 5$\frac{1}{4}$'s........... 96,750.00<br>Interest Income...... 583.33<br>  Cash............. 97,333.33 |
| DECEMBER 31, 1963<br>(a) To record accrued interest for 4 months, and (b) to accumulate bond discount applicable to current year. Accumulation: period held in current year, 3 months; total life of bond issue, 5$\frac{5}{12}$ years, or 65 months; current accumulation, $\frac{3}{65}$ x $3,250, or $150 (or 3 x $50, monthly accumulation = $150). | (a) Accrued Interest<br>   on Investment in<br>   Bonds.......... 1,750.00<br>    Interest Income. 1,750.00<br>(b) Investment in<br>   Atlas, Inc. 5$\frac{1}{4}$'s... 150.00<br>    Interest Income 150.00 |

| Transaction | Entry | | |
|---|---|---|---|
| JANUARY 1, 1964<br>To reverse 1963 accrued income. | Interest Income......<br>  Accrued Interest on<br>  Investment in Bonds | 1,750.00 | 1,750.00 |
| MARCH 1, 1964<br>Received semiannual interest. | Cash...............<br>  Interest Income.... | 2,625.00 | 2,625.00 |
| SEPTEMBER 1, 1964<br>Received semiannual interest. | Cash...............<br>  Interest Income.... | 2,625.00 | 2,625.00 |
| DECEMBER 31, 1964<br>(a) To record accrued interest for 4 months, and (b) to accumulate bond discount applicable to current year, $\frac{12}{12}$ x $3,250, or $600 (or 12 x $50, monthly accumulation = $600). | (a) Accrued Interest on<br>  Investment in<br>  Bonds..........<br>    Interest Income<br>(b) Investment in<br>  Atlas, Inc. 5¼'s...<br>    Interest Income. | 1,750.00<br><br><br>600.00 | <br><br>1,750.00<br><br><br>600.00 |

It is necessary to set some arbitrary minimum time unit in the amortization of bond premium or the accumulation of bond discount. The month is used in the text as the minimum unit. Transactions occurring during the first half of the month are treated as though they were made at the beginning of the month; transactions occurring during the second half are treated as though made at the start of the following month. Use of a longer term, such as the quarter or half year, is possible, although this offers less accuracy than the use of a shorter time unit.

Amortization of bond premium and accumulation of bond discount are recognized in the foregoing examples at the end of the investor's fiscal period and also at the time of bond redemption or sale. It would be possible to recognize amortization or accumulation whenever interest is received. But it would still be necessary to bring the amortization or the accumulation up to date at the end of the year when accrued interest is recognized. Instead of making the adjustment several times a year and for fractional periods, the adjustment is more conveniently made for a full year at the end of each fiscal year, except for the first and last years when fractional parts of a year are involved.

### Sale of bonds prior to maturity

Sometimes bonds held as a long-term investment are sold prior to their maturity. The book value of the bonds must be determined as of date of sale. This requires bond premium or discount adjustment to date of sale. The difference between the book value on the date of sale and the cash proceeds from the sale represents the net gain or loss. To illustrate a sale, assume that the bonds of Atlas, Inc. in the previous example are not held until maturity, but are sold at 97 plus accrued interest on February 1, 1965. Entries in 1965 are:

| Transaction | Entry |
|---|---|

| Transaction | Entry | | |
|---|---|---|---|
| JANUARY 1, 1965<br>To reverse 1964 accrued interest. | Interest Income....... 1,750.00<br>  Accrued Interest on<br>  Investment in Bonds | | 1,750.00 |
| FEBRUARY 1, 1965<br>To record accumulation of discount to date of sale:<br>  $\frac{1}{65}$ x $3,250, or $50. | Investment in Atlas, Inc.<br>  5¼'s................. 50.00<br>    Interest Income..... | | 50.00 |
| To record sale of bonds:<br>(a) Accrued interest,<br>  September 1–February 1... $2,187.50 | (a) Cash............. 2,187.50<br>    Interest  Income | | 2,187.50 |
| (b) Book value of bonds:<br>  Cost.................. $96,750.00<br>  Plus discount accumulation<br>  to date of sale:<br>    1963  $150.00<br>    1964   600.00<br>    1965    50.00     800.00<br>               $97,550.00<br>  Sales proceeds $97,000.00<br>  Less costs of sale   200.00  96,800.00<br>  Net loss................ $   750.00 | (b) Cash........... 96,800.00<br>  Loss  on  Sale  of<br>  Atlas, Inc. 5¼'s.. 750.00<br>    Investment  in<br>    Atlas, Inc. 5¼'s. | | 97,550.00 |

The two cash entries may be combined as a single compound entry. The bond interest income for January, 1965, is $487.50, consisting of interest received, $2,187.50, decreased by the interest relating to 1964, $1,750.00, and increased by discount accumulation for the current period, $50.00. This is the same as the monthly interest recognized in 1963 and 1964.

## Bond redemption prior to maturity

Bonds that are callable by the issuer prior to their maturity generally provide for the payment of a premium to the holder in the event this option is exercised. When bonds are called, Cash is debited for the call price received, the investment account is credited for the book value of the bonds called, and a gain or loss is reported for the difference. The contract with bondholders normally provides for the payment of accrued interest to the bond call date. When bonds are called on a regular interest payment date, the bondholder will receive the call price plus interest for a full period. Interest income is credited for the interest received.

## Bond conversion

When bonds are converted into another security, accounts are opened for the newly acquired security and the bond investment balance is closed. The procedures that are followed by the investor are similar to those previously described for the exchange of stock for other securities.

The newly acquired security is recorded at its market value, and the difference between this value and the book value of the bonds surrendered is reported as gain or loss. Before an exchange is recorded, the investment account should be brought up to date for discount accumulation or premium amortization. Interest collected at the time of the exchange is reported as interest income.

## Bond valuation

The market value of bonds varies with changes in the financial strength of the issuing company, changes in the level of interest rates, and shrinkage in the remaining life of the issue. In the absence of material price declines, bonds held as long-term investments are reported on the balance sheet at book value. This book value approaches par as the bonds move closer to maturity. To this extent, then, the accounting can be considered to follow a similar change that is taking place on the market as the bond life is reduced and a correspondingly lower valuation is attached to the difference between the actual rate and the market rate of remaining interest payments. Although investments are properly reported at book value, parenthetical disclosure of the aggregate market value of the securities is desirable as a means of making the statements more informative.

A material decline in bond value, however, as a result of unfavorable developments relating to the issuer cannot be ignored. Assume, for example, that the issuing company has found it impossible to meet redemption fund requirements, which suggests that it may have difficulties in paying off the obligation at its maturity. Even more serious, assume that there has been default on bond interest payments. When significant investment loss is indicated, entries to record the loss should be made. Such loss may be established through reference to current market quotations, investigation of prices at which other bonds can be sold, or special appraisal of the assets that are pledged as security on the bonded indebtedness.

When bonds are purchased *flat*, that is, when interest on bonds is in arrears and one price is paid for the bonds together with all accrued and unpaid interest, this price is recorded as the bond investment cost. Any amounts subsequently received on the bonds, whether designated as payments of principal or defaulted interest, should be treated as a recovery of investment cost as long as there is uncertainty of ultimate recovery of more than the amount invested. No interest should be accrued on the bonds until solvency of the debtor is restored and the regular receipt of interest is assured. Such bonds are reported at their unrecovered cost with full information as to the nature of the investment.

## Long-term notes and mortgages

Investments in long-term notes and mortgages have many character-istics in common with bond investments. During their lives they provide interest, and at their maturities they call for specified cash payments. Long-term notes and mortgages should be recorded at cost, or at their fair market value when acquired in connection with a sale of property. Any difference between an acquisition value and a maturity value calls for adjustments to income over the life of the investment. A note or mortgage may be acquired at a considerable discount when it involves a relatively large element of risk. Such acquisition raises the question of possible failure to recover the full amount of the obligation at maturity. When this possibility is foreseen, the investor may choose to carry the investment without accumulating the discount. If full payment is re-ceived at maturity, the discount would be recognized as interest at that time. Notes and mortgages should be analyzed in terms of installment maturities; the part that is due within one year is reported as a current asset, the balance as a long-term investment.

## Kind of funds

Cash and other assets set apart for certain common purposes are called *funds, sinking funds,* or *redemption funds.* Some funds are to be used for specified current purposes such as the payment of expenses or the dis-charge of current obligations and are appropriately reported as current assets. Examples of these are petty cash funds, payroll funds, interest funds, dividend funds, and withholding, social security, and other tax funds. Other funds are accumulated over a long term for such purposes as the acquisition or the replacement of properties, the retirement of long-term indebtedness, the redemption of capital stock, or possible future contingencies and are properly considered noncurrent and re-ported under the investment heading. Examples of these are bond re-tirement funds, preferred stock redemption funds, pension funds, funds for the acquisition of plant and equipment, and funds to meet costs arising from accidents, fires, and other contingencies.

A fund may be established through the voluntary action of manage-ment or it may be established as a result of contractual requirements. It may arise from a single deposit or from a series of deposits, or it may be composed of the sum of the deposits plus the earnings identified with such deposits. The fund may be used for a single purpose, such as the retirement of bonds at maturity, or it may be used for several related purposes, such as the periodic payment of interest on bonds, the retire-ment of bonds at various intervals, and the ultimate retirement of the remaining bonded indebtedness.

When a fund is voluntarily created by management, control of the fund and its disposition is an arbitrary matter depending upon the wishes of management. When a fund is created through some legal requirement, it must be administered and applied in accordance therewith. Such a fund is generally administered by one or more trustees under an agreement known as a *trust indenture*.

Although a fund that is to be applied to the retirement of debt may be controlled by a trustee, it should not be viewed as a reduction in debt unless it has been specifically agreed that payment to the trustee frees the transferor from any further obligation. Normally, the trustee plan is simply an arrangement for debt liquidation, and losses from fund misappropriation or from declines in the values of fund assets do not relieve the corporation of responsibility for full payment. Under such circumstances the fund calls for the same accounting that would be followed for a fund controlled by its owner.

## Fund accumulation

When a corporation is required by agreement to establish a fund for a certain purpose such as the retirement of bonds or the redemption of stock, the agreement generally provides that (1) fund deposits shall be fixed amounts or shall vary according to gross revenue, net income, or units of product sold, or (2) deposits shall be equal periodic sums which together with earnings will produce a certain amount at some future date. The latter arrangement is based on compound-interest factors, and compound-interest tables are used in determining the equal periodic deposits.

## Accounting for funds

Fund transactions involving investments in stocks and bonds call for recording and valuation procedures as described in the preceding pages. When a fund is administered by the company, fund transactions may be recorded currently on the company records. When a fund is administered by a trustee, fund transactions should be summarized by the trustee and periodic reports submitted to the company. This information can then be recorded on the company books. The trustee should maintain records enabling him to report on his fund stewardship. Such records are best kept in double-entry form.

The following example illustrates the accounting that may be employed for a fund. This example assumes the establishment of a fund for the retirement of bonds and gives the entries for the fund accumulation in the first year and for debt retirement in the last year.

| Transaction | Entry | | |
|---|---|--:|--:|
| **1964:**<br>JUNE 30, 1964<br>The Powell Corporation made the first of a series of 20 equal semiannual deposits of $40,000 to bond fund. | Bond Fund Cash.....<br>Cash............. | 40,000 | 40,000 |
| JULY 6, 1964<br>Purchased bond fund securities for $35,750, which includes accrued interest of $150. | Bond Fund Securities..<br>Bond Fund Income...<br>Bond Fund Cash.... | 35,600<br>150 | 35,750 |
| DECEMBER 1, 1964<br>Received interest on bond fund securities, $900. | Bond Fund Cash.....<br>Bond Fund Income. | 900 | 900 |
| DECEMBER 31, 1964<br>Paid bond fund custodian fees, $200. | Bond Fund Expenses..<br>Bond Fund Cash.... | 200 | 200 |
| Made second deposit of $40,000 to bond fund. | Bond Fund Cash.....<br>Cash............. | 40,000 | 40,000 |
| To record accrued interest on bond fund securities and cash deposits, $225. | Accrued Interest on Bond Fund Securities..<br>Bond Fund Income. | 225 | 225 |
| To record amortization of premium on bond fund securities, $100. | Bond Fund Income...<br>Bond Fund Securities | 100 | 100 |
| To close bond fund income and expense balances. | Bond Fund Income<br>Bond Fund Expenses<br>Profit and Loss..... | 875 | 200<br>675 |
| **1973:**<br>DECEMBER 31, 1973<br>Sold bond fund securities, book value after amortization entries, $1,060,000, for $1,100,000, including accrued interest, $8,000, total proceeds being added to bond fund cash on hand on this date of $15,000. | Bond Fund Cash.....<br>Bond Fund Securities<br>Bond Fund Income.<br>Gain on Sale of Bond Fund Securities..... | 1,100,000 | 1,060,000<br>8,000<br>32,000 |
| Paid bonded indebtedness from bond fund cash, $1,000,000. | Bonds Payable.......<br>Bond Fund Cash.... | 1,000,000 | 1,000,000 |
| Transferred bond fund cash on hand after payment of bonds to cash account. | Cash...............<br>Bond Fund Cash.... | 115,000 | 115,000 |
| To close nominal accounts relating to bond fund activities. | Bond Fund Income<br>Gain on Sale of Bond Fund Securities.......<br>Profit and Loss..... | 8,000<br><br>32,000 | 40,000 |

## Bond fund assets at the end of 1964 are as follows:

| | |
|---|--:|
| Bond Fund Cash................................... | $44,950 |
| Bond Fund Securities.............................. | 35,500 |
| Accrued Interest on Bond Fund Securities.................. | 225 |
| Total......................................... | $80,675 |

Bond fund income for 1964 is $875 and bond fund expense is $200; the difference, $675, represents the fund earnings. This amount is reported on the income statement as Other Revenue. A gain or a loss on the sale of fund securities would be recognized as an extraordinary item. The individual assets in the fund would be reported under the investments heading on the balance sheet.

The foregoing illustration assumed purchase of securities other than bonds originally issued by the company. Bond fund cash is commonly used to purchase a company's own bonds. Such fund use frequently operates to support a firm market price for the issue, since the company can enter the market whenever the market price makes retirement of the company's bonds attractive.

When a company retires its own bonds through bond fund cash, the liability is canceled, the fund cash account is credited, and a loss or gain on the retirement is recorded. For example, assume that the books of a company show bonds of $100,000 outstanding with an unamortized bond discount balance relating to this issue of $3,500. The company acquires and formally retires bonds with a face value of $20,000 at a cost of $19,500. The entry to record the bond retirement follows:

| | | |
|---|---|---|
| Bonds Payable. . . . . . . . . . . . . . . . . . . . . . . . . . . . . . . . . . . | 20,000 | |
| Loss on Bond Retirement. . . . . . . . . . . . . . . . . . . . . . . . | 200 | |
|     Bond Fund Cash. . . . . . . . . . . . . . . . . . . . . . . . . . . . | | 19,500 |
|     Unamortized Bond Discount. . . . . . . . . . . . . . . . . . . | | 700 |
| To record bond retirement as follows: | | |
|     Amount paid on retirement. . | $19,500 | |
|     Book value of bonds retired: | | |
|     face value of bonds, $20,000, | | |
|     less unamortized discount | | |
|     applicable to bonds, $700. . . | 19,300 | |
|     Loss on retirement . . . . . . . . . | $    200 | |

When bonds are acquired by a trustee and kept "alive," such bonds are sometimes carried on the books the same as any other investment. The treatment of bond reacquisition as an investment is not supportable in theory. Reacquired bonds, even though in the hands of a corporate agent, cannot be considered an asset by the corporation. Such bonds are, in effect, evidence of debt retirement. Reacquired bonds may be sold and thus provide additional cash, but this is also true of unissued bonds; both reacquired and unissued bonds are no more than instruments that may be used in future borrowing.

The treatment of bond reacquisition as a retirement by an entry similar to that given above may call for an increase in the deposit schedule to compensate for the loss of interest in the fund accumulation. The larger transfers to the fund, however, are accompanied by reduced interest payments in the absence of interest accruals on bonds reacquired by the trustee. If bonds are resold, the sale is treated just as an original issue, any premium or discount on the reissue being identified with the remaining life of the bond lot resold. The treatment of bond reacquisitions as bond retirement should be followed even though this calls for adjustments in a plan for systematic fund accumulation.

The accounting procedures described for the bond fund are applicable for other investment funds mentioned earlier.

## Funds and retained earnings appropriations

The creation of a fund is frequently accompanied by an appropriation of retained earnings. Although the two operations may be related, the nature and purpose of the fund and of the appropriation are different. The establishment of a fund insures the availability of assets for a specific purpose. The appropriation of retained earnings makes a portion of past earnings temporarily unavailable as a basis for dividend declaration; the latter action prevents working capital from being depleted by both fund accumulations and dividend payments.

Fund accumulation accompanied by periodic appropriations of retained earnings and the limitation of dividends may be required by the terms of the contract with the creditor group. On the other hand, such actions may be voluntarily authorized by management. In certain instances, funds and appropriated earnings may be maintained at identical balances; in other instances, such a relationship may not be required or authorized.

## Miscellaneous investments

Many assets could be named that are of an auxiliary character in terms of central business activities and are properly reportable under the investments heading. If such assets do not produce current interest, dividends, or other revenue, it is expected by management that they will ultimately have a favorable business effect in some other way. For example, a purchase of adjoining property is made in advance of needs because it is felt that such acquisition in the future will be possible only at considerably higher costs. Or a long-term loan is made to an old customer because it is believed that the loan will carry him through a financial crisis and he will continue as a profitable customer after the present strain has passed. Several investment items that are commonly found are considered in the remaining sections of this chapter.

### Cash surrender value of life insurance

Many business enterprises carry life insurance policies on the lives of their executives. It is recognized that the business has a definite stake in the continuing services of its officers. In some cases the insurance plan affords a financial cushion in the event of the loss of such personnel. In other instances, the insurance offers a means of purchasing a deceased owner's interest in the business, thus avoiding a transfer of such interest to some outside party or the need to liquidate the business in effecting settlement with the estate of the deceased.

Insurance premiums that exceed basic insurance charges produce a *cash surrender value* that is payable in the event of policy surrender and cancellation. If this cash surrender value belongs to the business, it should be reported as an investment. Insurance expense for a fiscal period is the difference between the amount paid for insurance and the increase in the cash surrender value of the policy. The increase in the cash surrender value is ordinarily relatively uniform after the first year of the policy. At the end of the first year there may be no cash surrender value, or, if there is such a value, it may be quite low, because the insurance company must recover certain costs in connection with selling and initiating the policy. The cost of life insurance to the business, then, may be considered correspondingly high during the first year of the policy because of the starting costs involved.

An insurance policy with a cash surrender value also has a *loan value*; this is the amount that the insurance company will permit the insured to borrow on the policy. When the insured uses the policy as a basis for a loan, the amount borrowed should be recorded as a liability and not as a reduction in the cash value. Such a loan may be liquidated by payments of principal and interest, or the loan may be continuing, to be applied against the insurance proceeds upon policy cancellation or ultimate settlement.

The loan that an insurance company will make on a policy is normally limited to the policy cash surrender value at the end of the policy year less discount from the loan date to the cash surrender value date. For example, assume a cash surrender value of $3,000 at the end of a fifth policy year. The maximum loan value on the policy at the beginning of the fifth policy year, assuming that the insurance premium for the fifth year is paid, is $3,000 discounted for one year. If the discount rate applied by the insurance company is 5%, the policy loan value is calculated as follows: $3,000 ÷ 1.05 = $2,857.14.

Although it would be possible for the insured to recognize policy loan values instead of cash surrender values, the latter practice is generally followed.

The insured may authorize the insurance company to apply any dividends that may be declared upon insurance policies to the reduction of the annual premium payment or to the increase in insurance cash surrender value, or he may collect such dividends in cash. Dividends should be viewed as a reduction in the cost of carrying insurance rather than as a source of supplementary revenue. Hence, if dividends are applied to the reduction of the annual premium, Insurance Expense is simply debited for the net amount paid. If the dividend is applied to the increase in the policy cash surrender value or if it is collected in cash, it should still be treated as an offset to the periodic expense of carrying the policy; the policy cash surrender value or Cash, then, is charged and Insurance Expense is credited. After a number of years, the periodic dividends plus increases in the cash surrender value may exceed the premium payments, thus resulting in revenue rather than expense on policy holdings.

Collection of a policy calls for cancellation of any cash surrender balance. Collection of a policy upon death of the insured requires the recognition of an increase in capital represented by the difference between the insurance proceeds and the balances relating to the insurance policy. The nature of the insurance policies carried and their coverage should be disclosed by appropriate comment on the balance sheet.

The entries to be made for an insurance contract are illustrated in the example that follows. The Andrews Manufacturing Company insured the life of its president, W. E. Andrews, on October 1, 1962. The amount of the policy was $50,000; the annual premiums were $2,100. The following table gives for each of the first three policy years the gross premium, the dividend, the net premium, the increase in cash value, and the net expense for the insurance.

| Year | Gross Premium | Dividend | Net Premium | Increase in Cash Value | Insurance Expense for Year |
|------|------|------|------|------|------|
| 1 | $2,100 | $—— | $2,100 | $ —— | $2,100 |
| 2 | 2,100 | —— | 2,100 | 1,150 | 950 |
| 3 | 2,100 | 272 | 1,828 | 1,300 | 528 |

The fiscal period for the company is the calendar year. Mr. Andrews died on July 1, 1965. The entries made in recording transactions relating to the insurance contract follow:

| Transaction | Entry |
|---|---|
| **OCTOBER 1, 1962**<br>Paid first annual premium, $2,100. | Prepaid Insurance.... 2,100.00<br>　Cash............. 　　　　2,100.00 |
| **DECEMBER 31, 1962**<br>To record insurance expense for Oct. 1–<br>Dec. 31: ¼ x $2,100, or $525. | Life Insurance Expense　525.00<br>　Prepaid Insurance.. 　　　　525.00 |
| **OCTOBER 1, 1963**<br>Paid second annual premium, $2,100.<br>　Premium...................... $2,100<br>　Less cash surrender value........ 1,150<br><br>　Net insurance charge.......... $　950 | Cash Surrender Value<br>of Life Insurance (as of<br>10/1/64)........... 1,150.00<br>Prepaid Insurance....　950.00<br>　Cash.............. 　　　　2,100.00 |
| **DECEMBER 31, 1963**<br>To record insurance expense for the year:<br>　¾ x $2,100 (Jan. 1–Sept.30)　$1,575.00<br>　¼ x $950　(Oct. 1–Dec. 31)　　237.50<br>　　　　　　　　　　　　　　$1,812.50 | Life Insurance Expense　1,812.50<br>　Prepaid Insurance.. 　　　　1,812.50 |
| **OCTOBER 1, 1964**<br>Paid third annual premium, $2,100.<br>　Premium..............　$2,100<br>　Less: Cash surrender value<br>　　　credit............. $1,300<br>　　　Dividend credit....　272　1,572<br><br>　Net insurance charge.......... $　528 | Cash Surrender Value<br>of Life Insurance (as of<br>10/1/65)........... 1,300.00<br>Prepaid Insurance....　528.00<br>　Cash.............. 　　　　1,828.00 |
| **DECEMBER 31, 1964**<br>To record insurance expense for the year:<br>　¾ x $950 (Jan. 1–Sept. 30).....　$712.50<br>　¼ x $528 (Oct. 1–Dec. 31).....　132.00<br>　　　　　　　　　　　　　　$844.50 | Life Insurance Expense　844.50<br>　Prepaid Insurance.. 　　　　844.50 |
| **JULY 1, 1965**<br>To record insurance expense for Jan. 1–<br>July 1: ½ x $528, or $264. | Life Insurance Expense　264.00<br>　Prepaid Insurance.. 　　　　264.00 |
| **JULY 1, 1965**<br>To record cancellation of policy upon death<br>of insured:<br>　Amount recoverable on policy:<br>　　Face of policy.............. $50,000<br>　　Premium rebate for period<br>　　July 1–Oct. 1 and current year<br>　　dividend..................　735<br>　　　　　　　　　　　　　　$50,735<br><br>　Cancellation of asset values:<br>　　Cash surrender value........ $ 2,450<br>　　Prepaid insurance..........　132<br>　　　　　　　　　　　　　　$ 2,582<br><br>　Gain on policy settlement....... $48,153 | Receivable from Insur-<br>ance Company....... 50,735.00<br>　Cash Surrender<br>　Value of Life Insur-<br>　ance Policy........ 　　　　2,450.00<br>　Prepaid　Insurance 　　　　132.00<br>　Gain on Settlement<br>　of　Life　Insurance<br>　Policy............. 　　　48,153.00 |

It should be observed in the example that cash surrender value increases are recognized on the books whenever a premium is paid. The periodic insurance premium includes a charge for the increase in the policy cash surrender value but such increase actually becomes effective as of the end of the policy year. Hence, anticipation of the cash surrender value on the date of the premium payment needs to be accompanied by a notation as to the effective date of such value. Anticipation of the cash surrender value should also be disclosed in presenting this asset on the balance sheet. If loan values instead of cash surrender values were recognized, no notation would be required since the loan values become effective immediately upon meeting premium requirements for the policy year. Dividends in the example reduce the insurance charge of the period in which they are applied against a premium. Actually the dividend applied against the premium for the third year accrues at the end of the second year and could be considered as a correction in the expense of the second year. Dividends received in the period of policy termination are recognized as a part of policy proceeds in final settlement rather than as a correction of insurance expense. The procedures that are illustrated involve certain concessions in theoretical accuracy but are normally preferred because of their practicality.

## Interests in real estate

Improved property purchased for supplementary income and possible price appreciation or for future use is shown under the investment heading. The expenses relating to such holdings should be deducted from any revenue produced by the property. Unimproved property is frequently acquired for possible future use or for sale. Land while unused makes no contribution to periodic revenue. This would suggest that any costs incident to its holding need not be deducted from current earnings but may be added to the investment balance. When the land is used for construction purposes or is sold, its cost will include all expenditures incident to its acquisition and holding. In reporting the land on the balance sheet, information should be provided in parenthetical or note form relative to any adjustments that may have been made to cost. Market or appraised values, when available, may also be reported parenthetically.

## Advances

Advances to subsidiaries are considered long-term investments when there is no evidence to indicate that amounts advanced will be collected currently. Such advances are sometimes presented on the balance sheet as additions to the investment in stock. But advances should be reported separately, since they represent claims against the subsidiary, while an investment in stock represents an ownership interest. Advances of a long-term character to other parties are also classified as investments.

## Deposits

Deposits to guarantee contract performance, to maintain various memberships, or to secure certain privileges or services, if not recoverable currently, are usually reported as investment items.

## Interests in partnerships

Interests in partnerships and joint ventures should be shown as investments on the books of the individual participants. An investment account is charged for the contribution made by the individual to the partnership. This account is charged for any further contributions and for profits of the partnership increasing the partner's individual interest; it is credited for withdrawals and for losses decreasing his interest.

## Interests in trusts and estates

An interest in a trust or an estate is reported as an investment on the beneficiary's books. The investment account is charged for any increases in this interest resulting from income and gains and is credited for any decreases resulting from expenses, losses, or asset distributions made to the beneficiary. Accounting for an interest in a trust or an estate, then, is similar to that for an interest in a partnership.

## Investments on the balance sheet

Investments are generally reported on the balance sheet after the current asset classification. The investment section should not include temporary investments held as a ready source of cash. Headings should be provided for the different investment categories and individual investments reported within such groupings. Detailed information relative to individual investments may be provided in separate supporting schedules. Investment costs should be supplemented by market quotations offered in parenthetical or note form. Information concerning the pledge of investments as collateral on loans should be provided. When investments are carried at amounts other than cost, the valuation that is employed should be described.

In reporting funds that are to be applied to specific purposes or paid to specific parties, disclosure should be made by special note of the conditions relative to their establishment and ultimate application. A fund arrearage or other failure to meet contractual requirements should be pointed out; the demand to be made upon current assets in the succeeding fiscal period by deposit requirements should also be disclosed when material. Offset of a fund balance against a liability item is proper only when an asset transfer to a trustee is irrevocable and actually serves to discharge the obligation.

The investment section of a balance sheet might appear as follows:

Investments:
  Affiliated companies:

| | | |
|---|---:|---:|
| Investment in Wilson Co., not consolidated, at cost (Investment consists of 90,000 shares representing a 90% interest acquired on July 1, 1960 for $1,500,000. Retained earnings of the subsidiary since date of acquisition have increased by $120,000; 90% of this amount, or $108,000, is identified with the parent company equity but is not included in the accounts.)...................... | $1,500,000 | |
| Advances to Wilson Co........................ | 115,000 | $1,615,000 |
| Miscellaneous stock investments, at cost (stock has an aggregate quoted market price of $112,000; stock has been deposited as security on bank loan — refer to notes payable, contra)......................... | | 100,000 |
| Bond retirement fund in hands of trustee, composed of: | | |
| Cash......................................... | $   15,000 | |
| Stocks and bonds, at cost (aggregate quoted market price, $420,000)............................ | 410,500 | |
| Dividends and interest receivable................ | 4,500 | 430,000 |
| Investment in land and unused facilities............. | | 65,000 |
| Cash surrender value of life insurance carried on officers' lives......................................... | | 12,500 |
| Total investments................................ | | $2,222,500 |

## QUESTIONS

**1.** Distinguish between (a) secured and unsecured bonds, (b) collateral trust and debenture bonds, (c) guaranteed bonds and income bonds, (d) convertible bonds and callable bonds, and (e) coupon bonds and registered bonds.

**2.** What is meant by bond market rate, nominal rate, and effective rate? Which of these rates changes during the lifetime of the bond issue?

**3.** Distinguish between the valuation standards applied to long-term and to short-term investments in bonds. What reasons can you offer for any differences?

**4.** Distinguish between straight-line and compound-interest methods of bond premium amortization. What arguments can be offered in support of each method?

**5.** A. C. McArthur acquires a second-mortgage note, face value $10,000, for $6,000. McArthur feels that in view of the risks involved on this paper, any future collections of both principal and interest should be treated as reductions in the investment balance until he has recovered $6,000. Thereafter, any collections of principal and interest can be regarded as earnings on the investment. What would be your comment on McArthur's stand?

**6.** Name and describe five funds that would be listed as current assets and five that would be listed as investments.

**7.** (a) Distinguish between a fund and an appropriation of retained earnings for such fund. (b) Would you normally recommend an appropriation of retained earnings in fulfilling the objectives of a fund?

**8.** Indicate the balance sheet classification for each of the following:

(a) Land used as parking area for customers.
(b) United States Treasury Bills to provide income for otherwise idle cash during the slack season.
(c) Land to provide for expansion program at least five years hence.
(d) A company's own bonds in a bond retirement fund.
(e) Accrued interest on company's own bonds in bond retirement fund.
(f) Advance to subsidiary company.
(g) Cash surrender value of insurance policy.
(h) A fund to be used to pay current bond interest.
(i) A preferred stock redemption fund.

## EXERCISES

**1.** (a) Assume that $100,000 Kern School District 3½% bonds are purchased for $97,523.45. Interest is payable semiannually and the bonds mature in 10 years. The purchase price provides a yield of 3.8% on the investment. What entries would be made for the receipt of the first two interest payments, assuming discount accumulation on each interest date by (1) the straight-line method and (2) the compound-interest method?

(b) Assume that the amount paid for the bonds is $106,518.28, a price to yield 2.75% on the investment. What entries would be made upon receipt of the first two interest payments, assuming premium amortization on each interest date by (1) the straight-line method and (2) the compound-interest method?

**2.** On June 1, 1964, Arthur Welk purchases Rupp Company bonds, face value $10,000, for $10,500 plus accrued interest. Bonds pay interest at the rate of 4½% semiannually on April 1 and October 1, and they mature on October 1, 1972. What are the entries that will be made on Welk's books to record (a) purchase of the bonds on June 1, (b) receipt of interest on October 1, and (c) adjustment for accrued interest at the end of the fiscal period, December 31, 1964? (Assume that bond premium is amortized by the straight-line method.)

**3.** F. A. Peterson acquired $15,000 of Murphy Motors 4% bonds on July 1, 1962. Bonds were acquired at 95; they pay interest semiannually on April 1 and October 1, and they mature on April 1, 1966. The fiscal period for Peterson is the calendar year; discount is accumulated on the bonds by the straight-line method. On March 1, 1965, Peterson sold the bonds for 98½ plus accrued interest. Give the entry to record the sale of the bonds on this date.

**4.** The Bronson Company has accumulated a bond retirement fund that shows the following balances on September 1, 1964:

| | | |
|---|---|---|
| Cash. . . . . . . . . . . . . . . . . . . . . . . . . . . . . . . . . . . . . | $ 110,000 | |
| Securities. . . . . . . . . . . . . . . . . . . . . . . . . . . . . . . . | 904,000 | $1,014,000 |

On this date securities were sold for $926,500 plus accrued interest, $10,250. Retirement fund cash was then applied to the retirement of bonds of $1,000,000 maturing on this date and accrued interest on the bonds of $22,500. The balance of the bond retirement fund cash was transferred to the cash account. Give the entries to record the above transactions.

**5.** The Benjamin Corporation insured the life of its president for $50,000. The policy was effective on January 1, 1961, and premiums were payable on the first of each year beginning on this date. The following table gives the data for the policy for the first four years:

| Year | Gross Premium | Dividend | Net Premium | Increase in Cash Value | Net Cost for Year |
|------|---------------|----------|-------------|------------------------|-------------------|
| 1 | $2,000 | $— | $2,000 | $ — | $2,000 |
| 2 | 2,000 | — | 2,000 | 1,100 | 900 |
| 3 | 2,000 | 266 | 1,734 | 1,250 | 484 |
| 4 | 2,000 | 266 | 1,734 | 1,350 | 384 |

The fiscal period for the company is the calendar year. The Benjamin Corporation paid the insurance premiums at the beginning of 1961, 1962, 1963, and 1964. The president of the company died on July 1, 1964, and the face value of the policy and also $1,130 representing premium refund and current year dividend became recoverable as of this date. Give all of the journal entries, including the periodic adjustments, that would be made on the books of the company relative to the above data for the period 1961–1964.

## PROBLEMS

**11-1.** Boyd and Bradley, Inc. acquired $10,000 of Carroll Sales Co. $4\frac{1}{2}\%$ bonds, interest payable semiannually, bonds maturing in 5 years. Bonds were acquired at $9,360, a price to yield approximately 6%.

*Instructions:* (1) Prepare tables to show the periodic adjustments to the investment account and the annual bond earnings, assuming adjustment by each of the following methods: (a) the straight-line method and (b) the compound-interest method.

(2) Give entries for the interest receipts and adjustments for the first year of bond ownership, assuming use of (a) the straight-line method, and (b) the compound-interest method.

**11-2.** The Daniels Co. acquired $10,000 of American Boat 5% bonds, interest payable semiannually, bonds maturing in 5 years. The bonds were acquired at $10,450, a price to yield approximately 4%.

*Instructions:* (1) Prepare tables to show the periodic adjustments to the investment account and the annual bond earnings, assuming adjustment by each of the following methods: (a) the straight-line method, and (b) the compound-interest method.

(2) Give entries for the interest receipts and adjustments for the first year of bond ownership, assuming use of (a) the straight-line method, and (b) the compound-interest method.

**11-3.** The Sells-Warner Insurance Co. made the following long-term bond investments during 1964:

| Date of Purchase | Investment | Interest Payment Dates | Maturity Date | Check Issued in Payment of Investment (Includes Accrued Interest) |
|---|---|---|---|---|
| March 1 | $15,000 Pacific Corp. 5's | March 1, Sept. 1 | March 1, 1974 | $15,000.00 |
| April 1 | 60,000 Lake County 3's | July 1, Jan. 1 | Jan. 1, 1973 | 57,825.00 |
| July 1 | 20,000 Bay Utilities 4½'s | June 1, Dec. 1 | June 1, 1967 | 20,407.50 |

*Instructions:* Give the entries to record the investments, the collections of interest in 1964, and also the adjustments that are required on December 31, 1964, the end of the company's fiscal year. Assume that entries for amortization and accumulation are made only at the end of the year.

**11-4.** On May 1, 1961, the Graham Co. acquired $20,000 of Milton Corp. 6% bonds at 98½ plus accrued interest. Interest on bonds is payable semiannually on March 1 and September 1, and bonds mature on September 1, 1964.

On May 1, 1962, the Graham Co. sold bonds of $8,000 for 100¾ plus accrued interest.

On July 1, 1963, $4,000 of bonds were exchanged for 1,000 shares of Milton Corp. no-par common, quoted on the market on this date at 4⅛. Interest was received on bonds to date of exchange.

On September 1, 1964, remaining bonds were redeemed.

*Instructions:* Give journal entries for 1961–1964 to record the foregoing transactions on the books of the Graham Co. including any adjustments that are required at the end of each fiscal year ending on December 31. (Show all calculations.)

**11-5.** On July 1, 1962, Knight Investors acquired $200,000 of Western Co. 4½% bonds at 97 plus accrued interest. Interest on bonds is payable semiannually on February 1 and August 1, and bonds mature on August 1, 1964.

On August 1, 1963, the Western Co. offered additional common stock for sale at par, $100, and offered bondholders the privilege of exchanging $1,000 bonds for 10 shares of stock. Knight Investors exchanged $100,000 in bonds for 1,000 shares of common on this date. Interest was received on bonds to date of exchange.

On April 1, 1964, bonds of $40,000 were sold at 99¼ plus accrued interest.

On August 1, 1964, bonds matured and collection was made on those held.

*Instructions:* Give journal entries for 1962–1964 to record the foregoing transactions on the books of Knight Investors, including any adjustments that are required at the end of each fiscal year ending on December 31. (Show all calculations.)

**11-6.** Carter and Cox, Inc. maintains a bond redemption and interest fund. Bonds acquired by the trustee of the fund are immediately canceled. Six per cent bonds of $1,000,000, interest payable semiannually on January 1 and July 1, were originally issued at face value. Bonds of $200,000 were retired prior to 1964. The bond fund on January 1, 1964, had a balance of $32,500, and transactions affecting the fund in 1964 are reported below. The trustee keeps no separate books, all fund transactions being reported on the company books.

Jan.   8 A deposit of $75,000 was made to the bond fund.
Mar. 16 Bonds of $50,000 were called at 101 plus accrued interest.
June 30 Interest checks for 6 months ending July 1 were mailed to bondholders.
July   8 A deposit of $75,000 was made to the bond fund.
Sept.  1 Bonds of $50,000 were purchased on the open market at 99½ plus accrued interest.
Nov.   1 Bonds of $30,000 were purchased at 99¾ plus accrued interest.
Dec. 31 Interest checks for 6 months ending January 1 were mailed to bondholders.
Dec. 31 Trustee's fees and bond fund expenses of $3,600 for the year were paid.

*Instructions:* Journalize the foregoing transactions.

**11-7.** The Sutton Co. has established a pension plan for employees. At the end of each period, Pensions Expense is debited and Estimated Amounts Payable under Pension Plan is credited for the estimated pension requirements. A pension fund is also maintained and is increased by semiannual deposits. Pension payments are recorded by charges to Estimated Amounts Payable under Pension Plan and credits to Pension Fund Cash. The balance in the pension fund and changes in the fund for 1964 follow:

Fund balance, January 1:

| | |
|---|---|
| Cash. . . . . . . . . . . . . . . . . . . . . . . . . . . . . . . . . . . . . . . . . . . . | $ 20,000 |
| U.S. Treasury 3's, interest payable May 1 and November 1, due May 1, 1976 (acquired at face value). . . . . . . . . . . | 150,000 |
| Harris Co. 1st Mortgage 6's, interest payable January 1 and July 1, due January 1, 1974 (face $80,000). . . . . . . | 82,400 |
| Accrued interest on U.S. Treasury 3's. . . . . . . . . . . . . . . . | 750 |

The pension fund transactions for 1964 are as follows:

Jan. 20 Cash of $60,000 was transferred to the pension fund.
Feb.   7 Purchased $50,000 of Woodland County 3% bonds, interest payable April 1 and October 1, at 96½ plus accrued interest. Bonds mature on April 1, 1968.
April  1 Received semiannual interest on Woodland County 3's.
May    2 Received semiannual interest on U.S. Treasury 3's.
June 30 Pension payments for 6 months were $15,200.
July   1 Received semiannual interest on Harris Co. 6's.
July   1 Purchased an additional $50,000 of Woodland County 3's, 1968 series, at 98½ plus accrued interest.

July 20 Cash of $60,000 was transferred to pension fund.

Sept. 25 Sold $20,000 of Harris Co. 6's for $21,250, which included accrued interest on the bonds to this date.

Oct. 1 Received semiannual interest on Woodland County 3's.

Nov. 1 Received semiannual interest on U.S. Treasury 3's.

Dec. 31 Pension payments for 6 months amounted to $16,600.

31 The balance of Estimated Amounts Payable under Pension Plan was increased by $112,500 for the year.

31 Received semiannual interest on Harris Co. 6's.

*Instructions:* Give the entries required for 1964 as a result of the above, including any adjustments that would be necessary at the end of the year. (Assume that straight-line accumulation and amortization procedures are followed with respect to all bonds in the pension fund, entries being made at the end of the year.)

**11-8.** On September 1, 1960, the United Boat Corporation insured the life of its president, C. H. Kellogg, for $100,000. The policy was dated September 1, 1960; the annual premium was $6,000. Total cash surrender values on the policy were stated as follows: at end of second policy year, $3,150; at end of third policy year, $6,750; at end of fourth policy year, $10,875.

The fiscal period for the company was the calendar year. Premium payments on the insurance policy were made by the company annually on September 1, 1960 through 1963. Dividend credits were applied against premiums as follows: September 1, 1962, $750; September 1, 1963, $825. Mr. Kellogg died on July 1, 1964, and collection of the face value of the policy as well as a premium refund and dividends totaling $1,625 was made on August 22.

*Instructions:* Give all of the journal entries, including the periodic adjustments, that would appear on the books of the company relative to the above data for the years 1960 to 1964.

**11-9.** On March 1, 1962, Smart and Tucker, Inc. insured each of its officers, H. E. Smart and W. E. Tucker, for $100,000. Policies of $100,000 were taken out on each officer effective March 1, 1962; the annual premium on each policy was $3,360. Total cash surrender values for each policy were stated as follows: at the end of second policy year, $1,680; at the end of third policy year, $3,840.

The fiscal period for the company was the calendar year. Premium payments on the insurance policies were made by the company annually on March 1, 1962 through 1964. Dividend credits were applied against premium payments on each policy on March 1, 1964, of $480. Mr. Smart died on September 1, 1964, and collection was made by the company of the face value of his policy together with a premium refund and dividends totaling $1,920.

*Instructions:* Give all of the journal entries, including the periodic adjustments, that would appear on the books of the company relative to the above data for the years 1962 to 1964.

# Chapter 12

# PLANT AND EQUIPMENT
## ACQUISITION, USE, AND RETIREMENT

### Nature of plant and equipment

The term *plant and equipment* is a classification heading for those tangible properties of a relatively permanent character that are used in the normal conduct of a business. Under this heading are included such items as land, buildings, machinery, equipment, and furniture. The term *fixed assets* is frequently used to designate plant and equipment, but as has already been observed, this term is also used in a broader sense to apply to both tangible and intangible properties used in a business.

As in the case of other noncurrent assets, plant and equipment items do not turn over as frequently as current assets. Plant items are acquired, used, and retired. Although plant and equipment as a class remains as long as the business continues, the individual items, with the exception of land, have a limited service life. The cost of plant items is assigned to operations by means of periodic depreciation charges. When an item is no longer of economic benefit to the business, its cost should have been fully absorbed through these periodic charges.

### Composition of plant and equipment

It is customary to classify plant assets in three principal groups: (1) land, (2) buildings, and (3) machinery and equipment. Land refers to earth surface and includes building sites, yards, and parking areas. When natural resources in the form of mineral deposits, oil and gas wells, and timber are found on land, these are frequently reported separately. Buildings refer to improvements permanently affixed to land and include not only structures in the form of factories, office buildings, storage quarters, and garages, but also structure facilities and appurtenances such as loading docks, heating and air conditioning systems, and walks and drives. Machinery and equipment consists of a wide variety of items including factory machines, hand and machine tools, patterns and dies, store and office equipment, and motor vehicles and other transport equipment. Items in the machinery and equipment group are frequently referred to as *personal property* or *personalty* as distinguished from the land and buildings group referred to as *real property* or *realty*.

### Capital and revenue expenditures

The proper treatment of expenditures incident to the acquisition and use of plant assets presents many accounting problems. Plant expenditures are made in anticipation of their favorable effects upon operations. In recording such expenditures, it must be determined whether favorable effects are limited to the current period or whether they extend into future periods. An expenditure that benefits only the current period is called a *revenue expenditure* and is recorded as an expense. An expenditure that benefits operations beyond the current period is called a *capital expenditure* and is recorded as an asset. A plant expenditure that is recorded as an asset is said to be *capitalized*.

Income cannot be accurately measured unless expenditures are properly identified and recorded as revenue or capital charges. An incorrect charge to an equipment item instead of to expense, for example, results in the current overstatement of earnings on the income statement and the overstatement of assets and capital on the balance sheet. As the charge is assigned to operations in subsequent periods, earnings of such periods will be understated; assets and capital on the successive balance sheets will continue to be overstated, although by lesser amounts each year, until the asset is written off and the original error is fully counterbalanced. On the other hand, an incorrect charge to expense instead of to an equipment item results in the current understatement of earnings and the understatement of assets and capital. Earnings of subsequent periods will be overstated in the absence of charges for depreciation; assets and capital will continue to be understated, although by lesser amounts each year, until the original error is counterbalanced.

Although all plant expenditures that will provide benefits beyond the current period should be capitalized, companies frequently adopt an arbitrary practice of charging expense for all expenditures that do not exceed a certain amount, perhaps $50 or $100. Such practice is adopted for the sake of expediency; the analysis of relatively small expenditures, as well as the application of depreciation procedures for them, is avoided. Adherence to such a practice is acceptable if it results in no significant misstatement of plant and equipment costs and periodic income.

### Valuation of plant and equipment

Plant and equipment items, just as all other facilities acquired by the business entity, are recognized initially at cost — the original bargained price for such resources. When payment for an asset is not made in the form of cash, the cash value of the consideration that is given in exchange must be established in arriving at cost. When it is not possible to arrive at a satisfactory cash value for the consideration that is transferred, the asset is reported at its present fair market value, or stated differently, the amount which would have been paid if it had been acquired in a cash transaction. A similar procedure is followed for assets acquired through gift or discovery.

The cost of a plant asset includes not only the original purchase price or equivalent value, but also the other expenditures required in obtaining and readying it for the purpose for which it was acquired. Any taxes and duties, freight and cartage, and installation and other expenditures related to the acquisition are added to the original outlay.

Plant assets are presented on the balance sheet at cost less the portion of cost that has been assigned to past revenues. Land is normally considered to have an unlimited service life, hence is properly reported at its original cost. In those special cases where agricultural land may lose its fertility through use or erosion or a building site may lose its utility through physical or environmental changes, reductions in cost to reflect the decline in asset usefulness may be appropriate. Natural resources are subject to exhaustion and are normally reported at cost less the portion of cost related to resources that have been removed. All other plant items are considered to have a limited service life and are normally reported at *cost less accumulated depreciation.* By *accumulated depreciation* is meant the portion of the asset cost that has been written off by periodic depreciation charges since the asset was acquired. The difference between asset cost and accumulated depreciation is referred to as the asset *book value.* Ordinarily no reference to market values or replacement values is made in presenting plant and equipment on the balance sheet. Plant assets are not intended for conversion into cash; accounting for these assets involves the accumulation of their costs and the appropriate assignment of such costs to production or revenue.

## Acquisition of plant and equipment

There are a number of different ways in which plant and equipment items are acquired and each presents special problems relating to asset cost. The acquisition of plant properties is discussed under the following headings: (1) purchase for cash, (2) purchase on deferred payment plan, (3) exchange, (4) issuance of securities, (5) self-construction, and (6) gift or discovery.

## Purchase for cash

Property that is acquired for cash is recorded at the amount of the cash outlay. Incidental outlays relating to its purchase or to its preparation for use are added to the original cost.

It was suggested in an earlier chapter that sound theory requires that discounts on purchases be regarded as reductions in costs:   earnings arise from sales, not from purchases.   In applying such theory, any available discounts on plant acquisitions should be treated as reductions in asset cost.   Charges resulting from failure to take such discounts should be reported as discounts lost or interest expense.   The treatment of discounts on plant acquisitions should not be affected by the exceptional practice that may be employed for reporting discounts on merchandise purchases.   Reasons of expediency that may support the treatment of discounts on merchandise purchases as revenue are not applicable in accounting for plant acquisitions.

A number of property items may be acquired for a lump sum.   Some of the assets may be depreciable, others nondepreciable.   Depreciable assets may have different useful lives.   If there is to be an accountability for the assets on an individual basis, the total purchase price must be allocated among the individual assets.   When part of a purchase price can be clearly identified with specific assets, such cost assignment should be made and the balance of the purchase price allocated among the remaining assets; when no part of the purchase price can be related to specific assets, the entire amount must be allocated among the different assets acquired.   Appraisal values or other evidence provided by competent independent authority should be sought to support such allocation.

To illustrate the allocation of a joint asset cost, assume that land, buildings, and equipment are acquired for $80,000.   Assume further that assessed values for the individual assets as reported on the property tax bill are considered to provide an equitable basis for cost allocation. The allocation is made as follows:

|  | Assessed Values | Cost Allocation According to Relative Assessed Values | Cost Assigned to Individual Assets |
|---|---|---|---|
| Real properties: |  |  |  |
| Land................ | $14,000 | 14,000/50,000 × $80,000 | $22,400 |
| Improvements (building) | 30,000 | 30,000/50,000 × $80,000 | 48,000 |
| Personal property (equipment)................ | 6,000 | 6,000/50,000 × $80,000 | 9,600 |
|  | $50,000 |  | $80,000 |

When the amount paid for a going business exceeds the values that can be identified with the specific tangible and intangible assets acquired, the excess is recognized as payment for goodwill.

An asset acquired in secondhand or used condition should be set up at its cost without reference to the balance that might be found on the seller's books.   Expenditures to repair, recondition, or improve the asset before it is placed in use should be added to cost.   It must be assumed that the buyer knew that additional expenditures would be required when he made the purchase.

### Purchase on deferred payment plan

When property is acquired on a deferred payment plan and interest is charged on the unpaid balance of the contract, such interest should be recognized as an expense. When a specific charge for interest is not made but the contract price exceeds the cash price at which the asset can be acquired, such excess should be regarded as the charge for deferring the payment. When a cash price is not quoted, the contract price on a deferred payment plan may still be considered to include a financing charge. In such a case the difference between the contract price and an assumed cash price, regarded as the future payments discounted at a going interest rate, would properly be recognized as interest. Recognition of interest under such circumstances is rare; however, special analysis and recognition of this factor is warranted when financing charges of a relatively large amount are implicit in the contract price.

Property may be acquired under a conditional sales contract whereby legal title to the asset is retained by the seller until payments are completed. The failure to acquire legal title may be disregarded by the buyer and the transaction recognized in terms of its substance — the acquisition of an asset and the assumption of a liability. The buyer has the possession and use of the asset and must absorb any decline in its value; title to the asset is retained by the seller simply as a means of assuring payment on the purchase contract. In reporting the asset on the balance sheet prior to full settlement, there should be disclosure by parenthetical remark or note that legal title to the asset still remains with the seller.

In order to conserve working capital and to obtain other benefits, business enterprises frequently lease plant and equipment items and pay a periodic rental for the services derived from the use of the assets. When the lease provides an option for the lessee to buy the asset, the lease contract may actually represent a deferred purchase arrangement which would call for reporting both the asset and lease obligation on the lessee's balance sheet.

### Acquisition by exchange

When one asset is traded for another, the new asset should be recorded at the fair market value of the asset given up; any difference between the fair market value of the asset given up and its book value should be recognized as a gain or loss on the exchange. When a cash payment is required on the acquisition, the new asset should be recorded at the sum of the cash paid and the fair market value of the asset exchanged. Any trade-in allowance should be carefully examined to determine whether it fairly measures the value of the asset exchanged. The use of a trade-in allowance that is inflated to provide a price concession will result in the overstatement of the newly acquired asset and also in the subsequent overstatement of depreciation charges. The newly acquired asset should be recorded at no more than the cash price that would be paid in the absence of a trade-in.

To illustrate an exchange, assume that machinery with an original cost of $5,000 and a book value of $2,000 is accepted at $1,600 in part payment on new machinery priced at $6,000. The following entry is made:

| | | |
|---|---:|---:|
| Machinery.......................................... | 6,000 | |
| Allowance for Depreciation of Machinery............ | 3,000 | |
| Loss on Trade of Machinery....................... | 400 | |
| Machinery...................................... | | 5,000 |
| Cash.......................................... | | 4,400 |

If, in the foregoing example, the machinery could have been acquired at a cash price of $5,600, this value should have been used in recording the asset. Although the trade-in allowance on the old machinery was stated at $1,600, the asset had an actual worth of no more than $1,200; the loss on the exchange was $800, the difference between the actual value of the asset given up, $1,200, and its book value, $2,000.

It was assumed in the example that the asset was exchanged at the beginning of a fiscal period. When a depreciable asset is exchanged within a fiscal period, depreciation should be recognized to the time of the exchange, and the entry to record the exchange should recognize the book value of the asset as of that date.

For federal income tax purposes, no gain or loss is recognized on the exchange of property held for productive use or investment solely for property of a like kind.[1] The tax basis of the new asset is measured by the book value of the asset given up increased by any cash paid on the trade. To illustrate, in the example just given, the loss cannot be recognized for tax purposes; instead the cost of the new machinery is regarded as $6,400, the book value of the asset exchanged, $2,000, plus the cash paid, $4,400. In determining taxable income, depreciation on the new asset is calculated on $6,400. The loss on the old asset is thus recovered in the form of additional depreciation over the life of the new asset.

The income tax method for reporting an asset acquired in an exchange cannot be supported as a sound accounting procedure. The life cycle of an old asset has ended and past periods should absorb the cost

---

[1] This rule does not cover stock in trade or stocks, bonds, or other evidences of indebtedness or interest.

of the asset; a new asset has been acquired and future periods should be charged with neither more nor less than its actual cost. The tax method is frequently applied in the accounts so that analysis and restatement of asset balances may be avoided in the preparation of income tax returns. However, such practice cannot be defended if it results in a significant misstatement of assets and periodic income.

A loss or a gain would be recognized for tax purposes as well as for accounting purposes when an old asset is sold for cash and a new asset is acquired in an independent transaction.

## Acquisition by issuance of securities

A company may acquire certain property in exchange for its own bonds or stock. When a market value for the securities can be determined, such value is assigned to the asset; in the absence of a market value for the securities, the fair market value of the asset would be sought.

Assets received in exchange for securities are properly valued at the par value of the securities only when the market value of the securities equals par value. If bonds or stock are selling at more or less than par value, the asset should be reported at such current cash value; bonds payable or capital stock should be credited at par and a premium or discount should be established for the difference. To illustrate, assume that a company issues 10,000 shares of its stock for land; the stock has a par of $10 and currently sells on the market at 8½. An entry should be made as follows:

| | | |
|---|---|---|
| Land......................................... | 85,000 | |
| Discount on Common Stock..................... | 15,000 | |
| Common Stock............................. | | 100,000 |

The value of the securities should be set as of the time of the exchange and at a price that is established by market transactions.

When securities do not have an established market value, appraisal of the assets by independent authority may be required in arriving at an objective determination of their fair market value. If satisfactory market values cannot be obtained for either securities that are issued or the assets that are acquired, values as established by the board of directors may have to be accepted for accounting purposes. For example, assume that a corporation issues stock in payment for certain mining property A market value cannot be established for the stock, and there are no means of arriving at a fair market value for the property received. If the board of directors values the property at $100,000, the property value and the issuing price of the stock are thereby set at this figure. Disclosure should be provided on the balance sheet of the source of the valuation. The assignment of values by the board of directors is normally not subject to challenge unless it can be shown that the board has acted fraudulently. Nevertheless, evidence should be sought to validate the fairness of original valuations and, if within a short time after an acquisition, the sale of stock or other information indicates that original valuations were erroneous, appropriate action should be taken to restate asset and capital accounts.

When a purchase price is made up of both cash and securities, similar standards for valuing properties apply. Any security discounts or premiums should be accounted for separately. When an asset is purchased for a given down payment plus a series of non-interest-bearing notes whose face values provide for interest charges, the asset cost should not include such charges.

### Acquisition by self-construction

Sometimes buildings or equipment items are constructed by a company for its own use. This may be done to save on construction costs, to utilize idle facilities, or to achieve a higher quality of construction.

When the cost of self-construction of a plant asset is less than the cost to acquire it through purchase or construction by outsiders, such difference for accounting purposes is not a profit but a *saving*. The construction is properly reported at its actual cost. The saving will emerge as profits over the life of the asset as lower depreciation is charged against periodic revenue. Assume, on the other hand, that the cost of self-construction is greater than bids originally received for such construction. There is generally no assurance that work under alternative arrangements might have been equal to that which was self-constructed, and in recording this transaction, just as in recording others, accounts should reflect those courses of action that were taken, not the alternatives that might have been selected. At the same time, if there is evidence indicating that cost has been excessive because of certain construction inefficiencies or failures, such excess is properly recognized as an extraordinary loss; subsequent periods should not be burdened with charges for depreciation arising from costs that could have been avoided.

### Acquisition by gift or discovery

When property is received through donation by a governmental unit or other source, there is no cost that can be used as a basis for its valuation. Even though certain expenditures may have to be made incident to the gift, these are generally considerably less than the value of the property. Here, cost obviously fails to provide a satisfactory basis for asset accountability as well as for future income measurement. In failing to recognize the property at the time of the donation; assets as well as capital will be understated. In subsequent periods, periodic net income will be overstated through the failure to record depreciation and amortization on donated properties having a limited term of usefulness. These misstatements will be accompanied by misrepresentations of the company's earning power reflected in the earnings-to-assets and earnings-to-capital relationships.

To avoid the foregoing consequences, property acquired through donation should be appraised and recorded at its fair market value. A donation is the source of the capital increase, hence a donated capital balance is credited. To illustrate, if the Beverly Hills Chamber of Commerce donates land and buildings appraised at $50,000 and $150,000 respectively, the entry on the books of the company acquiring the property would be:

| | | |
|---|---:|---:|
| Land........................................ | 50,000 | |
| Buildings.................................... | 150,000 | |
|     Donated Capital — Acquisition of Land and | | |
|     Buildings................................. | | 200,000 |

Depreciation of an asset acquired by gift should be recorded in the usual manner, the value assigned to the asset providing the basis for the depreciation charge.

If a gift is contingent upon some act to be performed by the donee, the contingent nature of the asset and the capital item should be indicated in the account titles. Account balances should be reported "short" or by special note on the balance sheet. When conditions of the gift have been met, both the increase in assets and in capital should be recognized in the accounts and on the financial statements.

Discoveries of valuable natural resources may be made on property that is owned. The presence of valuable resources, not previously known, materially enhances the value of the property. As in the case of a gift, cost fails to provide a satisfactory basis for asset valuation and income measurement. Here, too, an appraisal of the property is appropriate, and the property should be restated in terms of the estimated value of the discovered resources. In this case, a revaluation of properties is the source of the capital increase; appraisal capital, then, is recognized equal to the asset increase, a credit being made to an account such as Appraisal Capital — Discovery Value of Natural Resources.

### Interest during period of construction

In public utility accounting, interest during a period of plant construction is recognized as a part of asset cost. Interest, then, emerges as a charge for depreciation in the periods in which the properties are in-come-producing. Service rates established by regulatory bodies are based upon current charges and provide for a recovery of past interest in this manner.

The practice of capitalizing interest has been carried into accounting for the industrial unit. Support for this practice is made on the grounds that capital raised through borrowing is employed for construction purposes; furthermore, if buildings were acquired through purchase, a charge for interest would be implicit in the purchase price. On the other hand, it can be maintained that interest is a money cost, a cost that could have been avoided by raising capital through the sale of stock rather than through borrowing.

If interest is to be capitalized, the amount should be limited to that related to borrowed capital applied to construction. Thus, construction may be charged for the full interest charges on temporary construction loans. However, when bonds are issued, the charge to construction should be limited to interest on that part of the bonds proceeds applied to construction. When interest payments are capitalized, it follows that similar treatment should be applied to interest adjustments for debt discount and premium amortization.

### Other expenditures during period of organization and construction

Some have maintained that all charges for interest, taxes, and general and administrative services during a period of organization and con-struction should be capitalized. Support for such procedure is based on the theory that future periods are benefited by necessary initial costs and it is unreasonable to assume that losses have been incurred before sales activities begin. If the practice of capitalizing such initial expenditures is followed, the asset should be reported as noncurrent and should be written off against revenues in some systematic manner. In reporting the asset on the balance sheet, a note should be provided describing the expenditures that are summarized therein. Initial costs should not be reported as a part of plant and equipment. If this is done, the prop-erty items as well as periodic depreciation charges will be misstated.

### Plant asset records

Data concerning individual plant and equipment items are required in accounting for past activities and in planning future activities. Such data are also required for insurance, tax, and other purposes. Data requirements can be met only by detailed records that are systematically and efficiently maintained. Such records are variously termed "Unit

Plant Records," "Plant Ledger," and "Fixed Asset Control." They usually involve the controlling account principle, plant and equipment items being summarized in the general ledger and detail being recorded in subsidiary ledger form. Subsidiary ledger records are maintained to provide the significant data for each plant and equipment unit.

## Expenditures incurred during service life of plant and equipment items

During the lives of plant and equipment items, regular as well as special expenditures are incurred in their use. Certain expenditures are required to maintain and repair assets; others are incurred to increase their capacity or efficiency or to extend their useful lives. Each expenditure requires careful analysis to determine whether it should be assigned to revenue of the current period, hence charged to an expense account, or whether it should be assigned to revenue of more than one period, which calls for a charge to an asset account or to an allowance for depreciation account. In many cases the answer may not be clear or there may be alternatives, and the procedure that is ultimately chosen will be a matter of judgment.

The terms maintenance, repairs, betterments, improvements, additions, and rearrangements are used in describing expenditures that are made in the course of plant and equipment use. These are described in the sections that follow.

*Maintenance.* Expenditures to maintain assets in fit condition to perform their work are referred to as *maintenance*. Among these are expenditures for painting, lubricating, and adjusting equipment. Maintenance items are ordinary and recurring and do not improve the asset or add to its life; hence they are recognized as expenses.

*Repairs.* Expenditures to restore assets to a fit condition upon their breakdown or to restore and replace broken parts are referred to as *repairs*. When these expenditures are ordinary and recurring and are considered to benefit only current operations, they are charged to expense. When these are extraordinary and extend the life of the asset, they may be charged to the allowance for depreciation. The depreciation rate is then redetermined in view of changes in the asset book values and estimated life.

Repairs involving the overhauling of certain assets are frequently referred to as *renewals*. Substitutions of parts or entire units are referred to as *replacements*. Minor renewals or part replacements may be regarded as ordinary repairs; major renewals or part replacements fall into the category of extraordinary repairs. When the component parts of an asset have different lives and are carried separately, a part replacement would call for entries to cancel the book value related to the old part and to establish the new. Replacement of an entire unit would call for similar entries.

Repairs arising from flood, fire, or other casualty require special analysis. An expenditure to restore an asset to its previous condition should be reported as a loss from casualties. An expenditure that improves or enlarges the asset should be added to the asset balance, while an expenditure that extends the original life of the asset should be treated as a reduction in the allowance for depreciation.

*Betterments and improvements.* Changes in assets designed to provide increased or improved services are referred to as *betterments* or *improvements*. Installation of improved lighting systems, heating systems, or sanitary systems, represent such betterments. Minor expenditures for betterments may be recorded as ordinary repairs. Major expenditures call for entries to cancel the book value related to the old asset and to establish the new, or entries to reduce the allowance for depreciation related to the original asset.

*Additions.* Enlargements and extensions of existing facilities are referred to as *additions*. A new plant wing, additional loading docks, or the expansion of a paved parking lot, represent additions. Expenditures are capitalized, and this cost is written off over the service life of the addition.

*Rearrangements.* Movement of machinery and equipment items and reinstallations to secure economies or greater efficiencies are referred to as *rearrangements*. Costs related to rearrangements should be assigned to those periods that will benefit from such changes. When more than one period is benefited, an asset account, appropriately designated to indicate the nature of the cost deferral, should be established and this balance allocated systematically to revenue. When rearrangements involve reinstallation costs, the portion of asset book value related to an original installation should be canceled and the cost of the new installation added to the asset and written off over its remaining life.

## Nature of depreciation

In spite of expenditures for maintenance and repairs, the time ultimately comes when all plant and equipment items other than land can no longer make a favorable contribution to business activities and must be retired. The costs of such assets must be assigned to revenues over the limited duration of the assets' usefulness.

The Committee on Terminology of the American Institute of Certified Public Accountants has defined depreciation accounting as follows:

> *Depreciation accounting* is a system of accounting which aims to distribute the cost or other basic value of tangible capital assets, less salvage (if any), over the estimated useful life of the unit (which may be a group of assets) in a systematic and rational manner. It is a process of alloca-

tion, not of valuation. *Depreciation for the year* is the portion of the total charge under such a system that is allocated to the year. Although the allocation may properly take into account occurrences during the year, it is not intended to be a measurement of the effect of all such occurrences.[1]

It should be noted that the term *depreciation* is used in a specialized sense in accounting. It is the systematic allocation of cost in recognition of the exhaustion of asset life and is applicable only to those tangible assets that are used by the business. Depreciation is not used to designate a decline in market value as the term is popularly employed. Nor is the term used to designate the physical change in an asset — an asset may show little physical decline in the early years and may have significant physical utility even at the time of its retirement. It is not used to designate the charge for using up wasting assets, which is termed *depletion*, nor to designate the allocation of costs over a period of time for limited-life intangibles, which is termed *amortization*. Depreciation does not refer to a decrease in value assigned to marketable securities as a result of market decline, or to a decrease in value assigned to inventories as a result of obsolescence, spoilage, or other deterioration. The suggestion is frequently made that a term such as "property cost allocation" be used in place of "depreciation" to avoid any misinterpretation.

## Factors affecting useful life of the asset

Plant and equipment items have a limited useful life as a result of certain *physical* and *functional* factors. The physical factors that move a property item towards its ultimate retirement are (1) *wear and tear*, (2) *deterioration and decay*, and (3) *damage or destruction*. Everyone is familiar with the processes of wear and tear that render an automobile, a typewriter, or furniture no longer usable. The deterioration and the decay of an asset through aging, whether the asset is used or not, is also well known. Finally, fire, flood, earthquake, or accident may reduce or terminate the useful life of an asset.

The functional factors that limit the life of a property item are (1) *inadequacy* and (2) *obsolescence*. An asset may lose its usefulness when, as a result of altered business requirements, it can no longer carry the productive load and requires replacement. Although the asset is still usable, its inadequacy for present purposes has cut short its service life. An asset may also lose its usefulness as a result of consumer demand for new and different products or services, or as a result of technical progress and the availability of other assets that can be more economically employed. Here, obsolescence is the factor that operates to limit service life.

---

[1] *Accounting Research and Terminology Bulletins*, 1961 (New York: American Institute of Certified Public Accountants), *Accounting Terminology Bulletin No. 1*, p. 25.

Depreciation accounting calls for the recognition of both the physical and functional factors that limit the useful life of an asset. Physical factors are more readily apparent than functional factors in predicting the asset life. But, when certain functional factors hasten the retirement of an asset, these must also be recognized. Both physical and functional factors may operate gradually or may emerge in sudden fashion. Recognition of depreciation is usually limited to the conditions that operate gradually and are reasonably foreseeable. For example, a sudden change in demand for a certain product may make a plant item worthless, or an accident may destroy a plant item, but these are unforeseeable events that call for extraordinary charges if they materialize.

Since the service life of an asset is affected by maintenance and repairs, the policy that is operative with respect to these matters must be considered in estimating useful life. Low standards of maintenance and repair keep these charges at a minimum but may hasten the physical deterioration of the asset, thus requiring higher-than-normal allocations for depreciation. On the other hand, high standards of maintenance and repairs will mean higher charges for these items, but with a policy that prolongs the usefulness of assets, allocations for depreciation may be reduced.

Depreciation must be recognized on properties in use whether operations are profitable or not. The charge is required even though property values are rising. Costs have been incurred for the services to be provided by the items; these costs must be applied against the revenues to which they contribute.

## Determining the depreciation charge

Three factors must be recognized in arriving at the periodic charge for the use of a depreciable property item: (1) asset cost, (2) residual or salvage value, and (3) useful life.

*Asset cost.* The cost of a property item includes all of the expenditures relating to its acquisition and preparation for use. Expenditures considered to be related to revenues of future periods are capitalized and form the base for depreciation charges. These expenditures were considered earlier.

*Residual or salvage value.* The residual or salvage value of a depreciable asset is the amount which can reasonably be expected to be realized upon retirement of an asset. This may depend upon the retirement policy of the company as well as market conditions and other factors. If, for example, the company normally uses equipment until it is physically exhausted and no longer serviceable, the residual value, represented by the scrap or junk that may be salvaged, may be only nominal.

But if the company normally trades its equipment after a relatively short period of use, the residual value, represented by the value in trade, may be relatively high. In some cases the cost of dismantling and removing an asset may equal or exceed the residual value. From a theoretical point of view, any estimated residual value should be subtracted from cost in arriving at the depreciable cost of the asset; on the other hand, dismantling and removal costs that are expected to exceed ultimate salvage values should be added to cost in arriving at depreciable cost.

In practice both salvage values and dismantling and removal costs are frequently ignored in developing periodic depreciation charges. Disregard of these items is not objectionable when they are relatively small and not subject to reasonable estimate, and when it is doubtful whether any accuracy will be gained through such refinement of the depreciation estimate.

*Useful life.* The life of a property item may be expressed in terms of either an estimated time factor or an estimated use factor. The time factor may be a period of months or years; the use factor may be a number of hours of service or a number of units of output. The cost of the property item flows into production in accordance with the lapse of time or degree of use. The rate of cost flow may be modified by other factors, but basically depreciation must be measured on a time or use basis.[1]

## Recording depreciation

Periodic depreciation could be recorded by a charge to operations and a credit to the property item. Such practice would be consistent with that normally employed in the recognition of periodic charges for intangibles and other costs. However, it is customary to report the reduction in a depreciable asset in a separate valuation account. When cost allocation is reported in a separate account, original cost as well as that part of the cost already allocated to revenues can be provided on the balance sheet. This practice also serves to emphasize the estimates inherent in the allocation process.

A variety of titles are used to designate the valuation balance, such as Allowance for Depreciation, Accumulated Depreciation, and Depreciation Allocated to Past Operations. The term Reserve for Depreciation

---

[1]Prior to 1962 the Internal Revenue Service in *Bulletin "F"* offered a compilation of different assets and their probable useful lives on a time basis as found by normal experiences in various industries to assist taxpayers in establishing appropriate depreciation rates. This publication was superseded in July, 1962, by *Revenue Procedure 62-21*. While the original publication listed depreciation guidelines for thousands of individual items, the present guidelines are limited to 75 broad classes of property items. Guidelines are offered for assets related to business in general, for example, office furniture and equipment, transportation equipment, land improvements and buildings, and also for machinery and equipment and other asset groupings related to specific industries.

has also been widely used, but since this title may suggest the existence of a fund available for asset replacement, its use has been discouraged.

A separate valuation account is maintained for each asset or class of assets requiring the use of a separate depreciation rate. When a subsidiary ledger is maintained for plant and equipment, such record normally provides for the accumulation of depreciation allocations on the individual assets. Separate charges relating to individual property items in the subsidiary ledger support the plant and equipment balance in the general ledger; separate credits representing individual property item cost allocations in the subsidiary ledger support the allowance balance in the general ledger.

When a plant item consists of a number of units or structural elements with varying lives and such units are recorded separately, depreciation is recognized in terms of the respective lives of the different units. Retirement of an individual unit and its replacement by a new unit requires the cancellation of cost and allowance balances related to the old unit and recognition of the new.

### Methods of cost allocation

There are a number of different methods for the allocation of plant and equipment costs. The method that is to be used in any specific instance is a matter of judgment and should be selected only after a thorough study of the nature of the property item and the conditions that limit its use. The methods that follow are described in this chapter:

1. Straight-line method.
2. Service-life methods:
   a. Service-hours method
   b. Productive-output method
3. Decreasing-charge methods:
   a. Declining-balance method
   b. Sum of years'-digits method

The examples that follow assume the acquisition of a machine at a cost of $10,000 with a salvage value at the end of its useful life of $500. The following symbols are employed in the formulas for the development of depreciation rates:

$C$ = Asset cost
$S$ = Estimated salvage value
$n$ = Estimated life in years, hours of service, or units of output
$r$ = Depreciation rate per period, per hour of service, or per unit of output
$D$ = Annual depreciation charge

## Straight-line method

The *straight-line* method relates depreciation to the passage of time and recognizes equal periodic charges over the life of the asset. The depreciation charge is not affected by asset productivity, efficiency, or degree of use. In developing the periodic charge, an estimate is made of the useful life of the asset in terms of months or years. The difference between the asset cost and residual value is divided by the useful life of the asset in arriving at the cost to be assigned to each time unit.

Using data for the machine referred to earlier and assuming a 10-year life, annual depreciation is determined as follows:

$$D = \frac{C - S}{n}, \text{ or } \frac{\$10,000 - \$500}{10} = \$950$$

The depreciation rate is commonly expressed as a percentage to be applied periodically to asset cost. The depreciation rate in the example is calculated as follows: $(100\% - 5\%) \div 10 = 9.5\%$. This percentage applied to cost provides a periodic charge of $950. The rate may also be expressed as a percentage to be applied to depreciable cost — cost less residual value. Expressed in this way the rate is simply the reciprocal value of the useful life expressed in periods, or r (per period) $= 1 \div n$. In the example, then, the annual rate would be $1 \div 10$, or $10\%$, and this rate applied to depreciable cost, $9,500, gives an annual charge of $950. A table to summarize the process of cost allocation follows:

Asset Cost Allocation — Straight-Line Method

| End of Year | Debit to Depreciation | Credit to Allowance for Depreciation | Balance of Allowance for Depreciation | Asset Book Value |
|---|---|---|---|---|
| | | | | $10,000 |
| 1 | $ 950 | $ 950 | $ 950 | 9,050 |
| 2 | 950 | 950 | 1,900 | 8,100 |
| 3 | 950 | 950 | 2,850 | 7,150 |
| 4 | 950 | 950 | 3,800 | 6,200 |
| 5 | 950 | 950 | 4,750 | 5,250 |
| 6 | 950 | 950 | 5,700 | 4,300 |
| 7 | 950 | 950 | 6,650 | 3,350 |
| 8 | 950 | 950 | 7,600 | 2,400 |
| 9 | 950 | 950 | 8,550 | 1,450 |
| 10 | 950 | 950 | 9,500 | 500 |
| | $9,500 | $9,500 | | |

It was indicated earlier that residual value is frequently ignored when this is only a relatively minor amount. If this were done in the example, a ten-year life would call for the use of a $10\%$ rate; depreciation, then, would be recognized at $1,000 per year instead of $950.

In using the straight-line method, depreciation is a constant charge of each period and net income measurements become particularly sensitive to changes in the volume of business activity: with above-normal production, there is no increase in the depreciation charge; with below-normal production, revenue is still charged with the costs of assets standing ready to serve. When the life of a property item is affected primarily by the lapse of time rather than by degree of use, recognition of depreciation as a constant charge is particularly appropriate.

Straight-line depreciation is a widely used procedure. It is readily understood and frequently parallels observable asset deterioration. It has the advantage of simplicity and under normal plant conditions offers a satisfactory means of cost allocation. By normal plant conditions is meant (1) properties that have been accumulated over a period of years so that the total of depreciation plus maintenance is comparatively even from period to period, and (2) properties whose service potentials are being steadily reduced by functional as well as physical factors. The absence of either of these conditions may suggest the use of some other method.

### Service-life methods

Service-life methods view asset exhaustion as related primarily to asset use or output, and provide periodic charges that vary with the degree of such service. Service life for certain assets can best be expressed in terms of hours of service, for others in terms of units of production.

*Service-hours method.* The *service-hours method* is based on the theory that purchase of an asset represents the purchase of a number of hours of direct service. This method requires an estimate of the life of the asset in terms of service hours. Depreciable cost is divided by total service hours in arriving at the depreciation rate to be assigned for each hour of asset use. The use of the asset during the period is measured, and the number of service hours is multiplied by the depreciation rate in arriving at the depreciation charge. Depreciation charges fluctuate periodically according to the contribution that the asset makes in service hours.

Using asset data previously given and an estimated service life of 20,000 hours, the rate to be applied for each service hour is determined as follows:

$$r \text{ (per hour)} = \frac{C - S}{n}, \text{ or } \frac{\$10,000 - \$500}{20,000} = \$.475$$

Allocation of asset cost in terms of service hours is summarized in the table at the top of the next page.

Asset Cost Allocation — Service-Hours Method

| End of Year | Service Hours | Debit to Depreciation | | Credit to Allowance for Depreciation | Balance of Allowance for Depreciation | Asset Book Value |
|---|---|---|---|---|---|---|
| | | | | | | $10,000.00 |
| 1 | 1,500 | (1,500 × $.475) | $ 712.50 | $ 712.50 | $ 712.50 | 9,287.50 |
| 2 | 2,500 | (2,500 × $.475) | 1,187.50 | 1,187.50 | 1,900.00 | 8,100.00 |
| 3 | 2,500 | (2,500 × $.475) | 1,187.50 | 1,187.50 | 3,087.50 | 6,912.50 |
| 4 | 2,000 | (2,000 × $.475) | 950.00 | 950.00 | 4,037.50 | 5,962.50 |
| 5 | 1,500 | (1,500 × $.475) | 712.50 | 712.50 | 4,750.00 | 5,250.00 |
| 6 | 1,500 | (1,500 × $.475) | 712.50 | 712.50 | 5,462.50 | 4,537.50 |
| 7 | 3,000 | (3,000 × $.475) | 1,425.00 | 1,425.00 | 6,887.50 | 3,112.50 |
| 8 | 2,500 | (2,500 × $.475) | 1,187.50 | 1,187.50 | 8,075.00 | 1,925.00 |
| 9 | 2,000 | (2,000 × $.475) | 950.00 | 950.00 | 9,025.00 | 975.00 |
| 10 | 1,000 | (1,000 × $.475) | 475.00 | 475.00 | 9,500.00 | 500.00 |
| | 20,000 | | | $9,500.00 | $9,500.00 | |

It is assumed above that the original estimate of service hours is confirmed and the asset is retired after 20,000 hours which is reached in the tenth year. Such precise confirmation would seldom be found in practice.

It should be observed that straight-line depreciation resulted in an annual charge of $950 regardless of fluctuations in productive activity. When asset life is affected directly by the degree of use and when there are significant fluctuations in such use in successive periods, the service-hours method, which recognizes "hours used" instead of "hours available for use" normally provides the more equitable charge to operations.

*Productive-output method.* The *productive-output method* is based on the theory that an asset is acquired for the service that it can provide in the form of production output. This method requires an estimate of the total unit output of the property item. Depreciable cost divided by the total output gives the equal depreciation charge to be assigned for each unit of output. The measured production for a period multiplied by the depreciation charge per unit gives the charge to be made for depreciation. Depreciation charges fluctuate periodically according to the contribution that the asset makes in unit output.

Using the previous asset data and an estimated productive life of 2,500,000 units, the rate to be applied for each thousand units produced is determined as follows:

$$r \text{ (per thousand units)} = \frac{C - S}{n}, \text{ or } \frac{\$10,000 - \$500}{2,500} = \$3.80$$

Asset cost allocation in terms of unit output is summarized in the tabulation at the top of the next page.

## Asset Cost Allocation — Productive-Output Method

| End of Year | Unit Output | Debit to Depreciation | | Credit to Allowance for Depreciation | Balance of Allowance for Depreciation | Asset Book Value |
|---|---|---|---|---|---|---|
| | | | | | | $10,000 |
| 1 | 80,000 | ( 80 × $3.80) | $ 304 | $ 304 | $ 304 | 9,696 |
| 2 | 250,000 | (250 × $3.80) | 950 | 950 | 1,254 | 8,746 |
| 3 | 400,000 | (400 × $3.80) | 1,520 | 1,520 | 2,774 | 7,226 |
| 4 | 320,000 | (320 × $3.80) | 1,216 | 1,216 | 3,990 | 6,010 |
| 5 | 440,000 | (440 × $3.80) | 1,672 | 1,672 | 5,662 | 4,338 |
| 6 | 360,000 | (360 × $3.80) | 1,368 | 1,368 | 7,030 | 2,970 |
| 7 | 280,000 | (280 × $3.80) | 1,064 | 1,064 | 8,094 | 1,906 |
| 8 | 210,000 | (210 × $3.80) | 798 | 798 | 8,892 | 1,108 |
| 9 | 120,000 | (120 × $3.80) | 456 | 456 | 9,348 | 652 |
| 10 | 40,000 | ( 40 × $3.80) | 152 | 152 | 9,500 | 500 |
| | 2,500,000 | | | $9,500 | $9,500 | |

*Evaluation of service-life methods.* When quantitative uses of depreciable properties can be reasonably estimated and are readily measurable, the service-life methods provide highly satisfactory approaches to asset cost allocation. Depreciation is a fluctuating charge that tends to follow the revenue curve: high depreciation charges are assigned to periods of high activity; low depreciation charges are assigned to periods of low activity. When the useful life on an asset is affected primarily by the degree of its use, recognition of depreciation as a variable charge is particularly appropriate.

However, certain limitations in the use of the service-life methods need to be pointed out. Asset performance in terms of service hours or productive output may be difficult to estimate. Measurement solely in terms of such factors may fail to recognize special conditions that may be operative, such as increasing maintenance and repair costs, as well as possible inadequacy and obsolescence. Furthermore, when service life expires even in the absence of use, a service-life method may serve to conceal actual fluctuations in earnings; by relating periodic depreciation to revenues, the changes in operating results may be smoothed out, thus creating a false appearance of stability.

### Decreasing-charge methods

Decreasing-charge methods relate charges for depreciation to time rather than to services. But they provide for the highest depreciation charge in the first year of asset use and declining depreciation charges in ensuing years. Such plans are based largely on the assumption that there will be reductions in asset efficiency, output, or other benefits as the asset ages. Such reductions may be accompanied by increased charges for maintenance and repairs. Charges for depreciation decline, then, as the economic advantages afforded through ownership of the asset decline.

*Declining-balance method.* The *declining-balance method* provides decreasing charges by applying a constant percentage rate to a declining asset book value. The rate to be applied to the declining book value in producing the estimated salvage value at the end of the useful life of the asset is calculated by the following formula:

$$r \text{ (rate per period applicable to declining book value)} = 1 - \sqrt[n]{S \div C}$$

Using the previous asset data and assuming a 10-year asset life, the depreciation rate is determined as follows:

$$1 - \sqrt[10]{500 \div 10,000} = 1 - \sqrt[10]{.05} = 1 - .74113 = .25887, \text{ or } 25.887\%$$

Dividing the estimated salvage value by cost in the formula above gives .05, the value that the salvage value at the end of 10 years should bear to cost. The tenth root of this value is .74113. Multiplying cost and the successive declining book values by .74113 ten times will reduce the asset to .05 of its cost. The difference between 1 and .74113, or .25887, then, is the rate of decrease to be applied successively in bringing the asset down to .05 of its original balance. Since it is impossible to bring a value down to zero by a constant multiplier, a residual value must be assigned to the asset in using the formula. In the absence of an expected residual value, a nominal value of $1 can be assumed for this purpose.

Depreciation calculated by application of the 25.887% rate to the declining book value is summarized in the table that follows:

### Asset Cost Allocation —- Declining-Balance Method

| End of Year | Debit to Depreciation | | Credit to Allowance for Depreciation | Balance of Allowance for Depreciation | Asset Book Value |
|---|---|---|---|---|---|
| | | | | | $10,000.00 |
| 1 | (25.887% × $10,000.00) | $2,588.70 | $2,588.70 | $2,588.70 | 7,411.30 |
| 2 | (25.887% × $ 7,411.30) | 1,918.56 | 1,918.56 | 4,507.26 | 5,492.74 |
| 3 | (25.887% × $ 5,492.74) | 1,421.91 | 1,421.91 | 5,929.17 | 4,070.83 |
| 4 | (25.887% × $ 4,070.83) | 1,053.82 | 1,053.82 | 6,982.99 | 3,017.01 |
| 5 | (25.887% × $ 3,017.01) | 781.01 | 781.01 | 7,764.00 | 2,236.00 |
| 6 | (25.887% × $ 2,236.00) | 578.83 | 578.83 | 8,342.83 | 1,657.17 |
| 7 | (25.887% × $ 1,657.17) | 428.99 | 428.99 | 8,771.82 | 1,228.18 |
| 8 | (25.887% × $ 1,228.18) | 317.94 | 317.94 | 9,089.76 | 910.24 |
| 9 | (25.887% × $  910.24) | 235.63 | 235.63 | 9,325.39 | 674.61 |
| 10 | (25.887% × $  674.61) | 174.64 | 174.64 | 9,500.03 | 499.97 |
| | | | $9,500.03 | $9,500.03 | |

Instead of developing an exact rate that will produce a salvage value of $500, it is usually more convenient to approximate a rate that will provide satisfactory cost allocation; since depreciation involves estimate, there is little assurance that rate refinement will produce more accurate results. In the previous illustration, for example, the use of a rate of 25% is more convenient than 25.887%; differences are not material.[1]

*Sum of years'-digits method.* The *sum of years'-digits method* provides decreasing charges by applying a series of fractions, each of a smaller value, to depreciable asset cost. Fractions are developed in terms of the sum of the asset life periods. Assuming the asset previously described has an estimated 10-year life, periodic charges are developed by the sum of years'-digits method as follows:

| | Reducing Weights | Reducing Fractions |
|---|---|---|
| First year | 10 | 10/55 |
| Second year | 9 | 9/55 |
| Third year | 8 | 8/55 |
| Fourth year | 7 | 7/55 |
| Fifth year | 6 | 6/55 |
| Sixth year | 5 | 5/55 |
| Seventh year | 4 | 4/55 |
| Eighth year | 3 | 3/55 |
| Ninth year | 2 | 2/55 |
| Tenth year | 1 | 1/55 |
| | 55 | 55/55 |

Weights for purposes of developing reducing fractions are the years'-digits listed in reverse order. The denominator for the fraction is obtained by adding these weights; the numerator is the weight assigned to the specific year.[2] Depreciation calculated by applying the reducing fractions to depreciable cost is summarized in the table on page 325.

*Evaluation of decreasing-charge methods.* Decreasing-charge methods can be supported as reasonable approaches to asset cost allocation when the benefits provided by a property item decline as it grows older. These methods, too, are suggested when a property item calls for increasing maintenance and repairs over its useful life. When straight-line depreciation is employed, combined charges for depreciation, maintenance, and repairs will increase over the life of the asset; when decreasing-charge methods are used, combined charges will tend to be equalized.

[1]The declining-balance approach is acceptable for federal income tax purposes. The rate that is used, however, cannot exceed twice the appropriate straight-line rate computed without adjustment for salvage. An asset cannot be depreciated below a reasonable salvage value. The tax method is frequently referred to as the *double-declining balance method* to distinguish it from the method that is illustrated here. When the tax method is considered to provide a fair allocation of asset cost, its use in the accounts would also be proper.

[2]The denominator for the fraction can be obtained by dividing the sum of the digits for the first and last year by 2 and multiplying this value by the number of years of asset life. In the example, the denominator is calculated: $[(10 + 1) \div 2] \times 10 = 55$.

### Asset Cost Allocation — Sum of Years'-Digits Method

| End of Year | Debit to Depreciation | | Credit to Allowance for Depreciation | Balance of Allowance for Depreciation | Asset Book Value |
|---|---|---|---|---|---|
| | | | | | $10,000.00 |
| 1 | (10/55 × $9,500) | $1,727.27 | $1,727.27 | $1,727.27 | 8,272.73 |
| 2 | ( 9/55 × $9,500) | 1,554.55 | 1,554.55 | 3,281.82 | 6,718.18 |
| 3 | ( 8/55 × $9,500) | 1,381.82 | 1,381.82 | 4,663.64 | 5,336.36 |
| 4 | ( 7/55 × $9,500) | 1,209.09 | 1,209.09 | 5,872.73 | 4,127.27 |
| 5 | ( 6/55 × $9,500) | 1,036.36 | 1,036.36 | 6,909.09 | 3,090.91 |
| 6 | ( 5/55 × $9,500) | 863.64 | 863.64 | 7,772.73 | 2,227.27 |
| 7 | ( 4/55 × $9,500) | 690.91 | 690.91 | 8,463.64 | 1,536.36 |
| 8 | ( 3/55 × $9,500) | 518.18 | 518.18 | 8,981.82 | 1,018.18 |
| 9 | ( 2/55 × $9,500) | 345.45 | 345.45 | 9,327.27 | 672.73 |
| 10 | ( 1/55 × $9,500) | 172.73 | 172.73 | 9,500.00 | 500.00 |
| | | $9,500.00 | $9,500.00 | | |

Other factors that may suggest use of a decreasing-charge method include: (1) the anticipation of a significant contribution in early periods with the extent of the contribution to be realized in later periods less definite; (2) the possibility that inadequacy or obsolescence may result in premature retirement of the asset; in the event of premature retirement, depreciation charges will have absorbed what would otherwise require recognition as an extraordinary loss. Decreasing-charge methods are supported as conservative approaches to the cost allocation problem.

Decreasing-charge methods are frequently used for income tax purposes. Although total depreciation over the asset life is no greater than that provided by alternate methods, the recognition of higher depreciation in the early years of an asset's life serves to postpone the income taxes that would otherwise be payable and thus provides interest-free working capital to the business. The term *accelerated depreciation* is frequently employed to designate methods that are based on time factors but that provide higher charges in the early years of asset life and lower charges in later years.

### Group-rate and composite-rate methods

It was assumed in preceding discussions that depreciation is associated with individual property items and is applied to each separate unit. Such practice is commonly referred to as *unit depreciation*. Frequently, however, there may be certain advantages in associating depreciation with a group of properties and applying a single rate to the collective cost of the group. Group cost allocation procedures are referred to as *group depreciation* and *composite depreciation*.

*Group depreciation.* When useful life is affected primarily by physical factors, a group of similar items purchased at one time should have the same expected life, but in fact some will probably remain useful longer than others. In recording depreciation on a unit basis, the sale or retirement of an asset before or after its anticipated lifetime requires recognition of a loss or gain. Such losses and gains, however, can usually be attributed to normal variations in useful life rather than unforeseen disasters and windfalls.

The *group-depreciation* procedure treats a collection of similar assets as a single group. Depreciation is accumulated in a single valuation account and the depreciation rate is based on the average life of assets in the group. Because the allowance for depreciation account under the group procedure applies to the entire group of assets, it is not related to any specific asset. Thus, there are no "fully depreciated" assets when this method is used, and the depreciation rate is applied to the cost of all assets remaining in service, regardless of age, in arriving at the periodic depreciation charge.

When an item in the group is retired, no gain or loss is recognized; the asset account is credited with the cost of the item and the valuation account is charged for the difference between cost and any salvage. With normal variations in asset lives, the losses not recognized on early retirements are offset by the continued depreciation charges on those assets still in service after the average life has elapsed.

To illustrate, assume that 100 similar machines having an average expected useful life of 5 years are purchased at a total cost of $200,000. Of this group, 30 machines are retired at the end of four years, 40 at the end of five years, and the remaining 30 at the end of the sixth year. Based on the average expected useful life of 5 years, a depreciation charge of 20% is reported on those assets in service each year. The charges for depreciation and the changes in the group asset and allowance accounts are summarized as follows:

### Asset Cost Allocation — Group Depreciation

| End of Year | Debit to Depreciation (20% of Cost) | Asset Debit | Asset Credit | Asset Balance | Allowance for Depreciation Debit | Allowance for Depreciation Credit | Allowance for Depreciation Balance | Asset Book Value |
|---|---|---|---|---|---|---|---|---|
| | | $200,000 | | $200,000 | | | | $200,000 |
| 1 | $40,000 | | | 200,000 | | $ 40,000 | $ 40,000 | 160,000 |
| 2 | 40,000 | | | 200,000 | | 40,000 | 80,000 | 120,000 |
| 3 | 40,000 | | | 200,000 | | 40,000 | 120,000 | 80,000 |
| 4 | 40,000 | | $ 60,000 | 140,000 | $ 60,000 | 40,000 | 100,000 | 40,000 |
| 5 | 28,000 | | 80,000 | 60,000 | 80,000 | 28,000 | 48,000 | 12,000 |
| 6 | 12,000 | | 60,000 | – – – | 60,000 | 12,000 | – – – | – – – |
| | $200,000 | $200,000 | $200,000 | | $200,000 | $200,000 | | |

It should be noted that the depreciation charge is exactly $400 per machine-year. In each of the first four years, 100 machine-years of service are utilized, and the annual depreciation charge is $40,000. In the fifth year, when only 70 machines are in operation the charge is $28,000. In the sixth year when 30 units are still in service, a proportionate charge for such use of $12,000 is made. Under unit depreciation a loss of $12,000 would have been recognized at the end of the fourth year when 30 machines were scrapped prematurely. However, no charge for depreciation would have been recognized in the sixth year when the 30 machines remaining in service would have been fully depreciated.[1]

Application of the group depreciation procedure under circumstances such as the foregoing provides an annual charge that is more closely related to the quantity of productive facilities being used. Gains and losses due solely to normal variations in asset lives are not recognized, and operating results are more meaningfully stated. The convenience of applying a uniform depreciation rate to a number of similar items may also represent a substantial advantage.

*Composite depreciation.* The basic procedures employed under the group method for allocating the cost of substantially identical assets may be extended to include dissimilar assets. This special application of the group procedure is known as *composite depreciation.* The composite method retains the convenience of the group method, but because assets with varying service-lives are aggregated to determine an "average" life, it is unlikely to provide the reporting advantages found in the group method.

A composite rate is established by analyzing the various assets or classes of assets in use and calculating the depreciation that would be applicable to the group. The development of a composite rate based upon an analysis of the properties employed by a business unit is illustrated in the example that follows:

| Asset | Cost | Residual Value | Depreciable Cost | Estimated Life in Years | Annual Depreciation |
|-------|------|----------------|------------------|------------------------|---------------------|
| A | $ 2,000 | $ 120 | $ 1,880 | 4 | $ 470 |
| B | 6,000 | 300 | 5,700 | 6 | 950 |
| C | 12,000 | 1,200 | 10,800 | 10 | 1,080 |
|   | $20,000 | $1,620 | $18,380 |  | $2,500 |

Composite depreciation rate to be applied to cost: $2,500 ÷ $20,000, or 12.5%
Composite life of assets: $18,380 ÷ $2,500, or 7.35 years.

It will be observed that a rate of 12.5% applied to the cost of the assets, $20,000, results in annual depreciation of $2,500. Annual de-

---

[1] It should be observed that in the example the original estimates of an average useful life of 5 years is confirmed in the use of the assets. Such precise confirmation would seldom be the case. In instances where assets in a group are continued in use after their cost has been assigned to operations, no further depreciation charges would be recognized. On the other hand, where all of the assets in a group are retired before their cost has been assigned to operations, it would be necessary to recognize a loss on such retirement.

preciation of $2,500 will accumulate to a total of $18,380 in 7.35 years; hence 7.35 years may be considered the composite or average life of the assets. Composite depreciation would be reported in a single valuation account. Upon the retirement of an individual asset, the asset account is closed and the valuation account is charged with the difference between cost and residual value. As with the group procedure, no gains or losses are recognized at the time individual assets are retired.

After a composite rate has been set, it is ordinarily continued in the absence of significant changes in the lives of assets or asset additions and retirements having a material effect upon the rate. It is assumed in the example above that the assets are replaced with similar assets when they are retired. If they are not replaced, continuation of the 12.5% rate will misstate depreciation charges.

## Appraisal, retirement, and replacement systems

The charge to operations for asset use may be made on a basis other than the cost allocation processes described. Other systems include:

*Appraisal systems.* Asset accounts are charged for all expenditures relating to property acquisitions. At the end of each period assets are appraised, asset balances are reduced to the appraised values, and a charge is made to operations for such decrease. In appraising assets care must be exercised to assign values that reflect the portion of original cost that may reasonably be identified with remaining service utilities of the asset, not market values.

*Retirement systems.* Asset accounts are charged for all expenditures relating to property acquisitions. When property items are retired, asset accounts are credited for the cost of properties retired and a charge is made to operations for such cost less any amounts recovered as salvage.

*Replacement systems.* Asset accounts are charged for expenditures relating to original property acquisitions. Whenever original property items are replaced, a charge is made to operations for the cost of replacements less any amounts recovered as salvage on the properties replaced.

Depreciation systems such as the foregoing can be considered acceptable only when the use of standard depreciation procedures involve serious practical difficulties, such as in estimating useful lives, in distinguishing between replacements and repairs, and in handling recording routines. Systems should be reviewed periodically to provide assurance that they result in fair charges to revenue and that they do not serve as means for profit manipulation. The use of the above systems may be suggested in accounting for hand and machine tools of a manufacturing company, poles and related equipment of an electric utility, railroad ties of a railway, and dishes and silverware of a restaurant.

## Allowable depreciation for federal income tax purposes

The Internal Revenue Code allows taxpayers to use any reasonable method for computing depreciation, with certain limitations. The Code specifically names the following methods as acceptable:

*For all classes of depreciable property:*

1. The straight-line method
2. The declining-balance method, using an annual rate limited to one-and-one-half times the rate which would be applicable to the straight-line method unadjusted for salvage.

*For property having a useful life of 3 years or more which is acquired new after December 31, 1953, methods (1) and (2) and also the following:*

3. The declining-balance method, using an annual rate limited to double the straight-line rate unadjusted for salvage.
4. The sum of the years'-digits method.
5. Any other consistent method, provided accumulated depreciation over the first two-thirds of the useful life of the property does not exceed that obtained in (3) above.

## Depreciation accounting and property replacement

There has been a tendency on the part of many readers of financial statements to interpret depreciation accounting as somehow related to the accumulation of a fund for asset replacement. The use of such terms as "provision for depreciation" on the income statement and "reserve for depreciation" on the balance sheet have contributed to such misinterpretation.

It has been pointed out that the charge for depreciation originates from the recognition of the movement of a property item towards ultimate exhaustion. The nature of this charge is no different from those that are made to recognize the expiration of insurance premiums, patent rights, etc. It is true that revenue equal to or in excess of expenses for a period results in a recovery of such expenses; salary expense is thus recovered by revenue, as is insurance expense, patent amortization, and charges for depreciation. But this does not suggest that cash equivalent to the recorded depreciation will be available to meet the cost of property replacement. Resources from revenues may be applied to many uses: to the increase in receivables, inventories, or other working capital items; to the acquisition of plant or other noncurrent items; to the retirement of debt or the redemption of stock; and to the payment of dividends. If a fund is to be available for the replacement of property items, this calls for special authorization by management. A property replacement fund is seldom found, however, because its establishment would have to promise earnings exceeding those that might accrue from alternative uses of capital.

### Plant and equipment retirements

Properties may be retired by sale, trade, scrapping and removal, or abandonment. When properties are disposed of, both property and allowance accounts are canceled and a gain or loss is recognized for the difference between the amount recovered on the asset and its book value.

In recording a disposal, it is necessary to consider the practice that has been adopted for recognizing depreciation for fractional periods. Ordinarily, depreciation is recognized from the time of asset acquisition to the time of its retirement. In applying this method, depreciation, rather than being recognized on as short a period as a day or a week, would normally be calculated to the nearest month: no charge would be made for an asset that is used for less than half of a month; a charge for a full month would be recognized for an asset that is used for more than half of a month. This practice is assumed in the examples and problems in the text.

To illustrate the entries for asset retirement, assume that it is decided to sell certain machinery. The machinery was originally acquired on November 20, 1955, for $10,000 and had been depreciated at 10% per year. The asset is sold on April 10, 1964, for $1,250. The entries to record depreciation for 1964 and sale of the property item follow:

| | | |
|---|---|---|
| Depreciation of Machinery........................ | 250.00 | |
| Allowance for Depreciation of Machinery......... | | 250.00 |

To record depreciation for three months in 1964:
$10,000 × 10% × 3/12, or $250.00.

| | | |
|---|---|---|
| Cash......................................... | 1,250.00 | |
| Allowance for Depreciation of Machinery........... | 8,333.33 | |
| Loss on Sale of Machinery....................... | 416.67 | |
| Machinery.................................. | | 10,000.00 |

To record sale of machinery:

| | | |
|---|---|---|
| Cost........................... $10,000.00 | | |
| Depreciation to date of sale: | | |
| November 20, 1955–April 10, 1964 | | |
| (10% per year for 8-4/12 years)... | 8,333.33 | |
| Asset book value.................. $ 1,666.67 | | |
| Proceeds from sale ................ | 1,250.00 | |
| Loss on sale ...................... $ 416.67 | | |

The above entries can be combined in the form of a single compound entry as follows:

| | | |
|---|---|---|
| Cash........................................ | 1,250.00 | |
| Depreciation of Machinery................... | 250.00 | |
| Allowance for Depreciation of Machinery...... | 8,083.33 | |
| Loss on Sale of Machinery................... | 416.67 | |
| Machinery............................... | | 10,000.00 |

If a property item is scrapped or abandoned without cash recovery, a loss would be recognized equal to the asset book value; if the full cost of the asset has been written off, asset and allowance balances would simply be canceled.  If a property item is retired from active or standby service but is not immediately disposed of, asset and allowance balances should be closed and the salvage value of the asset established as a separate asset.

### Property damage or destruction

Special accounting problems arise when property is damaged or destroyed as a result of fire, flood, storm, or other casualty.  When a company owns many properties and these are widely distributed, the company itself may assume the risk of loss.  However, companies ordinarily carry insurance for casualties that may involve large sums.

When uninsured property items are damaged and expenditures are incurred in their restoration, such expenditures should be reported as an extraordinary loss.  When uninsured properties are partly or wholly destroyed, asset book values should be reduced or canceled and an extraordinary loss recorded for such reductions.  When property items are insured and these are damaged or destroyed, entries on the books must be made to report asset losses and also the insurance claims that arise from such losses.

## QUESTIONS

**1.** Distinguish between fixed tangibles and fixed intangibles.

**2.** (a) Define asset *cost*.  (b) How does one arrive at cost when the consideration is other than cash?  (c) What is asset *book value*?

**3.** (a) Distinguish between capital expenditures and revenue expenditures.  (b) Give five examples of each.

**4.** Which of the following items would be treated as a revenue expenditure and which as a capital expenditure?

    (a) Cost of installing machinery.
    (b) Cost of moving and reinstalling machinery.
    (c) Extensive repairs as a result of fire.
    (d) Cost of grading land.
    (e) Insurance on machinery in transit.
    (f) Bond discount amortization during construction period.
    (g) Cost of major overhaul on machinery.
    (h) New safety guards on machinery.
    (i) Commission on purchase of real estate.
    (j) Special tax assessment for street improvements.

**5.** Indicate the effects of the following errors on the balance sheet and the income statement in the current year and in succeeding years:

    (a) The cost of a depreciable asset is incorrectly recorded as a revenue expenditure.
    (b) A revenue expenditure is incorrectly recorded as a charge to a depreciable asset.

**6.** The Robinson Co. trades an asset for a similar new one, the trade-in value of the old asset being less than its book value. (a) What is the disposition of this difference for income tax purposes? (b) Would you recommend similar treatment in the accounts? Explain.

**7.** When the Bowman Corporation finds that the lowest bid it can get on the construction of an addition to its plant is $40,000, it proceeds to erect the building with its own workmen and equipment. (a) Assuming that the cost of construction is $35,000, how would you treat the savings? (b) Assuming a cost of $50,000, how would you suggest that the excess cost be treated?

**8.** What positions can be taken with respect to interest charges during a period of plant construction? Evaluate each position and state your preference.

**9.** Distinguish between (a) maintenance and repairs, (b) ordinary repairs and extraordinary repairs, (c) betterments and additions.

**10.** What is meant by depreciation accounting?

**11.** "The recognition of depreciation has no essential relation to the problem of replacement." Do you agree?

**12.** Distinguish between functional depreciation and physical depreciation.

**13.** Distinguish between inadequacy and obsolescence.

**14.** The policy of the Burke Co. is to recondition its plant each year so that it may be maintained in perfect repair. In view of the extensive periodic costs involved in keeping the plant in such condition, officials of the company feel that the need for recognizing depreciation is eliminated. Evaluate this argument.

**15.** Describe the calculation of periodic depreciation under each of the following methods:

(a) Straight-line.      (c) Productive-output.      (e) Sum of years'-digits.
(b) Service-hours.      (d) Declining-balance.

**16.** Evaluate each method listed in Question 15 above, indicating the circumstances under which the method would be particularly appropriate and the advantages found in its use.

**17.** (a) Distinguish between group depreciation and composite depreciation. (b) What entries are made for asset acquisitions and retirements under these methods? (c) What arguments can be presented for the adoption of such methods?

**18.** (a) Describe the allocation of plant charges to operations under (1) the appraisal system (2) the retirement system, and (3) the replacement system. (b) Do you recommend the use of such procedures?

## EXERCISES

**1.** Boyer, Inc. acquires a machine that is priced at $1,800. Payment of this amount may be made within 60 days; a 3% discount is allowed if cash is paid at time of purchase. Give the entry to record the acquisition, assuming:

    (a) Cash is paid at time of purchase.
    (b) Payment is to be made at the end of 60 days.
    (c) A deferred payment plan is agreed upon whereby a down payment of $200 is made with 12 payments of $150 to be made at monthly intervals thereafter.

**2.** On November 1, 1964, the Parker Corporation trades machinery acquired on January 5, 1961, for new machinery. The old machinery had a cost of $12,000 and had been depreciated on a 10-year life. The new machinery costs $8,000; $5,000 is allowed on the old machinery, the balance being paid in cash. (a) What entry is required to record the transaction? (b) What is the value of the new machine for income tax purposes?

**3.** The Cottle Company acquired land in exchange for 5,000 shares of its common stock, par $10, and cash of $25,000. The land was recorded at $75,000. The auditor ascertains that the company's stock was selling on the market at 6½ when the purchase was made. What correcting entry should be made?

**4.** The Swisher Co. enters into a contract with the Westlake Construction Co. for construction of an office building at a cost of $425,000. Upon completion of construction, the Westlake Construction Co. agrees to accept in full payment of the contract price Swisher Co. 6% bonds with a par value of $200,000 and common stock with a par value of $200,000. Swisher Co. bonds are selling on the market at this time at 95. How would you recommend that the building acquisition be recorded?

**5.** The Eastern Motors Corp. acquired land and old buildings at a cost of $40,000. Delinquent taxes of $6,000 were paid, as well as attorney's fees of $1,500 for title search, etc., in connection with the purchase of the property. Buildings were removed at a cost of $1,500, but $300 was realized from the sale of salvaged materials. From January 1 to April 1 buildings were constructed at a cost of $80,000. Buildings were occupied on April 1. Insurance on buildings taken out on January 1 was $2,400 for a 3-year period. How would land and buildings be carried on the books at the end of the year?

**6.** The Jones Company has a certain machine costing $50,000 with a useful life of 5 years and salvage value of $2,000. The estimated service life of the machine is 20,000 hours. In 1963 total service-hours amounted to 3,000; in 1964, 5,000. Compare depreciation charges for both years, using the straight-line, service-hours, and sum of years'-digits methods.

**7.** Wesley Sales acquires machinery at a cost of $10,000. The estimated life of the asset is 5 years, and it is believed that the asset will have to be scrapped at the end of this time with a value of approximately $100. Prepare a table of depreciation charges for the 5-year period if depreciation is recorded at a fixed percentage on the diminishing book value of the asset. (The fifth root of .01 = .398.)

**8.** The Warner Co. records show the following assets:

|            | Acquired | Cost    | Salvage Value | Estimated Useful Life |
|------------|----------|---------|---------------|-----------------------|
| Machinery  | 7/1/63   | $65,000 | $5,000        | 10 years              |
| Equipment  | 1/1/64   | 25,000  | 1,000         | 6 years               |
| Fixtures   | 1/1/64   | 15,000  | 3,000         | 4 years               |

What is (a) the composite life of the assets and (b) the composite depreciation rate on assets?

## PROBLEMS

**12-1.** An escrow statement received by Eastern Corp. in connection with the purchase of property on September 15, 1964, shows the following:

Charges:

| | |
|---|---:|
| Purchase price.................................... | $35,000 |
| Real estate taxes (paid by vendor and covering tax period, September 15, 1964–June 30, 1965)................. | 850 |
| Fire insurance paid by vendor and covering insurance period, September 15, 1964–Jan. 1, 1966)............. | 520 |
| Special assessment for street lighting (paid by vendor and covering tax period, September 15, 1964–June 30, 1965) | 15 |
| Termite inspection fees (fees were $150, ½ of fees were charged to vendee, as agreed)...................... | 75 |
| | $36,460 |

Credits:

| | |
|---|---:|
| Rentals on property (retained by vendor and covering rental period, September 15–November 1, 1964).......... | $    600 |
| Lease prepayment (retained by vendor and representing rental for month of December, 1965)................ | 200 |
| First mortgage note signed by vendee.................. | 25,000 |
| Cash deposited by vendee in escrow................... | 10,660 |
| | $36,460 |

*Instructions:* Give the entry that would be made by the Eastern Corp. to summarize the purchase of property as reported above. Assume that cost is apportioned to land and buildings in the ratio of assessed values as reported by the property tax bill, which are: land, $6,000, improvements, $8,000.

**12-2.** The following transactions were completed by the Palmer Co. during 1964:

Mar. 1.          Purchased real property for $75,825 which included a charge of $825 representing property taxes for March 1–June 30 that had been prepaid by the vendor. Thirty per cent of the purchase price is deemed applicable to land and the balance to buildings. A mortgage of $50,000 was assumed by the Palmer Co. on the purchase.

Mar. 2–30.  Previous owners had failed to take care of normal maintenance and repairs requirements on the building, necessitating current reconditioning at a cost of $6,500.

Apr. 1–May 15.  Garages in the rear of the buildings were demolished, $250 being recovered on the lumber salvage. The company itself proceeded to construct a warehouse. The cost of such construction was $10,000 which was almost exactly the same as bids made on the construction by independent contractors. Upon completion of construction, city inspectors ordered extensive modifications in the buildings as a result of failure on the part of the company to comply with the Building Safety Code. Such modifications, which could have been avoided, cost $2,500.

Nov. 5–20.  A fire of unknown origin destroyed the building show windows and entrance. The amount of the fire loss was estimated at $5,000, which included display merchandise of $600 and fixtures of $400, and the full amount of the loss was immediately recovered from the insurance company. A new entrance and windows of modern design were completed at a cost of $7,500.

Dec. 29–31.  The business was closed to permit taking the year-end inventory. During this period, required redecorating and repairs were completed at a cost of $450.

*Instructions:* Give journal entries to record each of the preceding transactions. (Disregard depreciation.)

**12-3.** The cost of a machine purchased by Potter, Inc. on April 1, 1964 is $25,000. It is estimated that the machine will have a $1,000 trade-in value at the end of its service life. Its life is estimated at 6 years; its working hours are estimated at 25,000; its production is estimated at 400,000 units. During 1964, the machine was operated 4,200 hours and produced 80,000 units.

*Instructions:* Compute the depreciation on the machine for 1964 by: (1) the straight-line method, (2) the service-hours method, (3) the productive-output method, (4) the sum of years'-digits method, and (5) the declining-balance method using an annual rate of 35%.

**12-4.** The Haney Supply Co. installs a processing line on November 1, 1963, at a cost of $30,000. It is estimated that the machinery will have an 8-year life, and that the cost of removing machinery at the end of this time will be equal to its scrap value. It is estimated that the machine will process 200,000,000 units during its useful life. During 1963 and 1964, 2,400,000 units and 22,000,000 units respectively were produced.

*Instructions:* Compute the depreciation on the machinery for the years ended December 31, 1963 and 1964, using (1) the straight-line method, (2) the productive-output method, and (3) the sum of years'-digits method.

**12-5.** The Ramsey Company had the following property transactions during the first two years of its operation:

| | Property Acquired | | Property Sold | |
| Year | Cost | Est. Life | Cost | Year Acquired |
|---|---|---|---|---|
| 1963 | $150,000 | 12 years | | |
| 1964 | 80,000 | 12 years | $30,000 | 1963 |

Depreciation was recorded on the books of the company at one-half of the full year's depreciation in the year of asset acquisition and at a full year's depreciation in the year of asset disposal. No residual value was considered.

*Instructions:* Based upon the above information show in T-account form the entries that would appear at the end of the two-year period in the allowance for depreciation account, assuming that depreciation is calculated by each of the following methods (show all calculations):

(1) Depreciation for the first one-third of asset life is to be recorded at one and one-half times the straight-line rate; for the second one-third, at the straight-line rate; and for the last one-third, at one-half of the straight-line rate.

(2) Depreciation is to be recorded on the asset declining balance at a rate that is double the straight-line rate.

**12-6.** The Paul Mfg. Co. acquired 20 similar machines at the beginning of 1960 for $30,000. Machines have an average life of 5 years and no residual value. The group-depreciation method is employed in writing off the cost of the machines. Machines were retired as follows:

1 machine at the end of 1962      12 machines at the end of 1964
4 machines at the end of 1963      3 machines at the end of 1965

*Instructions:* Give the entries to record the retirement of machines and the periodic depreciation for the years 1960–1965 inclusive.

**12-7.** Information relating to the equipment owned by James Whitson follows:

| | Cost | Estimated Salvage Value | Estimated Life in Years |
|---|---|---|---|
| Store Equipment | $17,500 | $ 500 | 10 |
| Office Equipment | 6,500 | 500 | 5 |
| Factory Equipment | 40,000 | None | 10 |
| Delivery Equipment | 16,000 | 4,000 | 4 |

*Instructions:* Calculate (1) a composite depreciation rate and (2) the composite life for the equipment owned.

# Chapter 13

# PLANT AND EQUIPMENT
## SPECIAL VALUATION PROBLEMS

### Changes in cost and depreciation

It was indicated in the preceding chapter that plant and equipment items are recorded at cost, that estimates are made of the useful lives of the assets, and that schedules are developed for the reasonable and systematic allocation of asset costs to periodic revenues. These are the normal procedures in accounting for plant and equipment. But during the course of asset use, certain circumstances may suggest revisions in cost allocation plans and, in some instances, actual departures from cost for asset valuation as well as for periodic allocations. These problems are considered in this chapter.

### Revisions in estimates of asset life

When an asset is retired, any errors in the estimates of asset life and asset residual value become evident, and recognition is made in the accounts at that time for any past overdepreciation or underdepreciation. If depreciation charges have been inadequate, the book value of the asset exceeds its residual value and a decrease in capital is recognized; if depreciation charges have been excessive, the book value is less than residual value and an increase in capital is recognized.

It may become evident during the life of a property item that depreciation was incorrectly estimated and that periodic charges have been inadequate or excessive. It may be found that asset life has been reduced by physical declines that exceed original expectations or by inadequacy or obsolescence that could not have been foreseen, or that life has been prolonged by high standards of maintenance and repairs or the absence of certain anticipated declines in usefulness. Under these circumstances, a choice must be made between the following procedures:

1. The book value may be accepted as it stands and such remaining book value allocated over the estimated remaining life of the asset.
2. A correcting entry may be made to restate accumulated depreciation on the basis of present evidence, and depreciation charges for the remaining life of the asset reported in accordance with such evidence.

To illustrate the foregoing procedures, assume that depreciation at 10% has been applied for a certain asset with an estimated life of 10 years. At the end of 5 years, when the book value of the asset is reduced to 50% of cost, it is determined that the asset has a remaining useful life of 10 years. If no change in prior depreciation is to be recognized in the accounts, the remaining asset cost will be distributed over the remaining life or at the rate of 5% a year (50% ÷ 10). If a correction for past overdepreciation is to be recognized, the asset book value will be increased to ⅔ of original cost and depreciation for the remaining life of the asset reported at the rate of 6⅔% a year (66⅔% ÷ 10).

The first position, which accepts existing book value as a basis for subsequent charges, has received wide support in practice. Those supporting this position maintain that cost once assigned to revenue is a permanent disposition of such cost and only unassigned cost is subject to future allocation. The correction of accounts for depreciation recognized in prior periods is considered unacceptable, since such revision will result in depreciation charges over the life of the asset whose total will differ from original depreciable cost.

Additional support for the first position is found in certain practical considerations. This is the general position that must be taken for income tax purposes; depreciation once allowed for tax purposes is not subject to later revision. When depreciation is reported on the books in accordance with income tax requirements, special account analysis and restatement of depreciation data is unnecessary in preparing tax returns.

Those taking the second position maintain that errors, no matter what their source, call for appropriate correction. The depreciation for each period should be the best estimate that can be made from the evidence at hand. Errors in past charges should not be corrected by compensating errors in subsequent charges; such a practice, it is maintained, will serve only to distort measurements of the past, present, and future.

## Recording corrections in accumulated depreciation

*Understatement of depreciation.* To illustrate the procedure that is followed when depreciation has been inadequate and a correction for past charges is to be made, assume that machinery, cost $15,000, has been depreciated by the straight-line method on an estimated 15-year life. After the machinery has been used for 5 years, it is determined that the asset can serve for only 5 more years. The annual depreciation, then, should have been $1,500 instead of $1,000, and the depreciation for the first 5 years has been understated by $2,500. The entry to correct the accounts is:

Corrections in Profits of Prior Periods — Understatement
of Depreciation (or Retained Earnings)............... 2,500
    Allowance for Depreciation of Machinery.........     2,500

Depreciation for the remaining years of asset life would be recorded at the revised rate of $1,500.

*Overstatement of depreciation.* To illustrate the procedure when depreciation has been excessive and a correction for past charges is to be made, assume that machinery, cost $15,000, has been depreciated by the straight-line method on an estimated 15-year life. After the machinery has been used 10 years, it is determined that the asset can be used for another 10 years. The annual depreciation, then, should have been $750 instead of $1,000 and the depreciation for the first 10 years has been overstated by $2,500. The entry to correct the account is:

| | | |
|---|---|---|
| Allowance for Depreciation of Machinery............ | 2,500 | |
| Corrections in Profits of Prior Periods — Overstatement of Depreciation (or Retained Earnings)....... | | 2,500 |

Depreciation thereafter would be recorded at the corrected annual rate of $750.

Correction of past depreciation is indicated for a fully depreciated asset that is continued in use, except when continued use involves extraordinary maintenance and repair charges that suggest little or no contribution on the part of the asset itself. For example, a fully depreciated asset may be continued in use by a business unit because of inability to finance a replacement. Inefficiencies and extraordinary charges may actually make the use of such an asset more costly than a new machine. Under these circumstances no value can be assigned to the property item. Cost and allowance balances for fully depreciated assets should not be offset until the property items are actually retired; financial statements should provide parenthetical or note references to fully depreciated assets still in use and included in the account totals.

## Changes in depreciation resulting from additions, betterments, and replacements

Depreciation charges may require revision during the life of plant and equipment items as a result of additional expenditures related to these properties. Expenditures that enlarge or improve property items and are reported as increases in the asset cost must be recognized in recording depreciation in subsequent periods. For example, assume that a machine with an estimated life of 20 years is acquired for $10,000. After the machine is used for 15 years, an expenditure of $2,000 is made that improves the machine but does not prolong its useful life. The entry for the betterment is:

| | | |
|---|---|---|
| Machinery..................................... | 2,000 | |
| Cash........................................ | | 2,000 |

Annual depreciation would now be calculated as follows:

| | | |
|---|---|---|
| Original asset: | $10,000 ÷ 20 | $500 |
| Betterment: | $ 2,000 ÷ 5 | 400 |
| Revised annual depreciation | | $900 |

Expenditures that rehabilitate certain assets or increase their service lives beyond original estimates, and are recorded by charges to the asset valuation account also affect the depreciation charges to be made in subsequent periods. To illustrate, assume in the previous example that the expenditure did not improve the asset but simply prolonged its remaining service life to 8 years. The expenditure to rehabilitate the asset is recorded as follows:

| | | |
|---|---|---|
| Allowance for Depreciation of Machinery............ | 2,000 | |
| Cash ....................................... | | 2,000 |

Depreciation for the remaining life of the asset is determined as follows:

| | |
|---|---|
| Asset cost....................................... | $10,000 |
| Less allowance for depreciation, $7,500, reduced by $2,000 as a result of asset rehabilitation.............................. | 5,500 |
| Book value to be written off during remaining 8 years...... | $ 4,500 |

Revised annual depreciation: $4,500 ÷ 8, or $562.50.

## Departures from cost

It was stated in Chapter 1 that the matching process is fundamental in accounting activity. It was further stated that this process consists of the measurement of revenue and the matching against revenue of expired costs. Costs related to future revenues are held back from current profit and loss recognition and deferred. Certain exceptions to this practice are accepted. Thus current assets, such as receivables, marketable securities, and inventories, are reported at less than cost when it is felt that realization of these assets may be limited to the lower amounts; long-term investments are reported at less than cost when declines in the values of these assets are significant and appear to be permanent; and properties acquired through donation or discovery are reported at their fair market values in providing satisfactory bases for asset reporting and income measurement. The introduction of appraisal values in the accounts for property items whose replacement values have changed materially since their acquisition represents a further departure from the cost concept; but this practice is considered acceptable only under exceptional circumstances.

## Replacement values for assets

In the early 1930's, companies experienced a severe fall in asset values. In addition, prices obtained for products sold had fallen to a point where they were insufficient to cover production costs if costs included depreciation based on the original asset costs. During the next three decades, companies experienced a continuous rise in property values. This rise was occasioned by a general increase in prices and in many cases by improvements in adjoining areas that increased land values significantly. In periods of both falling and rising prices, proposals have been made that current price levels be recognized in the valuation of property items.

*Price-level declines.* When the price level declines and recovery to previous levels is not expected, arguments in support of the recognition of such "permanent" declines take the following form: price decline and the ability to replace assets at materially lower prices results in a loss that may be compared to that from a fire or other casualty; to continue reporting property items at amounts that exceed the values of the economic utilities they afford would lead to distortions in financial position and income measurements. Recognition of lower replacement values on the records is advocated as being both realistic and conservative.

But those who support the continued use of cost claim that to adjust property accounts for price-level decline is to engage in normalizing costs and periodic income. This group maintains that the full burden of costs must be assigned to revenues in arriving at earnings that measure the sum total of management's activities.

Accountants generally have supported the continued use of cost in periods of price decline. There is agreement that write-downs are appropriate when it is clear that costs will not be recovered through future activities; however, write-downs simply in response to a declining price level are not encouraged.

*Price-level advances.* When a rise in the general price level is viewed as permanent, the argument is raised, as in the case of decline, that changes in the accounts must be recognized if financial position and charges to revenue are not to be distorted. Recognition of advances is supported not only as a means of making financial statements more informative and useful but also to insure the proper administration of business resources.

Here, too, the answer by accountants generally has been that adherence to cost is normally the best standard for the development of general purpose statements. Cost, it is maintained, is objective and verifiable, remains unalterable, and is readily understood. Cost, furthermore, is the relative factor in the process of matching sacrifice against achievement. Valuation data, on the other hand, are subjective and unverifiable, are continuously changing, and must be defined in terms of diverse valuation criteria. Accountants recognize that there may be occasions when special circumstances, such as the discovery of valuable resources or other special enhancement of values, call for the recognition of higher values. But the recognition of higher property values in the accounts simply in response to an advancing price level is discouraged.

## Use of appraisal data

Appraisal values for property items may be required for credit, tax, insurance, sale, or merger purposes. On the other hand, such values may be sought for use in the accounts. When appraisal values are required, they should be provided by reliable independent appraisers.

Appraisals by professional engineers or appraisers normally afford data relative to the cost of reproducing individual assets as follows:

1. *Reproduction cost*, which is the present amount required to reproduce the property new.
2. *Sound value*, which is the remaining fractional life of the asset applied to reproduction cost. Sometimes, sound value is expressed as a *condition percent* which is the present percentage relationship of sound value to reproduction cost.

It may frequently be more informative to obtain data relative to replacement cost rather than reproduction cost. Replacement cost suggests the cost of replacing existing capacity rather than reproducing identical facilities.

The purpose of obtaining appraisal data for use in the accounts may be either: (1) simply to correct account balances when the relationship of sound values to reproduction costs suggests that there has been past overdepreciation or underdepreciation; or (2) to bring accounts into agreement with current values. To illustrate such uses, assume the following: a property item was acquired at a cost of $60,000 and is being depreciated on an 8-year life or at a rate of $12\frac{1}{2}\%$; after being used for 4 years, the property is appraised at a reproduction cost of $100,000 and at a sound value of $60,000 or a condition percent of 60%.

Accumulated depreciation on asset cost is 50%. However, an asset decline to date of only 40% is indicated by the appraisal. If the latter decline measures primarily the physical deterioration of the asset, no change in original allocations may be indicated and future depreciation charges may be continued at $12\frac{1}{2}\%$. On the other hand, if the decline of 40% can be accepted as a measure of physical and functional decline, the appraisal may be regarded as indicating that past depreciation was excessive and that depreciation should be recognized at 10% per year. The allowance for depreciation, then, should be corrected and the revised rate used in recording depreciation subsequent to the correction. It will be assumed in the examples in this chapter that differences in appraisal and book depreciation indicate misstatements in prior depreciation and call for entries to correct the accounts.

If reproduction costs are to be reflected in the accounts, entries to correct accumulated depreciation would still be made. These are followed by entries to bring the account balances into agreement with appraised values.

Any changes that are reported in the accounts for asset cost as well as for related depreciation charges must be disregarded for income tax purposes. For tax purposes the basis for depreciation continues to be original cost; the basis for computing gain or loss on the disposal of the asset is the asset book value stated in terms of such cost.

### Asset devaluation recorded in the accounts

A write-down of plant and equipment cost reduces both the property item and retained earnings. The asset is credited and a nominal account or retained earnings is charged, depending upon whether the write-down is to be reflected on the income statement or on the retained earnings statement. In the case of depreciable assets, devaluation generally affects both the asset and the related allowance account balances.

To illustrate the write-down of a depreciable asset, assume the following data for a company's buildings:

| Cost | Asset Use to Date | Depreciation to Date | Allowance for Depreciation |
|---|---|---|---|
| $500,000 | 10 yrs. | 20% | $100,000 |

An appraisal of buildings establishes a present reproduction cost of $300,000 and a sound value of $240,000, or 80% of the reproduction cost. Since the appraisal confirms a 20% decline in the asset in 10 years, no correction in past depreciation charges is required. In recording the appraisal decrease in the accounts, then, changes are limited to the following:

| | Cost | Asset Use to Date | Depreciation to Date | Allowance for Depreciation |
|---|---|---|---|---|
| Original cost balances............... | $500,000 | 10 yrs. | 20% | $100,000 |
| Appraisal decrease.................. | (200,000) | | | (40,000) |
| Balances, per appraisal.............. | $300,000 | 10 yrs. | 20% | $ 60,000 |

The entry to revalue the asset follows:

| | | |
|---|---|---|
| Allowance for Depreciation of Buildings.......... | 40,000 | |
| Loss on Buildings Revaluation (or Retained Earnings)..................................... | 160,000 | |
| Buildings......................................... | | 200,000 |

Assume in the preceding example that the appraisal establishes a reproduction cost for the asset of $300,000 but a sound value of only $225,000 or 75% of such reproduction cost, depreciation of 25% being related to asset use for 10 years. Here, the appraisal indicates: (1) inadequate depreciation of $25,000 in the past in terms of cost; (2) a further reduction in the asset from a corrected book value of $375,000 to a sound value of $225,000. The changes are summarized below:

|  | Cost | Asset Use to Date | Depreciation to Date | Allowance for Depreciation |
|---|---|---|---|---|
| Original cost balances.............. | $500,000 | 10 yrs. | 20% | $100,000 |
| Correction in depreciation of prior periods......................... |  |  | 5% | 25,000 |
| Cost balances as corrected........... | $500,000 | 10 yrs. | 25% | $125,000 |
| Appraisal decrease.................. | (200,000) |  |  | (50,000) |
| Balances, per appraisal.............. | $300,000 | 10 yrs. | 25% | $ 75,000 |

The entries to accomplish these changes follow:

| Transaction | Entry |
|---|---|
| (1) To correct allowance for depreciation to 25% of cost, per appraisal. | Correction in Profits of Prior Periods — Understatement of Depreciation (or Retained Earnings)......................   25,000<br>    Allowance for Depreciation of Buildings      25,000 |
| (2) To reduce asset and depreciation allowance to a reproduction cost of $300,000, per appraisal. | Allowance for Depreciation of Buildings..   50,000<br>Loss on Buildings Revaluation (or Retained Earnings)..................... 150,000<br>    Buildings.........................      200,000 |

Depreciation after correction of the allowance balance would be recognized at 2½% per year as established by the appraisal.

## Quasi-reorganization

A situation may arise in which a company's properties were acquired at costs which do not permit a profit under current conditions. There may also be a deficit from previous operations or a retained earnings balance that is insufficient to absorb a reduction in the carrying value of the property items. Yet such a reduction may be warranted by current conditions and indeed may be necessary if the company is to be able to report profitable operations in future periods. The company erred in acquiring property which could not be employed profitably in the business, but it should be recognized that the mistake has already been made, and that future operations should not be burdened with past mistakes.

Under such circumstances a company may elect to write down property items and to accompany such action with a restatement of the capital structure, eliminating the deficit that is found after the write-off. The elimination of a deficit through a restatement of invested capital balances that provides, in effect, a "fresh start" accounting-wise on the part of the corporation, is called a *quasi-reorganization* or *corporate readjustment*. The quasi-reorganization procedure does not require recourse to the courts as in formal reorganization procedures; there is no change in the legal corporate entity or interruption in business activity.

To illustrate the nature of a quasi-reorganization, assume that the Baldwin Corporation has suffered losses from operations for some time and both current and future revenues appear to be insufficient to cover the depreciation on properties that were acquired when prices were considerably higher than at present. The company decides upon a restatement of assets and also the restatement of paid-in capital to remove the deficit and make possible the declaration of dividends upon a return to profitable operations. A balance sheet for the company just prior to this action follows:

Baldwin Corporation
Balance Sheet
June 30, 1964

| | | | | | | |
|---|---|---|---|---|---|---|
| Current assets | | | $ 250,000 | Liabilities | | $ 300,000 |
| Plant and equip- | | | | Stockholders' equity | | |
| ment | $1,500,000 | | | Capital stock, $10 par, | | |
| Less allowance for | | | | 100,000 shares . $1,000,000 | | |
| depreciation | 600,000 | 900,000 | | Less deficit | 150,000 | 850,000 |
| | | | | Total liabilities and stock- | | |
| Total assets | | | $1,150,000 | holders' equity | | $1,150,000 |

The quasi-reorganization is to be accomplished as follows:

1. Plant and equipment is to be reduced to its present sound value of $600,000 by reductions in the asset and allowance balances of 33⅓%.
2. Capital stock is to be reduced to a par of $5, $500,000 in capital stock thus being converted into "additional paid-in capital."
3. The deficit of $450,000 ($150,000 as reported on the balance sheet increased by $300,000 arising from the write-down of plant and equipment) is to be applied against the capital from the reduction of the par value of stock.

Entries to record the changes follow:

| Transaction | Entry | | |
|---|---|---|---|
| (1) To write down plant and equipment and allowance balances by 33⅓%. | Retained Earnings (Deficit) | 300,000 | |
| | Allowance for Depreciation | 200,000 | |
| | Plant and Equipment | | 500,000 |
| (2) To reduce the capital stock balance from $10 par to $5 par and to establish paid-in capital from reduction in stock par value. | Capital Stock ($10 par, 100,000 shares). | 1,000,000 | |
| | Capital Stock ($5 par, 100,000 shares) | | 500,000 |
| | Paid-In Capital from Reduction in Stock Par Value | | 500,000 |

| Transaction | Entry | | |
|---|---|---|---|
| (3) To apply the deficit after asset devaluation against paid-in capital from reduction in stock par value. | Paid-In Capital from Reduction in Stock Par Value.................. | 450,000 | |
| | Retained Earnings (Deficit)....... | | 450,000 |

The balance sheet after the quasi-reorganization is shown below.

Baldwin Corporation
Balance Sheet
June 30, 1964

| | | | | |
|---|---|---|---|---|
| Current assets............. | | $ 250,000 | Liabilities................. | $ 300,000 |
| Plant and equipment......... | $1,000,000 | | Capital stock, $5 par, 100,000 shares.................. | 500,000 |
| Less allowance for depreciation... | 400,000 | 600,000 | Paid-in capital from reduction in stock par value.... | 50,000 |
| Total assets............... | | $ 850,000 | Total liabilities and stockholders' equity......... | $ 850,000 |

Following the quasi-reorganization, the accounting for the company may be handled in a manner similar to that of a new company. Earnings subsequent to the quasi-reorganization, however, should be accumulated in a *dated retained earnings* account. On future balance sheets, retained earnings dated as of the time of account readjustment will inform readers of the date of such action and the fresh start in earnings accumulation.

## Asset appreciation recorded in the accounts

When appreciation is to be entered on the books, both the property and capital balances are increased. The capital increase, however, is still unrealized and must be designated as appraisal capital.

To illustrate the process of recording asset appreciation, assume that land, cost $50,000, is increased to an appraised value of $80,000. An entry is made as follows:

| | | |
|---|---|---|
| Land — Appraisal Increase..................... | 30,000 | |
| Appraisal Capital — Land.................... | | 30,000 |

Land would be reported on the balance sheet at its appraised value, $80,000. The appraisal capital should not be merged with other capital balances but should be reported separately on the balance sheet so that the reader of the statement is fully aware of the unrealized nature of such capital.

If the land is sold at a later date for $75,000, $25,000 of the recorded appreciation will have been realized. The gain is recognized and the appraisal capital is canceled by the following entry:

| | | |
|---|---|---|
| Cash. . . . . . . . . . . . . . . . . . . . . . . . . . . . . . . . . . . . . . . . . . | 75,000 | |
| Appraisal Capital — Land. . . . . . . . . . . . . . . . . . . . . . | 30,000 | |
| Land. . . . . . . . . . . . . . . . . . . . . . . . . . . . . . . . . . . . . . . | | 50,000 |
| Land — Appraisal Increase. . . . . . . . . . . . . . . . . . . . | | 30,000 |
| Gain on Sale of Land. . . . . . . . . . . . . . . . . . . . . . . . | | 25,000 |

With this entry, all evidence of the appraisal is canceled, and the account balances are the same as though the asset had been carried at its cost, $50,000, and subsequently sold for $75,000.

Appraisals of depreciable assets may indicate both corrections in accumulated depreciation as well as increased reproduction costs.   In recording devaluation, the effects of both a correction in accumulated depreciation and the asset write-down were reflected in retained earnings. In recording appreciation, however, a correction in accumulated depreciation affects retained earnings, but the asset write-up gives rise to appraisal capital. Entries, then, are required (1) to correct the allowance for depreciation in terms of cost and (2) to record the appraisal increase in the asset and also in the allowance for depreciation. Although appraisal increases may be reported directly in the asset and the allowance accounts, it is normally desirable to report these in separate accounts. Cost data are thus preserved and are available in the preparation of income tax returns where the effects of appraisals are ignored. Subsequent entries that require information concerning both cost and appraisal increases can be more conveniently prepared.

To illustrate the foregoing, assume the following data for buildings:

| Cost | Asset Use to Date | Depreciation to Date | Allowance for Depreciation |
|---|---|---|---|
| $200,000 | 20 yrs. | 40% | $80,000 |

At this time an appraisal of the property shows it to have a reproduction cost of $320,000 and a sound value of only $160,000, 50% of its useful life having expired. The appraisal thus indicates (1) inadequate depreciation in the past in terms of cost of $20,000; (2) an increase in the asset from a corrected book value of $100,000 to a sound value of $160,000. These changes are summarized as follows:

| | Cost | Asset Use to Date | Depreciation to Date | Allowance for Depreciation |
|---|---|---|---|---|
| Original cost balances. . . . . . . . . . . . . . . | $200,000 | 20 yrs. | 40% | $ 80,000 |
| Correction in depreciation of prior periods. . . . . . . . . . . . . . . . . . . . . . . . . | | | 10% | 20,000 |
| Cost balances as corrected. . . . . . . . . . . | $200,000 | 20 yrs. | 50% | $100,000 |
| Appraisal increase. . . . . . . . . . . . . . . . . . | 120,000 | | | 60,000 |
| Balances, per appraisal. . . . . . . . . . . . . . | $320,000 | 20 yrs. | 50% | $160,000 |

Entries to record the appraisal follow:

| Transaction | Entry | | |
|---|---|---|---|
| (1) To correct allowance for depreciation to 50% of cost, per appraisal. | Correction in Profits of Prior Periods — Understatement of Depreciation (or Retained Earnings)................ | 20,000 | |
| | Allowance for Depreciation of Buildings........................... | | 20,000 |
| (2) To increase asset and depreciation allowance to a reproduction cost of $320,000, per appraisal. | Buildings — Appraisal Increase...... | 120,000 | |
| | Allowance for Depreciation of Buildings — Appraisal Increase......... | | 60,000 |
| | Appraisal Capital — Buildings..... | | 60,000 |

## Depreciation on asset appreciation

When asset appreciation is recorded in the accounts, depreciation may continue to be recognized in terms of original cost, appraisal data finding expression only on the balance sheet. On the other hand, asset appreciation may be recognized in the calculation of periodic depreciation, net income being developed in terms of appraisal depreciation. Both procedures may be found in practice and arguments are advanced in support of each.

Those who would limit the use of appraisal values to the balance sheet insist that costs can arise only from expenditures; it is the past dollar cost that must be matched against dollars earned in arriving at net income. Depreciation accounting, it is maintained, should not be related to the problem of asset replacement. Asset replacement is a separate problem that calls for separate financial planning. Replacements at higher prices will be made on the assumption that future revenues will be sufficient to recover such outlays. Replacement considerations, then, should not be permitted to distort current income measurements.

Practical considerations, too, support the cost approach to depreciation. When depreciation is recorded in terms of cost, charges on the books show the depreciation actually allowable for income tax purposes. When depreciation is recorded on the basis of appraisals, charges must be restated in terms of cost in the preparation of tax returns.

Those who support charges for depreciation in terms of appraisal values insist that such a procedure must be employed if income measurements are to be meaningful. Comparative analyses of profit and loss data are possible only if current costs are matched against current revenues. Earnings measurements offer management a better guide to product pricing, dividend payments, and other operating policies. Those supporting charges in terms of appraisal values further maintain that a company is obliged to report charges on the income statement consistent with the representations for depreciable properties made on the balance sheet.

*Recording depreciation on cost.* When depreciation is based on original cost, the income statement reports operations on a cost basis, while only the balance sheet reflects appraisal values. Depreciation is recorded in the usual manner. A second entry is required, however, to recognize the shrinkage that has taken place in the recorded appreciation. Both the asset increase arising from the appraisal and the appraisal capital must be reduced. This is accomplished by a charge to appraisal capital and a credit to the allowance account reporting depreciation on the appraisal increase. The allocation of asset cost to operations is thus accompanied by a write-off of the appraisal increase.

To illustrate, assume that at the beginning of 1964, equipment acquired on January 1, 1961, is shown on the books at cost, $100,000, less an allowance of $37,500 representing depreciation at 12½% a year, or at a book value of $62,500. An appraisal on January 2, 1964, sets the reproduction cost of the equipment at $150,000 and its present sound value at 70% of this amount, or $105,000. Depreciation of 30% in 3 years reported by the appraisal indicates a depreciation rate of 10%. The following entries are required:

| Transaction | Entry | | |
|---|---|---|---|
| January 2, 1964<br>(1) To decrease allowance for depreciation to 30% of cost, per appraisal. | Allowance for Depreciation of Equipment..<br>  Corrections in Profits of Prior Periods —<br>  Overstatement of Depreciation (or Retained Earnings).................... | 7,500 | 7,500 |
| (2) To increase asset and depreciation allowance to a reproduction cost of $150,000, per appraisal. | Equipment — Appraisal Increase.........<br>  Allowance for Depreciation of Equipment<br>  — Appraisal Increase................<br>  Appraisal Capital — Equipment........ | 50,000 | 15,000<br>35,000 |
| December 31, 1964<br>(1) To record depreciation on cost of $100,000 at corrected rate of 10%, per appraisal. | Depreciation of Equipment..............<br>  Allowance for Depreciation of Equipment | 10,000 | 10,000 |
| (2) To reduce appraisal increase of $50,000 at rate of 10% consistent with reduction in asset at cost. | Appraisal Capital — Equipment.........<br>  Allowance for Depreciation of Equipment<br>  — Appraisal Increase................ | 5,000 | 5,000 |

Assuming that the asset is retired at the end of 1970, the allowance for depreciation at cost is offset against the asset account and the allowance for depreciation on the appraisal increase is applied against the asset appraisal increase account. All of the accounts related to the property item are thus closed.

*Recording depreciation on appraised values.* When depreciation is recorded on appraised values, the income statement reports charges consistent with the increased values assigned to assets. Depreciation on appraised values is recorded by a charge to expense and credits to the allowance accounts reporting depreciation on cost and on the appraisal increase. The entry to record depreciation may be accompanied by a second entry to recognize the portion of appraisal capital that may be regarded as realized through operations. This is accomplished by a charge to appraisal capital and a credit to retained earnings. The write-off of the asset in terms of appraised values is thus accompanied by the realization of appraisal capital, and retained earnings is reported at the balance that would have been shown in the absence of an appraisal. To illustrate, assume the facts given in the preceding illustration. The entries to record the revaluation are the same. Periodic entries to record depreciation are made as follows:

| Transaction | Entry | | |
|---|---|---|---|
| December 31, 1964 (1) To record depreciation on appraised value of $150,000 at corrected rate of 10%, per appraisal. | Depreciation of Equipment............... Allowance for Depreciation of Equipment Allowance for Depreciation of Equipment —Appraisal Increase................. | 15,000 | 10,000 5,000 |
| (2) To record realization of appraisal capital of $50,000 at rate of 10%, consistent with reduction in the asset appraisal increase. | Appraisal Capital — Equipment......... Retained Earnings.................. | 5,000 | 5,000 |

The first entry records depreciation on the appraised value. The second entry transfers appraisal capital to the retained earnings account. Appraisal capital then reflects the appraisal increase in the reduced book value of the asset, and retained earnings reports earnings based upon actual costs. When the asset is fully depreciated, the entire balance in the appraisal capital account will have been transferred to retained earnings by the periodic entries. Upon disposal of the asset, allowance for depreciation balances are applied against their respective asset accounts.

Instead of periodic transfers from appraisal capital to retained earnings, transfers may be made to a special revenue account which is ultimately combined with other profit and loss data and carried to retained earnings. The special revenue account is recognized on the income statement as an adjustment to the summary of operations to compensate for depreciation that is recognized at more than cost. When such a procedure is followed, operations can be viewed in terms of depreciation calculated on appraisal values, but both final net income and retained earnings balances are developed in accordance with historical cost.

Some accountants object to the transfer of appraisal capital to either revenue or retained earnings. They view appreciation proceeds as similar to devaluation procedures and would regard both asset and capital changes as of a permanent nature. Appraisal balances in asset accounts would be recognized for all further asset accounting including periodic allocations to operations; appraisal capital would be viewed as permanent capital with neither utilization nor sale of the asset affecting this balance. In answering such objection, it may be pointed out that the recognition of appraisal capital is necessitated by the presence of income which has definitely accrued to the benefit of stockholders but has not yet been *realized*. The subsequent utilization or sale of the asset gives rise to income that would normally be recognized in accordance with the accepted principles of income realization. At that point the increase in capital is no longer due to a subjective appraisal estimate, but is the result of actual arm's-length transactions, thus justifying its reclassification as retained earnings.

### Retained earnings appropriations in anticipation of asset replacements at a higher price level

Regardless of whether cost or appraisal depreciation is reported on the income statement, the practical problem of providing funds to take care of asset replacement at a higher price level still exists. In order to preserve resources for the replacement of assets at a higher price level, the board of directors may authorize the regular appropriation of retained earnings to withhold earnings from distribution as dividends.

If appropriations of retained earnings are made and funds provided by past earnings are ultimately applied to the replacement of assets at higher costs, appropriated balances may be allowed to stand indefinitely. On the other hand, appropriations may be returned to retained earnings and retained earnings used as a basis for a stock dividend increasing the permanent capital of the business to match the increased dollar investment in plant and equipment. Appropriations of retained earnings originate with the board of directors; the disposition of such balances is likewise a matter to be determined by the board of directors.

### Depletion

Natural resources, also called *wasting assets*, move towards exhaustion as the physical units that such resources comprise are removed and sold. The withdrawal of oil or gas, the cutting of timber, and the mining of coal, sulphur, iron, copper, or silver ore are examples of processes leading to the exhaustion of natural resources. The reduction in the cost or value of natural resources as a result of the withdrawal of such resources is referred to as *depletion*.

Depletion may be distinguished from depreciation in the following respects:

1. Depletion is recognition of the quantitative exhaustion taking place in a natural resource, while depreciation is recognition of the service exhaustion taking place in a plant and equipment item.

2. Related to (1), depletion is recognized as the cost of the material that becomes directly embodied in the product of the company; through depreciation, the cost of an asset may be allocated to production but the asset itself does not become a part of the finished product.

3. Depletion involves a distinctive asset that cannot be directly replaced in kind upon its exhaustion; depreciation involves an asset that is generally replaced upon its exhaustion.

The measurement of net income calls for the recognition of depletion. If the natural resource is sold directly upon its emergence or withdrawal, the recognition of depletion is, in effect, the recognition of cost of goods sold; if the natural resource is processed and stored before sale, depletion is initially recognized as a part of inventory cost.

When natural resources are acquired together with land for a lump sum, the total cost of the property must be allocated to the two property items. Separate accounts may be established for land and for the resources. The cost of the latter asset divided by the estimated quantity of resources that can profitably be removed gives the charge to be recognized for each unit removed, or the *unit depletion charge*. Depletion for the period is the measured number of units removed during the period multiplied by the unit depletion charge.

To illustrate, assume the following facts: land containing natural resources is purchased at a cost of $5,500,000. The land has a value after resource exploitation estimated at $250,000; the natural resource supply is estimated at 1,000,000 tons. The unit depletion charge and the total depletion charge for the first year, assuming the withdrawal of 80,000 tons, are calculated as follows:

Depletion charge per ton: ($5,500,000 — $250,000) ÷ 1,000,000, or $5.25
Depletion charge for the first year: 80,000 tons @ $5.25, or $420,000

When developmental costs, such as costs of drilling, sinking mine shafts, and constructing roads, are related to the exploitation of the resource, these should be added to the original cost of the property in arriving at the total cost subject to depletion. These costs may be incurred before normal activities begin. On the other hand, they may be continuing and hence may call for estimates in arriving at a depletion charge that is to be used uniformly for all recoverable units. When costs will be required in restoring land for use after the resources are exhausted, these should also be added to depletable cost.

The charge for resource exhaustion is recorded by a debit to Depletion and a credit directly to the resource account or to an allowance for depletion. If an allowance is established, it should be subtracted from the resource account in reporting the asset.

The charge for depletion, increased by labor and overhead relating to removal and processing, is reported in the cost of goods sold section of the income statement. If all of the units represented by the depletion charge are sold, depletion, labor, and overhead costs measure the cost of goods sold to be applied against revenue in arriving at gross profit on sales; if some of the units remain on hand, the total for depletion, labor, and overhead related to such units is recognized as inventory and subtracted from total costs in arriving at cost of goods sold. Depletion, therefore, is comparable to raw materials purchases in summarizing operations.

When buildings and improvements are constructed in connection with the exploitation of natural resources and their usefulness is limited to the duration of the project, it is reasonable to recognize depreciation on such properties on an output basis consistent with the charges to be recognized for the natural resources themselves. For example, assume that buildings are constructed at a cost of $250,000; the useful lives of the buildings are expected to terminate upon exhaustion of the natural resource consisting of 1,000,000 units. Under such circumstances, a depreciation charge of $.25 ($250,000 ÷ 1,000,000) should accompany the depletion charge that is recognized for each unit. When improvements provide benefits that are expected to terminate prior to the exhaustion of the natural resource, the cost of such improvements may be allocated on the basis of the units to be removed during the life of the improvements or on a time basis, whichever is considered more appropriate.

Depletion for tax purposes may differ from the amount reported on the books. Federal income tax laws permit the taxpayer to deduct annually a fixed percentage of gross income for depletion of oil and gas wells and minerals. Such *percentage or statutory depletion* is applicable only when it exceeds *cost depletion*. Under current law the depletion rate for oil and gas wells is 27½% of gross income and varies on minerals from 5% to 23% of gross income, but such deduction cannot exceed 50% of the taxable income from the property calculated without regard to the charge for depletion. The taxpayer is permitted to take percentage depletion as long as properties are income producing; there is no limitation on the total allowable depletion, and the sum of periodic depletion deductions may ultimately far exceed property cost.

### Dividends representing proceeds from wasting assets

When a company's stock in trade is its wasting assets, revenue represents a recovery of the cost of such wasting assets charged to operations, a recovery of other expenses, and earnings. When operations are to cease upon exhaustion of the resources, dividends need not be limited to net income but may be paid in amounts equal to such net income increased by the amount charged against revenue as depletion. To limit dividends to net income would be to retain the amount recovered from wasting assets, possibly in unproductive form, until the time the business is liquidated. In the absence of effective utilization of revenue proceeds for new properties or other productive purposes, such assets should be made available to stockholders. Amounts received by stockholders, then, would represent a distribution of earnings and in part a return of invested capital.

To illustrate the nature of the foregoing, assume that the Midas Mines Co. in 1964 issues capital stock in exchange for certain mineral properties valued at $100,000. During the course of the fiscal period, natural resources that cost $25,000 are sold for $50,000 and operating expenses of $10,000 are incurred. At the end of the period, the balance sheet reports the following:

Midas Mines Co.
Balance Sheet
December 31, 1964

| | | | | | |
|---|---|---:|---|---|---:|
| Cash...................... | | $ 35,000 | Liabilities.................. | | $ 5,000 |
| Receivables.................. | | 10,000 | Capital stock............... | | 100,000 |
| Mineral properties... | $100,000 | | Retained earnings........... | | 15,000 |
| Less allowance for | | | | | |
| depletion........... | 25,000 | 75,000 | | | |
| | | | Total liabilities and stock- | | |
| Total assets................. | | $120,000 | holders' equity.............. | | $120,000 |

Management, here, does not need to limit dividends to the retained earnings balance of $15,000, but may consider the limitation to be $40,000, or net income, $15,000, increased by the recovery of the asset depletion, $25,000. However, since revenue has not been fully realized in cash, and since some cash is required for a continuation of operations, dividends of a lesser amount would be in order. If a dividend of $28,000 is paid, it is regarded as representing first a distribution of earnings of $15,000, the balance a return of invested capital to owners. The return of invested capital is reported by a charge to a capital stock offset balance rather than by a charge to capital stock. The entry to record the $28,000 dividend distribution follows:

| Retained Earnings.............................. | 15,000 | |
| Capital Distributions to Stockholders............. | 13,000 | |
| Cash....................................... | | 28,000 |

The stockholders' equity after the distribution would be reported as follows:

| Capital stock..................................... | $100,000 |
| Less capital distributions to stockholders................. | 13,000 |
| Stockholders' equity................................ | $ 87,000 |

The distribution to stockholders of amounts equal to net income increased by the depletion charge is permitted by state laws. Such action is sanctioned on the theory that creditors are aware of the shrinking investment requirements that are peculiar to operations involving wasting assets not subject to replacement. As indicated in Chapter 10, when dividends are in part liquidating, stockholders should be informed of the portion of the dividend representing a distribution of corporate earnings and of the portion representing a return of invested capital.

## Plant and equipment on the balance sheet

Plant and equipment frequently constitutes a substantial portion of a company's total assets, and a separate listing on the balance sheet of the principal assets or groups of assets in this classification is normally desirable. Nondepreciable assets should not be combined with those that are subject to reductions for depreciation allowances. Depreciable assets should be reported at their cost or other basis, and allowances shown as subtractions from such amounts. The basis of an asset, whether cost or a value other than cost, should be disclosed. When there are significant differences in property costs and fair market values, it would be appropriate to disclose such differences by parenthetical remark or special note. When property is reported at an amount other than cost, the difference between the reported value and cost should be stated, together with an explanation of the source of such value and the authority for reporting such value in the accounts. When only summaries of plant and equipment items are provided, detail may be offered on supporting schedules.

Plant and equipment may be presented on the balance sheet as follows:

Plant and equipment:

| | | | |
|---|---|---|---|
| Tools, patterns, and dies, at inventoried value | | | $ 16,500 |
| Machinery and equipment, at cost (balance includes $40,000 of fully depreciated items still in use)................................ | | $184,000 | |
| Less allowance for depreciation............. | | 124,000 | 60,000 |
| Buildings, at cost......................... | | $320,000 | |
| Less allowance for depreciation............. | | 125,000 | 195,000 |
| Land, at cost of acquisition in 1946......... | | | 65,000 |
| Total plant and equipment.............. | | | $336,500 |

When appraisal increases have been recorded in the accounts, assets may be stated at appraised balances and costs reported parenthetically. It would be preferable, however, to offer information for both asset and allowance balances in a form such as the following:

| | Cost | Appraisal Increase | Book Value as Appraised | |
|---|---|---|---|---|
| Buildings............. | $100,000 | $ 75,000 | $175,000 | |
| Less allowance for depreciation............. | 40,000 | 30,000 | 70,000 | |
| Balance.............. | $ 60,000 | $ 45,000 | | $105,000 |

## QUESTIONS

**1.** What alternative procedures may be followed in the accounts upon determining that depreciation has been incorrectly estimated in past years? Evaluate each position.

**2.** How would you recommend that fully depreciated properties be carried in the accounts when they are still being used by the business?

**3.** Revision of past depreciation on properties and revision of account balances to conform to present replacement values of properties are two aspects of the same problem, the accurate statement of balance sheet data. Do you agree?

**4.** What are the arguments for and against the recognition of changes in plant and equipment values as a result of changes in the price level?

**5.** (a) When, in your opinion, would the recognition of a downward revision in the cost of plant items be appropriate? (b) When would you support an upward revision?

**6.** Distinguish between (a) reproduction cost and sound value, (b) appraisal capital and retained earnings, (c) appreciation and devaluation.

**7.** How will changes from cost to appraisal values affect the charges to be recognized on asset use and disposal for income tax purposes?

**8.** Define quasi-reorganization.

**9.** Assuming that appreciation is recorded in the accounts, what are the arguments in support of (a) depreciation in terms of cost and (b) depreciation in terms of appraised value?

**10.** The management of the Taft Corporation suggests that depreciation on assets that have been written up be recorded on the higher values in order to assure the availability of funds for the replacement of such assets. In your opinion, is this practice necessary and sufficient in meeting the problem?

**11.** Officers of the X Corporation feel that prices have reached a permanently higher level and thus insist that depreciation on plant and equipment be recognized in terms of higher reproduction costs if current earnings are to be accurately stated.  Officers of the Y Corporation feel that prices are too high and will ultimately decline and thus insist that current revenue be charged with a part of the cost of assets currently acquired if current earnings are to be accurately stated.  How would you reply to each of these proposals?

**12.** (a) Define wasting assets.  (b) Give five examples of wasting assets.

**13.** (a) Define depletion.  (b) What distinctions can be made between depletion and depreciation?

**14.** Justify the practice, followed in the case of a company with wasting assets, of adding the charge for depletion to net income in arriving at the amount available for dividends.

# EXERCISES

**1.** Machinery was acquired by the Morrison Co. on July 1, 1961, at a cost of $30,000, and was depreciated by the straight-line method on an estimated 8-year life.  On December 31, 1964, in reviewing account balances for purposes of making the adjustments for the past fiscal year, it was determined that the machinery will probably have a 10-year life. (a) Assuming that the asset book value is to be corrected for past over-depreciation, what entries would be made to correct the accounts and to record depreciation for 1964?  (b) Assuming that asset book value is not to be changed and such balance is to be allocated over the remaining life of the asset, what entry would be made to record depreciation for 1964?

**2.** The Winston Co. purchased land and an old building for $100,000. The land is estimated to be worth $80,000; the building is estimated to have a remaining life not to exceed 10 years. The building is used for 5 years and is then completely remodeled at a cost of $60,000. It is estimated that the building should have a life of 20 years from the date of such remodeling. Give the entries to be made for (a) purchase of land and building, (b) periodic depreciation, (c) cost of remodeling building, and (d) subsequent depreciation.

**3.** The Brooks Corporation owns office equipment costing $6,000 that has been used for 5 years and that has been reduced to a book value of $1,200, the estimated trade-in value at this time. Because of a shortage of new equipment for replacement, the company spends $1,500 over-hauling the old equipment. It is assumed that this expenditure will pro-long the life of the equipment by 3 years and that the trade-in value will remain the same. (a) What entry is made to record the expenditure? (b) What is the annual straight-line depreciation subsequent to the expenditure?

**4.** The Williams Co. shows property and stockholders' equity balances on January 1, 1964, as follows:

| Property Accounts | | Stockholders' Equity | |
|---|---|---|---|
| Plant and equipment.... | $1,650,000 | Capital stock (100,000 shares, $10 par)....... | $1,000,000 |
| Allowance for deprecia-tion................ | 350,000 | Premium on capital stock | 150,000 |
| | | | $1,150,000 |
| | | Less deficit............ | 200,000 |
| | | Total stockholders' equity | $ 950,000 |

On January 5, stockholders authorize that the property accounts be written down to their sound values as indicated by appraisal as follows:

| | |
|---|---|
| Plant and equipment........................... | $1,210,000 |
| Allowance for depreciation....................... | 265,000 |

They further authorize that the deficit after property restatement be applied against the premium on stock, and any excess against the capital stock account; capital stock outstanding is to be changed from $10 par to no-par. Give the entries that are required in recording the quasi-reorganization.

**5.** Machinery, reported on the books at $30,000 with a depreciation allowance of $8,000 and an estimated life of 15 years, was appraised on January 1 and found to have a reproduction cost new of $50,000 and an estimated total life of 20 years. What entries would be made to record the appraisal?

**6.** Machinery acquired on January 1, 1959, at a cost of $300,000 shows a depreciation allowance of $60,000 on January 1, 1964. On this date engineers and appraisers estimate that the machinery should have a remaining useful life of 25 years and a reproduction cost new of $450,000. (a) What entries should be made for the appraisal? (b) What entries should be made to record depreciation on this asset for the year 1964 if operations are (1) charged with cost and (2) charged with appraised values?

**7.** The Anderson Co. acquired buildings at the beginning of 1956 at a cost of $100,000 and is depreciating them on a 50-year basis. At the beginning of 1964 an appraisal indicates that the buildings have a reproduction cost of $200,000 and a sound value of $160,000 based on a 40-year life. The appraisal is recorded in the accounts, and depreciation for 1964 is recorded at cost. On January 3, 1965, the buildings are sold for cash, $175,000. What entries would be made on the books of the Anderson Co. for 1964 and 1965?

# PROBLEMS

**13-1.** The information that follows summarizes transactions of the Evans Mfg Co. relating to the acquisition of a machine:

Jan.   5, 1958. Purchased machine for $20,000; was allowed a 2% discount for making cash payment. The machine is estimated to have a 5-year life; its residual value is estimated at $1,600.

Dec. 31, 1960. The estimated life of the machine is revised from 5 years to 8 years, and the effect of such revision is recorded in the accounts. The estimated residual value is the same.

Jan. 10, 1962. Several major parts of the machine were replaced at a cost of $2,900: cost of such original parts is estimated at $2,000. Additional costs of $1,500 are incurred in overhauling the machine at this point, and it is estimated that the machine will have a 10-year life as a result of the replacements and overhaul. Residual value on a 10-year life is estimated at only $1,000.

Apr.   4, 1965. The machine is sold for $3,000.

*Instructions:* Give all the entries that would be made relative to machinery for the period 1958–1965, including the adjustments that are required to recognize depreciation by the straight-line method at the end of each calendar year.

**13-2.** Four machines are found in the shop of the Bartlett Engineering Co. at the beginning of 1964 as follows:

| Machine | Date Acquired | Cost, Including Installation | Estimated Useful Life | Estimated Salvage Value |
|---|---|---|---|---|
| A | Mar. 5, 1956 | $16,000 | 10 yrs. | $1,000 |
| B | April 1, 1958 | 8,000 | 10 yrs. | 400 |
| C | June 20, 1960 | 9,200 | 10 yrs. | 500 |
| D | Nov. 6, 1961 | 12,400 | 5 yrs. | 1,000 |

During 1964 the following transactions relating to machines are completed:

Jan. 2. Machine A, which had not been operating satisfactorily, was sold for $1,750. It was decided that the lives of Machines B and C probably would not exceed 8 years and that salvage values would be negligible and hence could be ignored; entries were made in the accounts to record the revised estimates.

Jan. 20. Machine E was purchased for cash at a cost of $12,000. The new machine is estimated to have a life of 10 years and no salvage value.

Feb. 8. Machine D was traded in for a larger machine costing $16,500. Machine D was accepted at a value of $8,500 for purposes of the trade-in, the balance of the purchase price being paid in cash. The new machine, to be referred to as Machine F, is recorded at $16,500. It is estimated to have a life of 10 years and a trade-in value of $1,500 at that time.

*Instructions:* (1) Give the journal entries that are required for 1964, including the adjustments for depreciation by the straight-line method at the end of the year (depreciation is calculated to the nearest month).

(2) Prepare a schedule showing the cost, depreciation allowance balance, and book value of machines on hand as of December 31, 1964.

**13-3.** The Murdock Sales Co. owns real estate acquired at the beginning of 1951. Account balances for this asset on January 2, 1961, appear as follows:

| | | |
|---|---:|---:|
| Land......................................... | | $40,000 |
| Buildings..................................... | $30,000 | |
| Less allowance for depreciation................ | 15,000 | 15,000 |
| | | $55,000 |

An appraisal of this property as of January 2, 1961, indicated that the land was worth $75,000, that buildings had a reproduction cost, new, of $45,000, and a present sound value of $30,000. A correction is made for past depreciation, and the appraisal is recorded in the accounts. On July 1, 1964, the company borrows $40,000, issuing a 10-year note secured by a mortgage on the property; interest at 6% is payable annually on July 1. On October 1, 1964, the company sells the land and buildings for $110,000, the purchaser assuming the mortgage note and accrued interest and making payment in cash for the difference.

*Instructions:* (1) Give the entry to record the asset appraisal on January 2, 1961.

(2) Give the entries to record straight-line depreciation in the years 1961-1963. (Operations are charged with depreciation at cost.)

(3) Give the entry to record the sale of property on October 1, 1964.

**13-4.** The following account balances relating to plant and equipment appear on the books of the Burnside Corporation on December 31, 1963:

| | | |
|---|---:|---:|
| Furniture and Fixtures........................... | $ 42,000 | |
| Allowance for Depreciation of Furniture and Fixtures.. | | $ 42,000 |
| Machinery....................................... | 240,000 | |
| Allowance for Depreciation of Machinery........... | | 120,000 |
| Buildings A and B............................... | 600,000 | |
| Allowance for Depreciation of Buildings A and B..... | | 112,500 |
| Land............................................ | 100,000 | |

Assets have been carried at cost since their acquisition. With the exception of Building B, completed on January 1, 1959, at a cost of $300,000, all of the assets were acquired on January 1, 1954. The straight-line method was used in recording depreciation; residual values were not recognized. The company now wishes to show plant and equipment items at their present sound value.

An appraisal firm submitted the following report on January 2, 1964:

| | Replacement Value (New) | Present Depreciated Value |
|---|---:|---:|
| Furniture and Fixtures................ | $ 60,000 | $ 10,000 |
| Machinery......................... | 300,000 | 100,000 |
| Buildings:  A, Constructed 1/1/54...... | 360,000 | 270,000 |
| B, Constructed 1/1/59...... | 330,000 | 288,750 |
| Land............................. | 250,000 | |

*Instructions:* (1) What is the estimated remaining life of each depreciable asset as determined from the appraiser's report?

(2) Prepare journal entries to give effect to appraisal values.

(3) Prepare the plant and equipment section of the balance sheet showing appraisal values.

(4) Give the adjusting entries for depreciation at the end of 1964, assuming that operations are charged with depreciation at cost.

(5) Give the adjusting entries for depreciation at the end of 1964, assuming that operations are charged with depreciation on the appraised values.

**13-5.** Right after its incorporation on July 1, 1960, the Home Corporation acquired plant and equipment for cash as follows:

| | Cost | Estimated Useful Life |
|---|---:|---:|
| Land..................................... | $ 80,000 | |
| Buildings............................... | 200,000 | 50 years |
| Machinery and Equipment.............. | 240,000 | 15 years |
| Office Furniture and Fixtures............ | 18,000 | 12 years |

At the end of 1962, it was decided that the estimated useful life used in calculating straight-line depreciation on plant items had been excessive. Correcting entries and depreciation calculated on the basis of the revised estimated life were authorized as follows:

| | Revised Estimate of Useful Life |
|---|---:|
| Buildings....................................... | 40 years |
| Machinery and Equipment..................... | 8 years |
| Office Furniture and Fixtures.................. | 10 years |

On April 27, 1963, additional machinery was acquired at $60,000 less a 5% discount for cash payment. Cost of freight was $2,000. Installation of machinery was completed at the end of June at a cost of $11,000. This machinery is estimated to have a 10-year life.

At the beginning of 1964, an appraisal of plant assets was made by professional appraisers. While no change was indicated in the life of the assets, it was ascertained that reproduction costs of those assets acquired in 1960 had increased by the following percentages:

| | |
|---|---|
| Land.................................. | 150% |
| Buildings................................ | 80% |
| Machinery and Equipment................. | 60% |
| Office Furniture and Fixtures.............. | 50% |

It was authorized that such appraisal increases be recorded in the accounts and that depreciation be recorded on the basis of appraisal values.

*Instructions:* (1) Give the journal entries relating to plant and equipment accounts for the period July 1, 1960, to December 31, 1964, including the entries for depreciation that are made at the end of each calendar year. (Assume that no changes are made in appraisal capital balances at the end of each year, since dividends are to be limited to net income based on appraisal depreciation.)

(2) Give the information that will appear in the plant and equipment and the appraisal capital sections of the balance sheet prepared as of December 31, 1964.

**13-6.** The Jerome Corp. was organized on January 2, 1964. It was authorized to issue 50,000 shares of common stock, par $20. On the date of organization it sold 20,000 shares at par and gave the remaining shares in exchange for certain land bearing recoverable ore deposits estimated by geologists at 800,000 tons. The property is deemed to have a value of $600,000.

During 1964 mine improvements totaled $17,500. Miscellaneous buildings and sheds were constructed at a cost of $22,500. During the year 35,000 tons were mined; 3,500 tons of this amount were on hand unsold on December 31, the balance of the tonnage being sold for cash at $5 per ton. Expenses incurred and paid for during the year, exclusive of depletion and depreciation, were as follows:

| | |
|---|---|
| Mining............................................. | $94,500 |
| Delivery............................................ | 9,250 |
| General and administrative............................ | 8,800 |

Cash dividends of $1 per share were declared on December 31, payable January 15, 1965.

It is believed that buildings and sheds will be useful only over the life of the mine; hence depreciation is to be recognized in terms of mine output.

*Instructions:* Prepare an income statement and a balance sheet for 1964. Submit working papers showing the development of statement data. Disregard income taxes.

# Chapter 14

# INTANGIBLES

## Nature of intangibles

The term *intangibles* is used in accounting to denote long-term property items without physical characteristics. From a strictly legal point of view, such assets as shares of stock, bonds, and claims against customers are regarded as intangibles. For the accountant, however, the term is limited to such properties as patents, copyrights, trademarks, franchises, leaseholds, and goodwill.

Intangible assets derive their values by affording special rights or advantages that are expected to contribute to the earnings of the business. Special rights contributing to earnings may be found, for example, in the ownership of patents; special advantages contributing to earnings may arise from the skill of employees, the ability of management, desirable location of the business, and good customer relationships — elements of a company's goodwill.

The "intangibles" designation is perhaps unfortunate since it has contributed to a general misunderstanding of the nature of these assets and to the accounting treatment that should be accorded them. Mere physical existence does not affect an item's economic significance. A factory building about to be razed may be reported on the balance sheet at little or no value despite its massive physical dimensions. On the other hand, patents without physical qualities could be the most valuable property item owned by a company. Intangible assets no less than tangible properties require a full accounting.

## Valuation of intangibles

In general, valuation for intangible assets should follow the standards employed for the tangible group. Intangibles should be recorded at cost. Cost should include all expenditures related to the development or the purchase of the assets. When an intangible is acquired in exchange for an asset other than cash, the fair market value of the asset exchanged or that of the intangible, whichever is more clearly determinable, should be used to record the acquisition. When shares of stock or bonds are issued in exchange for an intangible, the fair market value of the securities issued or the intangible acquired should be determined in recording the exchange. When several intangibles or a combination of tangible and intangible assets are acquired for a lump sum, this sum must be allocated to the individual assets in some equitable manner.

Costs are reported for intangible assets only when certain expenditures can be related to their acquisition. For example, no value should appear on the books for a franchise that is acquired without cost or for a company's goodwill developed over a period of years. But when an intangible asset without an accountable cost makes significant contribution to the earnings of a business, reference on the balance sheet to such right or advantage by means of a special note is appropriate.

The accounting for an intangible asset subsequent to its acquisition will depend upon the nature of the item. The AICPA Committee on Accounting Procedure classifies intangibles into two groups as follows:

> (a) Those having a term of existence limited by law, regulation, or agreement, or by their nature (such as patents, copyrights, leases, licenses, franchises for a fixed term, and goodwill as to which there is evidence of limited duration);
> (b) Those having no such limited term of existence and as to which there is, at the time of acquisition, no indication of limited life (such as goodwill generally, going value, trade names, secret processes, subscription lists, perpetual franchises, and organization costs).[1]

When an intangible asset has limited usefulness, its cost should be assigned to operations over its useful life. When an intangible has unlimited life and continued usefulness, cost is properly carried forward without change. Such procedures parallel those employed for tangible assets: the cost of a building with a limited life is charged to operations over the useful life of the building; land with an unlimited life and continued usefulness is carried forward at original cost.

### Intangibles with limited term of existence

The process of assigning the costs of intangibles with limited useful lives to operations in a systematic manner is called *amortization*. Legal or contractual circumstances may place an outside limit upon the term of usefulness of an intangible. In many cases this provides a definite period over which the cost of the asset may be amortized. When obsolescence and supersession are expected to shorten the practical duration of the asset, the amortization period should be reduced accordingly. Cost amortization is recorded by a charge to operations and a credit to the asset or to an asset valuation account.

When an amortization plan is adopted and subsequent events indicate a period of usefulness for the intangible that differs from the period originally estimated, the original amortization plan may be modified.

---

[1] *Accounting Research and Terminology Bulletins,* 1961 (New York: American Institute of Certified Public Accountants), *Accounting Research Bulletin No. 43,* p. 37.

Intangibles subject to amortization are reported on the balance sheet at unamortized cost or at original cost less a valuation account summarizing past accumulated amortization. If an intangible is reported at a value other than cost, full information concerning such valuation should be provided. The periodic amortization charge is reported as a manufacturing cost or an operating expense, depending upon the nature of the contribution made by the intangible.

Federal income tax regulations allow the taxpayer to write off the cost of an intangible by periodic charges when its use is definitely limited in duration. Periodic deductions would be recognized for income tax purposes on patents, copyrights, leaseholds, licenses, franchises, and similar properties.

### Intangibles without limited term of existence

When intangibles have unlimited or indefinite lives, partial or complete cost write-offs have been made as a result of: (1) the determination that the usefulness of such intangibles has become limited or has actually come to an end; (2) the adoption of a policy for the reduction or elimination of such intangibles.

When it becomes evident that an intangible has lost its usefulness and has become worthless, a write-off of the intangible is justified. When it is evident that a part of its usefulness has disappeared and its remaining usefulness is limited to a certain term, a partial write-off would be indicated, followed by amortization of the balance of the cost over the remaining period of usefulness.

The arbitrary write-off of an intangible when there is no indication of a loss of value is not supportable in theory. The write-off of an intangible that is making a continuing contribution to earnings is subject to the same criticism that can be made for the write-off of a tangible asset under similar circumstances. Notwithstanding such argument, arbitrary write-offs of intangibles have frequently been made in practice. In many instances, the write-offs have been made immediately after the acquisition of intangibles. In support of such practice, it has been argued that the limitation of intangible items is desirable as a conservative measure, since intangibles may lose their usefulness and, furthermore, may have little or no value upon the sale or liquidation of a business.

There is general agreement that when a partial or complete write-off of an intangible is made, such a charge should be absorbed by retained earnings and not by paid-in capital. When such a write-off is to be shown on the income statement, it should be reported as an extraordinary item. Only amortization charges for intangibles that are related to the revenue of the current period, then, should be reported in the operating section of the income statement; special write-offs of intangibles should be reported in the lower section of the income statement or on the retained earnings statement.

Accounting problems that are related to specific intangibles are discussed in the sections that follow.

## Patents

A patent is an exclusive right granted by the government to an inventor enabling him to control the manufacture, sale, or other use of his invention for a specified period of time. The United States Patent Office issues patents which are valid for seventeen years from the date of issuance. Patents are not renewable, although effective control of an invention is frequently maintained beyond the expiration of the original patent through new patents covering improvements or changes. The owner of a patent may grant its use to others under royalty agreements or may sell it.

The issuance of a patent does not necessarily indicate the existence of a valuable right. The value of a patent stems from whatever advantage it might afford its owner in excluding competitors from utilizing a process that results in lower costs or superior products. Many patents cover inventions which cannot be exploited commercially and may actually be worthless.

Patents are recorded at their acquisition costs. When a patent is developed through company-sponsored research, its cost includes such items as legal fees, patent fees, the cost of models and drawings, and related experimental and developmental expenditures. When a patent is purchased, it is recorded at its purchase price by the new owner.

The validity of a patent may be challenged in the courts. The cost of successfully prosecuting or defending original infringement suits is regarded as a cost of establishing the legal rights of the holder and may be added to the other costs of the patent. In the event of unsuccessful litigation, the litigation cost as well as other patent costs should be written off as a loss.

Patent cost should be amortized over the useful life of the patent. The legal life of a patent is used for amortization only when the patent is expected to provide benefits during its full legal life. The useful life of a patent is usually much shorter than its legal life because of obsolescence and supersession. New and more efficient inventions or changes in demand for certain products may result in loss of patent value; processes developed by competitors that are sufficiently different to qualify as new inventions yet so similar to a company's own process as to destroy the economic advantages enjoyed through patent protection may also result in the loss of patent value. In some instances, the useful life of a patent is expressed in terms of productive output rather than in years, and cost is assigned to operations on the basis of units produced.

The classification of the charge for patent amortization depends upon the nature and the use of the patent. A charge for patents that are used in the manufacturing process would be recognized as a manufacturing cost. A charge for patents that are used in shipping department activities would be recognized as a selling expense.

## Copyrights

Copyrights are exclusive rights granted by the federal government to the author or the artist enabling him to publish, sell, or otherwise control his literary, musical, or artistic works. The right to exclusive control is issued for a period of twenty-eight years, with the privilege of renewal for another twenty-eight years. Copyrights, like patents, may be licensed to others or sold.

The cost assigned to a copyright consists of all of the charges relating to the production of the work, including those required to establish the right. When a copyright is purchased, the copyright is recorded at its purchase price.

The useful life of a copyright is generally considerably less than its legal life. The cost of a copyright may be amortized over the number of years in which sales or royalties can be expected, or cost may be assigned in terms of the estimated sales units relating to such rights. As a conservative measure, costs of a copyright are frequently written off against first revenues from the copyright.

## Franchises

A franchise is a contract, often between a governmental unit and a private company, that gives the latter exclusive rights to perform certain functions or sell certain products or services. The rights may be granted for a specified number of years or in perpetuity; in certain instances, the rights may be revoked by the grantor.

The cost of a franchise includes any sum that may be paid specifically for a franchise as well as legal fees and other costs incurred in obtaining it. Although the value of a franchise at the time of its acquisition may substantially exceed its cost, the amount recorded for this item should be limited to actual outlays. When a franchise is purchased from another company, the amount paid is recorded as franchise cost.

When a franchise has a limited life, its cost should be amortized over such limited life. When the life of a franchise can be terminated at the option of the granting authority, the cost is best amortized over a relatively short period. The cost of a perpetual franchise that is of continuing economic value may be carried forward indefinitely. When the cost of a perpetual franchise is arbitrarily reduced or written off, the write-off should be treated as an extraordinary charge.

A franchise may require that periodic payments be made to the grantor. Payments may be fixed amounts or they may be variable amounts depending upon revenue, utilization, or other factors. Such payments should be recognized as charges to periodic revenue. When certain property improvements are required under terms of the franchise, the costs of the improvements should be capitalized and charged to revenue over the life of the franchise.

### Trademarks and trade names

Trademarks, together with trade names, distinctive symbols, labels, and designs are important to all companies that depend upon a public demand for their products. It is by means of such distinctive markings that particular products are differentiated from competing brands. In building up the reputation of a product, relatively large costs may be involved. The federal government offers legal protection for trademarks through their registry with the United States Patent Office. Prior and continuous use is the important factor in determining the ownership of a particular trademark. The right to a trademark is retained so long as continuous use is made of it. Protection of trade names and brands that cannot be registered must be sought in the common law. Distinguishing trademarks, trade names, and brands can be assigned or sold.

When a trademark is developed, its cost includes developmental expenditures such as designing costs, filing and registry fees, and also expenditures for successful litigation in the defense of such right. When a trademark is purchased, it is recorded at its purchase price.

Since the life of a trademark is not limited, its cost may be carried forward until it is determined that there has been a loss in value. However, cost is frequently amortized over a relatively short period on the theory that changes in consumer demand may limit the usefulness of the trademark.

### Research and development costs

Large enterprises engage in continuous research for the improvement of processes and formulas and the development of new and improved products. Expenditures for general research are frequently recorded as a part of regular manufacturing overhead, being regarded as a continuing charge of keeping abreast of current technological advance. When research is directed to particular improvements, it is appropriate to capitalize expenditures identified with such projects and report these on the balance sheet as research and development costs. When these activities are successful, costs as accumulated can be assigned to future periods that receive the benefits of such outlays. Expenditures on projects that are patentable are summarized and reported as patents; expenditures on projects that are not patentable but offer exclusive benefits may be summarized and reported as formulas or as special or secret processes. When activities directed to certain improvements prove unsuccessful, costs previously capitalized should be written off as a loss. Formulas and special processes are generally amortized over a relatively short period because any advantages offered through their possession may terminate at any time through discoveries by others.

Some companies follow the practice of charging all research expenditures to periodic revenue even though valuable rights are produced through research activities. When such practice is followed, the balance sheet fails to disclose the costs of special processes and improvements that will make significant contribution to future business success. The income statement fails to show charges for processes and improvements developed in prior periods, and in turn reflects charges that are applicable to future periods. For federal income tax purposes the taxpayer may elect to report expenditures for research and development either as (1) expenses that are deductible in the year paid or incurred, or (2) deferred costs to be amortized over a period of 60 months or more.

## Goodwill

Goodwill is generally regarded as the summation of all of the special advantages, not otherwise identifiable, related to a going concern. It includes such items as a good name, capable staff and personnel, high credit standing, reputation for superior products and services, and favorable location. Unlike most other assets, tangible or intangible, goodwill cannot be transferred without transferring the entire business.

From an accounting point of view, goodwill is recognized as the ability of a business to earn above-normal earnings with the identifiable assets employed in the business. By "above-normal earnings" is meant a rate of return greater than that normally required to attract investors into a particular type of business.

## Valuation of goodwill

Goodwill is recorded on the books only when it is acquired by purchase or otherwise established through a business transaction. The latter condition includes its recognition in connection with a merger or a reorganization of a corporation, a purchase or a partial purchase of a business, or a change of partners in a partnership. Recognition only under such circumstances assures an objective approach to the valuation of goodwill. To permit the recognition of goodwill on the basis of judgment and estimates by owners and other interested parties would open the doors to all manner of abuse and misrepresentation. Goodwill reported on the balance sheet arises from a purchase or a contractual arrangement calling for its recognition; above-normal earnings can be pointed to by management and owners as evidence of the existence of additional goodwill that has not found expression in the accounts.

In the purchase of a going business, the actual price to be paid for goodwill usually results from bargaining and compromises between the parties concerned. A basis for negotiation in arriving at a price for goodwill normally involves the following steps:

1. Projection of the level of future earnings.
2. Determination of appropriate rate of return.
3. Valuation of the net business assets other than goodwill.
4. Use of projected future earnings and rate of return in developing a value for goodwill.

***Projection of the level of future earnings.*** Past earnings ordinarily offer the best basis upon which to develop a specific value for goodwill. However, it is not these past earnings but projected future earnings that are being purchased. In considering past earnings as a basis for projection into the future, reference should be made to earnings most recently experienced. A sufficient number of periods should be included in the analysis so that a representative measurement of business performance is available.

In certain instances, it may be considered necessary to restate revenue and expense balances to give effect to alternative depreciation or amortization methods, inventory methods, or other measurement processes that may be considered desirable in summarizing past operations. Extraordinary gains and losses which cannot be considered a part of normal activities would be excluded from past operating results. Such items would include gains and losses from the sale of investments and plant and equipment, gains and losses from the retirement of debt, and losses from casualties.

The ordinary or normal earnings should be analyzed to determine their trend and stability. If earnings over a period of years show a tendency to decline, careful analysis is necessary to determine whether such decline may be expected to continue. There may be greater confidence in possible future earnings when past earnings have been relatively stable rather than widely fluctuating.

Any changes in the operations of the business which may be anticipated after the transfer of ownership should also be considered. The elimination of a division, the disposal of substantial property items, or the retirement of long-term debt, for example, could materially affect earnings.

The normal earnings of the past are used as a basis for estimating earnings of the future. Business conditions, the business cycle, sources of supply, demand for the company's products or services, price structure, competition, and other significant factors must be studied in developing data that will make it possible to convert past earnings into estimated future earnings.

***Determination of appropriate rate of return.*** The existence of above-normal earnings, if any, can be determined only by reference to a normal rate of return. The normal earnings rate is that which would ordinarily be required to attract investors in the particular type of business being acquired. In judging this rate, consideration must be given to such factors as money rates, business conditions at the time of the purchase, competitive factors, risks involved, entrepreneurial abilities required, and alternative investment opportunities.

In general, the greater the risk entailed in an investment, the higher the rate of return required. Because most business enterprises are subject to a considerable amount of risk, investors generally expect a relatively high rate of return to justify their investment. A long history of stable earnings or the existence of certain tangible assets that can be sold easily in the event of business failure might reduce the degree of risk in acquiring a business and thus reduce the rate of return required by a potential investor.

If goodwill is to be purchased, it should be looked upon as an investment and must offer the prospect of sufficient return to justify the commitment. Special risks are associated with goodwill. The value of goodwill is uncertain and fluctuating. It cannot be separated from the business as a whole and sold, as can most other business properties. Furthermore, it is subject to rapid deterioration and may be totally lost in the event of business sale or liquidation. As a result, a higher rate of return would normally be required on the purchase of goodwill than on the purchase of other business properties.

***Valuation of net business assets other than goodwill.*** Because goodwill is associated with the earnings that cannot be attributed to a normal return on identifiable assets, the ultimate evaluation of goodwill depends upon the valuation of those business properties that can be identified. In appraising properties for this purpose, current market values should be sought rather than the values reported in the accounts. Inventories and securities should be restated in terms of current market values. Receivables should be stated at realizable values. Plant and equipment items may require special appraisals in arriving at their present replacement or reproduction values. Care should be taken to determine that liabilities are fully recognized. Assets at their current fair market values, less the liabilities that are to be assumed, provide the net assets total which, together with estimated future earnings, are used in arriving at a purchase price for the business.

*Use of projected future earnings and rate of return in developing a value for goodwill.* A number of methods may be employed in arriving at a goodwill figure. Several of these will be described. Assume the following information for Company A:

Net earnings after adjustment and elimination of extraordinary and nonrecurring items:

| | |
|---|---|
| 1960 | $140,000 |
| 1961 | 90,000 |
| 1962 | 110,000 |
| 1963 | 85,000 |
| 1964 | 115,000 |
| Total | $540,000 |

Average net earnings 1960–1964 ($540,000 ÷ 5), $108,000.
Estimated future net earnings, $100,000.
Net assets as appraised on January 2, 1965, before recognizing goodwill, $1,000,000. (Land, buildings, equipment, inventories, receivables, $1,200,000; liabilities to be assumed by purchaser, $200,000.)

The average net earnings figure of $108,000 for the five-year period 1960–1964 was used in arriving at an estimate of the probable future net earnings. It is assumed that the prospective buyer after analyzing the assembled data concludes that future earnings may reasonably be estimated at $100,000 a year.

(1) *Capitalization of average net earnings.* The amount to be paid for a business may be determined by capitalizing expected future earnings at a rate that represents the required return on the investment. Capitalization of earnings as used in this sense means calculation of the principal value which will yield the stated earnings at the specified rate. This is accomplished by dividing the earnings by the specified rate.[1] The difference between the amount to be paid for the business as thus obtained and the appraised values of the individual property items may be considered the price paid for goodwill.

---

[1]This may be shown as follows: $P$ = principal amount or the capitalized earnings to be computed; $r$ = the specified rate of return; $E$ = expected annual earnings. Then, $E = P \times r$, and $P = E \div r$.

If, in the example, a return of 8% was required on the investment and earnings were estimated at $100,000 per year, the business would be valued at $1,250,000 ($100,000 ÷ .08). Since net assets with the exception of goodwill were appraised at $1,000,000, goodwill would be valued at $250,000. If a 10% return was required on the investment, the business would be worth only $1,000,000. In acquiring the business for $1,000,000, nothing would be paid for goodwill.

(2) *Capitalization of average excess net earnings.* In the foregoing method, a single rate of return was applied to the earnings in arriving at the value of the business. No consideration was given to the extent to which the earnings were attributable to net identifiable assets and the extent to which the earnings were attributable to goodwill. It would seem reasonable, however, to expect a higher return on an investment in goodwill than on the other assets acquired. To illustrate, assume the following facts:

|  | Company A | Company B |
|---|---|---|
| Net assets as appraised.................. | $1,000,000 | $500,000 |
| Estimated future net earnings............ | 100,000 | 100,000 |

If the estimated earnings are capitalized at a uniform rate of 8%, the value of each company is found to be $1,250,000. The goodwill for Company A is then $250,000, and for Company B, $750,000 as shown:

|  | Company A | Company B |
|---|---|---|
| Total net asset valuation (earnings capitalized at 8%)........................ | $1,250,000 | $1,250,000 |
| Deduct net assets as appraised........... | 1,000,000 | 500,000 |
| Goodwill............................ | $ 250,000 | $ 750,000 |

These calculations ignore the fact that the appraised value of the net assets identified with Company A exceeds that of Company B. Company A, whose earnings of $100,000 are accompanied by net assets valued at $1,000,000, would certainly command a higher price than Company B, whose earnings of $100,000 are accompanied by net assets valued at only $500,000.

Satisfactory recognition of both earnings and asset contributions is generally effected by (1) requiring a fair return on identifiable net assets, and (2) viewing any excess earnings as attributable to goodwill and capitalizing such excess at a higher rate that recognizes the degree of risk that characterizes goodwill. To illustrate, assume in the above cases that 8% is considered a normal return on identifiable net assets and that excess earnings are capitalized at 20% in determining the amount to be paid for goodwill. Amounts to be paid for Companies A and B would be calculated as follows:

|  | Company A | Company B |
|---|---|---|
| Estimated net earnings.................. | $ 100,000 | $ 100,000 |
| Normal return on net assets: | | |
| Company A — 8% of $1,000,000....... | 80,000 | |
| Company B — 8% of $ 500,000...... | | 40,000 |
| Excess net earnings.................... | $ 20,000 | $ 60,000 |
| Excess net earnings capitalized at 20%.... | ÷ .20 | ÷ .20 |
| Value of goodwill.................... | $ 100,000 | $ 300,000 |

|  | Company A | Company B |
|---|---|---|
| Value of net assets offering normal return of 8%............................. | $1,000,000 | $ 500,000 |
| Value of goodwill, excess net earnings capitalized at 20%.................. | 100,000 | 300,000 |
| Total net asset valuation............... | $1,100,000 | $ 800,000 |

(3) *Number of years' purchase.* Behind each of the capitalization methods described above, there is an implicit assumption that the superior earning power attributed to the existence of goodwill will continue indefinitely. The very nature of goodwill, however, makes it subject to rapid deterioration. A business with unusually high earnings may expect competition from other companies to reduce earnings over a period of years. Furthermore, the high levels of earnings may frequently be maintained only by special efforts on the part of the new owners, and they cannot be expected to pay for something they themselves must achieve.

As the goodwill being purchased cannot be expected to last beyond a specific number of years, one frequently finds that payment for excess earnings is stated in terms of "years' purchase" rather than capitalization in perpetuity. For example, if excess annual earnings of $20,000 are expected and payment is to be made for excess earnings for a five-year period, the purchase price for goodwill would be $100,000. If the excess annual earnings are expected to be $60,000 and the payment is to be made for four years' excess earnings, the price for goodwill would be $240,000.

Calculation of goodwill in terms of number of years' purchase will yield results identical to the capitalization method when the number of years used is equal to the reciprocal of the capitalization rate. Payment for five years' earnings, for example, is equivalent to capitalizing earnings at a 20% rate ($1 ÷ .20 = 5$). Payment of four years' earnings is equivalent to capitalization at a 25% rate ($1 ÷ .25 = 4$).

The years' purchase method has the advantage of conceptual simplicity. It is related to the common business practice of evaluating investment opportunities in terms of their "payback period" — the number of years it is expected to take to recover the initial investment.

(4) *Present value method.* The concept of the number of years' purchase can be combined with the concept of a rate of return on investment. The assumption here is that the excess earnings can be expected to continue for only a limited number of years, but an investment in these earnings should provide an adequate return, considering the risks involved. The amount to be paid for goodwill, then, is the discounted or present value of the excess earnings amounts that are expected to become available in future periods.

To illustrate the calculation of goodwill by the present value method, assume that the earnings of Company A exceed a normal return on the net identifiable assets used in the business by $20,000 per year. These excess earnings are expected to continue for a period of five years, and a return of 8% is considered necessary to attract investors in this industry. The amount to be paid for goodwill, then, may be regarded as the discounted value at 8% of five installments of $20,000 to be received at annual intervals. Present value tables may be used in determining the present value of the series of payments. The present value of 5 annual payments of $1 each, to provide a return of 8%, is found to be $3.992.[1] The present value of five payments of $20,000 each would then be calculated as $20,000 × 3.992, or $79,840.

It may be noted that the calculation of goodwill by the present value method, using a five-year period and an 8% return, produced approximately the same result as would have been obtained by purchasing four years' excess earnings, or by capitalizing these earnings at 25%. The years'-purchase method can be adjusted to provide for a return on investment by reducing the number of years' earnings below actual expectations. Similarly, the capitalization method can be adjusted to provide for the limited life-span of excess earnings by raising the capitalization rate above that normally considered appropriate. The principal advantage of the present value method is the explicit recognition of the anticipated duration of excess earnings together with the use of a realistic rate of return. Thus it focuses on the factors most relevant to the goodwill evaluation.

## Implied goodwill

When a lump sum amount is paid for an established business and no explicit evaluation is made of goodwill as illustrated in the preceding section, goodwill may still be recognized. In such case the identifiable net assets require appraisal, and the difference between the full purchase

[1] The present value of an ordinary annuity of 5 rents at interest of 8% is required. The calculation of present values is described in the authors' *Advanced Accounting.*

price and the value of identifiable net assets can be attributed to the purchase of goodwill.

Failure to recognize the payment for goodwill separately may result in attaching this cost to identifiable assets and thus cause their overvaluation. If this cost is attributed to depreciable assets, periodic depreciation charges and net earnings as well as financial position will be misstated. Failure to distinguish between costs of intangibles with a limited term of existence which are subject to amortization and those with an unlimited term of existence will result in similar misstatements.

When capital stock is issued in exchange for a business, the value of the stock determines the consideration that is paid for the assets. Care must be exercised so that what in effect represents a discount on the stock is not reported as goodwill. For example, assume that a company exchanges 100,000 shares of common stock, par $10, and selling on the market at 7½, for a business with assets appraised at $800,000 and liabilities of $200,000. The purchase should be recorded as follows:

| | | |
|---|---:|---:|
| Assets........................................ | 800,000 | |
| Goodwill..................................... | 150,000 | |
| Discount on Common Stock.................. | 250,000 | |
|     Liabilities................................. | | 200,000 |
|     Common Stock, $10 par.................. | | 1,000,000 |

If the discount is not recognized and goodwill is established at $400,000, both assets and invested capital will be misstated.

### Goodwill adjustment after acquisition

It has been maintained that when goodwill is acquired after sound and conservative determination and when its life is not limited, it should be carried on the books at cost indefinitely. This position is supported on the grounds that goodwill has an indeterminate life. Management, in the attempt to continue favorable operations, will maintain the value existing in the acquired goodwill. The intangible values originally acquired are considered to be perpetuated or supplanted by new business advantages.

It would seem that a stronger case can be made for the position of maintaining goodwill at original cost only as long as the advantages supporting its original recognition are continuing. With changes that suggest the impairment or the disappearance of the advantages represented by goodwill, reductions in this balance are just as appropriate as those for other assets whose capacities to contribute to future revenue have become limited or have disappeared. In applying the foregoing standard, a reduction in goodwill should be recognized as an extraordinary charge except when such charge can be related to operations.

In some instances goodwill may be considered to have a measurable life. Under such circumstances, the amortization of goodwill is just as appropriate as the amortization of other limited-life intangibles. For example, assume that $100,000 is paid for goodwill on the purchase of a business whose lease expires in ten years. If it is reasonable to assume that the business will not continue beyond the term of the lease, benefits identified with goodwill are limited to a ten-year period, and the cost of the intangible is properly charged to operations over this period. When goodwill is calculated as the present value of a certain number of years' excess earnings on the theory that earnings will tend to decline as a result of competition, changes in the business cycle, and the exhaustion of other goodwill factors, allocation of the cost of goodwill to operations during its estimated period of usefulness would also be appropriate.

Although there is theoretical support for maintaining goodwill on the records indefinitely when its value remains unimpaired, the practice of writing off this intangible is widespread. Goodwill is frequently reduced periodically or written off in total upon its acquisition or at some later date. When goodwill, or any other intangible, is arbitrarily written off before the end of its useful life, asset and capital balances are misstated and the ratio of earnings to invested capital is distorted. Earnings thus appear to be more favorable than is actually the case as a result of this "conservative" practice.

A deduction for the amortization or the write-off of goodwill is not allowed for federal income tax purposes. Goodwill, for tax purposes, is regarded as an asset of permanent character. Upon the sale or termination of a business, however, a deduction would be allowed for the portion of the asset not realized.

Goodwill is sometimes carried on published balance sheets at a nominal value such as one dollar. This may be the result of either of the following: (1) a company that has built up its own goodwill through successful operations may have recorded it on the books at this value to call attention to its existence without inflating asset and capital balances; (2) a company that has purchased goodwill may have arbitrarily written it down to this nominal figure. Similar practices are encountered with respect to patents, trademarks, copyrights, and other intangibles.

## Organization costs

In forming a corporation, certain expenditures are incurred including legal fees, promotional costs, stock certificate costs, underwriting costs, and incorporation fees. The benefits to be derived from these expenditures normally extend beyond the first fiscal period. Further, the recognition of such expenditures as expenses at the time of organization would commit the corporation to a deficit before it actually begins operations. These factors support the practice of recognizing the initial costs of organization as an intangible asset.

Expenditures relating to organization may be considered to benefit the corporation during its entire life. Thus, when the life of a company is not limited, there is support for carrying organization costs as an intangible asset indefinitely. On the other hand, in the absence of a disposal value, these costs must be applied to revenue before the ultimate net income emerging from business activities is determinable. This approach has led to the widespread practice of writing off organization costs within a relatively short period from the date of corporate organization. These charges when material in amount and when not assignable to current operations should be reported as an extraordinary charge.

It is sometimes suggested that operating losses of the first few years should be capitalized as organization costs or as goodwill. It is argued that the losses cannot be avoided in the early years when the business is being developed, and hence it is reasonable that later years should absorb these. Although losses may be inevitable, they do not necessarily carry any service potential. To report these losses as intangibles will result in the overstatement of assets and capital. Such practice cannot be condoned.

### Leaseholds and leasehold improvements

*Leaseholds* are personal property interests representing rights to the use of land or realty for a specified term. These rights are granted by property owners in consideration of specified rents through terms of a tenure contract called a *lease*. The terms of the lease and the use of the property by the lessee usually determine the accounting procedures to be followed in connection with the lease. Ordinarily, the leasehold is not recognized in the accounts of the lessee if the property is used in regular operations and if rentals under the lease are paid periodically. Periodic rents under the lease are charged to operations of the period covered by each installment.

Recent years have witnessed a sharp increase in *sale and lease-back* arrangements. Typically under such arrangements, a company acquires land and constructs buildings to meet its requirements, then sells the property to an investor and simultaneously leases it from the new owner. Occupancy and use of the property are continued without interruption. Such arrangements are entered into when they offer both investor and lessee financial and income tax advantages that are not found in alternative arrangements for the construction and use of facilities.

Although the possession of a lease with periodic rents may not require the recognition of asset or liability balances, it nevertheless confers special advantages and creates certain obligations during its lifetime. A lease transaction may have the effect of removing resources utilized in the operations of the business from the list of assets disclosed on the balance sheet. At the same time the contract may entail a financial burden equivalent to that of a mortgage or other debt which it replaces. When such factors are considered of particular significance, they must be disclosed by note on the financial statements.

Some accountants have taken the position that leases that provide "property rights" call for entries in the accounts. These persons would calculate the present values of all future rents and use this value in reporting the rights acquired under the leasehold as well as the debt related to such acquisition. In subsequent accounting, the asset balance would be written off by charges to operations; periodic payments under the lease would be recognized as reductions in the debt and in charges to interest expense. Present practice shows a preference for lease disclosure by parenthetical remark or note rather than by recognition in the accounts.

*Leasehold improvements* arise when property has been leased and additions, improvements, or alterations are made by the lessee. Improvements are usually identified with the original property and belong to the owner at the expiration of the lease. The lessee, however, enjoys the use of such improvements throughout the lease period. Under such circumstances, improvement costs are appropriately recorded by the lessee as leasehold improvements and are regarded as an intangible asset.

Improvement costs should be written off to operations over the life of the benefits. This period is the length of the lease or the life of the improvement, whichever is shorter. If occupancy is terminated before improvement costs have been fully amortized, the unamortized balance must be written off as an extraordinary loss. When leaseholds include renewal options but renewal is uncertain, the life of improvements should be regarded as limited to the original lease period. However, when renewal options carry significant advantages and extension is highly probable, it would be appropriate to spread leasehold costs over the extended period.

It is sometimes provided that the lessor, upon the termination of the lease, shall pay a certain amount for leasehold improvements turned over to him. The amount to be paid may be an agreed price, the cost of the property less depreciation for the period, or the appraised value of the property at time of transfer. When such a payment is involved, the amount to be charged to operations by the lessee is the cost of the improvements less the estimated amount recoverable upon termination of the lease.

In certain instances a lease contract may represent, in effect, an installment purchase of property. This would be the case, for example, when property is subject to purchase for a nominal sum upon conclusion of the lease, or when it is provided that periodic rentals may be applied to a purchase price for the leased property. When it is clearly evident that the transaction is in substance a purchase, both the asset and a corresponding liability should be recognized. Subsequent accounting would involve the recognition of payments on the obligation and charges for depreciation arising from the use of the property.

### Intangibles on the balance sheet

When a single long-term asset classification is given on the balance sheet, tangible and intangible subheadings should be provided and summaries developed for each group. When separate classifications are given for tangible and intangible assets, the intangible classification usually follows the tangible classifications. Each intangible should be listed separately. If an intangible has been acquired for a consideration other than cash, disclosure should be made of the properties or securities exchanged and the data used in arriving at the original cost assigned to the intangible. Disclosure should also be made of the valuation procedures that are employed for intangibles subsequent to their acquisition.

Intangible assets as they might appear on the balance sheet follow:

| Intangibles: | | |
|---|---:|---:|
| Goodwill, at original cost.................. | $220,000 | |
| Licenses, at costs less amortization based on estimated useful lives..................... | 18,000 | |
| Patents, acquired through issue of 12,000 shares of common stock with a market value of $12.50 per share and reported at such value, less amortization based on an estimated useful life of 10 years............................. | 107,500 | $345,500 |

## QUESTIONS

**1.** (a) List three intangibles that require no cost amortization under normal conditions. Under what circumstances should such balances be written off, and what accounting procedures should then be followed? (b) List three intangibles that require amortization under normal conditions. Indicate circumstances that might serve to accelerate the amortization process and state the accounting procedures to be followed in such cases.

**2.** State under what circumstances intangible cost is properly charged to (a) operating expenses, (b) extraordinary charges, (c) retained earnings.

**3.** (a) What items enter into the cost of a patent developed by a business? (b) What factors should be considered in establishing a schedule for amortization of patent cost?

**4.** Master Mechanics, Inc. maintains a shop for research and experimental work of various kinds. Costs of operating the shop are approximately $100,000 annually. Occasionally valuable patents are developed for factory use as a result of shop operations. What accounting treatment would you recommend for the expenditures of operating this department?

**5.** (a) Under what conditions may goodwill be reported as an asset? (b) The Barker Company engages in a widespread advertising campaign on behalf of new products, charging above-normal expenditures to goodwill. Do you approve?

**6.** What factors would one look for to support the existence of goodwill in making a purchase of a business?

**7.** Describe the procedure to be followed in arriving at a company's excess annual earnings for purposes of calculating an amount to be paid for goodwill.

**8.** Give four methods for arriving at a goodwill valuation, using estimated future earnings as a basis for such calculations.

**9.** (a) What are the principal arguments in favor of retaining goodwill on the books at cost? (b) What arguments can be raised in favor of writing off goodwill?

**10.** (a) What items are normally considered to compose the organization costs of a company? (b) Would you approve the inclusion of the following items: (1) common stock discount; (2) first-year advertising costs; (3) first-year loss from operations?

**11.** (a) Define (1) leasehold, (2) leasehold improvements. (b) What factors need to be considered in the amortization of costs identified with these intangibles?

**12.** The Wilson Co. acquires without cost a franchise considered to be of great value. How would you recommend that the intangible be reported on the balance sheet?

## EXERCISES

**1.** The Walter Co. developed patents at a cost of $8,500, and patent rights were granted at the beginning of 1959. It is assumed that the patents will be useful during their full legal life. At the beginning of 1961, the company paid $6,000 in successfully prosecuting an attempted infringement of these patent rights. At the beginning of 1964, $15,000 was paid to acquire patents that could make its own patents worthless; the patents acquired have a remaining life of 15 years but will not be used. (a) Give the entries to record the expenditures relative to patents. (b) Give the entries to record patent amortization for the years 1959, 1961, and 1964.

**2.** The Honeywell Mfg. Co. was incorporated on January 1, 1964. In reviewing the accounts in 1965 you find that the organization costs account appears as follows:

Organization Costs

|  | Debit | Credit | Balance |
|---|---|---|---|
| Discount on common stock issued............. | 45,500 |  | 45,500 |
| Incorporation fees.......................... | 1,250 |  | 46,750 |
| Legal fees relative to organization............ | 12,000 |  | 58,750 |
| Stock certificate cost....................... | 3,750 |  | 62,500 |
| Cost of rehabilitating building acquired at be-ginning of 1964 and estimated to have a re-maining life of 10 years.................. | 36,000 |  | 98,500 |
| Cost of leasing adjoining vacant lot for parking purposes for 10 years..................... | 6,500 |  | 105,000 |
| Advertising expenditures to promote company products.............................. | 24,000 |  | 129,000 |
| Amortization of organization costs for 1964 (20% of balance of organization cost, per board of directors' resolution)............. |  | 25,800 | 103,200 |
| Net loss for 1964 ......................... | 28,500 |  | 131,700 |

Give the entry or entries required to correct the account.

**3.** In analyzing the accounts of S. Bunn, Inc. in an attempt to measure goodwill, you find pre-tax earnings of $200,000 for 1964 after charges and credits for the items listed below. Plant and equipment is appraised at 50% above cost for purposes of the sale.

| Depreciation of plant and equipment..................... | $20,000 |
|---|---|
| Year-end bonus to president of company.................. | 15,000 |
| Gain on sale of securities.............................. | 20,000 |
| Gain on revaluation of securities....................... | 15,000 |
| Write-off of goodwill................................ | 45,000 |
| Amortization of patents and leaseholds.................. | 10,000 |
| Income tax refund for 1962............................ | 5,000 |

What is the "normal" pre-tax earnings figure for purposes of your calculations?

**4.** The appraised value of net assets of the Blumel Co. on December 31, 1964, was $60,000. Average net earnings for the past 5 years after elimination of extraordinary gains and losses were $10,000. Calculate the amount to be paid for goodwill under each of the following assumptions:

(a) Earnings are capitalized at 12½% in arriving at the business worth.

(b) A return of 8% is considered normal on net assets at their appraised value; excess earnings are to be capitalized at 12½% in arriving at the value of goodwill.

(c) A return of 10% is considered normal on net assets at their appraised value; goodwill is to be valued at 4 years' excess earnings.

(d) A return of 8% is considered normal on net identifiable assets at their appraised value. Excess earnings are expected to continue for 6 years. Goodwill is to be valued by the present value method using a rate of 10%. (The present value of 6 annual payments of $1 providing a return of 10% is $4.355.)

**5.** At the beginning of 1964 Michael Hartstein, Inc. acquired a 20-year lease on land and buildings from the Capital Development Co. at an annual rental of $12,500. Payment was made in 1964 of $25,000 representing rent for the first and last years of the lease. Modifications in the buildings were made by the lessee prior to occupancy at a cost of $44,000. Terms of the lease require that the buildings be restored to their original form by the lessee upon termination of the lease, and the cost of such changes is estimated at $18,000. (a) Give all of the entries that are required on the books of the lessee and of the lessor in 1964. (b) What items relative to the lease will appear on the balance sheets for the lessee and the lessor at the end of 1964?

## PROBLEMS

**14-1.** The Alloy Castings Co. spent $51,000 in developing a product, a patent being granted January 14, 1956. The patent had an estimated useful life of 10 years. At the beginning of 1960 the company spent $6,600 in successfully prosecuting an attempted infringement of the patent. At the beginning of 1961, the company purchased for $15,000 a patent which was expected to prolong the life of its original patent by 5 years. On July 1, 1964, a competitor obtained rights to a patent which made the company's patent obsolete.

*Instructions:* Give all of the entries that would be made relative to the patent for the period 1956–1964, including entries that record patent cost, annual patent amortization, and ultimate patent obsolescence. (Assume that the company's fiscal period is the calendar year.)

**14-2.** In your audit of the books of Cameron Corporation for the year ending September 30, 1964, you found the following items in connection with the company's patents account:

(a) The company had spent $85,000 during its fiscal year ended September 30, 1963 for research and development costs and charged this amount to its patents account. Your review of the company's cost records indicated the company had spent a total of $93,200 for the research and development of its patents, of which $8,200 was spent in its fiscal year ended September 30, 1962 and had been charged to expense.

(b) The patents were issued on April 1, 1963. Legal expenses in connection with the issuance of the patents amounting to $13,900 were charged to Legal and Professional Fees.

(c) The company paid a retainer of $6,000 on October 5, 1963, for legal services in connection with an infringement suit brought against it. This amount was charged to Deferred Costs.

(d) A letter dated October 15, 1964, from the company's attorneys in reply to your inquiry as to liabilities of the company existing at September 30, 1964, indicated that a settlement of the infringement suit had been arranged. The other party had agreed to drop the suit and to release the company from all future liabilities for $20,000. Additional fees due to the attorneys amounted to $400.

(e) The balance of the patents account on September 30, 1964, was $80,000. No amortization had been recognized on the patents for the fiscal year ended September 30, 1964.

*Instructions:* (1) From the above information prepare correcting journal entries as of September 30, 1964.

(2) Give the entry to record amortization on patents for the year ended September 30, 1964, assuming a life for patents of 17 years from the date of issuance.

**14-3.** West Coast Industries, Inc. assembles the following data relative to the Catalina Corp. in determining the amount to be paid for the net assets and goodwill of the latter company:

| | |
|---|---|
| Assets at appraised values (before goodwill)............... | $650,000 |
| Liabilities................................................. | 225,000 |
| Stockholders' equity...................................... | $425,000 |

Net earnings (after elimination of extraordinary items):

| | |
|---|---|
| 1960............... | $50,000 |
| 1961............... | 57,500 |
| 1962............... | 75,000 |
| 1963............... | 62,500 |
| 1964............... | 67,500 |

*Instructions:* Calculate the amount to be paid for goodwill under each of the following assumptions:

(1) Average earnings are capitalized at 12% in arriving at the business worth.

(2) A return of 10% is considered normal on net assets at appraised value; goodwill is valued at 5 years' excess earnings.

(3) A return of 8% is considered normal on net assets at appraised value; excess earnings are to be capitalized at 15%.

(4) Goodwill is valued at the sum of the earnings of the last 3 years in excess of a 10% annual yield on net assets. (Assume that net assets are the same for the 3-year period.)

(5) A return of 10% is considered normal on net identifiable assets at their appraised values. Excess earnings are expected to continue for 10 years. Goodwill is to be valued by the present value method using a 20% rate. (The present value of 10 annual payments of $1 providing a return of 20% is $4.192.)

**14-4.** The following data are assembled for Danish Bakers, Inc. and the French Pastries Co. as of July 1, 1964, in connection with a proposed merger of the two companies:

|  | Danish Bakers, Inc. | French Pastries Co. |
|---|---|---|
| Net assets other than goodwill per books as of July 1, 1964.......................... | $223,750 | $210,000 |
| Average pre-tax earnings per books, July 1, 1959 — June 30, 1964................. | 50,000 | 35,000 |

It is agreed that the values of the respective assets contributed, including goodwill, are to be determined on the following basis: 15% is to be considered a reasonable pre-tax return on the net assets other than goodwill; average pre-tax earnings for the period 1959–1964 in excess of 15% of the assets of July 1, 1964, are to be capitalized at 25% in calculating goodwill. Before determining the respective values, however, adjustments are to be made for the following items:

(a) Buildings of the Danish Bakers, Inc. are estimated to be worth $31,250 more than book value. Buildings have a remaining life of 25 years.

(b) The French Pastries Co. wrote off organization costs of $13,500 against earnings in 1961.

(c) The French Pastries Co. included in earnings a loss of $1,500 resulting from a fire in 1962 and a gain of $3,500 on the acquisition and retirement of bonds in 1963 at less than the book value of the liability.

*Instructions:* Prepare a statement to show for each party to the merger the determination of the amounts to be paid for (1) net assets other than goodwill and (2) goodwill.

**14-5.** Net income and net asset balances for a 5-year period for Samuel Carr's Motel follow:

| Year | Net earnings before income taxes | Net assets at end of year |
|---|---|---|
| 1960 | $50,000 | $390,000 |
| 1961 | 68,000 | 405,000 |
| 1962 | 85,000 | 444,000 |
| 1963 | 75,000 | 481,000 |
| 1964 | 82,000 | 520,000 |

Travel-Ami, Inc. agrees to purchase the motel at the beginning of 1965 and makes cash payment for the motel properties on the following basis:

10% is considered a normal return on motel investments.

Payment for goodwill is to be calculated by capitalizing at 20% the average annual pre-tax earnings that are in excess of 10% of average year-end net assets.

*Instructions:* Give the entry that would be made to record the acquisition of the motel net assets and the goodwill, net assets to be reported at the amounts shown on the original owner's books.

**14-6.** The Dempsey Corporation is considering the acquisition of the assets and business of the Jensen Corporation as of June 30, 1964. The Dempsey Corporation is willing to pay the appraised value of the net identifiable assets of Jensen plus a "reasonable amount" for goodwill. The net assets other than goodwill are appraised at $1,500,000 on June 30, 1964.

All-inclusive income statements prepared by the Jensen Corporation show the following pre-tax earnings for the five years preceding the proposed acquisition:

| Year ending June 30 | Pre-tax Earnings |
| --- | --- |
| 1960 | $187,000 |
| 1961 | 195,000 |
| 1962 | 170,000 |
| 1963 | 198,000 |
| 1964 | 210,000 |

Similar operating results are expected in the future except for items listed below.

(a) A review of Jensen Corporation accounting records reveals that plant and equipment acquired in July, 1959, at a cost of $200,000 has been depreciated on a straight-line basis with a 20-year useful life and no estimated salvage value. This equipment was included in the appraisal of net tangible assets at a current value of $300,000. Company engineers estimate that the equipment will probably be retired with a salvage value of $30,000 in approximately 12 years.

(b) Jensen had been paying $20,000 per year in interest charges on bonds that were redeemed at a gain of $10,000 on June 30, 1964. Funds for bond retirement were provided by sale in June, 1964 of the company's Consumer Products division for $400,000. This division had been a constant drain on profits, losing approximately $25,000 annually.

(c) Normal maintenance on plant and equipment of Jensen Corporation has been inadequate by approximately $14,500 annually.

Both parties agree that a return of 12% before taxes is normal on assets employed in the type of business engaged in by Jensen Corporation. Earnings in excess of this amount are expected to continue for another 5 years but since there is less certainty about excess earnings, a return of 20% is considered reasonable for an investment in above-normal pre-tax earnings.

*Instructions:* Prepare a summary showing how the amount to be paid for goodwill of the Jensen Corporation is determined using the present value method of calculating goodwill. (The present value of $1 per year for 5 years at 20% is approximately $3.)

# Chapter 15

# LONG-TERM LIABILITIES

## Nature of long-term liabilities

*Long-term* or *fixed liabilities* include all obligations that are not to be liquidated out of company resources classified as current. *Long-term debt* normally comprises the major element of a company's long-term liabilities. Such debt is found in the form of bonds, long-term notes, advances from affiliated companies, and long-term contract obligations. Other long-term liabilities include such items as taxes not currently payable, product warranties extending beyond the current period, claims in litigation that are not expected to be settled currently, obligations under long-term deposits, deferred compensation agreements, pension and other employee benefits payable, and deferred revenues making no claim upon current resources.

## Bonds payable

The power of a corporation to create bonded indebtedness is found in the corporation laws of the state and may be specifically granted by charter. In some cases formal authorization by a majority of stockholders is required before a board of directors can approve a bond issue.

Borrowing by means of bonds involves the issue of a number of certificates of indebtedness. Bond certificates may represent equal parts of the bond issue or they may be of varying denominations. Bonds of the business unit are commonly issued in $1,000 denominations, referred to as the bond face, par, or maturity value. Bonds may be unsecured or they may be secured by liens on real estate, equipment, or specific securities. An earlier discussion of long-term investments made reference to the various classes of bonds and their special features.

The group contract between the corporation and the bondholders is known as the *bond* or *trust indenture*. The indenture details the rights and obligations of the contracting parties, indicates the property that is pledged as well as the protection that is offered on the loan, and names the bank or trust company that is to represent the bondholders.

Bonds may be sold by the company directly to investors, or they may be underwritten by investment bankers or a syndicate. The underwriters may agree to purchase the entire bond issue or that part of the issue which is not sold by the company, or they may agree simply to manage the sale of the security on a commission basis.

Funds to meet short-term needs such as the financing of inventories and receivables are normally raised by the corporation through the issue of short-term notes. Funds to meet long-term needs, the acquisition of plant and equipment, for example, are normally raised by issuing bonds or capital stock. The issue of bonds instead of stock may be preferred by stockholders for the following reasons: (1) the charge against earnings for bond interest is normally less than the share of earnings that would otherwise be payable as dividends on a new issue of preferred stock or the sale of additional common stock; (2) present owners continue in control of the corporation; and (3) bond interest is a deductible expense in arriving at taxable income while dividends are not.

But there are certain limitations and disadvantages of financing through bonds. Bond financing is possible only when a company is in a satisfactory financial condition and can offer adequate security to a new creditor group. Furthermore, interest must be paid regardless of earnings and financial position. With operating losses and the inability of a company to raise sufficient cash to meet the periodic interest, bondholders may take legal action to assume control of company properties.

### Recording the bond issue

It was indicated in Chapter 11 that the sales price of a bond depends upon the interest rate it offers as compared with the interest rate on the money market. The market rate of interest varies with the nature of the credit risk and the length of the loan and fluctuates constantly with changes in the supply of money and the demand for money. Bonds will sell at face value only when they offer interest equal to the market rate at the time of sale; they will sell at a premium when they pay more than the market rate, and will sell at a discount when they pay less than the market rate. With the need for assigning an interest rate to bonds before they are actually sold, there is frequently a difference between the bond rate and market rate at the time of bond sale.

Although the investor usually records bonds at cost, the borrower normally records bonds at their face value — the amount that the company must pay at maturity. Hence, when bonds are issued at an amount other than face value, a bond discount or premium balance is established for the difference between the cash received and the bond face value. The discount or premium balance is written off to Bond Interest Expense over the life of the bond issue; periodic adjustments correct interest expense to the effective charge.

When bonds are issued in exchange for property, the transaction should be recorded at the cash price at which the bonds could be issued.

The yield that the bonds would have to provide is used in calculating a cash price. When difficulties are encountered in arriving at a cash price, the market or appraised value of the property acquired would be used. A difference between the face value of the bonds and the cash value of the bonds or the value of the property acquired is recognized as bond discount or bond premium.

When an entire bond issue is not disposed of at one time, alternative accounting procedures can be employed: (1) entries may be made only when bonds are sold and issued; or (2) an entry may be made upon approval of the issue recording bonds authorized and bonds unissued, and entries made thereafter to report changes in the unissued balance. In employing the latter method, the bond authorization is recorded by a charge to an unissued bonds account and a credit to an authorized bonds account. The subsequent sale and issuance of bonds is recorded by a charge to cash and a credit to the unissued bonds account. The amount of bonds issued is obtained by subtracting the unissued balance from the authorized balance.

In certain instances subscriptions are first obtained for bonds. Issue of the bond certificate is normally withheld until the full subscription price is collected.

To illustrate the entries for a bond issue, assume that a company is authorized to issue 6% debenture bonds of $500,000. Bonds of $300,000 are sold at 98 to investment bankers. Subscriptions for bonds of $100,000 at the same price are received from officers of the company who pay 25% of the subscription price. Collection is made from officers who have subscribed for bonds of $80,000 of the unpaid balance, and bonds fully paid for are issued. Entries are made as follows:

| Transaction | If authorized and unissued balances are not maintained | If authorized and unissued balances are maintained |
| --- | --- | --- |
| Received permission to issue $500,000 6% debenture bonds (500 bonds, $1,000 face value). | No entry | Unissued Bonds...........500,000<br>  Authorized<br>  Bonds Payable........500,000 |
| Sold bonds of $300,000 to investment bankers at 98. | Cash.........294,000<br>Discount on<br>Bonds Payable...6,000<br>  Bonds Payable......300,000 | Cash...........294,000<br>Discount on<br>Bonds Payable.....6,000<br>  Unissued Bonds.......300,000 |
| Received subscriptions for bonds of $100,000 at 98 accompanied by 25% down payment.<br>Received 25% of $98,000.............$24,500<br>Receivable—75% of $98,000.............73,500<br>            $98,000 | Cash..........24,500<br>Bond Subscriptions<br>Receivable......73,500<br>Discount on<br>Bonds Payable.....2,000<br>  Bonds Payable<br>  Subscribed........100,000 | Cash...........24,500<br>Bond Subscriptions<br>Receivable.......73,500<br>Discount on<br>Bonds Payable.....2,000<br>  Bonds Payable<br>  Subscribed.........100,000 |

| Transaction | If authorized and unissued balances are not maintained | If authorized and unissued balances are maintained |
|---|---|---|
| Received balance due on bonds of $80,000 subscribed for at 98—75% of $78,400, or $58,800. | Cash...........58,800<br>Bond Sub-<br>scriptions<br>Receivable.........58,800 | Cash.............58,800<br>Bond Sub-<br>scriptions<br>Receivable...........58,800 |
| Issued bonds of $80,000 to paid-up subscribers. | Bonds Payable<br>Subscribed.....80,000<br>Bonds Payable.......80,000 | Bonds Payable<br>Subscribed........80,000<br>Unissued Bonds........80,000 |

In reporting bonds on the balance sheet, bonds subscribed should be added to the bonds issued balance. The amount unissued should be reported parenthetically or as a subtraction from an authorized balance. Unissued bonds indicate a possible source of funds through sale or through pledge as security on other independent loans. The result of the bond transactions in the example may be reported as follows:

Long-term debt:
6% debenture bonds due March 1, 1974.............    $380,000
Add bonds subscribed...........................      20,000
                                                    _____
Bonds issued and subscribed......................              $400,000
(Bonds authorized but unissued, $120,000; $20,000
of this amount is reserved for bond subscribers.)

Bond Subscriptions Receivable is reported as a current asset when current collection is anticipated and cash is to become available as working capital. When bond proceeds are to be applied to some noncurrent purpose, neither the receivable nor the cash received from the issue of the bonds should be recognized as a current asset. For example, when terms of the bond issue require that bond proceeds be applied to the retirement of other debt or to the payment for plant and equipment, claims against subscribers as well as cash proceeds should be reported as noncurrent items with appropriate disclosure of the manner in which the cash will ultimately be applied.

Bond discount is frequently reported as a deferred cost and bond premium as a deferred revenue. Bond discount is viewed as a prepayment of interest by the company that is to be added to charges of future periods and bond premium as an advance by bondholders that is to be subtracted from interest charges of future periods. Although such practices are followed, sound theory calls for relating bond discount and premium to the bonds payable account: a discount should be subtracted from bonds reported at par; a premium should be added to bonds at par. Such procedure parallels that used in accounting for investments in bonds. The bond sales price determines the balance for the obligation to be reported at the time of the issue. As amortization of discount and premium balances is recorded, the obligation approaches its maturity amount. Amortization of a discount by charges to the bond interest expense account over the life of the issue raises interest expense to the effective amount and raises the book value of the obligation; periodic interest is viewed as the interest paid increased by the accrual of the discount to be paid at bond maturity. Amortization of a premium by credits to the bond interest expense account over the life of the issue reduces interest expense to the effective amount and reduces the book value of the obligation; periodic interest is viewed as the interest paid reduced by the return of a part of the premium originally advanced by bondholders.

The sale of bonds normally involves costs for legal services, printing and engraving, taxes, and underwriting. These costs should be summarized separately as issuing costs and charged to revenue over the life of the bond issue. However, issuing costs are frequently treated as deductions from bond proceeds, thus increasing the discount or reducing the premium that is recognized on the bond issue.

### Bond interest payments

When coupon bonds are issued, cash is paid by the company in exchange for interest coupons on the interest dates. Payments on coupons may be made by the company directly to bondholders, or payments may be cleared through a bank or other disbursing agent. Subsidiary records with bondholders are not maintained, since coupons are redeemable by bearers. In the case of registered bonds, interest checks are mailed either by the company or its agent. When bonds are registered, the bonds account requires subsidiary ledger support. The subsidiary ledger shows holdings by individuals and changes in such holdings. Checks are sent to bondholders of record as of the interest payment dates.

When an agent is to make interest payments, the company normally transfers cash to the agent in advance of the interest payment date. Since the company is not freed from its obligation to bondholders until payment has been made by its agent, it records the cash transfer by a charge to the account Cash Deposited with Agent for Bond Interest and a credit to Cash. On the date the interest is due, the company charges interest expense and credits accrued interest. Upon receipt from the agent of paid interest coupons, a certificate of coupon receipt and appropriate disposal, or other evidence that the interest was paid, the company charges accrued interest and credits the cash deposited with agent account.

### Premium and discount amortization procedures

As in the case of investments, either the straight-line method or the compound-interest or scientific method may be used for amortization of bond premium or discount. The straight-line method calls for writing off an equal amount of premium or discount each period. This procedure results in equal periodic interest charges. The compound-interest method calls for reporting interest at the effective rate. The effective rate provided by the bond issue must first be determined. This rate is then applied periodically to the bond carrying value in arriving at the charge to the interest expense account, the difference between the charge to expense and the amount paid being reported as a reduction in the premium or discount balance.

To illustrate the application of the straight-line and compound-interest methods of amortization, assume that 5-year bonds of $100,000, interest at 6% payable semiannually, are sold to yield 5%. This price as shown by bond tables is $104,376.03. The following tabulations show the differences in results through the use of the two methods:

### AMORTIZATION OF PREMIUM — STRAIGHT-LINE METHOD
$100,000 5-Year Bonds, Interest at 6% Payable Semiannually,
Sold at $104,376.03

| Interest Payment | A Interest Paid (3% of Face Value) | B Premium Amortization (1/10 × $4,376.03) | C Effective Interest (A − B) | D Unamortized Premium (D − B) | E Bond Carrying Value ($100,000 + D) |
|---|---|---|---|---|---|
| | | | | $4,376.03 | $104,376.03 |
| 1 | $3,000.00 | $437.60 | $2,562.40 | 3,938.43 | 103,938.43 |
| 2 | 3,000.00 | 437.60 | 2,562.40 | 3,500.83 | 103,500.83 |
| 3 | 3,000.00 | 437.60 | 2,562.40 | 3,063.23 | 103,063.23 |
| 4 | 3,000.00 | 437.60 | 2,562.40 | 2,625.63 | 102,625.63 |
| 5 | 3,000.00 | 437.60 | 2,562.40 | 2,188.03 | 102,188.03 |
| 6 | 3,000.00 | 437.60 | 2,562.40 | 1,750.43 | 101,750.43 |
| 7 | 3,000.00 | 437.60 | 2,562.40 | 1,312.83 | 101,312.83 |
| 8 | 3,000.00 | 437.60 | 2,562.40 | 875.23 | 100,875.23 |
| 9 | 3,000.00 | 437.60 | 2,562.40 | 437.63 | 100,437.63 |
| 10 | 3,000.00 | 437.63 | 2,562.37 | —— | 100,000.00 |

### AMORTIZATION OF PREMIUM — COMPOUND-INTEREST METHOD
$100,000 5-Year Bonds, Interest at 6% Payable Semiannually,
Sold at $104,376.03 to Yield 5%

| Interest Payment | A Interest Paid (3% of Face Value) | B Effective Interest (2½% of Bond Carrying Value) | C Premium Amortization (A − B) | D Unamortized Premium (D − C) | E Bond Carrying Value ($100,000 + D) |
|---|---|---|---|---|---|
| | | | | $4,376.03 | $104,376.03 |
| 1 | $3,000.00 | $2,609.40 (2½% of $104,376.03) | $390.60 | 3,985.43 | 103,985.43 |
| 2 | 3,000.00 | 2,599.64 (2½% of $103,985.43) | 400.36 | 3,585.07 | 103,585.07 |
| 3 | 3,000.00 | 2,589.63 (2½% of $103,585.07) | 410.37 | 3,174.70 | 103,174.70 |
| 4 | 3,000.00 | 2,579.37 (2½% of $103,174.70) | 420.63 | 2,754.07 | 102,754.07 |
| 5 | 3,000.00 | 2,568.85 (2½% of $102,754.07) | 431.15 | 2,322.92 | 102,322.92 |
| 6 | 3,000.00 | 2,558.07 (2½% of $102,322.92) | 441.93 | 1,880.99 | 101,880.99 |
| 7 | 3,000.00 | 2,547.02 (2½% of $101,880.99) | 452.98 | 1,428.01 | 101,428.01 |
| 8 | 3,000.00 | 2,535.70 (2½% of $101,428.01) | 464.30 | 963.71 | 100,963.71 |
| 9 | 3,000.00 | 2,524.09 (2½% of $100,963.71) | 475.91 | 487.80 | 100,487.80 |
| 10 | 3,000.00 | 2,512.20 (2½% of $100,487.80) | 487.80 | —— | 100,000.00 |

The use of the straight-line and compound-interest methods when bonds are issued at a discount is illustrated below. Here it is assumed that 5-year bonds of $100,000, interest at 4% payable semiannually, are sold for $95,625, a price that provides a yield of approximately 5%.

Even though it is possible that bonds may be retired prior to their maturity dates, such retirement cannot ordinarily be anticipated. Amortization schedules, then, are normally developed in terms of the full life of the bond issue. Early bond retirement will call for a cancellation of the bond premium or discount relating to the remaining life of the issue.

The investor in bonds normally employs straight-line amortization as a practical matter. With the acquisition of a number of different issues,

### AMORTIZATION OF DISCOUNT — STRAIGHT-LINE METHOD
$100,000 5-Year Bonds, Interest at 4% Payable Semiannually,
Sold at $95,625

| Interest Payment | A<br>Interest Paid<br>(2% of<br>Face Value) | B<br>Discount<br>Amortization<br>(1/10 × $4,375) | C<br>Effective<br>Interest<br>(A + B) | D<br>Unamortized<br>Discount<br>(D − B) | E<br>Bond Carrying<br>Value<br>($100,000 − D) |
|---|---|---|---|---|---|
|  |  |  |  | $4,375.00 | $ 95,625.00 |
| 1 | $2,000.00 | $437.50 | $2,437.50 | 3,937.50 | 96,062.50 |
| 2 | 2,000.00 | 437.50 | 2,437.50 | 3,500.00 | 96,500.00 |
| 3 | 2,000.00 | 437.50 | 2,437.50 | 3,062.50 | 96,937.50 |
| 4 | 2,000.00 | 437.50 | 2,437.50 | 2,625.00 | 97,375.00 |
| 5 | 2,000.00 | 437.50 | 2,437.50 | 2,187.50 | 97,812.50 |
| 6 | 2,000.00 | 437.50 | 2,437.50 | 1,750.00 | 98,250.00 |
| 7 | 2,000.00 | 437.50 | 2,437.50 | 1,312.50 | 98,687.50 |
| 8 | 2,000.00 | 437.50 | 2,437.50 | 875.00 | 99,125.00 |
| 9 | 2,000.00 | 437.50 | 2,437.50 | 437.50 | 99,562.50 |
| 10 | 2,000.00 | 437.50 | 2,437.50 | ——— | 100,000.00 |

### AMORTIZATION OF DISCOUNT — COMPOUND-INTEREST METHOD
$100,000 5-Year Bonds, Interest at 4% Payable Semiannually,
Sold at $95,625 to Yield Approximately 5%

| Interest Payment | A<br>Interest Paid<br>(2% of<br>Face Value) | B<br>Effective Interest<br>(2½% of Bond Carrying Value) | C<br>Discount<br>Amortization<br>(B − A) | D<br>Unamortized<br>Discount<br>(D − C) | E<br>Bond<br>Carrying<br>Value<br>($100,000 − D) |
|---|---|---|---|---|---|
|  |  |  |  | $4,375.00 | $ 95,625.00 |
| 1 | $2,000.00 | $2,390.63 (2½% of $95,625.00) | $390.63 | 3,984.37 | 96,015.63 |
| 2 | 2,000.00 | 2,400.39 (2½% of $96,015.63) | 400.39 | 3,583.98 | 96,416.02 |
| 3 | 2,000.00 | 2,410.40 (2½% of $96,416.02) | 410.40 | 3,173.58 | 96,826.42 |
| 4 | 2,000.00 | 2,420.66 (2½% of $96,826.42) | 420.66 | 2,752.92 | 97,247.08 |
| 5 | 2,000.00 | 2,431.18 (2½% of $97,247.08) | 431.18 | 2,321.74 | 97,678.26 |
| 6 | 2,000.00 | 2,441.96 (2½% of $97,678.26) | 441.96 | 1,879.78 | 98,120.22 |
| 7 | 2,000.00 | 2,453.01 (2½% of $98,120.22) | 453.01 | 1,426.77 | 98,573.23 |
| 8 | 2,000.00 | 2,464.33 (2½% of $98,573.23) | 464.33 | 962.44 | 99,037.56 |
| 9 | 2,000.00 | 2,475.94 (2½% of $99,037.56) | 475.94 | 486.50 | 99,513.50 |
| 10 | 2,000.00 | 2,486.50 ($2,000 + $486.50)[1] | 486.50 | ——— | 100,000.00 |

[1] 2½% of $99,513.50 is $2,487.84. However, use of 5% when the effective rate was not exactly 5% has resulted in a small discrepancy that requires adjustment upon recording the final interest payment. On the final payment the discount balance is closed and interest expense is increased by this amount.

the purchases and sales within the bond life, and the relatively minor differences in straight-line and compound-interest procedures, application of the simpler method is justified. But these considerations are not relevant in the case of the bond issuer. Here, only one or a few issues are involved and amortization schedules can be followed from the time of issuance of the bonds to their retirement. When large issues are involved, the difference between compound-interest amortization and straight-line amortization may be significant. Such circumstances support the use of the compound-interest method that provides for the accurate measure of expense in terms of a changing liability balance. Nevertheless, straight-line amortization is frequently found in practice and is accepted for income tax purposes. Remaining illustrations in this chapter assume the use of straight-line amortization.

## Accounting for bonds payable

When bonds are sold by a company between interest dates, the bond price is increased by a charge for accrued interest to the date of sale. Accrued Interest on Bonds Payable may be credited for the interest received from the investor; when interest for the full period is paid, the accrued interest balance is closed and Interest Expense is charged for the difference. It is also possible to credit Interest Expense for the accrued interest received. Payment of interest is then charged in full to Interest Expense. The latter procedure is used in subsequent illustrations.

Entries for the amortization of bond premium or discount may be made (1) at the time of each interest payment or (2) only at the end of the company's fiscal period. Normally, the latter procedure is more convenient since entries for amortization are made for the full year except for the first and last years when fractional parts of a year may be involved.

The entries for issuance of bonds and the payment of interest are illustrated in the example that follows. Assume that the Crescent Corporation decides to issue bonds of $100,000. Bonds are dated September 1, 1964, pay interest at 4½% semiannually on March 1 and September 1, and mature on September 1, 1974. Bonds are sold on December 1, 1964, at $94,150 plus accrued interest. The corporation adjusts and closes its books at the end of each calendar year. Since the bonds are issued on December 1, bonds have a life of only 9¾ years or 117 months. A schedule may be prepared to summarize discount amortization over the bond life. These data can then be used in making periodic adjustments.[1] The amortization schedule follows:

---

[1] Amortization procedures for bond discount are equally applicable to bond issue costs when these are carried separately.

## AMORTIZATION SCHEDULE — STRAIGHT-LINE METHOD

| Period | A<br>Int.<br>Paym't<br>(Includ.<br>Adj. for<br>Accruals) | B<br>Discount Amortization | | | C<br>Effective<br>Interest<br>(A+B) | D<br>Unamortized<br>Discount<br>(D−B) | E<br>Bond<br>Carrying<br>Value<br>($100,000<br>−D) |
|---|---|---|---|---|---|---|---|
| | | No.<br>of<br>Mos. | Fraction<br>of Disc.<br>to be<br>Amortized | Amt. of<br>Disc.<br>Amortization | | | |
| | | | | | | $ 5,850 | $ 94,150 |
| Dec. 1 (sales date)–Dec. 31, 1964 | $ 375 | 1 | 1/117 | $ 50 | $ 425 | 5,800 | 94,200 |
| Year Ended Dec. 31, 1965 | 4,500 | 12 | 12/117 | 600 | 5,100 | 5,200 | 94,800 |
| Year Ended Dec. 31, 1966 | 4,500 | 12 | 12/117 | 600 | 5,100 | 4,600 | 95,400 |
| Year Ended Dec. 31, 1967 | 4,500 | 12 | 12/117 | 600 | 5,100 | 4,000 | 96,000 |
| Year Ended Dec. 31, 1968 | 4,500 | 12 | 12/117 | 600 | 5,100 | 3,400 | 96,600 |
| Year Ended Dec. 31, 1969 | 4,500 | 12 | 12/117 | 600 | 5,100 | 2,800 | 97,200 |
| Year Ended Dec. 31, 1970 | 4,500 | 12 | 12/117 | 600 | 5,100 | 2,200 | 97,800 |
| Year Ended Dec. 31, 1971 | 4,500 | 12 | 12/117 | 600 | 5,100 | 1,600 | 98,400 |
| Year Ended Dec. 31, 1972 | 4,500 | 12 | 12/117 | 600 | 5,100 | 1,000 | 99,000 |
| Year Ended Dec. 31, 1973 | 4,500 | 12 | 12/117 | 600 | 5,100 | 400 | 99,600 |
| Jan. 1–Sept. 1, 1974 (maturity) | 3,000 | 8 | 8/117 | 400 | 3,400 | —— | 100,000 |
| | | 117 | 117/117 | $5,850 | | | |

## Entries on the corporation books in 1964 and 1965 follow:

| Transaction | Entry |
|---|---|
| **DECEMBER 1, 1964**<br>Sold $100,000 of 4½% bonds for $94,150, bonds maturing on September 1, 1974, 10 years from date of issue. Interest is payable semiannually on March 1 and September 1. Accrued interest received for the period September 1–December 1 is $1,125. | Cash.................. 95,275<br>Discount on Bonds Payable.............. 5,850<br>    Bonds Payable........ 100,000<br>    Bond Interest Expense. 1,125 |
| **DECEMBER 31, 1964**<br>(a) To record accrued interest for 4 months, and (b) to record amortization of bond discount applicable to current year. Amortization: bonds outstanding in current year, one month; total life of bond issue, 9¾ years or 117 months; current amortization, 1/117 of $5,850 = $50 (one month at $50). | (a) Bond Interest Expense............. 1,500<br>    Accrued Interest on Bonds Payable.... 1,500<br><br>(b) Bond Interest Expense   50<br>    Discount on Bonds Payable......... 50 |
| **JANUARY 1, 1965**<br>To reverse 1964 accrued interest. | Accrued Interest on Bonds Payable............... 1,500<br>    Bond Interest Expense. 1,500 |
| **MARCH 1, 1965**<br>Paid semiannual interest. | Bond Interest Expense... 2,250<br>    Cash............... 2,250 |
| **SEPTEMBER 1, 1965**<br>Paid semiannual interest. | Bond Interest Expense... 2,250<br>    Cash............... 2,250 |
| **DECEMBER 31, 1965**<br>(a) To record accrued interest for 4 months, and (b) to record amortization of bond discount applicable to current year, 12/117 of $5,850, or $600 (or 12 months at $50 a month, $600). | (a) Bond Interest Expense   1,500<br>    Accrued Interest on Bonds Payable.... 1,500<br><br>(b) Bond Interest Expense   600<br>    Discount on Bonds Payable......... 600 |

## Bond reacquisition prior to maturity

Corporations frequently reacquire their own bonds on the market when prices or other factors make such action desirable. Reacquisition of bonds prior to their maturity calls for the recognition of a gain or a loss for the difference between the bond carrying value and the amount paid. Payment of accrued interest on bond reacquisition is separately reported as a charge to Bond Interest Expense.

When bonds are reacquired, amortization of bond premium, discount, and issue costs should be brought up to date. Reacquisition calls for the cancellation of the bond face value together with any related premium, discount, or issue costs as of the reacquisition date.

When bonds are reacquired and canceled, Bonds Payable is debited. When bonds are reacquired but are held for possible future reissue, Treasury Bonds instead of Bonds Payable may be debited. It has already been indicated that treasury bonds are simply evidence of a liability that has been liquidated. Although treasury bonds may represent a ready source of cash, their sale creates new creditors, a situation that is no different from the debt created by any other type of borrowing. Treasury bonds, then, should be recorded at their face value and subtracted from the bonds payable balance in reporting bonds issued and outstanding. If treasury bonds are sold at a price other than face value, Cash is debited, Treasury Bonds is credited, thus reinstating the bond liability, and a premium or a discount on the sale is recorded, the latter balance to be amortized over the remaining life of this specific bond group. While held, treasury bonds occupy the same legal status as unissued bonds, and when an account is carried for unissued bonds, can be recorded with them. At the maturity of the bond issue, any balance in a treasury bonds or unissued bonds account is applied against Bonds Payable.

To illustrate bond reacquisition, assume that in the preceding example for the Crescent Corporation, bonds of $10,000 are reacquired at 98½ by the company on February 1, 1966. Entries at the time of bond reacquisition would be as follows:

| Transaction | Entry | |
|---|---|---|
| FEBRUARY 1, 1966<br>To record reacquisition of own bonds:<br>(a) Amortization of discount on bonds of $10,000 to date of purchase, 1/117 of $585, or $5 (or 1/10 of monthly amortization of $50). | (a) Bond Interest Expense. 5.00<br>Discount on Bonds<br>Payable.......... | 5.00 |
| (b) Payment of accrued interest, Sept. 1–Feb. 1, $10,000 at 4½% for 5 months. | (b) Bond Interest Expense. 187.50<br>Cash............. | 187.50 |

| Transaction | | Entry | |
|---|---|---|---|
| (c) Loss on bond retirement: | | (c) Bonds Payable | |
| Bonds at face value.......... | $10,000 | (or Treasury | |
| Discount on bonds....    $585 | | Bonds)..........10,000.00 | |
| Less amortization to | | Loss on Bond | |
| date of purchase, 14 | | Retirement.........365.00 | |
| months at $5........    70 | 515 | Cash............ | 9,850.00 |
| | | Discount on | |
| Book value of bonds.......... | $9,485 | Bonds Payable..... | 515.00 |
| Amount paid on reacquisition.. | 9,850 | | |
| Loss on bond retirement...... | $365 | | |

For income tax purposes a gain on bond reacquisition is fully taxable and a loss is fully deductible.

### Bond retirement at maturity

Most bond issues are payable at the end of a specified period. When bond discount or premium and issue cost balances have been satisfactorily amortized over the life of the bonds, bond retirement simply calls for a charge to the bonds payable account and a credit to cash. Any bonds not presented for payment at their maturity should be removed from the bonds payable balance and reported separately as Matured Bonds Payable; these are reported as a current liability except when they are to be paid out of a sinking fund. Interest does not accrue on matured bonds that have not been presented for payment.

If a bond fund is used to pay off a bond issue, any cash remaining in the fund may be returned to the cash account. Appropriations of retained earnings that may have been established during the life of the issue to express earnings restrictions may be returned to retained earnings.

### Serial bonds

Foregoing discussions were related to *term bonds* or bonds with a single maturity date. *Serial bonds* provide for a series of principal payments on periodic due dates. For example, a $500,000 bond issue may provide that stated bond blocks of $25,000 are to be paid off at the end of each year for 20 years. This plan provides for the gradual amortization of the debt.

The issuance of serial bonds eliminates the need for a bond sinking fund or for the appropriation of retained earnings. When a sinking fund cannot produce earnings at a rate equivalent to that paid on the bond issue, serial bonds are advantageous to the issuing company. Here cash that would otherwise be deposited in the fund is applied directly to the retirement of debt, and the payment of interest relating to that portion of the debt is terminated.

### Amortization procedures for serial bonds

When serial bonds are issued, the amortization schedule for bond premium or discount requires recognition of a declining debt principal. Successive bond years cannot be charged with equal amounts of premium or discount because of a shrinking debt and successively smaller interest payments.

Premium or discount on serial bonds may be amortized by a straight-line procedure or by a compound-interest procedure. The straight-line procedure is referred to as the *bonds-outstanding method* and calls for decreases in the amortization schedule proportionate to the decrease in the loan balance. The compound-interest procedure requires that the effective interest rate at which the bonds were issued be determined first. The charge for interest is then reported at the effective rate applied to the bond carrying value, the difference between the amount reported as expense and the amount of interest paid being reported as a reduction in the premium or discount balance.

*Bonds-outstanding method.* Amortization by the bonds outstanding method is illustrated in the example that follows. Assume that bonds of $100,000, dated January 1, 1964, are issued on this date for $101,350. Bonds of $20,000 mature at the beginning of each year. The bonds pay interest of 5% annually. The company's accounting period ends on December 31; the accounting period and the bond year thus coincide. A table showing the premium to be amortized each year is developed as follows:

AMORTIZATION SCHEDULE — BONDS-OUTSTANDING METHOD

| Year | Bonds Outstanding | Fraction of Premium to be Amortized | Annual Premium Amortization (Fraction × $1,350) |
|------|------|------|------|
| 1964 | $100,000 | 100,000/300,000 (or 10/30) | $ 450 |
| 1965 | 80,000 | 80,000/300,000 (or 8/30) | 360 |
| 1966 | 60,000 | 60,000/300,000 (or 6/30) | 270 |
| 1967 | 40,000 | 40,000/300,000 (or 4/30) | 180 |
| 1968 | 20,000 | 20,000/300,000 (or 2/30) | 90 |
|      | $300,000 | 300,000/300,000 (or 30/30) | $1,350 |

The annual premium amortization is found by multiplying the premium by a fraction whose numerator is the number of bond dollars outstanding in that year and whose denominator is the total number of bond dollars outstanding for the life of the bond issue. As bonds are retired, the amounts of premium amortization decline accordingly.

Periodic amortization may be incorporated in a table summarizing the interest charges and changes in bond carrying values as follows:

### AMORTIZATION OF PREMIUM — SERIAL BONDS
### BONDS-OUTSTANDING METHOD

| Date | A<br>Interest<br>Payment<br>(5% of<br>Face Value) | B<br>Premium<br>Amortiza-<br>tion | C<br>Effective<br>Interest<br>(A−B) | D<br>Principal<br>Payment | E<br>Bond Carry-<br>ing Value<br>Decrease<br>(B+D) | F<br>Bond<br>Carrying<br>Value<br>(F−E) |
|---|---|---|---|---|---|---|
| Jan.  1, 1964 |  |  |  |  |  | $101,350 |
| Dec. 31, 1964 | $5,000 | $450 | $4,550 | $20,000 | $20,450 | 80,900 |
| Dec. 31, 1965 | 4,000 | 360 | 3,640 | 20,000 | 20,360 | 60,540 |
| Dec. 31, 1966 | 3,000 | 270 | 2,730 | 20,000 | 20,270 | 40,270 |
| Dec. 31, 1967 | 2,000 | 180 | 1,820 | 20,000 | 20,180 | 20,090 |
| Dec. 31, 1968 | 1,000 | 90 | 910 | 20,000 | 20,090 | ——— |

*Compound-interest method.* Tables show that the above bonds were sold to yield approximately $4\frac{1}{2}\%$. Use of this rate results in the following interest charges and premium amortization:

### AMORTIZATION OF PREMIUM — SERIAL BONDS
### COMPOUND-INTEREST METHOD

| Date | A<br>Interest<br>Payment<br>(5% of<br>Face Value) | B<br>Effective<br>Interest<br>(4½% of Bond<br>Carrying<br>Value) | C<br>Premium<br>Amortiza-<br>tion<br>(A−B) | D<br>Principal<br>Payment | E<br>Bond Carry-<br>ing Value<br>Decrease<br>(C+D) | F<br>Bond<br>Carrying<br>Value<br>(F−E) |
|---|---|---|---|---|---|---|
| Jan.  1, 1964 |  |  |  |  |  | $101,350.00 |
| Dec. 31, 1964 | $5,000.00 | $4,560.75 | $439.25 | $20,000.00 | $20,439.25 | 80,910.75 |
| Dec. 31, 1965 | 4,000.00 | 3,640.98 | 359.02 | 20,000.00 | 20,359.02 | 60,551.73 |
| Dec. 31, 1966 | 3,000.00 | 2,724.83 | 275.17 | 20,000.00 | 20,275.17 | 40,276.56 |
| Dec. 31, 1967 | 2,000.00 | 1,812.45 | 187.55 | 20,000.00 | 20,187.55 | 20,089.01 |
| Dec. 31, 1968 | 1,000.00 | 910.99[1] | 89.01 | 20,000.00 | 20,089.01 | ——— |

[1] $4\frac{1}{2}\%$ of $20,089.01 is $904.01. However, use of $4\frac{1}{2}\%$ when the effective rate was not exactly $4\frac{1}{2}\%$ has resulted in a small discrepancy that requires adjustment upon the final interest payment. On the final payment the premium balance is closed and interest expense is reduced by this amount.

The straight-line method of amortization provides for the recognition of uniform amounts of amortization in terms of the par value of bonds outstanding. The compound-interest method provides for the recognition of interest at a uniform rate on the declining debt balance.

## Serial bond reacquisition prior to maturity

When serial bonds are reacquired prior to their maturities, it is necessary to cancel the unamortized premium or discount relating to that part of the bond issue that is liquidated. For example, assume the issuance of serial bonds previously described and amortization of the premium by the bonds-outstanding method as given on page 550. On April 1, 1965, $10,000 of bonds due January 1, 1967, and $10,000 of bonds due January 1, 1968, are reacquired at $100\frac{1}{2}$ plus accrued interest. The premium for the period January 1–April 1, 1965, relating to retired bonds, affects bond interest for the current period and will be written off as an adjustment to expense. The balance of the premium from the retirement date to the respective maturity date of the series retired must be canceled. The premium balance relating to retired bonds is calculated as follows:

Premium identified with 1965: $\dfrac{20,000}{80,000}$ $\times$ $360.00 $\times$ 9/12 $=$ $ 67.50

Premium identified with 1966: $\dfrac{20,000}{60,000}$ $\times$ $270.00 $=$ 90.00

Premium identified with 1967: $\dfrac{10,000}{40,000}$ $\times$ $180.00 $=$ 45.00

Premium identified with retired bonds ............ $202.50

Instead of the above procedure, the premium amortization per year on each $1,000 bond may first be calculated and this rate applied to bonds of each period that are canceled. The annual amortization rate per $1,000 bond is calculated as follows:

$$\frac{\$1,350 \text{ (total premium — life of bonds)}}{300 \text{ (total \$1,000 bonds outstanding — life of bonds)}} = \$4.50$$

The premium that is to be canceled may now be determined as follows:

| Year | Number of $1,000 Bonds $\times$ | Annual Premium Amortization per $1,000 Bond $\times$ | Fractional Part of Year = | Total Premium Cancellation |
|------|------|------|------|------|
| 1965 | 20 | $4.50 | 9/12 | $ 67.50 |
| 1966 | 20 | 4.50 | | 90.00 |
| 1967 | 10 | 4.50 | | 45.00 |
| | Premium identified with retired bonds.................... | | | $202.50 |

Bonds, carrying value $20,202.50, are retired at a cost of $20,100 resulting in a gain of $102.50. Payment is also made for interest on bonds of $20,000 for three months at 5%, or $250. The entry to record the retirement of bonds and the payment of interest on the series retired follows:

| | | |
|---|---|---|
| Bonds Payable (or Treasury Bonds)........... | 20,000.00 | |
| Premium on Bonds Payable................. | 202.50 | |
| Bond Interest Expense...................... | 250.00 | |
|     Cash..................................... | | 20,350.00 |
|     Gain on Bond Retirement................. | | 102.50 |

A revised schedule for the amortization of bond premium follows:

AMORTIZATION SCHEDULE — BONDS-OUTSTANDING METHOD
REVISED FOR BOND RETIREMENT

| Year | Annual Premium Amortization per Original Schedule | Premium Cancellation on Bond Retirement | Annual Premium Amortization Adjusted for Bond Retirement |
|------|------|------|------|
| 1964 | $ 450.00 | | $ 450.00 |
| 1965 | 360.00 | $ 67.50 | 292.50 |
| 1966 | 270.00 | 90.00 | 180.00 |
| 1967 | 180.00 | 45.00 | 135.00 |
| 1968 | 90.00 | | 90.00 |
| | $1,350.00 | $202.50 | $1,147.50 |

## Bond redemption prior to maturity

Provisions of the bond indenture frequently give the issuer the option of calling bonds for payment prior to maturity. Ordinarily, the call must be made on an interest payment date and no further interest accrues on the bonds not presented at this time. When only a part of the issue is to be retired, the bonds that are called may be determined by lot.

The inclusion of call provisions in the bond agreement is a feature favoring the issuer. The company is in a position to terminate the bond agreement and eliminate future interest charges whenever its financial position makes such action feasible. Furthermore, the company is protected in the event of a fall in the market interest rate by being able to retire the old issue from proceeds of a new issue paying a lower rate of interest. The bond contract normally requires payment of a premium if bonds are called. The bondholder is thus offered special compensation if his investment is terminated and he is faced with the problem of reinvesting his funds.

When bonds are called, the difference between the amount paid and the bonds redeemed together with related premium, discount, and issue cost balances is reported as a loss or a gain on retirement. To illustrate, assume that bonds of a corporation are callable at a 5% premium or at 105. Bonds of $20,000 are retired on this basis. At the time of call, bonds outstanding are shown at $100,000 with an unamortized discount on the issue of $2,500 and unamortized bond issue costs of $1,000. The following entry is made:

| | | |
|---|---:|---:|
| Bonds Payable (or Treasury Bonds)............... | 20,000 | |
| Loss on Bond Retirement........................ | 1,700 | |
|    Cash........................................ | | 21,000 |
|    Discount on Bonds Payable..................... | | 500 |
|    Unamortized Bond Issue Costs................. | | 200 |

Any interest paid at the time of call is reported as a charge to bond interest expense.

## Bond conversion

The option to convert bonds into capital stock is frequently included in the bond agreement. Ordinarily such conversion may take place only within a stated period and under certain conditions. Frequently, conversion is possible only on an interest payment date. Conversion terms may provide for the exchange of bonds for preferred or common stock on a par for par basis; if stock has a $100 par, then, a $1,000 bond would be convertible into 10 shares of stock. On the other hand, conversion terms may provide for exchange at a stated conversion price for shares.

terms may provide for exchange at a stated conversion price for shares. For example, it might be provided that each $1,000 bond could be exchanged for shares at a conversion price of $12.50; here, a $1,000 bond would be convertible into 80 shares of stock.

In some cases conversion prices for shares of stock increase at stated periods. Conversion privileges may terminate on a specified date. Conversion privileges are included to make bonds more attractive to the buyer. If corporate activities are successful, the bondholder may participate in this success by exchanging his bonds for stock.

Alternative procedures can be employed by the issuing company in recording the exchange of bonds for stock with a market value that differs from the bond carrying value:

1. Invested capital may be increased by an amount equal to the fair market value of the stock, a gain or a loss being recognized on the retirement of the bonds.
2. The bond carrying value may simply be assigned to the stock.

An increase in capital equal to the market value of the stock can be supported on the grounds that bondholders are actually paid an amount equal to the value of the stock given in exchange. The exchange of stock for bonds closes the transaction cycle relating to bonds and opens a new cycle relating to stock in which stock is recorded at the value that it would bring if sold on the open market. The gain or the loss is related to the bond issue since it arises from the termination of the bond contract. Neither advantage nor penalty is assigned to the new stock issue.

The assignment of the bond carrying value to the stock is supported on the theory that the company upon issuing the bonds is aware of the fact that bond proceeds may ultimately represent the consideration identified with stock. Thus, when bondholders exercise their conversion privileges, the value identified with the obligation is transferred to the security that replaces it.

To illustrate the entries for bond conversion, assume that a company's $1,000 bonds are convertible into 40 shares of its $20 par value common stock. Bonds of $10,000 are converted on this basis. At the time of conversion bonds outstanding are reported at $100,000 with an unamortized discount on the issue of $4,000. The common stock on this date is quoted at $30 per share.

If the quoted market value of the stock is to be used in recording the issue of stock, the entry to record the conversion would be as follows:

| | | |
|---|---:|---:|
| Bonds Payable.................................... | 10,000 | |
| Loss on Bond Conversion......................... | 2,400 | |
| Discount on Bonds Payable....................... | | 400 |
| Common Stock (400 shares, $20 par)............. | | 8,000 |
| Premium on Common Stock...................... | | 4,000 |

If the bond carrying value is to be used in recording the issue of stock, the entry would be as follows:

| | | |
|---|---:|---:|
| Bonds Payable..................................... | 10,000 | |
| Discount on Bonds Payable...................... | | 400 |
| Common Stock (400 shares, $20 par)............ | | 8,000 |
| Premium on Common Stock.................... | | 1,600 |

It should be observed that total capital is the same regardless of the value assigned to the stock. However, when market value was used in the first example, retained earnings of $2,400 became a part of the corporate paid-in capital.

## Bond refunding

Cash for the retirement of a bond issue is frequently raised through the sale of a new issue. This is referred to as *bond refunding;* the original issue is said to be *refunded.* Bond refunding may take place when an issue matures. Bonds may also be refunded prior to their maturity when the interest rate has dropped and the interest savings on a new issue will more than offset the costs of retiring the old issue. To illustrate, assume that a corporation has outstanding 6% bonds of $1,000,000 callable at 102 and with a remaining 10-year term, and similar 10-year bonds can be marketed currently at an interest rate of only 4½%. Under these circumstances it would be advantageous to retire the old issue with the proceeds from a new 4½% issue, since the future savings in interest will exceed by a considerable amount the premium to be paid on the call of the old issue.

The desirability of refunding may not be as obvious as in the preceding instance. In determining whether refunding is warranted in marginal cases, careful consideration must be given to such factors as the different maturity dates of the two issues, possible future changes in interest rates, changed loan requirements, different indenture provisions, income tax effects of refunding, and legal fees, printing costs, and marketing costs involved in refunding.

When refunding takes place before the maturity date of the old issue, the problem arises as to how to dispose of the call premium and unamortized discount and issue costs of the original bonds. Three positions are taken with respect to disposition of these items:

1. Such charges are considered a loss on bond retirement.
2. Such charges are considered deferrable and to be amortized systematically over the remaining life of the original issue.
3. Such charges are considered deferrable and to be amortized systematically over the life of the new issue.

The first position views bond retirement in refunding the same as any other debt cancellation. Payment of bonds terminates the old bond contract and any loss arising from such termination is assigned to the original loan period. The new bond issue is considered a new transaction with only its own costs assignable to future periods. Recognition of bond redemption charges as a loss finds support as a conservative measure, and is also the required procedure for income tax purposes.

The second position views the charges arising from bond retirement as the price paid for the option of entering into a new and more attractive borrowing arrangement. Such charges, then, are properly deferred so that they may be identified with the periods receiving the benefits from refunding — the unexpired term of the original issue. The remaining periods covered by the original issue will still realize a savings through reduced interest charges counterbalanced only in part by the amortization of redemption charges.

The third position views the charges from bond retirement as related to the benefits that are found in the new arrangement and hence as distributable over the entire life of the new issue even when this exceeds the life of the original bonds. The decision to refund the issue is made on the basis of the present arrangement as compared with the alternative borrowing plans that are available. Any charges relating to the new financing, then, should be absorbed over the full term of the new issue.

The authors believe that the strongest argument can be made for the first position. Here redemption charges are viewed as a loss in terminating an agreement that is no longer favorable rather than as costs for entering into more advantageous loan arrangements. The old loan cycle has ended; a new loan cycle has begun. To capitalize redemption charges would lend support to similar capitalization of the unrecovered book value of assets and removal charges when assets are retired upon acquisition of new assets. Either instance may be better viewed as a move into a new situation that calls for the recognition of losses that have accrued.

Recognition of a loss as compared with the deferral of redemption charges is illustrated in the example that follows. Assume that 6% bonds of $250,000 are retired from the proceeds of a new 4½% $300,000 issue. The original issue has 5 years to run; a discount balance of $3,000 is found on the date of refunding. Bonds are callable at 102. The new bonds have a 10-year life and are sold at 98. Entries are made as follows:

| | If Redemption Charges are Recognized as a Loss | | | If Redemption Charges Are Deferred | |
|---|---|---|---|---|---|
| JULY 1 Issued 4½% bonds of $300,000 at 98. | Cash......294,000 Discount on Bonds Pay-able........ | 6,000 | | Cash....... 294,000 Discount on Bonds Pay-able........ | 6,000 |
| | 4½% Bonds Payable... | | 300,000 | 4½% Bonds Payable.... | 300,000 |

| | If Redemption Charges are Recognized as a Loss | | | If Redemption Charges Are Deferred | | |
|---|---|---|---|---|---|---|
| JULY 1 Redeemed 6% bonds of $250,000, with unamortized discount of $3,000, at 102. | 6% Bonds Payable....250,000 Loss on Bond Redemption | 8,000 | | 6% Bonds Payable.....250,000 Bond Refund- ing Costs..... | 8,000 | |
| | Cash..... | | 255,000 | Cash...... | | 255,000 |
| | Discount on Bonds Pay- able...... | | 3,000 | Discount on Bonds Pay- able....... | | 3,000 |
| DECEMBER 31 Paid semiannual interest, 4½% of $300,000 for 6 months. | Bond Interest Expense.... | 6,750 | | Bond Interest Expense..... | 6,750 | |
| | Cash..... | | 6,750 | Cash ..... | | 6,750 |
| (a) To record discount amortization for 6 months on 10-year basis: 1/20 × $6,000 = $300. | Bond Interest Expense..... | 300 | | Bond Interest Expense..... | 300 | |
| | Discount on Bonds Pay- able...... | | 300 | Discount on Bonds Pay- able....... | | 300 |
| (b) To record deferred refunding costs amortization for 6 months on 5-year basis: 1/10 × $8,000 = $800. | No entry | | | Amortization of Bond Refunding Costs ......... | 800 | |
| | | | | Bond Refunding Costs........ | | 800 |

## Liability under pension plans

Plans for the payment of employee pensions and other retirement allowances have been widely adopted in recent years. Such plans involve the assumption of obligations that are deferred until employee retirement dates and will be settled over a period of years.

Many variations are found in the kinds of plans that are adopted and also in the financial arrangements that are made for payments to retired employees. Plans may be classified as *informal* wherein payments are determined at the time of retirement and are subject to change or discontinuance at the option of the employer, and *formal* wherein definite commitments are made for payments to be determined by formulas based upon length of service and earnings. Payments under the various plans may be made by direct outlays to retired employees, by the operation of self-administered funds, or by the payment of premiums to insurance companies or other agencies that assume full responsibility for the retirement payments. In accounting for a plan, both the nature of the plan and the arrangement for payments must be carefully considered.

*Informal plans.* In the absence of definite commitments for the payment of stated retirement benefits, entries to record pension costs can be made as monies are applied to this purpose. Accounting, then, is on a cash basis. Payments to employees are recorded by charges to expense and credits to Cash; similar entries are made if payments are made to an outside agency for the purchase of employee benefits. It would be possible, however, to employ an accrual method for pension costs when these can be satisfactorily estimated and it can be assumed that plans will be carried out even though the business is not legally required to do so.

*Formal plans.* When formal commitments have been made, it is generally agreed that the costs of providing such benefits for employees should be systematically accrued over the working years of such employees. An exact determination of periodic charges that will cover the pensions ultimately payable may not be possible. Estimates and assumptions together with actuarial calculations will have to be employed in arriving at such periodic charges.

When a pension plan is self-administered, the company normally recognizes the accrual of the pension obligations in the accounts and at the same time establishes a special trust fund to meet such obligations. The periodic accrual of pension benefits to employees is recorded by a charge to a pensions expense account and a credit to a pensions liability account. The transfer of cash to a pension fund is recorded by a charge to a pension fund cash account and a credit to Cash. The subsequent payment of pensions is recorded by a charge to the liability account and a credit to the pension fund cash account. The pensions expense should be reported with salaries and wages on the income statement for this is a part of the cost of employee services. The pension fund should be reported in the investment section of the balance sheet. The liability account may be designated Estimated Amounts Payable under Employee Retirement System in view of the estimates involved in its determination, and reported as noncurrent when pension fund cash will be applied to its payment. In the absence of a pension fund, the amount to be paid within one year would be reported as a current liability and the balance of the liability would be reported as noncurrent.

A company that pays premiums to an insurance company or other agency for assuming full pension responsibilities requires neither a trust fund nor the recognition of a liability for accrued pensions. Premiums under the plan are based upon the number of employees, their life expectancies, and the benefits to be provided upon their retirement. Entries are made periodically charging an expense account and crediting a liability account for the premiums payable to the outside agency. Payments to the agency are charged against the accrued liability; any premium accrued but unpaid at the end of the period is reported as a current liability.

Present day pension arrangements involve significant sums. The effects that such plans have on present and future earnings and financial position are material. Many companies follow cash-basis or tax-basis methods in the accounts that may fail to recognize adequately the obligations that have been assumed under pension plans. Such circumstances require that financial statements offer full disclosure as to the characteristics and the implications of the plans.

### Deferred revenues

Deferred revenues arise upon the receipt of cash or the recognition of some other asset before the asset may be considered earned. Cash received or receivables recognized for goods, services, or benefits to be supplied in future periods call for credits to deferred revenue accounts until commitments are fulfilled. Normally, costs are involved before revenues may be considered realized and the earnings from this source still remain to be determined.

It has already been indicated that when an obligation is to be liquidated through the use of existing current assets, it is properly reported as a current liability. The deferred credit classification on the balance sheet, then, should be limited to obligations that will not claim existing current assets in their liquidation. When a deferred revenue item involves an obligation covering a number of years, the amount of the obligation to be satisfied through existing current assets may be reported as current and the balance under the deferred revenues heading. However, when a balance is related to a number of years but the claim that it makes against existing current assets is considered only minor and incidental, the entire balance may be reported under the long-term heading. For example, the entire amount of rents collected in advance under a long-term lease would generally be reported under the deferred revenues heading. Costs emerging under such a claim will involve (1) depreciation related to leased properties and (2) periodic expenditures for taxes, repairs, insurance, etc., but the portion of the latter group to be paid currently would normally not be considered sufficiently important to call for special recognition. Items that are usually reported under the deferred revenues heading include leasehold and rental advances, interest received in advance, premiums received on long-term insurance contracts, fees received in advance on long-term service contracts, and deferred profits on installment sales when profits are to be recognized as earned only as installment receivables are collected.

### Long-term liabilities on the balance sheet

In reporting long-term liabilities on the balance sheet, the nature of the liabilities, maturity dates, interest rates, methods of liquidation. conversion privileges, and other significant matters should be indicated. When assets have been pledged to secure a liability, full particulars of the pledge should be indicated in the description of the obligation. This may be accompanied by identification on the asset side of the balance sheet of the specific assets pledged. When an agreement with a creditor limits the ability of a company to pay dividends, such limitation should be disclosed.

The portion of serial bonds that is payable within one year is reported as a current liability. Other long-term debt maturing within one year should be reported as a current liability only if retirement will claim current assets. If the debt is to be paid from a bond retirement fund or is to be retired through some form of refinancing, it would continue to be reported as noncurrent with an explanation of the method to be used in its liquidation.

Unissued bonds and treasury bonds may be combined since they both represent potential sources of funds without further authorization of bonds or mortgaging of properties. These may be reported parenthetically after listing bonds outstanding or as a subtraction item from the total bonds authorized. There should be disclosure of any treasury or unissued bonds that have been pledged on loans.

Long-term obligations other than long-term debt are generally listed separately or are reported under an Other Liabilities heading after the long-term debt classification. Deferred revenues are normally reported as the last liability classification. Contingent long-term debt, such as accommodation endorsements or guarantees of debt of affiliated companies, should be disclosed by parenthetical remarks in the liability section or by special notes.

Long-term liabilities may be reported on a balance sheet as of December 31, 1964, as follows:

Long-term debt:

| | | |
|---|---:|---:|
| 20-year, 5% first mortgage bonds outstanding, due January 1, 1976.............. | $210,000 | |
| Less unamortized bond discount......... | 4,500 | |
| | $205,500 | |
| (Authorized and unissued 5% first mortgage bonds, $40,000: pledged as security on short-term loans, $25,000; held in treasury, $15,000) | | |
| Serial 5% debentures, due May 1, 1966 to May 1, 1975, inclusive................ | $100,000 | |
| Purchase money obligations payable 1966 to 1970....,...................... | 55,000 | $360,500 |
| Deferred income tax liability............. | | 25,000 |
| Estimated employee retirement benefits and pensions payable...................... | | 120,000 |
| Deferred revenues: | | |
| Leasehold advances................... | | 50,000 |
| Total long-term liabilities............... | | $555,500 |

## QUESTIONS

**1.** What factors should be considered in determining whether cash should be raised by the issue of bonds or by the sale of additional stock?

**2.** Distinguish between:

(a) Secured and unsecured bonds.
(b) Callable and convertible bonds.
(c) Registered and coupon bonds.
(d) Term bonds and serial bonds.

**3.** (a) Distinguish between the straight-line and the scientific methods for premium and discount amortization on bonds payable. (b) Which method would you recommend? Why?

**4.** (a) What arguments can you offer for reporting discount on bonds payable and premium on bonds payable as deferred items? (b) What arguments can you offer for reporting these balances as bond valuation accounts?

**5.** The treasurer for the Gardner Co. proposes that treasury bonds be reported as an asset at the amount paid upon their acquisition What reply would you make to this proposal?

**6.** (a) Describe the bonds-outstanding method for premium or discount amortization. (b) How does this method differ from the compound-interest method of amortization?

**7.** What alternative accounting procedures may be employed in recording the exchange of capital stock for bonds in accordance with bond convertible features? What arguments can be made in support of each of the procedures?

**8.** Describe three methods for disposing of charges related to bonds retired through refunding. Give arguments pro and con for each method. Which method do you feel has the greatest merit?

**9.** What accounting differences would be suggested by informal arrangements involving voluntary retirement payments as compared with formal arrangements involving commitments for the payment of fixed amounts?

**10.** Comment on the following presentations and indicate what corrections you would make:

(a) Equipment, cost $100,000, on which installment notes of $90,000 are unpaid, is reported on the balance sheet at the company's net equity therein, $10,000.
(b) Treasury bonds, face value $50,000, cost $56,000 are reported as an asset at cost on the balance sheet.
(c) Advances from a subsidiary company are reported as a subtraction from the investment in the stock of the company in reporting the net investment in the subsidiary on the balance sheet.

## EXERCISES

**1.** (a) The Taft Corporation issues $100,000 of 4% debenture bonds on a basis to yield 4.8%, receiving $96,480. Interest is payable semiannually and the bonds mature in 5 years. What entries would be made for the first two interest payments, assuming discount amortization on interest dates by (1) the straight-line method and (2) the compound-interest method?

(b) If the sale is made on a 3½% yield, $102,275 being received, what entries would be made for the first two interest payments, assuming premium amortization on interest dates by (1) the straight-line method and (2) the compound-interest method?

**2.** On December 1, 1962, the Miller Company issues 10-year bonds of $100,000 at 102. Interest is payable on December 1 and June 1 at 6%. On April 1, 1964, the Miller Company retires 10 of its own $1,000 bonds at 99 plus accrued interest. The fiscal period for the Miller Co. is the calendar year. What entries are made to record (a) the issuance of the bonds, (b) the interest payments and adjustments relating to the debt in 1963, (c) the retirement of bonds in 1964, and (d) the interest payments and adjustments relating to the debt in 1964?

**3.** Wright, Inc. issues $100,000 of serial bonds on January 1, 1962, bonds of $10,000 being redeemable annually beginning on January 1, 1963. Bonds are sold for $97,250. Interest at 4% is payable semiannually on January 1 and July 1. On May 1, 1964, the bond series due on January 1, 1967, is retired at 99 plus accrued interest. What entry is made to record the bond retirement?

**4.** Alvin Gray is a holder of $10,000 of 10-year convertible bonds of the Clark Corporation that were issued by the company at 101. He has the option of converting each $1,000 bond into 10 shares of common stock, par value $100. The bond rate is 5% payable semiannually. The option is exercised by Gray 2½ years after the issuance of the bonds. (a) What entries are required on Gray's books and on the corporation's books to record the exchange in the absence of a market value for the stock? (b) If the stock had a market value of $120 per share at the time of exchange and this value is to be recognized, what entries would be made on the books of each party?

**5.** The Williams Company calls in a $200,000 6% bond issue that is not due for 4 years and on which there is unamortized bond discount of $3,200. The call price is 102. The company then issues 10-year 4¾% bonds of $250,000, which are sold at 99. List the methods that might be used for the disposition of charges relating to the bonds retired and give the entries for refunding that would be made in each case.

# PROBLEMS

**15-1.** The Cassidy Corporation issued $100,000 5% bonds, interest payable semiannually, bonds maturing 4 years after issue. The bonds were sold at $96,490, a price to yield 6% on the issue.

*Instructions:* (1) Prepare tables to show the periodic adjustments to the discount account and the annual bond interest assuming adjustment by each of the following methods: (a) the straight-line method and (b) the compound-interest method.

(2) Give entries for the interest payment and the discount amortization for the first year of the bond issue assuming use of (a) the straight-line method and (b) the compound-interest method.

**15-2.** Bronson and Cole, Inc. was authorized to issue 10-year, 5½% bonds of $1,000,000. The bonds are dated January 1, 1963, and interest is payable semiannually on January 1 and July 1. Checks for interest are mailed on June 30 and December 31. Bond sales were as follows:

April 1, 1963 　　$600,000 at 98½ plus accrued interest.
July 1, 1964 　　　$200,000 at 102.

On September 1, 1964, remaining unissued bonds were pledged as collateral on the issue of $150,000 of short-term notes.

*Instructions:* (1) Give the journal entries relating to bonds that would appear on the corporation's books in 1963 and 1964. (Straight-line amortization is used; an unissued bonds account is set up.)

(2) Show how information relative to the bond issue will appear on the balance sheet prepared on December 31, 1964. (Give balance sheet section headings and accounts and account balances appearing within such sections.)

**15-3.** The Jonathan Corporation received permission as of January 1, 1964, to issue 6% bonds of $6,000,000 maturing on January 1, 1974. The bonds are dated January 1, 1964, and interest is payable semiannually on January 1 and July 1. The bonds are callable at 102 plus accrued interest at any time after January 1, 1969.

On March 1, 1964, the corporation sold bonds of $3,000,000 at 103 plus accrued interest. Checks for interest were placed in the mail on June 30, 1964. The balance of the authorized issue was sold for cash on October 1, 1964, at 99½ plus accrued interest.

The corporation's fiscal period ends on November 30. Interest on bonds was accrued to this date, and bond amortization entries for the past fiscal year were recorded.

Interest checks were mailed on December 31, 1964.

*Instructions:* (1) Give the journal entries relating to the bonds that appear on the books for the year 1964. (The straight-line method is used for amortization; authorized bonds are not recorded in the accounts.)

(2) Assuming that the bonds are called in on July 1, 1969, give the journal entries to record the payment of interest and the bond retirement on this date.

**15-4.** The Morrison Co. was authorized to issue $5,000,000 of 6% debentures on April 1, 1963. Interest on the bonds is payable semiannually on April 1 and October 1. Bonds mature on April 1, 1973.

The entire issue was sold on April 1, 1963, at 98½ less costs of $25,000 involved on the issue. In 1964 bonds were purchased on the open market and retired as follows:

July 1          $200,000 at 98½ plus accrued interest.
November 1      $300,000 at 97½ plus accrued interest.

*Instructions:* Give the journal entries, including any adjustments relating to the issuance of bonds and interest on the obligation, that are required for 1963 and 1964. (The company's fiscal period is the calendar year.)

**15-5.** The Wilmington Company sold $1,000,000 of 5% debenture bonds on January 1, 1962, to an investment banking firm at 97½. The bonds have serial maturities; bonds of $200,000 are payable at annual intervals beginning on January 1, 1965. Interest is payable annually on January 1. Checks for principal and interest payments are mailed on December 31 of each year. On April 1, 1964, the company reacquired at 99 plus accrued interest bonds of $100,000 due January 1, 1965, and bonds of $100,000 due January 1, 1966. Bonds were formally retired.

*Instructions:* (1) Assuming discount amortization by the bonds-outstanding method and bond retirements as scheduled, prepare a table summarizing interest charges and bond carrying values for the bond life similar to that illustrated on page 399, supported by a schedule showing the calculation of amortization amounts.

(2) Prepare a similar table summarizing interest charges and bond carrying values for the bond life taking into consideration bond redemptions in advance of maturity dates as indicated.

(3) Record in journal form the retirement of bonds on July 1, 1964.

**15-6.** The Scoville Corporation plans to issue 4½%, 10-year bonds that are convertible into common stock within 5 years at the option of the bondholders. Each $1,000 bond may be exchanged for 15 shares of $50 par value stock, plus any accrued interest. Interest on bonds is payable on March 1 and September 1. Accrued interest is to be paid when the bonds are converted. The corporation's fiscal period is the calendar year.

Bonds of $1,500,000 are authorized and printed, and are dated March 1, 1962. Bonds unissued are recorded in the accounts. The issue does not take place until May 1, 1962, when bonds are disposed of at 102 plus accrued interest.

On August 1, 1963, holders of bonds of $400,000 elected to convert their holdings into stock; remaining bonds were converted into stock on

September 1, 1964. Paid-in capital was credited with the book value of bonds exchanged for stock.

*Instructions:* Give the necessary journal entries relating to the bond issue during the period 1962 to 1964, including any adjusting and reversing entries that may be required. Assume straight-line amortization.

**15-7.** The balance sheet for the Butler Corp. on December 31, 1963, the close of the fiscal period, shows the following accounts:

| | |
|---|---|
| Bond discount and issue costs .......................... | $ 14,000 |
| Accrued interest on bonds............................. | 22,500 |
| Bonds payable, due January 1, 1968, interest at 6% payable semiannually on January 1 and July 1................. | 750,000 |

On January 1, 1964, the following took place: cash of $975,000 was made available from the sale of $1,000,000 of 10-year, 4¾% bonds to Ward Underwriters. Cash from the new issue was used for retirement of the 6% bonds at a call price of 102 and for payment of accrued interest on this issue; the balance of cash was added to the general funds of the company. Interest on the new issue is payable January 1 and July 1.

*Instructions:* (1) Give the entries that would appear on the books of the corporation relative to bonds and bond interest for the year 1964, assuming that unamortized discount and call premium on the old issue are not to be identified with future fiscal periods.

(2) Give the entries that would appear on the books of the corporation relative to bonds and bond interest for the year 1964, assuming that unamortized discount and call premium on the old issue are to be amortized over the remaining life of the old issue.

**15-8.** At the beginning of 1964 the Leininger Co. entered into an agreement with employees to provide pensions and certain other benefits. The benefits were to be funded by an insurance company. The company agreed to pay the insurance company ten installments of $7,650 each in January of each year beginning with 1964 to cover present personnel for services performed since the time they joined the company. Such expenditures were viewed by the company as a means of encouraging employees to remain with the company and it was decided that for accounting purposes the installments should be recognized as periodic expenses over the 10-year period. In addition, costs for current services were to be calculated at semiannual intervals and payments were to be made to the insurance company in the month following accrual. Charges and payments relating to current service costs were as follows:

| | Charges | Payments |
|---|---|---|
| January 1 — June 30, 1964........ | $22,755 | |
| July 1 — December 31, 1964...... | 28,010 | $22,755 |

*Instructions:* (1) Give the entries that would be made relative to the pension plan in 1964.

(2) Indicate the account balances and any other data that would be reported relative to the pension plan on a balance sheet prepared on December 31, 1964.

# Chapter 16

# PAID-IN CAPITAL

### Forming the corporation

The corporation is an artificial entity created by law that has an existence separate from its owners and may engage in business within prescribed limits just as a natural person. The modern corporation makes it possible for large amounts of property to be assembled under one management. This property is transferred to the corporation by the individual owners because they believe the corporation will make effective and efficient use of it. In exchange for this property, the corporation issues ownership interests in the form of shares of stock. Managements elected by stockholders supervise the use, operation, and disposition of the property. Unless the life of the corporation is limited by law, it has perpetual existence.

Business corporations may be created under the corporation laws of any one of the fifty states or of the federal government. Since the states do not follow a uniform incorporating act, the conditions under which corporations may be created and under which they may operate are varied.

In most states at least three individuals must join in applying for a corporate charter. Application is made by submitting *articles of incorporation* to the secretary of state or other appropriate official. The articles must set forth the name of the corporation, its purpose and nature, the stock that is to be issued, those persons who are to act as first directors, and other data required by law. If the articles conform to the state's laws governing corporate formation, they are approved and are recognized as the *charter* for the new corporate entity.[1] Subscriptions to capital stock then become effective. A stockholders' meeting is called at which a code of rules or *by-laws* governing meetings, voting procedures, and other internal operations are adopted. A *board of directors* is elected, and the board appoints company administrative officers. Corporate activities may now proceed in conformance with laws of the state of incorporation and charter authorization. A complete record of the proceedings of stockholders' and directors' meetings must be maintained in a *minutes book.*

---

[1]When stock of a corporation is to be distributed outside of the state in which it is incorporated and exceeds a certain minimum dollar amount, it also requires registration with the Securities and Exchange Commission. The objective of such registration is to assure that all of the facts relative to the business and its securities will be adequately and honestly disclosed.

Corporations are classified as *public* when they represent governmental subdivisions or government-owned units and as *private* when they are privately owned. The private group includes *nonstock* companies where operations are of a nonprofit nature and stock is not issued, as in the case of hospitals, charities, and religious organizations, and *stock* companies where operations are for profit and stock is issued as evidence of an ownership interest. Corporations are also classified as *domestic* and *foreign;* a corporation is termed domestic in the state of its incorporation and foreign in all other states. A corporation whose stock is widely held and is available for purchase is known as an *open corporation;* a corporation whose stock is held by relatively few individuals and is not available for purchase is called a *close corporation.*

## Nature of capital stock

An ownership interest in a corporate entity is evidenced by shares of stock in the form of certificates. When a value is assigned to each share and is reported on the stock certificate, the stock is said to have a *par value;* stock without such an assigned value is called *no-par* stock.

Most companies issue a single class of stock. However, in assembling property for a corporation there may be advantages in issuing more than one kind of stock with varying rights and priorities. When a single class of stock is issued, shares are all alike and are known as *common stock.* When more than one class is issued, stock that is given certain preferences over the common issue is called *preferred stock.*

Unless restricted or withheld by terms of the stock contract, certain basic rights are held by each stockholder that are exercised pro rata according to the number of shares he owns. These rights are: (1) to share in distributions of corporate earnings; (2) to vote in the election of directors and in the determination of certain corporate policies; (3) to maintain one's proportional interest in the corporation through purchase of additional capital stock if issued, known as the *pre-emptive* right; and (4) to share in distributions of assets upon corporate liquidation.

If preferred and common stocks are issued, the special features of each class of stock are stated in the articles of incorporation or in the corporation by-laws and become a part of the stock contract between the corporation and its stockholders. One must be familiar with the over-all capital structure to understand fully the nature of the equity that is found in any single class of stock. Frequently the stock certificate describes the rights and restrictions relative to the ownership interest it represents, together with those pertaining to other securities issued. Shares of stock represent personal property and may be freely transferred by their owners.

### Legal or stated value of stock

When stock is issued by a corporation, a portion or all of the capital arising from the issue is designated *legal* or *stated capital*. State incorporation laws provide that dividends cannot reduce corporate capital below legal capital. Modern corporation laws normally go beyond these limitations and add that legal capital cannot be impaired by the reacquisition of capital stock. Creditors of a corporation cannot hold individual stockholders liable for claims against the company. But with a portion of the corporate capital restricted as to distribution, creditors can rely on the absorption by the ownership group of losses equal to the restricted capital before losses are applied to the creditors' equity.

When shares have a par value, the legal or stated capital is normally the aggregate par value of all shares issued and subscribed. When shares are no-par, laws of certain states require that the total consideration received for the shares, even when they are sold at different prices, be recognized as legal capital. Laws of a number of states, however, permit the corporate directors to establish legal capital by assigning an arbitrary value to each share regardless of issue price, although in some instances the value cannot be less than a certain minimum amount. The value that is fixed by the board of directors or the minimum value required by law is known as the share's *stated value*. No-par shares whose full proceeds must be regarded as legal capital are frequently referred to as *true* or *pure no-par stock* to distinguish these from no-par issues with a stated value.

The full amount invested by stockholders is recognized as *paid-in capital* or *invested capital*. The portion of the paid-in capital representing legal or stated capital is reported as *capital stock;* any amount in excess of that portion is reported as *additional paid-in capital* or *paid-in surplus*.

The sale of stock gives rise to corporate legal or stated capital. Legal capital may be increased by a stock dividend or by other appropriate action of the board of directors transferring additional paid-in capital or retained earnings to capital stock. Corporate legal capital is decreased by the formal retirement of capital stock. It may also be decreased by action of the board of directors reducing the par or stated value of shares as permitted by law.

### Par and no-par stock

When a corporation is authorized to issue stock with a par value, the incorporation laws of some states permit such issue only for an amount equal to or in excess of par. Par value may be any amount, for example, $100, $5, or 25 cents. Sale of the stock for an amount in excess of the par gives rise to a premium; the premium is added to capital stock at par in reporting total paid-in capital.

In certain states corporations may be permitted to sell stock at a discount. Capital stock is still reported at par, but the discount is reported as a subtraction item in presenting paid-in capital. Persons subscribing for stock at a discount fulfill their obligation to the corporation upon payment of the agreed price. However, the laws of the state may provide that if the assets of a corporation are insufficient to meet its obligations, creditors may hold stockholders personally liable for deficiencies up to the amounts of the discounts. Creditors are thus protected by the full legal capital as reported in the capital stock account.

Prior to 1912 corporations were permitted to issue only stock with a par value. In 1912, however, New York state changed its corporation laws to permit the issuance of stock without a par value, and since that time all other states have followed with similar statutory provisions. Today many of the common stocks as well as some of the preferred stocks listed on the large securities exchanges are no-par.

### Preferred stock

When a corporation issues both preferred and common stock, the preference attaching to preferred stock normally consists of a prior claim to dividends. A dividend preference does not assure stockholders of dividends on the preferred issue but simply means that dividend requirements must be met on preferred stock before anything may be paid on common stock. Dividends do not legally accrue; a dividend on preferred stock, as on common stock, requires the legal ability on the part of the company to make such a distribution, as well as appropriate action by the board of directors. Although preferred stockholders have a prior claim on dividends, such preference is usually accompanied by limitations on the amount of dividends they may receive.

Preferred stock is ordinarily issued with a par value. When preferred stock has a par value, the dividend preference is stated in terms of a percentage of par value. When preferred stock is no-par, the dividend must be stated in terms of dollars and cents. Thus holders of 5% preferred stock with a $50 par are entitled to an annual dividend of $2.50 per share before any distribution is made to common stockholders; holders of $5 no-par preferred stock are entitled to an annual dividend of $5 per share before dividends are paid to common stockholders.

A corporation may issue more than one class of preferred stock. Sometimes preferred issues are designated first preferred, second preferred, etc., with the first preferred issue having a first claim on earnings, the second preferred having a second claim, and so on. In other instances the claim to earnings on the part of several preferred issues may have equal priority, but dividend rates or other preferences may vary. Holders of the common stock may receive dividends only after the satisfaction of all preferred claims.

Other characteristics and conditions are frequently added to preferred stock in the extension of certain advantages or in the limitation of certain rights. Such factors may be expressed in adjectives modifying preferred stock, as cumulative preferred stock, participating preferred stock, convertible preferred stock, and redeemable preferred stock. More than one of these characteristics may be applicable to a specific issue of preferred stock.

*Cumulative and noncumulative preferred stock.* *Cumulative* preferred stock provides that, whenever the corporation fails to declare (*passes*) dividends on this class, such dividends accumulate and require payment in the future before any dividends may be paid to common stockholders. For example, assume that a corporation has outstanding 100,000 shares of 6% cumulative preferred stock, $10 par. Dividends were last paid through December 31, 1961, and the company wishes to resume payments at the end of 1964. The company will have to declare dividends on preferred for three years, or $180,000, before it may declare any dividends on common stock.

If preferred stock is *noncumulative*, it is not necessary to provide for dividends that were passed. A dividend omission on preferred stock in any one year means that it is irretrievably lost; dividends may be declared on common stock as long as the preferred stock receives the preferred rate for the current period. Preferred stock contracts normally provide for cumulative dividends. Courts have generally held that dividend rights on preferred stock are cumulative in the absence of specific conditions to the contrary.

*Participating and nonparticipating preferred stock.* Participating preferred stock receives the preferred rate and also shares dividends with common stock in accordance with certain participation features. Preferred stock may be *fully participating* and thus entitled to dividends at a rate or an amount per share equal to that paid to common after common is paid the preferred rate or amount, or it may be *participating* but limited to a certain maximum rate or amount. Since it is preferred stock, it still receives its regular dividend before amounts are available for common stock or for distribution on a participating basis. To illustrate, assume that a corporation has outstanding 5% fully participating preferred stock, par $100,000, and common stock, par $200,000. If dividends totaling $36,000 are to be distributed, dividends of 12% will be paid on both preferred stock and common stock. The apportionment is made as follows:

|  | Preferred ($100,000 par) | Common ($200,000 par) |
|---|---|---|
| To preferred, 5%.................. | $ 5,000 | |
| To common, up to preferred rate, 5%. | | $10,000 |
| To all shares ratably, 7% (balance to be paid, $21,000 ÷ par value of all stock outstanding, $300,000)....... | 7,000 | 14,000 |
| | $12,000 | $24,000 |

If the preferred stock was limited in participation to a maximum of 8%, it would receive $8,000, and common stock would receive the balance, or $28,000. When preferred stock is no-par, participation arrangements must be stated in dollar amounts rather than in percentages. A variety of participation arrangements is found on preferred issues.

When preferred stock is *nonparticipating*, dividends on this class are limited to the preferred rate or amount. Common stockholders may be paid any amount after payment of the preferred dividend for the current year. Preferred issues normally do not include participating features. Courts have generally held that preferred stock is nonparticipating when the stock contract does not specifically provide for participation.

*Convertible preferred stock.* Preferred stock is *convertible* when terms of the issue provide that it can be exchanged by its owner for some other security of the issuing corporation. Conversion rights generally provide for the exchange of preferred stock into common stock. Since preferred stock normally has a prior but limited right on earnings, large earnings resulting from successful operations accrue to the common stockholders. The conversion privilege gives the preferred stockholder the opportunity to exchange his holdings for stock in which his rights to earnings are not limited. Preferred stock may also be convertible into bonds. Here the investor has the option of changing his position from stockholder to that of creditor.

*Redeemable preferred stock.* Preferred stock is *redeemable* when the issue can be called in by the corporation at a stipulated price. This price may be set at par or the original issue price of the preferred, or at such amount increased by a redemption premium. Payment of any dividends in arrears as well as accrued dividends to the date of the call is also required.

*Asset and dividend preferences upon corporate liquidation.* Preferred stock is generally preferred as to assets upon corporate liquidation. Such a preference, however, cannot be assumed but must be specifically stated in the preferred stock contract. The asset preference for stock with a par value is an amount equal to par, or par plus a premium; in the absence of a par value it is a stated amount. Terms of the preferred contract may also provide for the full payment of any dividends in arrears upon liquidation, regardless of the retained earnings balance reported by the company. When this is the case and there are insufficient retained earnings or a deficit, such dividend priorities must be met from paid-in capital of the common issue; common stockholders receive whatever assets remain after settlement with the preferred group.

## Common stock

Strictly speaking, there should be but one kind of common stock. Common stock represents the residual ownership equity and carries the greatest risk. In return for the risk that it carries, it ordinarily shares in profits to the greatest extent if the corporation is successful. There is no inherent distinction in voting rights between preferred and common stocks. However, voting rights are frequently given exclusively to common stockholders as long as dividends are paid regularly on preferred stock; upon failure to meet preferred dividend requirements, special voting rights may be granted to preferred stockholders, thus affording this group a more prominent role in the management. In some states voting rights cannot be withheld on any class of stock.

Because of certain legal restrictions on preferred stock, some corporations have issued two types of common stock, known as Class A stock and Class B stock. One of the two types will have special preferences or rights that the other type does not have, such as dividend preferences or voting rights. The distinction between Class A and Class B stock, then, may be similar to that normally found between a company's preferred and common issues. The use of such classified common stocks has been so greatly abused that some stock exchanges have refused to list such issues, and this form of corporate financing has been largely discontinued.

## Recording issuance of capital stock

The capital stock of a corporation may be authorized but unissued; it may be subscribed for and held for issuance pending receipt of cash on stock subscriptions; it may be outstanding in the hands of stockholders; it may be reacquired and held by the corporation for subsequent resale or bonus distribution; it may be canceled by appropriate corporate action. An accurate record of the position of the corporation as a result of the exchanges of property between stockholders and the corporation must be maintained in the accounts. Each class of stock requires separate accounting.

*Recording the stock authorization.* The *authorized capital stock* of a corporation is the maximum number of shares that can be issued under the conditions set by the charter. Application to the state is required in obtaining any change in the original authorization. The amount of stock authorized may be recorded by a memorandum entry and then reported in memorandum form in the capital stock account.

*Recording the stock subscription.* The agreement to purchase stock, known as a *subscription*, states the number of shares subscribed for, the subscription price, terms of payment, and other conditions of the transaction. This is a legally binding contract on the subscriber and the corporation. By express provisions, however, the contract may be binding only if the corporation receives subscriptions for a stated number of shares. A subscription, while giving the corporation a legal claim for the contract price, also gives the subscriber the legal status of a stockholder unless certain rights as a stockholder are specifically withheld by law or by terms of the contract. Ordinarily stock certificates evidencing share ownership are not issued until the full subscription price has been received.

Upon receiving subscriptions, Capital Stock Subscriptions Receivable is debited for the subscription price, Capital Stock Subscribed is credited for the amount that is to be recognized as capital stock when subscriptions have been collected, and an additional paid-in capital account is credited for the amount of the subscription price in excess of par or stated value.[1] Subscriptions for par-value stock and for no-par stock with a stated value are recorded in a similar manner. When no-par stock is without a stated value, Capital Stock Subscribed is credited for the full amount of the subscription. If the laws of the state of incorporation permit stock with a par value to be sold at a discount and subscriptions are received on such a basis, Capital Stock Subscriptions Receivable is debited for the subscription price, Discount on Capital Stock is debited for the discount, and Capital Stock Subscribed is credited for the stock par value. A special *subscribers journal* may be used in recording capital stock subscriptions.

Capital Stock Subscriptions Receivable is a controlling account, individual subscriptions being reported in the subsidiary *subscribers ledger*. Subscriptions Receivable is regarded as a current asset only when the corporation expects to collect the balance currently. This is normally the case. When subscription amounts are due or are called for at different intervals, separate receivable or "call" balances may be established for amounts due on each collection date. Balances currently receivable are recognized as current assets; remaining balances are regarded as non-

---

[1]The term "Capital Stock" is used in account titles in the text when the class of stock is not specifically designated. When preferred and common designations are given, these are used in the account titles.

current. When subscription balances are to be collected only if cash is required and is called for by the company, these balances may be appropriately considered a subtraction item in reporting paid-in capital.

*Recording collection of subscriptions.* Subscriptions may be collected in cash or in other properties accepted by the corporation. When collections are made, the appropriate asset account is debited and the receivable account is credited. Credits are also made to subscribers' accounts in the subsidiary ledger.

*Recording the issue of stock.* The issuance of stock is recorded by a debit to Capital Stock Subscribed and a credit to Capital Stock. A *stockholders ledger* is controlled by the capital stock account; here separate accounts are maintained with each stockholder that report the number of shares issued. The issue of stock by the corporation calls for a credit to a stockholder's account for the shares issued. A transfer of stock ownership is recorded by a charge to the account of the person making the transfer and a credit to the account of the person acquiring the stock; since capital

| Transaction | Assuming stock is $10 par value | | |
|---|---|---|---|
| NOVEMBER 1 Received cash of $10,000 and equipment valued at $20,000 in exchange for 3,000 shares. | Cash.................. Equipment.............. Capital Stock......... | 10,000 20,000 | 30,000 |
| NOVEMBER 1–30 Received subscriptions for 5,000 shares at 12½ with 50% down payment, balance payable in 60 days. | Capital Stock Subscriptions Receivable........ Capital Stock Subscribed Premium on Capital Stock................ | 62,500 | 50,000 12,500 |
| | Cash.................. Capital Stock Subscriptions Receivable....... | 31,250 | 31,250 |
| DECEMBER 1–31 Received balance due on one half of subscriptions and issued stock to the fully paid subscribers, 2,500 shares. | Cash.................. Capital Stock Subscriptions Receivable....... | 15,625 | 15,625 |
| | Capital Stock Subscribed.. Capital Stock......... | 25,000 | 25,000 |
| Stockholders' equity after the above transactions: | Stockholders' Equity Paid-in capital: Capital stock, $10 par; authorized, 10,000 shares; issued and outstanding, 5,500 shares.... Capital stock subscribed, 2,500 shares................. Premium on capital stock...... | | $55,000 25,000 12,500 |
| | Total stockholders' equity...... | | $92,500 |

stock outstanding remains the same after transfer of individual holdings, general ledger accounts are not affected.

A *stock certificate book* also reports shares outstanding. Certificates in the book are usually serially numbered. As certificates are issued, the number of shares issued is reported on the certificate stubs. With ownership transfers, the original certificates submitted by the sellers are canceled and attached to the original stubs and new certificates are issued to the buyers. Frequently a corporation will appoint banks or trust companies to serve as *registrars* and *transfer agents.* These parties are assigned various responsibilities such as transferring stock certificates, maintaining the stockholders ledger, preparing lists of stockholders for meetings, and making dividend distributions.

## Issue of capital stock illustrated

The examples presented at the bottom of page 422 and below illustrate the entries for the sale of stock when: (1) stock has a par value,

| Assuming stock is no-par but has a stated value of $10 | | Assuming stock is no-par and has no stated value | |
|---|---|---|---|
| Cash.................. 10,000 | | Cash.................. 10,000 | |
| Equipment............ 20,000 | | Equipment............ 20,000 | |
| Capital Stock........ | 30,000 | Capital Stock........ | 30,000 |
| Capital Stock Subscriptions Receivable........ 62,500 | | Capital Stock Subscriptions Receivable........ 62,500 | |
| Capital Stock Subscribed.............. | 50,000 | Capital Stock Subscribed.............. | 62,500 |
| Paid-in Capital from Sale of Stock in Excess of Stated Value......... | 12,500 | | |
| Cash.................. 31,250 | | Cash.................. 31,250 | |
| Capital Stock Subscriptions Receivable....... | 31,250 | Capital Stock Subscriptions Receivable....... | 31,250 |
| Cash.................. 15,625 | | Cash.................. 15,625 | |
| Capital Stock Subscriptions Receivable....... | 15,625 | Capital Stock Subscriptions Receivable........ | 15,625 |
| Capital Stock Subscribed.. 25,000 | | Capital Stock Subscribed.. 31,250 | |
| Capital Stock......... | 25,000 | Capital Stock......... | 31,250 |
| Stockholders' Equity | | Stockholders' Equity | |
| Paid-in capital: | | Paid-in capital: | |
| Capital stock, $10 stated value; authorized, 10,000 shares; issued and outstanding, 5,500 shares.................. | $55,000 | Capital stock, no-par; authorized, 10,000 shares; issued and outstanding, 5,500 shares.... | $61,250 |
| Capital stock subscribed, 2,500 shares.................. | 25,000 | Capital stock subscribed, 2,500 shares.................. | 31,250 |
| Paid-in capital from sale of stock in excess of stated value..... | 12,500 | | |
| Total stockholders' equity...... | $92,500 | Total stockholders' equity....... | $92,500 |

(2) stock is no-par but has a stated value, and (3) stock is no-par and without a stated value. It is assumed that the Globe Corporation is granted permission to issue 10,000 shares of capital stock.

### Subscription defaults

If a subscriber defaults on his subscription by failing to make a payment when it is due, the corporation may (1) return to the subscriber the amount paid, (2) return to the subscriber the amount paid less any reduction in price or expense incurred upon the resale of the stock, (3) declare the full amount that the subscriber has paid as forfeited, or (4) issue to the subscriber shares equal to the number paid for in full. The practice that is followed will depend upon the policy adopted by the corporation within the legal limitations set by the state in which it is incorporated. To illustrate the entries under the different circumstances mentioned, assume the subscription of $10 par capital stock at 12½. One subscriber for 100 shares defaults after making a 50% down payment. Defaulted shares are subsequently resold at 11. The entries to record the default by the subscriber and the subsequent resale of the defaulted shares would be made as follows:

(1) *Assuming that the amount paid in is returned:*

| | | |
|---|---|---|
| Capital Stock Subscribed............................. | 1,000 | |
| Premium on Capital Stock............................ | 250 | |
|     Capital Stock Subscriptions Receivable............ | | 625 |
|     Cash......................................... | | 625 |
| Cash.................................................. | 1,100 | |
|     Capital Stock.................................. | | 1,000 |
|     Premium on Capital Stock...................... | | 100 |

(2) *Assuming that the amount paid in less the price reduction on the resale is returned:*

| | | |
|---|---|---|
| Capital Stock Subscribed............................. | 1,000 | |
| Premium on Capital Stock............................ | 250 | |
|     Capital Stock Subscriptions Receivable............ | | 625 |
|     Payable to Defaulting Subscriber (payment withheld pending stock resale)........................... | | 625 |
| Cash.................................................. | 1,100 | |
| Payable to Defaulting Subscriber.................... | 150 | |
|     Capital Stock.................................. | | 1,000 |
|     Premium on Capital Stock...................... | | 250 |
| Payable to Defaulting Subscriber.................... | 475 | |
|     Cash......................................... | | 475 |

(3) *Assuming that the full amount paid in is declared to be forfeited:*

| | | |
|---|---|---|
| Capital Stock Subscribed............................. | 1,000 | |
| Premium on Capital Stock............................ | 250 | |
|     Capital Stock Subscriptions Receivable............ | | 625 |
|     Paid-In Capital from Forfeited Stock Subscriptions.. | | 625 |
| Cash.................................................. | 1,100 | |
|     Capital Stock.................................. | | 1,000 |
|     Premium on Capital Stock...................... | | 100 |

*(4) Assuming that shares equal to the number paid for in full are issued:*

| | | |
|---|---:|---:|
| Capital Stock Subscribed........................ | 1,000 | |
| Premium on Capital Stock....................... | 125 | |
|     Capital Stock................................ | | 500 |
|     Capital Stock Subscriptions Receivable............ | | 625 |
| Cash........................................ | 550 | |
|     Capital Stock................................ | | 500 |
|     Premium on Capital Stock...................... | | 50 |

## Sale of security units for a lump sum

Corporations sometimes sell for a lump-sum price *security units* consisting of two or more classes of securities. In recording sales of this kind, the sales proceeds must be allocated among the different issues. When a sale consists of two different securities and there is a known market value for one, the sales price of the other may be determined by subtracting the known value from the sales price of the unit. To illustrate, assume that 1 share of common stock, par $100, is offered with each $1,000, 6%-bond at $1,050. If the common stock is selling for $80 per share, this value is assigned to common and the sales price applicable to the bonds is calculated as follows:

| | |
|---|---:|
| Unit price of $1,000 bond together with 1 share of common.. | $1,050 |
| Price identified with common share (market price)........... | 80 |
| Price identified with bond............................... | $  970 |

A discount should thus be identified with both the common shares and with the bonds. The entry to record the sale of 100 units would be:

| | | |
|---|---:|---:|
| Cash....................................... | 105,000 | |
| Discount on Common Stock.................... | 2,000 | |
| Discount on Bonds Payable.................... | 3,000 | |
|     Common Stock, $100 par..................... | | 10,000 |
|     Bonds Payable............................. | | 100,000 |

If two kinds of stock are offered as a unit, the procedure is similar. For example, assume that 2 shares of common, par $25, are offered with 5 shares of preferred, par $100, at $550 per unit. If the preferred stock has a market price of $96 per share, the sales price applicable to common stock is calculated as follows:

| | |
|---|---:|
| Unit price of 5 shares of preferred and 2 shares of common.... | $550 |
| Price identified with 5 shares of preferred (market price, $96 x 5). | 480 |
| Price identified with 2 shares of common.................... | $ 70 |

The entry to record the sale of 100 units, consisting of 500 shares of preferred and 200 shares of common, at $550 per unit would be:

| | | |
|---|---:|---:|
| Cash. . . . . . . . . . . . . . . . . . . . . . . . . . . . . . . . . . . . . . . . . | 55,000 | |
| Discount on Preferred Stock. . . . . . . . . . . . . . . . . . . . | 2,000 | |
|    Preferred Stock, $100 par . . . . . . . . . . . . . . . . . . . . . . | | 50,000 |
|    Common Stock, $25 par . . . . . . . . . . . . . . . . . . . . . . . | | 5,000 |
|    Premium on Common Stock . . . . . . . . . . . . . . . . . | | 2,000 |

If in the previous case the price charged for each unit had been $500, the common stock might have been designated a "bonus" and offered as an inducement on the purchase of preferred. The market price of the several issues should still be recognized, if determinable. Here the apportionment of proceeds would be made as follows:

| | |
|---|---:|
| Unit price of 5 shares of preferred and 2 shares of common . . . . | $500 |
| Price identified with 5 shares of preferred (market price, $96 x 5) . | 480 |
| Price identified with 2 shares of common . . . . . . . . . . . . . . . . . . . . | $ 20 |

The entry to record the sale follows:

| | | |
|---|---:|---:|
| Cash. . . . . . . . . . . . . . . . . . . . . . . . . . . . . . . . . . . . . . . . . | 50,000 | |
| Discount on Preferred Stock. . . . . . . . . . . . . . . . . . . . | 2,000 | |
| Discount on Common Stock. . . . . . . . . . . . . . . . . . . . | 3,000 | |
|    Preferred Stock, $100 par . . . . . . . . . . . . . . . . . . . . . . | | 50,000 |
|    Common Stock, $25 par . . . . . . . . . . . . . . . . . . . . . . . | | 5,000 |

If neither preferred nor common stock has a market price that can be applied in allocating the sales price, it may be necessary to charge the difference between the combined par values and the sales price to the account Discount on Preferred and Common Stocks. This balance should be reported as a subtraction item in presenting corporate invested capital, and should be closed when the sales price can be allocated to the individual securities. However, if the unit consists of bonds and stock and neither has a market value, it will be necessary to estimate the amount at which the bonds could be sold, since the sale of bonds at a figure other than face value requires discount or premium amortization in measuring periodic income.

## Stock issued for consideration other than cash

When stock is issued for consideration in the form of property other than cash, or for services, particular care is required in recording the transaction. When, at the time of the exchange, stock is sold by the company for cash or is quoted on the open market at a certain price, such price can be used in recording the consideration received and the capital increase. When means for arriving at the cash value of the securities are not available, it will be necessary to arrive at a value for the consideration that was acquired.

It may be possible to arrive at a satisfactory valuation of the property received in exchange for stock through an appraisal by competent outside authority. But such a solution may not be available in arriving at a valuation for consideration in the form of certain services as, for example, promotional services in organizing the corporation.

Normally the board of directors is given the right by law to establish valuations for consideration other than money that is received for stock. Such values will stand for all legal purposes in the absence of proof that fraud was involved in the action.    The assignment of values by the board of directors should be subject to particularly careful scrutiny. There have been instances where directors have assigned excessive values to the consideration for stock to avoid the recognition of a discount on the issue of stock or to improve the company's reported financial position. When the value of the consideration cannot be clearly established and the directors' valuations are used in reporting assets and invested capital, the source of the valuations should be disclosed on the balance sheet. When there is evidence that improper values have been assigned to the consideration received for stock, such values should be restated.

Stock is said to be *watered* when assets are overstated and capital items are correspondingly overstated.  On the other hand, the balance sheet is said to contain *secret reserves* when there is an understatement of assets or an overstatement of liabilities accompanied by a corresponding understatement of capital.  Such misstatements may be intentional or unintentional.  The accountant cannot condone either overstatement or understatement of net assets and capital.  It should be observed once more that any failures in accounting for assets are not limited to the balance sheet: the overstatement of assets will result in understatements of net income as asset cost is assigned to revenue; the understatement of assets will result in overstatements of net income as asset cost is assigned to revenue.

## Capital stock assessments

Laws of some states provide that a corporation requiring additional capital may levy assessments upon stockholders. Failure of a stockholder to comply with such special levies by the corporation may result in stock forfeiture.  If stock was originally issued at a discount, an additional capital contribution is recognized as a reduction in the discount; if legal capital requirements were fully met by original investments, assessments represent further increases in corporate paid-in capital. A capital stock assessment and its subsequent collection are recorded as follows:

| | | |
|---|---|---|
| Capital Stock Assessments Receivable.............. | 50,000 | |
|     Discount on Capital Stock (or Paid-In Capital from Stock Assessments)............................ | | 50,000 |
| Cash.......................................... | 50,000 | |
|     Capital Stock Assessments Receivable........... | | 50,000 |

Most states require that stock be issued as nonassessable.

### Issuance of stock in exchange for a business

A corporation, upon its formation or at some subsequent date, may take over a going business, issuing stock in exchange for the properties that are acquired. In determining the amount of the stock to be issued for business assets, the fair market value of the stock as well as the values of the properties acquired must be considered. Frequently the value of the stock transferred by the corporation will exceed the value of the tangible assets acquired because of the favorable earnings record of the business acquired. This excess may be considered as the amount paid for goodwill.

When a sole proprietorship or partnership is incorporated to secure the advantages of the corporate form of organization, the books of the old organization may be used after the changes that have taken place as a result of the incorporation are recorded, or a new set of records may be opened.

*If original books are retained.* If the partnership books are retained, entries are first made to indicate the changes in assets, liabilities, and the partners' interests prior to incorporation. A revaluation account may be charged with losses and credited with gains resulting from revaluations, and the balance in this account may subsequently be closed into the capital accounts in the profit and loss ratio. However, with relatively few changes in asset and liability balances, gains and losses may be reported directly in the capital accounts. In recording the issuance of stock in exchange for the partners' equities, the partners' capital accounts are charged and Capital Stock is credited. Subsequent corporate transactions are recorded in the old books that have become the records for the newly-formed corporation.

*If new books are opened for the corporation.* If new books are opened for the corporation, all of the accounts on the partnership books are closed and partnership assets and liabilities are recorded on the new records. In closing the partnership books, entries are made to record the transfer of assets and liabilities to the corporation, the receipt of capital stock, and the distribution of stock and cash in payment of partners' respective interests. If desired, it would be possible to record the revaluation of assets and the recognition of goodwill before recording the transfer of assets and liabilities.

### Stock reacquisition and retirement

A corporation may have the right to call certain classes of stock for redemption and may choose to exercise such right. In other cases, it may purchase stock on the open market and formally retire such shares.

Whether obtained through call or through purchase on the market, retirement of stock at a cost that differs from the original issuance price presents special accounting problems.

It is generally agreed that the reacquisition and retirement of stock cannot be considered to give rise to profit or loss. A company in issuing stock raises capital which it hopes to employ profitably; in reacquiring and retiring shares it reduces the capital that is to be employed in subsequent operations. Profit or loss arises from the utilization of resources that have been placed in the hands of the corporation, not from capital transactions between the company and its stockholders. Notwithstanding agreement on this matter, there are still certain problems that are raised in recording stock retirement. These are illustrated in the examples that follow.

Assume that a company has issued 1,000 shares of preferred stock, par $100, at 105. If the preferred stock is subsequently redeemed at its original issuance price of 105, preferred stock and premium account balances are simply charged for their full amounts and Cash is credited. All reference to the investment by the preferred stockholders is canceled.

Assume, however, that the stock is redeemed at a price of 102. Here, capital of $3,000 originally invested by the preferred stockholders is retained by the company. The redemption of the stock does not affect the nature of the capital remaining with the company; it is still capital that originated from an investment by stockholders. The redemption is recorded as follows:

| | | |
|---|---|---|
| Preferred Stock..................................... | 100,000 | |
| Premium on Preferred Stock..................... | 5,000 | |
| Cash............................................... | | 102,000 |
| Paid-in Capital from Preferred Stock Redemption | | 3,000 |

Assume the redemption of the same stock at a price of 110. Accountants are not in agreement as to the procedure that should be followed under these circumstances. There are some who would recognize the full payment as shrinkage in the corporate paid-in capital: after canceling paid-in capital from the original sale of the shares, the excess would be charged to a separate account recognized as a negative paid-in capital balance. All capital stock transactions, whether related to investment or to retirement, would thus be reflected as paid-in capital. Others would limit charges to paid-in capital to amounts originally credited when the shares were issued, and would charge retained earnings for any payment exceeding the original amount invested. However, the charge to retained earnings would be viewed not as a *loss* but as a *distribution of earnings*. Applying the latter approach in the example, an entry would be made as follows:

| | | |
|---|---:|---:|
| Preferred Stock.................................... | 100,000 | |
| Premium on Preferred Stock.................... | 5,000 | |
| Retained Earnings............................. | 5,000 | |
| Cash........................................ | | 110,000 |

This procedure is widely supported. Its use is assumed in subsequent illustrations in this chapter.

It should be observed that when stock is formally retired, there is a reduction in the corporate legal or stated capital. State laws normally do not bar the reduction of legal or stated capital when stock is issued subject to redemption and redemption is made at the price provided by terms of the stock issue.

### Treasury stock

When a company's own stock, paid for and issued, is reacquired and held in the name of the company, it is known as *treasury stock*. A company may acquire its own stock by purchase, by acceptance in satisfaction of a claim, or by donation from stockholders. Such shares may subsequently be sold or formally retired.

State laws normally provide that the reacquisition of stock must serve some legitimate corporate purpose and must be made without injury or prejudice to the creditors or to the remaining stockholders. In almost every state, it is provided that the legal or stated capital of the corporation may not be reduced by such reacquisition. Accordingly, purchases are limited to a company's retained earnings, or in some instances to the sum of its retained earnings and additional paid-in-capital balances, and reduce the amount that would otherwise be available for distribution as dividends. To illustrate the effects of such legislation, assume that the capital of a corporation is as follows:

| | |
|---|---:|
| Capital stock, $10 par, 100,000 shares outstanding........ | $1,000,000 |
| Retained earnings.................................... | 500,000 |

The company can declare dividends of $500,000 and creditors will continue to be safeguarded by the stockholders' investment of $1,000,000 as reported in the capital stock account. But assume the reacquisition by the company of a part of its outstanding stock for $400,000. If dividends of $500,000 were still permitted and were paid, protection to creditors would shrink to $600,000. With the company's ability to pay dividends reduced to $100,000 upon the purchase of treasury stock for $400,000, the original protection to the creditor group is assured; the sum of payments for treasury stock and dividends will not reduce net assets below the legal capital reported in capital stock, $1,000,000.

Despite the fact that the legal capital remains the same after the reacquisition of a company's stock by purchase, treasury stock cannot be viewed as an asset but must be regarded as a reduction in corporate capital. A company cannot have an ownership interest in itself; treasury stock confers upon the corporation no dividend, voting, or subscription rights. Treasury stock, as a matter of fact, may be regarded in exactly the same manner as unissued stock except for one matter: having already been issued in accordance with legal requirements governing legal or stated capital, its reissue is possible without the conditions that were imposed upon the original issue of stock.

The sale of treasury stock increases the number of shares outstanding. However, the legal capital, remaining unchanged upon its purchase, is not increased through its sale. If treasury stock is to be retired, such retirement is formalized by the preparation of a certificate or notice of reduction that is filed with appropriate state officials. Upon the formal retirement of shares, these revert to the status of unissued shares and there is a reduction in the corporate legal or stated capital. It may be observed that for federal income tax purposes, treasury stock transactions provide no taxable gain or loss; stock reacquisition as well as stock reissue or retirement are regarded as transactions related to a company's invested capital.

### Entries for treasury stock

A number of different methods have been suggested for recording transactions involving treasury stock. These methods are the products of two general approaches to the problem of treasury stock acquisitions:

1. The acquisition of treasury stock may be viewed as the retirement of outstanding stock.
2. The acquisition of treasury stock may be viewed as giving rise to a capital element whose ultimate disposition still remains to be resolved.

The two approaches are described in the following sections. Descriptions are accompanied by examples illustrating the alternate approaches.

*First approach: Treasury stock acquisition viewed as capital retirement.* The acquisition of treasury stock may be regarded as the withdrawal of a group of stockholders calling for the cancellation of capital balances identified with this group. It follows that the sale of treasury stock represents the admission of a new group of stockholders calling for entries to give effect to the investment by this group.

When the reacquisition of stock is viewed as stock retirement, alternative methods may be employed in reporting the reduction in the capital stock balance: (1) the capital stock account may be charged directly; (2) a treasury stock account may be charged and this balance treated as a subtraction item from capital stock. The alternative methods are illustrated on pages 432 and 433. The transactions for each case are described on pages 432 and 433.

| Transaction | First Approach: Treasury Stock Acquisition Viewed as Capital Retirement |
|---|---|
| | Treasury Stock Acquisition Reported as Reduction in Capital Stock |
| **1963**<br>Issue of stock, 10,000 shares, $10 par, at 15. | Cash.................. 150,000<br>   Capital Stock.........          100,000<br>   Premium on Stock...          50,000 |
| Net income for year, $30,000. | Profit and Loss........ 30,000<br>   Retained Earnings...          30,000 |
| **1964**<br>(1) Reacquisition of 1,000 shares at 16. | Capital Stock......... 10,000<br>Premium on Stock.....  5,000<br>Retained Earnings.....  1,000<br>   Cash...............          16,000 |
| (2) Sale of treasury stock at 20. | Cash................. 20,000<br>   Capital Stock........          10,000<br>   Premium on Stock...          10,000 |
| Stockholders' equity section after sale of treasury stock: | Stockholders' Equity<br>Capital stock..........  $100,000<br>Premium on stock......    55,000<br>Retained earnings......    29,000<br>                          $184,000 |

*Treasury Stock Reported as a Reduction in Capital Stock:*

Transaction (1): Treasury stock is acquired at a price that exceeds the original issuing price. Original credits to paid-in capital balances are canceled and Retained Earnings is charged for the excess as in the case of formal stock retirement.

Transaction (2): When the stock is resold at more than par, an entry is made as on an original sale at more than par. If the stock were resold at less than par, a discount balance might be established and recognized as a subtraction item in the presentation of paid-in capital; such discount would not be recoverable as a discount on original issue in view of the fact that the stock had once been issued and fully paid for. Instead of establishing a discount balance, the charge may be made to Retained Earnings. Such procedure would preserve capital at the legal or stated balance as reported by the capital stock account.

*Treasury Stock Account Used to Report Reduction in Capital Stock:*

Transaction (1): A treasury stock account instead of capital stock may be charged for the amount of the reduction in the capital stock. The treasury stock account subtracted from the capital stock account reporting the amount issued then gives the capital stock outstanding. Charges to other paid-in capital and retained earnings balances would be made as described in the preceding section.

Transaction (2): When the treasury stock is sold, the treasury stock account is credited for the amount at which treasury stock is carried, and any difference between the sales price and the carrying amount is treated as described in the preceding section.

| First Approach: Treasury Stock Acquisition Viewed as Capital Retirement | | | Second Approach: Treasury Stock Acquisition Viewed as Giving Rise to Capital Element Awaiting Ultimate Disposition | | |
|---|---|---|---|---|---|
| Treasury Stock Account Used to Report Reduction in Capital Stock | | | | | |
| Cash................ | 150,000 | | Cash................ | 150,000 | |
| Capital Stock....... | | 100,000 | Capital Stock........ | | 100,000 |
| Premium on Stock... | | 50,000 | Premium on Stock.... | | 50,000 |
| Profit and Loss........ | 30,000 | | Profit and Loss........ | 30,000 | |
| Retained Earnings... | | 30,000 | Retained Earnings... | | 30,000 |
| Treasury Stock........ | 10,000 | | Treasury Stock........ | 16,000 | |
| Premium on Stock..... | 5,000 | | Cash.............. | | 16,000 |
| Retained Earnings..... | 1,000 | | | | |
| Cash.............. | | 16,000 | | | |
| Cash................ | 20,000 | | Cash................ | 20,000 | |
| Treasury Stock...... | | 10,000 | Treasury Stock...... | | 16,000 |
| Premium on Stock... | | 10,000 | Paid-In Capital from Sale of Treasury Stock in Excess of Cost..... | | 4,000 |
| Stockholders' Equity | | | Stockholders' Equity | | |
| Capital stock.......... | | $100,000 | Capital stock.......... | | $100,000 |
| Premium on stock...... | | 55,000 | Premium on stock...... | | 50,000 |
| Retained earnings...... | | 29,000 | Paid-in capital from sale of treasury stock in excess of cost........ | | 4,000 |
| | | $184,000 | Retained earnings...... | | 30,000 |
| | | | | | $184,000 |

*Second approach: Treasury stock acquisition viewed as giving rise to capital element awaiting ultimate disposition.* The acquisition of treasury stock may be viewed as an application of cash to a capital purpose that has not been finally defined or consummated. Upon the purchase of treasury stock, a treasury stock account is charged for the cost of the purchase. This balance is recognized as a negative capital element that does not call for specific identification with paid-in capital or retained earnings at this time. If treasury stock is subsequently retired, the debit balance in the treasury stock account can be allocated to the appropriate capital balances as in the first approach. If the treasury stock is sold, the difference between acquisition cost and selling price is reported as an increase or decrease in capital. It is the retirement or the sale of treasury stock that makes possible a determination of the effect of treasury stock transactions upon corporate capital elements.

The application of this approach is illustrated above. The transactions in the example are described below.

Transaction (1): When treasury stock is purchased, it is recorded at its cost regardless of whether this cost is more or less than the original stock issue price. In a presentation of corporate capital at this time, treasury stock, consisting of a cost unallocated as to the different capital elements, would be reported as a subtraction from the sum of paid-in capital and retained earnings.

Transaction (2): When treasury stock is sold at more than its cost, the excess gives rise to paid-in capital arising from treasury stock transactions. If the treasury stock were sold at less than cost, the shrinkage in capital from treasury stock purchase and sale might be summarized in a separate account and the latter recognized as a subtraction item in the presentation of invested capital. Instead of recognizing a shrinkage in paid-in capital for the difference between the purchase and sales price, the charge may be made to Retained Earnings. Such procedure would preserve capital at the legal or stated balance as reported by the capital stock account.

Although there is theoretical support for each of the approaches presented, laws of the states may take different views relative to the effects of treasury stock transactions upon corporate capital. It has already been indicated that the state laws generally provide that legal or stated capital is not reduced by the repurchase by a company of its own shares. This provision is accompanied by restrictions on the availability of retained earnings and perhaps of additional paid-in capital for dividends. Upon the sale or retirement of treasury stock, some states cancel these restrictions, thus reinstating the reductions that were applied to specific capital balances. Other states do not cancel such restrictions but require that if treasury stock is sold, the proceeds from the sale be recognized as an increase in additional paid-in capital, and if treasury stock is retired, a transfer be made from the legal capital to additional paid-in capital.

When the procedures that have been illustrated on pages 432 and 433 conflict with the legal requirements relative to the status of treasury stock and to the effects upon capital balances upon its sale or retirement, they may be modified to meet such requirements. Ordinarily, the acquisition of treasury stock would call for use of the second approach and a charge to treasury stock at cost. On the balance sheet, however, treasury stock would be reported as a subtraction from retained earnings. Such procedure leaves legal capital balances unchanged while reporting the restriction on retained earnings. Alternatively, it would be possible to subtract treasury stock at cost from the sum of the capital balances and show the restriction upon retained earnings by special appropriation or by parenthetical remark.

### Acquisition of no-par treasury stock

Previous illustrations assumed the reacquisition and the resale of stock with a par value. The reacquisition of stock with a stated value provides no new problems; the stated value instead of the par value is used in reducing capital stock or in reporting treasury stock. When there is no stated or par value and the capital stock account has been credited with the proceeds from stock issued at different prices, a special problem arises. Under these circumstances, the capital stock offset is usually considered to be either (1) the original issuing price of the particular lot reacquired, or (2) the average price at which the stock of the company was originally issued.  For example, assume that no-par stock has been issued as follows:

| | |
|---|---:|
| 2,000 shares @ 18.................................... | $36,000 |
| 2,000 shares @ 20.................................... | 40,000 |
| 1,000 shares @ 22.................................... | 22,000 |
| 5,000 shares........................................ | $98,000 |

Assume that 1,000 shares are reacquired at 16½.  The acquisition is identified as the second lot sold, and treasury stock is to be recorded at the original issuing price.  The following entry is made:

| | | |
|---|---:|---:|
| Treasury Stock.............................. | 20,000 | |
| Cash........................................ | | 16,500 |
| Paid-in Capital from Stock Reacquisition........ | | 3,500 |

Assume that treasury stock is to be recorded at the average issuing price.  The average price per share is calculated as follows:

$98,000 (proceeds from sales) ÷ 5,000 (number of shares issued) = $19.60

The entry to record the acquisition would be:

| | | |
|---|---:|---:|
| Treasury Stock.............................. | 19,600 | |
| Cash........................................ | | 16,500 |
| Paid-in Capital from Stock Reacquisition........ | | 3,100 |

## Donated stock

Treasury stock may be acquired by donation from the stockholders. Shares may be donated so that the company may raise working capital through their sale.  In other instances shares may be donated so that the company may eliminate a deficit.  Ordinarily, all of the stockholders participate in the donation, each party donating a certain percentage of his holdings so that relative interests in the corporation remain unchanged.

Donations of stock with a par value are sometimes found where large blocks of stock were originally issued in exchange for properties of uncertain values, for example, mining properties, patents, and leaseholds. Such stock, which is considered fully paid, may be resold at any price without involving the purchaser in a possible liability to creditors for the difference between par and a lower purchase price.  Such a donation may represent a sacrifice on the part of the donors of the stock; frequently, however, it represents no more than return of a stock overissue.  The issuance of an excessive number of shares of stock for properties and the subsequent donation of stock that may be sold without a discount liability has been referred to as the "treasury stock subterfuge."

In the absence of any cost, the acquisition of treasury stock by donation may be reported on the corporation books by a memorandum entry.

Assuming that the assets of the company have been fairly valued, the sale of donated stock is recorded by a debit to cash and a credit to donated capital. If assets of the company have been overvalued, however, it would be improper to recognize an increase in capital arising from the sale of donated shares. Under these circumstances, the sale price for the stock should be employed as a basis for restating the company assets and paid-in capital.

To illustrate the latter instance, assume that the Sunset Mining Co. is formed to take over the mining properties of partners Adams and Burke, and the corporation issues 10,000 shares of no-par stock to the partners in exchange for the properties. A value of $250,000 is assigned to the properties and an entry is made for the acquisition as follows:

| | | |
|---|---|---|
| Mining Properties.............................. | 250,000 | |
|    Capital Stock............................... | | 250,000 |

Shortly after corporate formation, Adams and Burke donate 4,000 shares to the corporation, and the corporation resells these for $15 per share. If $15 can be regarded as a measure of the fair value of the stock exchanged for the properties, properties should be restated at $90,000, or $15 × 6,000, the number of shares actually exchanged for the properties. Upon the sale of the donated shares, then, entries should be made (1) to correct the property account and capital stock for both the stock overissue and the property overvaluation, and (2) to record the sale of the donated shares. These entries are:

| | | |
|---|---|---|
| Capital Stock................................ | 160,000 | |
|    Mining Properties........................... | | 160,000 |
| Cash........................................ | 60,000 | |
|    Capital Stock............................... | | 60,000 |

The balance sheet for the corporation would now show the following balances:

| | | | |
|---|---|---|---|
| Cash .................. | $60,000 | Capital stock, no-par, | |
| Mining properties. ....... | 90,000 | 10,000 shares outstanding................ | $150,000 |

## Stock rights and options

A company may grant rights and options to buy its stock. Such grants generally arise under the following circumstances:

1. A company requiring additional capital may offer stockholders subscription rights to make the purchase of additional shares attractive to them.
2. A company may provide subscription rights with the issue of various classes of securities to promote the sale of the latter.
3. A company may offer promoters, officers, or employees special subscription rights or options as compensation for services or other contributions.

*Rights issued to stockholders as means of increasing invested capital.* When rights are issued to stockholders, only a memorandum entry is made stating the number of shares that may be claimed under outstanding rights. This information is required so that the corporation may retain sufficient unissued or reacquired stock to meet the exercise of the rights. Upon surrender of the rights and payments as specified by the rights, the stock is issued. At this time a memorandum entry is made to record the decrease in the number of rights outstanding. At the same time an entry is made debiting Cash and crediting invested capital accounts for the amounts received under the terms of the offering. Information concerning outstanding rights should be reported on the balance sheet so that the effects of the exercise of future rights may be ascertained.

*Rights issued with various classes of securities to improve their marketability.* When rights are issued with the sale of other securities, recognition of the rights in the entry to record the sale will depend upon whether a value can be related to these rights. When rights have no value on the date of sale, the full sales price is identified with the sale of the other securities. When the rights are exercised, the stock is recorded as described in the previous section; if the rights are not exercised and are allowed to expire, no entry is required since no value was originally assigned to the rights. When rights do have a market value upon issuance, the sales price should be allocated between the rights and the other securities issued. The amount identified with the rights can be recognized by a credit to the account, Capital Stock Rights Outstanding. When the rights are exercised, the issue of stock is recorded at the sum of the value assigned to the rights and the amount of cash received; if the rights are not exercised and expire, the value assigned to the rights should be transferred to a paid-in capital balance.

*Stock options issued as compensation for services.* When stock options to promotors, officers, or other employees represent compensation for services, a charge should be recognized for compensation which is measured by the excess of the fair value of the stock on the date of the grant over the price that must be paid for the stock by the grantee. No charge is recognized when the price to be paid for the stock is equal to or more than the fair market value of the stock on the date of the grant. A charge for compensation would be accompanied by a credit to the account, Credit under Stock Option Plan. When options are exercised, the issue of stock is recorded at the sum of the value assigned to the stock options and the amount of cash received. When option plans are operative, the financial statements should report the number of shares under option, the option prices, the number of shares exercised, and the number of shares still exercisable.

## Stock conversions

Stockholders may be permitted by the terms of their stock agreement or by special action by the corporation to exchange their holdings for stock of other classes. In certain instances, the exchanges may affect only corporate paid-in capital accounts; in other instances, the exchanges may affect both paid-in capital and retained earnings accounts.

To illustrate the different conditions, assume that the capital of the Washington Corporation on December 31, 1964, is as follows:

| | |
|---|---:|
| Preferred stock, $100 par, 10,000 shares................ | $1,000,000 |
| Premium on preferred stock............................ | 100,000 |
| Common stock, $25 stated value, 100,000 shares......... | 2,500,000 |
| Paid-in capital from sale of common stock in excess of stated value....................................... | 500,000 |
| Retained earnings.................................... | 1,000,000 |

Preferred shares are convertible into common shares at any time at the option of the shareholder.

*Case 1:* Assume that conditions of conversion permit the exchange of each share of preferred for 4 shares of common. On December 31, 1964, 1,000 shares of preferred stock are exchanged on the above basis. The amount originally paid for the preferred, $110,000, is now the consideration identified with 4,000 shares of common stock with a total stated value of $100,000. The conversion is recorded as follows:

| | | |
|---|---:|---:|
| Preferred Stock ($100 par, 1,000 shares)......... | 100,000 | |
| Premium on Preferred Stock.................... | 10,000 | |
|    Common Stock ($25 stated value, 4,000 shares). | | 100,000 |
|    Paid-in Capital from Conversion of Preferred Stock into Common Stock................... | | 10,000 |

*Case 2:* Assume that conditions of conversion permit the exchange of each share of preferred for 3 shares of common. The conversion of 1,000 shares of preferred stock for common stock calls for the transfer of the paid-in capital balances related to preferred stock to the common equity; the excess of the book value of preferred holdings over the stated value of the common stock issued in exchange is recognized as paid-in capital relating to the latter issue. The conversion is recorded by the following entry:

| | | |
|---|---:|---:|
| Preferred Stock ($100 par, 1,000 shares).......... | 100,000 | |
| Premium on Preferred Stock.................... | 10,000 | |
|    Common Stock ($25 stated value, 3,000 shares)... | | 75,000 |
|    Paid-in Capital from Conversion of Preferred Stock into Common Stock....................... | | 35,000 |

*Case 3:* Assume that conditions of conversion permit the exchange of each share of preferred for 5 shares of common. In converting 1,000 shares of preferred for common, an increase in common stock of $125,000 must be recognized although it is accompanied by a decrease in the preferred equity of only $110,000; the increase in the legal capital related to the new issue can be accomplished only by a charge to retained earnings. The conversion, then, is recorded as follows:

| | | |
|---|---:|---:|
| Preferred Stock ($100 par, 1,000 shares).......... | 100,000 | |
| Premium on Preferred Stock.................... | 10,000 | |
| Retained Earnings............................ | 15,000 | |
|    Common Stock ($25 stated value, 5,000 shares).. | | 125,000 |

The problems relating to the conversion of bonds for capital stock were described in Chapter 15. When either stocks or bonds have conversion rights, the company must be in a position to issue securities of the required class. Unissued or reacquired securities may be maintained by the company for this purpose. Detailed information should be given on the balance sheet relative to security conversion features as well as the means for meeting conversion requirements.

### Recapitalizations

Corporate recapitalization occurs when an entire issue of stock is changed by appropriate action of the corporation. In some states recapitalizations including changes in the legal capital are possible by action of the board of directors and stockholders; in other states recapitalizations also require the approval of state authorities.

A common type of recapitalization is a change from par to no-par stock. If the capital stock balance is to remain the same after the change, the original capital stock account is closed and an account for the new issue is opened. Any premium relating to the original stock issue should be transferred to some other paid-in capital account appropriately labeled. If the capital stock balance is to exceed the consideration received on the original sale of the stock, a new capital stock account is credited for the value assigned to the new issue, original paid-in capital balances are closed, and the retained earnings account is charged for the difference. If the capital stock balance is to be reduced, the original account, as well as any premium account, is closed, a new capital stock account is credited for the value assigned to the new stock, and an appropriately titled additional paid-in capital account is credited for the difference.

To illustrate the foregoing, assume a capital for the Signal Corporation as follows:

| | |
|---|---:|
| Capital stock, $10 par, 100,000 shares | $1,000,000 |
| Premium on stock | 100,000 |
| Retained earnings | 250,000 |

Entries for each of the three possibilities are given below:

*Case 1:* Assume that the original stock is exchanged for no-par stock with a stated value of $10:

| | | |
|---|---:|---:|
| Capital Stock ($10 par, 100,000 shares) | 1,000,000 | |
| Premium on Stock | 100,000 | |
|    Capital Stock ($10 stated value, 100,000 shares) | | 1,000,000 |
|    Paid-in Capital from Exchange of Par for No-par Stock | | 100,000 |

*Case 2:* Assume that the original stock is exchanged for no-par stock with a stated value of $12.50:

| | | |
|---|--:|--:|
| Capital Stock ($10 par, 100,000 shares)........ | 1,000,000 | |
| Premium on Stock......................... | 100,000 | |
| Retained Earnings........................ | 150,000 | |
| Capital Stock ($12.50 stated value, 100,000 shares)............................. | | 1,250,000 |

*Case 3:* Assume that the original stock is exchanged for no-par stock with a stated value of $5:

| | | |
|---|--:|--:|
| Capital Stock ($10 par, 100,000 shares)......... | 1,000,000 | |
| Premium on Stock......................... | 100,000 | |
| Capital Stock ($5 stated value, 100,000 shares) | | 500,000 |
| Paid-in Capital from Reduction in Value Assigned to Stock......................... | | 600,000 |

Recapitalizations that involve revisions in the stated values of no-par shares or changes from no-par to a par value call for similar procedures.

Corporate recapitalization that is part of a plan for the elimination of a deficit is referred to as a *quasi-reorganization* and was described in Chapter 13.

## Stock splits and reverse stock splits

When the market price of shares is high and it is felt that a lower price will result in a better market and a wider distribution of ownership, a corporation may authorize that the shares outstanding be replaced by a larger number of shares. For example, 100,000 shares of stock, par value per share $100, are called in and exchanged for 500,000 shares of stock, par value $20. Each shareholder receives 5 new shares for each share owned. The increase in shares outstanding in this manner is known as a *stock split* or *stock split-up*. The reverse procedure, replacement of shares outstanding by a smaller number of shares, may be desirable when the price of shares is low and it is felt that there may be certain advantages in having a higher price for shares. The reduction of shares outstanding by combining shares is referred to as a *reverse stock split* or a *stock split-down*.

After a stock split or reverse stock split, the capital stock balance remains the same; however, the change in the number of shares of stock outstanding is accompanied by a change in the par or stated value of the stock. The change in the number of shares outstanding, as well as the change in the par or stated value, may be recorded by means of a memorandum entry. However, it would normally be desirable to establish a new account reporting the nature and the amount of the new issue. In any event, notations will be required in the subsidiary stockholders ledger to report the exchange of stock and the change in the number of shares held by each stockholder.

## Paid-in capital not designated as legal capital

Although it is common practice to report on the balance sheet a single value for additional paid-in capital, separate accounts should be provided in the ledger to identify the individual sources of such capital. Sources of additional paid-in capital and the accounts summarizing these are listed below.

| Source | Additional Paid-in Capital Account |
| --- | --- |
| Sale of stock in excess of par value | Premium on Stock (or Paid-in Capital from Sale of Stock in Excess of Par Value) |
| Sale of stock in excess of stated value | Paid-in Capital from Sale of Stock in Excess of Stated Value |
| Stock subscription defaults resulting in forfeiture of amounts paid in | Paid-in Capital from Forfeited Subscriptions |
| Assessments levied on stockholders | Paid-in Capital from Stock Assessments (except where stock was originally sold at a discount and stock assessments are considered to be proper credits to such discount) |
| Retirement of stock at less than original sales price | Paid-in Capital from Stock Redemption |
| Expiration of stock warrants or stock options | Paid-in Capital from Unexercised Warrants (or Stock Options) |
| Conversion of outstanding stock into a new issue with a smaller total par or stated value | Paid-in Capital from Stock Conversion |
| Reduction in corporate stated capital as a result of recapitalization | Paid-in Capital from Reduction in Value Assigned to Stock |
| Sale of treasury stock at more than cost | Paid-in Capital from Sale of Treasury Stock in Excess of Cost |
| Donation of stock or properties or forgiveness of corporate indebtedness by stockholders | Donated (or Paid-in) Capital from Contributions by Stockholders |
| Donation of properties or forgiveness of corporate indebtedness by governmental authorities or other outsiders | Donated (or Paid-in) Capital from Contributions by Governmental Authority (or others) |

Charges should be made to additional paid-in capital balances only when (1) transactions may be regarded as directly reducing such balances, or (2) there is an express authorization by the board of directors for such reduction. To illustrate (1) above, the redemption of a preferred stock issue calls for the cancellation of the capital stock balance and also any premium or other paid-in capital balance relating to the original issue; all reference to paid-in capital relating to the preferred stock should be canceled with the redemption of this class of stock. However, it would not be appropriate to charge some other paid-in capital balance with any part of the amount paid on the retirement of a preferred issue; to do so would be to obscure the data with respect to capital arising from other sources. To illustrate (2) above, authorization by the board of directors of the capitalization of a portion of a particular paid-in capital balance would call for a reduction in the additional paid-in capital account and an increase in the capital stock account.

Additional paid-in capital balances should not be charged with losses whether from normal operations or from extraordinary sources, nor should such paid-in capital be used for the cancellation of a deficit in the absence of formal steps taken to effect a quasi-reorganization.

The availability as a basis for dividends of paid-in capital that is not designated as legal capital depends upon the laws of the state of incorporation. In the absence of legal restrictions, such capital can be used as a basis for dividends. Laws may provide restrictions upon the use of all of the paid-in capital or upon the use of only certain kinds of paid-in capital. Separate accounts in the ledger summarizing paid-in capital by source make possible the ready determination of distributable capital. When capital other than retained earnings is used as a basis for dividends, stockholders should be informed by the corporation concerning the source of such distribution, since stockholders have the right to assume that dividends represent distributions of earnings unless they are notified to the contrary.

## QUESTIONS

**1.** Describe the essential nature of the corporation.

**2.** What are the four basic rights of stockholders?

**3.** Distinguish between: (a) a domestic corporation and a foreign corporation, (b) a stock corporation and a nonstock corporation, (c) an open corporation and a close corporation.

**4.** (a) Define legal or stated capital. (b) What limitations are placed upon the corporation by law to safeguard legal capital?

**5.** (a) What preferences are usually granted preferred stockholders? (b) What is redeemable preferred stock? (c) What is convertible preferred stock? (d) Distinguish between (1) cumulative and noncumulative preferred stock and (2) participating and nonparticipating preferred stock. (e) What limitations on stockholders' rights are generally found in preferred stock?

**6.** Describe each of the following records: (a) minutes book, (b) subscribers ledger, (c) stockholders ledger, (d) stock certificate book.

**7.** (a) How should cash proceeds be assigned to individual securities when two different securities are sold for a lump sum? (b) Would your answer differ if one of the securities is designated a bonus? Give reasons for your answer.

**8.** (a) What is meant by *watered stock?* (b) What are *secret reserves?* (c) The treasurer of one of your clients is in favor of secret reserves as a means of achieving "balance sheet conservatism." What is your comment?

**9.** What is the purpose of legislation limiting the reacquisition of a company's own stock to its retained earnings balance?

**10.** Distinguish between treasury stock and unissued stock.

**11.** The Waters Co. reports treasury stock as a current asset, explaining that it intends to sell the stock soon to acquire working capital. Do you approve of this reporting?

**12.** (a) Describe two approaches that may be taken in recording the reacquisition of treasury stock. (b) What are the entries in each case assuming that (1) stock is reacquired at more than the original issuing price? (2) stock is reacquired at less than the issuing price?

**13.** The Walsh Co. issues 10,000,000 shares of no-par common stock in exchange for certain mineral lands. Property is established on the books at $5,000,000. Shortly thereafter, stockholders donate to the corporation 20% of their shares. The stock is resold by the company at ten cents per share. What accounting problems do you see as a result of the stock donation and resale?

**14.** (a) What entries should be made on the books when stock rights are issued to stockholders? (b) What entries should be made when stock is issued on rights? (c) What information, if any, should appear on the balance sheet relative to outstanding rights?

**15.** (a) What is a stock split? (b) What are the reasons for a stock split?

**16.** List the different sources of "additional paid-in capital" and the accounts summarizing such items, and indicate for each account the circumstances that would call for a reduction in its balance.

**17.** The accountant for the Walter Corporation closes stock discount and deficit balances into paid-in capital from the sale of stock in excess of par and reports only the balance of the latter account on the balance sheet. Do you approve?

## EXERCISES

**1.** The Dayton Co. pays out dividends at the end of each year as follows: 1962, $50,000; 1963, $150,000; 1964, $240,000. Give the amount that will be paid per share on common and preferred stock for each year, assuming capital structures as follows:

(a) 200,000 shares of no-par common; 10,000 shares of $100, 6%, noncumulative, nonparticipating preferred.

(b) 200,000 shares of $10 common; 10,000 shares of $100, 6%, cumulative, fully participating preferred, dividends two years in arrears at the beginning of 1962.

(c) 200,000 shares of $10 common; 10,000 shares of $100, 6%, cumulative nonparticipating preferred.

(d) 200,000 shares of $10 common; 10,000 shares of $100, 6%, noncumulative preferred participating up to 7½%.

**2.** The Bushnell Corporation was organized and immediately sold its authorized stock of 100,000 shares at 12. Give the entries that are required for the issue of stock under each of the following assumptions:

(a) Shares have a $10 par value.

(b) Shares are no-par without a stated value.

(c) Shares are no-par with a stated value of $5 as assigned by the board of directors.

**3.** Ten shares of Beck, Ltd., with a par value of $100, are subscribed for at par. The subscriber defaults after he has paid $450. This stock is later sold for $950 cash. What entries are required if (a) no refund is made to the defaulting subscriber, (b) a refund is made of the cash paid less the discount allowed when the stock is resold?

**4.** Wells, Inc. sells 1,000 shares of its 5% cumulative preferred stock, par $100, to an investment group for $120,000, giving 1 share of common stock, par $50, as a bonus with each 2 shares of preferred. The market value of the preferred stock immediately following the sale is $105 per share. What is the entry for the sale?

**5.** Bonds of $1,000,000 are sold at face value, 5 shares of common stock, par $10, being offered as a bonus with each $1,000 bond. At the time the bonds are sold on this basis, stock is selling on the market at $12 per share. What entry would be made to record the sale of the bonds?

**6.** The ledger of Farris and Simpson shows the following data on December 31: Assets, $53,000; Liabilities, $23,000; Farris, Capital, $12,000; Simpson, Capital, $18,000. The partners decide to sell the business to Distributors, Inc. in exchange for 4,000 shares of that corporation's $10 par common stock. The market value of the stock at this time is $12. What entries are required (a) to record the purchase in the corporation accounts and (b) to close the books of the partnership? (c) How many shares in the new corporation will be distributed to each partner?

**7.** The Westmore Co. has 10,000 shares of preferred stock outstanding; stock had been issued at par, $100. On June 1, 1964, the company re-deemed 1,500 shares of preferred stock at 101½; on September 15, 1964, the company reacquired and retired 1,000 shares at 97. Give the entries to record the acquisition and the retirement of the preferred shares.

**8.** The capital accounts for the Bergstrom Co. were as follows on June 1, 1964:

| | |
|---|---:|
| Common stock, 100,000 shares, $10 par............... | $1,000,000 |
| Paid-in capital from sale of common at 12............. | 200,000 |
| Retained earnings....................................... | 500,000 |

On this date the company reacquired 5,000 shares of stock at 11; and in December of the same year it resold this stock at 14½. (a) What entries should be made for the stock acquisition and the resale if the purchase is viewed as a capital retirement with treasury stock being reported at par? (b) What entries should be made for the stock acquisition and the resale if the purchase is viewed as giving rise to a capital element awaiting ultimate disposition and treasury stock is reported at cost?

**9.** The Brock Exploration Co. issued 100,000 shares of no-par common stock to three partners in exchange for certain undeveloped mining properties. The properties were recorded at $1,000,000. Immediately thereafter, the partners donated to the corporation 25% of the shares to enable the company to raise working capital through the sale of these shares. The stock was resold at $7. What entries would be made on the corporation's books to record the stock donation and its resale? Assume that when the donated stock is resold, the properties are restated in accordance with the evidence available concerning share value.

**10.** Capital accounts for the Baxter Co. on December 31 are as follows:

| | |
|---|---:|
| Preferred stock, $50 par, 10,000 shares issued and outstand-ing..................................................... | $ 500,000 |
| Premium on preferred stock............................ | 50,000 |
| Common stock, $10 par, 100,000 shares issued and out-standing................................................. | 1,000,000 |
| Premium on common stock............................. | 126,000 |
| Retained earnings...................................... | 1,600,000 |

Preferred stock is convertible into common stock. Give the entry that is made on the corporation books assuming that 1,000 shares of preferred are converted under each assumption listed:

(a) Preferred shares are convertible into common on a share-for-share basis.
(b) Each preferred share is convertible into 7½ shares of common.
(c) Each preferred share is convertible into 4 shares of common.

**11.** The Matson Co. has 10,000 shares of common stock, par $10, out-standing. Proceeds from the sale of the stock were $120,000 and this is reflected in the paid-in capital balances. Give the entry that would be made on the company books for each assumption listed as follows:

(a) A stock split is effected, each shareholder receiving 4 shares of new stock, par value $2.50, for each share owned.
(b) A recapitalization is effected, each stockholder receiving 2 shares of new no-par stock with a stated value of $5 for each share owned.
(c) A recapitalization is effected, each shareholder receiving 1 share of new $5 par value stock for each share owned.
(d) A recapitalization is effected, each shareholder receiving 3 shares of new $5 par value stock for each share owned.

## PROBLEMS

**16-1.** The Hollingsworth Co. was organized on April 10, 1964, and was authorized to issue stock as follows:

200,000 shares of no-par common stock with a stated value of $10
5,000 shares of 5½% preferred stock with a par value of $100

Capital stock transactions through September 1, 1964, were as follows:

May 15 Subscriptions were received for 100,000 shares of common stock at 15 on the following terms: 10% was paid in cash at the time of subscription, the balance being payable in three equal installments due on the fifteenth day of each succeeding month.
June 1 All of the preferred stock was sold to an investment company for cash at 95 and stock was issued.
June 15 The first installment on subscriptions to 97,600 shares was collected. Terms of the subscription contract provided that defaulting subscribers have 30 days in which to make payment and obtain reinstatement; failure to make payment within the specified period will result in the forfeiture of amounts already paid in.
July 15 The second installment on common subscriptions was collected. Collections included receipt of the first and second installment on 400 shares from subscribers who defaulted on their first installment; however, subscribers to 500 shares defaulted in addition to subscribers already in default.
Aug. 15 The third installment on common subscriptions was collected. Collections included receipt of the second and third installment from subscribers to 400 shares who defaulted on their second installment. Stock certificates were issued to fully paid subscribers.
Sept. 1 Stock in default was sold to an investment company at 13.

*Instructions:* (1) Give the journal entries to record the transactions listed above.
(2) Prepare a balance sheet summarizing the transactions above.

**16-2.** The Olson Products Co. was incorporated on January 20, 1964, with authorized common stock of $1,000,000 and 6% cumulative preferred stock of $250,000, each class with a par value of $50.

Subscriptions were received for 6,000 shares of common stock at $60 a share, to be paid in four equal installments on March 1, April 1, May 1, and June 1. The first installment was paid in full. Subscribers for 200 shares defaulted on the second installment, and the amounts already received from these subscribers were returned. The second, third, and fourth installments were paid in full on their due dates by the remaining subscribers, and the stock was issued.

During March, preferred stock was offered for sale at $60, 1 share of common stock being offered with each subscription for 10 shares of preferred. On this basis subscriptions were received for all of the preferred stock. Subscriptions were payable in two equal installments: the first was payable by the end of March and the second was payable at any time prior to June 15. The first installment was paid in full. By June 1, $120,000 had been received on the second installment, and stock was issued to the fully paid subscribers.

*Instructions:* (1) Journalize the above transactions.
(2) Prepare a balance sheet as of June 1 reflecting the foregoing.

**16-3.** The Hawkes Corporation was organized on September 1, 1964, with an authorized capital stock of 100,000 shares of 5% cumulative preferred with a $25 par value and 500,000 shares of no-par common with a $20 stated value. During the balance of the year the following transactions relating to capital stock were completed:

Oct.  1  Subscriptions were received for 200,000 shares of common stock at 30, payable $10 down and the balance in two equal installments due November 1 and December 1. On the same date 10,000 shares of common stock were issued to George Hawkes in exchange for his business. Assets transferred to the corporation were valued as follows: land, $100,000; buildings, $115,000, equipment, $40,000; merchandise, $86,500. Liabilities of the business assumed by the corporation were: mortgage payable, $32,500; accounts payable, $12,500; accrued interest on mortgage, $375. No goodwill is recognized in recording the issuance of the stock for net assets.

Oct.  3  Subscriptions were received for 80,000 shares of preferred stock at 26, payable $10 down and the balance in two equal installments due on November 1 and December 1.

Nov.  1  Amounts due on this date were collected from all common and preferred stock subscribers.

Nov. 12  Subscriptions were received for 100,000 shares of common stock at 28, payable $10 down and the balance in two equal installments due December 1 and January 1.

Dec.  1  Amounts due on this date were collected from all common stock subscribers and stock fully paid for was issued. The final installment on preferred stock subscriptions was received from all subscribers except one whose installment due on this date was $8,000. State corporation laws provide that the company is liable for the return to the subscriber of the amount received less the loss on the subsequent resale of the stock. Preferred stock fully paid for was issued.

Dec.  6  Preferred stock defaulted on December 1 was sold for cash at 25¼. Stock was issued, and settlement was made with the defaulting subscriber.

*Instructions:* (1) Prepare journal entries to record the foregoing transactions.
(2) Prepare the capital section of the balance sheet for the corporation as of December 31.

**16-4.** Aiken, Barr, and Crane, partners sharing profits 2:2:1 respectively, draw up the following partnership balance sheet on November 1, 1964:

| Assets | | | Liabilities and Capital | | |
|---|---:|---:|---|---:|---:|
| | | | Liabilities | | |
| Cash ....................... | | $ 23,650 | | | |
| Accounts receivable .......... | | 40,000 | Notes payable................. | | $ 10,000 |
| Merchandise inventory ........ | | 44,000 | Accounts payable............. | | 17,600 |
| Furniture and fixtures.. | $16,500 | | | | |
| Less allowance for de- | | | Total liabilities............... | | $ 27,600 |
| preciation......... | 4,950 | 11,550 | Capital | | |
| | | | Aiken, capital........ | $36,600 | |
| | | | Barr, capital......... | 30,000 | |
| | | | Crane, capital........ | 25,000 | |
| | | | Total capital.................. | | 91,600 |
| Total assets.......... | | $119,200 | Total liabilities and capital...... | | $119,200 |

The partners incorporate on this date as ABC, Inc., with an authorized capital stock as follows:

Preferred stock, 10,000 shares, par $10
Common stock, 10,000 shares, par $10

The partners agree to the following:

(a) Adjustments are to be made in asset values as follows:
  (1) An allowance for doubtful accounts is to be established at 5% of accounts receivable.
  (2) Furniture and fixtures are to be raised to present replacement cost of $19,500 less a depreciation allowance of 30% on replacement cost.
  (3) Expenses of $650 have been prepaid and are to be recognized as an asset.
(b) Each partner is to be paid for his partnership equity as follows, it being assumed that stock has a value equal to its par:
  (1) 1,500 shares of preferred are to be allowed to each partner.
  (2) Remaining capital interests are to be paid for with common stock, in even multiples of 100 shares, each partner to be paid cash for his capital balance in excess of the highest 100-share multiple that can be issued.

The above adjustments and transactions are completed and shares not required for the settlement of the partners' interests are immediately sold at par.

*Instructions:* (1) Give journal entries to record the incorporation, assuming that it is to be reflected on the partnership books, no new books being opened by the corporation.
(2) Prepare a balance sheet for the corporation. (Assume that transactions are completed on November 1.)

**16-5.** The accounts of the Kelton Sales Co. at the beginning of 1964 showed the following issues of capital stock:

| | |
|---|---:|
| 20,000 shares at $12.00..................................... | $240,000 |
| 6,000 shares at $13.00..................................... | 78,000 |
| 4,000 shares at $13.50..................................... | 54,000 |

During 1964 the company reacquired 2,000 shares at $11, and these were resold at the beginning of 1965 at $14 per share.

*Instructions:* (1) Give the entries to record the acquisition and the resale of treasury stock for each assumption listed below if the treasury stock purchase is viewed as capital retirement and the treasury stock account is charged at par, stated value, or average, whichever is appropriate.

(a) Assume that the stock has a $10 par value.

(b) Assume that the stock is no-par with a stated value of $12.

(c) Assume that the stock is no-par and without a stated value.

(2) Give the entries to record the acquisition and the resale of treasury stock for each assumption listed in (1) above if the treasury stock purchase is viewed as a capital element awaiting ultimate disposition and the treasury stock account is charged for the amount paid.

**16-6.** The balance sheet for the Beverly Corporation on December 31, 1963, is as follows:

| | | |
|---|---:|---:|
| Assets............................................ | | $500,000 |
| Liabilities....................................... | | $239,500 |
| Stockholders' equity: | | |
| $1.50 Convertible preferred stock, $25 par.... | $ 60,000 | |
| Common stock, $10 par................... | 100,000 | |
| Premium on original sale of common at 12½. | 25,000 | |
| Retained earnings....................... | 80,000 | |
| | $265,000 | |
| Less treasury stock, common, 500 shares at cost | 4,500 | 260,500 |
| Total liabilities and stockholders' equity............... | | $500,000 |

During 1964 the following transactions were completed in the order given:

(a) 1,000 shares of common stock were reacquired by purchase at 8. (Treasury stock is recorded at cost.)

(b) 200 shares of common stock were reacquired in settlement of an account receivable of $2,000.

(c) Semiannual cash dividends of 50 cents on common stock and 75 cents on preferred stock were declared and paid.

(d) Each share of preferred stock is convertible into 3 shares of common stock; 400 shares of preferred stock were turned in for common stock; accrued dividends totaling $120 were paid to preferred stockholders exchanging their holdings.

(e) The 1,200 shares of the common treasury stock acquired during 1964 were sold at 12. The remaining treasury shares were exchanged for machinery with a fair market value of $5,900.

(f) 2,500 shares of common stock were issued in exchange for land appraised at $30,000.

(g) Semiannual cash dividends of 50 cents on common stock and 75 cents on preferred stock were declared and paid.

(h) Net income after income taxes was $25,000.

*Instructions:* (1) Give journal entries to record the transactions listed above. (For net income, simply give the entry to close the profit and loss account to Retained Earnings.)

(2) Prepare the stockholders' equity section of the balance sheet as of December 31, 1964.

**16-7.** Robert Safford, Inc. was organized on January 2, 1962, and was authorized to issue 100,000 shares of no-par stock. A stated value of $10 was assigned by the board of directors to each share, and shares were sold during 1962 as follows:

| | |
|---|---|
| January 14.................................. | 25,000 shares at 30 |
| February 19................................. | 20,000 shares at 35 |
| April 14.................................... | 5,000 shares at 40 |

The corporation paid regular quarterly dividends of 50 cents a share, the first quarterly dividend payable to stockholders of record March 15 and the remaining dividends at 3-month intervals thereafter during 1962. Dividends are paid on record date. Net income for the year was $375,000.

In 1963 the market price of its stock declined and the company reacquired its own stock as follows (treasury stock is recorded at cost):

| | |
|---|---|
| April 12.................................... | 2,000 shares at $32\frac{1}{2}$ |
| May 10..................................... | 1,000 shares at 28 |
| June 20.................................... | 4,000 shares at 24 |

The laws of the state provide that retained earnings must be reduced by an amount equal to the purchase price of treasury stock. The appropriation of retained earnings is canceled when treasury stock is sold and original invested capital restored.

In 1963 the company paid the first and second quarterly dividends of 50 cents to stockholders of record March 15 and June 15. For the year the company incurred an operating loss of $25,000.

In 1964 business conditions improved and the company, in order to obtain funds for expansion purposes, resold the 4,000 shares of treasury stock acquired June 20, 1963, as follows:

| | |
|---|---|
| February 5................................. | 3,000 shares at 32 |
| June 1..................................... | 1,000 shares at 36 |

The 1,000 shares of treasury stock acquired on May 10, 1963, were transferred to a creditor in settlement of a past-due account amounting to $35,500 on June 1, 1964. On this date stock had a market value of $36,000.

During 1964 the corporation paid regular dividends of 40 cents a share to stockholders of record March 15 and at quarterly intervals thereafter. A 50-cent extra dividend was paid on December 15. The net income for the year was $200,000.

*Instructions:* (1) Prepare journal entries to record the above transactions. (For annual profit or loss figures, simply give the entry to close the profit and loss account to Retained Earnings.)

(2) Construct the stockholders' equity section of the balance sheet as of December 31, 1962, December 31, 1963, and December 31, 1964.

# Chapter 17

# RETAINED EARNINGS

### Nature of retained earnings

The difference between assets and liabilities is proprietorship or capital, the owners' equity in assets. In a sole proprietorship, the owner's entire equity in assets resulting from investments, withdrawals, and profit and loss activities is reported in a single capital account. In a partnership, capital balances for the individual partners normally report partners' full equities resulting from investments, withdrawals, and profits and losses. It has already been indicated that, because of the nature of the corporate form, it is necessary to distinguish between the capital originating from the stockholders investment, designated as *paid-in* or *invested capital*, and the capital originating from earnings, designated as *retained earnings* or *earned surplus*.

Retained earnings is essentially the meeting place of the balance sheet accounts and the income statement accounts. In successive periods retained earnings are increased by earnings and decreased by dividends. As a result, the retained earnings balance represents the net accumulated earnings of the corporation. If the retained earnings account were affected only by earnings and dividends, there would be little confusion in its interpretation. But a number of factors tend to complicate the nature of retained earnings. Among these factors are: transactions between the corporation and its stockholders that affect retained earnings; stock dividends that result in transfers from retained earnings to paid-in capital; recapitalizations that result in transfers between retained earnings and capital stock; quasi-reorganizations and "fresh-start" retained earnings; legal restrictions upon retained earnings in protecting the stockholder and creditor groups; and contractual limitations upon the use of retained earnings for dividends. The nature of retained earnings is frequently misunderstood and this misunderstanding may lead to seriously misleading inferences in reading the balance sheet.

### Source of retained earnings

Retained earnings is the terminus of all profit and loss accounting. The retained earnings account is increased by profits from the sale of goods or services and is reduced by losses from these activities. The retained earnings account is also affected by: (1) extraordinary profit and loss items, including gains and losses arising from the sale of securities or plant assets and the retirement of debt, and charges arising from the write-off of worthless securities or other assets and the write-down of goodwill and other intangibles; (2) corrections in profits of prior periods.

Corporate earnings that are transferred to retained earnings originate from transactions with individuals or businesses outside of the company. No earnings are recognized in the construction of machinery or other plant items for a company's own use, even though the cost of such construction is below the price that would have to be paid outsiders for similar assets; self-construction at less than the asset purchase price is regarded simply as a savings in cost. No earnings are recognized on transactions with stockholders involving treasury stock; the purchase and sale of treasury stock are regarded as contractions and expansions of paid-in capital. The receipt of properties through donation and the recognition of appraisal increases in the accounts are not recognized as earnings; donations are regarded as giving rise to additional paid-in capital, while the appraisal increases are recognized as giving rise to a special unrealized capital element.

The earnings of a corporation may be distributed to the stockholders or they may be retained to provide for expanding operations. When earnings are retained, they may be appropriated so as to be reported as unavailable for dividend declaration. Appropriations may be returned to retained earnings after the purpose of the appropriation has been fulfilled. When operating losses or other charges to the retained earnings account produce a debit balance in this account, the debit balance is referred to as a *deficit*.

### Dated retained earnings

Any earnings after a corporate quasi-reorganization should be separately summarized and reported on the balance sheet as retained earnings dating from the time of such action. *Dated retained earnings* inform investors and others of the occurrence of a restatement of capital and the financial progress that has been made since that time.

### Dividends

*Dividends* are distributions to stockholders of a corporation in proportion to the number of shares that are held by the respective owners. Such distributions may take the form of (1) cash, (2) other assets, (3) evidences of corporate indebtedness, in effect, deferred cash dividends, and

(4) shares of a company's own stock. All of these involve reductions in retained earnings except dividends in corporate liquidation, which represent a return to stockholders of a portion or all of the corporate legal capital and call for reductions in invested capital.

Use of the term *dividend* without qualification normally implies the distribution of cash, with accumulated earnings as the source of such a distribution. Dividends in a form other than cash should be designated by their special form, and dividends that are declared from a capital source other than retained earnings should carry a description of their special origin. The terms *property dividend, scrip dividend,* and *stock dividend* suggest distributions of a special form; designations such as *liquidating dividend, dividend distribution of paid-in capital,* and *stock dividend of appraisal increment* identify the special origin of the distribution.

"Dividends paid out of retained earnings" is an expression frequently encountered. Accuracy, however, would require the statement that dividends are paid out of cash, which serves to reduce retained earnings. Earnings of the corporation increase net assets and also the stockholders' equity. Dividend distributions represent no more than asset withdrawals and reduce net assets and the stockholders' equity.

Among the powers that are delegated by the stockholders to the board of directors is that of controlling the dividend policy. Whether dividends shall or shall not be paid, as well as the nature and the amount of dividends, then, are matters that the board determines. In declaring dividends, the board of directors must observe the legal requirements governing the maintenance of legal or stated capital. These requirements vary with the individual states. In addition, the board of directors must consider the financial aspects of dividend distributions — the company asset position, present asset requirements, and future asset requirements. The board of directors, then, must answer two questions: Do we have the legal right to declare a dividend? Is such a distribution financially advisable?[1]

When a dividend is legally declared and announced, its revocation is not possible. In the event of corporate insolvency prior to payment of the dividend, stockholders have claims as a creditor group to the dividend, and as an ownership group to any assets remaining after all corporate liabilities have been paid. A dividend that was illegally declared

---

[1]Laws of the different states range from those making any part of capital other than that designated legal capital available for dividends to those permitting dividends only from retained earnings and under specified conditions. In most states dividends cannot be declared in the event of a deficit; in a few states, however, dividends equal to current earnings may be distributed despite a previously accumulated deficit. The availability of capital as a basis for dividends is a determination to be made by the attorney and not by the accountant. The accountant must report accurately the sources of each capital increase; the attorney investigates the availability of such sources as bases for dividend distributions.

is revocable; in the event of insolvency, such action is nullified and stockholders participate in asset distributions only after creditors have been paid in full.

## The formal dividend announcement

Three dates are essential in the formal dividend statement: (1) date of declaration, (2) date of stockholders of record, (3) date of payment. Dividends are made payable to stockholders of record as of a date that follows the date of declaration and precedes the date of payment. The liability for dividends payable is recorded on the declaration date and is canceled on the payment date. No entry is required on the record date, but a list of the stockholders is made up as of the close of business on such date. These are the persons who are to receive dividends on the payment date. A full record of the dividend action must be provided in the minutes book.

## Cash dividends

The most common type of dividend is a *cash dividend*. For the corporation, such dividends involve a reduction in retained earnings and in cash. A current liability for dividends payable is recognized on the declaration date; this is canceled when dividend checks are sent to stockholders. Entries to record the declaration and the payment of a cash dividend follow:

| | | |
|---|---:|---:|
| Retained Earnings............................ | 100,000 | |
| Cash Dividend Payable...................... | | 100,000 |
| Cash Dividend Payable....................... | 100,000 | |
| Cash........................................ | | 100,000 |

In declaring the dividend, the board of directors must consider the limitations set by the current position and the cash balance. For example, a corporation may have retained earnings of $500,000. If it has cash of only $150,000, however, cash dividends must be limited to this amount unless it converts certain assets into cash or borrows cash. If the cash required for regular operations is $100,000, the cash available for dividends is only $50,000. Although legally able to declare dividends of $500,000, the company can distribute no more than one-tenth of such amount at this time.

## Scrip dividends

If a corporation has retained earnings that may be used as a basis for dividend declaration but does not have sufficient funds at the time for a cash dividend, it may declare a *scrip dividend*, which consists of a written promise to pay certain amounts at some future date. The corporation can thus take regular dividend action although it is temporarily short of cash. Stockholders, in turn, are provided currently with instruments that they may sell for cash if they wish. Such dividends are rare.

Assume the declaration of a scrip dividend of $150,000, payable in six months together with interest at the rate of 6% for the period of payment deferment. The declaration is recorded as follows:

```
Retained Earnings............................    150,000
    Scrip Dividend Payable....................                150,000
```

When the scrip matures and scrip and interest payments are made, the entry is:

```
Scrip Dividend Payable.......................    150,000
Interest Expense.............................      4,500
    Cash.....................................                154,500
```

## Property dividends

A distribution to stockholders that is payable in some asset other than cash is generally referred to as a *property dividend* or *dividend in kind*. Frequently, the asset to be distributed is certain securities of other companies that are owned by the corporation. The corporation thus transfers to its stockholders its ownership interest in such securities.

A property dividend avoids the need for selling assets to pay dividends. When the value of the property exceeds its cost, the corporation is not required to recognize a "gain" for income tax purposes. However, stockholders are required to report dividend income equal to the fair market value of the asset acquired.

To illustrate the entries for a property dividend, assume that the State Oil Corporation owns 100,000 shares in the Valley Oil Co., cost $2,000,000, which it wishes to distribute to its stockholders. There are 1,000,000 shares of State Oil Corporation stock outstanding. Accordingly, a dividend of 1/10 of a share of Valley Oil Co. stock is declared on each share of State Oil Corporation stock outstanding. The entries for the dividend declaration and payment are:

```
Retained Earnings.......................    2,000,000
    Dividend Payable in Stock of Valley Oil Co.             2,000,000
Dividend Payable in Stock of Valley Oil Co...    2,000,000
    Investment in Stock of Valley Oil Co......              2,000,000
```

## Stock dividends

A corporation may distribute to stockholders additional shares of the company's own stock. Such a distribution is known as a *stock dividend*. A stock dividend permits the corporation to retain within the business net assets produced by earnings while at the same time offering stockholders tangible evidence of the growth of their equity.

Reference to a stock dividend usually implies (1) the capitalization of retained earnings and (2) a distribution of common stock to common stockholders. Such distributions are sometimes termed *ordinary stock dividends*. In certain states, stock dividends may be effected by the capitalization of certain paid-in capital or appraisal capital balances. In some instances, common or preferred stock is issued to holders of preferred stock or preferred stock is issued to holders of common stock. The latter distributions are sometimes referred to as *special stock dividends*.

The ordinary stock dividend makes a portion of retained earnings no longer available for distribution while raising the legal capital of the corporation. In recording the dividend, a charge is made to retained earnings and credits are made to appropriate paid-in capital balances. The stock dividend may be viewed as consisting, in effect, of two transactions: (1) the payment by the corporation of a cash dividend; and (2) the return of such cash to the corporation in exchange for stock.

In distributing stock as a dividend, the issuing corporation must meet legal requirements relative to the amounts to be capitalized. When stock has a par or a stated value, an amount equal to the value of the shares issued normally will have to be transferred to capital stock; when stock is no-par and without a stated value, the laws of the state of incorporation may provide specific requirements as to amounts to be transferred or they may leave such determinations to the corporate directors.

Although the amounts to be transferred to legal or stated capital balances upon the issuance of additional stock are set by law, the board of directors is not prevented from going beyond legal requirements and authorizing increases in both capital stock and additional paid-in capital balances. For example, assume that $100 par stock was originally issued at 120. Legal requirements may call for the capitalization of no more than the par value of the additional shares issued. The board of directors, however, in order to preserve the original capital stock and stock premium relationship, may authorize a transfer from retained earnings of $120 per share; capital stock, then, may be increased $100 and the premium balance $20 for every share issued. Or the board of directors may decide that the retained earnings transfer shall be made in terms of the fair value of shares, which exceeds the legal value. Here, too, the credit to capital stock is accompanied by a credit to a premium or other paid-in capital balance.

There have been suggestions that when stock dividends are so small in comparison with shares previously outstanding that they do not have any apparent effect upon share market value, capitalization of retained earnings should be made of an amount equal to the market value of the shares issued. Such corporate action would conform to the view that is taken by the public as to the amount of corporate earnings distribution. On the other hand, when the number of shares issued is so large that it has the effect of materially reducing share market value, the transaction takes the aspects of a split-up. Here, the shareholder is not likely to assume the capitalization of earnings as in the first instance, and there would be no need for the capitalization of an amount in excess of that required by law.[1]

The examples that follow illustrate the entries for the declaration and the issue of a stock dividend. Assume that the capital for the Bradford Co. on July 1 is as follows:

| | |
|---|---:|
| Capital stock, $10 par, 100,000 shares outstanding....... | $1,000,000 |
| Premium on stock.................................. | 100,000 |
| Retained earnings................................. | 750,000 |

The company declares a 10% stock dividend, or a dividend of 1 share for every 10 held. Shares are selling on the market on this date at $16 per share. The stock dividend is to be recorded at the market value of the shares issued, or $160,000 (10,000 shares at $16). The entries to record the declaration of the dividend and the issue of stock follow:

| | | |
|---|---:|---:|
| Retained Earnings............................ | 160,000 | |
|   Stock Dividend Distributable................. | | 100,000 |
|   Additional Paid-in Capital from Stock Dividend | | 60,000 |
| Stock Dividend Distributable................... | 100,000 | |
|   Capital Stock, $10 par...................... | | 100,000 |

Assume, however, that the company declares a 50% stock dividend, or a dividend of 1 share for every 2 held. Legal requirements call for the transfer from retained earnings to capital stock of an amount equal to the par value of the shares issued, and the stock dividend is recorded at this value. Entries for the declaration of the dividend and the issue of stock follow:

| | | |
|---|---:|---:|
| Retained Earnings............................ | 500,000 | |
|   Stock Dividend Distributable................. | | 500,000 |
| Stock Dividend Distributable................... | 500,000 | |
|   Capital Stock, $10 par. ..................... | | 500,000 |

If in this case the board of directors wished to maintain invested capital balances in their original relationship, authorization could be

---

[1]This is the position that is taken by the AICPA Committee on Accounting Procedure. The Committee, although reluctant to name a stock dividend percentage calling for retained earnings capitalization at the market value of the issue, does suggest that in stock distributions of recent years involving the issue of less than 20% to 25% of the number of shares previously outstanding, there would be but few instances where charges to retained earnings at the fair market value of additional shares would not be supportable. See *Accounting Research and Terminology Bulletins,* 1961 (New York: American Institute of Certified Public Accountants), *Accounting Research Bulletin No. 43,* pp. 49–54.

made for capitalization of the issue at $11 per share. Entries to record
the dividend declaration and stock issue would be:

| | | |
|---|---:|---:|
| Retained Earnings................................ | 550,000 | |
|    Stock Dividend Distributable................. | | 500,000 |
|    Additional Paid-in Capital from Stock Dividend. | | 50,000 |
| Stock Dividend Distributable.................... | 500,000 | |
|    Capital Stock, $10 par...................... | | 500,000 |

If a balance sheet is prepared after the declaration of a stock dividend
but before issue of the shares, Stock Dividend Distributable is reported
in the capital section as an addition to Capital Stock Outstanding. By
the declaration of the dividend, the corporation has reduced its retained
earnings balance and is committed to the increase of capital stock. The
stock that the corporation may still sell is limited to the difference between capital stock authorized and the sum of (1) capital stock issued,
(2) capital stock subscribed, (3) stock reserved for the exercise of stock
rights and stock options, and (4) stock dividends distributable.

## Liquidating dividends

A corporation will declare a *liquidating dividend* when the dividend is
to be considered a return to stockholders of a portion of their original
investments. Such distributions by the corporation represent reductions
of invested capital balances. Instead of actually charging capital stock
and additional paid-in capital balances, however, it is possible to charge
a separate account for the reduction in invested capital. This balance
is subtracted from the invested capital balances in presenting the stockholders' equity on the balance sheet.

Corporations owning wasting assets may regularly declare dividends
that are in part a distribution of earnings and in part a distribution of
the corporation's invested capital. Entries on the corporation books for
such dividend declarations should reflect the decrease in the two capital
elements. This information should be reported to stockholders so that
they may recognize dividends as representing in part income and in part
a return of investment.

## Dividends on preferred stock

When dividends on preferred stock are cumulative, the payment of a
stipulated amount on these shares is necessary before any dividends
may be paid on common. When the board of directors fails to declare
dividends on cumulative preferred stock, information concerning the
amount of dividends in arrears should be reported parenthetically or in
note form on the balance sheet. Or retained earnings may be divided on
the balance sheet to show the amount required to meet dividends in

arrears and the balance free for other purposes.  In this case retained earnings may be reported on the balance sheet in the following manner:

Retained earnings:
Required to meet dividends in arrears on pre-
    ferred stock............................. $40,000
Balance...................................  60,000

    Total retained earnings....................  $100,000

The board of directors may pay a portion of a cumulative preferred dividend or a portion of the total in arrears.  For example, 2% may be paid annually on 7% cumulative preferred stock, allowing 5% to accumulate for future payment.  Or a payment of $15 may be made on cumulative dividends in arrears of $50, leaving $35 as the balance in arrears.

## Dividends on no-par stock

Cash dividends on no-par stock must be expressed as a certain amount per share, since there is no par value upon which a percentage may be applied.  Dividends on stock with a par value are often expressed in the same manner.

When no-par stock is outstanding and the corporation desires to transfer an amount from Retained Earnings to Capital Stock, there is no need to declare a stock dividend.  The board of directors can simply take action to raise the stated value of the no-par stock.  An entry such as the following is made:

Retained Earnings............................ 500,000
Capital Stock...............................  500,000
    To raise $5 stated value on 100,000 shares of
    no-par stock to $10 in accordance with resolu-
    tion by board of directors.

## Extraordinary dividend distributions

In the case of common stock, a corporation may establish a policy of *regular dividends* and may provide for greater payments when warranted through *extraordinary dividends* or *extra dividends*.  For example, a corporation may have a regular rate of 50 cents a quarter or $2 a year per share on common stock.  In a particular quarter it may wish to declare a dividend of 80 cents a share.  Such a dividend may be expressed as a 50-cent regular dividend plus a 30-cent extra dividend.

## Appraisal capital

The problems and the procedures involved in recording an increase in plant assets after their valuation by independent appraisers and the authorization for use of this information in the accounts by the board of directors were described in Chapter 13. Charges to assets for increases established by appraisal were accompanied by credits to appraisal capital accounts. Such capital is separately designated in the capital section on the balance sheet. Readers of the statement are thus informed that property items are stated at amounts in excess of cost and that this action has resulted in an unrealized capital element.

Appraisal capital shrinks only as the asset value from which it emerged shrinks. Appraisal capital should never be used to absorb operating losses or the write-down of properties other than those values representing the source of such appraisal increase. Appraisal capital, representing unrealized earnings, is not properly used as a basis for cash dividends; however, its use as a basis for stock dividends is permitted in some states.

### Use of term "reserve"

It has already been indicated that the term *reserve* has been employed in a variety of different senses in accounting practice. It has been used in the following ways:

1. *As a valuation account.* The reserve designation has been employed to report a valuation account related to a balance sheet item. For example, deductions may be required from the face amount of assets in arriving at the amounts that they are expected to realize, as in the case of marketable securities, receivables, or inventories. Deductions may also be required from the face amount of assets in the recognition of cost expirations, as in the case of assets subject to depreciation, depletion, or amortization. When such reductions are related to current revenues, expense accounts are charged and asset valuation accounts are credited. Valuation accounts are ultimately applied against the items to which they relate. The accounts receivable valuation account is used to absorb accounts that prove to be uncollectible; the property valuation account is applied against the property item when the latter is disposed of or scrapped. It was suggested earlier that the term *allowance* should be substituted for the term *reserve* in designating valuation accounts.

2. *As an estimate of a liability of uncertain amount.* The reserve title has been employed to designate a liability of uncertain amount requiring an estimate. Estimates may be required for such items as unsettled claims for damages and injuries, premium claims outstanding, claims under guarantees for services and replacements, tax obligations, and obligations under pension plans. When such claims are related to current revenue, expense accounts are charged and liability accounts are credited. The liabilities are ultimately canceled through payment.

Designation of the accounts in this class as *estimated liabilities* rather than as *reserves* would clarify the nature of the items presented.

3. *As an appropriation of retained earnings.* The reserve title is used to indicate that retained earnings have been appropriated in accordance with legal or contractual requirements or as a result of authorization by the board of directors. The appropriation of retained earnings has no effect upon individual assets and liabilities nor does it change total capital; amounts are merely transferred from retained earnings to special retained earnings accounts and assets that might otherwise be distributed as dividends are thus kept within the business. The appropriation balance is no guarantee that cash or any other specific asset will be available in carrying out the purpose of the appropriation. Resources represented by retained earnings may have been applied to the enlargement of plant, to the increase of working capital, or possibly to the retirement of corporate indebtedness. If assets are to be made available for a particular purpose, special action relative to asset use would be required. When the purpose of the appropriation has been served, the appropriation balance is returned to Retained Earnings.

It was indicated in an earlier chapter that some authorities have recommended that the term *reserve* be limited to appropriations of retained earnings and that any alternative use of the term on the financial statements be discontinued. Others have gone further and have recommended abandonment of the term in financial statements. There can be little question that greater clarity in financial statement presentation would be promoted through abandonment of the term "reserve" and the adoption of more descriptive terminology.

## Retained earnings appropriations

Appropriations of retained earnings may be classified under the following headings:

1. *Appropriations to report legal restrictions on retained earnings.* Laws of the state of incorporation may require that a company, upon reacquiring its own stock, retain its earnings as a means of maintaining its legal capital. The restriction may be recognized in the accounts by the appropriation of retained earnings.

2. *Appropriations to report contractual restrictions on retained earnings.* Agreements with creditors or stockholders may provide for the retention of earnings within the company to protect the interests of these parties and assure redemption of the securities they hold. The restriction may be indicated in the accounts by the appropriation of retained earnings.

3. *Appropriations to report discretionary action by the board of directors in the presentation of retained earnings.* The board of directors may authorize

that a portion or all of the retained earnings be presented in a manner that will disclose the actual use in the present or the planned use in the future of the resources represented by this part of the stockholders' equity. Discretionary action on the part of the board of directors may then be the basis for appropriations.

A number of appropriated retained earnings accounts and the purposes for which such balances are established are listed below:

| Account | Purpose |
| --- | --- |
| (1) *Appropriations to report legal restrictions on retained earnings:*<br><br>Retained Earnings Appropriated for Purchase of Treasury Stock | To retain earnings upon the reacquisition of stock, so that resources of the business and the stockholders' equity may be maintained at original legal or stated balance. |
| (2) *Appropriations to report contractual restrictions on retained earnings:*<br><br>Retained Earnings Appropriated for Redemption of Bonds<br>Retained Earnings Appropriated for Bond Redemption Fund | To retain earnings so that resources may be available for the redemption of bonds or for transfer to a fund for bond redemption. |
| Retained Earnings Appropriated for Redemption of Preferred Stock<br>Retained Earnings Appropriated for Preferred Stock Redemption Fund | To retain earnings so that resources may be available for the redemption of preferred stock or for transfer to a fund for stock redemption. |
| (3) *Appropriations to report discretionary action by the board of directors in the presentation of retained earnings:*<br><br>Retained Earnings Appropriated for General Contingencies<br>Retained Earnings Appropriated for Possible Inventory Decline<br>Retained Earnings Appropriated for Self-Insurance | To retain earnings in the business so that resources may be available for use in meeting possible future losses. |
| Retained Earnings Appropriated for Increased Working Capital<br>Retained Earnings Appropriated for Plant Expansion | To report that resources from earnings are to be applied or have been applied to some particular business purpose and thus are unavailable for dividends. |

## Appropriations relating to stock reacquisitions

A legal restriction upon retained earnings arising upon the reacquisition of the company's own stock is recorded by a charge to Retained Earnings and a credit to an appropriately titled appropriations account.

Retained earnings thus replace the capital impairment arising from treasury stock acquisition. The appropriated balance may be returned to Retained Earnings when the legal restriction is removed. To illustrate, assume that a corporation reacquires its own stock and subsequently resells this stock. Retained earnings of $100,000 are restricted by law from use for dividends during the period treasury stock is held. The entries for the appropriation and for its subsequent cancellation follow:

| | | |
|---|---:|---:|
| Retained Earnings............................ | 100,000 | |
| Retained Earnings Appropriated for Purchase of Treasury Stock............................. | | 100,000 |
| Retained Earnings Appropriated for Purchase of Treasury Stock............................. | 100,000 | |
| Retained Earnings......................... | | 100,000 |

## Appropriations relating to bond redemption

A restriction upon retained earnings arising from a contract with creditors or stockholders is recorded by a charge to retained earnings and a credit to an appropriations account. When the restriction is removed, the appropriation is returned to retained earnings. To illustrate, assume that the corporation agrees to restrict retained earnings of $5,000,000 from dividend distribution during the full term of a bond issue. Entries when the loan is made and when it is liquidated follow:

| | | |
|---|---:|---:|
| Retained Earnings......................... | 5,000,000 | |
| Retained Earnings Appropriated for Redemption of Bonds............................. | | 5,000,000 |
| Retained Earnings Appropriated for Redemption of Bonds............................. | 5,000,000 | |
| Retained Earnings......................... | | 5,000,000 |

When the agreement with creditors provides for the periodic appropriation of earnings during the life of the obligation, entries similar to the first entry above would be made each period.

The appropriation of earnings may be accompanied by the segregation of assets in a special fund for retirement of the obligation at maturity. The establishment of the fund may be voluntary or it may be required by the bond indenture. A retained earnings appropriation that is accompanied by the segregation of assets in a special fund is said to be *funded*. This practice results not only in the limitation of dividends but also in the accumulation of resources to meet the obligation. Liquidation of the obligation by means of the redemption fund and the termination of the contract with creditors releases previously existing restrictions, and the appropriated retained earnings may be returned to a free status. It may be observed, however, that when proceeds from a bond issue are used for expansion purposes and when resources from profitable operations have been used to retire the bonds, the expansion has in effect been financed by earnings. Under these circumstances, the board of directors may choose to report retained earnings equivalent to the amount applied to expansion under the designation "Retained Earnings Appropriated for Plant Expansion," or it may choose to effect a permanent capitalization of such retained earnings by means of a stock dividend.

### Appropriations relating to stock redemption

Retained earnings may be appropriated at regular intervals as part of a plan to retire preferred stock from resources arising from earnings. The appropriation of earnings may be required by the contract with stockholders or it may be voluntary and established at the discretion of the board of directors. Stock may be reacquired out of cash or out of a redemption fund previously established by transfers from cash. In either case, upon the retirement of outstanding stock, the board of directors may authorize the return of the appropriation balance to retained earnings. However, it should be observed that retained earnings now take the place of the capital stock equity previously reported. In recognition of this factor, the board of directors may choose to designate these earnings as applied to the retirement of a previously existing stockholders' equity; on the other hand, it may choose to effect a permanent capitalization of such retained earnings by means of a stock dividend.

### Appropriations for possible future losses

Appropriations of retained earnings may be authorized by the board of directors in anticipation of possible future losses. Two examples of such appropriations are described in the following paragraphs: (1) the general purpose contingency appropriation and (2) the appropriation for self-insurance.

1. *Appropriation for general contingencies.* Company management may authorize that provision be made in the accounts for general undetermined contingencies. Such authorization calls for the appropriation of retained earnings to assure the availability of resources to absorb the losses if they materialize. The establishment of an asset valuation balance or a liability balance is not appropriate under these circumstances; the provision for contingencies is related to losses of the future that may or may not take place, not to losses of the past or of the present. In the event that the contingencies fail to materialize, the board of directors may authorize cancellation of the provision for contingencies, and the appropriated balance would then be returned to retained earnings. If the contingencies do materialize, the appropriated balance is still returned to retained earnings and the losses are assigned to the period in which they materialized.

To illustrate the foregoing, assume that management, in reviewing business conditions at the end of 1962, concludes that there may be a general business decline in the next year or two and authorizes that retained earnings of $500,000 be reported as an appropriation for general contingencies. In 1964 the company sells its marketable securities at a loss of $150,000. At the end of 1964, with prospects for business good, management decides that the provision for general contingencies is no longer required and should be canceled. The following entries record the appropriation for general contingencies, the recognition of the loss on the sale of securities, and the return of the appropriation to retained earnings.

| | | |
|---|---|---|
| 1962: Retained Earnings......................... | 500,000 | |
| Retained Earnings Appropriated for General Contingencies............................ | | 500,000 |
| 1964: Cash..................................... | 250,000 | |
| Loss on Sale of Marketable Securities......... | 150,000 | |
| Marketable Securities..................... | | 400,000 |
| Retained Earnings Appropriated for General Contingencies............................ | 500,000 | |
| Retained Earnings........................ | | 500,000 |

It should be observed that the appropriation for general contingencies established at the end of 1962 can be viewed only as a part of retained earnings; neither asset shrinkage nor liability can be recognized at this date. Since such provision is part of retained earnings, it must be established not by a charge to revenue in 1962 but by a charge to retained earnings. If revenue were charged, income of $500,000 in 1962 would by-pass recognition on the income statement and earnings for the year would be understated. Having established the appropriation by a charge to retained earnings, it would be improper to charge it for the losses resulting from the sale of securities in 1964. If this were done, losses of $150,000 in 1964 would by-pass recognition on the income statement and earnings for the year would be overstated. Any loss is recognized in the period in which it is incurred. The appropriation for contingencies is returned to retained earnings when the losses have been incurred or when they are no longer in prospect. The return is made directly to retained earnings and not through a revenue account since no revenue is involved in the transfer.

2. *Appropriation for self-insurance.* A company may face certain risks but may not obtain insurance on the theory that the assumption of these risks will prove less expensive in the long run than the cost of outside protection. When a company is self-insured, it may authorize that provision

be made in the accounts in anticipation of the losses that may have to be absorbed.

Self-insurance that involves definitely accruing obligations requires the establishment of liabilities through charges to periodic revenues. However, a self-insurance plan related to losses or casualties that cannot be considered to accrue would call for appropriations of retained earnings; charges to revenue would be made only when losses are actually incurred.

To illustrate, assume that a construction company decides to assume the risks for workmen's compensation. The company is satisfied that it can make reliable estimates of the amounts payable under compensation claims arising from employee accidents. Under these circumstances, the estimated amounts payable at the end of each period are recognized by a charge to an expense account and a credit to an estimated liability account; when payments are made in subsequent periods, the liability balance is charged and cash is credited. If payable estimates prove to be inadequate or excessive, correcting entries would be required. A fund may be established for payments to be made under the plan.

On the other hand, assume that a company with a number of branches throughout the country decides to act as self-insurer for any fire losses and authorizes that provision be made in the accounts for the losses that may have to be absorbed as a result of this policy. Fire loss cannot be considered to accrue; it is a contingency that may or may not occur. Until a fire occurs no loss has been incurred; the absence of a fire loss in one period does not increase the probability of loss in the next period. Under these circumstances, there is no support for the recognition in the accounts either of an asset valuation account or a liability account; any provision in the accounts for possible future losses would have to be regarded as an appropriation of retained earnings. Accounting for possible fire losses, then, would be similar to that employed for other contingencies. Appropriations arising from a policy of self-insurance must be established by a charge to retained earnings. Upon incurring a fire loss, a loss account is charged and the appropriate property accounts are credited. At the same time amounts in the appropriation account may be returned to retained earnings to absorb the losses that will be summarized in the latter account. When the appropriation account is credited for insurance premiums that would otherwise be paid and is charged for transfers to retained earnings based upon losses actually sustained, the balance in the account will measure the savings accruing to the company as a result of the self-insurance plan. The appropriation may be funded so that cash will be available for property replacement.

The two procedures described are illustrated below. It is assumed that a fund is maintained in each case to meet losses that emerge under the self-insurance plans.

| Transaction | Self-Insurance Considered to Involve Accruable Losses | Self-Insurance Considered to Involve Nonaccruable Losses |
|---|---|---|
| (a) Estimated liability under workmen's compensation self-insurance plan.<br><br>(b) Retained earnings appropriation under fire loss self-insurance plan. | (a)<br>Workmen's Compensation........ 20,000<br> Estimated Claims under Workmen's Compensation Plan......... 20,000 | (b)<br>Retained Earnings........... 20,000<br> Retained Earnings Appropriated for Self-Insurance — Fire Loss.... 20,000 |
| Establishment of fund to meet self-insurance plans. | Workmen's Compensation Fund... 20,000<br> Cash......... 20,000 | Property Replacement Fund...... 20,000<br> Cash......... 20,000 |
| (a) Workmen's compensation paid, $15,000.<br><br>(b) Fire loss: asset book value, $15,000; building replacement cost, $23,500; paid $15,000 from fund and $8,500 from regular cash balance. | (a)<br>Estimated Claims under Workmen's Compensation Plan........... 15,000<br> Workmen's Compensation Fund........ 15,000 | (b)<br>Fire Loss........ 15,000<br>Allowance for Depr. of Buildings. 6,500<br> Buildings...... 21,500<br><br>Retained Earnings Appropriated for Self-Insurance — Fire Loss........ 15,000<br> Ret. Earnings.. 15,000<br><br>Buildings........ 23,500<br> Prop. Replacement Fund.... 15,000<br> Cash......... 8,500 |

It should be observed that "self-insurance" is simply a policy of "no-insurance," since there is no indemnity in the event of loss. Management, in considering such a policy, should evaluate carefully such factors as the size of the organization and how this affects risk, the protective measures that are available in minimizing risk, and the probable savings that will accrue through such action. Self-insurance should be undertaken only when a company is financially prepared to assume the full responsibilities that are related to the risk-bearing role.

### Appropriations to describe business purposes served by retained earnings

Corporate officials may authorize appropriations to show the use of retained earnings within the business. For example, assume that earnings are to be retained by a company to finance the expansion of plant facilities. Or assume that resources from earnings have already been applied to plant expansion. In either instance, instead of continuing to report undistributed profits in retained earnings, which may be interpreted by stockholders as amounts available for dividends, the company may authorize transfers from retained earnings to a special account that describes the utilization of earnings. A permanent increase in a company's working capital position may likewise suggest an appropriation of earnings. Such appropriations may be carried forward indefinitely. On the other hand, in view of the permanent commitment of assets, the company may choose to effect a permanent capitalization of retained earnings by means of a stock dividend.

### Objections to appropriation procedures

There are some who have taken issue with the general practice of earmarking retained earnings through the appropriation procedure. These persons maintain that such practice may serve to confuse and mislead those using the financial statements. They suggest that when earnings are retained, the objectives of such retention are best explained by narrative materials accompanying the statements. Managerial policy, it is pointed out, arises from a number of complex factors; the equity section of the balance sheet is hardly the most practical vehicle for the description of such policy.

### The retained earnings statement

Those who wish to be completely informed on the financial position and the financial progress of a corporation require full information explaining the change in retained earnings balances on successive balance sheets. When the change in retained earnings for the period has resulted from no more than net income and dividends, a reconciliation of beginning and ending retained earnings balances can be provided on the balance sheet. Ordinarily, however, additional factors are responsible for the change, and a separate retained earnings statement is prepared.

The nature and form of the retained earnings statement depends upon the method of treating extraordinary gains and losses and corrections of past periods. When extraordinary items and corrections are reported on the income statement, the retained earnings statement reports only the retained earnings change as summarized on the income statement. When extraordinary items and corrections are considered to affect retained earnings directly, the retained earnings statement must be expanded to include them. If corporate paid-in capital balances have changed on successive balance sheets, these changes should be explained on a separate statement. Changes in appraisal capital balances would also call for a statement explaining the changes.

An income statement prepared in current operating performance form, and accompanying paid-in capital and retained earnings statements for the General Manufacturing Company for the year ended December 31, 1964, are illustrated on pages 469 and 470. The balance sheet for this company as of December 31, 1964, appears on pages 472 to 474.

Assume that the General Manufacturing Company prepares its income statement in all-inclusive form as shown on page 471. The retained earnings statement, then, shows only the increase reported by the income statement, the dividends, and the appropriations. In the illustration on page 471, the analysis of changes in appropriated and unappropriated retained earnings balances is prepared in columnar form.

General Manufacturing Company
Income Statement
For Year Ended December 31, 1964

| | |
|---|---:|
| Sales...................................................... | $1,500,000 |
| Net income before income taxes.......................... | $ 225,000 |
| Less income taxes applicable to net income (total tax provision, $112,500 less $7,500 applicable to extraordinary items)....... | 105,000 |
| Net income............................................... | $ 120,000 |

**Income Statement Prepared in Current Operating Performance Form**

General Manufacturing Company
Paid-in Capital Statement
For Year Ended December 31, 1964

| | Preferred Stock | Common Stock | Additional Paid-in Capital | Total |
|---|---|---|---|---|
| Paid-in capital, January 1, 1964...... | $500,000 | $250,000 | $205,000 | $ 955,000 |
| Add: Increase from sale of 10,000 shares of common stock, stated value $5, for $10.50 per share .. | | 50,000 | 55,000 | 105,000 |
| Increase from sale of treasury stock, cost $20,000, for $36,000.......... | | | 16,000 | 16,000 |
| Paid-in capital, December 31, 1964..... | $500,000 | $300,000 | $276,000 | $1,076,000 |

**Paid-in Capital Statement**

General Manufacturing Company
Retained Earnings Statement
For Year Ended December 31, 1964

| | | | |
|---|---|---|---|
| Retained earnings appropriated: | | | |
| Appropriated for purchase of treasury stock, balance, January 1, 1964................. | $60,000 | | |
| Deduct retained earnings restrictions removed upon sale of treasury stock in 1964 (see below)......................... | 20,000 | $ 40,000 | |
| Appropriated for contingencies, balance, January 1, 1964....................... | $50,000 | | |
| Add appropriation in 1964 (see below).... | 35,000 | 85,000 | |
| Appropriated retained earnings balance, December 31, 1964.... | | | $125,000 |
| Retained earnings unappropriated: | | | |
| Balance, January 1, 1964........................ | | $200,000 | |
| Add: Net income for year per income statement... | | 120,000 | |
| Gain on sale of securities......... $35,000 | | | |
| Less income taxes applicable to gain    8,750 | | 26,250 | |
| Transfer from appropriation for purchase of treasury stock (see above)................ | | 20,000 | |
| | | $366,250 | |
| Deduct: Loss on sale of land...    $ 5,000 | | | |
| Less income tax credit applicable to loss.....    1,250 | $ 3,750 | | |
| Organization costs written off... | 32,500 | | |
| Corrections in profits of prior periods—understatements of depreciation charges, 1961–1963.. | 20,000 | | |
| Cash dividends.............. | 50,000 | | |
| Transfer to appropriation for contingencies (see above)...... | 35,000 | 141,250 | |
| Unappropriated retained earnings balance, December 31, 1964. | | | 225,000 |
| Retained earnings, December 31, 1964....................... | | | $350,000 |

**Retained Earnings Statement to Accompany Income Statement in Current Operating Performance Form**

## Stockholders' equity on the balance sheet

The principles of balance sheet form and content discussed in preceding chapters are illustrated in the balance sheet for the General Manufacturing Company on pages 472 to 474.    Special attention is directed to the stockholders' equity section that is related to the income and capital statements just illustrated.

A reference to the notes accompanying financial statements would appear at the bottom of each statement.

General Manufacturing Company
Income Statement
For Year Ended December 31, 1964

| | |
|---|---:|
| Sales............................................................ | $1,500,000 |

| | | | |
|---|---:|---:|---:|
| Net income before income taxes............................. | | | $ 225,000 |
| Less income taxes applicable to net income (total tax provision, $112,500 less $7,500 applicable to extraordinary items)....... | | | 105,000 |
| Net income........................................... | | | $ 120,000 |
| Extraordinary items: | | | |
| Loss on sale of land............... | $5,000 | | |
| Less income tax credit applicable to loss..................... | 1,250 | $ 3,750 | |
| Organization costs written off............. | | 32,500 | |
| Corrections in profits of prior periods — understatement of depreciation charges, 1961–1963................................ | | 20,000 | $56,250 |
| Gain on sale of securities................. | $35,000 | | |
| Less income taxes applicable to gain...... | 8,750 | 26,250 | 30,000 |
| Net income and extraordinary items....................... | | | $  90,000 |

**Income Statement Prepared in All-Inclusive Form**

General Manufacturing Company
Retained Earnings Statement
For Year Ended December 31, 1964

| | Retained Earnings | | |
|---|---|---|---|
| | Appropriated for Purchase of Treasury Stock | Appropriated for Contingencies | Unappropriated |
| Balances, January 1, 1964. | $60,000 | $50,000 | $200,000 |
| Net income and extraordinary items per income statement ........... | | | 90,000 |
| Cash dividends... ...... | | | (50,000) |
| Earnings appropriated for contingencies......... | | 35,000 | (35,000) |
| Return to retained earnings of earnings previously restricted through ownership of treasury stock............... | (20,000) | | 20,000 |
| Balances, December 31, 1964, per balance sheet . | $40,000 | $85,000 | $225,000 |

**Retained Earnings Statement to Accompany Income Statement in All-Inclusive Form**

General Manufac
Balance
December

## Assets

| | | |
|---|---:|---:|
| Current assets: | | |
| Cash on hand and on deposit.................. | | $ 54,000 |
| U.S. Government securities at cost (market, $87,500)................................. | | 86,000 |
| Trade notes and accounts receivable — less allowance for bad debts, $2,600.................. | | 180,000 |
| Inventories (valuation at cost or market, whichever is lower, cost being calculated by the first-in, first-out method): | | |
| Raw materials and supplies.................. | $ 185,000 | |
| Goods in process........................... | 201,000 | |
| Finished goods............................. | 190,000 | 576,000 |
| Loans, advances, and accrued income items...... | | 20,000 |
| Prepayments including taxes, insurance, and sundry current items...................... | | 14,500 |
| Total current assets........................... | | $ 930,500 |
| Investments: | | |
| Fund consisting of U. S. Government securities to be used for property additions............... | $ 250,000 | |
| Land held for future expansion................ | 110,000 | 360,000 |
| Plant and equipment: | | |
| Property, plant, and equipment, at cost......... | $1,235,000 | |
| Less allowances for depreciation............... | 580,000 | 655,000 |
| Intangible assets: | | |
| Patents, formulas, and goodwill — less amortization (See Note A)......................... | | 120,000 |
| Other assets: | | |
| Advance payments on equipment purchase contracts..................................... | $ 25,000 | |
| Bond issue costs.............................. | 15,000 | |
| Developmental costs (See Note B)............. | 62,500 | 102,500 |
| Total assets................................... | | $2,168,000 |

The accompanying notes A through F are an integral part of this financial statement.

turing Company
Sheet
31, 1964

| Liabilities and Stockholders' Equity | | |
|---|---|---|
| **Liabilities** | | |
| Current liabilities: | | |
| Notes and accounts payable.............................. | | $ 52,500 |
| Estimated income taxes payable........................... | | 62,000 |
| Accrued payrolls, interest, and taxes...................... | | 23,500 |
| Serial debenture bonds due May 1, 1965................... | | 20,000 |
| Customers' deposits and sundry items..................... | | 24,000 |
| Total current liabilities................................. | | $ 182,000 |
| Contingent liabilities (See Note C) | | |
| Long-term debt: | | |
| Twenty-year 5½% first mortgage bonds......... | $ 260,000 | |
| Less unamortized discount on first mortgage bonds. | 10,000 | |
| | $ 250,000 | |
| Serial 5¾% debenture bonds due May 1, 1966, to May 1, 1974, inclusive...................... | 180,000 | 430,000 |
| Estimated employee pensions payable (See Note D)............ | | 60,000 |
| Deferred leasehold revenue (See Note E)..................... | | 110,000 |
| Total liabilities.......................................... | | $ 782,000 |
| **Stockholders' Equity** | | |
| Paid-in capital: | | |
| First preferred 5% stock, $25 par, cumulative and convertible into common, 10,000 shares authorized, 8,000 issued.......................... | $ 200,000 | |
| Second preferred 6% stock, $10 par, cumulative and redeemable, 50,000 shares authorized, 30,000 issued (See Note F)................. | 300,000 | |
| No-par common stock, $5 stated value, 100,000 shares authorized, 24,000 shares reserved for conversion of first preferred, 60,000 shares issued (treasury stock, 5,000 shares — deducted below) | 300,000 | |
| | $ 800,000 | |
| Additional paid-in capital: | | |
| From sale of common stock in excess of stated value................. $260,000 | | |
| From sale of treasury stock in excess of cost........................ 16,000 | 276,000 | |
| Total paid-in capital........................ | $1,076,000 | |
| Retained earnings: | | |
| Appropriated: | | |
| For purchase of treasury stock $40,000 | | |
| For contingencies......... 85,000 $125,000 | | |
| Unappropriated.................... 225,000 | | |
| Total retained earnings....................... | 350,000 | |
| | $1,426,000 | |
| Less common treasury stock, at cost (5,000 shares acquired at $8)............................. | 40,000 | |
| Total stockholders' equity........................ | | 1,386,000 |
| Total liabilities and stockholders' equity........... | | $2,168,000 |

General Manufacturing Company
Notes to Financial Statements — Year Ended December 31, 1964

Note A: Intangible assets are being amortized over the period of their estimated useful life, with the exception of goodwill, which is carried at
its original cost, $75,000. The balance of organization costs, $32,500,
was written off during the year.

Note B: Certain research and developmental costs in 1963 and 1964 relating
to new products that will be marketed beginning in 1965 have been
deferred and will be charged to subsequent revenue.

Note C: The Company is contingently liable on guaranteed notes and accounts
totaling $40,000. Also, various suits are pending on which the ultimate
payment cannot be determined. In the opinion of counsel and management, such liability, if any, will not be material. Retained earnings
have been appropriated in anticipation of possible losses.

Note D: The liability under the Company pension plan has been calculated
on the basis of actuarial studies.

Note E: The Company leased Market Street properties for a fifteen-year
period ending January 1, 1976. Leasehold payment received in advance is being recognized as revenue over the life of the lease.

Note F: Second preferred stock may be redeemed at the option of the board
of directors at $12\frac{1}{2}$ plus accrued dividends on or before December 31,
1966, and at gradually reduced amounts but at not less than $10\frac{1}{2}$
plus accrued dividends after January 1, 1972.

## Special measurements based on stockholders' equity

Reference is frequently made to two measurements that are based on
the stockholders' equity: (1) *book value per share*, as indicated by the balance sheet and (2) *earnings per share*, as indicated by the income statement.
These measurements are of interest to stockholders, present and prospective. The nature of these measurements and the problems involved in
their calculation are described in the remaining pages of this chapter.

## Book value per share

The *book value per share* measurement is the dollar equity in corporate
capital of each share of stock. It is the amount that would be paid on
each share assuming that the company were liquidated and the amount
available to stockholders was exactly the amount reported as the stockholders' equity.[1] The book value measurement is widely used as a factor
in evaluating stock worth. Both single values and comparative values
may be required, the latter to afford data relative to trends and growth
in the stockholders' equity.

When only one class of stock is outstanding, the calculation of book
value is relatively simple; the total stockholders' equity is divided by the

---

[1] It may be observed that financial analysts frequently follow the practice of subtracting
any amounts that are reported for intangibles from the total reported for the stockholders'
equity in calculating share book value.

number of shares of stock outstanding. When stock has been reacquired and a treasury stock balance is reported, this balance should be recognized as a subtraction item in arriving at the stockholders' equity, and the shares represented by the treasury stock should be subtracted from the shares issued in arriving at the shares outstanding. When shares of stock have been subscribed for but are unissued, capital stock subscribed should be included in the total for the stockholders' equity and the shares subscribed should be added to the shares outstanding. To illustrate, assume a stockholders' equity for the Mosich Corporation as shown below.

| | | |
|---|---|---|
| Capital stock, $10 par; 100,000 shares issued, 5,000 shares reacquired and held in treasury (see below).. | | $1,000,000 |
| Capital stock subscribed, 20,000 shares............. | | 200,000 |
| Additional paid-in capital........................ | | 350,000 |
| Retained earnings: | | |
| Appropriated................................ | $200,000 | |
| Unappropriated............................. | 450,000 | 650,000 |
| | | $2,200,000 |
| Less stock reacquired and held in treasury, 5,000 shares, reported at cost................................ | | 75,000 |
| Total stockholders' equity.................................... | | $2,125,000 |

The book value per share of stock is calculated as follows:

$2,125,000 (total capital) ÷ 115,000 (shares issued, 100,000, plus shares subscribed, 20,000, minus treasury shares, 5,000) = $18.48.

When more than one class of stock has been issued, it is necessary to consider the rights of the different classes of stockholders. With preferred and common issues, for example, the prior rights of preferred must first be determined and the portion of the stockholders' equity related to preferred stockholders calculated. The preferred stockholders' equity when subtracted from the total stockholders' equity gives the equity related to the common stockholders. The preferred equity divided by the number of preferred shares gives the book value of a preferred share; the common equity divided by the number of common shares gives the book value of a common share.

The portion of the stockholders' equity related to preferred would be that amount distributable to preferred stockholders in the event of corporate liquidation and calls for consideration of the liquidation value and also the special dividend rights of the preferred issue.

*Liquidation value.* Preferred shares may have a liquidation value equal to par, to par plus a premium, or to a stated dollar amount. Capital equal to this value for the number of preferred shares outstanding should be assigned to preferred. A preferred call price that differs from the amount to be paid to preferred stockholders upon liquidation would not be applicable for book value computations; the call of preferred stock is not obligatory, hence call prices are not relevant in the apportionment of values between preferred and common stockholders.

*Dividend rights.* (1) Preferred stock may have certain rights in retained earnings as a result of special dividend privileges. For example, preferred shares may be entitled to dividends not yet declared for a portion of the current year, assuming liquidation; here, a portion of retained earnings equal to the dividend requirements would be related to preferred shares. (2) Preferred stock may be cumulative with dividends in arrears. When terms of the preferred issue provide that dividends in arrears must be paid upon liquidation regardless of any retained earnings or deficit balance reported on the books, capital equivalent to the dividends in arrears must be assigned to preferred shares even though this impairs or eliminates the equity relating to common stockholders. When preferred stockholders are entitled to dividends in arrears only in the event of accumulated earnings, as much retained earnings as are available but not in excess of such dividend requirements are related to preferred stock. (3) Preferred stock may be participating. When retained earnings is subject to distribution on a participating basis, the portion distributable to preferred stock must be calculated and assigned to this equity.

The computation of book values for preferred and common shares is illustrated in the series of examples that follow. Examples are based upon the stockholders' equity reported by the Maxwell Corporation on December 31, 1964, which follows:

| | |
|---|---:|
| 6% Preferred stock, $50 par, 10,000 shares............. | $ 500,000 |
| Common stock, $10 par, 100,000 shares............... | 1,000,000 |
| Retained earnings................................ | 250,000 |
| Total stockholders' equity......................... | $1,750,000 |

*Example 1.* Assume that preferred dividends have been paid to July 1, 1964. Preferred stock has a liquidation value of $52 and is entitled to current unpaid dividends. Book values on December 31, 1964, are developed as follows:

| | | |
|---|---:|---:|
| Total stockholders' equity......................... | | $1,750,000 |
| Equity identified with preferred: | | |
| Liquidation value, 10,000 shares @ $52.... | $520,000 | |
| Current dividends, 3% of $500,000........ | 15,000 | 535,000 |
| Balance — equity identified with common............. | | $1,215,000 |
| Book values per share: | | |
| Preferred: $ 535,000 ÷ 10,000..................... | | $53.50 |
| Common: $1,215,000 ÷ 100,000................... | | $12.15 |

*Example 2.* Assume that preferred stock has a liquidation value of $52. Preferred is cumulative, with dividends 5 years in arrears that must be paid in the event of liquidation. Book values for common and preferred shares would be developed as follows:

| | | |
|---|---:|---:|
| Total stockholders' equity............................ | | $1,750,000 |
| Equity identified with preferred: | | |
| Liquidation value, 10,000 shares @ $52.... | $520,000 | |
| Dividends in arrears, 30% of $500,000..... | 150,000 | 670,000 |
| Balance — equity identified with common.............. | | $1,080,000 |
| Book values per share: | | |
| Preferred: $ 670,000 ÷ 10,000..................... | | $67.00 |
| Common: $1,080,000 ÷ 100,000.................... | | $10.80 |

*Example 3.* Assume that preferred stock has a liquidation value equal to its par value. Preferred is cumulative with dividends 10 years in arrears that are payable in the event of liquidation even though impairing the invested capital of the common shareholders. Book values for common and preferred shares are developed as follows:

| | | |
|---|---:|---:|
| Total stockholders' equity............................ | | $1,750,000 |
| Equity identified with preferred: | | |
| Liquidation value, 10,000 shares @ $50.... | $500,000 | |
| Dividends in arrears, 60% of $500,000...... | 300,000 | 800,000 |
| Balance — equity identified with common.............. | | $ 950,000 |
| Book values per share: | | |
| Preferred: $800,000 ÷ 10,000..................... | | $80.00 |
| Common:   950,000 ÷ 100,000..................... | | $ 9.50 |

*Example 4.* Assume that preferred stock has a liquidation value equal to its par value. Preferred stock participates ratably with the common stock after the common stock has received the preferred dividend rate. A preferred dividend of $1.50 has been paid for the first half of 1964 but no common dividends have been declared or paid.

The calculation of the portions of the retained earnings relating to the preferred and common issues on December 31, 1964, and the development of per-share book values are shown on the following page.

The nature and the limitations of the share book value measurements must be appreciated in using these data. Share book values are developed from the net asset values as reported on the books. Furthermore, calculations require the assumption of liquidation in the allocation of amounts to the several classes of stock. Book values of assets may vary materially from present fair values or immediate realizable values. Moreover, book values of property items are stated in terms of the "going concern;" the full implications of a "quitting concern" approach would call for many significant changes in the values as reported by the books.

Allocation of retained earnings to preferred and common shares:

|  | | To Preferred | To Common |
|---|---|---|---|
| Balance of retained earnings . . . . . . . . . | | $250,000 | |
| Less balance of current dividend requirements on preferred, 6% of $500,000 for 6 months. . . . . . . . . . . . . . . . . . . . | | 15,000 | $15,000 |
| | | $235,000 | |
| Less current dividend requirements on common, 6% of $1,000,000. . . . . . . . | | 60,000 | $ 60,000 |
| | | $175,000 | |
| Balance of retained earnings, distributable ratably to preferred and common, 11.6667% ($175,000, retained earnings available to both classes ÷ $1,500,000, par value of stock of both classes). Distributable to preferred, 11.6667% of $500,000. . . . . . . . . . . . . | | 58,333 | 58,333 |
| Distributable to common, 11.6667% of $1,000,000 . . . . . . . . . . . . . . . . . . | | $116,667 | 116,667 |
| Totals to common and preferred. . . . . . . . . . . . . . . | | $73,333 | $176,667 |

Calculation of book values:

| | | | |
|---|---|---|---|
| Total stockholders' equity. . . . . . . . . . . . . . . . . . . . . . . . . . . | | | $1,750,000 |
| Equity identified with preferred: | | | |
| Liquidation value, 10,000 shares @ $50 . . . . | | $500,000 | |
| Current dividends and retained earnings in participation with common (see above). . . . | | 73,333 | 573,333 |
| Balance — equity identified with common . . . . | | | $1,176,667 |
| Book values per share: | | | |
| Preferred: $ 573,333 ÷ 10,000. . . . . . . . . . . . . . . . . . . . | | | $57.33 |
| Common: $1,176,667 ÷ 100,000. . . . . . . . . . . . . . . . . . . | | | $11.77 |

### Earnings per share

The *earnings per share* measurement is the amount earned during a given period on each share of the capital stock outstanding. This measurement is frequently used as an index of stock worth. It is also used in judging the dividend policies of the company, the earnings per share being compared with the dividends per share during a period in obtaining the company's *payout percentage* or *payout ratio*.

When only one class of stock is outstanding, the entire net income is identified with these shares; net income, then, divided by the number of shares of stock outstanding gives the earnings per share. When preferred and common shares are outstanding, the claim that preferred shares have on net earnings should be deducted from net income in arriving at the earnings related to common. In the event of a net loss, a *loss per share* figure would be calculated. With cumulative preferred shares outstanding, preferred dividend requirements would be added to a net loss in arriving at the loss per share on common.

To illustrate the calculation of per-share earnings, assume net income of $1,500,000 and a single class of stock outstanding consisting of 1,000,000 shares. Per-share earnings are calculated as follows:

$$\$1,500,000 \div 1,000,000, \text{ or } \$1.50$$

However, assume the same earnings but two classes of stock outstanding as follows: 6% preferred stock, $100 par, 80,000 shares; and common stock, 1,000,000 shares. Preferred is cumulative and nonparticipating. Earnings per share are calculated as follows:

| | |
|---|---:|
| Net income..................................... | $1,500,000 |
| Current dividend requirements on preferred shares, 6% of $8,000,000..................................... | 480,000 |
| Net income identified with common shares............ | $1,020,000 |

Per-share earnings on common: $1,020,000 ÷ 1,000,000, or $1.02

Periodic earnings are frequently related to the number of shares of preferred stock outstanding. For example, in the preceding illustration, the relationship of earnings to preferred shares may be calculated as follows: $1,500,000 (net income) ÷ 80,000 (number of preferred shares) = $18.75. This value is commonly referred to as the "earnings per share on preferred stock." However, the inference to be drawn from this calculation differs from that which is found in the common share calculation. Division of residual earnings by the number of shares of common outstanding offers a measurement of the earnings that actually accrue on each common share; such earnings, if not made available to the common stockholders in dividends, will actually increase their equity in the corporation. Division of the total earnings by the number of shares of preferred outstanding, however, offers no more than the earnings protection that is available in meeting current dividend requirements on the preferred stock. In view of this difference, the AICPA Committee on Accounting Procedure has recommended that use of the term *earnings per share* be limited to earnings applicable to each share of common stock. Although the Committee agreed that it might be helpful to show the number of times or the extent to which the requirements of preferred dividends have been earned, it concluded that the term earnings per share was not applicable under conditions that involved only limited dividend rights for senior securities.[1]

When extraordinary items are reported separately either on the income statement or on the retained earnings statement, two per-share measurements are required: (1) per-share earnings before extraordinary charges and credits for the period, and (2) per-share effects of extraordinary charges and credits recognized during the period.

It should be observed that care must be exercised in using per-share earnings figures. These values are the products of the principles and practices employed in the accounting process and are subject to the same limitations that may be identified with the net income measurement as reported on the income statement.

## QUESTIONS

**1.** (a) What are the sources of retained earnings? (b) What dispositions may be made of retained earnings?

**2.** What circumstances give rise to a *dated retained earnings?*

**3.** Which of the following transactions are a source of capital? Indicate the class of capital in each case.
- (a) Operating profits.
- (b) Cancellation of a part of a liability upon prompt payment of the balance.
- (c) Reduction of par value of stock outstanding.
- (d) Discovery of an understatement of income in a previous period.
- (e) Release of Retained Earnings Appropriated for Purchase of Treasury Stock upon the sale of treasury stock.
- (f) Issue of bonds at a premium.
- (g) Purchase of the corporation's own capital stock at a discount.
- (h) Increase in the company's earning capacity, taken to be evidence of considerable goodwill.
- (i) Construction of equipment for the company's own use at a cost less than the prevailing market price of identical equipment.
- (j) Donation to the corporation of its own stock.
- (k) Sale of plant and equipment at a profit.
- (l) Gain on bond retirement.
- (m) Revaluation of plant and equipment resulting in
  - (1) decrease in allowance for depreciation as a result of overdepreciation in past periods, and
  - (2) increase in asset book value as a result of increase in asset replacement value.

---

[1] *Accounting Research and Terminology Bulletins,* 1961 (New York: American Institute of Certified Public Accountants), *Accounting Research Bulletin No. 49,* p. 34.

(n) Collection of stock assessments from stockholders.
(o) Discovery of valuable resources on company property.
(p) Conversion of bonds into common stock.
(q) Conversion of preferred stock into common stock.

**4.** What circumstances may call for the declaration of a scrip dividend?

**5.** (a) Define stock dividend. (b) What are the effects of a stock dividend on corporate capital accounts as compared with those of a stock split?

**6.** (a) What is a liquidating dividend? (b) Under what circumstances are such distributions made? (c) How would you recommend that liquidating dividends be recorded in the accounts of the corporation?

**7.** The Arden Co. is permitted by the state within which it is incorporated to distribute as dividends the sum of its net profit plus the amount charged against profits for depletion. How do you recommend that dividends be recorded (a) on the books of the corporation and (b) on the books of the stockholder?

**8.** What methods can be followed in reporting dividends in arrears on preferred stock on the balance sheet?

**9.** What objections would you raise for the use of revaluation capital (a) to absorb operating losses, (b) as a basis for cash dividends, and (c) as a basis for stock dividends?

**10.** Describe each of the following: (a) valuation reserve, (b) liability reserve, (c) retained earnings reserve.

**11.** Appropriations limiting the use of retained earnings may arise from (a) legal requirements, (b) contractual requirements, and (c) managerial policy. Give an example of each of the above.

**12.** What is meant by a funded appropriation?

**13.** (a) Describe a general purpose contingency appropriation. (b) How should it be established? (c) Assuming that certain contingencies materialize and that significant losses are incurred, how would you recommend that these be recorded, and what disposition should be made of the appropriation balance?

**14.** Management of the Rossmore Co., considering the possibility of a strike by employees, authorized the establishment of an appropriation for contingencies at the end of 1963 by a charge to revenue. The strike was called in 1964, and company losses incurred to the date of the strike settlement were charged against the appropriation. The company management points out that it exercised good judgment in anticipating strike losses and providing a cushion for such losses. What criticism, if any, can you offer of the accounting procedures followed by the company?

**15.** (a) What is meant by self-insurance? (b) Describe the accounting procedures in considering possible future charges and in recognizing such charges when they occur assuming that (1) self-insurance involves accruable losses and (2) self-insurance involves nonaccruable losses.

**16.** State where each of the following accounts will appear on the balance sheet:

(a) Reserve for Contingencies
(b) Reserve for Doubtful Accounts
(c) Reserve for Possible Inventory Decline
(d) Reserve for Self-Insurance — Fire Loss
(e) Reserve for Bond Retirement
(f) Reserve for Income Taxes
(g) Reserve for Undeclared Dividends
(h) Reserve for Increased Investment in Plant and Equipment
(i) Reserve for Depletion
(j) Reserve for Redeemable Coupons Outstanding
(k) Reserve for Repairs and Replacements

(l) Reserve for Purchase of Treasury Stock
(m) Reserve for Personal Injury Claims Pending
(n) Reserve for Unrealized Plant Appreciation
(o) Reserve for Leasehold Amortization
(p) Reserve for Restoration of Properties upon Termination of Lease
(q) Reserve for Sales Discounts
(r) Reserve for Reduction of Inventory to Market
(s) Reserve for Vacation Pay for Employees

**17.** Define book value per share. What problems arise in the calculation of book value per share when both preferred and common shares are outstanding?

**18.** Define per-share earnings. What problems arise in the calculation of per-share earnings when both preferred and common shares are outstanding?

**19.** How would you recommend that per-share earnings be reported when the income statement reports normally recurring items and also extraordinary items that are material in amount?

**20.** Which of the following transactions change total stockholders' equity? What is the nature of the change?

(a) Declaration of a cash dividend.
(b) Payment of a cash dividend.
(c) Retirement of bonds payable for which both a redemption fund and an appropriation had been established.
(d) Declaration of a stock dividend.
(e) Payment of a stock dividend.
(f) Conversion of bonds payable into preferred stock.
(g) The passing of a dividend on cumulative preferred stock.
(h) Donation by the officers of shares of stock.
(i) Operating loss for the period.

## EXERCISES

**1.** The retained earnings account for the Walker Company shows the following charges and credits. Give entries to correct the account.

## Retained Earnings

| | | | |
|---|---|---|---|
| Correction in profit of prior period................. | 1,500 | Jan. 1 Balance................. | 64,600 |
| Loss from fire............. | 850 | Premium on sale of common stock................... | 18,500 |
| Write-off of goodwill....... | 5,000 | Stock subscription defaults.. | 860 |
| Stock dividend........... | 20,000 | Gain on retirement of pre- | |
| Loss on sale of plant items.. | 12,400 | ferred stock at less than | |
| Officers compensation chargeable to profits of prior periods............ | 40,000 | issuance price........... | 3,600 |
| | | Gain on retirement of bonds at less than book value.... | 1,250 |
| Loss on retirement of pre- ferred shares at more than issuance price ......... .. | 10,200 | Revaluation of buildings: | |
| | | Overdepreciation in past.. | 6,000 |
| | | Increase from appraisal... | 20,000 |
| | | Gain on life insurance policy settlement............. | 2,200 |
| | | Refund of prior year's taxes. | 7,150 |

**2.** The capital accounts for the Burbank Co. on June 30, 1964, follow:

| | |
|---|---|
| Capital stock, $20 par, 100,000 shares................. | $2,000,000 |
| Premium on capital stock........................... | 800,000 |
| Retained earnings................................. | 4,500,000 |

Shares of the company's stock are selling at this time at 36. What entries would you make in each case below:

(a) A stock dividend of 5% is declared and issued.
(b) A stock dividend of 100% is declared and issued.

**3.** As a result of an agreement with bondholders, the Barney Co. is required to appropriate earnings of $200,000 at the end of each calendar year for the years 1959–1963. At the beginning of 1964, upon liquidation of the bonded indebtedness, the retained earnings appropriation is canceled. This is followed by the declaration and the issue of a 50% common stock dividend on 250,000 shares of $10 par common stock outstanding. Retained earnings are charged for the stock dividend at par. What entries are required for (a) periodic appropriations, (b) cancellation of the appropriation in 1964, and (c) capitalization of retained earnings by means of the stock dividend?

**4.** Suits for damages totaling $100,000 are pending against the Swift Co. on December 31, 1964. Counsel for the company advises that losses on such suits, if any, should not be material. However, company management authorizes that provision be made in the accounts for any possible loss up to $100,000. All of the suits are settled in 1965, payments of $14,500 being made. Give entries to record (a) the provision for losses authorized by management in 1964, (b) payments made in 1965, (c) cancellation of the provision for losses in 1965.

**5.** The Weisfield Co. reports appropriated retained earnings on its balance sheet at the end of 1964 at $480,000. Analysis of the account balances in support of this total discloses the following:

Reserve for contingencies — to meet estimated claims arising
    from accidents in 1964 for which the company is liable.... $ 22,500
Reserve for self-insurance — fire loss — to meet possible fire
    losses as a result of self-insurance on this contingency.... 30,000
Reserve for pensions — to meet estimated pension costs
    arising from contracts with employees................. 310,000
Reserve for revaluation of plant properties — arising from
    asset appraisal increases............................ 85,000
Reserve for possible declines on marketable securities — to
    meet possible future losses on marketable securities...... 20,000
Reserve for plant rehabilitation costs — to meet costs of re-
    habilitating plant at termination of lease in accordance
    with contractual requirements........................ 12,500

Which of the above items, if any, would you exclude from appropriated retained earnings? State how you would classify such items.

**6.** The stockholders' equity of Hall, Inc., on December 31, 1964, was:

Common stock, 50,000 shares, $10 par.................. $500,000
6% preferred stock, 5,000 shares, $25 par.............. 125,000
Additional paid-in capital............................ 75,000
Retained earnings.................................... 50,000
                                  $750,000

Calculate the book values per share of preferred stock and common stock under each of the following assumptions:

    (a) Preferred stock is noncumulative and nonparticipating, callable at $30, and preferred as to assets at $27.50 upon corporate liquidation.
    (b) Preferred stock is cumulative, nonparticipating, with dividends in arrears for 6 years; upon corporate liquidation, shares are preferred as to assets up to par, and must be paid any dividends in arrears before distributions may be made to common shares.
    (c) Preferred stock is fully participating with common stock; upon corporate liquidation any distributions beyond stock par values are to be made ratably on preferred and common shares.

**7.** The income statement for the Samson Co. for the year ended December 31, 1964, shows:

Net income before income taxes....................... $310,000
Income taxes applicable to net income................. 75,000

Net income.......................................... $235,000
Add extraordinary gain from sale of Springfield branch store
    (net of income taxes).............................. 205,000

Net income and extraordinary gain.................... $440,000

Calculate per-share earnings for 1964 under each of the following assumptions:

    (a) The company has only one class of stock, the number of shares outstanding totaling 200,000.
    (b) The company has shares outstanding as follows:
        5% cumulative, nonparticipating preferred, $100 par, 10,000 shares; common, $25 par, 200,000 shares.

## PROBLEMS

**17-1.** The balance sheet for the Morgan Corp. on December 31, 1964, reports the following balances:

| | |
|---|---|
| Common stock..................................... | $460,000 |
| Surplus........................................... | 274,000 |
| Stockholders' equity............................... | $734,000 |

The common stock account shows the following debits and credits since the time the company was organized in 1959:

*Credits:*
| | |
|---|---|
| 50,000 shares of common, $10 par................... | $500,000 |

*Debits:*
| | |
|---|---|
| 5,000 shares of common reacquired at 8.............. | 40,000 |
| | $460,000 |

A preferred stock balance was canceled in 1963 when preferred stock was reacquired and formally retired.   The surplus account shows the following credits and debits since date of organization:

*Credits:*
| | |
|---|---|
| Premium on issuance of common..................... | $150,000 |
| Gain on sale of unimproved properties................ | 40,000 |
| Appraisal of land and buildings at the end of 1964: | |
|    Adjustment for depreciation overstatement, 1959–1963. | 8,000 |
|    Increase in asset book value for appreciation......... | 50,000 |
| Net income, 1959–1964............................ | 168,000 |
| | $416,000 |

*Debits:*
| | | |
|---|---|---|
| Loss on bond retirement.................... | $12,000 | |
| Discount on issuance of preferred stock....... | 10,000 | |
| Payment on retirement of preferred stock issue in | | |
|    excess of par value...................... | 5,000 | |
| Fire loss................................. | 25,000 | |
| Cash dividends........................... | 90,000 | 142,000 |
| | | $274,000 |

*Instructions:* (1) Give journal entries to correct the capital accounts. Assume that treasury stock is to be carried at cost and an appropriation of retained earnings is to be reported equal to such cost.

(2) Prepare the stockholders' equity section of the balance sheet reflecting corrections in (1) above.

**17-2.** The stockholders' equity for the M and M Mfg. Co. on December 31, 1963, is shown on page 486.

During 1964, the following transactions affected the stockholders' equity:

Jan.   2   5,000 shares of preferred stock were called in for retirement at $26.50 in accordance with call provisions in the preferred contract.

Stockholders' Equity, December 31, 1963

| | | |
|---|---|---|
| 6% Preferred stock, $25 par, 20,000 shares authorized and issued (each share is callable at $26.50 and is convertible into 3 shares of common) | $500,000 | |
| Less discount on preferred stock | 50,000 | |
| | | $ 450,000 |
| Common stock, $5 par, 100,000 shares issued | $500,000 | |
| Premium on common from sale of stock at 8 | 300,000 | 800,000 |
| Total paid-in capital | | $1,250,000 |
| Retained earnings | | 350,000 |
| Total stockholders' equity | | $1,600,000 |

Mar. 2   5,000 shares of common stock were reacquired at $7.50; treasury stock is reported at cost.

Mar. 30   A 25¢ cash dividend was paid on common stock.

Apr. 20   Common stock reacquired on March 2 was sold at $9.00.

June 30   The semiannual dividend was paid on preferred stock.

July   1   4,000 shares of preferred stock were converted into common stock on a 3-for-1 basis in accordance with the conversion privilege in the preferred contract.

Sept. 30   A 25¢ cash dividend was paid on common stock, together with a 5% stock dividend. Common stock was selling on this date at $9.50, and retained earnings equal to the selling price of the stock issued were transferred to paid-in capital.

Dec. 31   The semiannual dividend was paid on preferred stock and a special dividend of 50¢ was paid on common stock.

Dec. 31   Net income for the year, $215,500, was transferred to retained earnings (debit Profit and Loss).

*Instructions:* (1) Record in journal form the transactions given above.

(2) Prepare the stockholders' equity section of the balance sheet as of December 31, 1964.

**17-3.** A condensed balance sheet for Wellington, Inc., as of December 31, 1961, appears below:

| | | | |
|---|---|---|---|
| Assets | $250,000 | Liabilities | $ 30,000 |
| | | 5% Preferred stock, $100 par | 50,000 |
| | | Common stock, $50 par | 100,000 |
| | | Premium on preferred stock | 5,000 |
| | | Retained earnings | 65,000 |
| | $250,000 | | $250,000 |

Capital stock authorized consists of: 500 shares of 5% cumulative, nonparticipating preferred stock with a prior claim on assets, and 10,000 shares of common stock.

Information relating to operations of the succeeding three years follows:

|                                                                 | 1962 | 1963 | 1964 |
|-----------------------------------------------------------------|------|------|------|
| Dividends declared on Dec. 20, payable on Jan. 10 of following year: | | | |
| Preferred stock............... | 5% cash | 5% cash | 5% cash |
| Common stock............... | { $1.00 cash<br>{ 50% stock* | $1.25 cash | $.50 cash |
| Credit balance in the profit and loss account after recording income tax liability for year...... | $30,000 | $15,000 | $25,000 |

*Retained earnings is reduced by the par value of the stock dividend.

1962: On July 1, land having a book value of $60,000 was appraised at $125,000. The board of directors authorized the recording of the appraisal in the accounts.

1963: On February 12 depreciation allowances were reduced by $36,000 following an income tax investigation. Additional income taxes of $10,000 for prior years were paid. On March 3, 200 shares of common stock were purchased by the corporation at $46 per share; treasury stock is recorded at cost and retained earnings are appropriated equal to such cost.

1964: On February 28, it was discovered that the merchandise inventory at the end of 1963 had been overstated by $4,800. On August 10 all of the treasury stock was resold at $56 per share and the retained earnings appropriation was canceled. By vote of the stockholders on September 12, each share of the common stock was exchanged by the corporation for 3 shares of no-par, each with a stated value of $20.

*Instructions:* (1) Give the journal entries affecting the capital accounts for the 3-year period ended December 31, 1964. Assume that corrections in profits of prior years are recorded directly in Retained Earnings.

(2) Prepare the stockholders' equity section of the balance sheet as it would appear at the end of 1962, 1963, and 1964.

**17-4.** The Bartlett Co. was organized on January 2, 1963, with authorized stock consisting of 10,000 shares of 6%, $100 par, nonparticipating preferred and 75,000 shares of no-par common. During the first two years of the company's existence, the following transactions took place:

1963
Jan.   2   Sold 4,700 shares of common stock at 6.
       2   Sold 3,800 shares of preferred stock at 110.
Mar.   2   Sold common stock as follows:
               3,400 shares at 9.
                 900 shares at 9½.
July  10   A near-by piece of land, appraised at $216,100, was secured for 800 shares of preferred stock and 14,000 shares of common. (Preferred stock was recorded at 110, the balance being assigned to common.)

Dec. 16　The regular preferred and a 50-cent common dividend were declared.
　　28　Dividends declared on December 16 were paid.
　　31　The profit and loss account showed a credit balance of $75,000, which was transferred to retained earnings.

1964
Feb. 27　The corporation reacquired 4,000 shares of common stock at 8. (State law requires that an appropriation of retained earnings be made for the purchase price of treasury stock. Appropriations may be returned to retained earnings upon resale of the stock.)
June 17　Resold 3,000 shares of treasury stock at 9¾.
July 31　Resold all of the remaining treasury stock at 9.
Sept. 30　The corporation sold 4,000 additional shares of common stock at 9¼.
Dec. 16　The regular preferred dividend and a 30-cent common dividend were declared.
　　28　Dividends declared on December 16 were paid.
　　31　The profit and loss account showed a credit balance of $60,000, which was transferred to retained earnings.

*Instructions:* (1) Journalize the foregoing transactions.

(2) Prepare the stockholders' equity section of the balance sheet as of December 31, 1964.

**17-5.** The balance sheet of the Hamner Corporation on December 31, 1963, is shown below:

Hamner Corporation
Balance Sheet
December 31, 1963

| Assets | | Liabilities and Stockholders' Equity | | |
|---|---|---|---|---|
| | | **Liabilities** | | |
| Cash......................... | $ 26,500 | Notes payable....... | $ 20,000 | |
| Notes receivable............... | 30,000 | Accounts payable.... | 15,250 | |
| Accounts receivable (net)........ | 22,000 | Preferred dividends | | |
| Merchandise inventory.......... | 40,000 | payable.......... | 2,500 | |
| Store furniture and fixtures...... | 7,500 | Mortgage payable.... | 50,000 | $ 87,750 |
| Building............. $81,500 | | | | |
| Less allowance for depr. 21,000 | 60,500 | **Stockholders' Equity** | | |
| | | 5% Preferred stock — | | |
| Land....................... | 60,000 | 5,000 shares, $10 par | $ 50,000 | |
| Organization costs............. | 15,000 | Common stock — | | |
| | | 10,000 shares, $10 | | |
| | | stated value....... | 100,000 | |
| | | Additional paid-in | | |
| | | capital*.......... | 14,000 | |
| | | Retained earnings.... | 9,750 | 173,750 |
| | ——— | Total liabilities and | | |
| Total assets.................. | $261,500 | stockholders' equity. | | $261,500 |

*Additional paid-in capital on the balance sheet consists of premium on preferred stock, $4,000, and paid-in capital from sale of common stock in excess of stated value, $10,000.

The following transactions affecting the stockholders' equity were completed in 1964:

Jan. 10  2,000 shares of 5% preferred stock were sold at 13.

     31  The following errors were discovered as of the end of 1963:

          Merchandise inventory was understated by $3,000.

          Depreciation had not been recorded on store furniture and fixtures. These had been purchased on April 1, 1961. Straight-line depreciation at 20% per year should be recognized.

          Building repairs of $2,500 made at the end of the year were improperly capitalized.

Feb.  2  5,000 shares of no-par common stock were sold for cash at 23.

Mar. 31  A semiannual dividend of 25 cents was declared and paid on common stock.

May 16  2,000 shares of no-par common stock were issued to Dwight Call in exchange for his going business. Assets taken over were recorded at the following values: land, $10,000; building, $20,000; merchandise inventory, $8,000; accounts receivable, $5,000. Accounts payable of $5,000 were assumed. Goodwill was recognized on the purchase equal to the difference between the net assets acquired and $42,000, the market value of the shares at the time of issue.

Aug. 15  500 shares of the company's own common stock were reacquired on the market for cash at 17. Stock was recorded at cost.

Sept. 30  A semiannual dividend of 25 cents and an extra dividend of 10 cents were declared and paid on common stock.

Oct.  3  The 500 shares of treasury stock were sold for cash at $20 per share.

Nov. 10  Merchandise, cost $10,000, was destroyed by fire. No insurance had been carried and the loss was charged to retained earnings.

Dec. 21  The 5% annual dividend was declared on preferred stock, payable January 12, 1965. The board of directors authorized an appropriation of retained earnings for plant expansion of $25,000.

     31  The credit balance of the profit and loss account after income taxes was $60,000; this was transferred to retained earnings.

*Instructions:* (1) Record the information above in journal entry form. (The corporation records corrections in profits of prior periods directly in retained earnings.)

(2) Prepare the stockholders' equity section of the balance sheet and statements of paid-in capital and retained earnings for the year ended December 31, 1964.

**17-6.** The stockholders' equity for the General Trucking Co. at the end of 1963 was composed of the following:

| | |
|---|---:|
| 5% Preferred stock, $100 par, 10,000 shares............. | $1,000,000 |
| Common stock, $1 stated value, 1,000,000 shares......... | 1,000,000 |
| Additional paid-in capital on issue of common stock...... | 3,400,000 |
| Retained earnings....................................... | 2,450,000 |
| Total stockholders' equity............................. | $7,850,000 |

Net income for 1964 was $800,000. At the end of 1964 the company issued a 10% stock dividend on common stock that was recorded at $8.25 per share, or $825,000, the market value of the shares at the time of declaration. Activities in 1964 also resulted in the following charges and credits to stockholders' equity accounts:

|  | Dr. | Cr. |
|---|---|---|
| Cash dividends on preferred stock ($5)......... | $ 50,000 | |
| Cash dividends on common stock (60 cents)..... | 600,000 | |
| Write-off of intangibles regarded of no future worth.................................... | 200,000 | |
| Gain on retirement of bonds (net of income tax charge related to gain)..................... | | $ 46,500 |
| Collection of life insurance on officer's life....... | | 200,000 |
| Increase in capital from treasury stock, common, purchased in 1964 and subsequently resold at more than cost............................. | | 12,500 |
| Payment of additional income taxes for 1958–1961 | 107,500 | |
| Uninsured casualties (net of income tax credit related to loss)............................. | 46,000 | |
| Loss on sale of investments (net of income tax credit related to loss)..................... | 21,000 | |
| Appraisal increment — increase in plant site acquired in 1940 to present appraised value... | | 800,000 |
| Retirement of 500 shares of preferred stock at 105. | 52,500 | |

*Instructions:* (1) Assuming that the income statement is prepared in current operating performance form, prepare a statement summarizing changes in retained earnings for 1964, and also a statement summarizing changes in paid-in capital similar to that illustrated on page 469.

(2) Prepare the stockholders' equity section of the balance sheet as of December 31, 1964.

**17-7.** The stockholders' equity for the Rollins Company on December 31, 1964, follows:

| | |
|---|---|
| 5% Preferred stock, $50 par, 20,000 shares............. | $1,000,000 |
| Common stock, $20 par, 100,000 shares................ | 2,000,000 |
| Additional paid-in capital........................... | 25,000 |
| Retained earnings................................... | 195,000 |
| Total stockholders' equity......................... | $3,220,000 |

*Instructions:* Calculate the book values of preferred shares and common shares as of December 31, 1964, under each of the following assumptions:

(1) Preferred dividends have been paid to October 1, 1964; preferred shares have a call value of $55, a liquidation value of $52.50, and are entitled to current unpaid dividends.

(2) Preferred shares have a liquidation value of par; shares are cumulative, with dividends 3 years in arrears and fully payable in the event of liquidation.

(3) Preferred shares have a liquidation value of par; shares are cumulative, with dividends 5 years in arrears and fully payable in the event of liquidation.

(4) Preferred shares have been paid 5% in 1964 but nothing has been paid on common; preferred is entitled to full participation ratably with common after common has been paid the preferred rate.

# Chapter 18

# FINANCIAL STATEMENT ANALYSIS
## USE OF COMPARATIVE DATA

### Statement analysis

The financial statements give vital information concerning the position of the business and the results of its operations. This information is important to the many groups that are interested in the business, including:

1. The owners — sole proprietor, partners, or stockholders.
2. The management.
3. The creditors.
4. Government — local, state, and federal (including regulatory, taxing, and statistical units).
5. Prospective owners and prospective creditors.
6. Stock exchanges, investment bankers, and stock brokers.
7. Trade associations.
8. Employees of the business and their labor unions.
9. The general public (including students and researchers).

Analysis of the data reported on the financial statements is necessary in reaching conclusions regarding the business and its activities. The nature of the analysis depends upon the questions that are raised. For example, inquiry concerning the working capital position of a company is answered by referring to the balance sheet and comparing current assets and current liabilities. Questions concerning a company's earnings growth or the trend of its dollar sales can be answered only by referring to income statements for a number of periods. Questions concerning the relationship of earnings to investment are answered by making use of both income statement and balance sheet data. The process of analysis involves the development of comparisons and the measurement of relationships. The results of analysis form the bases for conclusions that are reached and the policies that are adopted.

Analysis is generally directed toward reaching answers to three broad questions that are raised with respect to a business: (1) its solvency, (2) its stability, and (3) its profitability.

To be solvent, a business must be able to meet its liabilities as they mature. Statements are analyzed to determine whether the business is currently solvent and whether it can retain its solvency if it should experience a period of adversity. Such analysis includes studies of the relationship of current assets to current liabilities, the size and nature of the various creditor and ownership equities, the protection afforded the equity groups through the soundness of asset values, and the amounts and trends of periodic earnings.

Stability is measured by the ability of a business to meet interest and principal payment requirements on outstanding debt and also its ability to pay dividends to its stockholders regularly. In judging stability, data concerning operations and financial position require study. There must be a regular demand for the goods or services that are sold, and the margin on sales must be sufficient to cover operating expenses, interest, and dividends. There should be a satisfactory turnover of current assets and plant and equipment items. All of the business resources should be productively employed.

Profitability is measured by the success of a business in maintaining and increasing the owners' equity. The nature and the amount of earnings as well as their regularity and trend are all significant in this appraisal.

Although attention is normally directed to an evaluation of each of the foregoing factors, analysis must also serve the various groups that have individual questions of special interest. For example, management seeks guides to better controls, to more satisfactory purchasing, selling, and financing policies, and to more efficient utilization of resources. Creditors are interested not only in the position of a business as a going concern, but also in its position if it should be forced to liquidate. Owners may be interested in the ability of a business to obtain capital for growth purposes.

The various groups that are interested in the facts of business have looked to the accountant, not only for general purpose statements concerning financial position and the results of operations, but also for the special analyses of financial data that they may require. They have regarded the accountant as best qualified to develop analytical data in view of his knowledge of the conventions and processes that are applied in developing the statements that form the basis for analysis. It is not uncommon for the accountant to submit, along with the regular financial statements, comprehensive analyses of significant financial information that will assist individuals in reaching intelligent conclusions with respect to the business.

### Preliminary study of financial statements

If analytical data are to be reliable, they must be developed from financial statements that properly exhibit business position and operations.  As a first step, statements that are to be used as a basis for analysis should be carefully reviewed to determine whether they display any shortcomings or discrepancies.  In the course of the examination, the following questions should be asked: Is there full disclosure of all relevant financial data?  Have proper accounting principles and procedures been employed?  Have appropriate and consistent bases for valuation been used?  Are the data properly classified?  When necessary, statements should be corrected so that they report the full financial story in conformance with accepted accounting principles.

### Analytical procedures

Analytical procedures fall into two main categories: (1) comparisons and measurements based upon financial data for two or more periods, and (2) comparisons and measurements based upon the financial data of only the current fiscal period.  The first category includes the preparation of comparative statements, the determination of ratios and trends for data on successive statements, and special analyses of balance sheet and income statement changes.  The second category includes the determination of current balance sheet and profit and loss relationships and special analyses of earnings and earning power.  An adequate review of financial data usually requires both types of analysis.

The analytical procedures that are commonly employed are illustrated in this and the remaining chapters of the text.  Although individual analyses will be presented in statement and tabular forms, such data are frequently reported in graphic form for more effective presentation of significant relationships.  It should be emphasized that the analyses that are illustrated are simply guides to the evaluation of financial data.  Sound conclusions can be reached only through the intelligent use and interpretation of such data.

### Comparative statements

Financial data become more meaningful when they are compared with similar data for a prior period or for a number of prior periods.  Statements prepared in a form that reflects financial data for two or more periods are known as *comparative statements*.  Annual data can be compared with similar data for prior years.  Monthly or quarterly data can be compared with similar data for the previous months or quarters or with similar data for the same months or quarters of previous years.  Accounting authorities have strongly encouraged the preparation of statements in comparative form.  The Committee on Accounting Procedure of the AICPA in recommending that the use of comparative statements be extended, has commented:

The presentation of comparative financial statements in annual and other reports enhances the usefulness of such reports and brings out more clearly the nature and trends of current changes affecting the enterprise. Such presentation emphasizes the fact that statements for a series of periods are far more significant than those for a single period and that the accounts for one period are but an instalment of what is essentially a continuous history.

In any one year it is ordinarily desirable that the balance sheet, the income statement, and the surplus statement be given for one or more preceding years as well as for the current year. Footnotes, explanations, and accountants' qualifications which appeared on the statements for the preceding years should be repeated, or at least referred to, in the comparative statements to the extent that they continue to be of significance. If, because of reclassifications or for other reasons, changes have occurred in the manner of or basis for presenting corresponding items for two or more periods, information should be furnished which will explain the change. This procedure is in conformity with the well recognized principle that any change in practice which affects comparability should be disclosed.[1]

The number of companies submitting statements in comparative form has increased steadily in past years.[2]

## Comparative statements — horizontal analysis

Regardless of its financial strength at a given time, a company must operate successfully if it hopes to continue as a going concern. The income statement measures the effects of operations. These operations may be viewed over a number of periods by preparing the income statement in comparative form. The comparative statement may go beyond a simple listing of comparative values by offering analytical information in the form of dollar changes and percentage changes for the data that are presented. The absolute changes, together with the relative changes, are thus shown. The development of data measuring changes taking place over a number of periods is known as *horizontal analysis*. A comparative income statement for the Marshall Company reporting both dollar and percentage changes for a three-year period is illustrated on the following page.

The detail concerning cost of goods sold, operating expenses, and other revenue and expense items may be provided by expanding the statement or by preparing separate supporting schedules. A schedule reporting comparative cost of goods sold detail is illustrated on the next page.

---

[1]*Accounting Research and Terminology Bulletins,* 1961 (New York: American Institute of Certified Public Accountants), *Accounting Research Bulletin No. 43,* p. 15.

[2]In the AICPA list of 600 survey companies, the number of companies employing the comparative form for their customary certified statements was 540 in 1962 as compared with 256 in 1946. *Accounting Trends and Techniques in Published Annual Reports, Seventeenth Edition,* 1963 (New York: American Institute of Certified Public Accountants), p. 17.

Marshall Company
Condensed Comparative Income Statement
For the Years Ended December 31, 1962, 1963, and 1964

| | 1962 | 1963 | 1964 | Increase (Decrease) | | | |
| --- | --- | --- | --- | --- | --- | --- | --- |
| | | | | 1962–1963 | | 1963–1964 | |
| | | | | Amount | Per Cent | Amount | Per Cent |
| Gross sales | 1,000,000 | 1,750,000 | 1,500,000 | 750,000 | 75% | (250,000) | (14%) |
| Sales returns | 50,000 | 100,000 | 75,000 | 50,000 | 100% | (25,000) | (25%) |
| Net sales | 950,000 | 1,650,000 | 1,425,000 | 700,000 | 74% | (225,000) | (14%) |
| Cost of goods sold | 630,000 | 1,200,000 | 1,000,000 | 570,000 | 90% | (200,000) | (17%) |
| Gross profit on sales | 320,000 | 450,000 | 425,000 | 130,000 | 41% | (25,000) | (6%) |
| Selling expenses | 240,000 | 300,000 | 280,000 | 60,000 | 25% | (20,000) | (7%) |
| General expenses | 100,000 | 110,000 | 100,000 | 10,000 | 10% | (10,000) | (9%) |
| Total operating expenses | 340,000 | 410,000 | 380,000 | 70,000 | 21% | (30,000) | (7%) |
| Net operating income (loss) | (20,000) | 40,000 | 45,000 | 60,000 | —— | 5,000 | 13% |
| Other revenue items | 50,000 | 65,000 | 75,000 | 15,000 | 30% | 10,000 | 15% |
| | 30,000 | 105,000 | 120,000 | 75,000 | 250% | 15,000 | 14% |
| Other expense items | 10,000 | 20,000 | 20,000 | 10,000 | 100% | —— | |
| Net income before income taxes | 20,000 | 85,000 | 100,000 | 65,000 | 325% | 15,000 | 18% |
| Income taxes | 5,000 | 25,000 | 30,000 | 20,000 | 400% | 5,000 | 20% |
| Net income | 15,000 | 60,000 | 70,000 | 45,000 | 300% | 10,000 | 17% |

Marshall Company
Comparative Cost of Goods Sold Schedule
For the Years Ended December 31, 1962, 1963, and 1964

| | 1962 | 1963 | 1964 | Increase (Decrease) | | | |
| --- | --- | --- | --- | --- | --- | --- | --- |
| | | | | 1962–1963 | | 1963–1964 | |
| | | | | Amount | Per Cent | Amount | Per Cent |
| Merchandise inventory, January 1 | 105,000 | 125,000 | 330,000 | 20,000 | 19% | 205,000 | 164% |
| Purchases | 650,000 | 1,405,000 | 895,000 | 755,000 | 116% | (510,000) | (36%) |
| Goods available for sale | 755,000 | 1,530,000 | 1,225,000 | 775,000 | 103% | (305,000) | (20%) |
| Less merchandise inventory, December 31 | 125,000 | 330,000 | 225,000 | 205,000 | 164% | (105,000) | (32%) |
| Cost of goods sold | 630,000 | 1,200,000 | 1,000,000 | 570,000 | 90% | (200,000) | (17%) |

The effects of operations on financial position and the trends in financial position can be presented by means of a comparative balance sheet. Here, too, both dollar changes and percentage changes may be provided to show the absolute as well as the relative changes that have taken place. A comparative balance sheet for the Marshall Company for the three-year period, 1962-1964 inclusive, is illustrated on the following page.

Marshall Company
Condensed Comparative Balance Sheet
December 31, 1962, 1963, 1964

| | 1962 | 1963 | 1964 | Increase (Decrease) | | | |
| | | | | 1962–1963 | | 1963–1964 | |
| | | | | Amount | Per Cent | Amount | Per Cent |
| **Assets** | | | | | | | |
| Current assets............. | 673,500 | 955,500 | 855,000 | 282,000 | 42% | (100,500) | (11%) |
| Investments............... | 250,000 | 400,000 | 500,000 | 150,000 | 60% | 100,000 | 25% |
| Plant and equipment (net)... | 675,000 | 875,000 | 775,000 | 200,000 | 30% | (100,000) | (11%) |
| Intangibles................ | 100,000 | 100,000 | 100,000 | —— | — | —— | — |
| Other assets............... | 61,500 | 60,500 | 48,000 | (1,000) | (2%) | (12,500) | (21%) |
| Total assets................ | 1,760,000 | 2,391,000 | 2,278,000 | 631,000 | 36% | (113,000) | (5%) |
| **Liabilities** | | | | | | | |
| Current liabilities.......... | 130,000 | 546,000 | 410,000 | 416,000 | 320% | (136,000) | (25%) |
| Long-term liabilities – 4½% bonds................. | 300,000 | 400,000 | 400,000 | 100,000 | 33% | —— | — |
| Total liabilities............ | 430,000 | 946,000 | 810,000 | 516,000 | 120% | (136,000) | (14%) |
| **Stockholders' Equity** | | | | | | | |
| 6% Preferred stock......... | 250,000 | 350,000 | 350,000 | 100,000 | 40% | —— | — |
| Common stock............. | 750,000 | 750,000 | 750,000 | —— | — | —— | — |
| Additional paid-in capital.... | 100,000 | 100,000 | 100,000 | —— | — | —— | — |
| Retained earnings.......... | 230,000 | 245,000 | 268,000 | 15,000 | 7% | 23,000 | 9% |
| Total stockholders' equity.... | 1,330,000 | 1,445,000 | 1,468,000 | 115,000 | 9% | 23,000 | 2% |
| Total liabilities and stockholders' equity........... | 1,760,000 | 2,391,000 | 2,278,000 | 631,000 | 36% | (113,000) | (5%) |

Detail for the various asset, liability, and stockholders' equity categories may be provided by expanding the statement or by preparing separate supporting schedules as in the case of the income statement. A schedule reporting comparative current asset detail is given below.

Marshall Company
Comparative Current Assets Schedule
December 31, 1962, 1963, 1964

| | 1962 | 1963 | 1964 | Increase (Decrease) | | | |
| | | | | 1962–1963 | | 1963–1964 | |
| | | | | Amount | Per Cent | Amount | Per Cent |
| Cash..................... | 115,000 | 100,500 | 60,000 | (14,500) | (13%) | (40,500) | (40%) |
| Marketable securities........ | 100,000 | 150,000 | 150,000 | 50,000 | 50% | —— | — |
| Notes receivable........... | 10,000 | 40,000 | 50,000 | 30,000 | 300% | 10,000 | 25% |
| Accounts receivable........ | 328,500 | 350,000 | 380,000 | 21,500 | 7% | 30,000 | 9% |
| Total receivables......... | 338,500 | 390,000 | 430,000 | 51,500 | 15% | 40,000 | 10% |
| Less allowance for bad debts | 5,000 | 15,000 | 10,000 | 10,000 | 200% | (5,000) | (33%) |
| Net receivables.......... | 333,500 | 375,000 | 420,000 | 41,500 | 12% | 45,000 | 12% |
| Merchandise inventory....... | 125,000 | 330,000 | 225,000 | 205,000 | 164% | (105,000) | (32%) |
| Total current assets......... | 673,500 | 955,500 | 855,000 | 282,000 | 42% | (100,500) | (11%) |

Changes in retained earnings over a number of periods may be viewed by means of a comparative retained earnings statement. A comparative retained earnings statement for the Marshall Company appears as follows:

Marshall Company
Comparative Retained Earnings Statement
For the Years Ended December 31, 1962, 1963, 1964

|  | 1962 | 1963 | 1964 | Increase (Decrease) | | | |
|---|---|---|---|---|---|---|---|
|  |  |  |  | 1962–1963 | | 1963–1964 | |
|  |  |  |  | Amount | Per Cent | Amount | Per Cent |
| Retained earnings, Jan. 1.... | 240,000 | 230,000 | 245,000 | (10,000) | (4%) | 15,000 | 7% |
| Net income per income statement............... | 15,000 | 60,000 | 70,000 | 45,000 | 300% | 10,000 | 17% |
| Total.................... | 255,000 | 290,000 | 315,000 | 35,000 | 14% | 25,000 | 9% |
| Dividends: |  |  |  |  |  |  |  |
| Preferred stock............ | 15,000 | 21,000 | 21,000 | 6,000 | 40% | —— | — |
| Common stock........... | 10,000 | 24,000 | 26,000 | 14,000 | 140% | 2,000 | 8% |
| Total................... | 25,000 | 45,000 | 47,000 | 20,000 | 80% | 2,000 | 4% |
| Retained earnings, Dec. 31... | 230,000 | 245,000 | 268,000 | 15,000 | 7% | 23,000 | 9% |

Information concerning percentage changes on the comparative statements serves to point out certain relationships that require further investigation and possible action. For example, the comparative schedule of current assets shows an increase in notes receivable for 1963 of $30,000. The indication that this is a 300% increase serves to emphasize the significance of the change. Investigation may disclose that collections on account are slow and that customers are postponing payments by the issuance of notes. The comparative income statement reports an increase in sales returns for 1963 of $50,000. This information becomes more meaningful when gross sales are shown to have increased by 75% for the year while sales returns have increased by 100%. Investigation of the causes for the disproportionate increase appears warranted. The income statement also shows that in 1963 net sales went up 74% while cost of goods sold went up 90%; in 1964 net sales went down 14% while cost of goods sold went down 17%. These data suggest that wholesale price changes are not promptly reflected in the company's sales prices, and further study of the cost-price relationship appears warranted. When absolute amounts or relative amounts appear out of line, conclusions, favorable or unfavorable, are not justified until investigation has disclosed all of the reasons for the changes.

Percentage changes in the previous examples have been given in terms of the data for the year immediately preceding. With data covering more than two years, this procedure results in a changing base that makes the comparison of relative changes over the years difficult. When comparative data for more than two years are to be provided, it is generally desirable to develop all comparisons in terms of a base year. This may be the earliest year given, or some other year that is considered particularly appropriate. Each amount on the statement representing the base year is considered to be 100%. Each amount on all other statements is expressed as a percentage of the base-year amount. The set of percentages for several years may thus be interpreted as trend values or as a series of index numbers relating to the particular item. Assuming that the Marshall Company recognizes 1962 as the base year, comparative income statement data may be presented in the following manner:

Marshall Company
Condensed Comparative Income Statement
For the Years Ended December 31, 1962, 1963, and 1964

| | 1962 | 1963 | 1964 | Increase | (Decrease) | | |
|---|---|---|---|---|---|---|---|
| | | | | 1962–1963 | | 1962–1964 | |
| | | | | Amount | Per Cent | Amount | Per Cent |
| Gross sales............... | 1,000,000 | 1,750,000 | 1,500,000 | 750,000 | 75% | 500,000 | 50% |
| Sales returns.............. | 50,000 | 100,000 | 75,000 | 50,000 | 100% | 25,000 | 50% |
| Net sales.................. | 950,000 | 1,650,000 | 1,425,000 | 700,000 | 74% | 475,000 | 50% |
| Cost of goods sold.......... | 630,000 | 1,200,000 | 1,000,000 | 570,000 | 90% | 370,000 | 59% |
| Gross profit on sales........ | 320,000 | 450,000 | 425,000 | 130,000 | 41% | 105,000 | 33% |
| Selling expenses............ | 240,000 | 300,000 | 280,000 | 60,000 | 25% | 40,000 | 17% |
| General expenses........... | 100,000 | 110,000 | 100,000 | 10,000 | 10% | —— | — |
| Total operating expenses..... | 340,000 | 410,000 | 380,000 | 70,000 | 21% | 40,000 | 12% |
| Net operating income (loss)... | (20,000) | 40,000 | 45,000 | 60,000 | —— | 65,000 | —— |
| Other revenue items........ | 50,000 | 65,000 | 75,000 | 15,000 | 30% | 25,000 | 50% |
| | 30,000 | 105,000 | 120,000 | 75,000 | 250% | 90,000 | 300% |
| Other expense items........ | 10,000 | 20,000 | 20,000 | 10,000 | 100% | 10,000 | 100% |
| Net income before income taxes | 20,000 | 85,000 | 100,000 | 65,000 | 325% | 80,000 | 400% |
| Income taxes.............. | 5,000 | 25,000 | 30,000 | 20,000 | 400% | 25,000 | 500% |
| Net income................ | 15,000 | 60,000 | 70,000 | 45,000 | 300% | 55,000 | 367% |

When relationships for a certain base period can be considered "normal," a statement such as the one above serves as a clearer medium for interpretation than those previously illustrated. For example, the comparative income statement on page 775 shows that gross sales increased 75%, then dropped 14%; sales returns increased 100%, then decreased 25%. Analyses were based on data for the year immediately preceding. The illustration on page 498 shows that gross sales increased 75% and 50% in terms of 1962 amounts. It also shows that sales returns increased 100% and 50% as compared with 1962 amounts. It is thus shown that, while sales returns increased disproportionately as compared with sales in 1963, the increase was proportionate in 1964, both sales and sales returns increasing 50% in terms of 1962 data.

Analysis in terms of a base year is desirable, not only for the comparison of entire statements, but also for the comparison of various related single items, ratios, and other pertinent data. Data expressed in terms of a base year are well adapted for graphic presentation.

Data expressed in terms of a base year are frequently useful for comparisons with series summarizing similar data that are provided by business or industry sources or by governmental agencies. When the series that is to be used for making comparisons does not employ the same base period, it will have to be restated. Such restatement calls for the expression of each value in the series as a percentage of the value for the period that is recognized as the base year.

To illustrate, assume that net sales data for the Marshall Company for 1962-1964 are to be compared with a sales index for its particular industry. The industry sales indexes are as follows:

|  | 1962 | 1963 | 1964 |
|---|---|---|---|
| (1955 − 1957 = 100)................. | 124 | 157 | 146 |

Recognizing 1962 as the base year, industry sales and net sales for the Marshall Company may be expressed in comparative form as follows:

|  | 1962 | 1963 | 1964 |
|---|---|---|---|
| Industry sales index..................... | 100 | 127 | 118 |
| Marshall Company sales index........... | 100 | 174 | 150 |

Instead of comparisons of financial data in terms of a base year, comparisons can be made in terms of data averages for a period of years. Averages are first computed. Deviations from the averages for the individual years are then developed and presented in both absolute amounts and percentages. Such presentations may be particularly useful in defining trends and pointing out significant deviations from such trends.

Changes in the preceding examples were expressed in the form of percentages. Changes can be expressed in the form of ratios instead of percentages. A 50% increase in an item results in the designation of a ratio to the base figure of 1.50; a 25% decrease in an item results in a ratio to the base figure of .75. Plus and minus designations are thus avoided. Use of ratios instead of percentages is illustrated in the statement that follows:

Marshall Company
Condensed Comparative Income Statement
For the Years Ended December 31, 1962, 1963, and 1964

| | 1962 | 1963 | 1964 | Increase (Decrease) | | | |
| | | | | 1962–1963 | | 1962–1964 | |
| | | | | Amount | Ratio | Amount | Ratio |
|---|---|---|---|---|---|---|---|
| Gross sales................ | 1,000,000 | 1,750,000 | 1,500,000 | 750,000 | 1.75 | 500,000 | 1.50 |
| Sales returns.............. | 50,000 | 100,000 | 75,000 | 50,000 | 2.00 | 25,000 | 1.50 |
| Net sales.................. | 950,000 | 1,650,000 | 1,425,000 | 700,000 | 1.74 | 475,000 | 1.50 |
| Cost of goods sold.......... | 630,000 | 1,200,000 | 1,000,000 | 570,000 | 1.90 | 370,000 | 1.59 |
| Gross profit on sales........ | 320,000 | 450,000 | 425,000 | 130,000 | 1.41 | 105,000 | 1.33 |
| Selling expenses............ | 240,000 | 300,000 | 280,000 | 60,000 | 1.25 | 40,000 | 1.17 |
| General expenses........... | 100,000 | 110,000 | 100,000 | 10,000 | 1.10 | ——— | 1.00 |
| Total operating expenses..... | 340,000 | 410,000 | 380,000 | 70,000 | 1.21 | 40,000 | 1.12 |
| Net operating income (loss)... | (20,000) | 40,000 | 45,000 | 60,000 | ——— | 65,000 | ——— |
| Other revenue items........ | 50,000 | 65,000 | 75,000 | 15,000 | 1.30 | 25,000 | 1.50 |
| | 30,000 | 105,000 | 120,000 | 75,000 | 3.50 | 90,000 | 4.00 |
| Other expense items........ | 10,000 | 20,000 | 20,000 | 10,000 | 2.00 | 10,000 | 2.00 |
| Net income before income taxes | 20,000 | 85,000 | 100,000 | 65,000 | 4.25 | 80,000 | 5 00 |
| Income taxes.............. | 5,000 | 25,000 | 30,000 | 20,000 | 5.00 | 25,000 | 6.00 |
| Net income................ | 15,000 | 60,000 | 70,000 | 45,000 | 4.00 | 55,000 | 4.67 |

When a base figure is zero or is a minus value, it is possible to report a dollar change but the change cannot be expressed as a percentage. When a base figure is a positive value, however, a dollar change and also a percentage change can be stated. When ratio analysis is employed, ratios can be provided only when two positive values are given. The foregoing practices are illustrated in the examples below:

| Net Income (Loss) for Year Ended December 31 | | Increase (Decrease) | | |
| 1963 | 1964 | Amount | Per Cent | Ratio |
|---|---|---|---|---|
| $ 0 | $20,000 | $20,000 | ——— | ——— |
| 0 | ( 2,000) | ( 2,000) | ——— | ——— |
| ( 5,000) | 2,000 | 7,000 | ——— | ——— |
| ( 5,000) | ( 10,000) | ( 5,000) | ——— | ——— |
| 10,000 | 0 | ( 10,000) | (100%) | ——— |
| 10,000 | ( 2,000) | ( 12,000) | (120%) | ——— |
| 10,000 | 35,000 | 25,000 | 250% | 3.50 |
| 10,000 | 8,000 | ( 2,000) | ( 20%) | .80 |
| 10,000 | 10,000 | ——— | ——— | 1.00 |

Although comparisons in previous examples have been limited to annual data, it is frequently desirable to develop comparisons for shorter periods. It would be possible, for example, to prepare comparative statements for monthly or quarterly periods. Furthermore, in the case of profit and loss data, it may be desirable to compare a current month with the same month of preceding years, or cumulative data for the current year to date with cumulative data for the corresponding period of preceding years.

A number of companies have adopted the thirteen-month year, dividing the calendar year into thirteen equal periods of four weeks. Variations for the total number of days and number of Saturdays and Sundays found in the calendar months are thus eliminated in the development of comparative "monthly" statements. More reliable conclusions can be drawn from analyses developed from data for periods of comparable length.

### Comparative statements — vertical analysis

Comparative data may include analyses in terms of percentages or ratios based upon the related data of each individual period. For example, in presenting comparative operating data, it may be desirable to show the relationship in each period of cost of goods sold, operating expenses, other revenue and expense items, and income taxes to sales. This procedure is known as *vertical analysis*. Vertical analysis as applied to the comparative profit and loss data for the Marshall Company is illustrated on page 502. The net sales figure for each year is used as the base figure for that year and is expressed as 100%. If analysis were to be made by means of ratios, net sales would be expressed as 1.00 and revenue and expense items would be reported in terms of this base.

Although it may be impossible to specify a normal gross profit rate for the Marshall Company, it can be determined from the statement that a severe decline in the gross profit percentage took place in 1963 with a partial recovery in 1964. This would suggest that an analysis be made of the causes for the increase in the cost of goods sold percentage. Notwithstanding the reduction in the gross profit rate, the net income percentage on each dollar of sales increased in 1963 and again in 1964. This resulted from a reduction in the expense percentage per dollar of sales that more than compensated for the increase in the cost of goods sold percentage. The comparative statement points to certain relationships and trends that require further investigation in arriving at an explanation and an evaluation of the changes.

When supporting schedules are prepared for the detail relating to totals on the condensed income statement, individual items may be expressed in terms of net sales or in terms of the totals reported on the individual schedules. Sales salaries for the Marshall Company for 1964, for

Marshall Company
Condensed Comparative Income Statement
For the Years Ended December 31, 1962, 1963, and 1964

| | 1962 | | 1963 | | 1964 | |
|---|---|---|---|---|---|---|
| | Amount | Per Cent | Amount | Per Cent | Amount | Per Cent |
| Gross sales.................. | 1,000,000 | 105.3% | 1,750,000 | 106.1% | 1,500,000 | 105.3% |
| Sales returns................ | 50,000 | 5.3 | 100,000 | 6.1 | 75,000 | 5.3 |
| Net sales.................... | 950,000 | 100.0% | 1,650,000 | 100.0% | 1,425,000 | 100.0% |
| Cost of goods sold............ | 630,000 | 66.3 | 1,200,000 | 72.7 | 1,000,000 | 70.2 |
| Gross profit on sales........... | 320,000 | 33.7% | 450,000 | 27.3% | 425,000 | 29.8% |
| Selling expenses.............. | 240,000 | 25.3% | 300,000 | 18.2% | 280,000 | 19.7% |
| General expenses.............. | 100,000 | 10.5 | 110,000 | 6.7 | 100,000 | 7.0 |
| Total operating expenses........ | 340,000 | 35.8% | 410,000 | 24.9% | 380,000 | 26.7% |
| Net operating income (loss)...... | (20,000) | (2.1%) | 40,000 | 2.4% | 45,000 | 3.1% |
| Other revenue items........... | 50,000 | 5.3 | 65,000 | 3.9 | 75,000 | 5.3 |
| | 30,000 | 3.2% | 105,000 | 6.3% | 120,000 | 8.4% |
| Other expense items........... | 10,000 | 1.1 | 20,000 | 1.2 | 20,000 | 1.4 |
| Net income before income taxes.. | 20,000 | 2.1% | 85,000 | 5.1% | 100,000 | 7.0% |
| Income taxes................. | 5,000 | .5 | 25,000 | 1.5 | 30,000 | 2.1 |
| Net income.................. | 15,000 | 1.6% | 60,000 | 3.6% | 70,000 | 4.9% |

example, may be reported as a certain percentage of net sales of $1,425,000, with the selling expense schedule listing expenses adding up to 19.7%; or the salaries may be reported as a percentage of total selling expenses of $280,000, with the individual items on the schedule adding up to 100%.

Vertical analysis may be employed in presenting comparative balance sheets and retained earnings statements. On the balance sheet related items are expressed in percentages or ratios based upon the total assets or the total liabilities and stockholders' equity. A comparative balance sheet with percentage analysis for the Marshall Company is given on page 503.

When a supporting schedule is prepared to show the detail for a group total, individual items may be expressed as a percentage of the balance sheet base figure or as a percentage of the group total.

In preparing a comparative retained earnings statement, either the beginning or the ending retained earnings balance may be chosen as the base for analysis. Use of the beginning retained earnings balance as a base is illustrated on the following page.

Both horizontal and vertical analyses are required if business trends and financial and operating relationships are to be fully understood.

Marshall Company
Condensed Comparative Balance Sheet
December 31, 1962, 1963, 1964

| | 1962 | | 1963 | | 1964 | |
|---|---|---|---|---|---|---|
| | Amount | Per Cent | Amount | Per Cent | Amount | Per Cent |
| **Assets** | | | | | | |
| Current assets................ | 673,500 | 38% | 955,500 | 40% | 855,000 | 38% |
| Investments.................. | 250,000 | 14 | 400,000 | 17 | 500,000 | 22 |
| Plant and equipment (net)...... | 675,000 | 38 | 875,000 | 37 | 775,000 | 34 |
| Intangibles................... | 100,000 | 6 | 100,000 | 4 | 100,000 | 4 |
| Other assets.................. | 61,500 | 4 | 60,500 | 2 | 48,000 | 2 |
| Total assets.................. | 1,760,000 | 100% | 2,391,000 | 100% | 2,278,000 | 100% |
| **Liabilities** | | | | | | |
| Current liabilities............. | 130,000 | 7% | 546,000 | 23% | 410,000 | 18% |
| Long-term liabilities–4½ % bonds | 300,000 | 17 | 400,000 | 17 | 400,000 | 18 |
| Total liabilities............... | 430,000 | 24% | 946,000 | 40% | 810,000 | 36% |
| **Stockholders' Equity** | | | | | | |
| 6% Preferred stock............ | 250,000 | 14% | 350,000 | 15% | 350,000 | 15% |
| Common stock................ | 750,000 | 43 | 750,000 | 31 | 750,000 | 33 |
| Additional paid-in capital...... | 100,000 | 6 | 100,000 | 4 | 100,000 | 4 |
| Retained earnings ............ | 230,000 | 13 | 245,000 | 10 | 268,000 | 12 |
| Total stockholders' equity....... | 1,330,000 | 76% | 1,445,000 | 60% | 1,468,000 | 64% |
| Total liabilities and stockholders' equity..................... | 1,760,000 | 100% | 2,391,000 | 100% | 2,278,000 | 100% |

Marshall Company
Comparative Retained Earnings Statement
For the Years Ended December 31, 1962, 1963, and 1964

| | 1962 | | 1963 | | 1964 | |
|---|---|---|---|---|---|---|
| | Amount | Per Cent | Amount | Per Cent | Amount | Per Cent |
| Retained earnings, January 1.... | 240,000 | 100% | 230,000 | 100% | 245,000 | 100% |
| Net income per income statement. | 15,000 | 6 | 60,000 | 26 | 70,000 | 29 |
| Total....................... | 255,000 | 106% | 290,000 | 126% | 315,000 | 129% |
| Dividends: | | | | | | |
| Preferred stock.............. | 15,000 | 6% | 21,000 | 9% | 21,000 | 9% |
| Common stock.............. | 10,000 | 4 | 24,000 | 10 | 26,000 | 11 |
| Total...................... | 25,000 | 10% | 45,000 | 19% | 47,000 | 20% |
| Retained earnings, December 31. | 230,000 | 96% | 245,000 | 107% | 268,000 | 109% |

## Common-size statements

Comparative statements that give the vertical percentages or ratios for financial data without giving dollar values are known as *common-size statements*. Common-size statements may be prepared for the same business as of different dates or periods or for two or more business units as of the same date or for the same period.

A common-size income statement for the Marshall Company is given at the top of the next page. The statement is prepared simply by reporting the percentage figures that were shown on the comparative income statement on page 502. A common-size statement comparing balance sheet data for the Marshall Company with that of the Norris Company is given at the bottom of the next page. This statement provides a comparison of the relationships of balance sheet items for the two companies. It is readily seen, for example, that the relationship of the stockholders' equity to total assets is approximately the same for each company. Although the percentage of current liabilities to total assets for the Norris Company is somewhat higher than that for the Marshall Company, the ratio of current assets to current liabilities for the Norris Company exceeds significantly that of the Marshall Company. It would thus appear that the Norris Company has the stronger working capital position. Further inquiry, however, is necessary. Reference to the items composing working capital may show that Norris Company current assets consist primarily of slow-moving inventories, whereas Marshall Company current assets consist primarily of cash and marketable securities, and inventories are only a small part of the total. It may be further disclosed that while the inventories of both companies are reported on the last-in, first-out basis, this method was adopted by the Marshall Company some time prior to its adoption by the Norris Company and, as a result, inventories of the Marshall Company reflect costs that are significantly lower than those of the Norris Company.

In preparing common-size statements for two companies, one should be certain that the financial data for each company were originally developed in terms of comparable accounting methods, classification procedures, and valuation bases. Comparisons should be limited to companies that are engaged in similar activities. When financial policies of the two companies are different, such differences should be recognized in evaluating comparative reports. For example, one company may lease its plant and equipment while the other may purchase such properties; one company may resort to financing by means of long-term borrowing while the other may rely primarily on funds supplied by stockholders and by earnings. Operating results for the two companies under these circumstances cannot be wholly comparable.

### Statement accounting for variation in net income

As previously illustrated, the comparative income statement shows comparative balances, changes in individual profit and loss items, and also changes in the net income. Comparative income statement data may be used in the preparation of a statement accounting for the varia-

Marshall Company
Condensed Common-Size Income Statement
For the Years Ended December 31, 1962, 1963, and 1964

|  | 1962 | 1963 | 1964 |
|---|---|---|---|
| Gross sales............................... | 105.3% | 106.1% | 105.3% |
| Sales returns.............................. | 5.3 | 6.1 | 5.3 |
| Net sales................................. | 100.0% | 100.0% | 100.0% |
| Cost of goods sold......................... | 66.3 | 72.7 | 70.2 |
| Gross profit on sales...................... | 33.7% | 27.3% | 29.8% |
| Selling expenses.......................... | 25.3% | 18.2% | 19.7% |
| General expenses.......................... | 10.5 | 6.7 | 7.0 |
| Total operating expenses................... | 35.8% | 24.9% | 26.7% |
| Net operating income (loss)............... | (2.1%) | 2.4% | 3.1% |
| Other revenue items....................... | 5.3 | 3.9 | 5.3 |
|  | 3.2% | 6.3% | 8.4% |
| Other expense items...................... | 1.1 | 1.2 | 1.4 |
| Net income before income taxes............. | 2.1% | 5.1% | 7.0% |
| Income taxes............................. | 0.5 | 1.5 | 2.1 |
| Net income.............................. | 1.6% | 3.6% | 4.9% |

Marshall Company and Norris Company
Condensed Common-Size Balance Sheet
December 31, 1964

|  | Marshall Company | Norris Company |
|---|---|---|
| **Assets** | | |
| Current assets............................... | 38% | 64% |
| Investments................................ | 22 | — |
| Plant and equipment (net)................... | 34 | 35 |
| Intangibles................................ | 4 | — |
| Other assets................................ | 2 | 1 |
| Total assets................................ | 100% | 100% |
| **Liabilities** | | |
| Current liabilities........................... | 18% | 20% |
| Long-term liabilities......................... | 18 | 12 |
| Deferred revenues........................... | — | 2 |
| Total liabilities............................. | 36% | 34% |
| **Stockholders' Equity** | | |
| Preferred stock............................. | 15% | — |
| Common stock............................. | 33 | 46% |
| Additional paid-in capital.................... | 4 | 5 |
| Retained earnings........................... | 12 | 15 |
| Total stockholders' equity.................... | 64% | 66% |
| Total liabilities and stockholders' equity......... | 100% | 100% |

tion in net income. Here comparative data are assembled and presented in a manner that calls attention to the various constituent factors that were responsible for the change in net income. A statement accounting for the increase in the net income for the Marshall Company for 1964 over 1963 may be prepared from comparative operating data as follows:

Marshall Company
Statement Accounting for Variation in Net Income
1964 as Compared with 1963

| | | | | | |
|---|---|---|---|---|---|
| Net income for year ended December 31, 1963 | | | | | $60,000 |
| Net income was increased as a result of: | | | | | |
| Decrease in selling expenses | | | | | |
| 1963.................................. | | $300,000 | | | |
| 1964.................................. | | 280,000 | $20,000 | | |
| Decrease in general expenses | | | | | |
| 1963.................................. | | $110,000 | | | |
| 1964.................................. | | 100,000 | 10,000 | | |
| Increase in other revenue items | | | | | |
| 1964.................................. | | $ 75,000 | | | |
| 1963.................................. | | 65,000 | 10,000 | $40,000 | |
| Net income was decreased as a result of: | | | | | |
| Decrease in gross profit on sales: | | | | | |
| Decrease in net sales | | | | | |
| 1963.................................. | $1,650,000 | | | | |
| 1964.................................. | 1,425,000 | $225,000 | | | |
| Less decrease in cost of goods sold | | | | | |
| 1963.................................. | $1,200,000 | | | | |
| 1964.................................. | 1,000,000 | 200,000 | $25,000 | | |
| Increase in income taxes | | | | | |
| 1964.................................. | | $ 30,000 | | | |
| 1963.................................. | | 25,000 | 5,000 | 30,000 | 10,000 |
| Net income for year ended December 31, 1964 | | | | | $70,000 |

The statement shows that although reductions in net income resulted from a decrease in the gross profit on sales and an increase in income taxes, these were more than offset by a decrease in operating expenses and an increase in other revenue. It would appear, then, that increased operating efficiency was a significant factor in increasing net income.

It may be desirable to go further and analyze the change in the reported gross profit to determine the portion arising from a change in sales volume and the portion arising from a change in the sales price-cost of goods sold relationship or the gross profit rate. To illustrate the analytical procedures involved, assume that sales prices of the Marshall Company in 1964 are 10% above those in 1963. A schedule summarizing the change in gross profit can be prepared as follows:

Marshall Company
Schedule of Analysis of Variation in Gross Profit
To Accompany Statement Accounting for Variation in Net Income
1964 as Compared with 1963

| | | | |
|---|---|---|---|
| The decrease in gross profit was caused by: | | | |
| Decrease in volume of sales: | | | |
| Actual net sales, 1963......... | $1,650,000 | | |
| Net sales, 1964, at 1963 prices ($1,425,000 ÷ 1.10)........ | 1,295,455 | | |
| Volume decrease at 1963 prices....... | $ 354,545 | | |
| Gross profit rate, 1963, applied to volume decrease | | | |
| ($\frac{450,000}{1,650,000}$ × $354,545) equals decrease in gross profit | | | |
| resulting from decreased sales volume....... | | | $96,694 |
| Increase in gross profit rate: | | | |
| Increased sales price: | | | |
| Actual net sales, 1964....... | $1,425,000 | | |
| Net sales, 1964, at 1963 prices....... | 1,295,455 | $ 129,545 | |
| Less increase in cost of goods sold: | | | |
| Actual cost of goods sold, 1964....... | $1,000,000 | | |
| Cost of goods sold, 1964, on basis of 1963 cost percentage | | | |
| ($\frac{1,200,000}{1,650,000}$ × $1,295,455)....... | 942,149 | 57,851 | 71,694 |
| Decrease in gross profit....... | | | $25,000 |

The foregoing schedule shows that, while net sales decreased from $1,650,000 to $1,425,000, a decrease in sales volume of $354,545 actually took place in terms of 1963 sales prices. This would have resulted in a decrease in the gross profit of $96,694, were it not for sales price increases of $129,545 accompanied by cost increases of only $57,851 in terms of 1963 sales prices and costs. Increased sales prices, then, offer the explanation for the minor change in gross profit despite a relatively significant decrease in sales volume.

With this information, further inquiry into the relationships of volume, sales prices, and costs may be suggested. Attention may be directed to such matters as: the position of the company in the sales market; competitor's pricing policies; the level of operations that will provide lowest costs; and the possibility of a further decline in sales volume in the event of future price increases.

## Break-even point analysis

Financial statements are frequently analyzed to arrive at the level of sales that will cover all of the costs, referred to as the business unit's *break-even point*. At the break-even point the business would neither incur a loss nor make a profit.

Measurement of a company's break-even point requires a determination of its *variable costs*, those costs that fluctuate with the volume of sales, and its *fixed costs*, those costs that remain constant regardless of the volume of sales. In a retail business, variable costs include cost of goods sold, sales commissions, shipping supplies, and similar items that are affected by the volume of sales; fixed costs include store depreciation, property taxes, administrative salaries, and similar items that are not affected by the volume of sales. In a manufacturing business, variable costs include raw materials and direct labor; fixed costs include depreciation of factory properties, superintendents' salaries, and similar items that are not affected by production volume. Selling and administrative items that fluctuate with sales would be regarded as variable; selling and administrative items that are not affected by sales would be recognized as fixed. Since income taxes apply only after the break-even point is reached, this charge would not be included for purposes of break-even point analysis. In disregarding income taxes, any profit or loss that may be designated in relationship to the break-even point would be before adjustment for income taxes.

If all costs vary in direct proportion to sales and sales are made at a price in excess of such costs, there is no break-even point, for profit arises with the first sale. Whenever fixed costs exist, however, sales must cover both variable and fixed costs in reaching the break-even point. Stated differently, sales after covering variable costs serve to absorb fixed costs: the break-even point is reached when the excess of sales over variable costs just equals the amount of fixed costs. There is a profit only when the sales figure exceeds the sum of the variable and fixed costs.

The ratio of variable costs to the sales dollar is commonly referred to as the *variable cost ratio*. The part of the sales dollar after deducting variable costs that becomes available to cover fixed costs and to provide a profit is referred to as *marginal income*. Marginal income expressed in terms of the sales dollar is called the *marginal income ratio* or the *profit-volume ratio*, commonly designated the *P/V ratio*. Marginal income that exceeds fixed costs provides a profit. The amount by which total sales exceed sales at the break-even point is referred to as the *margin of safety*. The relationship of this excess to total sales is referred to as the margin of safety ratio, commonly designated the *M/S ratio*.

The break-even point can be arrived at by means of a graph or it can be arrived at mathematically. In either case two amounts must be known: (1) the total fixed costs of all categories — production, selling, general, and administrative; and (2) the relationship of variable costs of all categories to the sales figure. The break-even point can be determined graphically by plotting fixed and variable costs and sales information on a chart. When the maximum sales that can be achieved at full capacity or production are known, an analysis of profit and loss at any sales level can be developed. To illustrate, assume the following facts for the Eastern Manufacturing Company:

(a) Variable costs are 40% of sales.
(b) Total fixed costs are $180,000.
(c) Maximum sales volume at full capacity is $500,000.

These data are plotted on the graph given below.

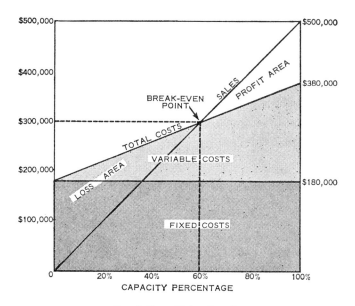

**Break-Even Point Graph**

The graph indicates that sales of $300,000 must be reached to break even; stated differently, 60% of full capacity must be achieved. This is the point where the total cost line and the sales line intersect. At this point variable costs are $120,000 (40% of $300,000) and fixed costs are $180,000.

The profit or loss at different sales volumes can also be determined from the graph. The lower the sales figure below the break-even point, the greater the loss; the higher the sales figure above the break-even point, the greater the profit. Sales of $250,000, for example, will result in a loss of $30,000 ($250,000 − [(40% of $250,000) + $180,000]); sales of $400,000 will produce a profit of $60,000 ($400,000 − [(40% of $400,000) + $180,000]).    Maximum sales will result in a profit of $120,000 ($500,000 − [(40% of $500,000) + $180,000]).  With sales at $400,000, a margin of safety of 25% would be achieved (sales in excess of sales at break-even point, $100,000 ÷ sales, $400,000).

If sales at the break-even point are to be arrived at mathematically, calculations are made in the following manner. Let S equal sales at the break-even point. Then S is equal to the sum of the variable costs, which are 40% of sales, plus the fixed costs of $180,000:

$$S = .40S + \$180,000$$
$$S - .40S = \$180,000$$
$$.60S = \$180,000$$
$$S = \$300,000$$

The break-even point can also be calculated by employing the P/V ratio described earlier. The P/V ratio or the portion of the sales dollar available for meeting fixed costs in the example above is .60 (sales, 1.00 − variable costs, .40). The following calculation is made:

$$S = \$180,000 \div .60$$
$$S = \$300,000$$

It should be noted that an increase in variable costs or in fixed costs or a decrease in sales price will raise the break-even point. On the other hand, a decrease in variable costs or in fixed costs or an increase in sales price will lower the break-even point. A change in the product sales mix, assuming that different products produce varying marginal income rates, will change the aggregate P/V ratio and thus also increase or decrease the sales volume necessary to break even.

Profit or loss at different sales volumes can also be arrived at mathematically. The M/S and P/V ratios are employed and the following calculation is made:

$$Sales \times M/S \times P/V$$

To illustrate, assume that sales of $400,000 are expected by the company previously referred to. The M/S ratio is .25 ([sales, $400,000 − sales at break-even point, $300,000] ÷ sales, $400,000); the P/V ratio is .60 (sales, 1.00 − variable costs, .40). The following calculation is made:

Profit at $400,000 sales level = $400,000 × .25 × .60, or $60,000.

In developing the graphs and also the measurements that have been illustrated, it is necessary first to classify costs as fixed or variable. Semivariable costs will have to be broken down into their fixed or variable components for this purpose. Break-even point analysis is based on the assumptions that the fixed costs will not vary regardless of the level of sales and that variable costs will vary in direct proportion to sales. Obviously, however, such exact conditions will seldom be found in practice. Fixed costs may vary to some degree depending upon sales; on the other hand, variable costs may not vary in direct proportion to sales as assumed. For example, economies of purchasing and production may serve to lower certain variable expenses; many expenses, both variable and fixed, may rise sharply upon reaching a certain point and may contract markedly below a certain level. When actual conditions vary from the assumptions that are required in developing the break-even analysis, the limitations that are found in such measurement should be recognized.

Many practical applications may be made of break-even analysis. Break-even information is useful in predicting the effect upon earnings of an increase or a decrease in sales volumes. For example, if it is predicted that operations of the Eastern Manufacturing Company, referred to on page 509, will reach 90% of capacity, profits would be estimated at $90,000 ($450,000 − [$180,000 + 40% of $450,000]). This information may be used in the determination of policy with respect to property acquisitions, loans, and dividend payments.

Break-even point analysis may be particularly valuable in making decisions concerning the expansion of plant facilities. For example, assume that the Eastern Manufacturing Company, in view of operations at 90% capacity or sales at $450,000, considers an expansion in plant facilities that will raise maximum sales possibilities to $800,000 but will raise fixed costs to $240,000. Assume variable costs are 40% of sales in either case. The following calculations may be made:

|  | Under Present Conditions | Under Proposed Conditions |
|---|---|---|
| Sales at break-even point (S): | S = .40S + $180,000, or $300,000 | S = .40S + $240,000, or $400,000 |
| Profit, assuming sales at 90% of present capacity or $450,000: | $450,000 − [(40% of $450,000) + $180,000], or $90,000 | $450,000 − [(40% of $450,000) + $240,000], or $30,000 |
| Sales necessary to reach profit of $90,000 (S'): | S'=.40S' + $180,000 + $90,000, or $450,000 | S' = .40S'+ $240,000 + $90,000, or $550,000 |
| Maximum profit at full capacity: | $500,000 − [(40% of $500,000) + $180,000], or $120,000 | $800,000 − [(40% of $800,000) + $240,000], or $240,000 |

In deciding whether expansion is warranted at this stage, the increased break-even point, the decreased profit if sales remain $450,000, and the increased sales required to produce the same profit would be weighed against the increased sales and profit potentials.

### Cash-flow and funds-flow analyses

Comparative balance sheet data show the change that·has taken place in a company's cash position and also in its working capital position. However, it may be of interest to determine the reasons for these changes. To what extent did such factors as earnings, property acquisitions, retirement of long-term debt, and the issuance of additional capital stock affect the company's cash and its working capital during the period? Analysis of comparative balance sheet data together with a review of financial and operating activities of the period will reveal the sources and the dispositions of cash and of working capital. Information with respect to the movement of cash and its effect upon the cash position of the business may be provided by means of a *cash-flow* statement; information with respect to the movement of working capital and its effect upon the working capital position of the business may be provided by means of a *statement of source and application of funds*. Because of the importance of these statements and the special problems that are involved in their preparation, they are considered separately in Chapter 20.

## QUESTIONS

**1.** What groups may be interested in a company's financial statements?

**2.** Explain how an understanding of accounting assists in the analysis and interpretation of financial statements.

**3.** What are the factors that one would look for in judging a company's (a) solvency, (b) stability, (c) profitability?

**4.** Distinguish between horizontal and vertical analytical procedures. What special purpose does each serve?

**5.** When data for more than two years are involved, what are the advantages of developing comparisons in terms of the earliest year given? What are the advantages of developing comparisons in terms of the preceding year?

**6.** What are the relative advantages of changes reported as percentages as compared with changes reported as ratios?

**7.** A company wishes to compare its sales for a number of years with a U. S. index of industrial production. What procedures will be required in developing such a comparison?

**8.** Mention some factors that may limit the comparability of financial statements of two companies in the same industry.

**9.** What is meant by a *thirteen-month year?* What advantages and disadvantages can you name in the use of such a year for accounting purposes?

**10.** What is meant by a *common-size* statement? What are its advantages?

**11.** What factors may be responsible for a change in net income from one year to the next?

**12.** What factors may be responsible for a change in a company's gross profit?

**13.** (a) The Marsh Co. reports an increase in gross profit in 1964 over 1963 of $60,000. What other information would be useful in the evaluation of this increase? (b) Give possible unfavorable factors that might accompany an increase in gross profit.

**14.** The Atlas Co. develops the following measurements for 1964 as compared with the year 1963. What additional information would you require before arriving at favorable or unfavorable conclusions for each item?

  (a) Net income has increased $50,000.
  (b) Sales returns and allowances have increased by $30,000.
  (c) The gross profit rate has increased by 5%.
  (d) Purchases discounts have increased by $5,000.
  (e) Cash has increased by $85,000.
  (f) Accounts receivable have increased by $150,000.
  (g) Inventories have decreased by $100,000.
  (h) Retained earnings have decreased by $300,000.

**15.** Distinguish between fixed costs and variable costs.

**16.** (a) What is meant by the P/V ratio? (b) What is meant by the M/S ratio? (c) Define marginal income.

**17.** (a) What is meant by a company's break-even point? (b) How is it calculated? (c) Suggest certain practical applications that can be made of break-even point analysis.

**18.** Assuming the same total revenue and cost figures at full production for two companies, what factors will cause a lower break-even point for one company than for the other?

## EXERCISES

**1.** Indicate the dollar change, the percentage change, and also the ratio that would be reported for each case below, assuming horizontal analysis:

Gain (loss) on sale of investments:

|     | 1963 | 1964 |     | 1963 | 1964 |
| --- | --- | --- | --- | --- | --- |
| (a) | $20,000 | $45,000 | (f) | $      0 | ($20,000) |
| (b) | 50,000 | 20,000 | (g) | (  5,000) | 5,000 |
| (c) | 0 | 30,000 | (h) | 5,000 | ( 20,000) |
| (d) | 40,000 | 0 | (i) | ( 10,000) | ( 10,000) |
| (e) | 20,000 | ( 30,000) | (j) | 10,000 | 10,000 |

**2.** Sales for the Webster Company for a five-year period and an industry sales index for this period are listed below. Convert both series into indexes employing 1960 as the base year.

|  | 1960 | 1961 | 1962 | 1963 | 1964 |
| --- | --- | --- | --- | --- | --- |
| Sales of Webster Company (in thousands of dollars) | $5,546 | $6,055 | $6,270 | $5,410 | $5,180 |
| Industry sales index (1950–52 = 100)....... | 188 | 208 | 214 | 195 | 181 |

**3.** Comparative data for the Winston Co. appear below:

|  | 1963 | 1964 |
|---|---|---|
| Sales.................................. | $5,000,000 | $6,875,000 |
| Cost of goods sold.................... | 3,000,000 | 4,262,500 |
| Gross profit on sales................. | $2,000,000 | $2,612,500 |

Assume that sales prices in 1964 average 25% above those for 1963. What part of the change in gross profit is due to a change in the sales volume and what part is due to a change in the gross profit rate?

**4.** It is determined that the variable costs for the Forrester Company are 40% of sales. Sales at capacity operations are $1,000,000. What are sales at the break-even point, assuming that total fixed costs are (a) $150,000, and (b) $450,000?

**5.** The total fixed costs for the Globe Mfg. Co. are $120,000; variable costs are 25% of the product sales price. Units sell for $5 each. (a) How many units must be sold for the company to break even? (b) How many units must be sold for the company to realize net income before income taxes of $100,000?

**6.** The Ray Co. has sales of $600,000, an M/S ratio of .40, and a P/V ratio of .30.

(a) What is the company's break-even point?
(b) What are the fixed costs?
(c) What is the net income before income taxes?

## PROBLEMS

**18-1.** Operations of the Lakewood Co. for 1963 and 1964 are summarized below:

|  | 1963 | 1964 |
|---|---|---|
| Sales..................................... | $205,000 | $260,000 |
| Sales returns............................. | 5,000 | 10,000 |
| Net sales................................. | $200,000 | $250,000 |
| Cost of goods sold........................ | 120,000 | 170,000 |
| Gross profit on sales..................... | $ 80,000 | $ 80,000 |
| Selling and general expenses.............. | 50,000 | 65,000 |
| Net operating income...................... | $ 30,000 | $ 15,000 |
| Other expense items....................... | 10,000 | 20,000 |
| Net income (loss) before income taxes..... | $ 20,000 | ($ 5,000) |
| Income taxes.............................. | 5,000 | |
| Net income (loss)......................... | $ 15,000 | ($ 5,000) |

*Instructions:* (1) Prepare a comparative income statement showing dollar changes and percentage changes for 1964 as compared with 1963.

(2) Prepare a comparative income statement offering a percentage analysis of component profit and loss items in terms of net sales for each year.

(3) Prepare a statement accounting for the variation in net income for 1964 as compared with 1963.

**18-2.** The financial position of Drummonds, Inc., at the end of 1963 and 1964 is summarized below:

| Assets | 1963 | 1964 |
|---|---|---|
| Current assets: | | |
| Cash on hand and on deposit................. | $    60,000 | $    40,000 |
| U.S. Government securities, at cost............ | 85,000 | 65,000 |
| Notes and accounts receivable, less allowance.... | 240,000 | 280,000 |
| Raw materials and supplies................... | 210,000 | 300,000 |
| Goods in process............................ | 160,000 | 210,000 |
| Finished goods.............................. | 300,000 | 450,000 |
| Miscellaneous prepaid items.................. | 20,000 | 20,000 |
| Total current assets........................ | $1,075,000 | $1,365,000 |
| Investments: | | |
| Bond redemption fund....................... | $ 300,000 | $ 350,000 |
| Investment in properties not in current use...... | 250,000 | 250,000 |
| Total investments.......................... | $ 550,000 | $ 600,000 |
| Plant and equipment at cost, less allowance........ | $ 800,000 | $ 750,000 |
| Intangibles..................................... | $ 150,000 | $ 125,000 |
| Other assets: | | |
| Unamortized bond issue costs................. | $    30,000 | $    25,000 |
| Machinery rearrangement costs............... | 20,000 | 15,000 |
| Total other assets.......................... | $    50,000 | $    40,000 |
| Total assets................................... | $2,625,000 | $2,880,000 |

| Liabilities | | |
|---|---|---|
| Current liabilities: | | |
| Notes and accounts payable.................. | $ 140,000 | $ 260,000 |
| Income taxes payable........................ | 20,000 | 40,000 |
| Accrued payrolls, interest, and taxes........... | 25,000 | 40,000 |
| Cash dividends payable...................... | 15,000 | 20,000 |
| Miscellaneous payables...................... | 5,000 | 5,000 |
| Total current liabilities..................... | $ 205,000 | $ 365,000 |
| Long-term debt — 10-year first mortgage bonds.... | 250,000 | 250,000 |
| Estimated employee pensions payable............. | 130,000 | 150,000 |
| Deferred revenues............................. | 30,000 | 25,000 |
| Total liabilities............................... | $ 615,000 | $ 790,000 |

Stockholders' Equity

| | | |
|---|---:|---:|
| Paid-in capital: | | |
| 4½% preferred stock, $25 par................ | $ 500,000 | $ 500,000 |
| No-par common stock, $10 stated value........ | 500,000 | 500,000 |
| Additional paid-in capital.................... | 650,000 | 650,000 |
| Total paid-in capital....................... | $1,650,000 | $1,650,000 |
| Retained earnings: | | |
| Appropriated............................... | $ 160,000 | $ 200,000 |
| Free....................................... | 200,000 | 240,000 |
| Total retained earnings..................... | $ 360,000 | $ 440,000 |
| Total stockholders' equity..................... | $2,010,000 | $2,090,000 |
| Total liabilities and stockholders' equity.......... | $2,625,000 | $2,880,000 |

*Instructions:* (1) Prepare a comparative balance sheet showing dollar changes and changes in terms of ratios for 1964 as compared with 1963.

(2) Prepare a common-size balance sheet comparing financial structure ratios for 1964 with those for 1963.

**18-3.** Financial statements for the Cunningham Mfg. Co. are given below and on pages 517 and 518.

Cunningham Mfg. Co.
Balance Sheets
December 31, 1962, 1963, 1964

| | 1962 | 1963 | 1964 |
|---|---:|---:|---:|
| **Assets** | | | |
| Current assets...................... | $ 760,000 | $ 990,000 | $1,215,000 |
| Investments........................ | 300,000 | 250,000 | 300,000 |
| Plant and equipment (net).......... | 1,050,000 | 980,000 | 1,350,000 |
| Intangibles........................ | 150,000 | 140,000 | 180,000 |
| Total assets...................... | $2,260,000 | $2,360,000 | $3,045,000 |
| **Liabilities** | | | |
| Current liabilities.................. | $ 310,000 | $ 370,000 | $ 320,000 |
| Long-term debt (5%).............. | 200,000 | 200,000 | 300,000 |
| Deferred revenues.................. | 20,000 | 30,000 | 25,000 |
| Total liabilities.................... | $ 530,000 | $ 600,000 | $ 645,000 |
| **Stockholders' Equity** | | | |
| 6% Cumulative, nonparticipating | | | |
| preferred stock, $50 par........... | $ 500,000 | $ 500,000 | $ 500,000 |
| Common stock, $50 par............. | 1,000,000 | 1,000,000 | 1,500,000 |
| Additional paid-in capital........... | 250,000 | 250,000 | 350,000 |
| Retained earnings (deficit).......... | ( 20,000) | 10,000 | 50,000 |
| Total stockholders' equity........... | $1,730,000 | $1,760,000 | $2,400,000 |
| Total liabilities and stockholders' equity | $2,260,000 | $2,360,000 | $3,045,000 |

Cunningham Mfg. Co.
Income Statements
For the Years Ended December 31, 1962, 1963, 1964

|  | 1962 | 1963 | 1964 |
|---|---|---|---|
| Gross sales.......................... | $1,800,000 | $2,400,000 | $2,800,000 |
| Sales returns........................ | 40,000 | 80,000 | 100,000 |
| Net sales........................... | $1,760,000 | $2,320,000 | $2,700,000 |
| Finished goods inventory, Jan. 1...... | $ 230,000 | $ 220,000 | $ 330,000 |
| Cost of goods manufactured.......... | 1,230,000 | 1,630,000 | 1,840,000 |
| Goods available for sale............. | $1,460,000 | $1,850,000 | $2,170,000 |
| Finished goods inventory, Dec. 31..... | 220,000 | 330,000 | 350,000 |
| Cost of goods sold.................. | $1,240,000 | $1,520,000 | $1,820,000 |
| Gross profit on sales................ | $ 520,000 | $ 800,000 | $ 880,000 |
| Selling expenses..................... | $ 400,000 | $ 480,000 | $ 560,000 |
| General and administrative expenses... | 160,000 | 170,000 | 180,000 |
| Total operating expenses............. | $ 560,000 | $ 650,000 | $ 740,000 |
| Net operating income (loss).......... | ($ 40,000) | $ 150,000 | $ 140,000 |
| Other revenue items................. | 30,000 | 30,000 | 40,000 |
|  | ($ 10,000) | $ 180,000 | $ 180,000 |
| Other expense items................. | 20,000 | 20,000 | 40,000 |
| Net income (loss) before income taxes... | ($ 30,000) | $ 160,000 | $ 140,000 |
| Income taxes....................... |  | 60,000 | 50,000 |
| Net income (loss)................... | ($ 30,000) | $. 100,000 | $ 90,000 |

Cunningham Mfg. Co.
Schedules of Cost of Goods Manufactured
For the Years Ended December 31, 1962, 1963, 1964

|  | 1962 | 1963 | 1964 |
|---|---|---|---|
| Raw materials inventory, Jan. 1....... | $ 180,000 | $ 160,000 | $ 210,000 |
| Raw materials purchases............. | 600,000 | 920,000 | 1,080,000 |
|  | $ 780,000 | $1,080,000 | $1,290,000 |
| Raw materials inventory, Dec. 31..... | 160,000 | 210,000 | 300,000 |

| | | | |
|---|---|---|---|
| Cost of raw materials used........... | $ 620,000 | $ 870,000 | $ 990,000 |
| Direct labor....................... | 360,000 | 440,000 | 510,000 |
| Manufacturing overhead............ | 300,000 | 360,000 | 380,000 |
| | $1,280,000 | $1,670,000 | $1,880,000 |
| Goods in process inventory, Jan. 1..... | 150,000 | 200,000 | 240,000 |
| | $1,430,000 | $1,870,000 | $2,120,000 |
| Goods in process inventory, Dec. 31 ... | 200,000 | 240,000 | 280,000 |
| Cost of goods manufactured.......... | $1,230,000 | $1,630,000 | $1,840,000 |

Cunningham Mfg. Co.
Retained Earnings Statements
For the Years Ended December 31, 1962, 1963, 1964

| | 1962 | 1963 | 1964 |
|---|---|---|---|
| Retained earnings (deficit), Jan. 1.......... | $ 10,000 | ($ 20,000) | $ 10,000 |
| Net income (loss) per income statement..... | ( 30,000) | 100,000 | 90,000 |
| | ($ 20,000) | $ 80,000 | $100,000 |
| Cash dividends: | | | |
| Preferred stock........................ | | $ 60,000 | $ 30,000 |
| Common stock........................ | | 10,000 | 20,000 |
| Total...................... | | $ 70,000 | $ 50,000 |
| Retained earnings (deficit), Dec. 31........ | ($ 20,000) | $ 10,000 | $ 50,000 |

*Instructions:* Prepare comparative statements for the three-year period showing dollar and percentage changes in terms of 1962, which is to be considered the base year.

**18-4.** (1) From the data for the Cunningham Mfg. Co. given in Problem 18-3, develop a comparative income statement for the three-year period, offering percentage analysis of component profit and loss items in terms of net sales for each period.

(2) Prepare a comparative schedule of cost of goods manufactured for the three-year period in support of the comparative income statement, offering percentage analysis of component cost of goods manufactured items in terms of the total cost of goods manufactured for each year.

**18-5.** From the data for the Cunningham Mfg. Co. given in Problem 18-3, prepare a condensed common-size balance sheet comparing financial structure percentages for the three-year period.

**18-6.** From the data for the Cunningham Mfg. Co. given in Problem 18-3, prepare statements accounting for the variation in net income (1) for 1964 as compared with 1962, and (2) for 1964 as compared with 1963.

**18-7.** Sales for Johnson Mfg. Co. and its chief competitor, the Wells Company, and the sales index for the industry, are given below:

|  | 1960 | 1961 | 1962 | 1963 | 1964 |
|---|---|---|---|---|---|
| Sales of Johnson Mfg. Co. (in thousands of dollars). | $6,640 | $7,420 | $7,760 | $8,600 | $8,580 |
| Sales of Wells Company (in thousands of dollars). | $9,440 | $9,610 | $9,650 | $9,710 | $9,450 |
| Industry sales index (1952 = 100)......... | 144 | 160 | 165 | 152 | 140 |

*Instructions:* (1) Convert the three series to index numbers using 1960 as the base year.

(2) Prepare a short report for the management of Johnson Mfg. Co. summarizing your findings.

**18-8.** Profit and loss data of Louie & Philips, Inc., for 1963 and 1964 follow:

|  | 1963 | 1964 |
|---|---|---|
| Sales..................................... | $2,688,000 | $3,450,000 |
| Cost of goods sold....................... | 1,920,000 | 2,760,000 |
| Gross profit on sales..................... | $ 768,000 | $ 690,000 |
| Operating expenses...................... | 500,000 | 550,000 |
| Net income............................ | $ 268,000 | $ 140,000 |

*Instructions:* Prepare a statement analyzing the variation in gross profit, giving as much information as can be determined concerning factors responsible for the change, under each of the following assumptions:

(1) No data are available relative to price and volume changes.

(2) Sales prices in 1964 are 20% above sales prices in 1963.

**18-9.** Total fixed costs for the Weston Mfg. Co. are $350,000; the variable costs are $300,000 at full capacity. The estimated sales price of goods sold at full capacity is $1,000,000. Assume that fixed costs are constant and that variable costs vary in direct proportion to sales. Income taxes are 30% on the first $25,000 and 52% on any amount in excess of $25,000.

*Instructions:* (1) Draw a chart showing the sales at the break-even point and net income after income taxes on sales beyond the break-even point.

(2) Calculate sales at the break-even point, assuming estimates to be the same except that the total costs of $650,000 at full capacity consist of fixed costs, $450,000, and variable costs, $200,000.

**18-10.** The following data are determined for the Harvey Co.: up to 40% activity or sales, the fixed costs are $500,000; above 40%, the fixed costs are $600,000. The variable costs are estimated as follows:

| Rate of Activity or Sales | Estimated Variable Costs | Rate of Activity or Sales | Estimated Variable Costs |
|---|---|---|---|
| 10%............ | $300,000 | 60%............ | $620,000 |
| 20%............ | 400,000 | 70%............ | 740,000 |
| 30%............ | 460,000 | 80%............ | 775,000 |
| 40%............ | 500,000 | 90%............ | 790,000 |
| 50%............ | 600,000 | 100%............ | 800,000 |

The sales at 100% capacity are assumed to be $2,000,000.

*Instructions:* Construct a chart and determine the approximate break-even point.

**18-11.** The Carolina Co. presents the following summary relating to current activities at capacity and estimated activities at capacity with proposed enlarged facilities:

| | With Present Facilities | | With Enlarged Facilities | |
|---|---|---|---|---|
| Sales.................... | | $1,000,000 | | $1,500,000 |
| Fixed costs.............. | $525,000 | | $750,000 | |
| Variable costs. ......... | 250,000 | 775,000 | 300,000 | 1,050,000 |
| Net income before income taxes | | $ 225,000 | | $ 450,000 |

*Instructions:* (1) Calculate the sales that are required at the break-even point under present and under proposed conditions.

(2) Calculate the sales that are required under proposed conditions in reaching present income at full capacity.

(3) Calculate the result from operations under proposed conditions if sales do not exceed the present dollar amount.

# Chapter 19

# FINANCIAL STATEMENT ANALYSIS
## SPECIAL RATIOS AND MEASUREMENTS

### Extensions of horizontal and vertical analysis

There are a great many special measurements that may be developed from financial statements and supplementary financial data. Such measurements may be divided into: (1) those that analyze balance sheet position, and (2) those that analyze operating results. Some of these measurements have special significance to particular groups, while others may be of general interest to all groups. Creditors, for example, are concerned with the ability of a company to pay its current obligations and seek information about the relationship of current assets to current liabilitities. Stockholders are concerned with dividends and seek information relating to the earnings per share that will form the basis for dividend declarations. Management is concerned with the liquidity of the merchandise stock and seeks information relating to the number of times goods have turned over during the period. All parties are vitally interested in the profitability of operations and wish to be informed about the relationship of earnings to both creditor and stockholder equities.

A number of measurements developed from the financial data for a single period will be described and illustrated in this chapter. These measurements represent extensions of the vertical analysis procedure. Measurements will also be provided in comparative form and will therefore represent the further application of the horizontal procedure. The analyses that are described and illustrated in this chapter should not be considered all-inclusive; other ratios and measurements may be useful to the various groups, depending upon their particular needs. It should be emphasized once again that sound conclusions cannot be reached from an individual ratio or measurement. But this information, together with adequate investigation and study, may lead to a satisfactory interpretation and evaluation of financial data. The analyses that are presented are based upon the financial statements for the Marshall Company for 1962, 1963, and 1964 that were given in the preceding chapter.

### Current ratio

A fundamental measurement in the analysis of balance sheet position is the comparison of current assets with current liabilities as of a certain date. Total current assets divided by total current liabilities gives the ratio of current assets to current liabilities, variously referred to as the *current ratio*, the *working capital ratio*, or the *banker's ratio*.

The current ratio is a valuable measure of the ability of a business unit to meet its current obligations. Since it is a measure of liquidity, care must be taken to determine that the proper items have been included in the current asset and current liability categories. Ordinarily a ratio of less than 2 to 1 for a trading or manufacturing unit is regarded as unsatisfactory. A comfortable margin of current assets over current liabilities suggests that a company will be able to meet maturing obligations even in the event of an unfavorable turn in business conditions and losses in the realization of such assets as marketable securities, receivables, and inventories.

In considering current condition, reference is frequently made to a company's *working capital*. This term may be used to indicate total current assets or simply the excess of current assets over current liabilities. When the term "working capital" is used to indicate total current assets, the term "net working capital" is used to represent the excess of current assets over current liabilities. Because of different uses of the term, the definition for working capital should be ascertained in interpreting working capital analyses. In this text working capital is used to denote the excess of current assets over current liabilities.

For the Marshall Company, working capital totals and current ratios for 1963 and 1964 are developed as follows:[1]

|  | 1963 | 1964 |
|---|---|---|
| Current assets............................... | $955,500 | $855,000 |
| Current liabilities............................ | 546,000 | 410,000 |
| Working capital............................. | $409,500 | $445,000 |
| Current ratio................................ | 1.8 : 1 | 2.1 : 1 |

Ratio calculations are sometimes carried out to two or more decimal places; however, ratios do not need to be carried out beyond one place unless some particularly significant interpretative value is afforded by the more refined measurement. The current ratio just given, as well as the other ratios to be described, can be expressed in terms of percentages. The ratios just given are expressed as percentages as follows:

|  | 1963 | 1964 |
|---|---|---|
| Current ratio.............................. | 175% | 209% |

---

[1]Comparative data for more than two years are generally required in evaluating financial trends. Analyses for only two years are given in the examples in this chapter, since these are sufficient to illustrate the comparative procedures involved.

From the standpoint of solvency it is more important to consider the ratio of current assets to current liabilities than the amount of working capital. For example, assume balance sheet data for Companies A and B as follows:

Company A: Current assets, $400,000; current liabilities, $50,000.
Company B: Current assets, $1,050,000; current liabilities, $700,000.

Both Company A and Company B have a working capital of $350,000, but Company A has a current ratio of 8:1 while Company B has a current ratio of 1.5:1. The short-term creditors of Company A are more certain of receiving prompt and full payment than those of Company B. On requests for short-term loans, bankers would probably be more favorable to Company A than to Company B.

It is possible, however, to overemphasize the importance of a high current ratio. Assume that a company is normally able to carry on its operations with current assets of $200,000 and current liabilities of $100,000. If the company finds itself with current assets of $500,000, current liabilities remaining at $100,000, its current ratio has increased from 2:1 to 5:1. The company may now have considerably more working capital than it actually requires. It should also be observed that certain unfavorable conditions may be accompanied by an improving ratio. For example, with a slowdown in business and postponement of programs for advertising, research, and plant and equipment repairs and replacements, a company's cash balance may rise. At the same time, slower customer collections may result in rising trade receivables, and reduced sales volume may result in rising inventories.

The amount of working capital required by a particular enterprise depends not only upon its size and its sales activity but also upon the character of its business. For example, a company that does business for cash and maintains a small inventory that turns over rapidly does not require as much working capital as a company with the same volume of business that sells goods on a credit basis and maintains a large inventory that turns over slowly. Working capital requirements may vary, too, depending upon the industry within which the enterprise is found. A construction company may require a large amount of working capital in financing construction activities; a public utility, on the other hand, may require only a small amount of working capital in its operations.

In analyzing working capital position, particular note should be taken of the valuation procedures used for the various assets and liabilities. Inventories reported on a last-in, first-out basis may be substantially below their market values during a period of rising prices; marketable securities reported at the lower of cost or market may be substantially below market; both receivables and payables reported at face or settlement amounts may be considerably above their present values. Special reference should also be made to estimated liabilities and to contingent liabilities in appraising the effects of possible payment requirements that may differ from reported amounts.

## Acid-test ratio

A test of a company's immediate solvency is made by comparing the sum of cash, marketable securities, notes receivable, and accounts receivable, commonly referred to as the *quick assets*, with current liabilities. The total of the quick assets when divided by current liabilities gives the ratio of quick assets to current liabilities, known as the *acid-test ratio* or *quick ratio*. Considerable time may be required in the conversion of raw materials, goods in process, and finished goods into receivables and then receivables into cash. A company with a satisfactory current ratio may be in an unsatisfactory condition in terms of immediate solvency when inventories form a significant part of the current asset total. This is revealed by the acid-test ratio. In developing the ratio, close inspection must be given to receivables and the securities included in the quick asset total. There may be instances where such items are actually less liquid than inventories.

Normally one looks for a ratio of quick assets to current liabilities of not less than 1 to 1. Again, however, special conditions applicable to the particular business must be evaluated. Questions such as the following should be considered: What is the composition of the quick assets? What special requirements are made by current activities upon these assets? How soon are the current payables due?

Acid-test ratios for the Marshall Company are calculated as follows:

|  | 1963 | 1964 |
|---|---|---|
| Quick assets: | | |
| Cash..................................... | $100,500 | $ 60,000 |
| Marketable securities...................... | 150,000 | 150,000 |
| Receivables (net)......................... | 375,000 | 420,000 |
| Total quick assets........................ | $625,500 | $630,000 |
| Total current liabilities..................... | $546,000 | $410,000 |
| Acid-test ratio............................ | 1.1 : 1 | 1.5 : 1 |

## Other measurements of working capital position

It may be desirable to develop other ratios in analyzing a company's working capital position. For example, it may be useful to show the relationship of total current assets to total assets, and of individual current assets such as receivables and inventories to total current assets. In the case of liabilities, it may be useful to show the relationship of total current liabilities to total liabilities, and of individual current liabilities to total current liabilities. Vertical analysis as applied to comparative statements in the previous chapter made available such data and also reported the changes and the trends in such relationships over a period of years.

The foregoing comparisons may provide information concerning the relative liquidity of total assets and the maturity of total obligations, as well as the structure of working capital and shifts within the working capital group. The latter data are significant, since all of the items within the current classification are not equally current. What may be considered reasonable relationships in the analysis of the working capital position will depend upon the particular enterprise.

## Analysis of receivables

There are special tests that may be applied in considering the liquidity of two significant working capital elements, receivables and inventories. In the case of receivables, analysis is directed to evaluation of both the amount and the quality of the receivables.

*Accounts receivable turnover.* The amount of receivables usually bears a close relationship to the volume of credit sales. The receivable position and approximate collection time may be evaluated by calculation of the *turnover of accounts receivable.* This rate is determined by dividing net credit sales for the period by the average notes and accounts receivable from trade debtors. In developing an average receivables figure, monthly balances should be used if available; the average is calculated from thirteen monthly balances, those of January 1, January 31, February 28, etc.

Assume in the case of the Marshall Company that all sales are made on a credit basis, that receivables arise only from sales, and that receivable totals for only the beginning and the end of the year are available. Receivable turnover figures are calculated as follows:

|  | 1963 | 1964 |
|---|---|---|
| Net credit sales........................ | $1,650,000 | $1,425,000 |
| Net receivables: | | |
|   Beginning of year.................... | $ 333,500 | $ 375,000 |
|   End of year......................... | $ 375,000 | $ 420,000 |
| Average receivables................... | $ 354,250 | $ 397,500 |
| Receivables turnover for year........... | 4.7 | 3.6 |

*Number of days' sales in receivables.* Average receivables are sometimes expressed in terms of average days' credit sales uncollected. The average time required to collect receivables is thus shown. For example, assume a business with 300 business or sales days per year. Annual dollar sales are divided by 300 to find average daily sales. Average receivables divided by average daily sales then gives the number of days' sales in average receivables. The latter procedure for the Marshall Company is illustrated below:

|  | 1963 | 1964 |
|---|---|---|
| Average receivables..................... | $ 354,250 | $ 397,500 |
| Net sales on account.................... | $1,650,000 | $1,425,000 |
| Average daily sales on account (net sales on account ÷ 300)...................... | $ 5,500 | $ 4,750 |
| Number of days' sales in average receivables. | 64 | 84 |

The same measurements can be obtained by dividing the number of days representing the year by the turnover rates. A comparable number of days for each year should be used in developing comparisons. Computations are generally based on the calendar year consisting of 365 days or a business year consisting of 300 days (365 days less Sundays and holidays).

In certain instances, instead of developing the number of days' sales in average receivables, it may be considered more useful to report the number of days' credit sales in receivables at the end of the period. Data in this form would be of special significance when an evaluation of the current position and particularly of the receivable position is sought. This information for the Marshall Company is presented below:

|  | 1963 | 1964 |
|---|---|---|
| Receivables at end of year.................. | $375,000 | $420,000 |
| Average daily credit sales................... | $ 5,500 | $ 4,750 |
| Number of days' sales in receivables at end of year...................................... | 68 | 88 |

What constitutes a reasonable number of days in receivables varies with the individual business. For example, if merchandise is sold on terms of net 60 days, 40 days' sales in receivables would not be unreasonable; but if terms are net 30 days, a receivable balance equal to 40 days' sales would indicate slow collections.

Sales activity just before the close of the period should be considered in interpreting the accounts receivable measurements. If sales are unusually light or heavy just before the end of the fiscal period, receivables are affected and the measurements, in turn, are distorted. When such unevenness prevails, it may be better to analyze accounts according to their due dates, as was illustrated in Chapter 6.

The problem of keeping accounts receivable at a minimum without losing desirable business is important. The company's investment in receivables usually does not provide revenue. The cost of carrying these accounts must be covered by the margin of profit made on sales. The longer the accounts are carried, the smaller will be the percentage return realized on invested capital. In addition, heavier bookkeeping and collection charges and increased bad debts must be considered.

To attract business, credit is frequently granted for relatively long periods. The element of cost involved in granting long-term credit should be recognized. Assume that a business has an average daily credit sales volume of $5,000 and the average amount of accounts receivable is $250,000. The latter figure represents the average daily credit business for 50 days. If collections and the credit period can be improved so that accounts receivable represent only 30 days' sales, then accounts receivable will be reduced to $150,000. Assuming a total cost of 8% to carry and service the accounts, the decrease of $100,000 in accounts would represent an annual savings of $8,000.

## Analysis of inventories

Procedures similar to those for evaluating receivables may be employed in evaluating inventory position. Both the number of times the average inventory has been replenished during a fiscal period, known as the *inventory turnover*, and the number of days' sales in average inventories may be computed from inventory and cost of goods sold data.

*Inventory turnover.* The amount of inventory carried in stock frequently bears a close relationship to the sales volume. The inventory position and the approximate disposal time may be evaluated by calculating the inventory turnover. The inventory turnover is calculated by dividing the cost of goods sold by the average inventory for the period. Whenever possible, monthly figures should be used in developing a representative average.

Assume for the Marshall Company that inventory balances for only the beginning and the end of the year are available. Inventory turnover figures are calculated as follows:

|  | 1963 | 1964 |
|---|---|---|
| Cost of goods sold...................... | $1,200,000 | $1,000,000 |
| Merchandise inventory: | | |
|    Beginning of year..................... | $ 125,000 | $ 330,000 |
|    End of year........................... | $ 330,000 | $ 225,000 |
| Average merchandise inventory............ | $ 227,500 | $ 277,500 |
| Inventory turnover for year.............. | 5.3 | 3.6 |

*Number of days' sales in inventories.* Average inventories are sometimes expressed in terms of average days' sales. Information is thus afforded concerning the average time it takes to dispose of the inventory. The number of days' sales in inventories is calculated by dividing the average inventory by the average daily cost of goods sold. When a turnover figure has been calculated, the number of days' sales can be obtained by dividing the days in the year by the turnover figure for the year. The latter procedure for the Marshall Company is illustrated below:

|  | 1963 | 1964 |
|---|---|---|
| Inventory turnover for year........................ | 5.3 | 3.6 |
| Number of days' sales in average inventory (assuming a business year of 300 days)...................... | 57 | 83 |

In certain instances, instead of developing the number of days' sales in average inventories, it may be considered more useful to report the number of days' sales in inventories at the end of the period. The latter measurement is determined by dividing the ending inventory by the average daily cost of goods sold. This information would be helpful in evaluating the current asset position and particularly the inventory position as of a given date.

A company with departmental classifications for merchandise will find it desirable to support the inventory measurements for the company as a whole with individual measurements for each department, since there may be considerable variation among departments. A company engaged in manufacturing may compute turnover rates for finished goods, goods in process, and raw materials. The finished goods turnover is computed by dividing the cost of goods sold by the average finished goods inventory. Goods in process turnover is computed by dividing the cost of goods manufactured by the average goods in process inventory. Raw materials turnover is computed by dividing the cost of raw materials used by the average raw materials inventory.

The same valuation methods must be employed for inventories if measurements developed from inventory figures are to be comparable. Maximum accuracy in developing measurements is possible if information relating to inventories and cost of goods sold is available in terms of physical units rather than dollar costs.

The effect of seasonal factors on the size of inventories at the end of the period should be considered in the inventory analyses. Inventories may be abnormally high or low at the end of the period. Many companies adopt a fiscal year that ends when operations are at their lowest point. This is referred to as a *natural business year*. Inventories will normally be at their lowest point at the end of such a period. The organization is able to take inventory and complete year-end closing most conveniently. Under such circumstances, monthly inventory balances should be calculated by the gross profit method in arriving at a representative average inventory figure.

The greater the rate of turnover of the stock of merchandise, the smaller is the amount of investment necessary for a given volume of business and consequently the higher is the rate of return on invested capital. This conclusion assumes that the enterprise can acquire goods in smaller quantities sufficiently often at no price disadvantage. If merchandise must be bought in very large quantities in order to get favorable prices, then the savings on quantity purchases must be weighed against the additional investment and the increased costs of storage and other carrying charges.

The financial advantage of an increased turnover figure may be illustrated as follows. Assume that the cost of goods sold for a year was $1,000,000, and the average inventory at cost was $250,000; the rate of turnover, then, was 4 times. Assume, further, that through careful buying the same volume of business can be maintained with turnover of 5 times, or an average inventory of only $200,000. If interest on the money invested in carrying the inventory is 6%, the savings on $50,000 will be $3,000 annually. The above does not include possible advantages gained from a decrease in merchandise spoilage and obsolescence, savings in storage costs, insurance, and taxes, and reduction in the risk of losses from price declines.

Inventory investments and turnover rates vary among different enterprises. The facts of each business unit must be judged in terms of the financial structure and the activities of the particular unit. Each business must plan an inventory policy that will avoid the extremes of a dangerously low stock that may impair sales volume and an overstocking of goods with a heavy capital investment attended by dangers that goods may become shop-worn or obsolete, that prices may fall, and that difficulties may arise in meeting the obligations arising from purchases.

### Further analysis of current assets and current liabilities

Turnover analysis applied to the specific receivable and inventory items can be applied to total current assets and to working capital. Current asset turnover is calculated by dividing net sales by average current assets. Working capital turnover is calculated by dividing net sales by the average working capital. The turnover figures may be viewed as the number of times current asset or working capital is replenished, or alternatively, as the number of sales dollars emerging for every dollar invested in current assets or in working capital. Increases in the turnover rates would generally indicate more effective utilization of current assets or working capital.

Procedures similar to those used in analyzing specific assets may also be used in analyzing specific liabilities. An accounts payable turnover rate, for example, may be developed by dividing purchases by the average payables balance, or the number of days' purchases in accounts payable may be developed by dividing accounts payable by the average daily purchases. Analysis of liabilities in terms of due dates may assist management in its cash planning activities.    Useful relationships may also be obtained by comparing specific assets or liabilities with other assets or liabilities or with asset or liability totals.   For example, data concerning the relationship of cash to accounts payable and of cash to total liabilities may be useful.

### Ratio of stockholders' equity to total liabilities

The relationship of the equities of the stockholder group and the creditor group in business assets may be measured in terms of ratios. The statements employing vertical analysis in the preceding chapter illustrated the development of such measurements.   Instead of expressing stockholder and creditor equities in terms of total assets, equities may be expressed in terms of each other.   For example, stockholders may have a 60% interest in total assets and creditors a 40% interest.  Here one can say that the ratio of the stockholders' equity to the creditors' equity is 1.5 to 1, or that the stockholders' equity is 150% of the total liabilities of the business.

Comparative data reporting stockholders' and creditors' equities in assets and the relationships of such equities to each other show the changes taking place in the sources of business capital.  As the stockholders' equity rises in relation to the creditors' equity, the margin of protection to the creditor group goes up.  From the stockholders' point of view, such an increase makes the organization less vulnerable to a decline in business and possible inability to meet obligations, and also serves to minimize the cost of carrying the debt.

However, it should not be overlooked that it is often advantageous to supplement funds invested by stockholders with a certain amount of funds provided by creditors.  The use of borrowed funds is known as *trading on the equity*, or applying *capital leverage*.  It is assumed that the additional earnings accruing to the business through use of borrowed funds will exceed the interest charges for such use.  When the rate earned on borrowed funds exceeds the rate paid on borrowings, the rate of return on the stockholders' equity rises and the stockholders realize a gain through trading on the equity; when the rate earned is less than that paid, the rate of return shrinks and the stockholders suffer a loss.

The effects of trading on the equity are illustrated in the example that follows.  Assume that a company with 10,000 shares of stock outstanding is able to borrow $1,000,000 at 6% interest.  The company estimates that pre-tax earnings will be $80,000 if it operates without the borrowed capital. Income taxes are estimated at 50% of earnings. The summary below reports the effects upon net income, assuming that borrowed capital earns (1) 10%, and (2) 4%.

|  | Results of Operations Without Borrowed Capital | Results of Operations If Borrowed Capital Earns 10% | Results of Operations If Borrowed Capital Earns 4% |
|---|---|---|---|
| Net operating income............... | $ 80,000 | $180,000 | $120,000 |
| Interest expense.................... |  | 60,000 | 60,000 |
| Net income before income taxes..... | $ 80,000 | $120,000 | $ 60,000 |
| Income taxes at 50%............... | 40,000 | 60,000 | 30,000 |
| Net income....................... | $ 40,000 | $ 60,000 | $ 30,000 |
| Number of shares outstanding....... | 10,000 | 10,000 | 10,000 |
| Earnings per share................ | $4 | $6 | $3 |

For the Marshall Company, relationships of the stockholders' equity to total liabilities are calculated as follows:

|  | 1963 | 1964 |
|---|---|---|
| Stockholders' equity..................... | $1,445,000 | $1,468,000 |
| Total liabilities........................ | $ 946,000 | $ 810,000 |
| Ratio of stockholders' equity to total liabilities | 1.5 : 1 | 1.8 : 1 |

In analyzing the relationship of the stockholders' equity to the creditors' equity, particular note should be made of any lease arrangements that represent primarily financing devices. Both the property rights provided under the leases and the liabilities that accompany such rights would need to be considered in arriving at a full evaluation of the status of equities, the relationships of equities, and changes in such equities from period to period.

### Ratio of plant and equipment to long-term debt

Comparisons may be made between plant and equipment and the total long-term debt. When plant and equipment items are pledged on the long-term obligations, this ratio indicates the protection afforded to the long-term creditor group, as well as the possibility for the expansion of long-term indebtedness on the basis of available security.

In the development of the ratio of plant and equipment to long-term debt, present sound values of plant and equipment instead of book values should be used whenever available, since the protection to creditors as well as the ability of the business to borrow is based on the present market values of the properties pledged. If a bond retirement fund is maintained consisting of a company's own obligations that have been reacquired but not retired, this fund should be subtracted from the long-term debt in developing the ratio; a bond retirement fund consisting of other investments, however, would represent additional security on the indebtedness rather than a reduction in debt and should be added to plant and equipment for purposes of this ratio. Long-term creditors generally limit their loans to a certain percentage of the value of properties pledged, so that there may be an adequate margin of safety in the event of business failure and a need to apply the security to the payment of the indebtedness.

For the Marshall Company, ratios of plant and equipment to long-term debt are as follows:

|  | 1963 | 1964 |
|---|---|---|
| Plant and equipment (net)................... | $875,000 | $775,000 |
| Long-term debt............................. | $400,000 | $400,000 |
| Ratio of plant and equipment to long-term debt. | 2.2 : 1 | 1.9 : 1 |

### Ratio of stockholders' equity to plant and equipment

The changes in the relationship of stockholders' equity to plant and equipment need to be considered in judging whether expansion is taking place through increases in the stockholders' equity or through borrowing. An increasing ratio indicates that plant and equipment acquisitions are being financed through funds supplied by the sale of stock or the retention of earnings, and normally this would be looked upon favorably. A declining ratio indicates that the increase of plant properties has exceeded the expansion in stockholders' equity. This may suggest possible overexpansion, excessive use of credit, and greater vulnerability to financial difficulties in the event of a decline in business.

For the Marshall Company, ratios of stockholders' equity to plant and equipment are as follows:

|  | 1963 | 1964 |
|---|---|---|
| Stockholders' equity...................... | $1,445,000 | $1,468,000 |
| Plant and equipment (net)................ | $ 875,000 | $ 775,000 |
| Ratio of stockholders' equity to plant and equipment........................... | 1.7 : 1 | 1.9 : 1 |

### Book value per share of stock

An important measurement of the stockholders' equity is afforded by a determination of the *book value per share*. This is the recorded dollar equity related to each share. The calculation of share book value was described in Chapter 17. It was indicated there that, when there is only one class of stock, book value per share is calculated by dividing the total stockholders' equity by the number of shares outstanding. When both common and preferred shares are outstanding, it is necessary to allocate the total stockholders' equity to the two classes of stock. Redemption or liquidation values and cumulative and participating features of the preferred issue must be considered in determining the portion of the stockholders' equity relating to preferred stock.

Both common and preferred stock of the Marshall Company are $10 par. The preferred stock is cumulative and nonparticipating, and no dividends are in arrears. The preferred stock has a liquidation value equal to its par value. The book values per share for common and preferred stock are calculated as follows:

|  | 1963 | 1964 |
|---|---|---|
| Total stockholders' equity............... | $1,445,000 | $1,468,000 |
| Equity related to preferred shares.......... | 350,000 | 350,000 |
| Equity related to common shares........... | $1,095,000 | $1,118,000 |
| Number of shares outstanding: Preferred.... | 35,000 | 35,000 |
|                              Common.... | 75,000 | 75,000 |
| Book value per share: Preferred........... | $10.00 | $10.00 |
|                       Common........... | $14.60 | $14.91 |

Retained earnings are sometimes reduced by the amount of intangible assets reported on the balance sheet for the purpose of share book value calculations. Such a procedure would be appropriate when intangibles are of doubtful value. Book value of the stock thus reported offers a more conservative appraisal of the stockholders' equity.

### Other measurements of balance sheet structure

A number of measurements of balance sheet structure other than those already described are developed in specific instances. Among these might be mentioned the ratio of individual noncurrent assets to total assets of the business or to total assets of the group, and individual noncurrent liabilities to total liabilities of the business or to total liabilities of the group. Relationships such as the foregoing may be presented directly on comparative statements by means of vertical analysis procedures.

### Ratio of net sales to total assets

Among the measurements that are developed from balance sheet and income statement data is the *ratio of net sales to total assets*, sometimes called the *assets turnover rate*. This ratio is calculated by dividing the net sales figure by the total assets that produced the sales. The resulting figure indicates the contribution that is made by total assets to sales.

With comparative data, judgments may be made concerning the relative effectiveness of asset utilization. A ratio increase may suggest the better utilization of assets, although a point may be reached where there is a strain on assets and a company is unable to achieve its full sales potential. An increase in total assets when accompanied by a ratio decrease may suggest an overinvestment in assets or their inefficient use.

In developing the ratio, long-term investments should be excluded from the asset total when these make no contribution to sales. If monthly figures for assets are available, they may be used in developing a representative average for total assets employed during the year. Sometimes the assets at the end of the year are used as a basis for the computation. When sales can be expressed in terms of units sold, ratios in terms of sales units per dollar invested offer more reliable guides to interpretation than sales dollars, since unit results are not affected by product sales prices.

Assume in the case of the Marshall Company that only asset totals for the beginning and end of the year are available and that sales cannot be expressed in terms of units. Ratios of net sales to total assets are computed as follows:

|  | 1963 | 1964 |
|---|---|---|
| Net sales.............................. | $1,650,000 | $1,425,000 |
| Total assets (excluding long-term investments): | | |
|     Beginning of year...................... | $1,510,000 | $1,991,000 |
|     End of year.......................... | $1,991,000 | $1,778,000 |
| Average total assets...................... | $1,750,500 | $1,884,500 |
| Ratio of net sales to average total assets..... | 0.9 : 1 | 0.8 : 1 |

## Ratio of net sales to plant and equipment

Related to the ratio just described is the *ratio of net sales to plant and equipment*, sometimes referred to as the *plant and equipment turnover* or the *fixed asset turnover*. Net sales, here, is divided by the investment in plant and equipment. The resulting figure indicates how effectively plant and equipment is utilized in terms of sales. With comparative data, judgments may be made concerning the relative efficiency of utilization of these assets and the effects on sales of increases or decreases in property totals. An increase in plant and equipment when accompanied by a ratio decrease may suggest overexpansion in plant facilities.

Assume for the Marshall Company that balances at the beginning and end of the year are used in measuring the average investment in plant and equipment. Ratios of net sales to plant and equipment are computed as follows:

|  | 1963 | 1964 |
|---|---|---|
| Net sales. . . . . . . . . . . . . . . . . . . . . . . . . . . . . . | $1,650,000 | $1,425,000 |
| Plant and equipment (net): |  |  |
| Beginning of year. . . . . . . . . . . . . . . . . . . . | $ 675,000 | $ 875,000 |
| End of year. . . . . . . . . . . . . . . . . . . . . . . . . | $ 875,000 | $ 775,000 |
| Average investment in plant and equipment. | $ 775,000 | $ 825,000 |
| Ratio of net sales to average plant and equip- |  |  |
| ment. . . . . . . . . . . . . . . . . . . . . . . . . . . . . . . | 2.1 : 1 | 1.7 : 1 |

When intangible assets contribute significantly to sales, these may be combined with plant and equipment in establishing the base for this measurement.

It may be pointed out that with increasing price levels and an unchanged sales volume in terms of units sold, the ratio of sales to plant and equipment may show regular improvement because sales prices are increasing while asset costs remain unchanged. In order to obtain a more meaningful ratio, the fair market values of property items rather than historical book values may be used.

**Rate of return on total assets**

The adequacy of earnings may be measured in terms of (1) the return on sales, (2) the return on total assets, and (3) the return on the stockholders' equity. There should be an adequate return in terms of each of the three standards if operating results are to be considered satisfactory. The return on sales was measured in the previous chapter where vertical analysis was applied to income statement data. The return on total assets and on the stockholders' equity are described in this and the following section.

The rate earned on total assets, frequently referred to as the *asset productivity rate*, is found by dividing the net income for the year by the total assets employed in the production of such income. If total assets by months are available, they should be used in developing an average for the year. Frequently, however, the assets at the beginning of the year or the assets at the end of the year are used for the calculation. In some instances it may be desirable to exclude revenue items arising from investments, such as interest, dividends, and rents, so that net income is limited to that resulting from trading operations. When this is the case, total assets should be reduced by the investments in developing the rate of return. Sometimes the rate of net operating income to total assets, or, perhaps, the rate of net income before income taxes to total assets, is developed in comparative form so that rates of return are not affected by financial management items or by changes in income tax rates.

Rates earned on total assets for the Marshall Company are determined as follows:

|  | 1963 | 1964 |
|---|---|---|
| Net income......................... | $ 60,000 | $ 70,000 |
| Total assets: | | |
|   Beginning of year.................... | $1,760,000 | $2,391,000 |
|   End of year....................... | $2,391,000 | $2,278,000 |
| Average total assets.................. | $2,075,500 | $2,334,500 |
| Rate earned on average total assets......... | 2.89% | 3.00% |

## Rate of return on stockholders' equity

The rate earned on the stockholders' equity is found by dividing the net income by the stockholders' equity. In the development of this rate, it is preferable to use the average stockholders' equity for a year calculated from monthly data, particularly when significant changes have occurred during the year as a result of the sale of additional stock, the retirement of stock, the payment of dividends, and the accumulation of earnings. Sometimes the beginning or the ending stockholders' equity is used for the measurement.

For the Marshall Company, rates earned on the stockholders' equity are calculated as follows:

|  | 1963 | 1964 |
|---|---|---|
| Net income........................... | $ 60,000 | $ 70,000 |
| Stockholders' equity: | | |
|   Beginning of year.................... | $1,330,000 | $1,445,000 |
|   End of year....................... | $1,445,000 | $1,468,000 |
| Average stockholders' equity............. | $1,387,500 | $1,456,500 |
| Rate earned on average stockholders' equity. | 4.32% | 4.81% |

## Times bond interest requirements were earned

Earnings may also be measured in terms of (1) their relationship to bond interest requirements, (2) their relationship to preferred dividend requirements, and (3) their availability to common stockholders.

The number of times that earnings cover the bond interest is calculated by dividing net income before any charges for bond interest or income taxes by the bond interest requirements for the period. The ability of the company to meet interest payments and the degree of safety afforded the bondholders is thus reported. The number of times interest charges were earned by the Marshall Company follows:

|  | 1963 | 1964 |
|---|---|---|
| Net income before income taxes............... | $ 85,000 | $100,000 |
| Add bond interest ($4\frac{1}{2}\%$ of $400,000).......... | 18,000 | 18,000 |
| Amount available in meeting bond interest requirements................................. | $103,000 | $118,000 |
| Number of times bond interest requirements were earned..................................... | 5.7 | 6.6 |

Net income before income taxes was used in the calculation above in view of the fact that income taxes apply only after bond interest is deducted and it is pre-tax income that affords the protection to the bond-holder group. However, the calculation is frequently made in terms of net income after income taxes. The latter procedure is employed because it is easier to apply, reference being made to the final net income figure on the income statement, it is consistent with other measurements employing net income, and it offers a more conservative approach in appraising the ability of the enterprise to meet periodic interest requirements. For the Marshall Company, net income balances after income taxes for 1963 and 1964 were $60,000 and $70,000 respectively. These balances would be raised by interest requirements for each year of $18,000, and divided by the same amounts, resulting in times-interest-earned calculations for 1963 and 1964 of 4.3 and 4.9 respectively.

In addition to calculations of interest coverage, calculations may be made of the number of times all fixed charges are covered in measuring a company's ability to meet its regularly recurring financial commitments such as management salaries, rents, taxes, and interest.

## Times preferred dividend requirements were earned

The number of times that earnings cover the preferred dividends is calculated by dividing net income for the year by the annual preferred dividend requirements. For the Marshall Company, calculations are:

|  | 1963 | 1964 |
|---|---|---|
| Net income................................ | $ 60,000 | $ 70,000 |
| Preferred dividend requirements (6% of $350,000) | $ 21,000 | $ 21,000 |
| Number of times preferred dividend requirements were earned...................... | 2.9 | 3.3 |

The relationship of earnings to preferred dividend requirements may also be indicated by dividing net income by the number of preferred shares outstanding. It should be recognized that this calculation does not show the amount of earnings to which preferred shares are entitled, but simply the amount of earnings that are available in meeting preferred dividend requirements.

For the Marshall Company, earnings available in meeting preferred dividend requirements are calculated as follows:

|  | 1963 | 1964 |
|---|---|---|
| Net income................................ | $ 60,000 | $ 70,000 |
| Number of shares of preferred outstanding..... | 35,000 | 35,000 |
| Earnings available in meeting preferred dividend requirements........................... | $1.71 | $2.00 |

Since preferred stock is 6%, $10 par, earnings required to cover preferred dividends would be 60 cents per share.

## Rate earned on common stockholders' equity

The rate earned on the common stockholders' equity is calculated by dividing the net income after preferred dividend requirements by the equity of the common stockholders. The average equity for common stockholders should be determined, although the rate is frequently based upon the beginning or ending common equity.

In the case of the Marshall Company whose preferred stock is non-participating, preferred dividend requirements are limited to 6%. The rate earned on the common stockholders' equity, then, is calculated as follows:

|  | 1963 | 1964 |
|---|---|---|
| Net income after income taxes............. | $ 60,000 | $ 70,000 |
| Less dividend requirements on preferred stock | 21,000 | 21,000 |
| Income related to common stockholders' equity................................. | $ 39,000 | $ 49,000 |
| Common stockholders' equity: | | |
| Beginning of year...................... | $1,080,000 | $1,095,000 |
| End of year........................... | $1,095,000 | $1,118,000 |
| Average common stockholders' equity...... | $1,087,500 | $1,106,500 |
| Rate earned on average common stockholder's equity................................. | 3.6% | 4.4% |

## Earnings per share on common stock

Earnings on common stock may be expressed in terms of the dollar amount relating to each share. In computing common share earnings, net income after the prior claim on earnings of preferred stock is divided by the number of common shares outstanding. In the case of the Marshall Company, earnings per share on common stock are computed as follows:

|  | 1963 | 1964 |
|---|---|---|
| Net income..................................... | $60,000 | $70,000 |
| Less dividend requirements on preferred stock.... | 21,000 | 21,000 |
| Income related to common stockholders' equity... | $39,000 | $49,000 |
| Number of shares of common stock outstanding... | 75,000 | 75,000 |
| Earnings per share on common stock............ | $ .52 | $ .65 |

## Price-earnings ratio on common stock

The market price of common stock may be expressed as a multiple of its earnings to provide a means of evaluating the attractiveness of common stock as an investment. In developing this measurement, referred to as the *price-earnings ratio*, market value per share of stock is divided by the annual earnings per share. Instead of using the average market value of shares for the period covered by earnings, the latest market value is normally used. Assuming market values for common stock of the Marshall Company at the end of 1963 and 1964 of $6.50 and $10.00 per share, price-earnings ratios would be calculated as follows:

|  | 1963 | 1964 |
|---|---|---|
| Market value per common share at end of year..... | $ 6.50 | $10.00 |
| Earnings per share............................. | $ .52 | $ .65 |
| Price-earnings ratio........................... | 12.5 | 15.4 |

As an alternative to the foregoing, earnings per share can be presented as a percentage based on the market value of the stock. Care should be taken to indicate that the earnings rate thus computed is stated in terms of the increase in the stockholders' equity as a result of profitable operations and not in terms of dividends actually paid to stockholders.

### Yield on common stock

A rate of return or *yield* in terms of actual distributions to common stockholders is found by dividing the annual dividends per common share by the latest market value per common share. For the Marshall Company, yields on the common stock are calculated as follows:

|  | 1963 | 1964 |
|---|---|---|
| Dividends for year per common share............. | $ .32 | $ .3467 |
| Market value per common share at end of year.... | $ 6.50 | $10.00 |
| Yield on common shares........................ | 4.9% | 3.5% |

### Distribution of earnings to creditor and ownership equities

Inasmuch as earnings are the ultimate source upon which the creditors and the owners of an enterprise must rely for a return of both principal and income, and because the different classes of security holders normally obtain different rates of return, a percentage analysis of the disposition of the earnings of a company may be of interest to all groups. In the case of the Marshall Company it is possible to prepare a summary of the distribution of earnings as follows:

|  | Equity Totals[1] | | Equity Percentage | | Amount of Earnings Paid and Accruing* to Equities | | Percentage Distribution of Total Earnings Paid or Accruing* to Equities | | Percentage Paid or Accruing* to Equities | |
|---|---|---|---|---|---|---|---|---|---|---|
|  | 1963 | 1964 | 1963 | 1964 | 1963 | 1964 | 1963 | 1964 | 1963 | 1964 |
| Bondholders (4½% long-term debt).......... | $ 400,000 | $ 400,000 | 22% | 22% | $18,000 | $18,000 | 23% | 20% | 4.5% | 4.5% |
| Preferred stockholders... | 350,000 | 350,000 | 19% | 19% | 21,000 | 21,000 | 27% | 24% | 6.0% | 6.0% |
| Common stockholders... | 1,087,500 | 1,106,500 | 59% | 59% | (24,000 | 26,000 | 31% | 30% | 2.2%[2] | 2.3% |
|  |  |  |  |  | (15,000* | 23,000* | 19%* | 26%* | 1.4%* | 2.1%* |
| Total................. | $1,837,500 | $1,856,500 | 100% | 100% | $78,000 | $88,000 | 100% | 100% | 4.2% | 4.7% |

[1]Average equities for the year are indicated in this illustration. It would be possible to base analyses on equities as of the beginning of the year or equities as of the end of the year.

[2]This percentage, while stated in terms of the common stockholders' equity, could be stated in terms of the par or stated value of the common stock or in terms of market value of the stock.

### Other measurements of operations

A number of other measurements of operations and operating results that are significant in various instances can be developed. Among these may be mentioned such ratios as gross profit to sales, net operating income to sales, net income to sales, individual manufacturing costs to cost of goods manufactured, individual selling expenses and individual general and administrative expenses to the totals for these groups. These relationships are generally presented by means of comparative statements offering horizontal and vertical analyses of profit and loss data.

### Interpretation of analyses

Analyses introduced in Chapter 18 and in this chapter are developed to help the analyst arrive at certain conclusions with regard to the business. It has already been stated that these are merely guides to the intelligent interpretation of financial data.

All of the ratios and measurements need not be used, but rather only those that will actually assist in the development of opinions with respect to the questions that have been raised by the analyst. The measurements that are developed need to be interpreted in terms of the conditions relating to the particular enterprise, the conditions relating to the particular industry in which the enterprise is found, and the conditions relating to the general business and the economic environment within which the enterprise operates. If measurements are to be of maximum value, they need to be compared with similar data developed for the particular enterprise for past periods, with similar measurements for the industry as a whole that may be regarded as standard, and with pertinent data relating to general business conditions and business and price fluctuations as these affect the individual enterprise. Only by intelligent use and integration of the foregoing sources of data can financial weaknesses and strengths be identified and reliable opinions be developed concerning business structure, operations, and growth.

### QUESTIONS

**1.** Define working capital and appraise its significance.

**2.** Distinguish between the current ratio and the acid-test ratio. What are usually considered minimums for each ratio?

**3.** Balance sheets for the Blake Corporation and the Carlson Corporation each show a working capital total of $500,000. Does this indicate that the short-term solvencies of the two companies are approximately equal? Explain.

**4.** Define (a) banker's ratio, (b) quick assets, (c) price-earnings ratio.

**5.** (a) How is the accounts receivable turnover calculated?  (b) How would you interpret a rising accounts receivable turnover rate?

**6.** (a) How is inventory turnover calculated?  (b) What precautions are necessary in arriving at the basis for the turnover calculation? (c) How would you interpret a rising inventory turnover?

**7.** (a) What is meant by *trading on the equity?* (b) Give figures to illustrate a gain accruing to owners through this practice.

**8.** "The ratio of stockholders' equity to total liabilities offers information concerning the long-term solvency of the business unit."  Explain.

**9.** Give rules for calculating share book values when a company has both common and preferred stock outstanding.

**10.** State the significance of each of the following measurements: (a) ratio of plant and equipment to long-term debt, (b) ratio of stockholders' equity to plant and equipment, (c) ratio of sales to total assets, and (d) ratio of sales to plant and equipment.

**11.** (a) What is meant by the *asset productivity rate?*  (b) How is it calculated?

**12.** Indicate how each of the following measurements is calculated and appraise its significance:

   (a) The number of times bond interest requirements were earned.
   (b) The number of times preferred dividend requirements were earned.
   (c) The rate of earnings on the common stockholders' equity.
   (d) The earnings per share on common stock.
   (e) The price-earnings ratio on common stock.
   (f) The yield on common stock.

**13.** (a) Distinguish between the *natural business year* and the *thirteen-month year.*  (b) What advantages are found in the adoption of each for accounting purposes?

## EXERCISES

**1.** The data that follow are taken from comparative balance sheets prepared for the Stanford Company:

|  | 1963 | 1964 |
|---|---|---|
| Cash. . . . . . . . . . . . . . . . . . . . . . . . . . . . . . . . . . . . . . . | $ 16,000 | $ 30,000 |
| Marketable securities. . . . . . . . . . . . . . . . . . . . . . . | 20,000 | 10,000 |
| Trade receivables (net). . . . . . . . . . . . . . . . . . . . . | 45,000 | 55,000 |
| Inventories. . . . . . . . . . . . . . . . . . . . . . . . . . . . . . . . | 60,000 | 75,000 |
| Prepaid expenses. . . . . . . . . . . . . . . . . . . . . . . . . . | 1,500 | 2,500 |
| Plant and equipment (net). . . . . . . . . . . . . . . . . . | 80,000 | 85,000 |
| Intangibles. . . . . . . . . . . . . . . . . . . . . . . . . . . . . . . . | 25,000 | 22,500 |
| Other assets. . . . . . . . . . . . . . . . . . . . . . . . . . . . . . | 5,000 | 6,000 |
|  | $252,500 | $286,000 |
| Current liabilities. . . . . . . . . . . . . . . . . . . . . . . . . . | $ 60,000 | $100,000 |

(a) **From the data given calculate** for both 1963 and 1964: (1) the working capital, (2) the current ratio, (3) the acid-test ratio, (4) the ratio of current assets to total assets, (5) the ratio of cash to current liabilities.

(b) Evaluate each of the above changes.

**2.** Statements for the Hancock Co. show the following balances:

|  | 1962 | 1963 | 1964 |
|---|---|---|---|
| Average receivables (net)........... | $ 30,000 | $ 40,000 | $ 60,000 |
| Net sales........................ | 345,000 | 390,000 | 480,000 |

Give any significant measurements that may be developed in analyzing the foregoing, assuming a 300-day business year and assuming that approximately one third of the sales are for cash, the balance being on account. What conclusions may be made concerning the receivables if sales on account are made on a 2/30, n/60 basis?

**3.** The average inventory for the ABC Company at cost price is $40,000; sales for 1964 were made at 20% above cost and totaled $300,000. (a) What was the inventory turnover rate? (b) What is the average age of the inventory, assuming a 300-day year?

**4.** Operating statements for the Wade Sales Co. show the following:

|  | 1962 | 1963 | 1964 |
|---|---|---|---|
| Sales........................ | $ 80,000 | $ 95,000 | $105,000 |
| Cost of goods sold: |  |  |  |
| Beginning inventory............. | $ 15,000 | $ 20,000 | $ 35,000 |
| Purchases.................... | 60,000 | 80,000 | 95,000 |
|  | $ 75,000 | $100,000 | $130,000 |
| Ending inventory............... | 20,000 | 35,000 | 55,000 |
|  | $ 55,000 | $ 65,000 | $ 75,000 |
| Gross profit on sales.............. | $ 25,000 | $ 30,000 | $ 30,000 |

Give whatever measurements may be developed in analyzing the inventory position at the end of each year. What conclusions would you make concerning the inventory trend?

**5.** The following data are taken from the Mason Corporation records for the years ending December 31, 1962, 1963, and 1964:

|  | 1962 | 1963 | 1964 |
|---|---|---|---|
| Finished goods inventory........... | $ 15,000 | $ 30,000 | $ 60,000 |
| Goods in process inventory......... | 40,000 | 40,000 | 40,000 |
| Raw materials inventory........... | 25,000 | 40,000 | 50,000 |
| Sales........................ | 360,000 | 340,000 | 400,000 |
| Cost of goods sold................ | 210,000 | 235,000 | 230,000 |
| Cost of goods manufactured........ | 200,000 | 250,000 | 260,000 |
| Materials used in production........ | 120,000 | 130,000 | 150,000 |

Calculate turnover figures for 1963 and 1964 for (a) finished goods, (b) goods in process, and (c) raw materials.

**6.** The total purchases of goods by the Bailey Wholesale Company during 1964 were $360,000. All purchases were on a 2/10, n/30 basis. The average balance in the vouchers payable account was $45,000. Was the company prompt, slow, or average in paying for goods? How many days' average purchases were there in accounts payable, assuming a 300-day year?

**7.** The capital accounts of the Mathews Corporation on December 31, 1964, are as follows:

| | |
|---|---|
| 6% Preferred stock, $50 par.......................... | $ 500,000 |
| Common stock, $10 par............................. | 1,000,000 |
| Additional paid-in capital.......................... | 200,000 |
| Retained earnings.................................. | 100,000 |

Give the book value per share for both preferred and common stock, assuming each of the following conditions:

(a) Preferred stock is cumulative and nonparticipating, with no dividends in arrears.
(b) Preferred stock is cumulative and nonparticipating, and dividends are in arrears since January 1, 1963.
(c) Preferred stock is cumulative and fully participating, with no dividend arrearages.
(d) Preferred stock is cumulative and fully participating, and dividends are in arrears since January 1, 1963.

**8.** The balance sheets for the Keller Company showed the following equities at the end of each year:

| | 1963 | 1964 |
|---|---|---|
| 4% Bonds payable...................... | $ 500,000 | $ 500,000 |
| 6% Nonparticipating preferred stock, $100 par.................................. | 500,000 | 600,000 |
| Common stock, $25 par................. | 1,000,000 | 1,200,000 |
| Additional paid-in capital............... | 100,000 | 100,000 |
| Retained earnings..................... | 200,000 | 300,000 |

Net income after income taxes was: 1963, $60,000; 1964, $105,000. Using the foregoing data, calculate for each year:

(a) The rate of earnings on the total stockholders' equity at the end of the year.
(b) The number of times bond interest requirements were earned.
(c) The number of times preferred dividend requirements were earned.
(d) The rate earned on the common stockholders' equity.
(e) The earnings per share on common stock.

## PROBLEMS

**19-1.** The balance sheet data for the Anderson Corp. on December 31, 1964, are given on the following page.

*Instructions:* From the balance sheet data, calculate the following:

(1) The amount of working capital.
(2) The current ratio.

(3) The acid-test ratio.
(4) The ratio of current assets to total assets.
(5) The ratio of stockholders' equity to total liabilities.
(6) The ratio of plant and equipment to bonds payable.
(7) The book value per share of preferred stock.
(8) The book value per share of common stock.

| Assets | | Liabilities and Stockholders' Equity | |
|---|---|---|---|
| Cash ........................ | $ 60,000 | Notes and accounts payable ... | $ 75,000 |
| Marketable securities ........ | 160,000 | Income taxes payable ........ | 15,000 |
| Notes and accounts receivable | | Accrued wages and interest ... | 5,000 |
| (net) ................... | 180,000 | Dividends payable .......... | 5,000 |
| Inventories ................ | 300,000 | Bonds payable ............. | 400,000 |
| Prepaid expenses ........... | 15,000 | Deferred revenues .......... | 10,000 |
| Bond redemption fund (secur- | | Common stock, $20 par ...... | 1,000,000 |
| ities of other companies) .... | 150,000 | Preferred stock, $10 par (non- | |
| Plant and equipment (net) .... | 930,000 | participating, noncumula- | |
| Intangibles ................ | 200,000 | tive) ..................... | 200,000 |
| Unamortized bond issue costs . | 5,000 | Retained earnings appropri- | |
| | | ated for plant expansion.... | 100,000 |
| | | Retained earnings.......... | 190,000 |
| | $2,000,000 | | $2,000,000 |

**19-2.** Comparative data for Morton-Good, Inc. for the three-year period 1962–1964 are presented below and on the following page.

### Income Statement Data

| | 1962 | 1963 | 1964 |
|---|---|---|---|
| Net sales........................... | $ 800,000 | $1,000,000 | $1,200,000 |
| Cost of goods sold.................. | 500,000 | 660,000 | 760,000 |
| Gross profit on sales................ | $ 300,000 | $ 340,000 | $ 440,000 |
| Selling, general, and other expenses.... | 280,000 | 300,000 | 350,000 |
| Net operating income............... | $ 20,000 | $ 40,000 | $ 90,000 |
| Income taxes...................... | 5,000 | 15,000 | 35,000 |
| Net income....................... | $ 15,000 | $ 25,000 | $ 55,000 |
| Dividends paid.................... | 15,000 | 30,000 | 40,000 |
| Net increase (decrease) in retained earn- | | | |
| ings............................. | — | ($ 5,000) | $ 15,000 |

### Balance Sheet Data

| Assets | 1962 | 1963 | 1964 |
|---|---|---|---|
| Cash.............................. | $ 50,000 | $ 35,000 | $ 55,000 |
| Trade notes and accounts rec. (net)... | 245,000 | 320,000 | 400,000 |
| Inventory (at cost)................. | 320,000 | 380,000 | 420,000 |
| Prepaid expenses................... | 20,000 | 10,000 | 30,000 |
| Plant and equipment (net) .......... | 650,000 | 600,000 | 680,000 |
| Intangibles........................ | 100,000 | 100,000 | 100,000 |
| Other assets....................... | 5,000 | 5,000 | 15,000 |
| | $1,390,000 | $1,450,000 | $1,700,000 |

Liabilities and Stockholders' Equity

| | | | |
|---|---|---|---|
| Trade notes and accounts payable..... | $ 130,000 | $ 165,000 | $ 205,000 |
| Wages, interest, dividends payable..... | 15,000 | 25,000 | 45,000 |
| Income taxes payable................ | 5,000 | 15,000 | 35,000 |
| Miscellaneous current liabilities....... | 10,000 | 15,000 | 10,000 |
| 5% bonds payable................... | 300,000 | 300,000 | 300,000 |
| Deferred revenues................... | 5,000 | 10,000 | 10,000 |
| 6% preferred stock, nonparticipating, $100 par...................... | 200,000 | 200,000 | 200,000 |
| No-par common stock, $10 stated value. | 400,000 | 400,000 | 500,000 |
| Additional paid-in capital............ | 200,000 | 200,000 | 260,000 |
| Retained earnings — appropriated.... | 60,000 | 60,000 | 80,000 |
| Retained earnings — free........... | 65,000 | 60,000 | 55,000 |
| | $1,390,000 | $1,450,000 | $1,700,000 |

*Instructions:* From the foregoing data, calculate comparative structural measurements for 1963 and 1964 as follows:

(1) The amount of working capital.

(2) The current ratio.

(3) The acid-test ratio.

(4) The trade receivables turnover rate for the year (all sales are on a credit basis).

(5) The average days' sales in trade receivables at the end of the year (assume a 300-day business year and all sales on a credit basis).

(6) The trade payables turnover rate for the year.

(7) The average days' purchases in payables at the end of the year.

(8) The inventory turnover rate.

(9) The number of days' sales in the inventory at the end of the year.

(10) The ratio of stockholders' equity to total liabilities.

(11) The ratio of plant and equipment to bonds payable.

(12) The ratio of stockholders' equity to plant and equipment.

(13) The book value per share of preferred stock.

(14) The book value per share of common stock.

**19-3.** Using the comparative data for Morton-Good, Inc. (Problem 19-2), calculate comparative operating measurements for 1963 and 1964 as follows:

(1) The ratio of net sales to average total assets.

(2) The ratio of net sales to average plant and equipment.

(3) The rate earned on net sales.

(4) The gross profit rate on net sales.

(5) The rate earned on average total assets.

(6) The rate earned on average stockholders' equity.

(7) The number of times bond interest requirements were earned (before income taxes).

(8) The number of times preferred dividend requirements were earned.

(9) The rate earned on average common stockholders' equity.

(10) The earnings per share on common stock.

**19-4.** Using the comparative data for Morton-Good, Inc. as given in Problem 19-2, prepare a summary of the distribution of earnings for the three-year period similar to that illustrated on page 539. Measurements are to be based on equity totals as of the end of each year.

**19-5.** Using the data for the Cunningham Mfg. Co. as given in Problem 18-3 on pages 516–518, calculate comparative structural measurements for 1963 and 1964 as follows:

(1) The amount of working capital.
(2) The current ratio.
(3) The acid-test ratio.
(4) The current asset turnover rate.
(5) The finished goods inventory turnover rate.
(6) The raw materials inventory turnover rate.
(7) The number of days' sales in average finished goods inventory (assume a 300-day business year).
(8) The number of days' raw materials requirements in average raw materials inventory.
(9) The ratio of stockholders' equity to total liabilities.
(10) The ratio of plant and equipment to long-term debt.
(11) The book value per share of the preferred stock.
(12) The book value per share of the common stock.

**19-6.** Using the data for the Cunningham Mfg. Co. as given in Problem 18-3 on pages 516–518, calculate comparative operating measurements for 1963 and 1964 as follows:

(1) The ratio of net sales to average total assets (excluding long-term investments).
(2) The ratio of net sales to average plant and equipment.
(3) The rate earned on net sales.
(4) The gross profit rate on net sales.
(5) The rate earned on average total assets.
(6) The rate earned on average stockholders' equity.
(7) The number of times long-term debt interest requirements were earned (before income taxes).
(8) The number of times preferred dividend requirements were earned.
(9) The rate earned on average common stockholders' equity.
(10) The earnings per share on common stock.

**19-7.** Using the comparative data for the Cunningham Mfg. Co. as given in Problem 18-3 on pages 516–518, prepare a summary of the distribution of earnings for 1963 and 1964 similar to that illustrated on page 539. Measurements are to be based on equity totals as of the end of each year.

**19-8.** Inventory and receivable balances and also gross profit data for the Crosser Company appear below:

|  | 1962 | 1963 | 1964 |
|---|---|---|---|
| Balance Sheet Data: |  |  |  |
| Inventory, December 31............. | $ 40,000 | $ 50,000 | $ 80,000 |
| Receivables, December 31.......... | 30,000 | 35,000 | 50,000 |
| Profit and Loss Data: |  |  |  |
| Net sales......................... | $210,000 | $270,000 | $300,000 |
| Cost of goods sold................ | 150,000 | 200,000 | 230,000 |
| Gross profit on sales.............. | $ 60,000 | $ 70,000 | $ 70,000 |

*Instructions:* Assuming a 300-day business year and all sales on a credit basis, calculate the following measurements for 1963 and 1964.

(1) The receivables turnover rate.
(2) The average days' sales in receivables at the end of the year.
(3) The inventory turnover rate.
(4) The number of days' sales in the inventory at the end of the year.

**19-9.** Stockholders' equities for the America Corporation at the end of 1963 and 1964 were as follows:

|  | 1963 | 1964 |
|---|---|---|
| 6% Pref. stock, par and liquidating value $50... | $100,000 | $100,000 |
| Common stock, $10 par..................... | 250,000 | 350,000 |
| Additional paid-in capital................... | 400,000 | 500,000 |
| Retained earnings......................... | 20,000 | 60,000 |

Give the book value per share of both common stock and preferred stock at the end of 1963 and at the end of 1964, assuming the conditions that are stated for each case below:

(1) Preferred is cumulative and nonparticipating; dividend requirements have been met on preferred annually.
(2) Preferred is cumulative and nonparticipating; the last dividend on preferred stock was paid for the year 1961.
(3) Preferred is cumulative and fully participating; dividend requirements have been met on preferred annually.
(4) Preferred is cumulative and fully participating; the last dividend on preferred stock was paid for the year 1961.

# Chapter 20

# FUNDS-FLOW AND
# CASH-FLOW REPORTING

## Nature and purpose of the funds statement

The financial statements that have been considered in detail in the preceding chapters are frequently supplemented by a *funds statement*. The latter is also variously referred to as *the statement of application of funds, the source and application of funds statement, the statement of financial operations, the statement of resources provided and applied, and the where-got, where-gone statement.*

The balance sheet provides a summary of a company's financial resources and the equities of the creditors and owners in such resources at the end of the period. Statements of income and capital summarize the activities that were responsible for the changes in capital during the period. The funds statement summarizes the activities that were responsible for the changes in the financial resources during the period. The funds statement in reporting the activities that generated resources and the uses to which such resources were directed offers the answers to such questions as: "What was responsible for the change in working capital?" "What was done with profits?" "How has expansion been financed?" "What amounts were raised by the sale of properties, the issue of bonds, the issue of stock?" "What was spent for plant and equipment, the liquidation of debt, the retirement of outstanding stock?" "Why aren't dividend payments larger?" "Why did working capital go down when profits were satisfactory?" "How was the bonded indebtedness paid off when operations resulted in a substantial loss?"

Stockholders, management, creditors, financial analysts, and others who refer to a company's financial statements are seriously concerned with a company's earnings history and earnings future; these parties are equally concerned with a company's financial resources and how these resources are being employed. Management, in particular, makes important use of the funds statement, not only as a means of appraising financial policies of the past but also as a tool for planning financial activities of the future. The number of businesses — both large and small — preparing the funds statement as an integral part of periodic reporting has grown larger each year. A number of companies now include the funds statement in the group of financial statements covered by the auditor's report.[1]  To be most useful, the statement should be prepared in comparative form for two or more years.  In many instances, the statement is particularly informative when prepared in cumulative form covering a number of years.

## "Funds" defined

*Funds* for purposes of the funds statement is defined in a number of ways, and the definition that is employed determines the character as well as the form of the statement.  Funds is generally used to denote working capital.  In its broadest sense, the term has been used to denote all financial resources.  In its narrowest sense, it has been used to denote no more than cash.  A fourth view of funds takes a position between the working capital view and the cash view, regarding funds as a company's net monetary assets or net quick assets — current assets excluding inventory and prepaid items, less current liabilities.

## Funds statement applying different fund concepts

The funds statement is prepared from comparative balance sheets supplemented by explanations for individual account changes.  To illustrate the process of analysis and the development of the funds statement applying each of the fund concepts suggested, assume balance sheet information for the Parker Company as follows:

| Assets | Dec. 31, 1963 | Dec. 31, 1964 | Liabilities and Stockholders' Equity | Dec. 31, 1963 | Dec. 31, 1964 |
|---|---|---|---|---|---|
| Cash................ | $100,000 | $ 75,000 | Accounts payable...... | $100,000 | $160,000 |
| Accounts receivable.. | 110,000 | 170,000 | Accrued expenses..... | 30,000 | 20,000 |
| Inventories......... | 160,000 | 195,000 | Long-term debt...... | 100,000 | 80,000 |
| Prepaid expenses..... | 20,000 | 10,000 | Preferred stock....... | | 100,000 |
| Plant and equipment. | | 130,000 | Common stock....... | 200,000 | 320,000 |
| Land.............. | 60,000 | 160,000 | Retained earnings.... | 20,000 | 60,000 |
| Totals........... | $450,000 | $740,000 | Totals........... | $450,000 | $740,000 |

*Funds defined as working capital.*  When funds are defined as working capital, balance sheet changes must be analyzed in terms of their effects upon the working capital pool.  Investigation of the balance sheet changes for the Parker Company for 1964 reveals the following:

The increase in plant and equipment reflects an application of funds of $130,000 to the purchase of plant and equipment items.

The decrease in long-term debt reflects an application of funds of $20,000 to the retirement of long-term debt.

---

[1] In the AICPA list of 600 survey companies, the number that included the funds statement in financial reports to stockholders was 228 in 1962 as compared with 116 in 1950; the number of funds statements that was covered by auditors' reports was 50 in 1962 as compared with 13 in 1950. *Accounting Trends and Techniques, Seventeenth Edition,* 1963 (New York:  American Institute of Certified Public Accountants), pp. 18, 21.

The increase in common stock reflects a source of funds of $120,000 from the sale of shares.

Retained earnings went up as a result of net income for the period. The increase in retained earnings, then, reflects a source of funds of $40,000 — working capital provided through sales exceeding the working capital consumed through cost of goods sold and expenses.

The increases in land and in preferred stock are found to be without funds significance. An examination of the account changes shows that land was acquired in exchange for preferred stock.

The foregoing analysis indicates an increase in working capital for the year of $10,000, funds of $160,000 being provided from the sale of common stock and from profitable operations and funds of $150,000 being applied to plant and equipment and to the retirement of long-term debt. This increase is confirmed by the working capital totals which are found to be $270,000 at the end of the year as compared with $260,000 at the beginning of the year. A statement for the Parker Company summarizing working capital changes for the year is given below. This statement, as well as the statements that are illustrated later, employs terms that are descriptive of the funds concept adopted in its preparation.

Parker Company<br>Statement of Source and Application of Working Capital<br>For Year Ended December 31, 1964

| | | |
|---|---:|---:|
| Working capital was provided by: | | |
| Sale of common stock................................... | $120,000 | |
| Operations............................................. | 40,000 | $160,000 |
| Working capital was applied to: | | |
| Acquisition of plant and equipment...................... | $130,000 | |
| Retirement of long-term debt........................... | 20,000 | 150,000 |
| Increase in working capital............................. | | $ 10,000 |

The increase in working capital is accounted for as follows:

| Working Capital Items | Dec. 31 1963 | Dec. 31 1964 | Increase (Decrease) |
|---|---:|---:|---:|
| Current assets: | | | |
| Cash...................................... | $100,000 | $ 75,000 | ($25,000) |
| Accounts receivable...................... | 110,000 | 170,000 | 60,000 |
| Inventories.............................. | 160,000 | 195,000 | 35,000 |
| Prepaid expenses........................ | 20,000 | 10,000 | ( 10,000) |
| Current liabilities: | | | |
| Accounts payable........................ | 100,000 | 160,000 | ( 60,000) |
| Accrued expenses....................... | 30,000 | 20,000 | 10,000 |
| Increase in working capital................. | | | $10,000 |

The statement that appears above consists of two sections. The first section reports working capital inflow and outflow and the change in working capital for the period. The second section reports the individual changes within the working capital pool and summarizes and reconciles such changes with the change reported in the first section. Although working capital has increased by $10,000, which may be regarded as favorable, significant changes have taken place within the working capital pool which may not be similarly regarded, and the ratio of current assets to current liabilities has changed from 3.0:1 to 2.5:1.

Instead of being prepared in two-section form, the statement may provide only the data in the first section and refer either to a separate supporting schedule or to the comparative balance sheet for the changes in individual working capital items.

Funds statements are most commonly prepared in accordance with the working capital concept for funds. References to the funds statement in this chapter and in the problems at the end of the chapter assume use of the working capital concept when no alternative concept is stated.

*Funds defined as all financial resources.* Funds may be regarded as all of the financial resources of the business unit — resources that are found not only in working capital but also in other sources including long-term debt and capital sources. The acquisition of properties in exchange for bonds or for stock while bypassing working capital is nevertheless recognized both as a source of funds (the issue of bonds or the issue of stock) and as an application of funds (the acquisition of properties). Properties acquired in exchange for other properties or received as gifts, as well as the settlement of debt or the liquidation of ownership interests through the transfer of properties, are similarly recognized. A funds statement for the Parker Company giving effect to the all financial resources concept follows:

Parker Company

Statement of Source and Application of Financial Resources

For Year Ended December 31, 1964

| | | |
|---|---:|---:|
| Financial resources were provided by: | | |
| Sale of common stock.................................. | $120,000 | |
| Issue of preferred stock............................... | 100,000 | |
| Operations........................................... | 40,000 | $260,000 |
| Financial resources were applied to: | | |
| Acquisition of plant and equipment..................... | $130,000 | |
| Acquisition of land................................... | 100,000 | |
| Retirement of long-term debt.......................... | 20,000 | |
| Increase in working capital........................... | 10,000 | $260,000 |

In comparing this statement with the statement on page 550, it will be observed that the exchange of stock for land receives recognition both as a source and as an application of resources. Furthermore, an increase in working capital is recognized as an application of resources —

resources put into working capital; a decrease in working capital would be recognized as a source of resources — resources released for alternative use. Resources provided and applied are thus shown equal in amount.

Many persons have expressed a strong preference for the all financial resources approach to funds. Such preference arises from the fact that the working capital approach, offering no more than a reconciliation of the change in working capital, can result in the omission of important financial changes. The all financial resources approach recognizes the effects of all of the financial activities during a period; reporting is complete and fully informative.[1]

*Funds defined as net monetary assets.* When funds are defined as net monetary assets, balance sheet changes require analysis in terms of their effects upon the company's pool of net monetary assets. Such analysis is similar to that employed when funds are viewed as working capital except for inventory and prepaid expense items. These do not qualify as monetary assets and require special treatment. Increases in these items can be recognized as funds applied since net monetary assets were reduced through their increase; decreases can be recognized as funds provided since net monetary assets were augmented through their decrease. However, it may be more appropriate to relate changes in inventories and prepaid expenses to the funds made available through profit and loss activities: increases in inventories and prepaid items may be regarded as reducing the net monetary assets made available from operations since expenditures for goods and services were actually greater than the charges applied against revenue in arriving at net income; decreases in inventories and prepaid expenses may be regarded as raising the net monetary assets made available from operations since expenditures for goods and services were actually less than the charges applied against revenue in arriving at net income.

A funds statement for the Parker Company giving effect to the net monetary assets concept is given on the opposite page.

Those supporting use of the net monetary asset concept point out that elimination of inventories and prepaid items from working capital provides a residual pool of relatively homogeneous items. It is suggested that greater validity from a conceptual as well as a practical view is

---

[1]Dr. Perry Mason in *Accounting Research Study No. 2*, " 'Cash Flow' Analysis and the Funds Statement," issued in 1961, and also the Accounting Principles Board in *Opinions of the Accounting Principles Board, No. 3*, "The Statement of Application of Funds," issued in October, 1963, recommend preparation of the funds statement using the all-financial-resources concept. It may be observed that the funds statement can be prepared as a reconciliation of the change in working capital and still include the recognition of gifts and exchanges. Such treatment requires adoption of the hypothesis that the receipt of the gift or the transfer of the item in exchange provides the company with current resources which are immediately applied to the acquisition of property, the liquidation of debt, or the retirement of capital stock.

Parker Company
Statement of Source and Application of Net Monetary Assets
For Year Ended December 31, 1964

| | | | |
|---|---|---|---|
| Net monetary assets were provided by: | | | |
| Sale of common stock...................... | | $120,000 | |
| Operations: | | | |
| Net income............................. | $40,000 | | |
| Add decrease in prepaid expenses............. | 10,000 | | |
| | $50,000 | | |
| Deduct increase in inventories............... | 35,000 | 15,000 | $135,000 |
| Net monetary assets were applied to: | | | |
| Acquisition of plant and equipment............. | | $130,000 | |
| Retirement of long-term debt.................. | | 20,000 | 150,000 |
| Decrease in net monetary assets................. | | | $ 15,000 |

The decrease in net monetary assets is accounted for as follows:

| Net Monetary Assets | Dec. 31 1963 | Dec. 31 1964 | Increase (Decrease) |
|---|---|---|---|
| Monetary assets: | | | |
| Cash...................................... | $100,000 | $ 75,000 | ($25,000) |
| Accounts receivable....................... | 110,000 | 170,000 | 60,000 |
| Current liabilities: | | | |
| Accounts payable......................... | 100,000 | 160,000 | ( 60,000) |
| Accrued expenses......................... | 30,000 | 20,000 | 10,000 |
| Decrease in net monetary assets.............. | | | ($15,000) |

found here. However, this presentation is subject to the same objection that is found in employing the working capital concept for funds: with analysis limited to changes in net monetary assets, important financial changes arising from gifts and exchanges may not be recognized.

*Funds defined as cash.* When the funds concept is employed to denote cash, balance sheet changes must be analyzed in terms of their effects upon the movement of cash. Cash is used in the same sense as that employed for cash recognized as a current asset — cash on hand and demand deposits in banks. A funds statement, then, serves to reconcile the beginning and ending cash balances. Such a reconciliation might be developed by simply classifying and summarizing cash receipts and disbursements reported in the cash account. However, the statement is prepared to point out the broad sources and uses of cash, and such items as cash collected from customers, cash paid for merchandise, and cash paid for expenses are submerged in a cash-from-operations category.

A statement for the Parker Company giving effect to the cash concept follows.

Parker Company
Statement of Cash Flow
For Year Ended December 31, 1964

| | | | | |
|---|---:|---:|---:|---:|
| Cash was provided by: | | | | |
| Sale of common stock..................... | | | $120,000 | |
| Operations: | | | | |
| Net income........................... | | $ 40,000 | | |
| Add: Decrease in prepaid expenses........ | $10,000 | | | |
| Increase in accounts payable........ | 60,000 | 70,000 | | |
| | | $110,000 | | |
| Deduct: Increase in accounts receivable..... | $60,000 | | | |
| Increase in inventories........... | 35,000 | | | |
| Decrease in accrued expenses..... | 10,000 | 105,000 | 5,000 | $125,000 |
| Cash was applied to: | | | | |
| Acquisition of plant and equipment......... | | | $130,000 | |
| Retirement of long-term debt.............. | | | 20,000 | 150,000 |
| Decrease in cash........................... | | | | $ 25,000 |

In developing a net monetary assets flow summary earlier, net income was adjusted for the changes in inventories and prepaid expenses to arrive at the contribution made by operations. In developing a cash flow analysis, net income is adjusted for changes in other current asset and current liability balances. In the example above, the following adjustments are required:

*Accounts receivable increase* — Net income is decreased since the cash receipts for goods and services sold were less than the revenue that was recognized in arriving at net income.

*Inventory increase* — Net income is decreased since purchases were greater than the charge that was made against revenue for cost of sales in arriving at net income.

*Prepaid expense decrease* — Net income is increased since the cash disbursements for expenses were less than the charges that were made against revenue for certain expenses in arriving at net income.

*Accounts payable increase* — Net income is increased since the cash disbursements for goods and services purchased were less than the charges that were made for these items in arriving at net income.

*Accrued expense decrease* — Net income is decreased since the cash disbursements for expenses were greater than the charges that were made against revenue for certain expenses in arriving at net income.

The cash-flow approach to the analysis of financial operations has received increasing attention in recent years. The statement is readily interpreted by the reader. It can be a highly useful tool for the forecasting and planning of cash. However, among its shortcomings, the statement fails to recognize non-cash gifts and exchanges that may be of significance in reviewing financial changes for the period. Furthermore, working capital analyses are still required in providing information concerning the effect of financial activities upon the working capital pool.

## Analysis of account changes in preparation of funds statement

As indicated earlier, the preparation of the funds statement requires comparative balance sheet information supplemented by explanations for account changes. Examples in the preceding sections were relatively simple and changes in account balances defined fund sources and applications. Ordinarily, however, more complex circumstances are encountered and it is not possible to rely on the net change in an account balance for a full explanation of the effect of that item on a company's funds. To illustrate, assume that comparative balance sheets report a $50,000 increase in bonds payable. Without further investigation, this might be interpreted as a source of funds of $50,000; but reference to the liability account may disclose that bonds of $100,000 were retired during the period while new bonds of $150,000 were issued. A further analysis of the transactions affecting the liability account may reveal that a call premium of $2,000 was paid on bonds retired and a discount of $7,500 was identified with the new issue. The funds statement, then, should report funds applied to bond retirement, $102,000, and funds provided by the new issue, $142,500.

Remaining pages of this chapter describe the nature of the analysis that is required as well as the procedures that are employed in developing the funds statement under the alternative funds concepts.

## Fund sources and applications

Decreases in noncurrent assets and increases in noncurrent liabilities and in capital items require analysis in calculating funds provided; increases in noncurrent assets and decreases in noncurrent liabilities and in capital items require analysis in calculating funds applied.

*Fund sources.* The following examples indicate fund sources and suggest the nature of the analysis that is necessary in determining the actual amounts provided.

1. *Decreases in noncurrent asset accounts.* Balances in land, equipment, investment, and other noncurrent asset accounts may decrease as a result of assets sold, thus representing fund sources. However, an analysis of the transactions that account for each change is necessary; disposal of investments at a profit, for example, provides funds that exceed the decrease in the asset account.

2. *Increases in noncurrent liabilities.* Balances in long-term note, bond, and other noncurrent liability accounts may increase as a result of amounts borrowed, thus representing fund sources. An analysis of the transactions that account for each change is necessary; issuance of bonds at a discount, for example, provides funds that are less than the increase in the bond account.

3. *Increases in capital.* Capital stock balances may increase as a result of the sale of stock, thus representing fund sources. However, the amounts received for shares must be determined, for these may differ from the increases in the capital stock balances. When an increase in retained earnings cannot be explained solely by the net income for the period, an analysis of the retained earnings account is necessary. An increase in retained earnings resulting from profitable operations is recognized as a source of funds; a decrease in retained earnings resulting from cash dividends is separately recognized as an application of funds.

*Fund applications.* The following examples indicate fund applications and suggest the nature of the analysis necessary in determining the actual amounts applied.

1. *Increases in noncurrent assets.* Balances in land, buildings, patents, and other noncurrent asset accounts may increase as a result of the acquisitions of such items, thus representing fund applications. An analysis of transactions that account for the change is necessary; the amount paid for patents, for example, is greater than the increase in the patents account balance when the account is reduced during the period for patents cost amortization.

2. *Decreases in noncurrent liabilities.* The balances in mortgage, bond, and other noncurrent liability accounts may show decreases resulting from retirement of obligations, thus representing fund applications. An analysis of transactions that account for each change is necessary; the amount paid bondholders, for example, exceeds the decrease in the bonds account when a call premium is paid upon bond retirement.

3. *Decreases in capital.* Capital stock balances may show decreases as a result of acquisition of shares previously issued, thus representing fund applications. However, the amounts paid for reacquired shares must be determined, for these may differ from the decreases in the capital stock balances. When a decrease in retained earnings cannot be explained solely by a net loss for the period, an analysis of the retained earnings account is necessary. A decrease in retained earnings resulting from operations at a loss is recognized as an application of funds; a further decrease resulting from cash dividends is separately recognized as an application of funds.

Changes in noncurrent and capital account balances must be analyzed and recognized as described regardless of the definition that is employed for funds. When the concept of funds is narrowed to denote net monetary assets or cash, changes in certain current asset and current liability balances are also recognized in arriving at the amount of funds made available through operations.

## Adjustments in developing amounts provided and applied

The preceding discussion has indicated that the changes in account balances require adjustment when they fail to report the amounts of funds actually provided or applied. When there are many adjustments or when adjustments are complex, use of working papers may facilitate the preparation of the funds statement. In employing working papers, special columns are provided for adjustments that modify account balance changes. The changes as adjusted may then be carried to columns summarizing fund sources and applications.

The adjustments that are required in developing fund data may be classified under three headings:

1. *Adjustments to cancel account changes that do not represent fund sources or applications.* Certain account changes may carry no fund flow implications. For example, properties may have been appraised and the appraisal changes recorded in the accounts. Intangible assets may have been written off against retained earnings. Fully depreciated assets may have been applied against allowance for depreciation balances. Errors of prior periods may have been discovered requiring changes in property and capital balances. Stock dividends may have been issued and retained earnings transferred to paid-in capital accounts. The foregoing items result in changes in account balances but such changes should be disregarded in reporting the flow of funds. When working papers are prepared adjustments are made to cancel account changes that do not require recognition on the funds statement.

2. *Adjustments to report the individual fund sources and applications when several transactions are summarized in a single account.* The change in the balance of an account may result from funds provided by several different sources or applied to several different purposes, or from a combination of funds provided and applied. For example, the change in the plant and equipment balance may reflect funds applied to the purchase of equipment and also to the construction of buildings. The change in the bonds payable balance may reflect both funds applied to the retirement of an old bond issue and funds provided by a new issue. The change in the capital stock balance may reflect both funds provided by the issue of shares and funds applied to the reacquisition and retirement of shares. When working papers are prepared, adjustments are made to report separately the different fund sources and applications.

3. *Adjustments to report individual fund sources and applications when such information is reported in two or more accounts.* The amount of funds that are provided or applied as a result of a certain transaction may be reflected in two or more accounts. For example, certain investments may have been sold for more than cost; the decrease in the investment account balance and the increase in earnings or in the retained earnings balance must be combined in arriving at the actual amount provided by the sale. Bonds may have been issued at a discount; the increase in the discount account balance must be applied against the increase in the bond account in arriving at the actual amount provided by the issue. Stock may have been retired at a premium; the decreases in the paid-in capital and retained earnings account balances must be combined in arriving at the actual amount applied to the retirement. When working papers are prepared, adjustments are made to combine related changes.

Retained Earnings is an example of an account that may be affected by all three types of adjustments. To illustrate, assume that a retained earnings account shows an increase for a year of $10,000. Inspection of the account discloses the following:

| Retained Earnings | | | | |
|---|---|---|---|---|
| Mar. 1 Goodwill written off........ | 20,000 | Jan. 1 Balance................. | 200,000 |
| July 10 Cash dividends............ | 30,000 | Dec. 31 Net income for year...... | 60,000 |

Goodwill was written off against Retained Earnings. Although both goodwill and retained earnings account balances show decreases of $20,000, the write-off is without funds significance. If working papers are prepared, the decreases in the account balances should be restored; the account changes from this action are thus canceled and receive no further consideration in developing the funds statement. Cash dividends of $30,000 are reported separately as an application of funds. This leaves $60,000 in the retained earnings account to be reported as a source of funds from profitable operations.

The net income figure offers only a part of the total funds made available if certain charges or credits to profit and loss carry no funds implications. For example, assume that depreciation of $20,000 is recorded in calculating net income. The entry for depreciation, although representing a proper charge in arriving at net income, is without funds significance; its effects, therefore, should be canceled. Funds from profitable operations, then, consist of $60,000, as reported, plus $20,000. If working papers are prepared, the increase in the allowance for depreciation is canceled and net income increased. To fully illustrate the nature of this adjustment, assume the following facts.

At the end of 1963, an attorney, in establishing a new office, invests cash of $15,000 and immediately acquires furniture and fixtures for $10,000. Furniture and fixtures are estimated to have a five-year life. Condensed comparative balance sheet and income statement data for 1963–1964 appear below:

| | Dec. 31 1963 | Dec. 31 1964 | |
|---|---|---|---|
| Working capital........................................ | $ 5,000 | | $14,500 |
| Furniture and fixtures.................................. | 10,000 | $10,000 | |
| Less allowance for depreciation........................ | | 2,000 | 8,000 |
| Capital................................................ | $15,000 | | $22,500 |
| | | | |
| Fees — received in cash or recognized as receivables........ | | | $20,000 |
| Expenses — paid in cash or recognized as payables.......... | | $10,500 | |
| — depreciation, recognized as reduction in furniture and fixtures balance........................ | | 2,000 | 12,500 |
| Net income............................................ | | | $ 7,500 |

Although there were no operating activities in 1963, funds of $10,000 were applied to the acquisition of furniture and fixtures and working capital changed from $15,000 to $5,000.   In 1964, the income statement reported net income of $7,500 after a charge against revenue for depreciation of $2,000.   However, operations provided working capital of $9,500 — fees providing working capital of $20,000 and expenses consuming working capital of $10,500.   To arrive at the net increase in working capital, revenue representing working capital inflow is reduced only by those expenses that involve working capital outflow or, alternatively, net income is raised by the charge for depreciation that involved no working capital outflow.   Break-even operations would have recouped working capital equivalent to the reduction in the furniture and fixtures balance; profitable operations served to increase working capital by both the amount of such reduction and the reported net income.

In calculating the funds provided by operations, net income must be increased by all changes that were recognized in arriving at net income but that involved no working capital outflow.   Net income is increased by such items as depletion, depreciation of plant and equipment items, and amortization of patents, research and development costs, leaseholds, bond payable discounts, and bond investment premiums.   Net income must be decreased by all credits that were recognized in arriving at net income but that involved no working capital inflow.   Net income is decreased by such items as the amortization of bond payable premiums and the accumulation of bond investment discounts.   When extraordinary gains and losses are included in the summary of operations, these should be related to their particular sources; funds provided by operations are thus limited to amounts produced by normal and recurring activities.

### Preparation of the funds statement — funds regarded as working capital

In the examples given earlier, funds statements were prepared directly from comparative account balances.   In the example to follow, comparative account balances require a number of adjustments and working papers are employed in developing the funds statement.   In this section it is assumed that the funds statement is to summarize changes in working capital.   The modifications in working papers and in statements under the alternative definitions for funds are illustrated in later sections.   Assume comparative balance sheets and supplementary data for Harper, Inc., as follows:

Harper, Inc.
Comparative Balance Sheet
December 31, 1963 and 1964

|  | December 31, 1963 | | December 31, 1964 | |
|---|---|---|---|---|
| **Current assets:** | | | | |
| Cash in banks and on hand.......................... | $ 65,000 | | $ 59,350 | |
| Accounts receivable (net) ........................... | 70,500 | | 60,000 | |
| Accrued income.................................... | 2,400 | | 250 | |
| Inventories........................................ | 76,500 | | 75,000 | |
| Prepaid operating expenses.......................... | 12,000 | $226,400 | 16,500 | $211,100 |
| Plant expansion fund investments (at cost)............. | | 106,000 | | 10,000 |
| **Plant and equipment:** | | | | |
| Office equipment.................................. | $ 26,000 | | $ 34,000 | |
| Less allowance for depreciation................... | 6,000 | $ 20,000 | 12,500 | $ 21,500 |
| Delivery equipment............................... | $ 38,800 | | $ 40,000 | |
| Less allowance for depreciation................... | 20,000 | 18,800 | 26,000 | 14,000 |
| Machinery and equipment.......................... | $ 80,000 | | $132,000 | |
| Less allowance for depreciation................... | 34,000 | 46,000 | 32,800 | 99,200 |
| Buildings......................................... | $225,000 | | $290,000 | |
| Less allowance for depreciation................... | 155,000 | 70,000 | 122,600 | 167,400 |
| Land............................................. | | 75,000 | 229,800 | 160,000 | 462,100 |
| Patents............................................. | | | 40,000 | | 35,000 |
| Total assets........................................ | | | $602,200 | | $718,200 |
| **Current liabilities** | | | | |
| Income taxes payable............................... | $ 9,500 | | $ 24,000 | |
| Accounts payable.................................. | 81,200 | | 72,000 | |
| Accrued salaries.................................. | 1,500 | | 5,000 | |
| Dividends payable................................. | | $ 92,200 | 4,400 | $105,400 |
| Bonds payable...................................... | | | $ 60,000 | |
| Less unamortized bond discount..................... | | | 2,700 | 57,300 |
| Total liabilities.................................. | | $ 92,200 | | $162,700 |
| **Stockholders' equity:** | | | | |
| Preferred stock.................................... | $100,000 | | $140,000 | |
| Common stock..................................... | 160,000 | | $240,000 | |
| Less treasury stock at par......................... | | | 12,000 | 228,000 |
| Additional paid-in capital.......................... | 40,000 | | 38,000 | |
| Retained earnings appropriated for plant expansion.... | 100,000 | | | |
| Retained earnings.................................. | 110,000 | 510,000 | 149,500 | 555,500 |
| Total liabilities and stockholders' equity .............. | | $602,200 | | $718,200 |

## Supplementary data:

### Changes in retained earnings during the year were as follows:

| | | |
|---|---|---|
| Balance, January 1, 1964...................................... | | $110,000 |
| Increases: | | |
| Net income and extraordinary items for the year................ | $ 36,000 | |
| Appropriation for plant expansion returned to retained earnings... | 100,000 | 136,000 |
| | | $246,000 |
| Decreases: | | |
| Cash dividends............................................. | $ 12,000 | |
| 50% stock dividend on common stock......................... | 80,000 | |
| Charge for inadequate depreciation in prior years on office equip... | 3,500 | |
| Acquisition of treasury stock for $15,000; par value of stock, $12,000, originally issued at premium of $2,000...................... | 1,000 | 96,500 |
| | | $149,500 |

### The income statement summarizes activities for 1964 as follows:

| | |
|---|---|
| Net income after income taxes................................................ | $30,300 |
| Add gain on sale of plant expansion fund investments......................... | 6,500 |
| | $36,800 |
| Deduct loss on trade of delivery equipment................................... | 800 |
| Net income and extraordinary items........................................... | $36,000 |

Plant expansion fund securities, cost $96,000, were sold for $102,500.

Delivery equipment was acquired at a cost of $6,000; $2,000 was allowed on the trade-in of old equipment that had a cost of $4,800 and a book value of $2,800, and $4,000 was paid in cash.

Fully depreciated buildings of $40,000 were demolished with no salvage value; new buildings were then constructed at a cost of $105,000.

Land was acquired for $85,000, the seller accepting in payment preferred stock, par $40,000, and cash of $45,000.

Machinery and equipment was overhauled and its life extended at a cost of $16,500, the cost being charged to the allowance for depreciation.

Amortization of patents cost and depreciation on plant and equipment were recognized as follows:

| | |
|---|---:|
| Patents............................................................. | $ 5,000 |
| Office equipment.................................................... | 3,000 |
| Delivery equipment.................................................. | 8,000 |
| Machinery and equipment............................................. | 15,300 |
| Buildings........................................................... | 7,600 |
| Total............................................................... | $38,900 |

Office equipment was acquired for cash, $8,000.

Machinery and equipment was acquired for cash, $52,000.

Ten-year bonds of $60,000 were issued at a discount of $3,000 at the beginning of the year; discount amortization for the year was $300.

Working papers for the preparation of the funds statement are given on pages 562 and 563.

In preparing working papers, items appearing on the comparative balance sheet are listed in the first pair of columns. Individual current items may be reported at their net amounts since these are recognized as a part of the working capital and require no adjustment. However, separate recognition is made of plant and equipment cost and depreciation allowance balances. Depreciation allowances, instead of being reported as credit balances in the debit section, may be more conveniently listed with liability and capital balances in the credit section. Similarly, negative long-term debt and negative capital balances are separately recognized and more conveniently listed with assets in the debit section. Net changes in account balances appear in the second pair of columns. Increases in assets, decreases in liabilities, and decreases in capital balances are shown in the debit column; decreases in assets, increases in liabilities, and increases in capital balances are reported in the credit column. A pair of columns for adjustments is provided where change balances can be eliminated or restated. After the adjustments have been recorded, adjusted balances are carried to the last two pairs of columns. Debit excesses in current asset and current liability items are reported in the working capital increase column; credit excesses are reported in the working capital decrease column. Remaining debit balances are reported in the funds applied column; remaining credit balances are

Harper,<br>Working Papers for Statement of Source<br>For Year Ended

| | Accounts<br>Debits | Balances | | |
|---|---|---|---|---|
| | | Dec. 31<br>1963 | Dec. 31<br>1964 | |
| 1 | Cash in banks and on hand.................................................... | 65,000 | 59,350 | 1 |
| 2 | Accounts receivable (net)..................................................... | 70,500 | 60,000 | 2 |
| 3 | Accrued income............................................................ | 2,400 | 250 | 3 |
| 4 | Inventories................................................................ | 76,500 | 75,000 | 4 |
| 5 | Prepaid operating expenses................................................... | 12,000 | 16,500 | 5 |
| 6 | Plant expansion fund investments.............................................. | 106,000 | 10,000 | 6 |
| 7 | Office equipment........................................................... | 26,000 | 34,000 | 7 |
| 8 | Delivery equipment......................................................... | 38,800 | 40,000 | 8 |
| 9 | Machinery and equipment.................................................... | 80,000 | 132,000 | 9 |
| 10 | Buildings................................................................. | 225,000 | 290,000 | 10 |
| 11 | Land..................................................................... | 75,000 | 160,000 | 11 |
| 12 | Patents................................................................... | 40,000 | 35,000 | 12 |
| 13 | Unamortized bond discount................................................... | .......... | 2,700 | 13 |
| 14 | Treasury stock, common, at par............................................... | .......... | 12,000 | 14 |
| 15 | .......................................................................... | 817,200 | 926,800 | 15 |
| | Credits | | | |
| 16 | Allowance for depreciation — office equipment.................................. | 6,000 | 12,500 | 16 |
| 17 | .......................................................................... | .......... | .......... | 17 |
| 18 | Allowance for depreciation — delivery equipment................................ | 20,000 | 26,000 | 18 |
| 19 | Allowance for depreciation — machinery and equipment.......................... | 34,000 | 32,800 | 19 |
| 20 | Allowance for depreciation — buildings........................................ | 155,000 | 122,600 | 20 |
| 21 | Income taxes payable....................................................... | 9,500 | 24,000 | 21 |
| 22 | Accounts payable.......................................................... | 81,200 | 72,000 | 22 |
| 23 | Accrued salaries........................................................... | 1,500 | 5,000 | 23 |
| 24 | Dividends payable.......................................................... | .......... | 4,400 | 24 |
| 25 | Bonds payable............................................................. | .......... | 60,000 | 25 |
| 26 | Preferred stock............................................................ | 100,000 | 140,000 | 26 |
| 27 | Common stock............................................................. | 160,000 | 240,000 | 27 |
| 28 | Additional paid-in capital.................................................... | 40,000 | 38,000 | 28 |
| 29 | Retained earnings appropriated for plant expansion............................. | 100,000 | .......... | 29 |
| 30 | Retained earnings.......................................................... | 110,000 | 149,500 | 30 |
| 31 | .......................................................................... | .......... | .......... | 31 |
| 32 | .......................................................................... | .......... | .......... | 32 |
| 33 | .......................................................................... | .......... | .......... | 33 |
| 34 | .......................................................................... | 817,200 | 926,800 | 34 |
| 35 | Funds provided by operations: | | | 35 |
| 36 | Net income and extraordinary items per income statement....................... | .......... | .......... | 36 |
| 37 | Add: Loss on trade of delivery equipment...................................... | | | 37 |
| 38 |      Depreciation and patents cost amortization............................. | | | 38 |
| 39 |      Bond discount amortization......................................... | | | 39 |
| 40 | Deduct: Gain on sale of plant expansion fund investments ...................... | | | 40 |
| 41 | Funds applied to dividends................................................... | | | 41 |
| 42 | Funds applied to purchase of treasury stock, common........................... | | | 42 |
| 43 | Funds provided by sale of plant expansion fund investments..................... | | | 43 |
| 44 | Funds applied to purchase of delivery equipment............................... | | | 44 |
| 45 | Funds applied to construction of buildings..................................... | | | 45 |
| 46 | Funds applied to acquisition of land.......................................... | | | 46 |
| 47 | Deduct: Preferred stock issued in part payment................................ | | | 47 |
| 48 | Funds applied to overhauling machinery and equipment......................... | | | 48 |
| 49 | Funds provided by issuance of bonds.......................................... | | | 49 |
| 50 | .......................................................................... | | | 50 |
| 51 | Decrease in working capital.................................................. | .......... | .......... | 51 |
| 52 | .......................................................................... | .......... | .......... | 52 |

Inc.
and Application of Working Capital
December 31, 1964

| | Net Changes | | Adjustments | | Funds | | Working Capital | | |
|---|---|---|---|---|---|---|---|---|---|
| | Dr. | Cr. | Dr. | Cr. | Applied | Provided | Increase | Decrease | |
| 1 | | 5,650 | | | | | | 5,650 | 1 |
| 2 | | 10,500 | | | | | | 10,500 | 2 |
| 3 | | 2,150 | | | | | | 2,150 | 3 |
| 4 | | 1,500 | | | | | | 1,500 | 4 |
| 5 | 4,500 | | | | | | 4,500 | | 5 |
| 6 | | 96,000 | (g) 96,000 | | | | | | 6 |
| 7 | 8,000 | | | | 8,000 | | | | 7 |
| 8 | 1,200 | | (h) 4,800 | (h) 6,000 | | | | | 8 |
| 9 | 52,000 | | | | 52,000 | | | | 9 |
| 10 | 65,000 | | (i) 40,000 | (j) 105,000 | | | | | 10 |
| 11 | 85,000 | | | (k) 85,000 | | | | | 11 |
| 12 | | 5,000 | (n) 5,000 | | | | | | 12 |
| 13 | 2,700 | | (p) 300 | (o) 3,000 | | | | | 13 |
| 14 | 12,000 | | | (f) 12,000 | | | | | 14 |
| 15 | | | | | | | | | 15 |
| 16 | | 6,500 | (e) 3,500 | | | | | | 16 |
| 17 | | | (n) 3,000 | | | | | | 17 |
| 18 | | 6,000 | (n) 8,000 | (h) 2,000 | | | | | 18 |
| 19 | 1,200 | | (n) 15,300 | (m) 16,500 | | | | | 19 |
| 20 | 32,400 | | (n) 7,600 | (i) 40,000 | | | | | 20 |
| 21 | | 14,500 | | | | | | 14,500 | 21 |
| 22 | 9,200 | | | | | | 9,200 | | 22 |
| 23 | | 3,500 | | | | | | 3,500 | 23 |
| 24 | | 4,400 | | | | | | 4,400 | 24 |
| 25 | | 60,000 | (o) 60,000 | | | | | | 25 |
| 26 | | 40,000 | (l) 40,000 | | | | | | 26 |
| 27 | | 80,000 | (d) 80,000 | | | | | | 27 |
| 28 | 2,000 | | | (f) 2,000 | | | | | 28 |
| 29 | 100,000 | | | (b) 100,000 | | | | | 29 |
| 30 | | 39,500 | (a) 36,000 | (c) 12,000 | | | | | 30 |
| 31 | | | (b) 100,000 | (d) 80,000 | | | | | 31 |
| 32 | | | | (e) 3,500 | | | | | 32 |
| 33 | | | | (f) 1,000 | | | | | 33 |
| 34 | 375,200 | 375,200 | | | | | | | 34 |
| 35 | | | | | | | | | 35 |
| 36 | | | | (a) 36,000 | | | | | 36 |
| 37 | | | | (h) 800 | | | | | 37 |
| 38 | | | | (n) 38,900 | | | | | 38 |
| 39 | | | | (p) 300 | | | | | 39 |
| 40 | | | (g) 6,500 | | | 69,500 | | | 40 |
| 41 | | | (c) 12,000 | | 12,000 | | | | 41 |
| 42 | | | (f) 15,000 | | 15,000 | | | | 42 |
| 43 | | | | (g) 102,500 | | 102,500 | | | 43 |
| 44 | | | (h) 4,000 | | 4,000 | | | | 44 |
| 45 | | | (j) 105,000 | | 105,000 | | | | 45 |
| 46 | | | (k) 85,000 | | | | | | 46 |
| 47 | | | | (l) 40,000 | 45,000 | | | | 47 |
| 48 | | | (m) 16,500 | | 16,500 | | | | 48 |
| 49 | | | | (o) 57,000 | | 57,000 | | | 49 |
| 50 | | | 743,500 | 743,500 | 257,500 | 229,000 | 13,700 | 42,200 | 50 |
| 51 | | | | | | 28,500 | 28,500 | | 51 |
| 52 | | | | | 257,500 | 257,500 | 42,200 | 42,200 | 52 |

reported in the funds provided column. The net effect of activities upon working capital is summarized in the funds columns and this change is carried to the working capital columns bringing the latter into balance.

Explanations for the individual adjustments that are recorded on the working papers for Harper, Inc., on pages 562 and 563 follow. The letter preceding each explanation corresponds with that used in reporting the elimination on the working papers.

(a) Net income reported in retained earnings is transferred to a section where funds provided by operations is to be summarized by the following adjustment on the working papers:

| | | |
|---|---|---|
| Retained earnings................................... | 36,000 | |
| Funds provided by operations: Net income and extra-ordinary items per income statement................ | | 36,000 |

"Funds provided by operations" is reported on a separate line below the comparative balance sheet detail. Since a number of adjustments may be required in arriving at the net amount of funds provided by operations, adequate space should be allowed after this line for such adjustments. Additional items requiring recognition but not related to the summary of operations are listed below the space allowed for such summary.

(b) The transfer of retained earnings appropriated for plant expansion to retained earnings has no funds significance and the changes in the account balances are canceled by the following adjustment:

| | | |
|---|---|---|
| Retained earnings............................... | 100,000 | |
| Retained earnings appropriated for plant expansion .. | | 100,000 |

(c) The cash dividends reported in retained earnings are reported separately as an application of funds by the following adjustment:

| | | |
|---|---|---|
| Funds applied to dividends....................... | 12,000 | |
| Retained earnings............................. | | 12,000 |

(d) The transfer of retained earnings to capital stock as a result of the common stock dividend has no funds significance and the changes in the account balances are canceled by the following adjustment:

| | | |
|---|---|---|
| Common stock.................................. | 80,000 | |
| Retained earnings............................. | | 80,000 |

(e) The charge to retained earnings and credit to the allowance for depreciation—office equipment upon the recognition of inadequate depreciation for prior years has no funds significance and the changes in the account balances are canceled by the following adjustment:

| | | |
|---|---|---|
| Allowance for depreciation—office equipment........ | 3,500 | |
| Retained earnings............................. | | 3,500 |

(f) The acquisition of treasury stock, common, for $15,000 was recorded by a charge to treasury stock at par, $12,000, a charge to additional paid-in capital, $2,000, and a charge to retained earnings, $1,000. Funds applied to the acquisition of treasury stock are summarized by the following adjustment:

| | | |
|---|---|---|
| Funds applied to purchase of treasury stock, common.. | 15,000 | |
| Treasury stock, common (at par)................ | | 12,000 |
| Additional paid-in capital...................... | | 2,000 |
| Retained earnings............................. | | 1,000 |

Instead of recognizing the application of funds on a separate line, it would be possible to transfer charges from additional paid-in capital and retained earnings accounts to the treasury stock account; the sum of the charges to this account, $15,000, would then be extended to the funds applied column. Although such procedure may be followed whenever two or more balances account for a single source or application of funds, it is generally more satisfactory to transfer related balances to a separate line where a full description of the transaction can be provided.

Charges to retained earnings of $136,000 and credits of $96,500, or net charges of $39,500, have canceled the retained earnings credit excess of $39,500 reported in the net changes column; fund sources and applications affecting the retained earnings balance have been fully identified and given appropriate recognition.

(g) The sale of plant expansion fund investments was recorded by a credit to the asset account at cost, $96,000, and a credit to a nominal account that was included in the summary of operations, $6,500. Since the effect of the sale was to provide funds of $102,500, this is reported on a separate line and both the reduction in the investments balance and the extraordinary gain included in the summary of operations are canceled. The adjustment follows:

| | | |
|---|---:|---:|
| Plant expansion fund investments.................. | 96,000 | |
| Funds provided by operations: Gain on sale of plant expansion fund investments....................... | 6,500 | |
| Funds provided by sale of plant expansion fund investments....................................... | | 102,500 |

If the gain on the sale of the investments had not been recognized on the income statement but had been reported directly in Retained Earnings, the latter balance instead of funds provided by operations would have been charged.

(h) Delivery equipment was purchased for $6,000; $2,000 was allowed on the trade-in of old delivery equipment, cost $4,800, with a book value of $2,800, and $4,000 was paid in cash. The loss of $800 on the equipment traded in was recognized by a charge to a nominal account that was included in the summary of operations. Since the effect of the trade was to apply funds of $4,000, this is reported on a separate line and the changes in the delivery equipment balance and in the allowance for depreciation on delivery equipment are canceled together with the extraordinary loss included in the summary of operations. The following adjustment is made:

| | | |
|---|---:|---:|
| Funds applied to purchase of delivery equipment...... | 4,000 | |
| Delivery equipment (old)......................... | 4,800 | |
| Allowance for depreciation — delivery equipment... | | 2,000 |
| Delivery equipment (new)...................... | | 6,000 |
| Funds provided by operations: Loss on trade of delivery equipment.............................. | | 800 |

(i) The write-off of the cost of fully depreciated buildings against the allowance for depreciation is without funds significance, and the changes in the account balances are canceled by the following adjustment:

| | | |
|---|---:|---:|
| Buildings........................................ | 40,000 | |
| Allowance for depreciation — buildings........... | | 40,000 |

(j) The buildings account reports a debit excess of $65,000 raised by an adjustment of $40,000. The sum of the debits represents the cost of constructing buildings. The cost of new buildings is reported separately as an application of funds by the following adjustment:

| | | |
|---|---:|---:|
| Funds applied to construction of buildings........... | 105,000 | |
| Buildings....................................... | | 105,000 |

This adjustment could be omitted and the $105,000 balance for buildings simply carried to the funds applied column. However, the adjustment is made in the interest of clarity; the account change is transferred to a separate line and a full description of the transaction provided.

(k) and (l) Land was acquired at a price of $85,000; payment was made in preferred stock, par $40,000, and cash, $45,000. Adjustments may be made on the working papers as follows: (k) the increase in the land balance, $85,000, is reported separately as an application of funds; (l) the increase in the preferred stock balance, $40,000, is transferred to the section summarizing the acquisition of land and is reported as an offset to the charge recognized in (k) in arriving at the funds applied to the acquisition. The adjustments are:

| | | |
|---|---:|---:|
| Funds applied to acquisition of land................. | 85,000 | |
| Land........................................ | | 85,000 |
| Preferred stock................................. | 40,000 | |
| Funds applied to acquisition of land: Preferred stock issued in part payment......................... | | 40,000 |

(m) The cost of overhauling machinery and equipment that was charged to the allowance for depreciation balance is reported separately as an application of funds by the following adjustment:

| | | |
|---|---:|---:|
| Funds applied to overhauling machinery and equipment | 16,500 | |
| Allowance for depreciation — machinery and equipment......................................... | | 16,500 |

(n) The changes in the allowances for depreciation and in the patents account resulting from the recognition of depreciation and patents amortization are canceled and funds provided by operations are increased by the charges made against earnings that did not involve fund outflow by the following adjustment:

| | | |
|---|---:|---:|
| Patents......................................... | 5,000 | |
| Allowance for depreciation—office equipment........ | 3,000 | |
| Allowance for depreciation — delivery equipment..... | 8,000 | |
| Allowance for depreciation — machinery and equipment............................................ | 15,300 | |
| Allowance for depreciation—buildings.............. | 7,600 | |
| Funds provided by operations: Depreciation and patents cost amortization....................... | | 38,900 |

(o) Bonds payable was credited $60,000 and unamortized discount on bonds charged $3,000 when bonds were issued. Funds provided by the bond issue are summarized by the following adjustment:

| | | |
|---|---:|---:|
| Bonds payable.................................. | 60,000 | |
| Unamortized bond discount...................... | | 3,000 |
| Funds provided by issuance of bonds............. | | 57,000 |

(p) The change in the bond discount account for discount amortization is canceled and funds provided by operations increased by the charge against earnings that did not involve fund outflow by the following adjustment:

| | | |
|---|---:|---:|
| Unamortized bond discount....................... | 300 | |
| Funds provided by operations: Bond discount amortization....................................... | | 300 |

Office equipment of $8,000 and machinery and equipment of $52,000 were acquired during the year. No adjustments are made to the asset accounts since balances reflect only the single changes.

Adjusted balances together with the additional data established on the working papers are now extended to the funds and working capital columns and the working capital change is calculated. The funds statement is then drawn up from the working papers.

Harper, Inc.
Statement of Source and Application of Working Capital
For Year Ended December 31, 1964

| | | | |
|---|---:|---:|---:|
| Working capital was provided by: | | | |
| Operations: | | | |
| Net income and extraordinary items per income statement............................... | | $ 36,000 | |
| Add: Loss on trade of delivery equipment...... | $    800 | | |
| Depreciation and amortization......... | 38,900 | | |
| Bond discount amortization............ | 300 | 40,000 | |
| | | $ 76,000 | |
| Deduct gain on sale of plant expansion fund investments............................... | | 6,500 | $ 69,500 |
| Sale of plant expansion fund investments........ | | | 102,500 |
| Issuance of bonds........................... | | | 57,000 |
| | | | $229,000 |
| Working capital was applied to: | | | |
| Acquisitions of plant and equipment: | | | |
| Land ($85,000, less preferred stock issued in part payment, $40,000)........................ | $ 45,000 | | |
| Buildings.............................. | 105,000 | | |
| Machinery and equipment................. | 52,000 | | |
| Office equipment........................ | 8,000 | | |
| Delivery equipment...................... | 4,000 | $214,000 | |
| Overhauling machinery and equipment......... | | 16,500 | |
| Purchase of treasury stock, common........... | | 15,000 | |
| Dividends............................... | | 12,000 | 257,500 |
| Decrease in working capital................. | | | $ 28,500 |

The decrease in working capital is accounted for as follows:

| Working Capital Items | Dec. 31 1963 | Dec. 31 1964 | Increase (Decrease) |
|---|---:|---:|---:|
| Current assets: | | | |
| Cash in banks and on hand................ | $ 65,000 | $ 59,350 | ($  5,650) |
| Accounts receivable (net)................. | 70,500 | 60,000 | ( 10,500) |
| Accrued income......................... | 2,400 | 250 | (  2,150) |
| Inventories............................. | 76,500 | 75,000 | (  1,500) |
| Prepaid operating expenses............... | 12,000 | 16,500 | 4,500 |
| Current liabilities: | | | |
| Income taxes payable.................... | 9,500 | 24,000 | ( 14,500) |
| Accounts payable....................... | 81,200 | 72,000 | 9,200 |
| Accrued salaries........................ | 1,500 | 5,000 | (  3,500) |
| Dividends payable....................... | ——— | 4,400 | (  4,400) |
| Decrease in working capital................ | | | ($28,500) |

Some persons object to the presentation of funds provided by operations in the form just illustrated. This form, they maintain, implies that the depreciation of assets generates funds. Actually, it is revenue that provides funds but the net income balance fails to report the full amount provided because of charges for depreciation. This difficulty can be overcome by listing individual revenues and expenses but excluding items and amounts that do not involve current fund inflow or outflow. It is also possible to omit the detailed adjustments for operations or provide these on a supporting schedule where they can be described.

*Special problems.* The analyses that are required in developing the funds statement may be simple or complex. In each instance where a noncurrent asset, a noncurrent liability, or a capital account balance has changed, the question should be asked: "Does this indicate a change in working capital?" Frequently the answer to this question is obvious, but in some cases careful analysis is required. The following items require special mention:

1. Assume that retained earnings are reduced upon the declaration of a cash dividend that is payable in the following period. Declaration of the dividend has increased current liabilities and thus reduced working capital. Subsequent payment of the dividend will have no effect upon the amount of working capital, simply reducing both cash and the current liability. Declaration of a dividend, then, should be reported as funds applied. The reduction in working capital will be confirmed in the summary of working capital balances.
2. Assume that a long-term obligation becomes payable within a year, and requires change to the current classification. Such a change calls for a recognition of funds applied. The change in classification has resulted in a shrinkage of working capital; subsequent payment will have no effect upon the amount of working capital. The reduction in the non-current liability can be reported as "Funds applied to long-term obligations maturing currently." Working capital balances will confirm the reduction in working capital.
3. In the previous examples, prepaid expenses were classified as current assets and therefore treated as working capital items in the analysis of the change in working capital. Prepaid expenses are sometimes listed under a separate heading or reported with noncurrent assets. Such treatment calls for the special analysis of the prepaid expenses just as for other items classified as noncurrent, since their exclusion from the current group makes them part of the explanation for the change that took place in the current classification.

*Alternative form of working papers.* When the funds statement reports the changes in working capital, adjustments apply only to noncurrent assets and liabilities and to capital balances. Since adjustments do not affect the working capital items, it is possible to substitute working capital totals for the individual items for each year on the working papers. With the working capital change already calculated and reported, there is no need for a special pair of columns for this purpose; the difference between funds provided and funds applied is ultimately reported as a balancing figure in the funds columns and reconciled with the working capital change already listed. Working papers may be further simplified by eliminating comparative balance sheet data and beginning with account balance changes in the following manner:

| Accounts | Net Changes | | Adjustments | | Funds | |
|---|---|---|---|---|---|---|
| | Dr. | Cr. | Dr. | Cr. | Applied | Provided |
| Decrease in working capital.. (followed by changes in non-current asset, noncurrent liability, and capital accounts) | | 28,500 | | | | |
| Decrease in working capital... | | | | | 257,500 | 229,000 28,500 |
| | | | | | 257,500 | 257,500 |

## Preparation of the funds statement — funds regarded as all financial resources

If, in the example in the preceding section, the funds statement was to be prepared as a summary of changes in all financial resources, working papers would be similar to those illustrated on pages 562–563 except for the recognition given to the acquisition of land in exchange for preferred stock and cash, and the acquisition of delivery equipment in exchange for old equipment and cash. In each case, the full cost of the property item would be reported on the working papers as resources applied; the stock that was issued and also the equipment traded would be recognized as sources of funds and would be reported on the working papers as resources provided. A funds statement would be prepared as follows:

Harper, Inc.
Statement of Source and Application of Financial Resources
For Year Ended December 31, 1964

| | | |
|---|---|---|
| Financial resources were provided by: | | |
| Decrease in working capital........................... | $ 28,500 | |
| Operations........................................... | 69,500 | |
| Sale of plant expansion fund investments.............. | 102,500 | |
| Issuance of bonds.................................... | 57,000 | |
| Issuance of preferred stock........................... | 40,000 | |
| Exchange of delivery equipment...................... | 2,000 | $299,500 |
| | | |
| Financial resources were applied to: | | |
| Acquisition of plant and equipment: | | |
| Land................................ $ 85,000 | | |
| Buildings............................ 105,000 | | |
| Machinery and equipment............... 52,000 | | |
| Office equipment....................... 8,000 | | |
| Delivery equipment.................... 6,000 | $256,000 | |
| | | |
| Overhauling machinery and equipment................ | 16,500 | |
| Purchase of treasury stock, common................... | 15,000 | |
| Dividends............................................ | 12,000 | $299,500 |

## Preparation of the funds statement — funds regarded as net monetary assets

If Harper, Inc., was to define funds as net monetary assets, working papers would be similar to those illustrated on pages 562 and 563 except for the recognition given to the changes in inventories and prepaid expenses. Instead of recognizing these changes as a product of fund inflow and outflow, the changes would be recognized as a part of such flow. The decrease in inventories would be added to net income in the operations section on the working papers; the increase in prepaid expenses

Harper, Inc.
Statement of Source and Application of Net Monetary Assets
For Year Ended December 31, 1964

| | | | |
|---|--:|--:|--:|
| Net monetary assets were provided by: | | | |
| Operations: | | | |
| Net income and extraordinary items per income statement......................................... | | $36,000 | |
| Add: Depreciation and amortization................ | $ 38,900 | | |
| Bond discount amortization................ | 300 | | |
| Loss on trade of delivery equipment......... | 800 | | |
| Decrease in inventories.................... | 1,500 | 41,500 | |
| | | $77,500 | |
| Deduct: Gain on sale of plant expansion fund investments........................... | $ 6,500 | | |
| Increase in prepaid operating expenses.... | 4,500 | 11,000 | $ 66,500 |
| Sale of plant expansion fund investments............ | | | 102,500 |
| Issuance of bonds............................... | | | 57,000 |
| | | | $226,000 |
| Net monetary assets were applied to: | | | |
| Acquisitions of plant and equipment: | | | |
| Land ($85,000 less preferred stock issued in part payment, $40,000)............................ | $ 45,000 | | |
| Buildings..................................... | 105,000 | | |
| Machinery and equipment..................... | 52,000 | | |
| Office equipment............................. | 8,000 | | |
| Delivery equipment.......................... | 4,000 | $214,000 | |
| Overhauling machinery and equipment............. | | 16,500 | |
| Purchase of treasury stock, common.............. | | 15,000 | |
| Dividends....................................... | | 12,000 | 257,500 |
| Decrease in net monetary assets..................... | | | $ 31,500 |

The decrease in net monetary assets is accounted for as follows:

| Net Monetary Assets | Dec. 31 1963 | Dec. 31 1964 | Increase (Decrease) |
|---|--:|--:|--:|
| Monetary assets: | | | |
| Cash in banks and on hand................ | $65,000 | $59,350 | ($ 5,650) |
| Accounts receivable (net).................. | 70,500 | 60,000 | ( 10,500) |
| Accrued income......................... | 2,400 | 250 | ( 2,150) |
| Current liabilities: | | | |
| Income taxes payable..................... | 9,500 | 24,000 | ( 14,500) |
| Accounts payable........................ | 81,200 | 72,000 | 9,200 |
| Accrued salaries......................... | 1,500 | 5,000 | ( 3,500) |
| Dividends payable........................ | | 4,400 | ( 4,400) |
| Decrease in net monetary assets............... | | | ($31,500) |

would be subtracted from net income. Net income as adjusted would then summarize the net monetary assets made available by operations. A funds statement would be prepared as shown on page 570.

## Preparation of the funds statement — funds regarded as cash

If Harper, Inc., wishes to summarize cash flow, working papers would be prepared as illustrated on pages 572 and 573. Adjustments are the same as those described on pages 564–566 but are supplemented by adjustments to state dividends and profit and loss activities in terms of cash. The charge for cash dividends declared is adjusted for the change in the dividends payable balance in arriving at the cash applied to dividends during the period. Net income as previously adjusted to reflect the working capital change is further adjusted for the differences that are found in net monetary items other than cash. A statement of cash flow prepared from the working papers appears below.

Harper, Inc.

Statement of Cash Flow

For Year Ended December 31, 1964

| | | | |
|---|---:|---:|---:|
| Cash was provided by: | | | |
| Operations: | | | |
| Net income and extraordinary items per income statement....................................... | | $ 36,000 | |
| Add: Loss on trade of delivery equipment........ $ | 800 | | |
| Depreciation and amortization............. | 38,900 | | |
| Bond discount amortization............... | 300 | | |
| Decrease in accounts receivable............ | 10,500 | | |
| Decrease in inventories................... | 1,500 | | |
| Decrease in accrued income.............. | 2,150 | | |
| Increase in income taxes payable........... | 14,500 | | |
| Increase in accrued salaries............... | 3,500 | 72,150 | |
| | | $108,150 | |
| Deduct: Gain on sale of plant expansion fund investments.......................... $ | 6,500 | | |
| Decrease in accounts payable........... | 9,200 | | |
| Increase in prepaid operating expenses... | 4,500 | 20,200 | $ 87,950 |
| Sale of plant expansion fund investments.......... | | | 102,500 |
| Issuance of bonds.............................. | | | 57,000 |
| | | | $247,450 |
| Cash was applied to: | | | |
| Acquisitions of plant and equipment: | | | |
| Land ($85,000, less preferred stock issued in part payment, $40,000)........................... | $ 45,000 | | |
| Buildings..................................... | 105,000 | | |
| Machinery and equipment..................... | 52,000 | | |
| Office equipment............................. | 8,000 | | |
| Delivery equipment........................... | 4,000 | $214,000 | |
| Overhauling machinery.......................... | | 16,500 | |
| Purchase of treasury stock, common.............. | | 15,000 | |
| Dividends..................................... | | 7,600 | 253,100 |
| Decrease in cash................................. | | | $ 5,650 |

| | Accounts | Balances | | |
|---|---|---|---|---|
| | Debits | Dec. 31, 1963 | Dec. 31, 1964 | |
| 1 | Cash in banks and on hand....................... | 65,000 | 59,350 | 1 |
| 2 | Accounts receivable (net)...................... | 70,500 | 60,000 | 2 |
| 3 | Accrued income............................... | 2,400 | 250 | 3 |
| 4 | Inventories.................................... | 76,500 | 75,000 | 4 |
| 5 | Prepaid operating expenses..................... | 12,000 | 16,500 | 5 |
| 6 | Plant expansion fund investments................ | 106,000 | 10,000 | 6 |
| 7 | Office equipment.............................. | 26,000 | 34,000 | 7 |
| 8 | Delivery equipment............................ | 38,800 | 40,000 | 8 |
| 9 | Machinery and equipment...................... | 80,000 | 132,000 | 9 |
| 10 | Buildings..................................... | 225,000 | 290,000 | 10 |
| 11 | Land......................................... | 75,000 | 160,000 | 11 |
| 12 | Patents....................................... | 40,000 | 35,000 | 12 |
| 13 | Unamortized bond discount..................... | ............ | 2,700 | 13 |
| 14 | Treasury stock, common, at par................. | ............ | 12,000 | 14 |
| 15 | ................................................ | 817,200 | 926,800 | 15 |
| 16 | Credits | | | 16 |
| 17 | Allowance for depreciation — office equipment....... | 6,000 | 12,500 | 17 |
| 18 | ................................................ | ............ | ............ | 18 |
| 19 | Allowance for depreciation — delivery equipment ..... | 20,000 | 26,000 | 19 |
| 20 | Allowance for depreciation—machinery and equipment. | 34,000 | 32,800 | 20 |
| 21 | Allowance for depreciation—buildings............... | 155,000 | 122,600 | 21 |
| 22 | Income taxes payable........................... | 9,500 | 24,000 | 22 |
| 23 | Accounts payable.............................. | 81,200 | 72,000 | 23 |
| 24 | Accrued salaries............................... | 1,500 | 5,000 | 24 |
| 25 | Dividends payable............................. | ............ | 4,400 | 25 |
| 26 | Bonds payable................................ | ............ | 60,000 | 26 |
| 27 | Preferred stock................................ | 100,000 | 140,000 | 27 |
| 28 | Common stock................................ | 160,000 | 240,000 | 28 |
| 29 | Additional paid-in capital...................... | 40,000 | 38,000 | 29 |
| 30 | Retained earnings appropriated for plant expansion.... | 100,000 | ............ | 30 |
| 31 | Retained earnings............................. | 110,000 | 149,500 | 31 |
| 32 | ................................................ | ............ | ............ | 32 |
| 33 | ................................................ | ............ | ............ | 33 |
| 34 | ................................................ | ............ | ............ | 34 |
| 35 | ................................................ | 817,200 | 926,800 | 35 |

| | | |
|---|---|---|
| 36 | Cash provided by operations: | 36 |
| 37 | Net income and extraordinary items per income statement..................... | 37 |
| 38 | Add: Loss on trade of delivery equipment..................................... | 38 |
| 39 | Depreciation and patent cost amortization............................. | 39 |
| 40 | Bond discount amortization........................................ | 40 |
| 41 | Decrease in accounts receivable, less estimated uncollectibles.............. | 41 |
| 42 | Decrease in inventories............................................ | 42 |
| 43 | Decrease in accrued income........................................ | 43 |
| 44 | Increase in income taxes payable.................................... | 44 |
| 45 | Increase in accrued salaries........................................ | 45 |
| 46 | Deduct: Gain on sale of plant expansion fund investments..................... | 46 |
| 47 | Decrease in accounts payable....................................... | 47 |
| 48 | Increase in prepaid operating expenses.............................. | 48 |
| 49 | Cash applied to dividends....................................................... | 49 |
| 50 | Deduct: Increase in dividends payable........................................ | 50 |
| 51 | Cash applied to purchase of treasury stock, common............................. | 51 |
| 52 | Cash provided by sale of plant expansion fund investments...................... | 52 |
| 53 | Cash applied to purchase of delivery equipment................................ | 53 |
| 54 | Cash applied to acquisition of land............................................ | 54 |
| 55 | Deduct: Preferred stock issued in part payment........................... | 55 |
| 56 | Cash applied to overhauling machinery and equipment.......................... | 56 |
| 57 | Cash provided by issuance of bonds............................................ | 57 |
| 58 | Cash applied to construction of buildings...................................... | 58 |
| 59 | ................................................................................ | 59 |

Inc.
Statement of Cash Flow
December 31, 1964

| | Net Changes | | Adjustments | | Cash | | |
| | Dr. | Cr. | Dr. | Cr. | Applied | Provided | |
|---|---|---|---|---|---|---|---|
| 1 | ........... | 5,650 | ........... | ........... | ........... | 5,650 | 1 |
| 2 | ........... | 10,500 | (r) 10,500 | ........... | | | 2 |
| 3 | ........... | 2,150 | (w) 2,150 | ........... | | | 3 |
| 4 | ........... | 1,500 | (t) 1,500 | ........... | | | 4 |
| 5 | 4,500 | ........... | ........... | (u) 4,500 | ........... | | 5 |
| 6 | ........... | 96,000 | (g) 96,000 | ........... | | | 6 |
| 7 | 8,000 | ........... | | | 8,000 | ........... | 7 |
| 8 | 1,200 | ........... | (h) 4,800 | (h) 6,000 | | | 8 |
| 9 | 52,000 | ........... | | | 52,000 | ........... | 9 |
| 10 | 65,000 | ........... | (i) 40,000 | (j) 105,000 | ........... | | 10 |
| 11 | 85,000 | ........... | | (k) 85,000 | | | 11 |
| 12 | ........... | 5,000 | (n) 5,000 | | | | 12 |
| 13 | 2,700 | ........... | (p) 300 | (o) 3,000 | | | 13 |
| 14 | 12,000 | ........... | | (f) 12,000 | | | 14 |
| 15 | ........... | | | | | | 15 |
| 16 | ........... | | | | | | 16 |
| 17 | ........... | 6,500 | (e) 3,500 ⎫ | | | | 17 |
| 18 | ........... | | (n) 3,000 ⎭ | | | | 18 |
| 19 | ........... | 6,000 | (n) 8,000 | (h) 2,000 | | | 19 |
| 20 | 1,200 | ........... | (n) 15,300 | (m) 16,500 | | | 20 |
| 21 | 32,400 | ........... | (n) 7,600 | (i) 40,000 | | | 21 |
| 22 | ........... | 14,500 | (x) 14,500 | | | | 22 |
| 23 | 9,200 | ........... | | (s) 9,200 | | | 23 |
| 24 | ........... | 3,500 | (v) 3,500 | ........... | | | 24 |
| 25 | ........... | 4,400 | (q) 4,400 | ........... | | | 25 |
| 26 | ........... | 60,000 | (o) 60,000 | ........... | | | 26 |
| 27 | ........... | 40,000 | (l) 40,000 | ........... | | | 27 |
| 28 | ........... | 80,000 | (d) 80,000 | ........... | | | 28 |
| 29 | 2,000 | ........... | | (f) 2,000 | | | 29 |
| 30 | 100,000 | ........... | | (b) 100,000 | | | 30 |
| 31 | ........... | 39,500 | (a) 36,000 | (c) 12,000 ⎫ | | | 31 |
| 32 | ........... | | (b) 100,000 | (d) 80,000 ⎪ | | | 32 |
| 33 | ........... | | | (e) 3,500 ⎪ | | | 33 |
| 34 | ........... | | | (f) 1,000 ⎭ | | | 34 |
| 35 | 375,200 | 375,200 | ........... | ........... | | | 35 |
| 36 | ........... | ........... | ........... | ........... | ........... | ........... | 36 |
| 37 | ........... | ........... | ........... | (a) 36,000 | ........... | ........... | 37 |
| 38 | ........... | ........... | ........... | (h) 800 | ........... | ........... | 38 |
| 39 | ........... | ........... | ........... | (n) 38,900 | ........... | ........... | 39 |
| 40 | ........... | ........... | ........... | (p) 300 | ........... | ........... | 40 |
| 41 | ........... | ........... | ........... | (r) 10,500 | ........... | ........... | 41 |
| 42 | ........... | ........... | ........... | (t) 1,500 ⎫ | ........... | 87,950 | 42 |
| 43 | ........... | ........... | ........... | (w) 2,150 ⎪ | | | 43 |
| 44 | ........... | ........... | ........... | (x) 14,500 ⎪ | | | 44 |
| 45 | ........... | ........... | ........... | (v) 3,500 ⎭ | | | 45 |
| 46 | ........... | ........... | (g) 6,500 | ........... | | | 46 |
| 47 | ........... | ........... | (s) 9,200 | ........... | | | 47 |
| 48 | ........... | ........... | (u) 4,500 | ........... | | | 48 |
| 49 | ........... | ........... | (c) 12,000 ⎫ | | | | 49 |
| 50 | ........... | ........... | | (q) 4,400 ⎭ | 7,600 | | 50 |
| 51 | ........... | ........... | (f) 15,000 | ........... | 15,000 | ........... | 51 |
| 52 | ........... | ........... | (g) 102,500 | ........... | ........... | 102,500 | 52 |
| 53 | ........... | ........... | (h) 4,000 | ........... | 4,000 | | 53 |
| 54 | ........... | ........... | (k) 85,000 ⎫ | | | | 54 |
| 55 | ........... | ........... | | (l) 40,000 ⎭ | 45,000 | | 55 |
| 56 | ........... | ........... | (m) 16,500 | ........... | 16,500 | | 56 |
| 57 | ........... | ........... | | (o) 57,000 | ........... | 57,000 | 57 |
| 58 | ........... | ........... | (g) 105,000 | ........... | 105,000 | ........... | 58 |
| 59 | ........... | ........... | 793,750 | 793,750 | 253,100 | 253,100 | 59 |

The working papers and the cash-flow statement just illustrated developed the net amount of cash provided by operations. It would be possible to prepare a detailed explanation of the cash provided by operations by applying profit and loss adjustments to the individual profit and loss items rather than to the result of operations. This detail may be developed by expanding the operations section of the working papers. The operations section of the working papers just illustrated can be expanded as shown below. Adjustment (a) instead of reporting the net result of operations as summarized on the income statement, lists the individual profit and loss items. The adjustments that are required in developing the cash flow from operations are then applied to the individual profit and loss items.

| | Accounts | | Adjustments | | Cash | | |
|---|---|---|---|---|---|---|---|
| | | | Dr. | Cr. | Applied | Provided | |
| 36 | Cash provided by operations: | | | | | | 36 |
| 37 | Sales................................... | | | (a) 750,000 | | | 37 |
| 38 | Add: Decrease in accounts receivable................ | | | (r) 10,500 | | 760,500 | 38 |
| 39 | Cost of goods sold........................... | (a) | 550,000 | | | | 39 |
| 40 | Add: Decrease in accounts payable................. | (s) | 9,200 | | | | 40 |
| 41 | Deduct: Depreciation on machinery and equipment .... | | | (n) 27,900 | | | 41 |
| 42 | Decrease in inventories..................... | | | (t) 1,500 | 529,800 | | 42 |
| 43 | Selling and general expenses........................ | (a) | 146,400 | | | | 43 |
| 44 | Add: Increase in prepaid operating expenses........... | (u) | 4,500 | | | | 44 |
| 45 | Deduct: Depreciation on office equipment............ | | | | | | 45 |
| 46 | and delivery equipment................... | | | (n) 11,000 | | | 46 |
| 47 | Increase in accrued salaries................. | | | (v) 3,500 | 136,400 | | 47 |
| 48 | Other revenue — interest income ..................... | | | (a) 4,600 | | | 48 |
| 49 | Add: Decrease in accrued income ................... | | | (a) 2,150 | | 6,750 | 49 |
| 50 | Other expense — interest expense ..................... | (a) | 3,900 | | | | 50 |
| 51 | Deduct: Bond discount amortization ................ | | | (p) 300 | 3,600 | | 51 |
| 52 | Gain on sale of plant expansion fund investments ........ | | | (a) 6,500 | | | 52 |
| 53 | To cancel gain .............................. | (g) | 6,500 | | | | 53 |
| 54 | Loss on trade of delivery equipment ..................... | (a) | 800 | | | | 54 |
| 55 | To cancel loss..................................... | | | (h) 800 | | | 55 |
| 56 | Income taxes..................................... | (a) | 24,000 | | | | 56 |
| 57 | Deduct: Increase in income taxes payable ............. | | | (x) 14,500 | 9,500 | | 57 |

Cash made available through operations as summarized above may be presented on the statement of cash flow as follows:

Cash was provided by:
Operations:
Receipts — Sales................... $760,500
Other revenue — interest
income................ 6,750 $767,250

Payments — Cost of goods sold...... $529,800
Selling and general ex-
penses................ 136,400
Other expense — inter-
est expense........... 3,600
Income taxes......... 9,500 679,300 $ 87,950

## QUESTIONS

**1.** Describe the statement of source and application of funds. What information does it offer that is not provided by the income statement? What information does it offer that is not provided by the comparative balance sheet?

**2.** What different definitions are found for funds as used for the funds statement? Describe the funds statements under each of the different fund concepts. Which approach do you support?

**3.** Name a source of funds originating from a transaction involving (a) noncurrent assets, (b) noncurrent liabilities, (c) capital stock, (d) retained earnings. Name an application of funds identified with each group.

**4.** What three classes of adjustments are usually necessary in the preparation of working papers for a funds statement?

**5.** Give five working-paper adjustments to cancel book entries that have no effect upon funds.

**6.** Give five working-paper adjustments that summarize changes in two or more accounts in stating a source or application of funds.

**7.** Give five examples where a single account change may provide a basis for recognizing both a source and an application of funds.

**8.** (a) What adjustments are applied to the net income figure when the funds statement summarizes the working capital flow? (b) What adjustments are applied to net income when the funds statement summarizes net monetary asset flow? (c) What adjustments are applied to net income when the cash flow approach is adopted?

**9.** The Warner Co. in 1964 had its worst year, operations resulting in a substantial loss. Nevertheless, without the sale of property items, borrowing, or the issue of additional stock, the company's working capital increased significantly. What possible explanation can you suggest for such increase?

**10.** (a) Give five adjustments that raise the net income figure in calculating working capital provided by operations. (b) Give five adjustments that reduce the net income figure in calculating working capital provided by operations.

**11.** Indicate how each of the following would be reported on a funds statement assuming: (a) funds are regarded as working capital; (b) funds are regarded as all financial resources.

(1) Land and buildings are acquired for 40% cash and a mortgage note for the balance.

(2) Fully depreciated machinery is written off.

(3) Long-term notes are due within the year and their classification is changed to current.

(4) Capital stock is issued in exchange for land.

(5) In an examination of past income tax returns, the government asserts certain tax deficiencies and these are recognized on the company books by charging retained earnings and crediting a current liability.

**12.** Jerome Thatcher maintains that the use of reducing-charge methods for depreciation results in a greater amount of funds made available for use by the business in the earlier years of an asset's life than the use of the straight-line method for depreciation. Evaluate this argument.

## EXERCISES

**1.** The balance sheets of the Rohr Company at the end of 1963 and 1964 follow:

|  | 1963 | 1964 |
|---|---|---|
| Cash........................................... | $ 20,000 | $ 15,000 |
| Accounts receivable (net)....................... | 45,000 | 50.000 |
| Merchandise inventory.......................... | 40,000 | 65,000 |
| Prepaid expenses............................... | 10,000 | 5,000 |
| Buildings and equipment........................ | 70,000 | 85,000 |
| Allowance for depreciation — buildings and equipment | (7,500) | (17,500) |
| Land.......................................... | 45,000 | 80,000 |
|  | $222,500 | $282,500 |
| Accounts payable............................... | $ 40,000 | $ 50,000 |
| Accrued expenses............................... | 12,500 | 10,000 |
| Notes payable—bank............................ | 30,000 |  |
| Mortgage payable.............................. |  | 30,000 |
| Capital stock, $10 par.......................... | 150,000 | 185,000 |
| Retained earnings (deficit)...................... | (10,000) | 7,500 |
|  | $222,500 | $282,500 |

Land was acquired for $35,000 in exchange for capital stock, par $35,000, during the year; equipment of $15,000 was acquired for cash. Cash dividends of $10,000 were charged to retained earnings during the year; the transfer of net income to retained earnings was the only other entry in this account.

Prepare the following statements without the use of working papers:

(a) A funds statement applying the working capital concept of funds.
(b) A funds statement applying the all financial resources concept of funds.
(c) A funds statement applying the net monetary assets concept of funds.
(d) A statement of cash flow.

**2.** State how each of the following transactions will be reflected on the funds statement:

(a) Marketable securities are purchased for $12,000.
(b) Equipment, book value $6,000, is traded for new equipment costing $15,000; a trade-in value of $5,000 is allowed on the old equipment, the balance of the purchase price to be paid in twelve monthly installments.

(c) Buildings are acquired for $60,000, the company paying $25,000 cash and signing a mortgage note payable in 5 years for the balance of the purchase price.

(d) Uncollectible accounts of $650 are written off against the allowance for bad debts.

(e) As part of a quasi-reorganization, Capital from Reduction in Stock Stated Value of $210,000 is established by a reduction in the capital stock balance, and plant and equipment items of $185,000 are then written off against this account.

(f) 5% bonds of $150,000 are issued at 99, part of the proceeds being applied to the retirement of 6% bonds of $50,000 at 102.

(g) Cash of $100,000 was paid on the purchase of business assets consisting of: merchandise, $40,000; fixtures, $15,000; land and buildings, $25,000; and goodwill, $20,000.

(h) A cash dividend of $5,000 is declared, payable at the beginning of the following year.

**3.** Give the adjustments needed for working papers for a funds statement upon analysis of the following account:

Retained Earnings

| 1964 | | | 1964 | | |
|---|---|---|---|---|---|
| June | 1 Stock dividend......... | 200,000 | Jan. | 1 Balance.............. | 760,000 |
| | 1 Goodwill written off..... | 100,000 | Mar. 20 Correction for understate- | | |
| Aug. | 5 Discount on sale of treas- | | | ment of inventory at | |
| | ury stock, par $150,000, | | | end of 1963.......... | 12,000 |
| | for $125,000........... | 25,000 | Mar. 25 Gain on sale of X Co. | | |
| Dec. | 5 Cash dividends........ | 50,000 | | stock (cost, $60,000).... | 20,000 |
| | 31 Appropriated for contin- | | July | 1 Gain on redemption of | |
| | gencies.............. | 100,000 | | bonds of $200,000 at 96 | 8,000 |
| | 31 Balance.............. | 325,000 | | | |
| | | 800,000 | | | 800,000 |
| | | | 1965 | | |
| | | | Jan. | 1 Balance.............. | 325,000 |

**4.** From the information that follows, give the necessary adjustments to clear the changes in the accounts listed in preparing working papers for a funds statement for 1964.

| | Dec. 31, 1963 | Dec. 31, 1964 |
|---|---|---|
| Tools....................................................... | $ 12,000 | $ 14,000 |
| Machinery.................................................. | 45,000 | 39,000 |
| Allowance for Depreciation of Machinery................ | 16,000 | 15,500 |
| Delivery Equipment....................................... | 15,000 | 18,000 |
| Allowance for Depreciation of Delivery Equipment........ | 6,000 | 6,500 |
| Buildings.................................................. | 100,000 | 100,000 |
| Allowance for Depreciation of Buildings.................. | 62,500 | 68,500 |
| Land....................................................... | 40,000 | 25,000 |
| Patents.................................................... | 4,500 | 3,500 |
| Goodwill................................................... | 50,000 | — |
| Discount on Bonds Payable................................ | 6,000 | — |
| Bonds Payable............................................. | 100,000 | — |
| Capital Stock.............................................. | 250,000 | 350,000 |
| Treasury Stock............................................ | — | 22,000 |
| Retained Earnings Appropriated for Bond Retirement Fund. | 100,000 | — |
| Retained Earnings......................................... | 180,000 | 147,700 |

### Retained Earnings

| | | | |
|---|---:|---|---:|
| Stock dividend.................. | 100,000 | Balance...................... | 180,000 |
| Loss on scrapping of machinery, | | Gain on sale of land, cost $15,000, | |
| cost $6,000, for which an allow- | | sold for $18,000............. | 3,000 |
| ance of $4,500 had been provided | 1,500 | Gain on trade of delivery equip- | |
| Premium on purchase of treasury | | ment, cost $4,000, book value, | |
| stock, par $22,000............. | 8,000 | $2,500, allowance of $3,200 being | |
| Goodwill...................... | 50,000 | received on new equipment cost- | |
| Unamortized discount, $4,000, call | | ing $7,000.................. | 700 |
| premium, $2,500, on bond retire- | | Retained earnings appropriated | |
| ment........................ | 6,500 | for bond retirement fund...... | 100,000 |
| Cash dividends................. | 10,000 | Net income for year........... | 40,000 |
| Balance....................... | 147,700 | | |
| | 323,700 | | 323,700 |
| | | Balance...................... | 147,700 |

The income statement reports depreciation of buildings, $6,000; depreciation of machinery, $4,000; depreciation of delivery equipment, $2,000; tools amortization, $4,000; patents amortization, $1,000; and bond discount amortization, $2,000.

**5.** A summary of revenues and expenses for the Warden-West Corporation for 1964 follows:

| | |
|---|---:|
| Sales.................................. | $1,000,000 |
| Cost of goods manufactured and sold........ | 650,000 |
| Gross profit............................. | $ 350,000 |
| Selling, general and administrative expenses.. | 200,000 |
| Net income before income taxes............. | $ 150,000 |
| Income taxes............................ | 65,000 |
| Net income ............................. | $ 85,000 |

Net changes in working capital items for 1964 were as follows:

| | Net changes | |
|---|---:|---:|
| | Dr. | Cr. |
| Cash......................................... | $26,000 | |
| Trade receivables (net)....................... | 40,000 | |
| Inventories.................................. | | $15,000 |
| Prepaid expenses (selling and general)........... | 2,500 | |
| Accrued expenses (75% of increase related to manu- | | |
| facturing activities and 25% to general operating | | |
| activities).................................. | | 6,500 |
| Income taxes payable......................... | | 12,000 |
| Trade payables.............................. | | 30,000 |

Depreciation on plant and equipment for the year totaled $140,000; 70% was related to manufacturing activities and 30% to general and administrative activities.

Prepare a summary reporting in detail the cash provided and applied through profit and loss activities for the year.

## PROBLEMS

**20-1.** Condensed balance sheet data for Wallace, Inc., follow:

| Assets | Dec. 31, 1963 | Dec. 31, 1964 | Liabilities and Stockholders' Equity | Dec.31, 1963 | Dec. 31, 1964 |
|---|---|---|---|---|---|
| Cash................. | $ 30,000 | $ 10,000 | Accrued expenses.. | $ 5,000 | $ 7,500 |
| Current receivables...... | 50,000 | 60,000 | Current payables.. | 40,000 | 52,500 |
| Inventory.............. | 60,000 | 75,000 | Bonds payable.... | 50,000 | 40,000 |
| Prepaid expenses........ | 10,000 | 12,500 | Capital stock, at par | 100,000 | 125,000 |
| Land, bldgs., and equip.. | 85,000 | 125,000 | Additional paid-in capital......... | 10,000 | 15,000 |
| Allowance for depr...... | (25,000) | (30,000) | Retained earnings . | 5,000 | 12,500 |
| Totals................. | $210,000 | $252,500 | Totals............ | $210,000 | $252,500 |

Land and buildings were acquired in exchange for capital stock; the assets were recorded at $30,000, their appraised value. Equipment was acquired for $10,000 cash. Net income for the year transferred to retained earnings was $25,000; cash dividends accounted for the remaining change in retained earnings.

*Instructions:* Prepare the following (working papers are not required):
(1) A funds statement applying the working capital concept of funds.
(2) A funds statement applying the all financial resources concept of funds.
(3) A funds statement applying the net monetary assets concept of funds.
(4) A statement of cash flow.

**20-2.** Comparative balance sheet data for the firm of Bay and Bay are given below:

Bay and Bay
Comparative Balance Sheets

| Assets | Dec. 31, 1963 | Dec. 31, 1964 | Liabilities and Capital | Dec. 31, 1963 | Dec. 31 1964 |
|---|---|---|---|---|---|
| Cash................. | $ 3,600 | $ 4,500 | Accrued expenses...... | $ 2,200 | $ 2,600 |
| Current receivables..... | 10,500 | 8,800 | Current payables...... | 8,250 | 8,100 |
| Inventory............. | 31,600 | 45,000 | Long-term note....... | | 6,000 |
| Prepaid expenses....... | 1,650 | 1,200 | Paul Bay, Capital...... | 20,600 | 17,700 |
| Furniture and fixtures... | 16,000 | 23,500 | Thomas Bay, Capital... | 20,850 | 35,550 |
| Allowance for depr...... | (11,450) | (13,050) | | | |
| Totals................. | $51,900 | $69,950 | Totals................ | $51,900 | $69,950 |

Net income for the year was $15,000 which was transferred in equal amounts to the partners' capital accounts. Further changes in the capital accounts arose from additional investments and withdrawals by the partners. The change in the furniture and fixtures account arose from a purchase of additional furniture; part of the purchase price was paid in cash and a long-term note was issued for the balance.

*Instructions:* Prepare the following (working papers are not required):
(1) A funds statement applying the working capital concept of funds.
(2) A funds statement applying the all financial resources concept of funds.
(3) A funds statement applying the net monetary assets concept of funds.
(4) A statement of cash flow.

**20-3.** The following data were obtained from the books and records of the Walsh Co.:

| | Net changes in 1964 | |
| --- | --- | --- |
| | Dr. | Cr. |
| Current assets................................ | $ 51,500 | — |
| Plant and equipment (net)................... | 25,000 | — |
| Goodwill.................................... | — | $ 20,000 |
| Current liabilities........................... | — | 45,000 |
| Bonds payable.............................. | — | 100,000 |
| Bond discount.............................. | 3,800 | — |
| Preferred stock............................. | 100,000 | — |
| Common stock.............................. | — | 50,000 |
| Retained earnings........................... | 9,700 | — |
| Appraisal capital........................... | 25,000 | — |
| | $215,000 | $215,000 |

| Retained Earnings | | |
| --- | --- | --- |
| Premium on retirement of preferred stock........................ 5,000 | Balance, Jan. 1................. | 55,000 |
| | Gain on sale of land............ | 35,000 |
| Stock dividend on common stock... 50,000 | Net income after income taxes.... | 43,800 |
| Cash dividends paid during year... 13,500 | | |
| Goodwill written off.............. 20,000 | | |

Ten-year bonds of $100,000 were issued on July 1, 1964, at 96, proceeds being used in the retirement of preferred stock. Land, cost $30,000 and recorded on the books at an appraised value of $55,000, was sold for $65,000. The cash proceeds from the sale were applied to the construction of new buildings costing $88,000. Depreciation recorded for the year was $8,000.

*Instructions:* Prepare a funds statement applying the working capital concept of funds. (Working papers are not required.)

**20-4.** The following data were taken from the books and records of the Thomas Company:

Balance Sheet Data

| | December 31 | | | |
| --- | --- | --- | --- | --- |
| | 1963 | | 1964 | |
| Current assets (net)......................... | | $148,300 | | $165,200 |
| Plant and equipment........................ | $96,000 | | $100,500 | |
| Less allowance for depreciation............. | 30,000 | 66,000 | 34,000 | 66,500 |
| Investments in stocks and bonds............. | | 30,000 | | 27,000 |
| Goodwill................................... | | 25,000 | | 1 |
| | | $269,300 | | $258,701 |
| Current liabilities........................... | | $ 45,800 | | $ 58,800 |
| Bonds payable.............................. | | 50,000 | | — |
| Unamortized bond discount.................. | | (1,250) | | — |
| Preferred stock ($100 par).................. | | 50,000 | | — |
| Common stock ($10 par).................... | | 100,000 | | 150,000 |
| Additional paid-in capital................... | | — | | 30,000 |
| Retained earnings........................... | | 24,750 | | 19,901 |
| | | $269,300 | | $258,701 |

Retained Earnings

| | | | |
|---|---|---|---|
| Goodwill written off.............. | 24,999 | Balance........................ | 24,750 |
| Premium on retirement of preferred | | Net income and extraordinary items | |
| stock ........................ | 1,000 | per income statement......... | 36,150 |
| Cash dividends................. | 15,000 | | |

Income Statement Data

| | | |
|---|---|---|
| Net income ........................................... | | $40,650 |
| Add gain on trade of equipment........................ | | 1,500 |
| | | $42,150 |
| Deduct: Loss on sale of securities.................. | $2,500 | |
| Loss on retirement of bonds............... | 3,500 | 6,000 |
| Net income and extraordinary items............... | | $36,150 |

Fully depreciated equipment, original cost $10,500, was traded in on new equipment costing $15,000; $1,500 was allowed by the vendor on the trade-in. One hundred shares of Banks Co. preferred stock, cost $15,000, held as a long-term investment, were sold at the beginning of the year. Additional changes in the investments account resulted from the purchase of Carl Co. bonds. The company issued common stock in April, and part of the proceeds was used to retire preferred stock at 102 shortly thereafter. On July 1 the company called in its bonds outstanding, paying a premium of 5% on the call. Discount amortization on the bonds to the date of call was $250. Depreciation for the year on plant and equipment was $14,500.

*Instructions:* Prepare working papers and a funds statement applying the working capital concept of funds.

**20-5.** The following information is assembled for the Benson Corporation:

Balance Sheet Data

December 31

| | 1963 | | 1964 | |
|---|---|---|---|---|
| Cash (overdraft in 1963)................... | | ($ 5,625) | | $ 45,875 |
| Accounts receivable...................... | | 68,625 | | 50,000 |
| Inventories.............................. | | 62,000 | | 80,000 |
| Plant and equipment..................... | $95,000 | | $130,000 | |
| Less allowance for depreciation........... | 20,000 | 75,000 | 21,500 | 108,500 |
| Investments............................. | | 20,000 | | 8,000 |
| Patents................................. | | 30,000 | | — |
| | | $250,000 | | $292,375 |
| Accounts payable......................... | | $ 40,000 | | $ 45,000 |
| Bonds payable........................... | | 20,000 | | 50,000 |
| Premium on bonds payable................. | | — | | 2,375 |
| Preferred stock ($100 par)................. | | 50,000 | | |
| Common stock ($10 par).................. | | 100,000 | | 150,000 |
| Premium on common stock................. | | | | 20,000 |
| Retained earnings........................ | | 40,000 | | 25,000 |
| | | $250,000 | | $292,375 |

### Retained Earnings

| 1964 | | | 1964 | | |
|---|---|---|---|---|---|
| Oct. 15 | Cash dividends......... | 12,500 | Jan. 1 | Balance............... | 40,000 |
| Dec. 12 | Premium on retirement of | | Dec. 31 | Net income and extraor- | |
| | preferred stock.......... | 5,000 | | dinary items per income | |
| | | | | statement............. | 2,500 |

Income Statement Data for Year Ended December 31, 1964:

| | | | |
|---|---|---|---|
| Net income......................................... | | | $34 000 |
| Add gain on sale of investments......................... | | | 3,000 |
| | | | $37,000 |
| Deduct: | | | |
| Premium on retirement of bonds..................... | $ 1,000 | | |
| Loss on disposal of equipment....................... | 3,500 | | |
| Patents written off................................. | 30,000 | 34,500 | |
| Net income and extraordinary items..................... | | | $ 2,500 |

Equipment, cost $10,000, book value, $4,000, was scrapped, salvage of $500 being recovered on the disposal. Additional equipment, cost $45,000, was acquired during the year. Securities, cost $12,000, were sold for $15,000. Patents of $30,000 were written off against profits. 7% bonds, face value $20,000, were called in at 105, and new 10-year, 5% bonds of $50,000 were issued at 105 on July 1. Preferred stock was retired at a cost of 110 while $50,000 in common stock was issued at 14. Depreciation on plant and equipment for the year was $7,500.

*Instructions:* (1) Prepare working papers and a funds statement applying the working capital concept of funds.

(2) Prepare a statement of cash flow.

**20-6.** A comparative balance sheet for the Stillwell Company appears as follows:

| | December 31 | |
|---|---|---|
| | 1963 | 1964 |
| Cash............................................. | $ 135,000 | $ 190,000 |
| Marketable securities.............................. | 120,000 | 130,000 |
| Accounts and notes receivable, less allowances for bad debts........................................ | 220,000 | 250,000 |
| Inventories........................................ | 300,000 | 360,000 |
| Investments in stock of subsidiary companies (at cost)... | 335,000 | 240,000 |
| Buildings and equipment, less allowance.............. | 800,000 | 1,040,000 |
| Patents and goodwill............................... | 140,000 | 36,000 |
| Unamortized bond discount and issuance costs......... | 30,000 | 21,600 |
| | $2,080,000 | $2,267,600 |
| Accounts and notes payable......................... | $ 145,000 | $ 180,000 |
| Miscellaneous accrued liabilities including taxes........ | 65,000 | 88,200 |
| 4% Mortgage bonds................................ | 500,000 | 400,000 |
| Preferred stock ($25 par, each share convertible into two shares of common)............................... | 250,000 | 210,000 |
| Common stock ($10 par)........................... | 300,000 | 432,000 |
| Additional paid-in capital........................... | 200,000 | 288,000 |
| Retained earnings.................................. | 620,000 | 669,400 |
| | $2,080,000 | $2,267,600 |

An analysis of balance sheet changes discloses the following:

(a) Stock owned in the Mitchell Co., a partially owned subsidiary, was sold for $200,000. Stock had originally cost $95,000.

(b) The entire goodwill of $100,000 was written off the books in 1964.

(c) The patents had a remaining life of ten years on December 31, 1963, and are being written off over this period.

(d) Mortgage bonds mature on January 1, 1974. On July 1, 1964, bonds of $100,000 were purchased on the market at $103\frac{1}{2}$ and formally canceled.

(e) The decrease in preferred stock outstanding resulted from the exercise of the conversion privilege by preferred stockholders.

(f) 10,000 shares of common stock were sold during the year at $18.

(g) During the year equipment that cost $60,000 and that had a book value of $12,000 was sold for $8,600. Depreciation of $64,000 was taken during the year on buildings and equipment. Additional changes in the buildings and equipment balance resulted from the purchase of equipment.

(h) The net income for the year transferred to retained earnings was $107,000.

(i) Dividends paid during the year totaled $50,000.

*Instructions:* (1) Prepare working papers and a funds statement applying the working capital concept of funds.

(2) Prepare a cash flow statement.

**20-7.** Financial data for the Reardon Manufacturing Co. are presented below.

Reardon Manufacturing Co.
Comparative Balance Sheet
December 31, 1963 and 1964

| | 1963 | | 1964 | |
|---|---|---|---|---|
| **Assets** | | | | |
| Cash................................... | | $ 35,000 | | $ 78,550 |
| Accounts receivable...................... | $27,625 | | $ 53,000 | |
| Less allowance for bad debts............. | 2,125 | 25,500 | 2,500 | 50,500 |
| Inventories............................. | | 40,000 | | 54,000 |
| Office supplies.......................... | | 1,500 | | 1,000 |
| Miscellaneous prepaid expenses (sell. and gen.) | | 3,000 | | 3,500 |
| Investments in outside companies........... | | 16,000 | | 27,000 |
| Machinery.............................. | $75,000 | | $ 95,000 | |
| Less allowance for depreciation.......... | 40,000 | 35,000 | 44,000 | 51,000 |
| Buildings............................... | $90,000 | | $124,500 | |
| Less allowance for depreciation.......... | 36,000 | 54,000 | 40,000 | 84,500 |
| Land................................... | | 40,000 | | 80,000 |
| Goodwill............................... | | 50,000 | | |
| | | $300,000 | | $430,050 |
| **Liabilities and Stockholders' Equity** | | | | |
| Accounts payable........................ | | $ 34,000 | | $ 30,000 |
| Miscellaneous accrued expenses (sell. and gen.) | | 4,000 | | 6,500 |
| Estimated income taxes payable............ | | 10,000 | | 15,000 |
| Bonds payable.......................... | $50,000 | | $175,000 | |
| Less bond discount...................... | 4,250 | 45,750 | 10,875 | 164,125 |
| Capital stock ($10 par).................. | | 100,000 | | 125,000 |
| Additional paid-in capital................. | | 30,000 | | 35,000 |
| Retained earnings....................... | | 76,250 | | 54,425 |
| | | $300,000 | | $430,050 |

Reardon Manufacturing Co.
Condensed Statement of Income and Retained Earnings
For Year Ended December 31, 1964

| | | |
|---|---:|---:|
| Sales........................................................ | | $215,400 |
| Deduct: Cost of goods sold (includes depreciation of machinery, | | |
| $7,500, and depreciation of buildings, $6,000)......... | $118,000 | |
| Selling, general, administrative, and other expenses...... | 40,225 | |
| Income taxes.................................... | 18,000 | 176,225 |
| Net income......................................... | | $ 39,175 |
| Balance of retained earnings at beginning of 1964................. | | 76,250 |
| | | $115,425 |
| Add: Gain on sale of investments in outside companies............ | | 6,500 |
| | | $121,925 |
| Deduct: Loss on disposal of machinery......................... | $ 1,500 | |
| Cash dividends....................................... | 16,000 | |
| Goodwill written off................................. | 50,000 | 67,500 |
| Balance of retained earnings at end of 1964...................... | | $ 54,425 |

Ten-year bonds of $50,000 had been issued on July 1, 1962, at 90. Additional ten-year bonds of $125,000 had been issued on July 1, 1964, at 94.

Machinery that was no longer required was sold for $6,000 in 1964; the machinery had an original cost of $11,000 and accumulated depreciation on the date of the sale totaled $3,500.

Fully depreciated storage quarters were dismantled during the year, and buildings, cost $2,000, were written off against the allowance for depreciation of buildings account. Investments in outside companies that cost $12,000 were sold at the beginning of the year for $18,500, and additional securities were subsequently acquired during the year. Additional capital stock was issued by the company during the year at 12 in order to raise working capital.

*Instructions:* (1) Prepare working papers and a funds statement applying the working capital concept of funds.

(2) Prepare working papers and a statement of cash flow that includes profit and loss detail.

# APPENDIX

Statements of several well-known corporations are given on the pages that follow. Statements of financial position and operations together with accompanying statement notes as presented in the corporate annual reports are reproduced. These statements illustrate practical applications of contemporary accounting standards and concepts.

A summary is presented preceding each set of statements pointing out matters of particular interest in viewing the statements. The forms, procedures, and items that are pointed out are not necessarily examples of good reporting or unsatisfactory reporting; rather, these are matters of interest that call for evaluation in terms of the accounting framework as a whole as developed in the text.

Reference to the statements and statement items may be made throughout the course as various phases of statement structure, form, and content are considered.

Statements are included for the following companies:

(1) Radio Corporation of America
(2) United Air Lines
(3) The Standard Oil Company (An Ohio Corporation)
(4) Houston Lighting & Power Company
(5) Scott Paper Company
(6) General Electric

# RADIO CORPORATION OF AMERICA

The following features are of interest in reviewing the financial statements and accompanying notes taken from the annual report of Radio Corporation of America for 1963.

Four financial statements are presented: (1) Consolidated Earnings, (2) Consolidated Financial Position, (3) Consolidated Reinvested Earnings, and (4) Consolidated Statement of Funds. The first three statements are presented in comparative form. The annual report also includes a "Ten Year Financial Review" in which significant balance sheet and income data are presented in condensed form together with analytical ratios and measurements relating thereto. This summary is not reproduced.

**Consolidated Earnings.** Earnings data are presented in single-step form except for income taxes and a special gain that are presented as separate items.

**Consolidated Financial Position.** The statement of consolidated financial position is prepared in conventional account form. Asset, liability, and stockholders' equity items make reference to special notes that offer full explanations for the balances reported.

**Consolidated Reinvested Earnings.** The consolidated reinvested earnings statement reconciles beginning and ending reinvested earnings balances reported on comparative balance sheets. Reinvested earnings reported at the beginning of the year are increased by net profit and by the special gain (net of tax) for the year and are reduced by cash dividends and stock dividends declared during the year.

**Consolidated Statement of Funds.** A consolidated statement of funds is included as a part of the regular financial statements and is covered in the report of the independent public accountants. The funds statement explains the change for the latest year in "cash funds" defined as cash and short-term investments.

**Notes to Financial Statements.** Notes to financial statements provide detail relating to a number of important matters including federal income taxes in dispute, terms of long-term debt contracts, a company incentive plan, stock options outstanding, a stock-split becoming effective in 1964, and changes in capital surplus for the year.

*Radio Corporation of America*

## CONSOLIDATED EARNINGS

|  | Years Ended December 31 | |
| --- | --- | --- |
|  | **1963** | **1962** |
| **Products and Services Sold** | | |
| Products and services sold—commercial | $1,218,429,000 | $1,127,958,000 |
| U.S. Government sales | 560,635,000 | 614,788,000 |
| Interest | 7,933,000 | 4,234,000 |
| Dividends and other | 2,280,000 | 4,666,000 |
|  | 1,789,277,000 | 1,751,646,000 |
| **Cost of Operations** | | |
| Wages and salaries | 683,394,000 | 685,222,000 |
| Retirement plan contributions | 11,312,000 | 9,916,000 |
| Social security, insurance, and other employee benefits | 46,254,000 | 43,451,000 |
| Total employment costs | 740,960,000 | 738,589,000 |
| Materials and services purchased | 818,769,000 | 819,714,000 |
| Depreciation | 46,541,000 | 40,977,000 |
| Rent | 22,558,000 | 20,979,000 |
| Interest on long term debt | 10,449,000 | 10,090,000 |
| State, local, foreign, and miscellaneous taxes | 14,367,000 | 13,362,000 |
|  | 1,653,644,000 | 1,643,711,000 |
| **Profit Before Federal Taxes on Income** | 135,633,000 | 107,935,000 |
| **Federal Taxes on Income** | 69,600,000 | 56,400,000 |
| **Net Profit for Year** | 66,033,000 | 51,535,000 |
| **Gain on Sale of Whirlpool Corporation Stock**, less federal tax of $2,320,000 | | 6,960,000 |
| **Total Net Profit and Capital Gain** | $ 66,033,000 | $ 58,495,000 |

## CONSOLIDATED FINANCIAL POSITION

### ASSETS

|  | December 31 | |
| --- | --- | --- |
|  | **1963** | **1962** |
| **Current Assets** | | |
| Cash | $   79,485,000 | $  108,254,00 |
| Short term investments, at cost (approximate market) | 249,731,000 | 108,900,00 |
| Receivables—U. S. Government | 70,580,000 | 116,889,00 |
| —Other (less reserve: 1963, $8,545,000; 1962, $8,750,000) | 197,619,000 | 190,900,00 |
| Inventories, at lower of cost or market | | |
| Plant inventories and Government contracts (less progress payments: | | |
| 1963, $33,865,000; 1962, $33,023,000) | 93,599,000 | 98,804,00 |
| Finished goods | 91,988,000 | 88,582,00 |
| Prepaid expenses | 34,282,000 | 31,527,00 |
| **Total Current Assets** | 817,284,000 | 743,856,00 |
| **Investments** | | |
| Foreign subsidiaries, at or below cost (underlying net assets: | | |
| 1963, $30,975,000; 1962, $34,241,000) | 16,160,000 | 20,169,00 |
| RCA Credit Corporation, at cost plus undistributed earnings | 3,022,000 | 4,847,00 |
| Whirlpool Corporation common stock, 166,747 shares at cost | 3,109,000 | 3,109,00 |
| Other investments, at or below cost | 17,040,000 | 18,387,00 |
| RCA common stock held in treasury, at cost (Notes 3 and 4) | | |
| 1963, 64,604 shares; 1962, 89,028 shares | 3,592,000 | 4,140,00 |
| **Total Investments** | 42,923,000 | 50,652,00 |
| **Plant and Equipment** | | |
| Land and buildings | 165,897,000 | 160,275,00 |
| Machinery and equipment, including equipment leased to customers | 353,643,000 | 327,299,00 |
| Total, at cost (less accumulated investment tax credit: | | |
| 1963, $2,898,000; 1962, $1,294,000) | 519,540,000 | 487,574,00 |
| Less: Accumulated depreciation | 250,261,000 | 223,184,00 |
| **Net Plant and Equipment** | 269,279,000 | 264,390,00 |
| **Total Assets** | $1,129,486,000 | $1,058,898,000 |

*Radio Corporation of America*

| LIABILITIES AND SHAREHOLDERS' EQUITY | December 31 | |
| --- | --- | --- |
| | **1963** | **1962** |
| **Current Liabilities** | | |
| Accounts payable and accruals................................................................ | $ 227,919,000 | $ 231,940,000 |
| Federal taxes on income (Note 1)................................................ | 69,873,000 | 50,417,000 |
| Dividends payable on preferred and common stock.................................... | 9,427,000 | 5,816,000 |
| Total Current Liabilities................................. | 307,219,000 | 288,173,000 |
| **Other Liabilities** | | |
| Long term debt (Note 2)................................................ | 255,118,000 | 255,261,000 |
| Incentive plan awards payable, and unawarded balance | | |
| (1963, $1,367,000; 1962, $729,000) (Note 3)........................................ | 10,447,000 | 7,390,000 |
| Deferred federal taxes on income, related to depreciation........................ | 25,947,000 | 18,655,000 |
| Total Other Liabilities................................. | 291,512,000 | 281,306,000 |
| **Shareholders' Equity** | | |
| Capital stock, no par, at stated value | | |
| $3.50 cumulative first preferred stock, shares authorized 920,300, outstanding 900,824 (preference on liquidation $100 per share, $90,082,400)................................. | 14,575,000 | 14,575,000 |
| Common stock, authorized 18,500,000 shares (Notes 4 and 5) | | |
| Issued (1963, 17,531,957 shares; 1962, 17,418,763 shares including 2% stock dividend paid in February, 1963)................................. | 35,064,000 | 34,837,000 |
| Capital surplus (Note 6)................................................ | 180,583,000 | 176,245,000 |
| Reinvested earnings (Note 2)................................................ | 300,533,000 | 263,762,000 |
| Total Shareholders' Equity................................. | 530,755,000 | 489,419,000 |
| Total Liabilities and Shareholders' Equity................................. | $1,129,486,000 | $1,058,898,000 |

## CONSOLIDATED REINVESTED EARNINGS

| | Years Ended December 31 | |
|---|---|---|
| | **1963** | **1962** |
| Reinvested Earnings at Beginning of Year | $263,762,000 | $244,984,000 |
| Net Profit for Year | 66,033,000 | 51,535,000 |
| Gain on Whirlpool Corporation Stock, less Tax | | 6,960,000 |
| | 329,795,000 | 303,479,000 |
| **Cash Dividends Declared** | | |
| Preferred stock, $3.50 per share | 3,153,000 | 3,153,000 |
| Common stock, 1963, $1.50 per share; 1962, $1.00 per share | 26,109,000 | 16,945,000 |
| **2% Stock Dividend Declared on Common Stock** | | |
| 339,187 shares at $57.84 per share | | 19,619,000 |
| | 29,262,000 | 39,717,000 |
| Reinvested Earnings at End of Year (Note 2) | $300,533,000 | $263,762,000 |

## CONSOLIDATED STATEMENT OF FUNDS

| | Year Ended December 31, 1963 | |
|---|---|---|
| **Cash Funds Provided by** | | |
| Operations | | |
| Net profit for year | $ 66,033,000 | |
| Provisions not requiring current cash funds | | |
| Depreciation | 46,541,000 | |
| Deferred taxes, related to depreciation .. | 7,292,000 | |
| Offsetting investment tax credit... | 1,604,000 | |
| Total available from operations | | $121,470,000 |
| Sale of common shares under options | | 6,120,000 |
| Reduction in receivables and other net current assets | | 57,680,000 |
| Reduction in investments and increase in other debt... | | 9,087,000 |
| Total Cash Funds Provided | | 194,357,000 |
| **Cash Funds Used for** | | |
| Dividends declared on preferred and common stock | 29,262,000 | |
| Plant and equipment, less $6,998,000 book value of disposals | 53,033,000 | |
| Total Cash Funds Used | | 82,295,000 |
| **Increase in Cash Funds** | | |
| Cash and short term investments, December 31, 1963 | 329,216,000 | |
| Cash and short term investments, December 31, 1962 | 217,154,000 | |
| Net Increase in Cash Funds | | $112,062,000 |

*Radio Corporation of America*

# NOTES TO FINANCIAL STATEMENTS

1. **Federal taxes on income:** Federal income tax returns of RCA and its consolidated subsidiaries have been audited through 1957 and tax liabilities for those years have been substantially settled. RCA has suits pending in the Court of Claims against the United States for recovery of excess profits taxes paid for the years 1940-44. No recognition has been given to these claims in the financial statements.

2. **Long term debt:** Long term debt outstanding at December 31, 1963 included:

Promissory notes

| | |
|---|---|
| 3%, due 1970 to 1974 | $100,000,000 |
| 3¾%, due 1973 to 1977 | 50,000,000 |
| 5⅝%, due 1977 to 1986 | 100,000,000 |
| Purchase money mortgages payable in installments to 1986 | 5,118,000 |
| Total | $255,118,000 |

The terms of the promissory notes include limitations on the payment of cash dividends and the purchase of the Corporation's capital stock. At December 31, 1963, reinvested earnings of $124,469,000 were free of such limitations.

3. **RCA Incentive Plan:** The RCA Incentive Plan, which was approved by the shareholders in 1954 and again in 1959, provides that the maximum credit which can be made to the Incentive Reserve in any year cannot exceed the lesser of (a) 15% of Incentive Plan Net Earnings after deducting 5% of Capital Employed, or (b) 25% of dividends paid by the Corporation in such year. The following summary shows for the year 1963 the credit calculated by the Independent Public Accountants as required by the Plan.

| | |
|---|---|
| Net Profit for Year | $66,033,000 |
| Add: Provision for incentive awards | 6,901,000 |
| Interest on long term debt | 10,449,000 |
| Incentive Plan Net Earnings | 83,383,000 |
| Less: 5% of Capital Employed ($746,799,000) | 37,340,000 |
| Incentive Plan Base | $46,043,000 |
| Maximum Credit to Incentive Reserve Based on Earnings— 15% of Incentive Plan Base | $ 6,906,000 |
| Maximum Credit to Incentive Reserve Based on Dividends— 25% of dividends paid in year ($45,270,000) | $11,317,000 |

For 1963 the maximum credit as computed above was $6,906,000 and the Incentive Committee directed that $6,901,000 be credited to the Incentive Reserve. This credit, together with $729,000 credited to the Incentive Reserve in previous years but unawarded and carried forward for awards in subsequent years, made a total of $7,630,000 available for awards for 1963 of which the Incentive Committee determined that $6,263,000 be awarded for 1963. The consolidated balance sheet at December 31, 1963 includes in accounts payable and accruals the portions of incentive awards which are payable in cash within one year. The remainder of the incentive awards, payable in cash and RCA common stock, is included in awards payable. Payment of any deferred installment is contingent under the earning out provisions of the Plan.

4. **Stock options:** In 1957 and 1960 the shareholders approved a stock option plan and an amendment, respectively, under which options may be granted to key employees selected by a committee of the Board of Directors for the purchase within a maximum period of ten years, at a price not less than fair market value at date of grant, of up to 600,000 shares of common stock from the Corporation's treasury or from authorized but unissued shares. Options which have been granted are exercisable in cumulative annual installments of 20%, beginning with 20% at date of grant.

At December 31, 1962, options were outstanding on 420,626 shares and 29,035 shares were available for future grant, under the 1957 plan. During 1963, options for 37,000 shares were granted, options for 20,231 shares were canceled, and options for 113,194 shares were exercised at prices ranging from $26.68 to $64.13 and averaging $39.88. At December 31, 1963, options, which expire at various dates in 1964 to 1973, inclusive, were outstanding on 324,201 shares, of which options on 168,204 were then exercisable, and 12,266 shares were available for future grant. Options outstanding were at prices per share ranging from $26.70 to $73.25 and averaging $54.57.

At December 31, 1962 there was outstanding an option, exercisable on or before June 30, 1965, to purchase 59,944 shares of common stock at $45.86 per share, based on 95% of market price on date of grant, granted to an officer in 1955 and approved by shareholders in 1956. During 1963, the option was exercised as to 35,000 shares, leaving 24,944 shares under the option at December 31, 1963.

The foregoing numbers of shares and prices have been adjusted for 2% stock dividends declared in the years 1959 to 1962, inclusive.

5. **Common stock:** On January 31, 1964, and therefore not reflected in the 1963 financial statements, each share of common stock was split into three shares and the total authorized number of shares of common stock was increased from 18,500,000 shares to 80,000,000 shares. The stated value of the common stock was reduced from $2 a share to $.66⅔ a share. There was no change in the total stated value of common stock issued or in capital surplus and reinvested earnings accounts.

6. **Capital surplus:** Capital surplus was increased by a net amount of $4,338,000 during the year 1963 as a result of the following transactions in RCA common stock: issuance of 113,194 shares under stock options for $4,288,000 more than stated value; sale of 35,000 treasury shares under a stock option for $87,000 more than cost; distribution of 14,424 treasury shares under the RCA Incentive Plan at award values $37,000 less than cost.

## INDEPENDENT PUBLIC ACCOUNTANTS' CERTIFICATE

To the Shareholders of
Radio Corporation of America

We have examined the accompanying statement of financial position of RADIO CORPORATION OF AMERICA AND CONSOLIDATED SUBSIDIARIES at December 31, 1963 and the related statements of earnings, reinvested earnings, and funds for the year then ended. Our examination was made in accordance with generally accepted auditing standards, and accordingly included such tests of the accounting records and such other auditing procedures as we considered necessary in the circumstances. It was not practicable to confirm amounts due from the United States Government, as to which we satisfied ourselves by means of other auditing procedures.

In our opinion, the statements mentioned above present fairly the financial position of Radio Corporation of America and Consolidated Subsidiaries at December 31, 1963 and the results of their operations for the year then ended, in conformity with generally accepted accounting principles applied on a basis consistent with that of the preceding year.

*Arthur Young & Company*

New York, N. Y.
February 14, 1964

| | |
|---|---|
| **Transfer Agents** | The Corporation Trust Company, 120 Broadway, New York, N.Y. 10005 |
| | The First National Bank of Chicago, Dearborn, Monroe and Clark Streets, Chicago, Ill. 60690 |
| **Registrars, Preferred Stock** | The Chase Manhattan Bank, 80 Pine Street, New York, N.Y. 10005 |
| | Continental Illinois National Bank and Trust Company of Chicago, 231 South La Salle Street, Chicago, Ill. 60690 |
| **Registrars, Common Stock** | Chemical Bank New York Trust Company, 20 Pine Street, New York, N.Y. 10015 |
| | Continental Illinois National Bank and Trust Company of Chicago, 231 South La Salle Street, Chicago, Ill. 60690 |
| **General Counsel** | Cahill, Gordon, Reindel & Ohl, 80 Pine Street, New York, N. Y. 10005 |
| **Annual Meeting** | May 5, 1964, at 10:30 A.M., Pacific Daylight Time, in Studio 2 of the National Broadcasting Company, 3000 West Alameda Avenue, Burbank, Calif. 91505 |

## UNITED AIR LINES

The following features are of interest in reviewing the financial statements and accompanying notes taken from the annual report of United Air Lines for 1963.

Three sets of statements are presented under the headings: (1) Statements of Earnings, (2) Statements of Financial Position, and (3) Statements of Surplus. The first two statements are prepared in comparative form. The annual report also includes: (1) a summary headed "10 Year Statement of Financial Position," offering asset, liability, and stockholders' equity balances at the end of each year for the period 1954–1963; (2) a summary headed "10 Year Comparative Statistics," offering financial, operating, and personnel statistics and analyses for the period 1954–1963. The report also includes a "Statement of Source and Disposition of Funds." Funds are defined as working capital. The supplementary statements have not been reproduced.

**Statements of Earnings.** The statement of earnings is prepared in multiple-step form and offers all-inclusive reporting. Separate designations are provided for (1) earnings from operations before income taxes, (2) earnings before income taxes, (3) net earnings, and (4) net earnings and gain on sale of aircraft.

**Statements of Financial Position.** The statement of financial position is prepared in conventional account form. Valuation procedures are described in stating assets. Maturity dates are indicated for all debt balances. Notes relating to balance sheet items are reported at the bottom of the statement. The notes include information relating to commitments for the purchase of aircraft, terms of a credit agreement with banks, transfer of a self-insurance appropriation to earned surplus, requirements for the redemption of preferred shares, and grants, exercises, and cancellations relative to stock option plans in effect.

**Statements of Surplus.** Two surplus statements are provided: (1) a Statement of Capital Surplus Invested that summarizes changes in capital surplus from the sale of shares at amounts in excess of par value, the conversion of debentures, and the issue of stock dividends; (2) a Statement of Earned Surplus that summarizes changes in earned surplus arising from net earnings and a special gain for the year, the return of an earned surplus appropriation balance, and cash and stock dividends on preferred and common shares.

## STATEMENTS OF EARNINGS

*for the years ended December 31*

| | 1963 | 1962 |
|---|---|---|
| **OPERATING REVENUES:** | | |
| Passenger ........................... | $562,595,018 | $542,732,008 |
| Freight ............................. | 30,171,686 | 28,063,829 |
| Mail ................................ | 19,508,639 | 18,692,827 |
| Express ............................ | 6,381,526 | 6,527,003 |
| Other revenue, net .................... | 4,126,988 | 4,131,599 |
| Mutual Aid Agreement provision ......... | 80,513 | (5,894,463) |
| | $622,864,370 | $594,252,803 |
| **OPERATING EXPENSES:** | | |
| Flying and ground operations ........... | $319,721,844 | $305,418,756 |
| Maintenance ........................ | 114,999,806 | 109,862,065 |
| Depreciation and amortization ........... | 63,882,600 | 69,535,814 |
| Sales and advertising .................. | 61,102,515 | 60,655,430 |
| General and administrative ............. | 25,697,237 | 24,199,771 |
| | $585,404,002 | $569,671,836 |
| **EARNINGS FROM OPERATIONS** | | |
| before income taxes ................. | $ 37,460,368 | $ 24,580,967 |
| **OTHER DEDUCTIONS (INCOME), NET:** | | |
| Interest on long-term debt .............. | $ 11,036,134 | $ 13,603,352 |
| Interest capitalized .................... | (1,934,408) | (1,084,282) |
| Other. net .......................... | 156,712 | (668,694) |
| | $ 9,258,438 | $ 11,850,376 |
| **EARNINGS before income taxes** .......... | $ 28,201,930 | $ 12,730,591 |
| **INCOME TAXES on above earnings** ........ | 14,188,000 | 6,390,000 |
| **NET EARNINGS** ...................... | $ 14,013,930 | $ 6,340,591 |
| **GAIN ON SALE OF AIRCRAFT after tax** ... | 697,613 | 1,388,568 |
| **NET EARNINGS AND GAIN ON SALE OF AIRCRAFT** ............. | $ 14,711,543 | $ 7,729,159 |

## STATEMENTS OF FINANCIAL POSITION

*as of December 31*

| ASSETS | 1963 | 1962 |
|---|---|---|
| **CURRENT ASSETS:** | | |
| Cash | $ 31,724,453 | $ 34,634,820 |
| Receivables, less reserve | 71,105,361 | 72,060,449 |
| Flight equipment expendable parts, at average cost, less depreciation reserve (1963, $4,633,515; 1962, $4,541,397) | 23,102,513 | 21,974,505 |
| Maintenance and operating supplies, at average cost | 5,923,117 | 5,815,996 |
| Prepaid expenses | 2,243,093 | 3,976,832 |
| | $134,098,537 | $138,462,602 |

**OPERATING PROPERTY AND EQUIPMENT:**

| | Flight Equipment | Land and Buildings | Other Equipment | | |
|---|---|---|---|---|---|
| Original cost— | | | | | |
| 1963 | $729,930,970 | $63,585,060 | $55,392,140 | $848,908,170 | |
| 1962 | 701,063,167 | 59,938,523 | 52,535,990 | | $813,537,680 |
| Depreciation reserves— | | | | | |
| 1963 | 294,324,169 | 27,279,419 | 30,134,681 | 351,738,269 | |
| 1962 | 274,081,502 | 25,468,251 | 26,219,504 | | 325,769,257 |
| | | | | $497,169,901 | $487,768,423 |

| OTHER ASSETS: | 1963 | 1962 |
|---|---|---|
| Jet aircraft introductory costs, being amortized | $ 1,103,247 | $ 1,599,610 |
| Investments and miscellaneous | 3,019,443 | 2,952,383 |
| | $ 4,122,690 | $ 4,551,993 |
| | $635,391,128 | $630,783,018 |

**NOTES:**

Commitments for purchase of aircraft and other capital equipment approximated $173,971,000 at December 31, 1963.

At December 31, 1963, under terms of a credit agreement with a group of 34 banks, an additional $95,000,000 may be borrowed as needed prior to December 31, 1965. This commitment and the amount of the term loan notes outstanding were reduced $60,000,000 on February 5, 1964, concurrent with the sale of $60,000,000, 5% notes due February 1, 1984. Effective July 1, 1964, the interest rate on the term loan notes increases from ¼% to ½% above the prime rate.

In 1963, $5,000,000 appropriated in 1959 was returned to earned surplus from the reserve for self-insured risks.

| LIABILITIES AND STOCKHOLDERS' EQUITY | 1963 | 1962 |
|---|---|---|
| **CURRENT LIABILITIES:** | | |
| Long-term debt maturing within one year ....................... | $    2,592,000 | $    2,592,000 |
| Accounts payable and accrued liabilities ...................... | 96,432,550 | 90,721,119 |
| Customer deposits under air travel plan ...................... | 8,444,325 | 8,149,800 |
| Advance sales of tickets for transportation ................... | 15,715,400 | 13,809,478 |
| Accrued Federal income taxes ............................. | 1,221,414 | 1,241,108 |
| Accrued interest on long-term debt .......................... | 2,613,880 | 2,583,076 |
| | $127,019,569 | $119,096,581 |
| **LONG-TERM DEBT:** | | |
| 3½% sinking fund debentures due 1967 ...................... | $    4,776,000 | $    6,368,000 |
| 3¾% sinking fund debentures due 1974 ..................... | 13,500,000 | 14,500,000 |
| 4% sinking fund debentures due 1981 ....................... | 120,000,000 | 120,000,000 |
| 4¼% subordinated convertible debentures due 1976 ............ | 1,486,000 | 1,486,000 |
| 4⅞% subordinated convertible debentures due 1985 ........... | — | 24,998,400 |
| 4¾% term loan notes (see note below) ..................... | 85,000,000 | 112,000,000 |
| | $224,762,000 | $279,352,400 |
| **RESERVES:** | | |
| Reserve for self-insured risks (see note below) ................. | $    5,373,580 | $    8,964,962 |
| Reserve for deferred Federal income taxes .................... | 55,070,431 | 40,354,495 |
| | $  60,444,011 | $  49,319,457 |
| **STOCKHOLDERS' EQUITY:** | | |
| Cumulative preferred stock, $100 par value, authorized 600,000 shares; 5½% Series of 1960, outstanding 149,460 shares (see note below) | $  14,946,000 | $  15,423,000 |
| Common stock, $10 par value; authorized 10,000,000 shares (see note below); outstanding 6,484,211 shares .............. | 64,842,110 | 53,254,160 |
| Capital surplus invested ................................. | 102,028,804 | 76,201,777 |
| Earned surplus ....................................... | 41,348,634 | 38,135,643 |
| | $223,165,548 | $183,014,580 |
| | $635,391,128 | $630,783,018 |

Redemption of 4,770 shares of cumulative preferred stock is required annually by June 1.

At the beginning of the year 152,888 shares of common stock were reserved for options granted. During the year options for 35,529 shares were exercised; options for 23 shares were cancelled; and options granted were increased 8,240 shares for a stock dividend declared during the year. At the end of the year 125,576 shares were reserved for options granted. In addition 8,817 shares of common stock were reserved for convertible debentures and 496,022 shares for warrants.

## STATEMENTS OF SURPLUS

*for the year ended December 31, 1963*

### CAPITAL SURPLUS INVESTED

| | |
|---|---:|
| Balance December 31, 1962 ................................... | $ 76,201,777 |
| Add — Amount arising from sale of common stock .................... | 295,989 |
| Amount arising from conversion of 4⅞% subordinated convertible debentures ........................................... | 16,430,875 |
| Excess of adjusted market value over par value of stock issued as stock dividend ........................................ | 9,100,163 |
| Balance December 31, 1963 ................................... | $102,028,804 |

### EARNED SURPLUS

| | |
|---|---:|
| Balance December 31, 1962 ................................... | $ 38,135,643 |
| Add — Net earnings and gain on sale of aircraft per accompanying statement | 14,711,543 |
| Return of 1959 appropriation for self-insured risks .............. | 5,000,000 |
| | $ 57,847,186 |
| Deduct — Cash dividends on 5½% preferred stock — $5.50 per share ..... | $ 835,148 |
| Cash dividends on common stock — $.50 per share ........... | 2,857,114 |
| Stock dividend on common stock — 6% per share ........... | 12,806,290 |
| | $ 16,498,552 |
| Balance December 31, 1963 ................................... | $ 41,348,634 |

### OPINION OF INDEPENDENT ACCOUNTANTS

TO THE STOCKHOLDERS AND BOARD OF DIRECTORS, UNITED AIR LINES, INC.:

We have examined the statement of financial position of United Air Lines, Inc. (a Delaware corporation) as of December 31, 1963, and the related statements of earnings and surplus for the year then ended. Our examination was made in accordance with generally accepted auditing standards, and accordingly included such tests of the accounting records and such other auditing procedures as we considered necessary in the circumstances. We had made a similar examination for the year ended December 31, 1962.

In our opinion, the accompanying statements of financial position and statements of earnings and surplus present fairly the financial position of United Air Lines, Inc. as of December 31, 1963 and 1962, and the results of its operations for the years ended those dates, in conformity with generally accepted accounting principles consistently applied during the period.

Chicago, Illinois
February 14, 1964

*Arthur Andersen & Co.*

# THE STANDARD OIL COMPANY (AN OHIO CORPORATION)

The following features are of interest in reviewing the financial statements and the accompanying notes taken from the annual report of the Standard Oil Company (An Ohio Corporation) for 1963.

Three financial statements are presented: (1) Consolidated Balance Sheet, (2) Consolidated Income Statement, and (3) Stockholders' Interest Statement. The balance sheet and income statement are prepared in comparative form. The annual report includes two summaries headed "Ten-Year Financial Review" and "Ten-Year Operating Review" in which significant financial data as well as stockholder and employee data for the years 1954 through 1963 are presented in comparative form. The annual report also includes a summary headed "Financing Expansion and Replacement" that reports the source and application of funds for the year. Funds are defined as Cash and U.S. Government Securities. The supplementary statements have not been reproduced.

**Consolidated Balance Sheet.** The balance sheet is prepared in the conventional account form. Valuation procedures are described in reporting assets. Detail is provided concerning payment dates for long-term debt.

**Consolidated Income Statement.** The income statement is prepared in single-step form. Extraordinary gains and losses are included in the statement, providing all-inclusive reporting.

**Stockholders' Interest Statement.** The stockholders' interest statement offers a full reconciliation of the changes for the year in preferred and common stock balances, capital in excess of par value, and net income employed in the business. The statement summarizes the changes in capital balances arising from the issue of stock in exchange for properties, the sale of stock under stock options, the reacquisition of stock by purchase, net income for the year, and dividends declared for the year.

**Notes to Financial Statements.** Notes to the financial statements are limited to two items: (1) capital stock, including retirement provisions relating to the preferred class and the number of preferred and common shares held as treasury stock; (2) stock option plans, including grants, exercises, and cancellations during the year.

# CONSOLIDATED BALANCE SHEET

## ASSETS

| | December 31 | |
| --- | ---: | ---: |
| | **1963** | **1962** |
| **CURRENT ASSETS** | | |
| Cash. . . . . . . . . . . . . . . . . . . . . . . . | $ 26,300,720 | $ 27,169,850 |
| U. S. Government securities—at cost, approximating market . . . | 49,499,152 | 32,561,071 |
| Accounts receivable, less estimated uncollectibles . . . . . . . . | 66,606,450 | 62,562,027 |
| Inventories | | |
| Crude oil, refined products, and merchandise— | | |
| cost, last-in, first-out—less than market . . . . . . . . . . | 49,609,979 | 44,568,032 |
| Materials and supplies—average cost . . . . . . . . . . . | 4,819,856 | 5,427,932 |
| | $196,836,157 | $172,288,912 |
| **INVESTMENTS AND OTHER ASSETS** | | |
| Securities of other companies—at cost . . . . . . . . . . . . | $ 6,864,370 | $ 5,932,261 |
| Notes receivable and advances . . . . . . . . . . . . . . . | 9,217,736 | 3,698,582 |
| Prepaid expenses and deferred charges . . . . . . . . . . . | 5,555,667 | 5,034,886 |
| | $ 21,637,773 | $ 14,665,729 |
| **PROPERTY, PLANT, AND EQUIPMENT—at cost** . . . . . . . | $538,667,122 | $518,247,457 |
| Less accumulated depreciation and depletion . . . . . . . . . . | 288,634,932 | 273,527,614 |
| | $250,032,190 | $244,719,843 |
| | $468,506,120 | $431,674,484 |

## THE STANDARD OIL COMPANY *(AN OHIO CORPORATION)*
### AND SUBSIDIARIES

**LIABILITIES AND STOCKHOLDERS' INTEREST**

|  | December 31 1963 | 1962 |
|---|---|---|
| **CURRENT LIABILITIES** | | |
| Accounts payable . . . . . . . . . . . . . . . . . . . . . | $ 46,292,230 | $ 37,237,601 |
| Salaries, wages, and commissions. . . . . . . . . . . . . . | 6,037,329 | 6,713,170 |
| Accrued taxes, other than taxes on income . . . . . . . . . | 15,269,680 | 14,490,962 |
| Accrued federal and foreign taxes on income. . . . . . . . . | 20,662,138 | 13,199,384 |
| Current maturities on long-term debt, less | | |
| $2,573,000 in treasury in 1963. . . . . . . . . . . . . . | 977,000 | 1,550,000 |
| | $ 89,238,377 | $ 73,191,117 |
| **LONG-TERM DEBT—excluding current maturities** | | |
| Note payable ($300,000 due annually). . . . . . . . . . . . | $ 1,200,000 | $ 1,500,000 |
| Sinking Fund Debentures—3%, ($2,000,000 due annually, | | |
| balance in 1968) less $141,000 in treasury in 1963 . . . . . . | 15,859,000 | 17,239,000 |
| Sinking Fund Debentures—4¼%, ($1,250,000 due annually) . . . | 21,250,000 | 22,500,000 |
| | $ 38,309,000 | $ 41,239,000 |
| **STOCKHOLDERS' INTEREST** | | |
| Capital stock—Notes A and B | | |
| Preferred—cumulative, $100 par value . . . . . . . . . . . | $ 17,245,600 | $ 17,360,600 |
| Common —$10 par value . . . . . . . . . . . . . . . . . | 54,228,440 | 48,608,980 |
| | $ 71,474,040 | $ 65,969,580 |
| Capital in excess of par value of capital stock . . . . . . . . | 96,155,321 | 70,864,979 |
| Net income employed in the business . . . . . . . . . . . . | 173,329,382 | 180,409,808 |
| | $340,958,743 | $317,244,367 |
| | $468,506,120 | $431,674,484 |

*See notes to financial statements.*

# CONSOLIDATED INCOME STATEMENT

| | Year ended December 31 | |
| --- | --- | --- |
| | **1963** | **1962** |
| **INCOME** | | |
| Sales and operating revenue . . . . . . . . . . . . . . . . . . | $568,310,817 | $515,364,916 |
| Less gasoline and oil excise taxes . . . . . . . . . . . . . | 122,807,156 | 117,691,111 |
| Net sales and operating revenue . . . . . . . . . . . . . . | $445,503,661 | $397,673,805 |
| Sales of purchased crude oil . . . . . . . . . . . . . . . . | 55,227,793 | 34,112,197 |
| Miscellaneous income—includes profit from sales of assets . . . . | 6,367,415 | 4,369,449 |
| | $507,098,869 | $436,155,451 |
| **COSTS AND EXPENSES** | | |
| Materials, merchandise, operating and other expenses . . . . . . | $324,678,652 | $276,144,393 |
| Salaries, wages, and employee benefits . . . . . . . . . . . | 80,697,896 | 75,361,171 |
| Taxes and other payments to governments . . . . . . . . . . | 33,785,575 | 25,961,106 |
| Depreciation of facilities. . . . . . . . . . . . . . . . . | 19,638,861 | 19,063,194 |
| Depletion of oil and gas producing properties . . . . . . . . . | 5,333,435 | 6,872,908 |
| Nonproductive wells and surrendered mineral leases . . . . . . | 7,474,306 | 5,537,463 |
| Abandonment of refining facility . . . . . . . . . . . . . . | —0— | 1,344,002 |
| Debenture and other interest . . . . . . . . . . . . . . . | 1,603,527 | 1,649,629 |
| | $473,212,252 | $411,933,866 |
| **NET INCOME** . . . . . . . . . . . . . . . . . . . | $ 33,886,617 | $ 24,221,585 |

## NOTES TO FINANCIAL STATEMENTS

**A—CAPITAL STOCK** Authorized capital stock consists of 302,818 shares of preferred stock, issuable in series, and 7,500,000 shares of common stock. At December 31, 1963, 172,456 shares of Series A, 3¾% preferred stock, and 5,422,844 shares of common stock were outstanding. The outstanding shares excluded 4,922 shares of preferred and 41,442 shares of common stock in treasury. Provisions of the preferred stock require annual retirement of 2% of the aggregate number of shares theretofore issued.

**B—STOCK OPTION PLANS** Restricted Stock Option Plans authorize the issuance of common stock to executives and key employees at not less than the market price on the dates options are granted. Options granted under the Plans become exercisable in equal annual amounts beginning one year from date of grant, and generally expire no later than ten years from date granted. Under these Plans, at the beginning and end of 1963, options were outstanding for 61,708 and 114,610 shares, and reserved for future options were 165,000 and 100,650 shares. During 1963, options were granted for 64,350 shares, exercised for 9,502 shares, and cancelled for 1,946 shares. The foregoing were adjusted to reflect the 10% stock dividend paid in June, 1963.

## THE STANDARD OIL COMPANY *(AN OHIO CORPORATION)*

### AND SUBSIDIARIES

# STOCKHOLDERS' INTEREST STATEMENT

| | Capital Stock | | Capital in Excess of Par Value | Net Income Employed in the Business | Total Stockholders' Interest |
|---|---|---|---|---|---|
| | Preferred— $100 Par Value | Common— $10 Par Value | | | |
| **BALANCE AT DECEMBER 31, 1962** | $ 17,360,600 | $ 48,608,980 | $ 70,864,979 | $180,409,808 | $317,244,367 |
| Net income. . . . . . . . . . | | | | 33,886,617 | 33,886,617 |
| Dividends | | | | | |
| Paid in cash | | | | | |
| Preferred stock, $3.75 a share | | | | (647,929) | (647,929) |
| Common stock, 62½¢ a share in first quarter and 65¢ quarterly thereafter  . . . . | | | | (13,294,316) | (13,294,316) |
| Paid in common stock | | | | | |
| 10% on common stock— 492,877 shares  . . . . . . | | 4,928,770 | 21,844,325 | (26,773,095) | |
| Common stock issued in connection with purchase of substantially all the assets of Pro-phy-lac-tic Brush Company—66,667 shares . . . . | | 666,670 | 3,241,683 | | 3,908,353 |
| Common stock sold under stock option plans—9,502 shares— Note B. . . . . . . . . . . . | | 95,020 | 323,502 | | 418,522 |
| Stock purchased for treasury | | | | | |
| Preferred—1,150 shares. . . . . | (115,000) | | | | (115,000) |
| Common—7,100 shares. . . . . | | (71,000) | (119,168) | (251,703) | (441,871) |
| **BALANCE AT DECEMBER 31, 1963** | $ 17,245,600 | $ 54,228,440 | $ 96,155,321 | $173,329,382 | $340,958,743 |

(Decreases shown in parentheses.)

### ACCOUNTANTS' REPORT

Board of Directors
The Standard Oil Company
Cleveland, Ohio

We have examined the consolidated financial statements of The Standard Oil Company, an Ohio corporation, and subsidiaries for the year ended December 31, 1963. Our examination was made in accordance with generally accepted auditing standards, and accordingly included such tests of the accounting records and such other auditing procedures as we considered necessary in the circumstances.

In our opinion, the accompanying balance sheet and statements of income and stockholders' interest present fairly the consolidated financial position of The Standard Oil Company and subsidiaries at December 31, 1963, and the consolidated results of their operations for the year then ended, in conformity with generally accepted accounting principles applied on a basis consistent with that of the preceding year.

ERNST & ERNST

Cleveland, Ohio
February 14, 1964

## HOUSTON LIGHTING & POWER COMPANY

The following features are of interest in reviewing the financial statements and accompanying notes taken from the annual report of the Houston Lighting & Power Company for 1963.

Three financial statements for the year are presented: (1) Statement of Income, (2) Statement of Earned Surplus, and (3) Balance Sheet. Each statement is prepared in comparative form. Financial statements are accompanied by a schedule of long-term debt. The annual report also includes a "Summary of Operations" that offers financial and operating detail covering a 10-year period, 1954–1963. This summary is not reproduced.

**Statement of Income.** The income statement is prepared in multiple-step form. Operating revenues are followed by operating revenue deductions to arrive at a net operating revenues balance. This is followed by other income and income deductions in arriving at the net income for the year.

**Statement of Earned Surplus.** The balance of earned surplus at the beginning of the year is increased by the net income for the year and is decreased by cash dividends on preferred and common shares for the year.

**Balance Sheet.** The balance sheet is prepared in a form that is common to public utilities. Assets and liabilities are presented to emphasize total utility plant and the sources of utility plant financing. The assets are listed in the following order: (1) utility plant, (2) current assets, and (3) deferred debits. Liabilities are listed as follows: (1) capital stock and surplus, (2) long-term debt, (3) current liabilities, (4) deferred credits, (5) reserves, (6) accumulated deferred federal income taxes, and (7) contributions in aid of construction. Commitments in the form of construction contracts are entered short at the end of the liability section.

**Notes to Financial Statements.** Two notes accompany the financial statements: (1) a note explaining a stock split during the year; (2) a summary offering an analysis of the long-term debt total on the balance sheet.

## statement of income  *for the years ended December 31, 1963 and 1962*

|  | 1963 | 1962 |
|---|---|---|
| OPERATING REVENUES | $155,192,588 | $141,649,198 |
| OPERATING REVENUE DEDUCTIONS: | | |
| Operating expenses, excluding fuel and maintenance | 22,948,943 | 20,018,110 |
| Fuel | 26,956,648 | 25,417,598 |
| Maintenance | 7,584,420 | 6,773,766 |
| Provision for depreciation of electric plant | 15,718,949 | 15,260,686 |
| Federal income taxes: | | |
| Current | 33,270,773 | 29,531,837 |
| Investment tax credit deferred to future years, less amortization | 660,432 | 332,163 |
| Reduction of deferred income taxes, relating to accelerated amortization | (462,009) | (92,232) |
| Other taxes | 9,368,904 | 8,830,257 |
| TOTAL OPERATING REVENUE DEDUCTIONS | 116,047,060 | 106,072,185 |
| NET OPERATING REVENUES | 39,145,528 | 35,577,013 |
| OTHER INCOME | 442,625 | 265,946 |
| GROSS INCOME | 39,588,153 | 35,842,959 |
| INCOME DEDUCTIONS: | | |
| Interest on long-term debt | 8,456,250 | 7,781,250 |
| Amortization of premium and expense on long-term debt (net) | 39,099 | 39,213 |
| Other interest | 101,328 | 629,486 |
| Interest charged to construction — credit | (630,086) | (112,411) |
| Other | 119,094 | 108,126 |
| TOTAL INCOME DEDUCTIONS | 8,085,685 | 8,445,664 |
| NET INCOME | $ 31,502,468 | $ 27,397,295 |

## statement of earned surplus  *for the years ended December 31, 1963 and 1962*

|  | 1963 | 1962 |
|---|---|---|
| BALANCE AT BEGINNING OF YEAR | $ 87,235,676 | $71,704,174 |
| NET INCOME FOR THE YEAR | 31,502,468 | 27,397,295 |
| TOTAL | 118,738,144 | 99,101,469 |
| LESS CASH DIVIDENDS: | | |
| Preferred | 389,588 | 389,588 |
| Common | 13,973,967 | 11,476,205 |
| TOTAL DIVIDENDS | 14,363,555 | 11,865,793 |
| BALANCE AT END OF YEAR | $104,374,589 | $87,235,676 |

# Houston Lighting & Power Company

## ASSETS

| | 1963 | 1962 |
|---|---|---|
| **UTILITY PLANT:** | | |
| Electric plant, at original cost | $577,876,815 | $542,315,409 |
| Electric plant acquisition adjustments, at cost | 3,150,414 | 3,150,414 |
| TOTAL UTILITY PLANT | 581,027,229 | 545,465,823 |
| Less accumulated provision for: | | |
| Depreciation of electric plant | 114,833,224 | 103,242,334 |
| Amortization of electric plant acquisition adjustments (prior to 1945) | 1,465,307 | 1,465,307 |
| TOTAL | 116,298,531 | 104,707,641 |
| NET UTILITY PLANT | 464,728,698 | 440,758,182 |
| **CURRENT ASSETS:** | | |
| Cash in banks — On demand | 7,939,733 | 5,479,783 |
| Working funds and special deposits | 85,042 | 78,567 |
| Temporary cash investments: | | |
| Certificates of deposit | | 8,000,000 |
| United States Treasury Bills (at cost plus amortization of discount) | 16,899,624 | 14,919,654 |
| Accounts receivable — Customers and others (less accumulated provision for uncollectible accounts, $101,247 in 1963 and $74,192 in 1962) | 9,428,479 | 9,576,573 |
| Materials and supplies (at average cost — less accumulated provision for inventory adjustments, $54,937 in 1963 and $49,877 in 1962) | 4,139,097 | 3,635,146 |
| Prepayments | 392,234 | 441,869 |
| TOTAL CURRENT ASSETS | 38,884,209 | 42,131,592 |
| **DEFERRED DEBITS** | 572,052 | 840,345 |
| **TOTAL** | $504,184,959 | $483,730,119 |

# Balance Sheet December 31, 1963 and 1962

## LIABILITIES

| | 1963 | 1962 |
|---|---|---|
| CAPITAL STOCK AND SURPLUS: | | |
| Preferred stock, cumulative; no par; authorized, 500,000 shares — $4 series (entitled upon liquidation to $100 a share), outstanding, 97,397 shares ..........................$ | 9,739,700 | $  9,739,700 |
| Common stock; no par; authorized, 30,000,000 shares; outstanding, 20,252,127 shares (Note 1).................. | 100,177,449 | 100,177,449 |
| TOTAL CAPITAL STOCK .......................... | 109,917,149 | 109,917,149 |
| Earned surplus ...................................... | 104,374,589 | 87,235,676 |
| TOTAL CAPITAL STOCK AND SURPLUS................ | 214,291,738 | 197,152,825 |
| LONG-TERM DEBT — First mortgage bonds (Note 2) ......... | 230,000,000 | 230,000,000 |
| CURRENT LIABILITIES: | | |
| Accounts payable .................................... | 7,157,713 | 5,836,776 |
| Customers' deposits .................................. | 1,966,033 | 2,107,941 |
| Taxes accrued ....................................... | 23,392,762 | 23,023,142 |
| Interest accrued .................................... | 2,507,661 | 2,516,323 |
| Other .............................................. | 4,784,053 | 4,337,420 |
| TOTAL CURRENT LIABILITIES..................... | 39,808,222 | 37,821,602 |
| DEFERRED CREDITS: | | |
| Unamortized premium (less expense) on long-term debt ...... | 390,333 | 351,234 |
| Customers' advances for construction .................... | 647,502 | 524,266 |
| Unamortized investment tax credit ...................... | 1,087,530 | 332,163 |
| Other .............................................. | 719,754 | 616,231 |
| TOTAL DEFERRED CREDITS........................ | 2,845,119 | 1,823,894 |
| RESERVES: | | |
| Injuries and damages ................................. | 50,000 | 50,000 |
| Employees' provident ................................. | | 76,825 |
| Insurance ........................................... | 1,000,000 | 500,000 |
| TOTAL RESERVES ............................. | 1,050,000 | 626,825 |
| ACCUMULATED DEFERRED FEDERAL INCOME TAXES — Relating to accelerated amortization ...................... | 11,685,244 | 12,147,253 |
| CONTRIBUTIONS IN AID OF CONSTRUCTION............ | 4,504,636 | 4,157,720 |
| CONSTRUCTION COMMITMENTS — $14,000,000 | | |
| TOTAL ................................$ | 504,184,959 | $483,730,119 |

# Notes to Financial Statements

1. During 1963, the Company's articles of incorporation were amended to increase the authorized shares of common stock to 30,000,000 shares, and on May 1, 1963 two additional shares of common stock were issued for each share outstanding so as to effect a 3 for 1 stock split.

2. Long-term debt consists of the following:

FIRST MORTGAGE BONDS:

| | |
|---|---:|
| 2⅞% series, due 1974 | $ 30,000,000 |
| 3¼% series, due 1981 | 20,000,000 |
| 2¾% series, due 1985 | 30,000,000 |
| 3¼% series, due 1986 | 30,000,000 |
| 4¾% series, due 1987 | 40,000,000 |
| 3% series, due 1989 | 30,000,000 |
| 4⅞% series, due 1989 | 25,000,000 |
| 4½% series, due 1992 | 25,000,000 |
| TOTAL LONG-TERM DEBT | $230,000,000 |

*Accountants' Opinion*

HOUSTON LIGHTING & POWER COMPANY:

We have examined the balance sheet of Houston Lighting & Power Company as of December 31, 1963 and the related statements of income and earned surplus for the year then ended. Our examination was made in accordance with generally accepted auditing standards, and accordingly included such tests of the accounting records and such other auditing procedures as we considered necessary in the circumstances.

In our opinion, the accompanying balance sheet and statements of income and earned surplus present fairly the financial position of the Company at December 31, 1963 and the results of its operations for the year then ended, in conformity with generally accepted accounting principles applied on a basis consistent with that of the preceding year.

HASKINS & SELLS
*Certified Public Accountants*

Houston, Texas
February 5, 1964 .

## SCOTT PAPER COMPANY

The following features are of interest in reviewing the financial statements and the accompanying notes taken from the annual report of Scott Paper Company for 1963.

Three financial statements are presented: (1) Consolidated Operations, (2) Consolidated Financial Position, and (3) Stockholders' Investment. Each statement is presented in comparative form. The financial statements are accompanied by a statement of Source and Application of Funds, which is reproduced, and an "Historical Financial Summary" providing condensed balance sheet and income statement data for a 10-year period, which is not reproduced.

**Consolidated Operations.** The operations statement lists revenues and costs and expenses in single-step form in arriving at a net income before taxes balance. This balance is reduced by income taxes to provide a net income balance. Net income is then reduced by dividends on preferred shares and dividends on common shares to provide a balance representing the amount reinvested in the business.

**Consolidated Financial Position.** Assets, liabilities, and capital are presented in modified "financial-position" form. Net current assets (working capital) is reported and this balance is increased by long-term assets. The statement then summarizes the equities of bondholders and stockholders in the "asset less current liability" balance.

**Stockholders' Investment.** A shareholders' investment statement summarizes changes in the equities of the preferred and common shareholders. Income for the year reinvested in the business as summarized on the operations statement is added to the common stockholders' equity in arriving at the total investment identified with the common stockholders.

**Notes to the Financial Statements.** Notes to the financial statements provide information relating to such matters as inventory valuation, the nature of plant assets, differences in financial and income tax reporting, redemption and conversion features of bonded debt outstanding, stock-option plans, and long-term leases held by the company.

Scott Paper Company

## CONSOLIDATED OPERATIONS

| | 1963 | 1962* |
|---|---|---|
| Sales, less discounts and allowances.......................... | $370,039,920 | $354,449,607 |
| Scott's share of the earnings of foreign affiliates.............. | 2,559,598 | 2,224,573 |
| | $372,599,518 | $356,674,180 |
| Costs and expenses | | |
| Materials, labor and other product costs................ | $228,490,207 | $218,722,191 |
| Marketing and distribution............................. | 55,220,700 | 53,940,218 |
| Research, administration and general................... | 21,596,240 | 19,411,291 |
| Interest................................................ | 956,312 | 1,134,176 |
| | $306,263,459 | $293,207,876 |
| Income before taxes........................................ | $ 66,336,059 | $ 63,466,304 |
| Provision for taxes on income | | |
| State and foreign....................................... | $ 1,810,000 | $ 1,915,000 |
| Federal................................................ | 28,270,000 | 28,855,000 |
| | $ 30,080,000 | $ 30,770,000 |
| Net income................................................ | $ 36,256,059 | $ 32,696,304 |
| Dividends on preferred shares.............................. | 349,759 | 395,588 |
| Amount earned on common shares........................... | $ 35,906,300 | $ 32,300,716 |
| Dividends on common shares................................ | 21,786,262 | 20,937,636 |
| Remainder reinvested in the business...................... | $ 14,120,038 | $ 11,363,080 |

Costs and expenses include depreciation and depletion
of $18,789,919 in 1963 and $17,587,173 in 1962.

*The accompanying notes are an integral part of these statements.*

*Restated—see note 3*

Scott Paper Company

# CONSOLIDATED FINANCIAL POSITION

| | December 31 | |
|---|---|---|
| | 1963 | 1962 |
| CURRENT ASSET | | |
| Cash................................................. | $ 10,073,370 | $ 11,501,423 |
| Marketable securities, at cost............................ | 18,771,305 | 13,129,644 |
| Receivable from | | |
|     Customers......................................... | 28,000,766 | 27,709,605 |
|     Others............................................ | 3,192,037 | 4,249,213 |
| Inventories............................................. | 53,610,023 | 52,215,538 |
| Prepaid items.......................................... | 4,958,560 | 4,557,718 |
| | $118,606,061 | $113,363,141 |
| Less—CURRENT LIABILITIES | | |
| Payable to suppliers and others........................... | $ 26,172,297 | $ 25,822,234 |
| Dividend declared on preferred shares.................... | 79,762 | 97,523 |
| Estimated taxes on income............................... | 25,857,105 | 22,653,222 |
| | $ 52,109,164 | $ 48,572,979 |
| NET CURRENT ASSETS | $ 66,496,897 | $ 64,790,162 |

| | 1963 | 1962 | | |
|---|---|---|---|---|
| PLANT ASSETS, at cost... | $352,236,124 | $333,455,476 | | |
|     Less depreciation... | 165,351,566 | 149,853,955 | | |
| | | | 186,884,558 | 183,601,521 |
| TIMBER RESOURCES, at cost less depletion................... | | | 24,559,249 | 27,082,918 |
| INVESTMENTS IN AFFILIATED AND OTHER COMPANIES....... | | | 50,167,337 | 39,921,010 |
| PATENTS, TRADEMARKS AND GOODWILL..................... | | | 1 | 1 |
| OTHER ASSETS........................................... | | | 1,996,097 | 2,017,302 |
| TOTAL ASSETS LESS CURRENT LIABILITIES.................. | | | $330,104,139 | $317,412,914 |
| PROVIDED BY | | | | |
|     HOLDERS OF 3% CONVERTIBLE DEBENTURES........... | | | $ 27,257,700 | $ 35,168,900 |
|     SHAREHOLDERS (see following page)................... | | | 302,846,439 | 282,244,014 |
| | | | $330,104,139 | $317,412,914 |

*The accompanying notes are an integral part of these statements.*

## SHAREHOLDERS' INVESTMENT

|  | December 31 | |
|---|---|---|
|  | 1963 | 1962 |
| **Cumulative Preferred Shares Without Par Value** | | |
| Authorized—128,231 shares | | |
| Outstanding | | |
| $3.40 series—56,461 shares (1962—63,251 shares) stated at | $  5,723,734 | $   6,412,070 |
| $4.00 series—31,770 shares (1962—43,760 shares) stated at | **3,177,000** | 4,376,000 |
| Investment of preferred shareholders...................... | $  8,900,734 | $ 10,788,070 |
| **Common Shares Without Par Value** | | |
| Authorized—40,000,000 shares | | |
| Issued—26,627,905 shares (1962—26,262,911 shares).......... | **$154,615,332** | $145,237,109 |
| Income reinvested in the business | | |
| At beginning of year.......................................... | **126,218,835** | 114,855,755 |
| From year's operations....................................... | **14,120,038** | 11,363,080 |
| At end of year................................................. | **140,338,873** | 126,218,835 |
| In Treasury, at cost—31,000 shares............................ | **(1,008,500)** | |
| Investment of common shareholders........................ | **$293,945,705** | $271,455,944 |
| **Total Investment of Shareholders** | **$302,846,439** | $282,244,014 |

*The accompanying notes are an integral part of these statements.*

## NOTES TO THE FINANCIAL STATEMENTS

**NOTE 1** Inventories, stated at the lower of cost or market, were:

|  | 1963 | 1962 |
|---|---|---|
| Finished and in process | | |
| Paper.................................................... | $  20,981,823 | $  19,502,161 |
| Pulp...................................................... | **5,076,759** | 5,934,427 |
| Logs and pulpwood........................................... | **13,703,693** | 12,720,642 |
| Other materials and supplies................................ | **13,847,748** | 14,058,308 |
|  | $  53,610,023 | $  52,215,538 |

**NOTE 2** Plant asset accounts are summarized as follows:

|  | 1963 | 1962 |
|---|---|---|
| Land and rights of way........................................ | $   3,832,606 | $   3,780,277 |
| Buildings...................................................... | **48,122,594** | 47,600,024 |
| Machinery and equipment..................................... | **300,280,924** | 282,075,175 |
|  | **$352,236,124** | $333,455,476 |

Currently anticipated expenditures for major plant expansion amount to $60,000,000. Expenditures in connection with this program are estimated at $36,000,000 in 1964 and $24,000,000 in 1965.

**NOTE 3** The consolidated statements include the accounts of all wholly owned domestic and Canadian subsidiaries. In addition the Company includes in income its share of the earnings of its foreign and domestic affiliates which are at least 50% owned. Prior to 1963 such share was shown as a separate item of income in the statement of consolidated operations. Effective in 1963 this presentation was modified to show separately only the Company's share of the earnings of those affiliates (all foreign) which are engaged in the production and sale of products to customers other than Scott. This modification had no effect upon net income since the Company's share of the earnings of its other affiliates (all domestic and engaged in the supplying of pulp and timber to Scott) has been reflected under appropriate captions in the statement of consolidated operations of the Company and its subsidiaries. The statement of consolidated operations for 1962 has been restated to reflect this modified presentation. Taxes which may become payable if undistributed earnings of the affiliates are received as dividends have not been provided because of the continuing use of such earnings in expansion programs of those companies.

|  | 1963 | 1962 |
|---|---|---|
| Investments in affiliates—stated at book amounts of underlying net assets* |  |  |
| Foreign..................................................... | $25,283,763 | $20,081,842 |
| Domestic (principally Brunswick Pulp & Paper Company) | 18,630,595 | 15,273,389 |
|  | $43,914,358 | $35,355,231 |
| Other investments—stated at cost............................ | 6,252,979 | 4,565,779 |
|  | $50,167,337 | $39,921,010 |

*The stated amounts of these investments exceeded cost by $9,704,768 at December 31, 1963 and by $4,364,039 at December 31, 1962.

**NOTE 4** Depreciation computed for tax purposes currently exceeds depreciation reflected in these statements. Accordingly, the statement of consolidated financial position includes in estimated taxes on income at December 31, 1963, $10,100,000 ($3,300,000 for 1963, $4,400,000 for 1962 and $2,400,000 for prior years) which may be payable in future years if tax depreciation becomes less than depreciation recorded for financial purposes.

**NOTE 5** The 3% Convertible Debentures are dated March 1, 1956 and become due March 1, 1971. They are redeemable (at Company option) in whole or in part at any time on 30 days' notice; the redemption price is $101.60 to February 29, 1964, $101.40 to February 28, 1965 and decreases each March 1 thereafter. The Debentures may be surrendered for conversion into common shares at $25.66⅔ principal amount of debentures per common share; at December 31, 1963, 1,061,988 common shares were reserved for this purpose. Conversions to December 31, 1963 totaled $71,427,400; of this amount $7,911,200 was effected in 1963 by issuance of 308,018 common shares and cash payment of $7,487.

**NOTE 6** At December 31, 1963 officers and other key employees held options granted under the Company's stock option plan for the purchase of 1,301,544 of the Company's common shares. Option prices range from $25.66⅔ to $42.00 per share with an overall average price of $31.83 per share. Such options with respect to 370,511 shares are presently exercisable and become exercisable with respect to an additional 155,788 shares at various dates in 1964. Options to purchase shares at an average price of $25.89 per share were exercised in 1963 to the extent of 56,976 shares.

**NOTE 7** The Company has under long-term lease its executive office building, research and engineering center, certain warehouses and other facilities constructed at a total cost of approximately $24,000,000. The leases extend for periods up to 40 years with rentals totaling approximately $1,600,000 annually through 1976 and reduced amounts thereafter. The Company has options to purchase the properties under specified conditions.

**NOTE 8** The current status of the Federal Trade Commission's order of December 16, 1960 directing Scott to divest itself of properties acquired through the merger with Soundview Pulp Company in 1951 and the merger with Hollingsworth & Whitney Company and the acquisition of the assets of Detroit Sulphite Pulp & Paper Company in 1954 is commented upon in the section headed Legal Matters

# OPINION OF INDEPENDENT ACCOUNTANTS

*To the Board of Directors and The Shareholders of Scott Paper Company:*

In our opinion, the foregoing statements present fairly the consolidated financial position of Scott Paper Company and its subsidiaries at December 31, 1963 and the results of their operations for the year, in conformity with generally accepted accounting principles applied on a basis consistent with that of the preceding year. Our examination of these statements was made in accordance with generally accepted auditing standards and accordingly included such tests of the accounting records and such other auditing procedures as we considered necessary in the circumstances.

Philadelphia
January 21, 1964

Price Waterhouse & Co.

# SOURCE AND APPLICATION OF FUNDS

(000 Omitted)

|  | 1963 | 1962 | 1961 | 1960 | 1959 |
|---|---|---|---|---|---|
| **SOURCE OF FUNDS** | | | | | |
| From operations | | | | | |
| Income before taxes.......... | **$66,336** | $63,466 | $60,126 | $55,610 | $48,867 |
| Depreciation and depletion... | **18,790** | 17,587 | 16,014 | 14,444 | 13,699 |
|  | **$85,126** | $81,053 | $76,140 | $70,054 | $62,566 |
| Sale of Scott's interest in B. C. Forest Products Ltd., to Brunswick Pulp & Paper Co.. | | | 15,530 | | |
| Exercise of employee stock options................. | **1,475** | 1,246 | 371 | | |
| Other transactions............... | **2,452** | 3,991 | 2,283 | 3,057 | 3,159 |
|  | **$89,053** | $86,290 | $94,324 | $73,111 | $65,725 |
| **APPLICATION OF FUNDS** | | | | | |
| Taxes on income................. | **$30,080** | $30,770 | $28,985 | $27,250 | $23,625 |
| Dividend payments............... | **22,136** | 21,333 | 18,969 | 17,898 | 16,602 |
| Expenditures for plant assets.... | **20,111** | 14,462 | 23,279 | 33,935 | 15,661 |
| Expenditures for timber resources | **1,537** | 4,657 | 2,414 | 3,240 | 1,008 |
| Investments in affiliated and other companies*............ | **10,246** | 3,865 | 12,784** | 3,805 | 3,915 |
| Acquisition of preferred shares.. | **1,818** | 269 | | | |
| Acquisition of common shares... | **1,009** | | | | |
| Other transactions............... | **409** | 245 | 1,443 | 80 | 45 |
|  | **$87,346** | $75,601 | $87,874 | $86,208 | $60,856 |
| **WORKING CAPITAL INCREASE OR (DECREASE)...................** | **$1,707** | $10,689 | $ 6,450 | ($13,097) | $ 4,869 |

*Includes Scott's share in the undistributed earnings of the affiliated companies.

**Includes $10 million invested in Brunswick Pulp & Paper Company.

# GENERAL ELECTRIC

The following features are of interest in reviewing the financial statements and the accompanying notes taken from the annual report of General Electric for 1963.

Two financial statements are presented: (1) Consolidated Statement of Current and Reinvested Earnings, and (2) Consolidated Statement of Financial Position. The statements are prepared in comparative form. The annual report also includes a "10 Year Summary" in which significant financial, operating, employee, and stockholder data for the years 1954–1963 are presented in condensed form together with ratios and measurements that are useful in the interpretation of these data. This summary has been reproduced and follows the financial statements for the current period. A summary of working capital changes for the year is provided in a special section of the annual report referred to as a "1963 Financial Summary."

**Consolidated Statement of Current and Reinvested Earnings.** A combined earnings and reinvested earnings statement is provided. Income data are presented in multiple-step form with balances reported for earnings resulting from sales, earnings before income taxes and renegotiation, and net earnings. Dividends declared for the year are reported as a deduction from net earnings to arrive at the amount of earnings reinvested for the year. The latter balance is then added to reinvested earnings at the beginning of the year and provides the balance of reinvested earnings at the end of the year. The earnings statement is accompanied by summaries of earnings per share and dividends per share.

**Consolidated Statement of Financial Position.** Assets, liabilities, and capital are presented in modified "financial-position" form. Assets and liabilities are listed and an excess of assets over liabilities, reserves, and minority interest — referred to as ownership — is presented. The ownership is then expressed in terms of common stock issued, amounts in excess of par value received for stock, and earnings reinvested in the company. Assets, liability, and ownership items are reported in condensed form and detail is provided in the form of supplementary schedules.

**Notes to Financial Statements.** Notes to financial statements offer an analysis of a number of significant aspects of company position and operations: (1) the basis of consolidation is explained; (2) the effects of price adjustments to customers are described; (3) valuation procedures for marketable securities and inventories are stated; operations of sales finance subsidiaries are described; provisions that are found in long-term debt contracts are described; the contingent liability arising from the sale of installment receivables on a full recourse basis is described.

# General Electric 1963 Financial Statements

## Consolidated Statement of Current and Reinvested Earnings     For the year

|  | 1963 | 1962 | 1961 |
|---|---|---|---|
| **SALES of products and services to customers** . . . . . . . | $4,918,715,661 | $4,792,732,530 . | $4,456,815,169 |
| **Deduct operating costs:** | | | |
| Inventories at January 1 (costs carried over from prior year) . . | 722,774,339 | 648,447,738 | 655,161,191 |
| Wages, salaries and employee benefits . . . . . . . . . . | 2,121,621,077 | 2,040,782,602 | 1,903,613,703 |
| Materials, supplies and all other costs not shown separately . . | 2,275,962,051 | 2,290,816,062 | 2,062,921,379 |
| Depreciation (wear and obsolescence of plant and equipment) | 127,694,800 | 127,056,005 | 117,879,850 |
| Taxes, except those on income . . . . . . . . . . . . | 43,046,566 | 43,043,084 | 39,379,845 |
| Less—Inventories at year-end (costs carried over to next year) | −742,964,766 | −722,774,339 | −648,447,738 |
|    —Wages, salaries and employee benefits directly reimbursed by Atomic Energy Commission . . . . . . | −111,216,185 | −106,220,875 | −105,451,984 |
| **Total costs applicable to sales** . . . . . . . . . . . | 4,436,917,882 | 4,321,150,277 | 4,025,056,246 |
| **EARNINGS RESULTING FROM SALES** . . . . . . . . . | 481,797,779 | 471,582,253 | 431,758,923 |
| **Add nonoperating income:** | | | |
| Net earnings of General Electric Credit Corporation . . . . . | 8,709,216 | 8,666,884 | 9,539,960 |
| Dividends received from foreign nonconsolidated subsidiaries . | 2,055,497 | 1,787,671 | 2,602,548 |
| Other nonoperating income—net . . . . . . . . . . . . | 64,810,473 | 39,559,568 | 51,192,811 |
| Less—Interest on debentures and other financial charges . . . | −8,036,966 | −8,254,046 | −8,776,894 |
| **Nonoperating income—net** . . . . . . . . . . . . . | 67,538,220 | 41,760,077 | 54,558,425 |
| **EARNINGS BEFORE INCOME TAXES AND RENEGOTIATION** . | 549,335,999 | 513,342,330 | 486,317,348 |
| Deduct—Federal and Canadian income taxes, and renegotiation | 274,600,000 | 244,000,000 | 241,700,000 |
|    —Other income taxes . . . . . . . . . . . . . . | 3,181,541 | 2,646,568 | 2,453,274 |
|    —Minority interest in subsidiary's net earnings . . . . | 915,702 | 851,993 | 85,117 |
| **NET EARNINGS applicable to common stock** . . . . . . . | 270,638,756 | 265,843,769 | 242,078,957 |
| Deduct—Dividends declared for year . . . . . . . . . . | 183,124,154 | 177,460,824 | 176,440,908 |
| Amount added to reinvested earnings for year . . . . . . . | 87,514,602 | 88,382,945 | 65,638,049 |
| Reinvested earnings January 1 . . . . . . . . . . . . . | 1,093,043,238 | 1,004,660,293 | 939,022,244 |
| **REINVESTED EARNINGS December 31** . . . . . . . . . | $1,180,557,840 | $1,093,043,238 | $1,004,660,293 |
| Earnings per share . . . . . . . . . . . . . . . . . | $3.00 | $2.97 | $2.72 |
| Dividends declared per share . . . . . . . . . . . . . | $2.05 | $2.00 | $2.00 |
| Dividends paid per share . . . . . . . . . . . . . . . | $2.00 | $2.00 | $2.00 |

Reference should be made to Notes on pages 618 and 619

**Consolidated Statement of Financial Position**

| | December 31 1963 | December 31 1962 |
|---|---|---|
| Cash on hand and in banks . . . . . . . . . . . . . . . . . . . | $ 383,308,940 | $ 81,861,808 |
| Marketable securities (short-term investments readily convertible to cash) . . . | 237,809,454 | 263,939,952 |
| Receivables* (money owed to the Company by customers, to be paid within a year) . | 698,274,792 | 716,040,558 |
| Inventories (materials, and products being made or completed and ready for sale) . | 742,964,766 | 722,774,339 |
| | 2,062,357,952 | 1,784,616,657 |
| **Deduct:** Collections from customers on contracts in progress and anticipated price adjustments on contracts . . . . . . . . . . . . . . . . . . | 188,108,055 | 228,123,379 |
| CURRENT ASSETS (cash, or items generally convertible to cash within a year) . . | 1,874,249,897 | 1,556,493,278 |
| Investments and advances* (mainly securities of wholly owned companies not consolidated, plus loans to them) . . . . . . . . . . . . . . . | 284,628,100 | 257,963,496 |
| Plant and equipment less accumulated depreciation* (original cost of land, buildings and equipment—less estimated cost consumed by wear and obsolescence) . . . | 694,768,299 | 712,917,860 |
| Other assets* (long-term receivables, special funds, etc.) . . . . . . . . . . | 161,485,018 | 319,612,876 |
| TOTAL ASSETS (items owned at the end of the year) . . . . . . . . . . | 3,015,131,314 | 2,846,987,510 |
| Notes payable by consolidated subsidiaries . . . . . . . . . . . . . . | 150,000 | 50,000 |
| Accounts payable* (money owed for materials and services supplied by others) . | 203,163,325 | 209,478,404 |
| Dividends payable to share owners . . . . . . . . . . . . . . . . . | 49,197,136 | 44,399,899 |
| Taxes accrued (taxes owed to local, state, Federal and Canadian governments) . . | 260,119,319 | 252,418,277 |
| Other costs and expenses accrued* (amounts to be paid for wages, interest, etc.) . | 313,836,712 | 279,393,028 |
| CURRENT LIABILITIES (amounts generally due within the year ahead) . . . . . | 826,466,492 | 785,739,608 |
| 3¹/₂% debentures due May 1, 1976 (amount owed on long-term borrowings) . . . . | 203,008,000 | 222,472,000 |
| Other liabilities* (long-term payables, etc.) . . . . . . . . . . . . . | 86,417,398 | 61,550,493 |
| Remainder of premium received from 1956 sales of debentures . . . . . . . . | 687,314 | 785,622 |
| Miscellaneous reserves (provision for future payment of costs incurred to date) . . | 34,054,459 | 36,042,392 |
| Minority share owners' interest in Canadian General Electric Company, Ltd. . . . | 18,907,834 | 18,074,474 |
| TOTAL LIABILITIES, reserves and minority interest (amount owed at year end) . . | 1,169,541,497 | 1,124,664,589 |
| Excess of Assets over Liabilities, Reserves and Minority Interest—Ownership . . | $1,845,589,817 | $1,722,322,921 |
| This ownership (share owners' equity) is evidenced by: | | |
| Common stock* (issued shares of stock, each with a par value of $5) . . . . . . | $ 452,435,485 | $ 449,444,830 |
| Amounts in excess of par value received for stock* . . . . . . . . . . . | 212,596,492 | 179,834,853 |
| Earnings reinvested in the Company . . . . . . . . . . . . . . . . | 1,180,557,840 | 1,093,043,238 |
| TOTAL SHARE OWNERS' EQUITY . . . . . . . . . . . . . . . . . . . | $1,845,589,817 | $1,722,322,921 |

*Details shown on page 618

## Details of Items in Statements

| | DECEMBER 31 | |
|---|---:|---:|
| | **1963** | **1962** |
| **Receivables:** | | |
| From nonconsolidated subsidiaries . . . . . . | $ 11,381,366 | $ 10,523,243 |
| Other, less reserves . . . . . . . . . . . | 686,893,426 | 705,517,315 |
| | $ 698,274,792 | $ 716,040,558 |
| **Investments and Advances:** | | |
| General Electric Credit Corporation—Equity . . . . | $ 86,468,016 | $ 77,758,800 |
| —Advances . . . | 15,000,000 | 20,000,000 |
| Other sales finance subsidiaries—Equity and advances . | 202,601 | 98,318 |
| Foreign nonconsolidated subsidiaries—Investments . . | 52,892,318 | 51,344,662 |
| —Advances . . | 36,952,477 | 39,279,492 |
| General Electric common stock at cost . . . . . | 28,780,456 | 27,442,642 |
| Miscellaneous securities at cost . . . . . . . . | 71,832,232 | 49,539,582 |
| | 292,128,100 | 265,463,496 |
| Less: Reserve . . . . . . . . . . . | 7,500,000 | 7,500,000 |
| | $ 284,628,100 | $ 257,963,496 |
| **Plant and Equipment:** | | |
| Plant and equipment at cost . . . . . . . . . | $1,751,507,242 | $1,723,347,324 |
| Less: Accumulated depreciation and amortization . . | 1,056,738,943 | 1,010,429,464 |
| Cost less accumulated depreciation and amortization . | $ 694,768,299 | $ 712,917,860 |
| **Other Assets:** | | |
| Long-term receivables, less reserve . . . . . . . | 29,354,807 | $ 168,715,247 |
| Equipment leased to others—net . . . . . . . . | 50,654,148 | 53,687,030 |
| Advances to vendors and distributors . . . . . . | 12,833,431 | 22,465,955 |
| Funds for employee benefit plans—per contra in | | |
| Other Liabilities . . . . . . . . . . . | 19,193,154 | 22,187,564 |
| Deferred charges, less reserve . . . . . . . . | 12,580,415 | 11,482,094 |
| Loans and advances to employees . . . . . . . | 4,821,482 | 4,843,242 |
| All other . . . . . . . . . . . . . | 32,047,581 | 36,231,744 |
| | $ 161,485,018 | $ 319,612,876 |
| **Accounts Payable:** | | |
| Trade payables . . . . . . . . . . . | $ 151,186,604 | $ 159,992,187 |
| Payables representing collections from | | |
| employees and others . . . . . . . . . | 51,399,284 | 48,975,189 |
| Accounts payable to nonconsolidated subsidiaries . | 577,437 | 511,028 |
| | $ 203,163,325 | $ 209,478,404 |
| **Other Costs and Expenses Accrued:** | | |
| Payrolls accrued . . . . . . . . . . . | $ 36,299,911 | $ 30,791,865 |
| Interest expense accrued . . . . . . . . . | 1,197,202 | 1,327,486 |
| Other costs and expenses accrued— | | |
| includes liabilities for replacements under | | |
| guarantees, renegotiation, allowances to | | |
| customers, employee benefit costs, etc. . . . . . | 276,339,599 | 247,273,677 |
| | $ 313,836,712 | $ 279,393,028 |
| **Other Liabilities:** | | |
| Noncurrent accounts payable and other accruals . . | $ 67,224,244 | $ 39,362,929 |
| Liability for employee benefit plans— | | |
| per contra in Other Assets . . . . . . . . | 19,193,154 | 22,187,564 |
| | $ 86,417,398 | $ 61,550,493 |
| **Common Stock ($5 par value):** | | |
| Balance January 1 . . . . . . . . . . . | $ 449,444,830 | $ 446,728,235 |
| Shares issued under General Electric | | |
| Stock Option Plans . . . . . . . . . | 1,853,110 | 1,451,675 |
| Shares issued under General Electric | | |
| Savings and Security Program . . . . . . . | 1,137,545 | 1,264,920 |
| Balance December 31 . . . . . . . . . . | $ 452,435,485 | $ 449,444,830 |
| Issued shares Dec. 31 (105,000,000 authorized) . . . | 90,487,097 | 89,888,966 |
| **Amounts in Excess of Par Value** | | |
| **received for stock:** | | |
| Balance January 1 . . . . . . . . . . . | $ 179,834,853 | $ 151,813,595 |
| Premium received on shares issued . . . . . . | 29,427,040 | 25,765,816 |
| Net Increase from dispositions of treasury stock . . . | 3,334,599 | 2,255,442 |
| Balance December 31 . . . . . . . . . . | $ 212,596,492 | $ 179,834,853 |

## Notes to Financial Statements

**Basis of consolidation** — These financial statements and accompanying schedules represent a consolidation of the accounts of the Parent Company – General Electric – and those of all wholly owned subsidiary companies dealing primarily in United States or Canadian currencies, except sales finance subsidiaries.

All significant intercompany items have been eliminated.

Canadian accounts were converted to U. S. dollars on a dollar-for-dollar basis. To revalue fixed assets in Canada to historical U. S. dollar cost, and other net assets to the year-end exchange rate, $7,269,293 was carried in Miscellaneous Reserves at the close of 1963. Net assets in Canada at December 31, 1963, totaled $125,002,371 after this revaluation.

Net sales billed for 1963 were reduced by $17.8 million and for 1962 by $50 million, representing provision for price adjustments to customers on sales of certain products which were subjects of antitrust cases, and costs were increased by $8.1 million for other related adjustments.

Expenses directly reimbursed by the Atomic Energy Commission for atomic projects at Richland, Wash., Schenectady, N.Y., and St. Petersburg, Fla., are not included in sales or costs.

Marketable securities were carried at the lower of amortized cost or market value. Carrying value was substantially the same as market value.

Inventories were carried at cost, exclusive of certain indirect manufacturing expenses and intercompany profits. Carrying value was not in excess of market. Cost of substantially all inventories in the United States was determined on a last-in, first-out (LIFO) basis. Inventories of Canadian components, with net value of $75.3 million before exchange revaluation, were valued on a first-in, first-out (FIFO) basis.

**Investments and advances** — Carrying value of U. S. and Canadian sales finance subsidiaries represents the Company's equity in, and advances to, these subsidiaries, and all of their earnings are included in the consolidated statements for General Electric Credit Corporation at right form a part of these notes. Jelco Corporation had borrowings from banks of $16,397,838 at the close of 1963.

Carrying value of foreign nonconsolidated subsidiaries represents cost of investments in, and advances to, these companies. Only dividends received from these subsidiaries are included in the Company's statement of current earnings.

Investment in General Electric common stock at the close of 1963 represented the cost of 372,983 shares being held for corporate purposes, such as requirements for the General Electric Savings and Security Program and Incentive Compensation Plan. On December 31, 1963 these shares had a quoted market value of $32,496,144.

On December 31, 1963 the fair value of miscellaneous securities was approximately $125 million. General Electric Company 3½% debentures mature May 1, 1976, with interest payable on May 1 and November 1. The indenture provides for sinking fund payments of $13 million annually through 1975. The Company, at its option, may make additional annual payments of up to $13 million, and also may redeem all or part of the bonds at any time upon payment of redemption premiums ranging downward from 2.45%. The underlying indenture also includes certain limitations on pledge, mortgage, or disposition through sale and leaseback of manufacturing properties. Re-acquired debentures with face value of $54,853,000 held in treasury in anticipation of future sinking fund requirements have been deducted from unretired debentures which totaled $257,861,000 at the end of 1963.

Contingent liabilities — At the close of 1963, the Company was contingently liable to a number of financial institutions for $263.8 million of installment receivables, including interest collectible in the future, which had been sold to such institutions on a full recourse basis.

No specific provision has been made for possible future costs arising from antitrust matters.

## General Electric Credit Corporation
## Consolidated Financial Statements

### Financial Position

| | DECEMBER 31 | |
|---|---|---|
| | **1963** | **1962** |
| Cash . . . . . . . . . . . . . . . . . . | $ 28,197,289 | $ 34,926,460 |
| Receivables, less reserve and deferred income (a) . . | 772,509,184 | 662,363,476 |
| Prepaid interest and discount . . . . . . . . | 2,832,948 | 2,455,938 |
| Other assets . . . . . . . . . . . . . | 4,150,686 | 2,610,441 |
| Total assets . . . . . . . . . . . . | 807,690,107 | 702,356,315 |
| Notes payable to: | | |
| General Electric Company . . . . . . . . | 15,000,000 | 20,000,000 |
| Others . . . . . . . . . . . . . . | 563,201,347 | 484,026,300 |
| Others—subordinated . . . . . . . . . | 65,000,000 | 50,000,000 |
| Accounts and drafts payable . . . . . . . . | 32,408,151 | 27,662,417 |
| Deferred payments to dealers . . . . . . . . | 35,207,247 | 33,308,059 |
| Accrued Federal taxes on income . . . . . . | 5,812,146 | 6,077,087 |
| Other accrued liabilities . . . . . . . . . | 4,593,200 | 3,523,652 |
| Total liabilities . . . . . . . . | 721,222,091 | 624,597,515 |
| Assets less liabilities—equity . . . . . . . | $ 86,468,016 | $ 77,758,800 |
| | | |
| Equity represented by: | | |
| Par value of common stock . . . . . . . | $ 20,000,000 | $ 20,000,000 |
| Reinvested earnings . . . . . . . . . . . | 66,468,016 | 57,758,800 |
| Equity—held by General Electric Company . . . . . | $ 86,468,016 | $ 77,758,800 |
| | | |
| (a) Reserve for receivable losses . . . . . . | $ 14,350,000 | $ 12,300,000 |
| Deferred income . . . . . . . . . . | 98,580,066 | 82,446,703 |

### Current and Reinvested Earnings

| | 1963 | 1962 | 1961 |
|---|---|---|---|
| Volume of time sales and inventory financing . . . . . . . . | $975,989,206 | $914,544,426 | $820,615,545 |
| Gross earned income . . . . . . . . . | $ 79,548,207 | $ 71,334,832 | $ 65,177,962 |
| Expenses—Operating and administrative . . . . . . . | 39,128,626 | 34,517,369 | 30,455,192 |
| —Interest and discount . . . . . | 22,205,365 | 18,855,579 | 14,912,810 |
| —Federal income taxes . . . . | 9,505,000 | 9,295,000 | 10,270,000 |
| Net earnings for the year . . . . . | 8,709,216 | 8,666,884 | 9,539,960 |
| Deduct: Transfer to common stock for par value increase . . . . . . . | — | —8,900,000 | |
| January 1 reinvested earnings . . . . . | 57,758,800 | 57,991,916 | 48,451,956 |
| December 31 reinvested earnings . . . . | $ 66,468,016 | $ 57,758,800 | $ 57,991,916 |

### Independent Auditors' Report

to the share owners and board of directors of General Electric Company.

We have examined the consolidated statement of financial position of General Electric Company and subsidiaries as of December 31, 1963 and the related statement of current and reinvested earnings for the year then ended. Our examination was made in accordance with generally accepted auditing standards, and accordingly included such tests of the accounting records and such other auditing procedures as we considered necessary in the circumstances.

In our opinion, the accompanying consolidated statements, subject to the anti-trust litigation referred to at left, present fairly the financial position of General Electric Company and subsidiaries at December 31, 1963 and the results of their operations for the year then ended, in conformity with generally accepted accounting principles applied on a basis consistent with that of the preceding year.

Peat, Marwick, Mitchell & Co.

Seventy Pine St., New York 5, N. Y., Feb. 20, 1964

# 10 year summary

| Per-share amounts in dollars; Other dollar amounts in millions | 1963 | 1962 | 1961 | 1960 |
|---|---|---|---|---|
| Net sales billed . . . . . . . | $4,918.7 | $4,792.7 | $4,456.8 | $4,197.5 |
| Orders price index (1957-59=100) | 87 | 90 | 92 | 97 |
| | | | | |
| Net earnings . . . . . . . . | $270.6 | $265.8 | $242.1 | $200.1 |
| Earnings per share . . . . . . | 3.00 | 2.97 | 2.72 | 2.26 |
| Earnings as a percentage of sales . | 5.5% | 5.5% | 5.4% | 4.8% |
| Earned on capital invested (a) . . | 13.6% | 14.1% | 13.7% | 11.9% |
| | | | | |
| Cash dividends declared . . . . | $183.1 | $177.5 | $176.4 | $175.5 |
| Dividends declared per share . . | 2.05 | 2.00 | 2.00 | 2.00 |
| No. of shares issued—Dec. 31 . . | 90,487,097 | 89,888,966 | 89,345,647 | 88,860,183 |
| Average number of share owners . | 503,516 | 446,919 | 440,938 | 416,950 |
| Market price range per share (b) . | 87½-71¾ | 78½-54¼ | 80¾-60½ | 99⅞-70¼ |
| | | | | |
| Current assets . . . . . . . | $1,874.3 | $1,556.5 | $1,452.5 | $1,478.5 |
| Current liabilities . . . . . . | 826.5 | 785.7 | 782.0 | 705.6 |
| Total assets . . . . . . . . | 3,015.1 | 2,847.0 | 2,704.5 | 2,551.3 |
| | | | | |
| Long-term debt and notes payable | 204.1 | 223.4 | 229.6 | 250.5 |
| Share owners' investment . . . | 1,845.6 | 1,722.3 | 1,603.2 | 1,513.4 |
| Total capital invested (c) . . . . | 2,049.7 | 1,945.7 | 1,832.8 | 1,763.9 |
| | | | | |
| Plant expenditures . . . . . . | 111.9 | 125.4 | 145.2 | 136.9 |
| Depreciation and amortization . . | 127.7 | 127.1 | 117.9 | 116.0 |
| Total taxes and renegotiation (d) . | 320.8 | 289.7 | 283.5 | 229.1 |
| | | | | |
| Total employee compensation (e) . | 2,121.6 | 2,040.8 | 1,903.6 | 1,848.2 |
| Average number of employees . . | 262,882 | 258,174 | 249,100 | 250,621 |
| Average compensation per employee, in dollars (e) . . . | $8,071 | $7,905 | $7,642 | $7,374 |

| 1959 | 1958 | 1957 | 1956 | 1955 | 1954 |
|---|---|---|---|---|---|
| $4,349.5 | $4,120.8 | $4,335.7 | $4,090.0 | $3,463.7 | $3,334.7 |
| 101 | 100 | 99 | 93 | 86 | 89 |
| | | | | | |
| $280.2 | $242.9 | $247.9 | $213.8 | $208.9 | $204.4 |
| 3.19 | 2.78 | 2.84 | 2.46 | 2.41 | 2.36 |
| 6.4% | 5.9% | 5.7% | 5.2% | 6.0% | 6.1% |
| 16.7% | 15.7% | 16.9% | 15.3% | 17.8% | 19.2% |
| | | | | | |
| $174.3 | $173.7 | $173.2 | $172.4 | $145.9 | $131.4 |
| 2.00 | 2.00 | 2.00 | 2.00 | 1.70 | 1.53 |
| 88,282,899 | 87,681,422 | 87,396,796 | 87,143,662 | 86,875,994 | 86,660,618 |
| 404,431 | 395,493 | 377,555 | 362,122 | 338,563 | 277,047 |
| 99⁷/₈-74 | 79³/₈-57 | 72³/₈-52³/₈ | 65¹/₂-52³/₄ | 57³/₄-46¹/₄ | 48¹/₂-29 |
| | | | | | |
| $1,567.3 | $1,407.9 | $1,353.0 | $1,268.7 | $1,056.1 | $1,056.5 |
| 739.3 | 700.4 | 733.4 | 676.4 | 708.9 | 686.7 |
| 2,561.5 | 2,420.9 | 2,361.3 | 2,221.1 | 1,903.1 | 1,815.3 |
| | | | | | |
| 278.0 | 306.3 | 303.1 | 308.5 | 92.0 | 51.9 |
| 1,457.7 | 1,311.0 | 1,231.2 | 1,143.4 | 1,089.8 | 1,020.0 |
| 1,735.7 | 1,617.3 | 1,534.3 | 1,451.9 | 1,181.8 | 1,071.9 |
| | | | | | |
| 91.3 | 104.1 | 153.6 | 205.2 | 161.4 | 170.6 |
| 119.9 | 124.5 | 119.9 | 108.7 | 97.4 | 86.4 |
| 313.1 | 282.1 | 300.3 | 247.2 | 206.5 | 230.4 |
| | | | | | |
| 1,783.7 | 1,640.2 | 1,715.3 | 1,643.8 | 1,372.4 | 1,250.9 |
| 246,840 | 249,718 | 282,029 | 280,497 | 250,306 | 243,622 |
| | | | | | |
| $7,226 | $6,568 | $6,083 | $5,860 | $5,483 | $5,135 |

(a) Net earnings for the year—before interest on money borrowed—as a percentage of total capital invested at the close of each year.
(b) Represents high and low market price on New York Stock Exchange for each year.

(c) Represents total share owners' investment (ownership) plus long-term debt and notes payable as of December 31 each year.
(d) Excludes certain excise and sales taxes, which are not included in sales or costs, and

social security taxes, which are listed under employment costs.
(e) Includes Company cost of vacations, holidays, pensions, insurance, social security taxes, and all other employee benefits.

# INDEX